The
Debt-FREE & Prosperous Living
Basic Course

By John Cummuta

Sixth Edition — Complete Revision

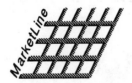

Marketline Press, Wauzeka, Wisconsin

The *Debt-FREE & Prosperous Living*
Basic Course

Sixth Edition

Twenty-second Printing 1996
Printed in the United States of America

ISBN 1-883113-07-5

Distributed by Financial Independence Network Limited, Inc. (FINL)
310 Second Street
Boscobel, WI 53805
608-375-3100

Contents

The *Debt-FREE & Prosperous Living* "Financial Freedom Strategy" by John Cummuta

Part One — The Strategy

First of all, let us be completely honest: there is only one real definition of *"Financial Freedom"* — that is to be dependent on NO ONE. And that is the goal of the *Debt-FREE & Prosperous Living* program — to help you be completely independent of any job, any person and certainly independent from any need for government support, EVER. It is what I call getting "Un-vulnerable."

This program is built on the premise that the ideal situation would be to have NO bills and to have a substantial income at the same time — without having to work for it. In other words, I want to help you achieve, IN AS SHORT A TIME AS POSSIBLE, a situation where you own your home and your car(s), you have NO installment debt — and you have enough money in investments that you can live off the interest.

THAT IS TRUE FINANCIAL INDEPENDENCE!

To achieve this goal, you have to follow a new strategy. It is nearly impossible to reach this kind of freedom doing things the way you have always been taught — the way you see everyone else doing them. You first need to understand how you have been misled over the years, then you need to design an efficient and sound strategy, to use the money you earn to get you to your goal in the shortest period of time.

You will notice, as we go through the concepts that follow, that many of them run completely counter to "Conventional Wisdom." That

A Whole New Outlook on Life

Notes

Key Points	Details

is because <u>conventional wisdom is wrong</u>. And it is generally wrong because it is "wisdom" that has been promoted by the businesses that profit greatly from our doing what is good for them — not for us. These businesses have most Americans paying hundreds of thousand of dollars, over the years, for services they do not really need. Or, at least, for products and services that DO NOT provide the happiness, bliss and security that they're promised to give us.

How We've Been Misled

If you are like most folks, you will find yourself actually angry when you finish reading these pages. It will be like a veil has been lifted from your eyes and you will see for the first time how the entire way our economy works is designed to make you work yourself to exhaustion — simply to accumulate wealth for the companies you do business with — NOT FOR YOU.

The most staggering example of this is a home mortgage. If you buy a home with a 30-year conventional or adjustable rate mortgage, <u>you will pay for that loan about THREE TIMES</u>. Just multiply out your payment times 360 months and you will see that the total is about 3 times the value of the money you borrowed.

That means that two-thirds of that total is INTEREST. Interest is the profit the mortgage company makes for lending you the money to buy the house. And they feel that you should pay them back THREE TIMES. **That's 200% interest!**

Let's put some real numbers to this.

If you buy a $250,000 home, with a $200,000 mortgage, you will end up paying about $600,000 over 30 years. THIS MEANS THAT YOU WILL PAY <u>NEARLY A HALF MILLION DOLLARS</u> IN INTEREST!

Now let these words soak into your mind and heart: You will have to work...week after week...year after year...to earn FOUR HUNDRED THOUSAND DOLLARS — <u>Just so you can give it to the bank to make them rich</u>! Ask yourself — do they deserve almost a half million dollars

Notes

Key Points	Details

of your hard-earned wealth more than you do? Are they doing you such a tremendous favor that you should wear yourself out over three decades to generate nearly a half million dollars, **to add to their wealth?**

That's YOUR MONEY. You work for it. You pay taxes on it. Yet they end up with it. It's not fair. In fact it is legal robbery, and I am dedicated to helping you dump these leeches and begin turning the tide of your wealth-building power toward YOUR benefit instead of theirs.

I am going to help you craft a strategy for yourself and your family that will keep the maximum amount of the wealth you produce IN YOUR HANDS. The power of retaining and investing the money you waste on mortgage interest alone could change your life completely.

Just think about that four hundred thousand dollars. If you put it into mutual funds that averaged 10% interest per year, you could enjoy a $40,000-a-year retirement income WITHOUT EVER TOUCHING THE PRINCIPAL! You would never have to work again, and the exciting thing is that we're not even talking about your having to make any extra money to make this happen for you. This four hundred thousand (or whatever it works out to for you) is money you are going to earn anyway. We're just giving you control of who ends up with it: you or THEM.

By the way, if you have an accountant who tells you that you should never pay off your mortgage, *"Because it's the last tax shelter for the average consumer,"* GET A NEW ACCOUNTANT. Think about what they're saying. Let me translate it for you. They're really saying, *"Keep on paying a dollar of interest to get back 28 cents in tax deductions."*

Friend, if you are willing to trade a dollar for 28 cents, you can invest with me for the rest of your life!

Notes

Key Points	Details

Car loans. Next to a home mortgage, the greatest form of legal robbery is auto loans. You will notice how the banks and finance companies are willing to give you up to five, six and in some cases even more years to pay off a car these days. That's because the loan is just like a mini home mortgage — ONLY THE INTEREST RATE IS HIGHER. If car finance companies thought they could get away with it, they would offer you 30-year loans on cars. They'd love to get three times the price of the car, and suck your wealth dry in the process.

Insurance. It has been said that in no other expense area do people spend so much of their money with so little understanding of the value of what they're buying.

The first thing you need to do is admit that your insurance agent (even if they are your brother or sister) is probably not trying to find a way to protect you from life's "icky" things — *with NO concern for their own profit.* And even if you do believe that they are completely selfless, let's consider the insurance companies they work for.

INSURANCE COMPANIES DO NOT LOSE MONEY ON INSURANCE POLICIES! Sure, some of them go out of business by making rotten outside investments — but they do not lose a penny on their insurance programs. That is a simple fact. The truth is that, when they sell you an insurance policy, they are gambling (with the odds in their favor) that bad things <u>will not</u> happen to you, and you (silly if you think about it) are gambling that bad things <u>will</u> happen to you. THE INSURANCE COMPANIES NEVER LOSE IN THIS GAME.

Sure, there are a small number of people who pay a few dollars in premiums, then make a big claim. While it may appear that the insurance company loses money in this situation, the fact is that they have<u>thousands</u> of other people paying premiums, to whom nothing bad is happening. So they simply take the profit they are making on most people, and easily cover the benefits they have to pay out to the few unfortunate ones. And they know, whenever they sell you a policy, that you are thousands of times more likely to be one of the fortunate ones who cost them nothing, but make them thousands!

Let's Look at More Ways You're Getting Ripped Off

Notes

Key Points	Details

They only bet on sure things. Which means that, if they are willing to sell you a policy, it is only because history has proven to them that they are going to win. Another way to say it is that, if they are willing to sell it to you — YOU PROBABLY DON'T NEED IT. In fact, <u>their mathematicians (called actuaries) have statistically calculated that you probably will never need it, or they would never sell it to you.</u>

While there are some areas of your life that you do want to cover with the correct types of insurance, one thing you can be sure of is that you almost certainly do not want exactly what they want to sell to you.

I'll get into specific suggestions about how to properly buy insurance in a later section.

A Few More Misapplied Strategies

As I did the research for developing this unique *Financial Freedom Strategy*, I was amazed at how many of the financial "Rules" we are taught (or just pick up) ARE WRONG! And they are not just a little wrong. They can be deadly to our ever achieving real financial independence, in a desirable time-frame.

The two untrue "Truths" that I found most difficult to break my own addiction to were the principles of *"Saving money, a little at a time, as you go along through life,"* and *"You need to use credit to develop and maintain a good credit rating."*

Saving money as you go along. Every time you get financial advice, it usually includes instruction to build a little nest-egg on the side, while you work your way through life. Many "Authorities" will counsel you to save 10% of your income as an investment for the future. They call it *"Paying yourself first."*

Now, in and of itself this is not bad advice. It is just the way it's most often applied that causes people to move sluggishly toward their goals — instead of taking the shortest, fastest course. **Efficiency comes from focusing on ONE task at a time.**

Notes

Key Points	Details

Our *Financial Freedom Strategy* has proven the fastest, safest route to your financial goals: *first* you eliminate ALL debt — *then* you save.

You need a good Credit Rating. Believe it or not we are going to help you get to a point where you won't care what your credit rating is, BECAUSE YOU WON'T NEED IT. You will HATE credit, and you will never need the assistance of a lender again. As you can see, we are already flying in the face of the "Truths" you've been led to believe all your life.

Actually, most Americans were never taught — by family or by the education system—how to manage their financial resources throughout the various stages of their lives. So they have become the unwitting students (and slaves) of Madison Avenue advertisers and the money-lending companies behind them.

Think about it. Where did you receive your personal financial training? Haven't you really been trained by TV and other advertising media on how you should live, what you should buy to show that you have arrived at a certain status level, and what kind of American Dream you should be chasing?

Are you not instructed by the media what kind of car you should be driving to look successful? Are you not shown what kind of house you should live in to be really happy, or what kind of clothes will make you socially acceptable? And doesn't everyone who's anyone go on a cruise every year?

Even if you watch supposedly "Information-Only" financial programs, the experts you are listening to are usually just salespeople for investment companies.

I, on the other hand, am a teacher without any investment products to tout. I simply wish to show you a strategy that can get you to complete financial independence in the shortest period of time. I am trying to help you put into play what you already know deep inside — a bigger home or faster car will not make you nearly as happy as will the absence of the pressures brought on by the monthly payments that come with these things.

I want to help you reach a point where you are driving an acceptable, attractive car and living in a comfortable home — but you

Notes

Key Points	Details

have NO PAYMENTS TO MAKE ON ANYTHING BUT FOOD, HEAT AND MINIMUM LEGAL TAXES. At that point you will be insulated from layoffs, economic downturns, inflation and all the other woes that mentally and emotionally squeeze the average worker. You will be beyond it, in a place that few people reach — because they are continually misled to waste their wealth.

A New Strategy

The new strategy I am proposing is not based on assumptions or generalities, but rather on pure mathematics and probability. Sounds scientific, doesn't it? Well it's really pretty simple and straightforward. It is founded on the premise that <u>you want to get debt-free and start building wealth in the shortest period of time</u> — while protecting yourself from the bad things that have a *reasonable* probability of actually happening to you.

The key to achieving debt-freedom is **the management of compound interest in your life**. You will begin to see, as you study this course, that compound interest is more powerful than you probably imagine — and right now it is likely stacked 100% AGAINST you. Our system is based on a *mathematical process* that <u>first shorts out this compound interest working *against* you</u>. It then teaches you to turn the "financial funnel" around so you can later maximize the power of compound interest working FOR you.

The key to protecting yourself from the bad things that might happen to you involves *Mathematical Probability*. This means that you "probably" need to employ only those kinds of insurance that protect you from <u>catastrophic occurrences</u>, where the expense could wipe you or your survivors out. It is "probably" more cost-effective to assume the risk of insuring yourself from life's minor illnesses and accidents, by maximizing the deductibles on your policies. "Probability" shows us that this is most often cheaper than paying an insurance company higher premiums, month after month, to cover those minor costs for you.

Notes

Key Points	Details

We'll talk more specifically about this in a later section.

The real good news about insurance is that, after you have followed the *Financial Freedom Strategy's* investment recommendations, you will soon have the resources to protect yourself from almost everything you are now buying insurance for — and you will need little or no insurance other than for personal liability.

The three major stages of our *Financial Freedom Strategy* are:

Stage 1. Pay off ALL debt first

Stage 2. Operate strictly on a cash basis

Stage 3. Then focus ALL available cash on wealth-building

There's also a fourth stage that more and more Americans are choosing. We call it The New Paradigm. It involves not only leaving the fast lane, but taking the exit ramp. These people are choosing to leave fast-paced, high-pressure metropolitan lifestyles for more relaxed, less-expensive and safer small town lives. But this doesn't mean "living off the land." I live in a small Illinois town, in a comfortable split-level home, on an acre of woods, with my boat in the river that's about a mile from my driveway. This is not a bad way to live. So...if it fits you...

Stage 4. Move to a cheaper, safer, more enjoyable location

By following the three or four stages of this strategy, you will attain REAL independence in a relative handful of years — and you will never need credit again. Most people following this strategy are completely debt-FREE, including their home mortgage, in 4 to 6 years. And then they're onto quickly building retirement wealth with all the monthly money they had previously been wasting on debt payments.

ASK YOURSELF: How much better off will you be, 4 to 6 years from today, if you continue on the course you're on now?

Notes

Key Points	Details

PHASE 1

Pay Off ALL Debt First

In the next few pages I will begin describing exactly how you will pay off all your debts. The system is fool-proof...except for one thing — <u>YOUR commitment</u>. I cannot come over to your house and make you faithfully follow the steps of this plan. And while putting this system to work in your life won't be unbearably hard, it will be challenging. Only your commitment will keep you on the course — and to steel that commitment, I want you to give yourself some good reasons to follow through on *your* plan for Financial Freedom.

Before you go any further, turn to the *Your Retirement Lifestyle To-Do List* in Appendix E at the back of this book. On it I want you to list all the things you have always wanted to do, but never had the time to do. This is a list of the dream life you will live when this plan has worked its magic for you. Nothing is unimportant — put it all down.

When you have finished the list, either cut it out of the book or photocopy it and hang it somewhere where you will see it all the time — preferably where you sit to do your bills. Any time you feel your resolve starting to flag, run to this list and read it again. And every time you do, just remember that — should you give up — THE HUGE BALL OF DEBT YOU ARE JUST BARELY CARRYING NOW WILL BE MORE THAN YOU CAN BEAR IN YOUR OLDER YEARS. IN FACT, IT MAY CRUSH YOU LIKE IT HAS OTHERS.

Notes

Key Points	Details

Before you can actually begin paying off bills I first need to help you uncover what I call your *"Accelerator Margin,"* so you can focus its leverage on paying off your debts. The *Accelerator Margin* is the amount of money that you will add to the monthly payment of one bill after another — until they are all paid off. Then you will take the whole monthly amount that used to be going to all your bills, and focus it on your mortgage payment <u>until your house is paid off</u>. For most people the entire process takes between four and six years, sometimes less.

If you are not yet making mortgage payments on a house, you will use this first step to pay off all revolving credit debt (bank cards, store charge cards, gas cards with any balance on them, car loans, and so on) — then you will put all the monthly money you have freed up by paying off your bills into moderate- to low-risk investments, to build up a down-payment for your home.

Then, as soon as you get into your new house, you will immediately start the process of paying off the mortgage!

Don't save any money until all debt is gone? This sounds like heresy, but it is what I recommend with this strategy. Of course some people's circumstances require special consideration, but the bottom line is that **you will achieve a lot more, a lot faster, by focusing your total available dollars on bill payoff,** than you will by spreading it thin, trying to pay off bills while simultaneously trying to save some of your income. If you want to put a thousand dollars or so into the bank as an emergency backup fund that's fine, but you want to get 100% of your available income paying off bills as soon as you can.

HERE'S WHY: Let's say that you currently need $4,000 net income

Finding The Money For Bill Payoff

Don't Save Until ALL Debt is Gone

Notes

Key Points	Details

each month to cover your bills and expenses. Let's further say that you can presently put together an *Accelerator margin* of $400 — ten percent of your monthly income.

If you use the logic that you want to build up a six-month cash reserve *before* you start putting all your *Accelerator Margin* into eliminating debts, then you need to save six times $4,000 (your monthly requirement), or $24,000 to give you six month's worth of cash. If you divide the $400 you have available each month into the $24,000 cash reserve amount you plan to save up, you'll find that it will take you 60 months or **FIVE FULL YEARS JUST TO BUILD YOUR CASH RESERVE — BEFORE YOU CAN EVEN START ELIMINATING YOUR DEBT.**

But, if you follow my Financial Freedom Strategy to the letter, you could be completely debt-FREE in those same five years by **PAYING OFF ALL DEBT FIRST, AND SAVING SECOND!**

Then look how your situation will have changed. Let's suppose that — after you have paid off your mortgage, car payment and other credit payments — you could get along on just $1,000 a month. That would mean that you would only need $6,000 (instead of $24,000) in your six-month emergency fund. AND, you would now have about $3,000 a month to put away (because you have no bills to pay) — so **it would take you only TWO MONTHS to save up your six-month emergency money INSTEAD OF FIVE YEARS!**

The bottom line is that, the first way (the traditional way) you could save up your emergency fund in five years — but still have all your bills. Our way, it would take you five years and two months — but you would have your emergency fund saved up AND HAVE NO BILLS!

When I first formulated these strategies out of ideas I had gathered from a variety of financial education sources, my wife and I sat down and worked out the same numbers I will have you work out a little later. We

We Were Stunned

Notes

Key Points	Details

were stunned. Bills on which we had been paying the minimum payment — month after month for years — were eliminated in LESS THAN A YEAR! <u>From that point on we were able to more than DOUBLE our mortgage payment, for a total payoff time-frame of only 4 years and 7 months</u>.

Imagine our excitement. We had 26 years left on our mortgage, and we had planned on just paying it out like most folks. Sure, we had heard about mortgage reduction plans, but never really thought seriously about using one, because we could never find the extra money to do it with. Plus, even 15 or 20 years seemed like forever.

But with the total bill payoff strategy I had developed (and will show you in this book), we found the extra money by paying off all our charge accounts. Then — <u>using the same money we had been paying on credit cards and car leases each month</u>, we accelerated the payoff of our home to just over four years.

When I worked out the numbers I was dumbfounded.

If we had continued using our income the way we had been, we would have eventually paid off the house and we would have maybe put a few bucks in the bank. But it would have taken a quarter of a century...and it would have funneled hundreds of thousands of our hard-earned dollars to the mortgage company!

With the *Financial Freedom Strategy*, 26 years from now we will own the same (or a similar) house, and with the money that would have gone to the mortgage company going into our own investments — we will be millionaires! ALL THIS IS BEING DONE WITH THE SAME INCOME WE HAVE NOW. THIS WILL <u>NOT</u> REQUIRE ANY ADDITIONAL MONEY TO MAKE IT WORK!

But for the strategy to be effective, <u>you must concentrate your finances at one point of attack at a time</u>. In the first stage you will be paying off bills, so you do not want to weaken the mathematics by trying to save a portion of your income at the same time. Saving comes in stage two, <u>after your bills and your home are paid off</u>.

If you need any further motivation to convince you to focus all your money in the payoff direction, consider the **interest** on both the bill-payoff and the savings sides of the equation.

Notes

Key Points	Details

The power of compound interest is incredible. In fact, when asked what was the greatest invention he had ever seen, Albert Einstein responded, *"Compound Interest."* Mayer Amschel Rothschild, the German merchant who founded the greatest banking dynasty in history, called compound interest, *"The Eighth Wonder of the World."*

But this power can be working *for* you or *against* you. Right now it is likely pumping money the wrong way — and at a tremendous rate.

If you are putting money into a savings or money market account at say 4% or 5% interest, or even a fund that produces 8% or 9% — while you are simultaneously paying 20% or more on credit interest — you are moving backwards at a rate of 11% to 15% a year. And when you compound that over several years, it becomes a staggering loss of your wealth.

While savings account interest rates may be higher or lower at the time you read this manual, the relationship between the interest rates on money you're receiving interest on and money you're paying interest on will almost always be disproportionate — and not in your favor.

Without confusing the issue with the relatively inconsequential effects of taxes, it should be obvious that — if you use a dollar to pay off a bill where you are being charged 20% interest, you are making more on your money than if you put it in an investment where you are earning a lower rate. In other words, you can make 20% (or 18%, or whatever your credit cards charge) on your money by using every available dime to pay off all your credit cards.

> NOTE: Investing your money into paying off a debt where interest is charged on the outstanding monthly balance gives you a return <u>exactly equal</u> to investing the same money into an interest-earning account with the same interest rate. The main difference is that the return on investment is GUARANTEED to stay at the interest rate being charged to you, when you are paying off credit debt. Whereas interest rates in most growth investments fluctuate. In other words, every dollar used to prepay the balance of say an 18.9% credit card is earning a GUARANTEED, after-tax return of 18.9%!

That means that every dollar you put into savings or investments, instead of bill payoff, is earning you **less** of a return than it could. In short, you do not want to invest until <u>after</u> you have NO credit debt.

Notes

Key Points	Details

Even when it comes to your mortgage, where the interest rate is lower than credit card levels, you are still getting an above-average return on your money by using it to pay the mortgage off. This is because, to compare apples to apples, you must only compare the GUARANTEED return you would receive by prepaying your mortgage with investments that would also GUARANTEE their return. Growth mutual funds do not qualify, because they do not guarantee their return. In fact, you can lose money in these funds.

The safest investments that qualify would be U.S. Treasury instruments, such as long-term bonds. You will find that long-term bonds generally offer slightly less interest than the current mortgage interest rates. So prepaying your mortgage still gives you a higher return on your money than the best comparable investment.

Plus, the bottom-line goal of everything we are working for is to make you **"Un-vulnerable"** in the shortest possible time. And nothing helps you feel more un-vulnerable than knowing that you DO NOT HAVE TO MAKE A MORTGAGE PAYMENT. No one can foreclose on you and take your home away. Your increased sense of security is at least as important as the monetary returns of any strategy.

When you own your house outright, you are insulated from the stresses of potential layoffs, inflation and all the other bad things that can happen in the economy. If all you have to bring in each month is enough money to eat and pay the light bill, you are much less threatened by turns of events that emotionally paralyze other people. Just this reduction in stress could literally add years to your life...**and they will be _fun_ years.**

And do not worry about the loss of your mortgage interest tax deduction, or concern yourself with any other tax consequences. This is a strategy designed to make you completely independent in the shortest period of time, which will put a lot more money back in your hands than will saving a few pennies on your taxes. Once you understand where your money is really going you will realize that the same people who try to steal all your wealth through interest charges also want you to waste all your time being distracted by the tax consequences of how you use your money. They don't want you to figure out that interest can take as much of your money as taxes do over your lifetime.

Besides, if you are like most Americans, you don't have much to tax-shelter anyway. Wait till you really have something to protect, then concern yourself with tax-reduction tactics.

Notes

Key Points	Details

Later we will focus on some less obvious methods for reducing expenses, but for now consider all the ways that come to your mind on how you can trim your expenditures — to maximize the amount you can put into the payoff process.

Look for ways to reduce your insurance premiums, your car payment, possibly your house payment, your food and entertainment expenses, and even ways to save money when you are buying clothes and other personal and household needs.

The bottom line for this stage of the strategy is to focus ALL AVAILABLE MONEY into your bill payoff process. This does not mean that you can't ever go to the show or out to dinner. What it does mean is that you must understand the trade-offs. If you go out to dinner, that might mean adding a month onto the payoff time-line for a certain bill — thereby delaying, to some extent, the day when you will be completely debt-FREE. If it is worth it to you to make that trade, go ahead.

On the other hand, beware of the initial urge to shut off all forms of fun completely. You will get frustrated and quit your plan entirely. Be willing to indulge yourself now and again — just KNOW what you are trading and make sure it is worth it to you.

By the way, at Financial Independence Network Limited, we publish a companion newsletter to this book. It too is called *Debt-FREE & Prosperous Living*, and it provides an ongoing, training and information base to its subscribers. The way we see it, this book provides the overall *strategy* and the monthly newsletter provides the ongoing *tactics* to most successfully implement the *Financial Freedom Strategy* in your life.

If you didn't receive information about subscribing to the *Debt-FREE & Prosperous Living* newsletter when you got this book, you can call and request a FREE information package from our offices at 1-800-321-FINL.

Reduce All Your Spending to the Minimum

Notes

Key Points	Details

PHASE 2

Operate on a *Strictly-CASH* Basis

You will NEVER need credit again! Within months of paying off your debts — by investing what had been going to debt-elimination payments — you will become your own bank...your own credit card company, so you will never need to use the "Other Guys" again.

We have been taught in this economy to believe in credit. In fact, **we have been indoctrinated that we cannot live without credit**. Every step of the way we are told to get and keep a "good credit rating." Why? So we can get more credit, that's why.

But the actual truth is that credit is not your friend. Yes, you probably will need it to buy your first home. But even that could be accomplished without credit if you had sufficient patience.

Think about this for a moment: **WHEN SOMEONE OFFERS YOU CREDIT — THEY ARE NOT <u>GIVING</u> YOU ANYTHING.** If they offer you a $5,000 Gold Visa card, THEY ARE NOT GIVING YOU $5,000. They are not adding a single dime into your life. They are simply moving up the date at which you can spend money that YOU WILL HAVE TO EARN — and then charging you a terrible price (also money you will have to earn) for letting you "use" $5,000 of their money

So, the net effect is that — when someone offers you credit — they will actually REDUCE, not add to, the money will have to spend OVER YOUR LIFETIME.

Notes

Key Points	Details

Credit does only one thing: **it takes <u>more</u> money away from you** than the actual value (purchase price) of the thing you buy on credit. Usually a lot more. And that extra money you are giving to the credit company is the same money that should be invested to produce your future retirement income.

That is the sad reality of it. People are literally giving away their future (retirement) wealth — to have a few extra "Things" right now. But the true cost of using credit is much greater than they think. So they drown in credit interest and wake up one day, old and wanting to stop working, only to realize that they cannot stop — because they still owe more and more interest on more and more debt.

The Internal Revenue Service conducts an ongoing study of people who reach retirement age with little or nothing — financial failures. And **the <u>number one</u> reason cited by these people as the cause of their financial ruin was THEIR INABILITY TO DELAY GRATIFICATION**. In other words, they had to have everything RIGHT NOW instead of waiting until they could afford it. So they bought it on credit, <u>and gave away their futures</u>.

But it does not have to be that way for you, because once you break the credit habit, you are free to operate totally on cash — and invest thousands for your happy retirement.

What It's Like to Operate on CASH

You'll begin to see the benefits of operating 100% on cash even before you pay off your mortgage. Imagine that you have paid off all your charge account debts, and you are paying off your mortgage balance by adding in all the dollars that used to be wasted each month on credit account payments. Then one day the washing machine breaks.

Here is where most people would pull out a credit card to get it repaired, but you will just take the money you were going to add to your mortgage payment that month and <u>use it to pay cash</u> for the washing machine repair.

Notes

Key Points	Details

Now imagine that you have paid off your mortgage and you are putting ALL the money that used to be wasted on revolving credit debt and your mortgage payments into investments. Then suppose your car dies.

Here is where most people would crawl to the bank and apply for a car loan, but you just hold off on your investments for one month and <u>buy a good used car for cash</u>. Or, if necessary, you pull a little out of your liquid investment account and <u>buy a better car — CASH</u>.

Let's go for broke. Imagine that you want to buy a new home.

Here is where most people grovel into the mortgage company offices, beg for awhile, and show everything but their blood tests to prove that they are worthy of paying hundreds of thousands of dollars in pure profit to the mortgage company for the privilege of using some of their money. <u>But you just sell the house that you now own 100%, add a little from your liquid investment account (if necessary) and buy your new home CASH</u>.

Then, the next month, you go right back to putting the full amount into your investments again.

What About Impulse Buying?

Impulse buying is one of the most wealth-draining habits Americans get into. I call it "Malling," because that's where it most frequently takes place. You know, the *"I've had a tough week so I deserve to buy myself something"* syndrome. And, because it's so easy and painless, you flop down the old credit card to pay for it.

Well, you will find that it is much harder to spend cash on something you don't really need than it was to just whip out the plastic to buy it. But if you really need...or even really <u>want</u> something...you *can* buy it cash at this stage of your financial life. And what freedom that will be, because you can fully enjoy each purchase without the nagging pressure and guilt of having to pay for it for months and years into the future.

Notes

Key Points	Details

Let me give you an example of what I mean by "nagging pressure." Suppose you bought $2,000 worth of furniture on a typical* credit card, and paid only the minimum monthly payments requested by the credit card company, it would take you **31 years and 2 months** to pay it off. Plus — in addition to the original $2,000 cost for the furniture — **you would have paid $8,202 in interest!** Long after you had thrown the furniture out, you would be draining your wealth away paying for it.

In this example, using a credit card would cause you to pay **FIVE TIMES the furniture's value!** And you would have to work, many extra months, to earn the $8,202 — just to help build the wealth of the credit card company rather than your own wealth. Doesn't it make you mad when you see these numbers, and realize that they are being used against YOU right now?

When you operate on cash, the process becomes its own buying regulator. You will think longer and harder about each purchase, and you will therefore be a lot less likely to buy things you do not need. And when you do buy something, it will be only the size or amount necessary — because you will be feeling the full payment at the time of purchase rather than in little bite-sized pieces over the next several decades of bill paying.

* **19.8% interest with a $40 annual fee**

How Bad It Really Is to Use Credit Cards

Notes

Key Points	Details

PHASE 3

Then, Focus ALL Available Resources On Building Wealth

Once you have paid off all your debts, both credit accounts and home mortgage, you then want to take the same total amount you were paying on the bills and focus that into wealth-producing investments.

For starters, your wealth-building strategy should consider both *possibilities* and *probabilities*.

It is *possible* that something unforeseen might come up, like a breakdown in your car or a major appliance, so you should start the wealth-building process by putting about a half year's worth of required income into a liquid (easily convertible to cash) account such as a money market account or an assets management account. This way you can easily withdraw any amount you might need to meet an emergency. I use a *Schwab One* account from Charles Schwab & Co., Inc..

The *Schwab One* account lets you deposit money, then write checks against that money just like a bank. But the account is also a one-stop brokerage and portfolio management account for making and managing all the investments I will recommend later in this book, and in my monthly newsletter.

You can also get a Visa debit card with your *Schwab One* account. I will explain the important advantages of a debit card later. You can

Notes

Key Points	Details

manage your *Schwab One* account by either going into a local Schwab office, by using their *Telebroker®* automated telephone system, or by trading "on-line" with their *StreetSmart®* PC software system, which lets you buy and sell investments, get quotes or research financial information right from the convenience of your Personal Computer.

> **NOTE: I get nothing for recommending Schwab. It is simply that my entire *Financial Freedom Strategy* is based on the premise that you are like me, and do not want to have to deal with a lot of complexities to invest and build retirement wealth. I don't want to have to transact with each mutual fund company individually, yet I also do not want to pay full commissions for using a broker (Schwab offers over 200 popular mutual funds at zero commission). Other brokerage companies offer similar services, but I have looked around and have concluded that the *Schwab One* account offers the most services and conveniences, with the least complexity, at reasonable costs. For information about the *Schwab One* account, call 1-800-435-4000 any time night or day.**

Make sure that, which ever type of account you choose for your emergency cash fund that it is both interest-bearing and liquid (easily withdrawn). Next, you can begin concentrating ALL your investment money each month into less liquid but higher-growth investments. I recommend that you invest in mutual funds. These can be stock funds, bond funds or other types of investments that are managed by professionals with proven track records. I do not recommend that you do your own individual-stock investing. I have never met any nonprofessional investor who — over time — came out ahead of the better mutual fund managers.

Of course, if you find the research and drama of selecting your own investments to be rewarding, in and of itself, by all means...do it.

Some mutual funds have produced annual growth rates exceeding 40%. Of course, they occasionally have off years where they end up with negative growth (a nice way of saying the investors lost money). But overall, mutual funds do very well, and should provide you with true wealth-building power for your hard-earned money — while freeing you from having to personally research each individual company or security you might consider investing in.

The time-proven fact is that, over decades, you can't beat the money-growing power of the U.S. stock market — and the simplest way

Notes

Key Points	Details

for most people to invest in the market is through mutual funds.

> **NOTE: Throughout the investment stage of your *Financial Freedom Strategy* plan you will, of course, maintain the necessary insurance to cover you from catastrophic occurrences, such as a totalled car or open-heart surgery.**

What About Taxes on My Investments?

While you consider investments, also consider the effects of taxes on the growth of your investments. Many experts try to make this sound like an incredibly complex issue, but essentially there are three kinds of investments when it comes to this issue: tax-free (also called tax-exempt), tax-deferred and non-tax-deferred.

Tax-free investments are usually debt obligations of a governmental body. The most popular are tax-free municipal bonds. They are free from federal income taxes, and in some states they are free of state income taxes as well (called double tax-free). These investments yield lower returns than taxable investments, but you must consider the value of not having to pay the taxes on your growth.

Tax-deferred investments let the interest accumulate in your account without your having to pay current taxes on the interest income or capital gains. The most common forms of tax-deferred investment plan are the Individual Retirement Account (IRA), the Keogh (for self-employed) and the 401(k) plans offered by many employers. A tax-deferred plan should definitely be a part of your investment strategy, because the increased value of having the full interest compound each month is incredible (see the IRA growth table in Appendix E). It can make a difference of hundreds of thousands of dollars in your future wealth.

Tax-deferred investments usually come with some kind of tax penalty if you pull the money out before your retirement. The whole idea behind these types of investment products is that, when you normally begin withdrawing the money later in life, you will be in a lower income bracket and the taxes will therefore be lower than they would be if you

Notes

Key Points	Details

paid them now, when you are in your higher (than retirement) earning years. But you can be sure that YOU WILL PAY TAXES ON THE MONEY ONE WAY OR ANOTHER — AT ONE TIME OR ANOTHER.

The income taxes on non-tax-deferred investments must be paid in the tax year the gain is realized.

What you are after is maximum "After-Tax" growth in your wealth, so when you compare tax-free, tax-deferred and taxable investments, compare the after-tax gain on the taxable investment with the yield of the tax-favored investment.

When you figure out how much money you are blowing in interest by using credit cards, financing cars for 4 to 6 years, and paying out a 30-year mortgage, you will need smelling salts. But then when you see what that same money can do for you once it is rerouted in a direction where the compound interest works FOR you, you will have to be restrained so you don't hurt yourself bouncing off the ceiling.

Like I said earlier, when my wife and I worked out our debt-elimination and wealth-building plan we were at first angered by how much of our wealth the banks and mortgage company had been siphoning off. But then when we realized that THE SAME MONEY WE WERE ALREADY SPENDING EVERY MONTH COULD PAY OFF THE SAME HOUSE WE WERE ALREADY PAYING FOR — PLUS EARN US NEARLY $4 MILLION IN THE SAME AMOUNT OF TIME WE WOULD HAVE BEEN PAYING ON THE MORTGAGE, we felt like a thousand pound weight had been removed from our shoulders.

You see, the reason I had begun researching these systems and methods in the first place was that I had come to believe what I thought at the time was a fact: *that if I did not find some "magic bullet" to make me hundreds of thousands of dollars, I would probably have to keep working until the day I died.*

Here's Where the Money You Used to Waste on Credit Card, Auto and Mortgage Payments Can Make You Rich

Notes

Key Points	Details

What scared me was that I was already making good money — but no matter how much I earned, we still seemed to be constantly bouncing off the bottom. We had a nicer TV and newer cars, but we were still not financially independent. We were still just living from month to month.

In fact, we were actually worse off than when I had made less money, because now we had larger payments and bigger balances on everything. This meant that I was trapped — I <u>had to continue bringing in BIG BUCKS</u> just to pay the bills...just to keep what we had...and little or nothing was building for the future.

This was REAL pressure, because I knew that I had to maintain this high income level at all costs, or we would be in serious trouble. I was definitely not feeling financially "Independent." In fact, I was feeling even more *dependent* than when I had a smaller income. I was feeling **<u>vulnerable</u>** to the economy, to my employer, to anything that could upset my income stream.

Then, when developed this system and discovered that there really was a WAY to achieve financial independence — a way that did not even require a bunch of extra money, but was simply a method of redirecting the money we were already bringing in — I got excited. It was a system that could not only get us out of debt, but could make us rich — USING THE INCOME WE WERE ALREADY MAKING. For the first time I felt like we really had a chance to live out the kind of future we had hardly dared dream about before.

And then I realized that a side benefit of the strategy was that I WOULD NEVER NEED CREDIT AGAIN.

Sound Like a Dream?

It's not a dream.

Never needing credit is just the way that people who are not up to their necks in debt can live. In fact, <u>in most situations, people using cash can live better than people operating on credit</u>.

Notes

Key Points	Details

Did you ever hear the saying, "Money Talks?"

It really does...when it's real money. It is not nearly so loud when you have to ask for financing. But if you have the dough, you can often strike bargains that are never available to the credit addict.

Just as a recent example: I bought a Pontiac Grand Prix a few months ago, from a dealer — and **I got it for HALF PRICE!** I know that I only paid half price, because I verified it with *Consumer Reports* magazine's auto pricing service.

I got the car, which was used but in nearly-new condition, for half price because I stood in the dealership with my CHECKBOOK. I tapped the checkbook on the salesman's desk and said, *"I'm going to write a check to buy a car today. Now I can write the check here...or I can walk across the street and write a check at the dealer over there. You decide."*

Well...they decided alright. They decided to not let real money get out the door, and I drove away in a wonderful car with all the trimmings — FOR HALF PRICE! Someone interested in that same car — but asking for bank financing — would have had no bargaining leverage, so they would have paid nearly the asking price. Then they would have been taken to the cleaners with the finance charges, and ended up paying thousands more than I did for the same car.

CASH IS KING!

Even when it comes to buying homes...or maybe I should say ESPECIALLY when it comes to buying homes.

In today's economy, more and more people are losing their homes. This is not your fault, but it could be your good fortune...if you have CASH. You can visit the sheriff's tax sales in your county (or parish in Louisiana) and often buy homes for pennies on the dollar. Some of these houses are incredible values, and when you've bought one, YOU OWN IT. You continue to operate on cash, with no mortgage payments.

Watch your local newspaper for auctions. You would be amazed what you can buy at these sales, IF YOU HAVE CASH. You could easily furnish a home, buy a car, buy a boat, buy computers or almost anything else you can imagine. But it all goes to the man or woman with cash.

Notes

Key Points	Details

When you are in debt, you are actually forced to live like you make LESS income than you actually do — because when you made those credit purchases in the past, you committed a portion of the income you are making today.

So, if eighty percent of your after-tax income goes to credit debt payments (including your house), **those purchases from the past are forcing you to live on only twenty percent of your present income.** Someone who is completely debt-FREE, and making exactly the same income as you, has that eighty percent to spend or invest. **They get to live on 100%, because they operate on CASH.**

However, before you can get to the cash stage, you have to move through the bill and mortgage elimination stages. And there are some significant obstacles to watch out for. The obstacles that helped get you into the dilemma you are in today.

Our economic "system" in this country has trained us to think in terms of monthly payments. When we go to buy a TV set, or a car, or even a home, we think in terms of how much of a monthly payment can we afford. This gets us in deep, deep trouble.

You see, we don't even think about the overall cost of the purchase. Is it good for us? Are we being ripped off? Is it absurd to pay 21% interest on a TV, or to pay nearly three times for our home over the course of a 30-year mortgage?

And you know why we never think beyond the monthly payment?

Because, *"Everyone's buying with monthly payments, so it must be the right thing to do. Dad bought his cars and the house I grew up in this way, so it must be right. Shucks, everyone pays 30 years for a house. How else could anyone afford one...huh?"*

I had a friend once tell me that — if they had offered him ten-year

Using Credit Actually LOWERS Your Standard of Living

The Monthly Payment Trap

Notes

Key Points	Details

financing on a recently purchased new car — he probably would have taken it, because it would have given him lower MONTHLY PAYMENTS.

We go out into the marketplace to buy something and the only two numbers we consider are our monthly income and the total of our monthly expenses. Or we look at a specific credit card to see how much room there is before we go over our limit. Whatever is left over is SPENDABLE CREDIT! It is almost like it is our patriotic duty to keep our monthly payments equal to our income.

Merchants and the money-lending companies behind them have us trained to look at the wrong part of the equation. Read my lips: **IT DOES MATTER HOW MUCH THE TOTAL COST IS!** It matters to your future wealth, and it matters more than you probably imagine.

As I write this page, I am looking at a full-color insert that a local Chicago-area furniture store stuffed in the Sunday paper. For each suite of furniture there are big red numbers that give a monthly payment...with a little cross after the number. Then, if you search, you find...in tiny black numbers...the full price. At the bottom of the front page, in big yellow letters in a bright red box, it says "NO MONEY DOWN."

This ad typifies how merchants use our "monthly payment" and "Gotta have it now" weaknesses against us.

First of all, the meaning of the little cross after each bright red monthly payment amount is found in a small patch of ridiculously small print at the bottom of the last page of this mini catalog. There we find that the "Low Monthly Payments" are based on an Annual Percentage Rate interest of **31.5%**! Then, to add insult to injury, the "Low Monthly Payments" also require **10% down!**

But didn't they say "NO MONEY DOWN" on the front page? Yep. They just sort of lied...that's all. On the same page where, in bright

That is Absolutely the WRONG Way to Look at it

Notes

Key Points	Details

letters, they say "NO MONEY DOWN," they also show me "low monthly payments" that require a down-payment! Of course, I am not supposed to really find this out until I'm in the showroom, where the salesperson will have me in a headlock...while my wife is saying, *"Oh, honey, wouldn't this look great in our bedroom?"*

And...if I ever get around to reading the fine print on the sales contract, that is where I would probably discover the **31.5% interest rate.** But, by then both my wife and I are envisioning the wonderful (junk) furniture in our home, and we're too psyched up to be put off by the interest rate on the "low monthly payments."

Let's examine one example from their catalog, a bedroom set that has a "Low Monthly Payment" of "ONLY $54.51 per month." Right next to that it says, "SALE...$949" in itsy-bitsy letters. Well, thanks to their **31.5% interest rate**, I would end up paying $1,253.50 for that $949 bedroom set — over 23 months. **That is an extra $304.50 in interest — just for using their "Easy Monthly Payments!"**

Think about this: **EVERY PENNY OF INTEREST YOU PAY IS MONEY YOU HAVE TO EARN...MONEY THAT SHOULD BE CONTRIBUTING TO YOUR WEALTH...BUT INSTEAD YOU ARE DONATING IT TO THE WEALTH-BUILDING OF THE BANK OR FINANCE COMPANY.** Do you really think that they deserve it more than you and your family do?

The bottom-line truth is that **you are only going to be able to create a certain amount of wealth in your life**, and you cannot afford to waste ANY of that wealth-creation power on making banks rich. You need to keep as much of it as possible for yourself!

It still amazes me when I think back about how I would routinely sign mortgage papers, reading the financing disclosure pages that told me how much interest I would be paying over the life of the loan — and I never seemed to wonder how I would replace the hundreds of thousands of dollars I was promising the mortgage company.

You know — two hundred thousand dollars is not that easy to come by. And I'm sure that I could find better uses for it than the mortgage company could. Of course, now I know that using financing was damaging both my short- and long-term financial interests. Credit stinks!

Notes

Key Points	Details

And if that is not clear enough, let me state for the record that — with the possible exception of getting your hands on your first home — you DO NOT EVER WANT TO USE CREDIT FOR ANYTHING.

President Reagan was not quite right when he used to say that Communism was the focus of all evil in the world. I believe that Credit is the focus of all evil. I have seen debt crush more people, ruin more marriages, destroy more healthy minds and bodies, and shorten more lives than anything else I have witnessed in my time.

And maybe more tragic, I have seen the stress of bills demand so much attention from people that they never find the time or mental freedom to enjoy all the good people and things God has placed in their lives.

Notes

Key Points	Details

Part Two — The Specifics

Now we're going to start putting the philosophy we've been discussing to work The first step in applying the Financial Freedom Strategy is to find your initial *"Accelerator Margin."* This is the money that will prime your debt payoff pump. It is buried in your current monthly expenditures, and in the savings opportunities we will discuss in this manual, and which we also teach about in our monthly *Debt-FREE & Prosperous Living* newsletter.

The *Accelerator Margin* does not have to be a lot of money. It is like the snowball that you begin rolling down hill. By the time you get to the bottom, it has become a boulder-sized ball that you can make a snowman with. But it all started with a little snowball.

The amount you are shooting for in putting together your *Accelerator Margin* is 10% of your net, monthly, household income. In other words, if you bring home $2,000 a month, you are trying to put together a $200 *Accelerator Margin*. If you think you *cannot* afford that, keep reading and we will show you how it can be done. On the other hand, if you can afford more, DO IT. This is not a game you want to stretch out. The goal is to pay off ALL debts in the shortest period of time. That is the fastest track to true financial independence.

Let's first look at places where extra money might be hidden, in wasted purchases or monthly expenditures. As we mentioned before, you can blow a lot of money just in the way you buy your car(s), your home, and your insurance. So we will concentrate on these, because they offer the highest monthly potential for finding hidden *Accelerator Margin* money.

Step One Towards Debt Elimination

Notes

Key Points	Details

Obviously, you do not buy a car every day, but you probably will buy one at some point over the next few years, and what I'm sharing with you is a "Lifetime Strategy." I am therefore including some tips on how NOT to buy a car, so when you do...you won't simply hand over thousands of dollars that should be building <u>your</u> economic freedom. Most car dealers are plenty rich enough without your tossing your hard-earned money on their pile.

Here we go:

1. Don't ever buy a brand new car. Buy nothing newer than two years old. *The reason:* a new car loses nearly half its value in the first two years. Yet you can buy two-year-old cars that are in "Like-New" condition, and with plenty of life left in them. Plus, the first owner will get all the bugs worked out under the warranty. Let the poor sucker who bought it new take the 50% bath on the car's depreciation — not you. Buying a brand new car is simply throwing thousands of dollars down the chute. If you are hooked on new-car smell, they sell spray cans of the stuff at auto-parts stores.

2. Do not ever take more than 36 months financing on a car. I offer this tip with some reservation. My first suggestion is to NEVER buy a car with borrowed money. But if you are absolutely stuck, and must take a loan out — do not let it be for more than 36 months. People who take longer loans always owe more than the car is worth, until the last few months. Later in the book I will show you how to <u>pay off</u> your car loans — and my advice is to NEVER FINANCE ANOTHER ONE AS LONG AS YOU LIVE.

3. Do not ever take "Credit Life Insurance" on a car loan or a mortgage. This is incredible, if you really think it through. The car dealer or mortgage company is asking <u>you</u> to pay for an insurance policy on which <u>THE BANK is the beneficiary</u>, and on which the dealer or mortgage company makes a commission when they sell it to you. **You can better protect your heirs with a term life insurance policy that will produce enough money to pay off the car(s) and the house.** And if you already have credit life, (check all your loan papers) CANCEL IT. When you do, watch how your monthly payments **drop**. THAT IS ACCELERATOR MARGIN MONEY — ADD IT INTO THE MONEY YOU WILL PAY OFF YOUR BILLS WITH.

Notes

Key Points	Details

NOTE: whenever I recommend that you cancel any insurance, for which I also indicate a more cost-effective replacement (as I did in #3 above), ALWAYS GET THE REPLACEMENT POLICY IN FORCE <u>BEFORE</u> YOU CANCEL THE COVERAGE YOU WILL BE DROPPING.

4. Never take ANY Extended Warranties of any kind. Like most other forms of insurance, warranty policies are never likely to be needed by the person paying for them. If it was likely that your car, stereo, washer, microwave, TV would have the troubles covered by the warranty, THEY WOULD NOT SELL IT TO YOU. And if a salesperson tries to make it sound like a warranty is *"Free,"* ask them specifically if there is ANY charge to you for that coverage — either up front or in your payments. Cancel ALL extended warranties and get refunds for the unused time on them. I used to buy extended warranties on everything I purchased, until one day I realized that...I HAVE NEVER MADE A CLAIM ON ONE IN MY ENTIRE LIFE. With savings I have since realized, I could afford to fix any of the once-covered products that might break.

5. Do not buy ANY after-market products or services from a car dealer. <u>Cars come from the factory with rust protection already on them,</u> so do not get talked into buying undercoating or any other rust protection. And if you see anything on the sticker like, "Market Adjustment" that is just a secret name for **additional pure profit** for the dealer. It has NO VALUE to you, you get nothing for this money. Avoid buying dealer-installed sound systems. You can buy stereos a lot cheaper from electronics stores, and frequently get the installation for Free. You should <u>never</u> pay any "Documentation Fees." This is the dealer actually charging YOU for his people to do the paperwork on your purchase. The dealer should also pay shipping, freight, delivery or "Prep" charges — NOT YOU.

6. Life Insurance. The purpose of life insurance is NOT to make your survivors rich should you die. It is to assure them a continuance of your income stream, should you stop producing it yourself. What you want to do is buy pure "Term" life insurance, with a sufficient death benefit that it would generate your present monthly income if it were invested in a good mutual fund. The next step is to put together a Trust (your banker or lawyer can help) that will be the beneficiary of your life insurance. The trust will

Notes

Key Points	Details

invest the money from your insurance policy, and pay your survivors the monthly interest as a continuation of your income stream. By the way, once you have sufficient investments to produce the required income stream should you die, YOU WILL NO LONGER NEED LIFE INSURANCE.

NEVER, NEVER, NEVER consider any kind of insurance that supposedly builds a cash value or contains an investment program along with the life benefit. "Whole Life" or any other type of "Cash Value" life insurance is one of the most incredible legal rip-offs I have ever come across. Most people do not know this, but the Cash Value that you build up in a whole life policy over the years BELONGS TO THE INSURANCE COMPANY —NOT TO YOU OR YOUR BENEFICIARIES! Do you believe that? They sell it to you like you are building up an investment, but if you want to touch any of the "cash" you have to **Borrow** it, and pay it back **with interest**. And when you die, they do not pay your survivors the policy's death benefit PLUS the cash value you have supposedly built up. They just pay the death benefit...AND KEEP THE CASH VALUE. The reason they sell "Cash Value" or other "Investment" types of life insurance so hard is that they are COMMISSION RICH policies to sell. There isn't nearly as much commission to be made on selling Term insurance.

Just remember it this way: ALL types of "Cash Value" or "Universal Life" policies are bad for your wealth building. You can do much better by buying the best value term policy for the coverage you really need, and **investing the rest into your debt-elimination and wealth-building plan**.

7. It is the same with automobile insurance. If you naively accept all the coverages your insurance agent starts suggesting, you will likely end up paying hundreds of dollars a year more than you need to. Insurance companies have many crafty ways of making you pay twice for the SAME coverage. **For example:** "Uninsured and Under-insured Motorist" coverage. This is your insurance company getting you to pay premiums for coverage you are probably already paying for under the "Medical" section of your policy. Let me quote from State Farm Insurance's Car Policy booklet (I have State Farm insurance) under the description for UNINSURED MOTOR VEHICLE - COVERAGE U: "We will pay damages for **bodily injury** an insured is legally entitled to

Notes

Key Points	Details

collect..." Now I'll quote from the same booklet under MEDICAL EXPENSES - COVERAGE C: "We will pay reasonable medical expenses, for ***bodily injury*** caused by accident..." Sounds awfully familiar doesn't it? It seems to me that your "Medical" coverage would suffice — and that asking you pay a separate premium to cover the same ***bodily injury*** expenses, simply because those injuries are the fault of an uninsured or underinsured motorist, is putting double burden on you, the policyholder, to guarantee the insurance company twice the premiums to pay for the same injuries. What your insurance company is actually saying here is that — if the other motorist is at fault...and they have insurance... they would have to pay for your injuries. But, since they don't have insurance, your insurance company will have to pay — and they don't like that. So they're going to make YOU pay premiums for bodily injury coverage that <u>the other motorist isn't willing to pay for</u>...to make sure that your insurance company doesn't lose any money on the deal. You're being penalized for being the good guy who carries proper car insurance.

NOTE: Many states mandate Uninsured Motorist and Underinsured Motorist minimum coverages. <u>Make sure that you obey these laws</u>. Also, Uninsured/ Underinsured Motorist coverage may allow you to recover other damages resulting from an accident with an uninsured person, such as loss of income. Such an accident is probably unlikely, but if this one area of coverage is important to you, then you may want to maintain higher UM coverages. It's a matter of "which way do you want to bet?" As in other examples, let me remind you that you should never drop a coverage until you have compensating coverage IN FORCE <u>before</u> you cancel the existing coverage. I personally carry the minimum Uninsured/Underinsured Motorist coverage mandated by Illinois law.

Now let's talk about the "Medical" coverage on your car insurance policy. You likely already have a medical (health insurance) policy that covers you and your family <u>both in and out of the car — 24 hours a day</u>. Non-dependents that might be hurt in your vehicle would be taken care of by the liability portion of your policy, so — if you have a solid health insurance package, the "Medical" coverages on your car insurance may well be redundant. You can only get repaired of your bodily injuries once, yet — if you have health insurance at work, "Medical" coverage on your car insurance and "Uninsured/Underinsured" coverage on your

Notes

Key Points	Details

car insurance — YOU WILL BE INSURED THREE TIMES TO COVER THE ONE SET OF EXPENSES! And YOU will be paying for at least two of them on your car insurance.

Your agent will probably also recommend "Road Service" and "Rental Car" coverages, because they know you will never even remember you have them should you get into the highly unlikely situations where these coverages would actually pay you anything. Most people either have Road Service coverage through an auto club, they flat forget they have this coverage on their car insurance, or — most likely — they never need it. The "Rental Car" coverage is of almost no value, because it pays so little (State Farm pays $10 a day) and because it is frequently a duplication of coverage provided under the "Comprehensive" coverage on the same policy.

8. Personal liability insurance. You are probably carrying a couple of separate liability coverages, one on your auto and another on your home owner's policy. The purpose of liability insurance is so that — should you or your property injure someone to the point where they would sue you — the insurance would pay rather than the court ordering you to sell your home and other assets to satisfy the judgement against you. Generally speaking, unless there are unusual circumstances involved, you probably only need liability coverage equal to about <u>twice your networth</u> — to make your insurance twice as attractive as your home and other possessions to a potential plaintiff. And you want the highest deductibles available, so as to keep the premiums to a minimum. Do not waste premium money betting that you <u>will</u> have an accident or liability claim. Bet that you will not — the insurance company is betting you won't...and they are rarely wrong.

If you have your auto and home-owner's insurance through the same company, look into dropping your auto and home liability coverages to the minimums allowed and getting a $1 million "Umbrella" liability policy that will cover you under all circumstances.

I made ALL OF THE ABOVE changes in my auto and liability coverages during lunch one day, and I am saving $261 a year — while maintaining more than adequate protection.

Notes

Key Points	Details

9. Medical insurance is the same. If you pay for part or all of your medical (health) insurance coverage, <u>take the highest possible deductible you can stand</u>. Unless you or a family member is particularly prone to illness, all you really need medical insurance for is to protect you from the huge bills that can come from a major illness. Bills that could drain your savings and investments. If you insist on having coverage that will pay for every sniffle — YOU WILL <u>REALLY</u> PAY THROUGH THE NOSE! In most cases, the increased premiums you will pay over a year, for a lower deductible or for more coverage, will cost you more than carrying a higher deductible and covering your incidental medical expenses yourself would cost.

These are just a few suggestions of areas where I know you are paying more each month than you have to. And every dollar you are wasting on these excess expenditures is a dollar that is not currently free to be in your *Accelerator Margin*.

Once you see how much just a few extra *Accelerator Margin* dollars can speed up your debt elimination, you will become as ruthless as I am to find every possible penny. Besides, it is YOUR money. Why should you give one penny more than you must to anyone other than to you and your loved ones?

Look at every expense area you have. Are you really using all the premium (extra charge) Cable TV channels you are paying for each month? Could you brown-bag it to lunch more often than you do? Do you pay someone to cut the grass or shovel the snow, when you could do it yourself? Are you paying $25 to have JiffyLube change your oil, when you could do it for less than half that. Are you paying a premium to eat frozen/precooked meals, when you could cook more nutritious meals from scratch — for a fraction of the cost? Are you paying full price for all your groceries, when your weekly newspaper is stuffed with discount coupons?

I am not talking about living like a Tibetan Monk. I am just suggesting that there is money flowing out of your hands each month that could get you out of debt faster. If it is worth it to you to become truly debt-FREE, find it.

I'll give you a tool to help you find unnecessary expenditures: it's called **CIA**. No, that doesn't stand for Central Intelligence Agency. It

Notes

Key Points	Details

represents **Convenience, Indulgence** and **Appearance**.

We waste money on **Conveniences** like eating the expensive frozen prepared meals instead of making less expensive meals ourselves. When we pay other to do tasks that we could easily do much more cheaply ourselves. When we take the kids to McDonalds after the little league game instead of making a snack at home. When we waste $5 a day on eating lunch outside of work, rather than taking a few minutes to make a lunch to take to work in the morning.

We waste money on **Indulgences** when we go to the mall after a hard day or week, because we "deserve" some kind of treat. That treat generally uses up money we really don't *need* to spend — and it is frequently charged on a credit card, which makes the cost higher and the indulgence more damaging. We indulge ourselves with expensive credit-card dinners (again usually prompted by a hard week). We waste money on indulgences when we buy expensive toys, usually on credit, to help us make up for the "tough" life we live. These indulgences drain more from the average American's financial resources than they might imagine. Most people are stunned when they research and compile indulgences expenditures.

We waste money on **Appearances** when we try to keep up with the Joneses. Let me tell you something — the Joneses are going bankrupt. Everything they have is in hock, and if they lost their income, they would probably be homeless in a month or two. They are living an illusion, and you will be too if you try to compete with them. Forget trying to impress people with your possessions. Wait until you're retired early — then they'll really be impressed!

Examine your life ruthlessly, to see where you are wasting money on **CIA**, and eliminate those wastes. You will probably be able to find the majority of your *Accelerator Margin* from this examination alone.

Notes

Key Points	Details

Before I tell you how to pay off all the bills you have, let us make sure that you cannot make any more. **CUT UP AND THROW AWAY <u>ALL</u> YOUR CREDIT CARDS**, with the possible exception of travel cards that cannot carry a balance (like *American Express*) and gasoline cards for road emergencies when you do not have cash with you. But NEVER, NEVER, NEVER ADD TO THE ROLLING BALANCES OF THESE GAS CARDS.

<u>**There is NO justification for keeping the credit cards — NONE.**</u> If you find yourself trying to make excuses, think of how an alcoholic would sound explaining why they should be able to keep a fully-stocked bar...WHILE THEY ARE SIMULTANEOUSLY TRYING TO GIVE UP LIQUOR! **GIVE UP THE PLASTIC!**

You'll hear yourself using the old *"What if an emergency comes up"* excuse, or the *"I just use them during the month, then pay them off as soon as the bill comes in"* reason. Later I'll be showing you how you will be able to handle emergencies without the help of Visa or MasterCard. And I'll be giving you alternative ways to have the convenience of a credit card without the ability to get into debt.

In terms of the *"I pay the full bill off when it comes in"* argument, the truth is that using a credit card — even with the intention of paying the whole thing off when it comes in — frequently causes people to spend more than they would if they were writing a check or laying down cash, because plopping down the plastic is TOO PAINLESS, and too convenient for impulse buying. Impulse buying hurts your financial health.

> **DEFINITION: For the purposes of this course, a *"Bill"* is a debt <u>that can be completely paid off</u>. Monthly, ongoing costs such as utilities are *"Expenses,"* and although you want to minimize them, they are not to be included in this debt-elimination program, because they can never be totally paid off.**

Paying Off Your Bills — Including Your Mortgage

Notes

Key Points	Details

The first thing you want to do is get all your bills together. Now write down each account's total balance and its corresponding required monthly payment on the ***Calculating Bill Payoff*** form in Appendix E at the back of this manual. When you have them all written down, divide the *"Total Balance"* amounts by their respective *"Monthly Payments"* and put the answers in column 4.

For example: let's say you have a Visa card with a $500 balance, and a minimum monthly payment of $25. You would divide $500 by $25 and get an answer of 20. The answer does not mean anything in and of itself, but it is the first step in determining the proper order in which to pay off all your bills.

Do this for each bill, and mark the answer to each division in the appropriate column-4 box on the ***Bill Payoff*** form.

Next, starting with the lowest division answer, number the bills from "1" to whatever number of bills you have to pay off. Put these answers in the *"Priority"* column. For example, if you had two bills (say the Visa above and a department store charge) — and the Visa division gave you the answer of 20, while the other came out at 17 — the department store account would be number "1" and the Visa account number "2".

These numbers indicate the order in which you should pay off your bills. You would pay off the department store first and the Visa account second.

You do not care which account has the highest interest rate, because this system so accelerates bill payoff that you will not be paying enough months of interest for it to make a significant difference. <u>You are going to beat the banks at their interest game, and turn off the blood they have been sucking out of your financial life</u>.

Notes

Key Points	Details

OK, it is time to start rolling the bill-payoff snowball down hill.

Add the full *"Accelerator Margin"* you have accumulated to the regular payment **for bill number "1"** each month until the bill is completely paid off. For example, if you put together a $200 *Accelerator Margin* and added it to the Visa account we talked about above, you would completely pay the bill off in just over two months! **Imagine, a bill that you would normally be adding to and paying down for the rest of your life could be GONE in just over two months**.

Even if you could only add a $100 *Accelerator Margin*, the Visa bill would be completely paid off in just four months.

Then the next month you take ALL of what you had been paying on the Visa account, the $200 *Accelerator Margin* plus the $25 normal Visa payment, and you add all of it ($225) to the regular payment of bill number "2". If that bill had a monthly payment of say $50, you would be paying a total of $275 each month on that bill. It too would likely be gone in a few months, and you would then be adding the full $275 to the payment of bill number 3 — and so on down through all your consumer credit bills.

By the time you get to larger bills, like your car payment, your *Accelerator Margin* will have grown to an impressive amount. Both you and whoever gave you your car loan will be amazed at how quickly you'll pay it off.

When you have knocked off all the regular revolving credit accounts, including any car payments, you will be ready for the big one — **your mortgage payment**. In many cases people have completely eliminated all their debt except their mortgage by the end of their first year on the plan. They will then frequently have an *Accelerator Margin* that is equal to their mortgage payment, sometimes as much as twice their mortgage payment.

Now Watch the Power of Mathematics Working For You

Notes

Key Points	Details

Don't be demoralized if it takes you a little longer to get through the bills that precede your mortgage. Many people take longer than a year to get to the mortgage and still end up debt-free in a total of between 5 and 6 years. **That still beats 30 years by a long shot!**

> **NOTE: Contact your mortgage company directly and ask for SPECIFIC instructions on how to make *additional principal prepayments* along with your regular monthly payment. Ask them to mail written guidelines to you if they have them. In most cases, the *Additional Principal Prepayment* forms in Appendix E will work.**

When you add your now-large *Accelerator Margin* to your mortgage, you'll begin knocking off principal at an incredible rate. Your equity in your home will skyrocket — for two reasons:

> **1. 100% of your Accelerator Margin is reducing your principal balance (adding to your equity — the portion of the house you own).**

> **2. The portion of your regular monthly payment that is interest will be falling dramatically, because it is calculated each month on the "remaining unpaid balance." Since your Accelerator Margin is pounding down this unpaid balance, the interest calculation will be performed each month on a smaller and smaller balance amount. So more and more of your regular monthly payment amount will also be applied to the unpaid balance, further accelerating the payoff process.**

When Will You Be Completely Debt-FREE?

To get a rough idea of how long it would take you to get completely out of debt — INCLUDING YOUR MORTGAGE — we will use the *Debt-Elimination Time Calculator* form in Appendix E.

First total up all your debt balances. This number, including your mortgage balance, will be an impressive amount. But you will be encouraged when you see what happens as we short-circuit the devastating

Notes

Key Points	Details

impact of compound interest working against you — by paying these bills off by the shortest mathematical route.

Next, total up ALL your monthly net income. Forget about what was going into savings, because you are going to <u>stop saving for right now</u>. I even recommend that you consider temporarily suspending any savings that are coming out of your paycheck at work and add that monthly amount to your *Accelerator Margin*. **You want to get as much monthly income working on the pay-down as possible.** Your money will do you a lot more good paying off 20% debt load than it will earning 5%, 6%, or 8% in savings.

> **NOTE: many people ask me about 401(k) plans they have at work. The 401(k) is a great retirement investment plan, because you're probably earning around 50% on your money just from your employer's contribution. Plus the growth of the total investment accumulates tax-deferred until you begin taking distributions in retirement. What I recommend is that you MINIMIZE the amount you are putting into your 401(k) until your debts are completely paid off, so you can use that monthly income for debt-elimination — THEN RAISE YOUR CONTRIBUTION TO THE MAXIMUM PERCENTAGE OF YOUR PAY THAT IS ALLOWED.**

Now locate your approximate total debt amount in the *Total Debt Amount* column, along the left edge of the *Debt-Elimination Time Calculator* chart in Appendix E. Then run your finger across to the right until you reach your approximate total monthly amount available for paying on ALL your bills — including your mortgage. This income amount should include both your *Accelerator Margin* and the normal minimum monthly payments on all your bills, <u>but not the money that will go towards non-debt, monthly expenses like food, utilities, gasoline and insurance</u>.

When you have located this monthly amount, follow that column up to the line at the top of the table and you will see the approximate number of years it will take you to get COMPLETELY OUT OF DEBT.

This chart will show you why you want to put the most you can into your monthly payoff *Accelerator Margin*. The lower the monthly amount you can muster against your total credit debt load, <u>the longer it will take you to pay it off</u>. **And the longer the payoff takes, the greater the portion of YOUR money that will be going towards interest rather than principal.**

Notes

Key Points	Details

Most people come out at around 5 years, but the more you can put into the process the shorter that time-frame. Let's see an example of how it might work:

If your debt, including your mortgage, totalled $100,000 — and the total monthly income (including all *Accelerator Margin* amounts) you had available for paying on your debt was $2,500 — you would first locate $100,000 in the left-most column, then look across to the right and find "2536". This is the amount closest to the $2,500 you have available each month. Then run your finger up to the top of that column and your answer is **4 years! All your debts — INCLUDING YOUR HOME — would be paid off in just 4 years.**

Be honest with yourself — what plan do you currently have, or have you ever heard about, that could get you totally debt-free in that short a time?

To get a handle on how brief that time is, simply think back four years. Doesn't it seem like just yesterday? Well that is how quickly you will be looking back and remembering how hard it was carrying your heavy load of debt around.

Another feeling you will have at that time is COMPLETE FREEDOM AND "UN-VULNERABILITY." That is not to say that you will quit your job or radically change your life. You might...you might not. The point is that, for the first time in your life, YOU WILL BE IN A POSITION TO MAKE THAT CHOICE.

No boss will be able to hold your job over your head, because you will not go bankrupt if you lose your job. You could easily live on unemployment or savings until you found other work, or you could even work at McDonald's, if you had to, and still be OK. Or maybe you'd just choose to move to a less-expensive area and start a home-based business. **The important thing is that the pressure would be off you, AND YOU'D HAVE OPTIONS.**

Think about how many people (maybe yourself included) are sweating out the economy, or their company's stability, all the time. According to a recent NBC television report, America has lost 25% of its jobs in just the last ten years, and is still losing 2,200 jobs every day!

People are nervous, uneasy, stressed.

Notes

Key Points	Details

Layoffs start coming around and people panic because they know that **they cannot survive without their <u>whole</u> paycheck <u>every month</u>.** But when you have no debts, all you need to worry about is eating, heating and paying taxes. That takes a lot less money each month than you are spending now, so even a small savings account could sustain you for a relatively long period of time. No need to panic.

Once you begin building your investments — WHICH STARTS HAPPENING THE MONTH AFTER YOUR MORTGAGE IS GONE — you will quickly build up a more-than-sufficient emergency reserve. After just a few months, you'll have as much in the bank as any credit card would ever offer you as a credit line — so you can be your own credit card or bank from that moment on. By the end of the first year, you'll have more in your savings and investments than you probably dare to dream of right now.

As I mentioned earlier, when my wife and I first worked out our plan, we were stunned. If we would continue paying our bills and our house according to the way good little consumers are supposed to — 26 years down the road we would own our home and have maybe (I'm being optimistic) $100,000 put away.

<u>Taking the same money</u>, but using our debt-elimination and wealth-building strategy — 26 years down the road we will <u>own the same house</u>, plus have **$3.8 million in investments!** All this with the SAME MONEY WE EARN AND SPEND RIGHT NOW! You pay it out one way and you end up with the house and a little money (maybe). Pay the same money out the *Financial Freedom Strategy* way and you end up with the SAME HOUSE, <u>and you are a millionaire</u>.

Which way would you choose?

That's what I thought.

Now let's get back to your bill payoff plan. Once you have worked out your *Accelerator Margin*, plot out how long it will take to pay off the first bill, then how long it will take to pay off the next bill, with all the money continuing to roll down the list against subsequent bills. Record the date that each bill will be gone in column 6 on the ***Calculating Bill Payoff Order*** form in Appendix E. Then go to the ***Your Wealth-Building Plan*** form in Appendix E and calculate the date that you will be COMPLETELY <u>DEBT-FREE</u>.

Notes

Key Points	Details

You should track your progress every month against this ***Bill Payoff Order*** schedule. This will help you to avoid frittering away money on nonessentials, while you *think* you are paying off your bills. If you know when a bill is supposed to be paid off — and it is not — you know that you have been undisciplined in following your plan (or you had an emergency that required the *Accelerator Margin* that month). And you know exactly how far off schedule you are. Remember, our goal is not to fool ourselves into thinking that we are addressing the problem — it is to GET THE JOB DONE!

Assuming that you will follow your payoff plan, you will soon be in a position to say *"Good-bye Forever"* to credit, credit ratings, and all the headaches and humiliation that go with credit.

By the way, DO NOT let yourself slip into the negative emotional trap that *"this is some kind of super-restrictive BUDGET."* This is not a *budget* — it is a *spending plan* or a *resource allocation plan* that simply guides you in how to best *use* your financial resources. It is not a *restrictive* approach to using money, but rather it is an *aggressive* approach to building a future of YOUR OWN design. Most importantly, it is making you "Un-vulnerable," and eventually...Rich.

You are NOT giving things up. In fact, you are GAINING a few important things, like control and ownership of your own life — and freedom of choice about what you do with the rest of that life — not to mention the hundreds of thousands of dollars of interest you otherwise would have paid to creditors.

Now You'll Be Operating TOTALLY on a Cash Basis

Once you get out of debt, **you can operate on 100% cash...and never use credit at all.**

If the TV breaks down, take a small part of what you are now investing each month and get the TV fixed. If it cannot be repaired, take a little more money and get a new one.

Need a new car? Hold off on your investing schedule for a couple months and buy one CASH.

Notes

Key Points	Details

Need a new home? Sell the one you OWN, add a little from your savings and investments if necessary, and buy a new one CASH!

You will soon never need credit or a credit rating again.

NOTE: your credit rating is unfortunately used for other things these days, such as a qualification factor for a job or even a promotion. So don't irresponsibly damage your credit rating if you can avoid it, just because you think it now has no purpose. I disagree with the ways people are using our credit records, but I cannot change the rules by myself. We must therefore deal with reality as it exists. We can, however, voice our opinions about how our credit records should and should not be used, to our Congressperson and Senators.

If Your Job Requires You to Use a Credit Card

If you feel you need something like a Visa card or MasterCard, then get an "Off-line Debit Card" from your bank. If no bank in your area offers the off-line debit card, you can get a Visa debit card with a *Schwab One* account from Charles Schwab & Co. This card, sometimes called a "Checking Card," is different from the on-line ATM debit cards that many local merchants will accept these days.

The card I'm talking about looks and works like a regular Visa or MasterCard credit card, but instead of building up debt (on which interest is charged), the money is taken directly from your checking account. In other words, using the debit card is just like writing a check, but with the convenience of a credit card. The purchase transaction goes through the ACH (Automatic Clearing House) system just like checks do, so it generally won't show up on your account for two or three days. Whereas, the on-line, local ATM debit card purchases are instantaneously deducted from your checking account. More than 50 million Americans are now using debit cards

If your bank does not offer an off-line debit card, check with other banks in your area. If none of the banks around you offer one, contact FINL at 815-356-8800 and we will put you in touch with a bank that does.

Notes

Key Points	Details

You can also use an *American Express* card, because you are supposed to pay the full balance on it every month. However, Gold and Platinum *American Express* card-holders are frequently offered lines of credit. <u>DO NOT ACCEPT ONE</u>.

Now that you are out of debt and operating 100% on CASH, you can take <u>ALL the money you were putting on your mortgage payoff and concentrate it ALL on wealth-production</u>. This monthly amount should now include what was your mortgage payment, plus the payments amounts from all the other bills that you paid off before the mortgage, and your original *Accelerator Margin* — combined.

If you do not yet have a six-month income cushion in a liquid investment such as a money-market or brokerage account, build that up first. Since your monthly income needs are now much lower (no more debt), you should be able to put six months worth away in just a few months. Then it will be time to start focusing on investment vehicles that will give you the best possible return — with the relative safety of having your money in the hands of experienced investment managers.

I am talking about Mutual Funds.

There are people who will try to sell you on their special *"Insider," "Contrarian"* or *"Scientific"* investing systems — all of which will supposedly make you *"Rich...Rich...Rich"* beyond your wildest dreams. These systems *"Can't lose,"* so their purveyors say. Why, you could *"double your money overnight."* They may even tell you that mutual funds are for babies...folks who do not have nerve enough to do *"Real"* individual-security investing.

Well, they are wrong on all counts. Most super-duper, can't-lose deals are only good for the insiders, and unless you are a broker for the company making the stock offering, or an owner of the company whose stock is being offered — you are NOT one of the insiders. You are just one of the suckers who is going to help make THEM *"Rich...Rich...Rich."*

Let's Start Building Your Wealth

Notes

Key Points	Details

The other point is that <u>mutual funds ARE real investments</u>. When you buy shares in a mutual fund, you are, in essence, buying stock in a company whose business is investing — they use your money to buy stocks, bonds, precious metals, money market instruments or whatever asset or security the fund is designed to invest in. As the values of the securities your mutual fund manager has purchased for you go up, your wealth increases.

It is just like owning stock in IBM. If the demand for IBM stock goes up, the value of your shares increases. When you buy shares in a mutual fund, and the securities the fund manager purchases with your money go up in value (overall), the value of your mutual fund shares increases. Or, if the fund intends to keep share values constant, you will be given more shares to compensate for the growth of the internal securities.

But the main reason I recommend mutual funds is that they give you every benefit you should be looking for in your investing strategy. Remember, one of the main concepts behind our *Financial Freedom Strategy* is "Simplicity with Safety." Mutual fund investing is simple and quite a bit safer than investing in individual securities yourself.

While your brother-in-law or some newsletter financial guru may be able to show you how he made a fortune by putting all his eggs in Afghan silkworm farms, a turn in the silk market could wipe him out overnight. Mutual funds, on the other hand may not always offer you the biggest gains available on the planet — but they WILL offer you solid return potential, while giving you considerable protection against crashing and burning into ash.

Another important point is that my focus with this strategy is to give you a plan to follow <u>that DOES NOT require your becoming a financial expert</u>. That is another beauty of mutual funds: they come with built-in experts who will do all the complicated stuff for you.

Now let's see what mutual funds are and how they work.

Notes

Key Points	Details

Mutual funds began in Europe early in the nineteenth century, with the first U.S. mutual fund forming in 1924. They are just what they sound like: a fund created by people "mutually" pooling their money for the purpose of investing it. The people who have pooled their money (bought shares) in the fund are actually the "Owners" of a company (the fund), and their company goes out and invests in other companies, government debt instruments, money markets and the like.

The owners of this investing company (the shareholders in the mutual fund) then participate in the profits or losses from these investments, proportionately to their number of shares in the fund. Mutual fund shareholders include individuals like you and me, as well as institutions such as banks, insurance companies and pension funds.

One of the great benefits of putting your money into a mutual fund is that its investments are being coordinated by an experienced *fund manager*, who generally has years of documented success in the market. He or she also has a staff of specialists who continually monitor and analyze all the information that can impact the performance of the fund's investments.

THIS LEVEL OF EXPERIENCE AND BREADTH OF RESOURCES ARE FAR BEYOND WHAT YOU OR I COULD LIKELY HOPE TO HAVE IF WE ARE INVESTING ON OUR OWN.

Another big advantage of putting your money into mutual funds is that they automatically give you *diversification* — something that most investors will tell you is crucial to protecting your assets.

Mutual funds invest in a variety of stocks, bonds or other securities, and therefore are insulated from being devastated by a drop in a single investment. For example, if the fund invests equally in 100 different stocks, five of those stocks could lose all their value, and the worst effect would be that your asset value would be reduced by 5%.

What Exactly Are Mutual Funds?

Notes

Key Points	Details

Because those five stocks only represent 5% of the fund's holdings. Whereas, if you had invested the same amount of money that you put into the mutual fund into one of the five companies that failed — you could have lost part or ALL of your money.

And, if you think about it, the mutual fund has 95 other investments in this example that will likely hold their value or go up. So it is possible that the overall gains in these other stocks would more than recover the losses from the five that fail. With this example mutual fund you would still probably have made a profit, even though some of the securities the fund invested in dropped in value. Investing in the individual stocks themselves, you would have risked losing everything.

It is highly unlikely that you or I could afford to spread our risk as broadly as a mutual fund automatically does for us. Most mutual funds are invested in at least 100 securities. For you to accomplish the same amount of diversification would take a considerable amount of money. Even if the average price per share across the 100 companies was just $25, it would cost you $25,000 just to buy ten shares of each stock. And that's before considering brokerage commissions. Whereas, you could invest in a mutual fund for as little as $1,000, and get the same 100-stock diversification protection as would have cost you $25,000 in this example.

To assure this important diversification for mutual fund investors, government regulations forbid a fund from investing more than 5% of its assets in a single company. And the fund cannot own more than 10% of any company's total capitalization. The benefit for you and me is that, single stocks within a fund may rise and fall, but no one company's securities can represent a large enough percentage of our mutual fund to sink it. This helps keep our money at minimum risk.

Most mutual funds are a part of what is called a *family* of funds A mutual fund family is simply a group of separate mutual funds marketed by the same overall management company. You will usually find several funds from the *Fidelity* family, for example, in the Mutual Fund Update in each month's issue of the *Debt-FREE & Prosperous Living* newsletter.

If you intend to make your mutual fund purchases directly on your own (as opposed to through a broker like Charles Schwab, Olde Discount and others), you will want to simplify managing your investments and moving money between funds (when the economy dictates), by looking for fund families that offer funds in the *Stock, Bond, precious metals* and

Notes

Key Points	Details

Money-Market categories. That way it will be simpler to switch from one kind of fund to another when necessary. When you move money from one fund to another, within the same family of funds, the movement will be less complicated and cheaper.

> **NOTE: this is one reason why I recommend the *Schwab One* account, because it allows you to switch your money between funds of <u>different families</u> with the same ease as switching within a family. It is accomplished with a single phone call and the transaction appears on a single monthly statement. Schwab is not the only brokerage firm offering this service, but they do offer these switching transactions, AT NO COMMISSION OR FEE, on a larger number of mutual funds than any other broker I've found.**

Another advantage of investing in mutual funds, versus trying to do your own individual-security investing, is what we could call *economies of scale*. Since the fund manager is running a big company, he or she saves money on all the clerical, analytical and other specialty help needed to be successful. And having all these economists, consultants and other specialists gives the fund manager access to more powerful and timely information than you or I would likely have available to us.

Yet another advantage of mutual fund investing is that *the fund does all the paperwork for you.* You will get regular statements, either monthly or quarterly, showing your investments and redemptions (buying and selling shares), and any income you have received during that time. You will be able to compare these summaries with the individual confirmations you received each time you made a transaction.

At tax time you will be issued a Form 1099, which shows your exact tax liability, from your income and capital gains, over the previous calendar year. Be aware that a copy of each Form 1099 is also sent to the IRS, so don't think you can "forget" to include any gains from your investments and avoid the wrath of Uncle Sam.

Another benefit of mutual funds, that fits in precisely with our *Financial Freedom Strategy*, is that — because the fund manager is minding the store for you — you can generally relax while your assets are growing in value...paying you income...or both. That makes mutual funds the perfect investment for retirement. You travel, play golf, or what ever else floats your bass-boat, meanwhile your experienced fund manager and his or her staff of specialists are hard at work making you richer.

Notes

Key Points	Details

Of course, one of the major reasons for investing is to have your money make money. You'll be glad to know that mutual funds are no slackers when it comes to growth.

For example: if you had invested in the *Fidelity Magellan* fund ten years ago, and continually plowed your dividends and capital gains back into more shares in the fund, your investment would have grown an average of nearly **29% annually over those ten years!**

Compare that to your bank passbook, bank money-market account, bank Certificates of Deposit (CD's), or ANY SO-CALLED INSURANCE POLICY WITH AN ATTACHED INVESTMENT VEHICLE. And, if you had made those fund share purchases through (and had the shares held within) a *brokerage* account, for example, your investments would have been insured for $500,000 should the broker go bankrupt. Compare that to the $100,000 FDIC cap you always hear the banks bragging about.

But just to give that 29% growth figure I quoted some tangible value, consider that — had YOU put money into the *Fidelity Magellan* fund just ten years ago — **every thousand dollars you invested would be worth $17,558 today! A $15,000 investment back then would be worth MORE THAN A QUARTER MILLION DOLLARS TODAY!**

And that is with the safety, diversity and simplicity of a mutual fund. That is also without your having to become a financial genius, timing the market and throwing the dice. It's comparatively safe, it's simple, and it lets you sleep. The three S's: *Safe, Simple, Sleep*. Those are key ingredients to the type of lifestyle I want to live — and the kind I believe you want to live too.

There are essentially two types of mutual funds: *Open-End funds* and *Closed-End funds*. Most mutual funds you will hear about, and almost all we will tell you about here and in the monthly *Debt-FREE & Prosperous Living* newsletter are open-end funds.

Types of Mutual Funds

Notes

Key Points	Details

Open-end funds can issue and sell new shares to the public as long as there are people willing to buy them. In other words, the pool of investors can grow indefinitely for an open-end fund. There are both pros and cons to this ability of the fund to get big.

The main advantage is that a large fund has the resources to increase diversity, and therefore protect its shareholders from being adversely affected by a drop in any single stock or even a single industry. But that same "Larger Pie" situation precludes a larger fund from benefiting in a dramatic way from a gain in any stock or sector of the market.

For example: if a large fund has 5% of its holdings in the health care sector, while a smaller fund has 25% of its investments in health care companies, a big gain in the health care stocks would have a much greater positive effect on the smaller fund than the larger one.

Conversely, should health care take a beating, shareholders in the smaller fund would feel the impact more keenly than those in the larger fund.

When an open-end fund sells shares, it is issuing new shares. This is called a *primary distribution*, and because these are new shares, the Security and Exchange Commission (SEC) requires the fund to offer all potential investors a **prospectus**. This is a document detailing data about the fund's financial soundness, as well as its purpose and strategy.

> NOTE: Another advantage of managing your mutual fund investments through a *Schwab One* account is that you can call Schwab toll-free for a prospectus on any mutual fund from any fund family.

The prospectus is structured according to government specifications, so you can imagine what delightful reading it is. But it does contain information that you need to understand, to make an enlightened investment decision.

How to Read a Mutual Fund Prospectus

Notes

Key Points	Details

You should never invest in a mutual fund based solely on the company's advertising. The prospectus is the only place where the fund's feet are held to the fire to tell the truth, about specific aspects of the fund, using specific language. So understanding this fine-print document is imperative for every responsible investor.

As an example, we'll run through the prospectus for the *Schwab Money Market Fund.*

1. KEY FEATURES OF THE FUNDS

This is a quick capsulization of the fund's objectives, automatic investment features, liquidity, costs, management, shareholder services and reporting.

2. SUMMARY OF EXPENSES

This is where you will be told about Loads. Loads are sales commissions you pay, either upon purchasing shares in the fund or upon redeeming shares. You want "No-Load" funds. There is no proven performance advantage for funds that charge loads -- so why pay them? This section will also tell you about 12b-1 fees. These are charges the fund withdraws from your account to help them cover their marketing expenses. They should never be above 1%, and on money funds or index funds, they should be below a half percent. Total operating expenses of a money fund should be under 1%, and should not exceed 2% regardless of the fund type.

3. CONDENSED FINANCIAL INFORMATION

This is a table of data and ratios that detail fund performance over a period of previous years. You should always be aware that past performance is no guarantee of future performance. But — I'll add — it sure beats a dart from across the room.

4. INVESTMENT OBJECTIVES AND POLICIES

Here's where you find out what the fund does with shareholder's money. It tells you how they plan to invest, and what they expect to accomplish. For example, if a fund invests in stocks, its objective will be *"capital appreciation."* This section also tells you how the fund manager expects to handle volatile market situations. If the policy is to stay *"fully*

Notes

Key Points	Details

---

invested at all times," you can expect significant ups and downs in the fund's performance. But, if the fund moves substantial portions of its assets into treasury instruments when the going gets rough in the stock market, the ride will be smoother...and the potential gains somewhat lower. You know — nothing ventured (risked) nothing gained.

5. SECURITIES AND INVESTMENT TECHNIQUES

This section explains which types of securities the fund can hold, and what percentage of each type. It also describes the fund's authority to borrow money.

6. MANAGEMENT OF THE FUNDS

The record of the fund manager is an important factor in choosing a mutual fund. Funds advertise their best performance numbers, over their most productive recent years. However, many times the fund manager whose leadership produced that performance has moved along to another position. Look for management stability (more than three years) — **and that the current manager is the one who generated the performance they're bragging about.**

You'll also find the information here about the fees and expenses the manager charges the fund.

7. DISTRIBUTIONS AND TAXES

This section will tell you how the fund will determine how much money it has made or lost, how frequently they'll make that calculation, and how frequently they will pay out or reinvest your share of that money. This is also where you'll find the fund's intentions as to taxable distributions of income or gains to fund shareholders. You'll also be told about your potential federal, state and local tax liabilities from the fund's proceeds.

8. SHARE PRICE CALCULATION

Just like it sounds, this section describes how the fund determines a share's Net Asset Value (NAV). See Closed-end Funds on page 57 for a definition of NAV.

Notes

Key Points	Details

---

9. HOW THE FUNDS SHOW PERFORMANCE

This section explains how the fund's marketing people come up with the performance figures shown in their ads and other promotional materials.

10. TAX-ADVANTAGED RETIREMENT PLANS

Most mutual fund families offer a service whereby you can invest money into their various funds through the tax-advantaged structure of an IRA, Keogh or other Corporate Retirement Plan. In other words, the money you put into your IRA could be invested in the mutual funds you designate — and the growth would then compound tax-free. This section of the prospectus explains how that can be done.

11. GENERAL INFORMATION

This is information about the fund company, and about other funds they offer.

12. HOW TO PURCHASE SHARES

In the case of Schwab's funds, the prospectus explains that you must have a brokerage account with Schwab (such as a *Schwab One*) to purchase shares in their funds. This section also describes any minimum initial purchase amount requirements, as well as ongoing purchase minimums.

13. HOW TO EXCHANGE BETWEEN FUNDS

Commonly called *"Switching,"* this section tells how you can move your invested money between funds within the company's family of funds.

14. HOW TO REDEEM SHARES

This section tells how to sell your shares back to the fund, and how the redemption price is calculated.

While formats may vary somewhat, these data should be available in every mutual fund's prospectus. Read it, understand it, then invest with confidence.

Notes

Key Points	Details

Some funds are strategically positioned to undertake higher risks for greater potential gains, while others are not quite so venturesome, and will therefore generate somewhat lesser gains (as well as lesser potential losses). The front page of a fund's prospectus will tell you the fund's investment objective, such as *Aggressive Growth, Growth* or *Income*. Usually the higher the "Growth" potential, the higher the risk.

As I said earlier, when you buy shares in an **open-end** fund, you are buying new shares directly from the fund. When you sell shares, you are selling them back to the fund, not to other investors. When you invest, you are increasing the fund's asset pool, and when you sell back shares, the money comes out of the asset pool to pay you back. You will generally have your money within a couple days of selling your shares.

Closed-end funds, on the other hand issue a specific, limited number of shares. These shares are then traded like stocks, on exchanges, and their value — from day to day — is determined by marketplace supply and demand.

Unlike open-end funds, where the value of your shares are determined by the collective value of the underlying investments being made by the fund manager, the market value of a closed-end fund share is based on the demand (or lack thereof) <u>for the share in the fund itself</u>.

This can work in your favor if the fund is doing well, and demand is high, but you could also find yourself in a situation where — even though the securities the fund is holding are doing well — the demand for shares in the fund are weak, <u>so the value of your shares drop</u>.

The value of a mutual fund share — whether the fund is open-end or closed-end — is its Net Asset Value, or just NAV. The NAV is simply the total assets of the mutual fund divided by the total number of shares outstanding. If the fund has a assets of $100 million, and there are a million shares distributed, each share has a NAV of $100.

When demand for shares in a close-end fund is not strong, shares will trade at a *discount* off of the NAV. If demand is high, shares in the fund will trade at a *premium* above the NAV. Trading closed-end fund shares takes more skill and knowledge than does open-end fund trading. If a closed-end fund is trading at a premium, you must know whether market circumstances justify the higher price. If shares are trading at a discount, you must know if it's enough of a bargain.

Notes

Key Points	Details

"Loads," in mutual fund terms, are *Sales Fees* or *Commissions* that you are required to pay, to either buy or sell shares in a given mutual fund.

Load funds add these commissions or sales charges onto your purchase, or more correctly, they take it out of the money you are investing — unless you specifically add additional money to cover the load. And these charges can be substantial, running up to 8.5%. **That would be $850 on a $10,000 investment!**

But the effect of the load can be worse than just $850, because — when you invest the $10,000 — whoever sold you the shares would take out their $850 and actually only invest $9,150 for you in the fund. That means that, not only would you lose the $850, but you would also lose all the dividends and capital gains you might have realized on the shares that the $850 could have bought you. Over the course of ten years, in a fund netting just 12% growth, that would cost you $2,805 in future assets, because they took the $850 load out of your $10,000 investment.

Loads are strictly *sales commissions* for the stockbroker, insurance salesperson or financial planner who sold you the shares. Loads do nothing to increase your investment, or even the size of the fund's asset pool.

Funds charging loads of 7.25% to 8.5% are called *full-load* funds. I do not recommend buying any of these. History has not shown these funds to perform any better than *no-load* funds, so there does not seem to be any redeeming value for the penalty of having to pay the sales commissions.

Funds charging about 3% to 5% loads are considered *mid-load* funds. You will find some of these offered through the mail and in magazine ads, as opposed to through commissioned salespeople. Most through-the-mail funds are no-load.

Notes

Key Points	Details

When I talk about loads, in most cases I am talking about *front loads*, which mean commissions that are skimmed off your investment before it gets invested. There are also funds that charge their load on the back end, when you sell the shares. These *redemption fees*, as they are often called, can run up to 6%. Most commonly they are reduced by 1% or so each year that you hold the shares — so that after six or seven years you could sell them without having to pay any load.

But keep in mind that back-end loads or redemption fees are being charged on your money after it grows. That means that, while 6% might seem lower than 7.25% or 8.5%, it is most often being calculated on a larger asset, and therefore can be quite a chunk of change...**your change.**

Some mutual funds will charge you up to 1.25% for what are called 12b-1 fees. These are nothing more than the fund's way of charging you to help pay their marketing costs. A true no-load will either not have this charge at all or it will be less than .25%. But be careful. Some funds that claim to be no-loads do charge marketing fees greater than .25%, and because these fees are not *legally* considered commissions (loads), they get away with using the "No Load" label. **READ THE PROSPECTUS!**

A true *no-load* fund is one on which you pay NO sales fees, redemption fees, exit fees or marketing fees.

Low-load funds are marketed just like no-loads, except that they charge a 1% to 2% fee to cover the costs of advertising, handling your telephone questions, printing and mailing of sales materials and so on. Some of these funds can be good, so do not completely discount them. When you feel more comfortable in evaluating the true value of one fund versus another, you can determine for yourself whether a given fund's potential might be worth a couple percent for their overhead costs. But, for the most part, I will stick to recommending no-load funds to you.

However, as we all know, in life...nothing is perfect. There are a couple *potential* disadvantages to no-load funds. One we at FINL can help with, the other needs to be evaluated when you make your investments.

The first potential disadvantage is that no-loads do not have a lot of money for advertising (because they are not getting it from you and me), so you will need to find them rather than waiting for them to find you. This is the one we can help you with. If you subscribe to our monthly *Debt-FREE & Prosperous Living* newsletter, we'll keep you advised as

Notes

Key Points	Details

to which funds we consider to be good opportunities. The *Mutual Fund Update* column lists the top mutual funds, which have been concurrently recommended by five or more of the top-performing investment newsletters in America — within the preceding 30 days.

The second potential disadvantage of smaller no-load funds is that, because they cannot afford to do big-time advertising, they may remain small, and therefore never gain the economies of scale enjoyed by the larger funds. They may also have a hard time attracting the more successful money managers away from larger funds. This possible downside is something you just need to be aware of as you watch your investments from year to year. If one of your funds seems to be going nowhere, it may be time to look for a faster growing fund.

There are five basic categories of mutual funds: *stock funds, stock and bond funds, specialty funds, bond funds* and *money-market funds*.

Stock funds are mutual funds that buy stock in other companies. Stock is *equity* in the company, which means that you are a part *owner* of the businesses your mutual fund owns stock in.

Normally stock funds are designed for Growth, some are designed for *Aggressive Growth*. These types of funds should be a portion of every investor's portfolio, but the percentage of one's assets invested in the more aggressive stock funds should decrease with the investor's age and lowering capital-risk tolerance.

Young investors who are looking for large capital appreciation over the long-term, and who have time to recover from possible losses from riskier funds, should keep 50% to 80% of their assets in *Growth* and *Aggressive Growth* funds. But as the investor ages (approaches and reaches retirement), assets should be shifted more towards income-producing funds, with a small portion (minimum 10% to 20%) remaining in growth funds, to keep the portfolio ahead of inflation.

Mutual Fund Categories

Notes

Key Points	Details

International stock funds buy only foreign (non-USA) stocks. *Global stock funds* buy stocks from all around the world, including the U.S. These types of funds usually invest conservatively, in major, proven corporations.

Stock and bond funds, sometimes called *balanced funds*, split their holdings between stocks and bonds. Bonds differ from stocks in that — while stocks are actual *ownership* in a company — bonds are essentially *loans* to the company. Stock is equity in the company, bonds are debt instruments where the holder of the bond does not own any of the company, but the company (or government body) owes the bond holder the money...and pays interest on that debt throughout the "maturity" period.

Balanced funds can be good for your retirement years, because they offer the security and income production of bonds, while still providing some growth through their stock component.

Specialty funds include such things as *sector funds* and funds that invest in hard assets like *gold* and other *precious metals*.

Sector funds are mutual funds that invest all or most of their asset pool in companies in a single industry or segment of an industry. There are sector funds for high technology, transportation, health care and so on.

The idea behind sector funds is that, while the stock market overall may be down or listless, a specific industry may be hot. In the late 1980s and the beginning of the 1990s such sectors as health care and pharmaceuticals were hot. So, if you had gotten into a related sector fund as that sector started its climb, you would have enjoyed incredible growth, sometimes exceeding 100% per year.

The obvious downside is that, if you mis-time your move into a sector fund, you can lose money just as quickly. And most often — by the time the average citizen is hearing about how hot a sector is — it is already cooling down and the smart money is on the way out.

Gold and precious metals funds are volatile and highly speculative. These funds are closely influenced by commodity prices and political pressures, and can be a bad dream for the unprepared investor. The rule of thumb in this investment category is: *Only invest money you can afford to lose.*

Notes

Key Points	Details

Bond funds have historically meant *good solid income generators*. However, interest rates have tremendous influence over the market value of bonds, and interest rates have been on a roller coaster in recent years. A rule of thumb is that, for every point short-term interest rates rise, long-term government bonds lose 10% - 12% of their capital value. Of course you would only realize that loss of you sold your bonds.

Another factor with government bonds is that they are backed by an increasingly insolvent government. Some day in the not-to-distant future, people holding government bonds are going to wake up to find them dramatically devalued. The government brags that their debt instruments are backed by the *full faith and credit of the U.S. government,* but what they forget to remind you is that the federal government is backed by YOU. If they run out of rope, they will just stick their hands in your pocket, and one easy way to do that is give you back less than they promised on things like bonds.

Of course, we can still head that train off at the pass by electing people who will REALLY cut the deficit and pay down the national debt.

Another element of bond investing that you should know is that not all bonds are created equal. There are many bond mutual funds available today which own more speculative, riskier bonds — what some people call *junk bonds*. The polite term is *High-Yield bonds*. These are simply bonds from less proven companies, who are willing to pay higher interest rates to attract money — but the investor is usually lending money to a company that has not proven its ability to hang together through tough times...and may not be able to cover their interest obligations or even pay back the principal when those tough times come. The word is "Risk." If you can tolerate it, there are some good "High-Yield" mutual funds out there.

The primary overall risk to the bond fund investor is rising interest rates. Like I said above, for each percentage point the Prime Rate rises, bonds lose about 10% of their market value. **But the reverse is also true**. So getting into bond funds is a GREAT idea when interest rates have topped off and are beginning to fall. Then, for each point they fall, your bonds will increase 10% in value!

A secondary shortcoming of bonds is that, with the exception of junk bonds, most do not pay after-tax interest rates that are much above inflation. So, to make bonds work for you, you need to time your entry

Notes

Key Points	Details

into bond funds when the Prime Rate is beginning to fall, so you can benefit from both their income generation AND their value appreciation.

There are many types of bond funds, such as *municipal bond funds, high-grade corporate bond funds, high-grade tax-exempt bond funds, high-yield corporate bond funds*, and so on. While defining each of these fund types is beyond the scope of this Basic Course, you can find many good books on mutual funds, at both your local library and book store, that can make you a veritable mutual fund wizard.

Each fund type has its own pros and cons, and each fits a different investment circumstance. For instance, if you are in a high tax bracket, you may find that tax-free municipal bonds give you solid returns without adding to your tax woes.

Money-market funds invest primarily in short-term IOU's from banks and America's strongest, most stable corporations. Some invest in short-term notes from the federal, state and local governments.

Many of these funds let you write checks directly out of your account, but these checks are normally limited to amounts over $500.

Money-market mutual funds pay higher (frequently much higher) interest rates than the so-called money-market accounts offered by banks and Savings & Loans. Most brokerage accounts, like my *Schwab One*, let me select a money-market fund in which they will park any money I don't have invested in other funds. So, as I pull money out of one investment, they put it into my pre-selected money-market fund. There it stays until I give them another order to buy shares of some other mutual fund.

To make wise choices in mutual fund investing, you will need a listing of available funds and their long-term performance. And you want this listing to be a comparison of apples-to-apples.

NOTE: *Schwab One* account holders can get a free *Mutual Fund Performance Guide*, which list over 600

Locating And Investing In The Best Mutual Funds

Notes

Key Points	Details

funds, and compares them in several different areas of cost and performance. Another great source of mutual fund information is Gerald Perritt's *The Mutual Fund Encyclopedia*. It's available from Dearborn Financial Publishing, Inc. • 520 North Dearborn Street • Chicago, IL 60610-4354. The retail price is $34.95.

You will also find useful mutual fund comparisons in *Forbes, Money, Business Week, Barrons* and *Consumer Reports,* among other publications. Each of these magazines publishes an annual mutual fund ranking, comparing the important indicators of each fund's costs and performance.

These rankings usually look back over the last 10-year period, to compare track records, but remember that **past performance is no guarantee of a mutual fund's future success. However, the longer a fund has produced superior performance, the longer it is likely to do so in the future.**

Beware of new funds with no track record, EVEN IF THEY'VE HAD SPECTACULAR STARTS.

To find even more detailed information about various funds, check your library for a copy of *The Wiesenberger Investment Companies Service*.

As I touched on earlier, one determining factor in your choice of funds is *where are you in relation to your desired retirement date?* If there are 15 or 20 years to go for you before you want to retire, you should consider more *aggressive growth* types of funds. With that much time before you intend to stop working, you are not concerned about present income generation from your investments. But, as you approach retirement, you will want to shift into funds that produce more income, and are not as risky with your money as some of the *growth* funds can be.

The Financial Freedom Investing Strategy

Notes

Key Points

Details

Also as I indicated earlier, another important consideration in choosing the right category of fund is *what are interest rates doing?* If the Prime Rate is FALLING, you should generally be in bond funds. If it is low — say under 8% or 9% — and not increasing with any momentum, you should be in stock funds. If it is CLIMBING, money-market funds will give you the best protection from the economic squeeze

Dollar-Cost Averaging

Even with these switching strategies, you should add the critical ingredient of *consistency* into your investing. Investing should be a process, not one adrenaline-packed event after another. One proven method of investing that provides automatic growth through consistency is commonly called *Dollar-Cost Averaging*. What it means is to simply invest the same amount regularly — such as a fixed monthly investment amount. Pick the best funds to be in, based on the current interest rate situation or other pertinent market conditions, then invest the same or an increasing amount, month after month after month. Do not worry whether the market is up or down.

Here is why Dollar-Cost Averaging can keep you ahead of the game. Suppose you decide to invest $300 a month. When you first start buying shares in a given fund, they are priced at $15. You get 20 shares for your $300. Now let's suppose the share price slips to $10. You again invest your $300, but this time it buys you 30 shares. When the price gets back up to $15, you have 50 shares worth $750 — BUT YOU ONLY PAID $600 FOR THEM. Dollar-Cost Averaging put you ahead $150.

Dollar-Cost Averaging makes you buy MORE shares when the price drops, so — over all — you come out ahead. The reason is that, over time, the stock market has historically continued to rise, despite short-term ups and downs. Since there is every reason to believe that this trend will continue into the foreseeable future, your cheaply-bought shares will likely be worth more...and you will have more of them because you bought some of the cheaply during the market dips.

Notes

Key Points	Details

Follow these basic mutual fund investing rules and you should enjoy a lifetime of successful wealth-building. Wealth-building that is Safe, Simple, and lets you Sleep.

Of course, **all of this starts ONLY AFTER ALL YOUR DEBT IS ELIMINATED.**

When Can You Retire?

To give you an example of how quickly your investments can add up — and how quickly you could retire on the interest income, turn to the ***Wealth-Building/Retirement Calculator*** in Appendix E.

Find the approximate amount you will be investing each month, after ALL your debts are paid off. This amount should be the total of ALL of what used to be your monthly bill payment amounts, including your mortgage payment, plus your initial *Accelerator Margin*.

Now follow that line across to the number of years you plan to continue putting this amount into your investments. There you will find the approximate total amount that would be built up in your investment accounts, and after the dash you will see the approximate monthly interest payment or distribution you could receive from your investments —<u>each month for the rest of your life</u>.

Now that sounds like REAL financial independence to me. No bills, you own your home, and you have good money coming in every month, <u>whether you work or not</u>.

A quick look at the numbers on the chart shows that — if you were to maintain a strong monthly investment pattern — you could retire quite comfortably in as few as 5 years. That is reality, my friend, not the baloney you hear from get-rich programs and schemes. And it certainly beats living on Social Security or working till you die.

Notes

Key Points	Details

What I consider to be one of the major benefits of getting out of debt and on a cash basis is that you are then able to help the people in your life who really need it. Whether it is an aging parent, a sibling in trouble, or starving children around the world...you will have the resources to help.

Many people really want to help others, but they get frustrated when they can hardly take care of their own needs. By following our debt-elimination and wealth-building strategy, you can quickly get to a point where you have the option to share as much of your wealth as you please.

After all, you really cannot take it with you...BUT YOU DO NOT HAVE TO LEAVE ALL YOUR WEALTH IN THE HANDS OF BANKS, INSURANCE COMPANIES, CREDIT CARD COMPANIES AND MORTGAGE COMPANIES. YOU should decide how much of your wealth you want to spend on yourself, how much you want to leave behind...and to whom it should go.

Following this program WILL get you to that point in the shortest possible time.

You are really just beginning the process of becoming truly financially FREE. And, as you continue this exciting transformation of your life — you need never be on your own. We want to be your built-in support group.

You Can Help Those Who Need You

Being a Part of The FINL Family

Notes

Key Points	Details

Financial Independence Network Limited, Inc. (FINL), the distributor of this course, is not just a company that sells books and cassettes. We are an group of people whose sole purpose is helping you achieve financial "Un-vulnerability." And we've developed a variety of programs and tools to get the job done. This Basic Course is just one of them. It's just a starting point. It's basic training, like bootcamp, but it is not the whole picture.

While you can probably take the straightforward concepts taught in this Basic Course and apply them successfully without any "Advanced" information, I have found that achieving financial independence is an ongoing process. It involves a continual accumulation of knowledge to maximize my control over all the areas where I use money in my life.

A few examples include buying or selling my house (a mistake here can cost you thousands); buying, selling and maintaining a car; buying insurance; buying investments; buying groceries; buying...well almost anything I might buy. Each transaction will have an effect on my overall financial freedom strategy. Then there are the legal implications of wealth, bankruptcy, estates, probate, wills, trusts, and so on. All these detailed and constantly-changing subjects are beyond the scope of this course.

That is why — as I mentioned earlier — I publish a second component to the *Debt-FREE & Prosperous Living* educational system. It is the monthly *Debt-FREE & Prosperous Living* newsletter. In its pages we fill in all the blanks that may be left by the broad-stroke nature of this course. If you feel that you are gaining all the knowledge you need right now to begin and maintain your debt-elimination and wealth-building process, JUST IGNORE THESE FEW PARAGRAPHS.

But, if you think you might like more ongoing support in your efforts, then consider the Basic Course your launching pad. Subscribing to the *Debt-FREE & Prosperous Living* newsletter would provide you with ongoing "mid-course corrections." In this manual I have told you a lot of things to do...but in some cases not precisely HOW to do them.

The main reason for that is because those specific steps or tactics change from year to year — sometimes from month to month or even week to week. Personal finances and wealth-building are inescapably affected by government, and those rascals never rest if there is an opportunity to change a law and get at more of your money.

Notes

Key Points	Details

But the *Debt-FREE & Prosperous Living* newsletter will keep you up to date on any changes that might affect the way you should implement your debt-elimination and wealth-building plan as time goes on.

Our goal at FINL is to do everything we can to help you through your own personal financial revolution. I know that I have challenged you to go against the grain, and that is not easy. So I want myself and my staff to be there for you, to help you manage the transition — and even the conversion of those who may be your critics as you begin to change the way you use money.

> **NOTE: If you do get any flak for taking a radically different financial path, remember that 96% of the people in this country DO NOT achieve financial independence (IRS study) — so if you look around you at how other people are managing their finances...and do the exact opposite...you have a 96% chance of being right!**

We want to share the load of this against-the-grain journey with you, so call us anytime at 815-356-8800 (during business hours Central Time). I consider my team to be both your partners in achieving financial freedom and your resources for the support and tools necessary to get the job done.

We will beat the system — together. This is more than just a financial *system* to us...it is our *mission*. To us it's a *cause!*

I know this has been a rather blatant commercial. Forgive me if I pushed too hard, but I want you to be fully aware of the help available to you. Enough said.

Over the years ahead, you are going to become more and more free, through applying these principles, and I hope that during that time we can get together at one of our meetings or seminars around the country. Just think about how much fun it will be to gather at a conference where everyone there is unburdened by life's major pressure source — financial problems.

Then, like the old Christmas movie, we will all be able to say *It's a Wonderful Life.*

Notes

Key Points	Details

The following sections of this manual include excerpts from our newsletter, to help you follow through with the concepts you've learned up to this point. They offer more specific tactics to implement the strategies we've covered so far.

You'll also find all the tables and charts that have been referenced in the text, as well as other resources I thought would be useful for you. Please read through these articles. They contain valuable and ACTIONABLE information that you can put to use starting today.

And...if you were ever going to begin getting TOTALLY FINANCIALLY FREE...wouldn't today be a good day to start?

Valuable Resources in the Following Pages

Notes

Key Points	Details

Appendix A
Phase 1 — Debt Elimination

The information in this appendix is comprised of Stage 1 articles from the *Debt-FREE & Prosperous Living* monthly newsletter. They are reprinted here to give you additional tips and tactics to more successfully complete Phase 1 of the *Financial Freedom Strategy*. The authors include: John Cummuta, Lois Cummuta, Michael DiFrisco and Gary Eden.

Any references to the *Personal Financial Success* Basic Course refer to editions of this course book prior to the third printing.

Notes

Key Points	Details

▶Consumer
COST-CUTTING

GROCERY COUPONS— ARE THEY WORTH THE BOTHER?

I'm asked this question over and over and frankly I'm really surprised each time I hear it. Yes, Yes and Yes is always my answer. How do I answer the skeptics? Proof...and here it is. My shopping trip from 6/29/91 broken down for you.

I have the average, all-American family: myself, my husband, one daughter, one son, one dog, and one cat — so my bill will be pretty average. The total bill for this weekly trip was $187.16 *before* my coupons were deducted. After all my discount coupons were subtracted, the check I wrote was for only $162.16. That's a CASH SAVINGS of $25.00!

Considering that this was a typical weekly shopping trip, I'm saving my family in the neighborhood of $100 a month.

"Wow," you say — but that's not all. Because, after I got home I mailed

in proof of purchase for several products, for another $11.00 in rebates.

Plus, to put the icing on the cake, in my grocery sack were two items which I

"I'm saving my family in the neighborhood of $100 a month."

---

received absolutely FREE: A jar of mayonnaise, worth $2.19 and a *Disney* magazine for my son priced at $1.95. I got these two items for free, just for buying things I was going to buy anyway: a can of coffee and 2 tubes of toothpaste. These special offers were on two coupons I had cut from the Sunday paper.

But it gets even better than that, because I had previously picked up coupons for both the coffee and the toothpaste, so I actually paid a lot less for both products — and got the mayonnaise

and *Disney* magazine for FREE besides. That's how to multiply your value when you're shopping!

Another question I often hear is, "Clipping and organizing coupons takes too much time." Well, I spent only about 30 minutes preparing for this typical weekly shopping trip, and I saved $36.00 by investing those 30 minutes of time. That means that my coupon clipping and organizing time was worth $72.00/hour!

I don't know about you, but my regular job doesn't pay me anywhere near that amount. So was it too much time, or was it WELL worth it?

If you're still not convinced, or if it still sounds a little complicated, stay with me in the months ahead as I talk about my "Couponing Adventures." We'll explore things like:

- How you get started
- How to get organized
- What coupons to look for
- What size products you should buy
- How to get the rebate dollars

And more.

I'm even going to talk about my "Shopping Adventures" outside the grocery store. In other words, we'll explore how to save money on some of the other things you buy regularly.

Consumer COST-CUTTING

LET'S GET ORGANIZED —TO SAVE MORE AT THE GROCERY STORE

Sound Impossible? It really isn't. It can actually be fun — and just like everyone tells you, it's good for you because the more organized you are the more money you save. Now, isn't that incentive enough. Let me tell you how I did it.

Each week or month I'd end up with coupons from FINL and other sources that I hadn't used yet. You know...I would come home from my shopping trips and always find a coupon, scrunched at the bottom of my purse, and it would be for something I'd just bought and could have saved money on. It really made me mad because it would happen consistently each week.

It got so frustrating that I wanted to give up and say I just can't do it! It's too much work! But I thought of the REAL money I'd be throwing away. So I made my stand. I decided that I

wasn't going to let my disorganization get the best of me.

As soon as I'd made the commitment I began to see how simple it could be. I knew I needed something that would somehow separate items with coupons of similar items. So one day when I was in the school supply/business section at K-Mart I saw one of those expandable canceled check files, divided into 12 sections. Perfect! I typed up some labels and I was organized.

It was really as easy as that. My categories are: Dairy Products, Frozen Foods, Canned Goods, Cereal/Breakfast Items, Paper/Plastic Products, Salad Dressing/Mayo/Oil, Pet Products, Coffee, Juice, Tea, Cleaning/Laundry Products, Health Products, Cooking/Snacks and Miscellaneous. These are just the categories I chose. Your family may require a different set of categories. Baby Items, for example is a category you might need, while you may

not need Pet Products.

As my coupons grew and my skill level increased (yours will too) I found I needed even more organization to make things easier and quicker. So I put 3" x 5" index cards between each category, to create sub-categories. For example: under the Cereal/Breakfast category I titled mine Cereal, Pancake/Syrup, Frozen Breakfast, and Bread. In the Health Products I had sub-categories of Drugs, Toothpaste/Mouthwash,

> **"I saw one of those expandable canceled check files, divided into 12 sections. Perfect! I typed up some labels and I was organized."**

Deodorant/Soap/Shampoo Feminine Products. I keep all Restaurant/Fast Food coupons in Misc.

Experiment. You may have a better idea. Believe me, I've seen it all in the checkout line: envelopes, shoe boxes, and those specially-designed, fancy coupon organizers. However, I've found the really serious couponers need more room than those store-bought organizers provide.

But, however you accomplish it, please be organized. Don't be like my worst

nightmare when I got behind a woman who had her flyer from the Sunday paper, and was flipping through pages and ripping out the coupons right at the checkout!

Give yourself a goal, and give yourself a reward. If I put all that effort into saving that money, I want to show something for it. I treat myself each month with something for me, something that's not a need, like a plant for the house or a new pair of shoes. Or one of my favorite — treat your family and yourself to a night of not cooking. Now that's truly a rewarding way to SAVE. Think of it — you're actually taking money from your food budget and using it in your entertainment budget, and it's not costing you a thing.

So have a goal, get organized, and don't think of grocery shopping as drudgery. You're getting something out of it, knowing you'll have something to show for it besides empty bags. Next time you walk out with your receipt, walk away with something more, a smile.

Consumer COST-CUTTING

T'IS THE SEASON FOR SAVINGS

You've heard people say, "The best is saved for last", well I'd change that to, "the best savings"! Sure, you can find sales any day of the week, but the best sales are those "final sales". That's where you can really CASH IN on the savings.

If you're really serious about saving money, you'll be watching the department stores for "final sales" and saving big money — 50% and MORE. The Fall season has begun, and when everyone else is buying sweaters, we shoppers are at our best because it's the end of summer season sale time, and we're buying summer things — for a fraction of their regular prices.

A real shopper loves it when the competition is toughest and the bargains are on the line. I was there to fight the crowds when the doors opened on the day of "THE SALE" — the day when the stores take "Sale" items and mark

them down an additional percentage, usually from 25% to 75% off of the already reduced price.

The entrance doors were packed with shoppers anticipating the store opening time — that's when the game begins. It was really fun. How can I say "Fun?" you might ask. Well the real fun is when you go home and see what bargains you got compared to what people paid for them just weeks earlier.

At a recent sale at one of the top department stores in the Chicagoland area, *Marshall Fields*, I bought four CHAUS designer items: three pairs of shorts, two of these were linen walking shorts marked down to $4.97 and one cotton pair for only $2.97 each. They were originally priced at over $29.00. I also got a pair of designer knit pants, with an original price tag of $32.00, marked down to $2.97.

In other words, I bought a total value of $119.00 worth of designer clothes and paid only $15.88! That's a savings of 87%.

Then I went to the shoe department for that perfect color, which I needed to match a dress. Original price for these *Evan Picone* designer shoes was $95.00 — my price $26.97. That's 72% off!

The point of all this is to say that, to buy clothes for yourself or your family — on a budget — doesn't mean you have to shop at Walmart (and look like it). You can buy the same high-quality designer clothes that the people who are blowing

> "The entrance doors were packed with shoppers anticipating the store opening time — that's when the game begins. It was really fun."

their money buy — only you don't have to pay the ridiculous prices. By the way, designer clothes really are better made (in most cases). They look better and they'll last longer than cheap substitutes.

The Secret of Big Department Store Savings

I'm going to let you in on the secret to these kind of savings: timing, timing, timing. This is the time of year — the changing of the season — and regular department stores are the places to find the great bargains.

Outlet stores and the new outlet malls are great places to shop if you want to save 30% on items you have to buy in between the season-changing sales at department stores. But for the real discounts (70% to 80% reductions), watch the calendar and shop the department store clearance sales.

Cashing in at the cashier doesn't only mean the grocery store, I'm serious about saving money no matter what kind of store I'm shopping at. I want quality in the things I buy, both in feeding and clothing my family, but I want to pay as little as possible. If you shop smart you can "Have it all". I do.

See you at the mall!

COST-CUTTING

PRESENTS FOR ME? IT'S NOT EVEN MY BIRTHDAY!

If your family is anything like mine, you have family get-togethers for birthdays and holidays. We pick names for Christmas — we put everyone's name in a hat and each person picks one name, so one person buys for one other person. We set a dollar amount. This way everyone has a present to open on Christmas Eve and we don't have to buy for each and every person.

We have a different system for birthdays. We still buy for everyone, but with things being the way they are economically for everyone we've limited our gifts to $5.00. Actually, it's not the gift that really matters, it's the thought, plus the fun of opening lots of presents. With the families still growing, and an abundance of little ones (and more on the way) I needed to think about ways of saving money here too.

Here's how I do it

I've found a way to get presents with very little money — and many times, with no cost at all! Many companies offer small items when you purchase their products or a combination of several products. These are then redeemed through the mail. All I do is watch the newspapers, bulletin boards and product labels for special promotions, buy the required products, then send in the UPC codes and cash register receipts with minimal postage and handling fee (if needed). I've received all kinds of fun things, to keep or give away as gifts.

When I get them in the mail I can't wait to open the package and see what I got this time. It's like opening presents even when it's not my birthday.

For example:
- I bought the required size batteries, and received a very cute stuffed reindeer, and his nose lights up (batteries not included). This went into my son's Christmas stocking last year.

- I purchased some boxes of macaroni & cheese and mailed away for several small play dinosaurs (my 3 year old nephew loved them).

- I purchased Pudding Cups and received a cool pack for lunch boxes (my niece is just starting first grade).

- I got enough small plastic picture frames to give away on Mothers day to all of the "Mom's" with their child's pictures in them, just for buying packages of hot dogs. Everyone thought I was so clever.

- I've gotten a small corning ware serving dish for buying butter (this was a perfect size for serving shrimp cocktail sauce, or vegetable dip — so I couldn't part with it.

- For buying plastic garbage bags, I saved enough labels to send away for a very nice picnic basket that was perfect for a new bride's shower gift.

There's always something these companies are ready to GIVE away, and I'm right there to take it. If you're serious about saving money any way you can — you should be too.

AVOID PAYING FULL PRICE
Here's some useful advice on making the most of bargain hunting.
1. Be aware of current prices and styles. Don't end up paying more for something at an outlet store because you aren't aware of its relative value.

2. When you're shopping for bargains, have specifics in mind or you'll be faced with overwhelming choices.

3. Consider the options: factory outlet stores, resale shops, auctions, garage and yard sales, and discount shops.

4. Make shopping a pleasant experience by wearing comfortable clothes and shopping with a friend.

5. Buy in bulk and buy off-season when possible.

6. Don't be afraid to bargain—especially if you discover a flaw in the item you are purchasing.

7. Don't buy anything just because it's a bargain and don't be pressured into buying. When in doubt, don't do it. Buy in bulk and buy off-season when possible.

Consumer
COST-CUTTING

$25 TO $50 OF <u>FREE</u> MONEY EVERY MONTH?

Does this sound familiar?

I go to the mailbox with a sick feeling in my stomach, because I know there'll be one or more bills in the pile. How much will it be today? And they're always higher than I think they'll be, whether it's the electric bill or the trash collection fee.

But that's all changed now! These days I go to the mail box to find that the total amount is due — TO ME. What am I taking about? Refunding! Every day or so I get refund checks, from product manufacturers, for buying products — products I was going to buy for my family anyway.

Here's How it Works

Every week I check the "Food" section of the newspaper. The coupon inserts they put in the Sunday paper are usually packed with refund opportunities. I also check mag-

azines, as well as the local grocery store, drug store, even discount stores. These businesses usually have one wall or corner where they post rebate forms.

It's important to find originals of these coupons, because the manufacturers

will not accept photocopies. The coupons you find will range from products you are going to be buying soon to things you'll need one of these days, like batteries for instance.

Follow the instructions on the form carefully. Many companies require more qualifiers than others. For some you'll need the UPC

(Universal Product Code) bar code; some may require a box top, box bottom or a combination of various portions of the package, plus the original cash register receipt as proof of purchase; some only ask for one of the above. There are even those that only ask you to fill out a form with couple of questions on it. I once got a quality pair of mens socks worth $5.00 for just filling out a form.

When a manufacturer makes this offer they really want to tempt you so they will frequently accompany the form with a cents-off discount coupon. I like to keep my coupon attached to the rebate form, so when I'm in the grocery store and looking for the product, I have all the brand and size/quan-

tity information I need right there in front of me.

The combat zone of the supermarket aisle is no place to have to rely on your memory. You need to know exactly what you need, how many you need, if you need to buy a companion product or a particular size, which is most often the case. You have to send in exactly what they

want, and send it in by a certain date.

Refunding also gives you a great opportunity to try a product that you probably would not have chosen if they were not offering a rebate. In fact, this is exactly why the manufacturers offer these rebate checks. They hope you'll like their product so much that you'll buy it again. So it's a good deal for everyone. You buy their product, which makes them happy, and they give you cash back, which makes you happy.

As the title suggests, this can amount to a nice sum of money coming back to you. You can see by the checks in the photo, received over a period of just two weeks, that this is no nickel and dime deal. I'm getting about $50.00 month for just a few minutes of my time! That kind of change can go a long way towards building your Accelerator Margin, to pay off your debts faster.

I send out maybe two or three forms each week. The key is to be consistent. Think of it this way: that's two or three checks coming back to me, every week.

Everyday is a good day when there's a check for me in the mail. And now I don't mind asking myself "How much is it going to be in the mailbox today?" The more the merrier. Now it will be a Merry (100% CASH) Christmas!

"IT DOESN'T GET ANY BETTER THAN THIS"

Manufacturers want you to try their products, so they use several methods to influence your choices:

They Offer Trial Size Products

Almost always the offer is in the form of a coupon. Most often it will say something like "Free trial size or 49 cents off regular size." It has been my experience that you'll need to redeem these coupons right away. They usually have a relatively quick expiration date.

When a manufacturer puts out a trial size they usually offer it for less than $1.00. Some people like to buy these trial sizes to try the product without having to spend the money for the full size, and many of these smaller packages are great for traveling.

When you receive one of these "Trial Offer" coupons, remember that you're not the only person who got one. Many of your neighbors got the same coupon and they're out redeeming it. It's not uncommon to have the stores sell out of a popular size quickly.

Although it's not as common a practice as it was a few years ago, some manufacturers still mail sample sized products right to your house, everything from soap to cereal.

Grocery Stores' Demos

Here's another increasingly popular way for the manufacturer to get their new products noticed. This is where the manufacturer either sponsors or co-sponsors a demonstrator at the store location. You'll see them with their table of samples. These demonstrators cook the product and have it hot and ready for a taste test. They offer everything from ice cream to vegetable dips, and of course who isn't always ready for a bite of pizza while walking around the supermarket.

Usually these in-store offers are accompanied by a store sale, plus — to even further tempt you — a cents off coupon. Sometimes manufacturers are just trying to build customer awareness of their new product. When it's impractical to offer a sample, they will often have an "Expert" there to hand out advice and/or recipes, plus offer coupons on products that the store has on promotional sale.

Don't be shy. Take advantage of these demo and sample offers when you get them. They're a great way to see if a product is something you like, or if it may even be an improvement over what you're using now. And with "Sampling," you don't need to pay full price for the product and risk being disappointed when it does not live up to your expectations.

Free Product if You Buy a Companion Product

This is becoming more common. for example a meat company might offer free eggs if you buy their breakfast sausage, or you'll see a free milk offer if you buy a certain cereal, or maybe free tuna if you buy mayonnaise.

BOGO (Buy-One-Get-One Free)

For example: let's say that your local grocery store is offering a BOGO on Rice Krispies. Let's also say that you have a manufacturers coupon offering a free gallon of milk if you buy a box of Rice Krispies. To make it even more interesting, we'll say that you also have a coupon for 50 cents off on the milk.

That means for buying one box of Rice Krispies you'll get a free box of Rice Krispies, plus a free gallon of milk! The Rice Krispies might have cost $2.98, but you also got an additional free box valued at $2.98 plus a gallon of milk valued at $2.88. That means it cost you $2.48 for $8.84 worth of groceries. That's a savings of $6.36!

"Try Us Free"

This type of promotion is very popular now. It's when you buy a product and the manufacturer then offers to refund the entire purchase price to you. It's a great offer, but it can be even better if they offer to refund you a set specific amount of money. They usually use an established retail purchase price, let's say $1.79 for deodorant. But let's see how you can make their deal even sweeter.

Suppose you can find the deodorant at a discount store or on sale and can purchase it for $1.49. This doesn't change their offer of refunding you the full $1.79. It just means you're going to end up with the free product and a 30 cent profit to boot.

Now suppose you not only found the deodorant on sale, but you also had clipped a discount offer for the product and had it in your file. Let's say it's for another 30 cent off. The end result is that you'll pay $1.10 for deodorant, and them the manufacturer will refund you the full $1.79. You got the product free and made a 69 cent profit. It doesn't get any better than this.

Consumer COST-CUTTING

SAVE BIG ON WINTER CLEARANCE SALES

Well, we survived another Holiday, the house is back to normal and everyone is talking about dieting and Spring. The stores are already displaying their Spring items. Winter clearance sales are well under way. Now is the time to scout the racks of clearance clothes and save big.

This is the season when I do my heaviest clothes buying. Because I live in the Chicago area, it's relatively cooler here most of the year. Even during most of the Spring and Fall we can wear varying degrees of winter clothes, sweaters, jackets, wool skirts and slacks. So when I purchase winter items for myself and my family I get the longest use out of them. That means the more I buy now the less I need to buy for myself and the kids for next fall, when things are the most expensive.

This may not be practical for people living in other parts of the country where it is warmer most of the year. They would reverse the cycle and do their heavier shopping during the late summer for summer clearance items.

I know what you may be thinking, well I don't know what size those growing little ones will wear next year. You can't save money by guessing and buying the wrong size. But there is so much you can buy now, most of them higher-ticket items too. Stick to the things that you know they will be able to wear, winter coats, gloves, sweaters, shirts. The fashions right now make this not as big a problem as it was during other fashion trends. Everyone's wearing things BIG.

Buying clothes for myself actually helps me with my diet. There I am, in the dressing room, standing in front of those three-way mirrors trying on the size I was before the holidays. That's when I can SEE that I need to take off those pounds. And, of course, this cannot only save you money on food and replacing perfectly good clothing, but it's healthier to stay at a consistent weight.

I know women who have three sizes in their wardrobe. One for when they've let themselves gain a few pounds, one for when their dieting and one for when they have lost their excess weight. Remember, it takes only 10 pounds to go up or down a dress size.

It Gets Better Every Day

The closer to Spring we get, the more the stores want to make room for the new items and the more they mark the old items down. This means more savings for our clothing budget, more money in our pockets. So it's not too late to get those bargains.

Remember, if you're paying off old debt at this time, it may not be the time to buy new things for yourself, but to only buy what you absolutely need for the kids. They're not going to stop growing and you can't stop buying things for them.

Shop smart and save now. There's a season for everything, and this is the season for SAVING.

▶ Consumer
COST-CUTTING

SOME FACTS ABOUT COUPONS

More than 3,000 manufacturers currently offer coupons, in this country alone. Total coupon distribution has nearly tripled over the last 10 years. With a growth rate of more than 190 percent over the decade it's no surprise that the United States is the largest coupon market in the world.

The growth in couponing is taking place primarily because:

• The manufacturers realize that consumer promotions increase and maintain brand sales.

• Coupons produce results, and they can be more strategically targeted and distributed than the traditional price cuts.

• Coupons have the ability to introduce or increase sales volume for "New and Improved" products.

• And now, because of bar codes and other computer-readable coding, the redemption of coupons can be effectively tracked — in some cases back to individual consumers.

Retailers take advantage of this marketing potential by supporting and even initiating coupon efforts. They run their own coupon specials along with the manufacturers so as to entice the customer into their particular store, by offering additional savings. There is a great deal of retailer interest in coupon promotions, because they produce results and because the retailer can leverage the power of the manufacturer's offer with add-on specials of his own.

Because of coupon effectiveness, manufacturer promotion spending has shifted from traditional media advertising to consumer promotions.

A growing type of promotion is where manufacturers have in-store demonstrations. They hire people to hand out samples of their product, usually along with cents-off coupons. Everyone benefits from this kind of advertising. The store, the manufacturer and the consumer. This kind of demo really helps increase sales and promotes the product, and it's becoming an increasingly popular and effective use of those tightly watched promotion dollars.

More manufacturers than ever are now using cents-off coupons, while the use of money-back offers/cash refunds, sweepstakes and premiums are on the decline. People want immediate help at the checkout counter. They would rather have the money in their pocket now than have to collect UPC codes and mail them in and wait for a refund. Also there is the rising cost of postage. If the rebate offered is a $1.00 refund, this means it costs the consumer 29 cents to get $1.00 back. Sometimes people think twice about whether it's worth the bother. Of course I say, "Yes"! Those dollars add up.

The average duration of all coupons decreased by one month over the last three years, from 5.9 months in 1988 to 4.9 months in 1990. We need to watch our expiration dates very closely. I know the stores I shop in keep an eye on them.

Read The Paper to See Why Coupons Are So Popular

One of the biggest contributing factors to the increase of couponing is the economy. It has been proven that coupons are redeemed more heavily in times of economic recession. Given the current economic climate, one would anticipate an even greater growth in coupon redemption in the months and years ahead.

My philosophy is that we need to shop smart and take advantage of every way possible to save money. If the product manufacturers want to pay me to try their products, I'm all for it. It's money — and I'll take it from every direction. Remember, the more you DON'T SPEND at the store, the more you'll have for debt elimination and wealth building.

> **Given the current economic climate, one would anticipate an even greater growth in coupon redemption in the months and years ahead.**

▶ Consumer
COST-CUTTING

GETTING WHAT'S YOURS AT THE CHECKOUT

This past week I went to the store and I did what I always do — check my receipt for accuracy. When I'm at the grocery store I'm making mental notes of the prices I'm paying for everything, so when I check the receipt later I know what I should have paid.

This week oranges were on sale for $.99/lb. but when I checked my receipt I found I had been charged $1.19/lb. When I returned to the store, I told the lady that I was charged too much. She looked annoyed, then she asked, "When did you buy them? Oh it was last week? Well...the price was probably different and they always change on Friday."

I assured her they were $.99 when I purchased them. She just did not want to check the price, it was too much bother for her, but I persisted and finally a different woman came to my rescue and called the produce department to verify that oranges had indeed been $.99 lb when I purchased them. She refunded my money, apologizing for the inconvenience.

So — if you find a mistake — rule number one is: don't let anyone try to talk you out of YOUR money. Like Sergeant Friday from Dragnet, you're only interested in the facts, not a checkout clerk's opinions.

The Great Coupon Disappearance Mystery

Another thing to watch for when redeeming coupons is to make sure the checkout person gives you credit for ALL the coupons you have.

I have, on several occasions, checked my receipts and found that I was supposed to have received a free item that I didn't get credit for. If you have a lot of items you're buying, and the checkout person has to check down through a long list of items to find the free one, it may be tempting for them to just skip that coupon.

What I do to make it easier for them is to point out the free items as I put them on the counter. "This item will be a free item, I have a coupon for it." They can then make a mental note of the cost or have a general idea of where on the receipt they will have to look later for the price. This makes it more likely that they will give me full credit for my free items.

A quick and simple check system for making sure you get credited for all your coupons is to count the number of coupons you're handing to the checkout person, then verify on the receipt that you got credit for that many coupons. It's usually best to do this BEFORE you leave the store. Mistakes are always easier to correct with the same person who committed them, and reasonably soon after the crime.

Remember this is real MONEY we're talking about. A $1.50 coupon is worth $1.50 in CASH. I want to make sure they give me full credit.

I have invested time in clipping the coupons or selecting them from my FINL menu. Then I've watched over them to make sure I use them before they expire, and to make sure I select the proper size and brand. This is a fair amount of work, and I expect a return on my investment, just like my other investments. So I'm not going to leave the success of my money-saving efforts to a checkout person who doesn't have near as much to gain...or lose. Don't you agree?

SAVINGS INSPIRA-TION FROM EXPERT "COUPONERS"

'd like to take this time to thank all of you who write in with suggestions, ideas and testimonials of how you're saving money. In this column I'm going to share one of these exciting letters.

It comes from the Keith Jones family of Spartanburg, South Carolina. They are averaging savings of $100 - $115 a month. In addition to that they have $12 - $27 a month coming back, in the form of rebates.

Their secret weapon? Organization! They keep organized by using a bulletin board. They call it their "Coupon Board". Everything is out in the open so they don't miss a rebate date, or let any coupon expire before they take advantage of the savings. This helps them keep coupons together with associated rebate forms so they don't get separated. No money-saving opportunities get by this clever family.

When they return from the store, the Joneses highlight their receipt, marking the date, the store and any items purchased for rebate. This is a great idea. It helps avoid the problem of receipts getting all mingled together, making it difficult and time-consuming to go through every receipt, line by line, to find which rebate item is on which receipt. No lost time with this organized family.

Check the sidebar for a sample of their well documented savings.

I was really impressed with one receipt they sent me. They had purchased 57 items on one shopping trip, and when I added up the number of coupons they redeemed it came to 74. That means that they had successfully used not only manufacturers' coupons but they had also saved addition dollars with in-store coupons.

Using this technique they actually saved twice. Their bill came to $94.39 but they wrote a check for only $64.09, a savings of $30.30. That's 1/3 off their bill. Another receipt they sent me was for a grocery purchases totalling $153.49. They wrote the check for just $109.60. Saving $51.57. Another savings of 1/3 of the entire bill. On this one they purchased 101 items but redeemed 142 coupons. Most of the coupons listed were average coupons of $.25 per coupon.

I like to think I've seen some good couponers in my time, but my hat is off to the Jones family. I'm impressed! □

Shopping Date	Total $ Check	Total $ Purchased	Total $ Saved	Number of Items	Number of Coupons
12/23/91	$109.60	$153.49	$51.57	101	142
1/14/92	68.37	93.61	25.24	47	39
3/04/92	36.48	54.76	18.28	37	26
3/11/92	57.21	74.27	17.06	45	42
3/17/92	64.09	94.39	30.30	57	74
3/27/92	16.27	23.76	7.49	14	15
3/28/92	78.02	106.02	28.00	63	40
Total	**$252.07**	**$353.32**	**$101.13**		

COOK UP YOUR OWN SAVINGS

I want to talk a little about an often over-looked way of saving money at the grocery store. Today we live in a society where we're all busy and don't have time to spare. So often a woman is either the head of the household or she works full-time for a second income. She just doesn't have time to cook. So what's a mother to do?

The answer most people choose is to buy already-prepared, microwavable meals!

However, if we stopped to analyze the cost of these conveniences, we'd be shocked to learn how very expensive they are. Most of us just buy them and don't even stop to consider the real cost — over time. Frozen dinners are now priced at over $3.00 each. If you have a family of four for example, that's more than $12.00 per meal.

An Opportunity to Save Money

Let's consider what's in the average frozen dinner. They usually offer very small por-tions made from chicken, fish, and occasionally a lesser grade of beef. Sometimes you don't get any meat at all, just pasta. That way they can stick a fancy Italian name on it, make it cheaper, and pull in a greater profit.

But the purpose of the Personal Financial Success system is to keep all the profit for yourself. We're trying to help you keep as much of the money you earn as possible, so let's not give it away to food processing companies — just because they whipped up a little pasta and cheese sauce.

When you consider that you could serve four healthy 6 oz steaks at home for the same $12.00 you're paying for the frozen slop in a box, you start to realize just how much you're really spending for heat-and-serve convenience.

Consider the healthy choice of chicken. If you buy it on sale you can serve a complete meal to your family for less than $5.00. Put another way you can almost figure it will cost about half or less to prepare a meal yourself, than it will to serve factory-prepared, oven-ready dinners.

I was really shocked to see how much a frozen Kids TV dinner costs these days. Since my kids are grown, I don't have occasion to be buying them, but I checked out their prices for this article. Almost $2.00 for less than 7 oz. of food! A few chicken nuggets, a couple of fries, a tiny bit of corn and — big deal — you get a cookie.

You could buy a whole box of chicken nuggets for less than $3.00, a large bag of fries for $.89, a can of corn for $.33 and a whole box of cookies for $1.00. That would be enough to last 5 meals and you'd only spend $5.33. That would be less than half of what it costs to buy the same ingredients in single children's frozen meals — and you still have the con-venience of heat-and-serve.

Don't forget, along with the food you're also paying for the packaging. Think of the waste just in the garbage to be hauled away when you fill bag after bag with frozen dinner containers. And now that some communities are charg-ing per bag of garbage, we have to consider even this cost when purchasing gro-ceries.

I work full-time, so I'm all for convenience, but if I'm going to spend the kind of money you pay for factory-prepared meals, I'd rather have it served to me at a restaurant table.

Time is money! We need to think of ways to spend the time instead of our hard earned money — then use the money to eliminate our debt and build retirement wealth. Buying expensive, "Fast" food now, and having to pay for it with a reduced lifestyle later is not a reason-able trade-off. □

"CONVENIENCE" FOOD RIP-OFFS

• Gorton's Microwave Baked Scrod with Bread Crumbs costs $3.19 for a 6-ounce package. That comes out to $8.51 per pound. But since the bread crumbs account for about 2 ounces, the real price for the frozen fish is $12.76/lb. The price for fresh scrod: $4.99/lb.

• Like butter on your veggies? Add it yourself. A package of frozen peas cost about 50 cents more than the same size of but-terless peas.

Consumer
COST-CUTTING

IT PAYS TO WAIT

I've been noticing a trend lately involving products that are being advertised on TV. The ones that have the half-hour commercials (called infommercials), usually seen early on weekend mornings.

The trend I've noticed is that, after a relatively short period of time, I start seeing these same products being advertised by local discount stores, at substantially reduced prices. And I know it's the same product, because they'll usually brag in the discount store ad, "As Seen On TV."

Due to the huge difference in price, along with a few other less obvious benefits, I thought I would talk about it this month.

Everyone knows that television advertising is expensive, so we can assume that the costs of these half-hour programs are passed on to the people calling in and buying the products. Sometimes even the television station takes a percentage of the profits.

If you order direct from TV, in addition to the higher price, there's also shipping and handling charges to pay. And, if you read the incredibly small print (that's usually on the screen for a second or two), you'll be waiting a month or more to get your step exerciser, juice machine, car polish or whatever.

Patience Pays Off

If you can resist the impulse to buy immediately you will enjoy several advantages:

First and most important is the savings. Look at the chart below and compare a few of these products.

Another advantage to waiting to find these products locally is that it will allow you to inspect each item yourself. How is it constructed? Does it look durable? How does it compare to other similar items on the same shelf?

Third, if you decide a product doesn't live up to your expectations or you get a defective item and need to return it, you save time and expense here too. It's cheaper because you don't have to pay postage or shipping back to the manufacturer, and you don't have to wait 4 - 6 weeks for a refund check. You just take your receipt to the store and the cash is handed to you.

Giving a product the "test of time" means there has been time in the market place to test whether this item is a proven winner or it fizzles out as a "dud". After all, the marketplace is the only true judge.

It's just like most other items you think about purchasing, if you don't have to be the first on your block to own it, patience will get you the best price — as well as a bit more peace of mind in knowing that others have been satisfied with the product before you laid your money down. ☐

 INSIGHTS

HOW TO BE A SMART CONSUMER

How to Get the Most for Your Money and Avoid Consumer Problems Before you Buy:

- Think about what you need and what product or service features are important to you.
- Compare brands. Ask for work-of-mouth recommendations and look for formal product comparison reports. Check your local library for magazines and other publications that contain product comparisons.
- Compare stores. Look for a store with a good reputation and plan ahead to take advantage of sales.
- Check with your local Better Business Bureau (BBB) to find out if the company is reputable.
- Check for any extra charges, such as delivery fees, installation charges, and service costs.
- Read warranties to understand what you must do and what the manufacturer must do if you have a problem.

- Read contract terms carefully. Make sure all blank spaces are filled in before you sign a contract.
- Ask the sales person to explain the store's return or exchange policy.
- Do not assume an item is a bargain just because it is advertised as one.

After you buy:

- Read and follow the instructions on how to use the product or service.
- Use the product only for the purpose outlined by the manufacturer in the instructions.
- Read and understand the warranty. Keep in mind that you may have additional warranty rights in your state. Check with your state or local consumer office for more information.
- Keep all sales receipts, warranties, and instructions.
- If trouble develops, report the problem to the company as soon as possible. Trying to fix the product yourself may cancel the warranty.
- Keep a file of your efforts to resolve the problem. It

should include the names of the individuals you speak with and the date, time and outcome of the conversation. Also, keep copies of the letters you send to the company and any replies they send to you.

How to Handle Your Own Complaint

As a consumer you have the right to expect quality products and services at fair prices. If something goes wrong, there are things you can do to resolve the problem. Here are some suggestions for handling your own complaint:

Collect records:

Start a file about your complaint. include copies of sales receipts, repair orders, warranties, cancelled checks, and contracts which will back up your complaint and help the company resolve your problem.

Go back to where you made the purchase:

Contact the person who sold you the item or performed the service. Calmly and accurately explain the problem and what action you would like taken. If that person is not helpful, ask for the supervisor or manager and restate your case. A large number or consumer problems are resolved at this level. Chances are, yours will be too.

Allow each person you contact time to resolve your problem before contacting someone else for help.

Don't give up:

If you are not satisfied with the response at the local level, don't give up. Call or write a letter to the person responsible for consumer complaints at the company's headquarters. Many companies have toll-free telephone numbers. Often these toll-free "800 numbers are printed on the product's package. check your local library for a directory of toll-free telephone numbers. Or, call 1 (800) 555-1212 to learn whether a company has a toll-free telephone number. If you're writing a letter, send your letter to the consumer office or to the president of the company.

Describe the problem:

When you complain to a company, be sure to describe the problem, what (if anything) you have already done to resolve it, and what you think is a fair solution. Do you want your money back? Would you like the product repaired? Do you want the product exchanged?

How to Write a Complaint Letter

The following books may help you locate useful company and brand name information:

- Standard & Poor's Register of Corporations, Directors and Executives
- Standard Directory of

(continued next page)

Advertisers
- Thomas Register of American Manufacturers
- Trade Names Directory

- The letter should include your name, address, home and work telephone numbers, and account number, if appropriate.
- Make your letter brief and to the point. List all the important facts about your purchase, including the date and place you made the purchase and any information you can give about the product — such as the serial or model number.
- If you are writing to complain about a service you received, describe the service and who performed it.
- State exactly what you want done about the problem and how long you are willing to wait to resolve it. Be reasonable.
- Include copies of all documents regarding your problem.
- Be sure to send COPIES, not originals.
- Don't write any angry, sarcastic, or threatening letter. The person reading your letter probably was not responsible for your problem, but may be very helpful in resolving it. Type your letter if possible. If it is hand-written make sure it is neat the easy to read.
- Keep a copy of all letters to and from the company.

Information obtained from the U.S. Office of Consumer Affairs Consumer's Resource Handbook. Free copies of the handbook are available by writing: Handbook, Consumer Information Center, Pueblo, Colorado 81009.

THINK UTILITY BILLS ARE A "FIXED" COST? THINK AGAIN.

Even if you own a modest-sized home, chances are great that you could be saving money on your utility bills each month. It's a fact, Americans are the greatest wasters of energy in the world. As energy costs have skyrocketed in the last few decades, we continue to let dollars fly out leaky windows and disappear down drains.

So where should you start? The Department of Energy estimates that 48% of your energy dollar goes to heat and cool your house. We spend another 16% heating water. Keeping our food fresh takes about 12%, while the remaining 24% goes into lighting, cooking and running appliances. So let's start with the house itself.

- Light a candle near doors and windows and see if air leaks make the flame flicker. Caulk and weatherstrip the doors and windows that need it. For a small outlay of cash to weatherstrip, you could save 10% or more on your heating and cooling bills.

- Insulate the floors over unheated areas in your home such as garages or crawl spaces. Adding insulation is easy and can cut your energy bills significantly.

- If you have any high-ceilinged rooms, use a ceiling fan in the winter. The cost to run one is minimal compared to the 30% savings you can realize on your heating bills.

- If you use your fireplace, close the damper immediately after the fire's out. 8% of the heat in your house can escape through the chimney.

- Remember this: You can save 2% on your heating bills for every degree you turn the thermostat down. So wear a sweater and save! Also, if you're going to be away from the house — even for a few days — turn the thermostat down. Before a party, you can also turn the thermostat down. The body heat generated by your guests will make up the difference.

- Boil water in a closed pot or kettle. It will boil about twice as fast.

- Use toaster ovens and microwaves whenever practical. They're more efficient than your big range and stove.

- Clean the condenser coils on your refrigerator. At least once every few months, pull the fridge away from the wall and brush or vacuum all the dust and dirt from the coils. Air needs to circulate freely around the coils to keep the refrigerator running efficiently.

- You can save 10% by letting your dishes air dry in the dishwasher. If you don't have an "air-dry" switch, turn the unit off after the cleaning cycle is done.

- Don't forget the good ol' clothesline. When the weather's right, hang your laundry out to dry.

- Put an insulation blanket around your hot water heater. They cost about $15.00 but will save up to 10% on your water heating bills.

- Do an "energy audit" of your house, room by room.

HOW TO RETIRE SUCCESSFULLY... OR HOW NOT TO

Loren Dunton is the President and Founder of the National Center for Financial Education, founder of the Society for Financial Counselling, the International Association for financial Planning, and the College for Financial Planning.

In a letter he recently sent me he described how, over years of counselling retirees, he found a set of characteristics that defined the "Haves" and the "Have-nots."

The Haves, of course, are those who retired with the means to enjoy their remaining years, through travel and other recreational activities. While the Have-nots are those who are living out lives of quiet desparation — dependent on their children, or scraping by in run-down hotels, or still working at menial jobs so they can survive on Social Security.

What suprised him the most in analyzing these two groups of people were not their dissimilarities, but rather their similarities. He had expected to find that those retiring in comfort and leisure had earned a lot more money during their working lives, but that was not so. However, there were definite differences in the way these two groups had lived their lives.

Prominent characterisitics in the track records of the

HAVE NOTS were:

• Renting instead of buying

• Being antagonistic to budgeting (we call it planned spending)

• Making impulsive expenditures

• Buying new cars more often

• Loaning money out carelessly

• Greater indulgence of their children

I would add a few additional facts to Loren's findings. The Internal Revenue Service conducts an ongoing study that indicates the most prevalent cause of financial failure in America is the inability to delay gratification. The "I have to have it NOW" syndrome.

Another chief factor in reaching retirement empty-handed is debt. In fact, I believe that this is the number one cause. You can't get ahead of the financial game in this country while carrying a load of debt. The government steals quite enough from us. If we also let Citibank and their clones suck 20% and more out of our wealth each year, we are in fact working for them — not for ourselves and our families.

Finally, I have found that a major cause of the inability to get on financial track is the misguided concept of trying to save a little on the side, while continuing to buy on credit and service that debt. It's just plain dumb to be earning between 5% and say 12% on your money, while paying up to 21%. You just can't win that game.

This is where most "Conventional" financial advice — even from the priciest newsletters and financial planners — leads you astray. They all tell you to save 10% of your income, while continuing to do everything else the same way everyone around you is doing it. They concentrate on teaching all the intricate details of how to invest that 10%, but they miss the main causes of financial failure. Your chief problem is NOT that you're not putting enough money into your financial bucket — but rather that there is a huge hole in the bucket...and the government, banks and other business have their buckets under the hole in yours.

So this "Save a little while buying on credit and paying off debt" advice is WRONG. Need proof? Federal statistics indicate that 96% of Americans DO NOT achieve financial independence. So doing what other people are doing has a 96% chance of being stupid.

On the other hand, I've found that the best plan to help you make the most financial progress in the shortest period of time is another American trait — the military concept of

"Massing of Forces."

The *Personal Financial Success* Financial Freedom Strategy is based on the principle of massing your financial forces on ONE THING AT A TIME. You first eliminate ALL debt. Then you begin operating 100% on CASH, never to use credit again. Finally, you focus ALL your financial forces on building real wealth. Using this focused strategy, you will accomplish all three steps faster than you ever believed possible.

Back to Loren's Findings

As you might expect, the "Haves" did not make the same mistakes as the "Have-nots." But more than that, they could all point to some "experience" in their lives that put them on the road to financial freedom.

In many cases it was a parent or grandparent who had taken the time to teach them the real course to having more money at retirement. Others indicated that an information source or consultant had made a strong impression on them that financial prudence led to freedom. In your case it will be the day you subscribed to F.I.N.L..

He also noticed that the "Haves" appeared to be what he called "Fixer-uppers," meaning that they saved a lot of money by doing things themselves, and they kept older cars running rather than blowing their wealth on new ones.

The "Haves" also saw and avoided the trap of

(continued next page)

"Keeping up with the Joneses." They somehow realized the truth that the Joneses end up bankrupt.

But the number one characteristic he found in the financially successful people was that somewhere along the road they DEVELOPED A PLAN to get them to financial freedom. And that's exactly what F.I.N.L. and the *Personal Financial Success* system are all about.

Our plan is simple, and it works. Many financial newsletters and advisors will suggest plans that sound like a space shuttle mission. These may seem reasonable to people who have spent their whole lives learning the nuances of stocks, bonds and the like, but to the average citizen...they're just too complicated.

And the real truth is that many of those so-called financial experts are just re-stating principles they read in the other guy's newsletter. They're all saying the same things. But we're not. We are telling you the simplest way to get to complete financial freedom in the shortest time.

I hate to sound negative, because it's not my nature, but the world is changing. American industry has more world-wide competition than ever before, and the business boom cannot go on forever. That's why we can't seem to get out of this recession.

You need to start thinking a little defensively. That's why our strategy is to get you to where you are no longer financially vulnerable FIRST, and as quickly as possible. Then you can get agressive in your investing if you want to.

I believe that if you follow our plan, you'll sleep a lot better...a lot sooner.

YOUR MONEY: WHERE TO KEEP IT ONCE YOU'VE GOT IT

Emergency or vacation savings:
Either a money-market mutual fund or a savings account in an insured bank.

College savings:
If the child you are saving for is still young, stock-owning mutual funds that invest for growth are best. If your child is starting high school, put the "freshman-year" money into a four-year CD and do the same each year.

Home down-payment money:
If you plan to purchase you new home in about two years, put it in a two-year CD. Continue to put new savings into that CD if the bank allows, or into a bank or money-market account.

Retirement savings:
If you're still relatively young, put most of your money into stock-owning mutual funds. If you're middle-aged, put at least half into stock-owning funds and the other half into bonds or bond mutual funds.

A lump-sum payment from a pension fund:
At retirement put at least 30 to 40 percent into stock-owning mutual funds for growth or leave it in your employer's diversified stock fund. Invest the rest of the payout in bonds or bond mutual funds.

Reducing Your DEBT

WHERE DOES YOUR MONEY ACTUALLY GO?

How many times have you come home from work on a payday and said to yourself, "Where does all this money go?" "How come I never seem to have any left over?"

Well, in this column I'm going to show you a typical American family of four, and we'll see how their hard-earned income is stolen from them.

Let's start with the premise that they have an annual household income of $50,000. This may seem like a lot to you, or it may be less than your income-earners bring home. If your situation is more or less than this example, just estimate how these figures would translate to your household income.

Let's Look At a Lifetime

The average American works for about 40 years, so this typical family will end up earning about $2 million over their working lives ($50,000/yr times 40 years). That sounds like a lot of money, doesn't it? You'd think that someone could get along rather nicely if they're bringing home $2 million, wouldn't you? They would be...if they could keep it. But there are powers out there who are determined to take that wealth away from them...away from YOU.

First there's the government. Over their 40 working years, this family will pay more than three-quarters of a million dollars in taxes. And that's based on today's tax rates. We all know that governments at all levels are continually looking for more ways to tax us. But just using today's tax rates, this family is down to having to

live out their forty years (as well as save for the future) on $1.25 million.

However, the next thief is waiting in the wings.

Interest payments and over-payments on insurance will eat away another half million dollars of their wealth, over their 40 working years. That's right. The insurance companies, banks and mortgage companies are second only to the government in stealing your wealth.

Imagine, a full 25% of all the wealth you'll earn will be taken away by people who make you think that they're doing you a favor by lending you money or "protecting" your interests! Of course, when you follow the F.I.N.L. Financial Freedom Strategy, you'll cut these thieves off at the pass, and keep that half million for building your future retirement wealth.

But let's get back to our typical family. Between the government and interest, they are now reduced to living for 40 years on just $750,000...of the $2 MILLION that they'll actually earn! These hard-working citizens, who earn $50,000 a year, will have to figure out how to live on just $18,750 a year — because that's all the insurance companies, banks and government will let

> ..."the typical American family will end up earning about $2 million over their working lives..."

them keep. And out of that $1,562 per month they'll have to eat, buy cars, pay their utilities, clothe themselves and their children, educate their children, maintain their home and cars, enjoy whatever recreation they can — and (don't laugh) invest money for their retirement.

Is there any wonder why we can't find any money left at the end of the month? This is why you must develop the discipline and commitment to follow the financial strategies taught in the *Personal Financial Success* Basic Course and this newsletter. We'll help you eliminate the insurance and interest thieves completely, and we'll show you how to dramatically reduce what the government thieves take from your wealth. Then we'll show you how to quickly put your money to work, SO THAT THE BANKS, INSURANCE COMPANIES...AND EVEN THE GOVERNMENT ARE PAYING YOU!

And the F.I.N.L. business opportunity just gives you a way to make more money even faster, so you can accelerate your journey to true financial independence.

DO YOU HAVE A DEBT PROBLEM?

By the strictest *Personal Financial Success* definition, if you have ANY debt you have a debt problem. However, this program is really for those who are recovering from debt and building a new personal economy, so it is more likely that you do still have some debt. In fact, this may be your first issue of this newsletter, and you may be just beginning your debt-elimination journey.

So let's look at debt as a problem, just like drinking or drugs can be, and see what the signs are that YOU may be experiencing a debt problem.

IS THIS YOU?

Is the month over already? Do you find yourself getting bills for the new month, but you haven't finished paying last month's commitments yet? Are you surprised to find a bill from last month not yet paid? Do you frequently feel that there are more bills than you thought?

Do you have a lot of unopened business mail? Do you avoid knowing exactly how much money you really have — or don't have — by putting off paying bills? Do you put off paying them by just letting them pile up unopened?

Do you rarely balance your checkbook? Do you fool yourself by leaving a "Little extra in there," so you can justify never keeping a running balance after each check?

Do you delay writing checks till the last moment? Do you use this tactic to fool yourself into thinking that there's more money in your account than is really yours?

Do you put the minimum downpayments on credit purchases? Of course, we believe that you should never buy anything on credit. But we're talking about your tendencies prior to joining our program, so the question is whether you tend to put the minimum down, so that you appear to have a lot of money in your checking account, while still buying whatever you want?

Do you spread your debt around? Do you charge purchases on a number of credit cards and store accounts, so you can fool yourself by saying that no particular bill is really that big?

Do you find yourself taking frequent cash advances on credit cards? Do you use the excuse that this is just to squeeze you through till your next paycheck?

Do you frequently borrow "a few bucks" from friends or family to, "Tide you over?" Are you regularly running out of money before you run out of week or month?

Do you tell yourself that having and using credit is the "Adult Thing to Do?" In your mind, do you connect being a grownup and charging things? Do you tell yourself that if one credit card is good, then a half dozen would be great — then you sign up for them, because "The more credit cards you can get the more prosperous you must be?"

Have you ever had a credit account cancelled? Have non-payment or late payments gotten you in trouble more than once?

Do you have credit cards and accounts for which you do not know the terms of their agreements?

Do you usually pay just the minimum requested payment on your credit accounts?

Do you go shopping when bills depress you?

If you find yourself saying "Yes" to more than one of these questions, you may very well have a debt problem. More precisely, a money management problem.

If you now hear your mind making excuses for you like, "I've never been good with numbers," or "I'm a woman and women aren't supposed to understand high-finance," or "I was never taught about how to manage money," you probably have a debt problem or money management problem. Not spending more than you make does not take the mathematical prowess of a rocket scientist — and gender has nothing to do with intelligence and common sense.

If you agree that you have a debt problem, then you're going to have to face it. And you're going to have to deal with it now, because it won't go away on its own. The sooner you attack the problem, the sooner you'll beat it. And the first step is to eliminate the use of credit.

As we've urged in the past, just cut up the cards and begin the pay-off plan that you work out in your *Personal Financial Success* Basic Course. Don't wait, just do it.

The key to success in any endeavor is to TAKE ACTION. As you see the bills go away...the ones you swore would be with you till you died...you'll feel more and more empowered to control the course of your life.

> **"The first step in getting rid of your debt problem is to eliminate the use of credit."**

CREATING TAX DEDUCTIONS

If there's one reality you are forced to confront each spring it's the realization that taxes are the single biggest expense you'll ever face in life.

But unlike the other "wealth siphons" you've read about in the pages of this newsletter and the *Personal Financial Success* Basic Course, there's not a heck of a lot you can do about shaking the U.S. Government's Internal Revenue Service off your back. They'll always be there, with there collective hands out waiting to collect what's theirs.

In the *Financial Dollars and Sense* column each month, Steven Homberg outlines specific tips, suggestions and organizational skills to help yield a lower tax bill come April 15. Another tactic you can employ now to give you greater tax deductions next year is to turn some of your "normal" activities into tax deductible strategies.

In his book *Financial Self Defense*, author Charles Givens gives a list of guidelines for these deductions. They've been adapted and modified (in keeping with the *Personal Financial Success* principles you've been soaking in) and are presented here:

CURRENT NONDE-DUCTIBLE ACTIVITY	TAX DEDUCTIBLE ACTIVITY
You rent.	Purchase your home. Use the *Personal Financial Success* plan to accelerate your mortgage payments. During that period, the mortgage interest will be tax deductible and your property taxes will always be tax deductible.
You use your home computer only for personal activities.	Use your personal computer to prepare your personal taxes, for a small side business or to help you market the F.I.N.L program. A portion will become tax deductible.
You take trips and vacations but get no tax deductions.	Try to plan your travel around business-related conventions, seminars or job interviews.
You give your children allowances and other gifts of cash.	Pay your kids a salary for helping you in your small business.
You help your children with the purchase of a home.	Buy the home WITH your children. This will allow you to deduct part of the depreciation and other related expenses.
You have money taken out of your paycheck for savings or investments.	After you have reduced your debt according to the *Personal Financial Success* plan, have some of your paycheck go into an IRA or company retirement plan and take a deduction for that contribution.
You use your health club or country club membership for exercise and relaxation only.	Use the club as a place to talk to other members about the F.I.N.L. program. A portion of your dues will become deductible.

Your F.I.N.L.
MONEY WATCH

FACING SOME STARTLING FINANCIAL REALITIES

DID YOU KNOW? Only five out of every one hundred Americans will be financially prepared for retirement. One reason why is that the average American will spend about 12% of its income on health care, up from 9% a decade ago. At this rate, a family will pay about 17% ($1.00 out of every $6.00) of its income on health care by the year 2000.

The life savings of an average 50-year-old is only $2300, and 90% of people facing retirement are worried about their ability to meet daily living expenses.

This will mean a substantial cut in your retirement benefits, increased dependence upon family and the government, not to mention a drastic reduction in your standard of living.

America is aging at a rapid rate due to longer life expectancy and the matur-

ing of the baby boomers. By the year 2000, 21% of the nation's work force will be over 65, compared to 12% now. Individuals age 75 and older should increase by 52%, from seven million in 1985 to eleven million by the year 2000.

The number of individuals contributing to the Social Security System is expected to have dropped in excess of 30%. Social Security may be drastically reduced, or eliminated, due to increased demand and limited resources.

Unlike their parents, baby boomers to date have not saved their money. They grew up thinking high inflation would last forever. They bought expensive cars and mortgaged their homes as high as their lenders would allow. In so doing, they are the most pervasive credit users in history.

Currently savings are at the lowest level since World War II. As of March, 1991, the national savings rate was

3.7% compared to 7.3% in 1972. To reverse this trend, Americans will have to increase their personal savings or face the prospect of poverty in retirement.

Now that you are aware of this problem, what should you do? First — get out of debt! Then, look for sources of money you can free up to start an investment program. Increase the deductible on your auto and home insurance.

Replace your whole life insurance policies with term insurance. Change your own car oil and replace the filters yourself. Do everything possible to get yourself out of debt and become financially independent. (Follow the Financial Freedom Strategies you are learning through the *Personal Financial Success* Basic Course and this newsletter). Be as diligent and persistent in your efforts to invest for your future as though your life depended on it, because in reality it does.

HOW DUMB WAS I?

I just bought a 1988 Pontiac Bonneville for $7,000 cash! It's a great car with all the comforts, and it feels and drives like brand new. Before you start thinking that I've got tons of cash lying around to do this kind of thing, let me assure you that I saved for quite awhile to put that $7,000 together, but the point is that I'm driving a very nice car — AND I HAVE ZERO PAYMENTS!

That's why I now wonder how dumb I used to be.

You see, before my conversion to the principles we preach in the F.I.N.L. Financial Freedom Strategy, I used to be a regular American consumer. I was leasing two cars: a 1986 Oldsmobile Ninety-Eight Regency and a 1987 Corvette. Because I had a successful home-based business, I rationalized that leasing was a "Smart Business Move." But let me just use the Olds to show you how "Un-smart" leasing really was (and still is).

A couple days ago, while driving my new (to me) Bonneville, I realized that it is the equivalent Pontiac model to the Oldsmobile Ninety-Eight Regency I used to drive. Then I remembered the terms under which I "Possessed"

that Olds. I paid $463 monthly lease payments for FOUR YEARS, and when the lease ended I was told that I could own the car for a payoff of only $7,000!

That $7,000 to "Own" a 1986 Olds was the same amount I just paid to own my 1988 Bonneville! For the same money I have a car that's essentially the same vehicle, but TWO YEARS NEWER. However, that's not what really eats at me.

What burns me is that I paid the leasing company $22,224 (48 months of lease payments) for the privilege of driving THEIR CAR...and if I wanted it to be MY car...I still had to pay them the current market value (actually more) for the car. So the $22,224 WAS COMPLETELY WASTED!

That was $22,224 OF MY WEALTH that I just gave away to the leasing company, so they could make more profit. Generous, wasn't I? Well, it's actually worse than that. Because if I had put that $22,224 in a mutual fund producing just 10% growth annually, in ten years my $22,224 would have become $60,161. And in twenty years it would have multiplied to $162,859!

That means that I really gave away between $60,000 and $160,000 of MY FUTURE

WEALTH, just to drive a car that I WOULD STILL HAVE TO PAY FOR IF I WANTED TO OWN IT!

My friend, BEWARE of auto leasing commercials. They are so seductive. They tell you that you could be driving a brand new car, with all the bells and whistles, for just "X" dollars a month and, "NO MONEY DOWN." But the truth is that you will be giving away many tens of thousands of dollars of your future wealth, just for the privilege of driving that car. And it works out the same if you finance a new car "Purchase." Even with the special 2.9% deals. Read the fine print — the 2.9% interest is only good for the first year or two of the loan. Find out what it jumps up to, then plan on lying down for a moment to recover.

Emotion vs. Practicality

It might help to drop down off the emotional cloud for a moment to consider this question: WHAT IS A CAR?

Isn't it really just a means of getting from here to there? Sure it's nice to smell the new interior (although you can get that smell in a spray can now), but is it worth $100,000 or more of your future wealth? Isn't it also true that the car you now own can go 55 miles an hour just like a new one? And isn't it many times a matter of ego to buy a "New" car? Is stroking your ego worth $100,000 or more of your future wealth?

"But," you might ask, "what about the 'Dependability' of a new car verses the cost of having to repair and maintain my present car — or to buy a used car?"

Unless you have the worst lemon of a car on the continent, it's not likely to cost you $2,400 to $3,600 a year to maintain it. But that's what it would cost you to lease or finance the purchase of even a small "New" car.

And in just two years of making payments on a small to medium "New" car, you'll pay out more than I paid for my Bonneville. Then you'll be driving a little Chevy or something and I'll be driving the roomy, comfortable...yes, even luxurious Bonneville — and I'll have NO payments, while you'll still have two or three years of several hundred dollars a month left to go. And the car you'll be driving will have lost about HALF its value over those two years.

Think about it. I was dumb...but you don't have to be. Save up and buy a decent car CASH. Then, a year or two later when you've saved up more cash, sell the car you have and buy a better one CASH. That's how I did it after I got smart. I started with a Chevette, moved up to a Ford Tempo, and most recently up to the Bonneville.

Cash really works. And it leaves your future wealth in YOUR future, not that of the finance company!

> "My friend, BEWARE of auto leasing commercials. They are so seductive."

THROW THE BUMS OUT!

If you've been a subscriber to F.I.N.L. for any length of time, you know that I usually speak my mind, and that my goal is to help you protect yourself from the wealth-sucking leeches that are continually looking for more ways to steal the money you work so hard for.

Well there's no way I could discuss this subject without talking about Washington, D.C.

You Need to Understand That They're NOT On Your Side

The bottom line fact about the government, particularly at the federal level, is that they would like to take ALL your money. They would like you to work like a plow horse, all week long, and then hand your full check over to them. They do not care whether you live or die. But if you decide to live — they want all your money.

The reason they've become such a bunch of buzzards is that the system is flawed. The way our electoral process works, these characters (many of whom start out as nice, idealistic people) know that — whatever else happens — THEY MUST GET RE-ELECTED! From the moment they get into office, they're working on greasing the skids to keep the big office and all its perks.

So they concentrate on getting as many federally-funded goodies for their state or district as they possibly can — whether or not these expenditures are really good for the country at large.

"But that's what they're supposed to be doing," you might say.

Wrong!

When they take office, they swear an oath to the United States of America. That means that they're supposed to do what's good for ALL of us. But, in many cases, they do what appears to be good for their district or state...AT THE EXPENSE OF THE REST OF THE TAX PAYERS.

When you multiply that money-wasting scenario by the 535 little nippers running around Capitol Hill, you have a massive budget deficit...and 535 wealth-sucking leeches looking for ways to pay for all the bribes they've voted to their constituents.

Here's Just One of Their Latest Schemes

A friend told me today that Congress is now trying to eliminate some of the tax deductions for operating a business out of your home. I don't believe they can pull this one off, but the important thing is that they're making the attempt. You need to understand what this action means.

It means that, while they flap their gums about America being the Land of Opportunity — where anyone can build their personal fortune — in reality, Congress (and their bureaucrats) do everything they can to make that impossible. They tell you and me to go out and build the American Dream — and then the moment we start to succeed, they start penalizing us at every turn.

They do it through oppressive taxes, through stupid regulations, and through being just so inefficient as an organization that they screw up everything they have anything to do with. They see us as a bottomless well of resources to keep funding their inefficiencies. I don't know about you, but I say fire the bums!

They Produce NOTHING

The government does not produce a penny of the Gross National Product. They don't create a single job. In fact, even big business doesn't create jobs any more in America. Small Business is creating 100% of the new jobs, and therefore the new revenue generated in this country. And that means you and me.

We're the heroes. We're the ones contributing something to the welfare of America. The politicians and bureaucrats, on the other hand, are sucking the wealth we generate away from us to fund their own re-election campaigns and their grandiose lifestyles. If they want to prove me wrong, they should change the laws to limit themselves to ONE TERM, so they don't have to bother working for re-election, so they can be free to do what's right for the WHOLE country — AND SO THEY HAVE TO COME BACK OUT HERE AND LIVE UNDER THE STUPID LAWS THEY CREATE.

I suggest that you write to your Senator and Representative, and tell them that you will not stand for their taking away the incentives for starting a small businesses in the home. Then tell them that you're sick and tired of their spending your money irresponsibly, and then coming back to the trough to find more ways to steal more of it from you, to continue funding their irresponsibility.

That's what I'm doing! And — although the system seems to corrupt whomever we send up there — I'll remember the worst of the bandits this November at the ballot box.

Oh yeah, one more thing I'm doing, and I ask you to join me: pray for them. I'm serious.

▶ Reducing Your
DEBT

WHAT ECONOMIC RECOVERY?

Have you ever felt that the economy is really in whatever condition the media decide they want it to be in? That they keep projecting whatever economic picture they've decided on, until we all start behaving in accordance with it? And then that the economy eventually becomes a self-fulfilling prophecy...it becomes what they conditioned us to believe it was all along?

Well, now they're trying to make us believe that a recovery is underway. They now have experts on who say that "leading economic indicators show strengthening...inventories are down... housing starts are up," and a bunch of other meaningless baloney.

Why do I say, "meaningless baloney?" Well, last week Digital Equipment Corporation, one of the largest companies in America, announced layoffs of over 30,000 people this year! Do you think those people are feeling encouraged by the economic recovery?

Let's bring it closer to home. Do you think your job is any more secure today than it was last year at this time? Do you think the boom days we enjoyed from World War II to the late 1980's will return any time soon? DO YOU THINK YOUR PERSONAL ECONOMY IS IN GOOD SHAPE?

Your Personal Economy Is the ONLY One You Live In

Many Americans are lulled into thinking that their own financial security is somehow identical to the "state of the U.S. economy." But the fact is that each of us lives within our own economy, and one economy could be terrible even when the nation's economy is in fairly good shape — or it could be flying high while the rest of the country fights recession, inflation or whatever other maladies the media can cook up.

The bottom line is the issue of RESPONSIBILITY. If you are ever going to change the doomed course of your personal economy, YOU MUST ACCEPT 100% RESPONSI-BILITY FOR IT. Your financial situation is NOT the responsibility of the President, the Congress, inflation rates, your mother or any other outside influences. YOU are 100% responsible for your own economic situation!

Once you accept that fact, you instantly gain tremendous power to change it. You see, when you sit there thinking that the President, Congress, your mother or anyone else but you is controlling the quality of your financial situation, you can simply sit on your hands and complain. But the moment you admit what is true whether you admit it or not — that you are the ONLY one who is responsible for your personal economy — YOU IMMEDIATELY HAVE 100% CONTROL TO IMPROVE IT!

You Can Have a Better Life Than You Ever REALLY Dreamed

Everyone fantasized about having millions of dollars, but in their heart of hearts they see themselves trapped on the same financial road as everyone around them. You, however, have taken a step that irreversibly sets you on a new path. You have subscribed to this newsletter, and you now know the truth — THAT YOU CAN TAKE ABSOLUTE CONTROL OF YOUR FINANCES... AND END UP ON EASY STREET.

It's true. It's not a fantasy. Anyone can do it if they first work out the numbers, then FOLLOW the plan. You can have true financial freedom — probably earlier in your life than you ever thought possible.

There's one catch.

You have to MAKE yourself be strong. You can't lean on mommy, your boss or anyone else. YOU have to make YOU do what this plan demands. YOU have to make yourself trim your excess expenditures and put the maximum amount humanly possible onto your bill pay-off process. YOU have to make yourself cut up your credit cards and NEVER get in debt another penny as long as you live. YOU need to look yourself in the mirror and admit that the two or three pizzas, the rented videos, and the movies or meals out each week ARE NOT ALL NECESSARY TO SUSTAIN LIFE...at least not for now.

For now you MUST put all the leverage you can muster against your debt, so you can completely eliminate it in the shortest period of time. Later, after the few years this takes, you will have the cash to make much more liberal buying decisions — but right now you are on a mission.

ONLY YOU can make yourself do these things. I can't come to your house and shake my finger at you when you blow money that could be paying off your debt. But I won't have to live your debt-ridden future years either — YOU WILL.

YOU are responsible. YOU have control. YOU have the power of our Financial Freedom Strategy in your hands, to not only create a "Recovery" for your personal economy, but to make it flourish. I pray you really do it. □

Reducing Your DEBT

"BUT I DON'T HAVE ANY EXTRA MONEY TO PAY OFF DEBT WITH!"

The bad news is that you obviously cannot pay off your debt any time soon without putting some extra money into the equation. The good news is that you probably have money you can pull together for this purpose — money you're dribbling away on much less important expenditures.

Every time someone has come to me pleading that they had no extra money to pay off debt with, I've uncovered — after brief questioning — wasted dollars in their monthly spending. Sometimes this has added up to hundreds of frittered-away dollars every month. And after these people saw how unimportant their money-wasting expenditures were, when compared to their long-term financial independence, they immediately redirected this money flow into their debt-elimination and wealth-building plans.

You Can Feed Your Face OR Your Future

One of the biggest money wasters in your life is your mouth. Americans blow more money on food than almost all other money-wasters combined. When one of my brothers complained that he couldn't use our debt-elimination plan because he didn't have any extra money, we sat at his kitchen table (after removing a pizza delivery box) and figured out that his family was spending over $100 a month on fast food and eating out.

While recreational eating may be pleasurable, you should ask yourself whether it's worth trading your older years for. Will you be happy in your retirement with no money... but with plenty of dreams about meals you ate in restaurants years before? Will the memories of lunches you went out for with your co-workers, two or three times a week, make the cheap, tasteless meals you'll be forced to eat in your later years more satisfying? Be honest with yourself, because these are the trade-offs you're making every day.

Think of all the times each week and month that you buy food out, when you could take less expensive food from home. When you go to watch your son's little league game, you could pack a snack from home rather than going to McDonald's. When you go to the show you could pop corn at home and bring it with. And you could bag lunch from home every day, saving lunches out for truly special occasions. If you'll sit down and honestly figure these types of savings out for yourself, I'll bet you'll be stunned by the dollars you blow on these types of purchases. This is money that could be parlayed into thousands and thousands of retirement dollars for you and your family. Isn't that a better use of the money?

The High Cost of Entertainment

Another surprisingly high monthly money waster for my brother was renting videos and going out to the movies. He found that he was spending around $75 a month on videos and theaters.

While entertainment is an important part of a balanced lifestyle, some forms of recreation are more expensive than others. Renting recent video movies and, worse yet, going out to see current movies in the theater can be serious money-drainers. Two trips to the theater for a family of four, and a couple video rentals a week can cost you about $60 a month. throw in monthly cable TV charges and the cost of pay-per-view programs and you can easily approach $100 a month.

But let's be conservative and say that your eating out and movie watching costs you $100 a month combine (it was costing my brother $175 a month), let's see what you're really trading for treating yourself to these extras.

You're Giving Away Your Future Wealth

Let's say we invest the $100 a month, that the average family might save by preparing their own snacks and lunches and reducing video entertainment purchases, into a mutual fund producing 12% interest. While $100 may not seem like a lot, the mutual fund will turn it into nearly $100,000 over 20 years. And left to compound for 30 years — this money you may be dribbling away each month could grow to $308,097.32!

Imagine that. Nearly a third of a million dollars.

That's what you're really giving away when you go out to the movies more than you really NEED to, when you go out to a restaurant for lunch instead of brown bagging it, or when you buy several premium channels on your cable TV. Let's be frank. I'm not asking you to live like a monk or give up any of the real necessities of life. I'm talking about things that all provide momentary pleasure — for which you are trading hundreds of thousands of future dollars and many years of retired pleasure and comfort for. □

Reducing Your DEBT

DO IT YOURSELF

The F.I.N.L. debt-elimination system, taught in the *Personal Financial Success* Basic Course, is a mathematical process that converts every extra dollar you invest in it into quicker financial freedom. Every dollar you put into the process gets you debt-free and building wealth sooner. Every dollar you do not put into the process keeps you in debt longer, and it lessens the amount of investment money on which compound interest is calculated.

So you want to put every single dollar you can into your debt-elimination system, and you should leave no stone unturned in scraping together your Accelerator Margin.

Places We Still Waste Money

While not all of the money-saving opportunities in this article will apply to you, some — maybe many — will hit the nail on the head.

The main point is that you need to change your mindset to be just like Scrooge. You want to hold onto every possible penny of your income, so you can focus it all against your debt — and then into building your wealth.

I'm going to run through some simple areas where you may be spending money you really don't have to. Let's call them "Leisure Costs," because these are tasks where we could do the work ourselves and save money, but it's becoming more fashionable to go for the convenience of "Having it done for us."

Now I know that not all of these will fit you, but if you find yourself saying, "I can't find any extra money in my budget to do this debt-elimination thing," then you should absolutely consider every suggestion in this article — then try to think of others. The alternative is to stay in debt and eventually go down the tubes, living out your life in poverty. You choose.

Here are a few suggestions to get you started:

1. Changing our oil. Jiffy Lube, Minute Lube and a host of other quick-oil-change franchises have turned an under $10 task into a $20 to $30 expense.

2. Cleaning our carpets. You can rent a cleaning machine at the local hardware or discount store for a lot less than hiring someone to come in and do it for you.

3. Growing our own vegetables. Having a garden is a good way to cut your grocery bill, and working in it helps melt away the tensions of the day.

4. Washing our own car. We could probably use the exercise anyway.

5. Mowing our own lawn. See number four above.

6. Doing our own hair. This applies more to women, but I'm sure that beautyshop expenses can add up if unchecked.

7. Cook our own meals. Lois dealt with this in her *Consumer Cost Cutting* column a couple months back. The bottom line was that you could save quite a few dollars, EVERY MONTH, by cooking from-scratch meals rather than going with frozen dinners or already-prepared foods.

8. Do our own laundry. This may or may not apply to you, but there are many people who claim to have no money for paying down their debt, yet they routinely drop their laundry off at the cleaner's every week.

These are but a few opportunities to slice a few unnecessary dollars out of our expenses, so we can add them to our Accelerator Margin, and pay off our debt all that much sooner.

I find that, when people get a handle on how dramatically our debt-elimination and wealth-building system can change their lives, they get fanatical about identifying every possible dollar they can add into the process. It becomes their mission, indeed their obsession, because they realize that these dollars are the same ones that can assure them a comfortable retirement — and their retirement becomes more important than helping the carpet cleaner or the car wash make a profit.

If you haven't yet read through your *Personal Financial Success* Basic Course, and calculated out your bill pay-off schedule, DO IT TODAY. Every day you wait is another day that your wealth is going to your creditors instead of to YOUR future! □

Saving On INSURANCE

WHEN YOUR INSURANCE COMPANY NEEDS INSURANCE

Insurance companies with names like Executive Life, Executive Life of New York, First Capital and Fidelity Bankers Life, Mutual Benefit Life, Travelers, Aetna and Mutual of New York have all had rough sledding over the past year. Some have been taken over by state insurance regulators, others have had their claims-paying-ability ratings downgraded.

In either case, it's not good news for their policy-holders.

Get Your Insurance Straight

If you've been a subscriber to *Personal Financial Success* for any length of time, you know that we focus on helping you become totally financially-self-reliant. We want to show you a way to use every weapon in your financial arsenal — and ONLY IN ITS MOST EFFICIENT MODE OF OPERATION.

That's why the *Personal Financial Success* Basic Course and the monthly insurance columns in this newsletter tell you to ONLY USE INSURANCE AS PURE INSURANCE, AND NOT TRY

TO MAKE INSURANCE PURCHASES DO DOUBLE DUTY AS INVESTMENTS. You will always be better off if you pay only for insurance when you're buying an insurance policy, and only pay for an investment when you're buying an investment.

We do understand that some investments, particularly annuities, are bought through insurance companies — but when you want an annuity, don't ham-string it by trying to make the same purchase simultaneously buy you life insurance. Put that money to work ONLY as an investment and buy separate TERM LIFE INSURANCE.

If you do that, you will most likely not be in the position many people find themselves today: having "Cash Value" life insurance policies with companies where the "Cash" might not be safe, or even recoverable any more.

If That's You...

Here are some quick tips, in case you find yourself with a "Cash Value" policy or investment with an insurer whose future is not secure.

WHOLE LIFE POLICIES: Most whole life policies have a provision that if you don't pay the premium, the company will simply deduct it from your built-up cash value and continue the life insurance coverage. You can read your policy or call the company to see if this is true for your policy. If it is, stop making premium payments to the insurance company and start making them to an investment (preferably an already established mutual fund). You will continue to have life insurance, and if the company recovers to the point where you can "cash the policy out," do it, and invest the money into a real investment. BUT BEFORE YOU CASH OUT THE POLICY — MAKE SURE YOU HAVE TERM LIFE INSURANCE IN EFFECT WITH ANOTHER CARRIER.

With most insurance policies that accumulate "Cash Values" (also known as the world's worst return on investment), they have what are called surrender charges if you try to take your money out. You need to weigh the level of risk in staying with your current insurer (are they in trouble?), plus the increased return you could get by investing that money in a real investment, against the penalty the insurance company will exact for your having the gall to take back your own money!

ANNUITIES: This is an investment where you have two potential penalties for pulling your money out. One is the surrender charge exacted by the insurance company itself, the other is the tax liability and penalty due because an annuity is a tax-deferred investment that you're not supposed to

removed before you start taking retirement distributions. But, if the company you have your annuity with is in trouble, you should examine these risks and make an informed decision.

First of all, most annuity surrender charges work on a sliding schedule over time. For example, the surrender charge might be 6% the first year, declining by 1% per year. So after you've held the annuity for at least six years, there would be no surrender charge from the insurance company to get your money out.

The IRS doesn't work that way. However, they will give you a period of time to put the full amount back into another tax-deferred annuity with another carrier. You may find that the more stable carriers are not offering the highest rates of return in the marketplace...but...maybe that's why they're still stable.

When it's time to annuitize (start taking distributions), you can choose any company you want to convert the lump sum you've built up in your annuity into monthly income disbursements. But keep in mind that, once you choose a company, you're stuck with it for life. So choose wisely. Look for companies with an A+ rating.

Where Do I Get These Ratings?

Throughout this article we've mentioned an insurance company's "rating." You can find these ratings in the *Best Review* from A.M. Best. It's available at your local library.

☐

Saving On
INSURANCE

TALKING TURKEY ABOUT HEALTH INSURANCE

Are your health insurance premiums making you sick?

Every day we read in the papers about how health insurance costs keep rising and more companies are either reducing benefits or are refusing to do business in your area altogether. It seems that every month we are paying more for our medical coverage. State and Federal government are both looking for answers. Is the Canadian system best? Should the government provide coverage? Should the insurance solution remain in the private sector? The big question is: how can all the benefits we read about be funded?

Let's look at the alternatives. Many insurance companies today are offering a wide range of deductibles from as low as $100-annually to $5,000-and even higher. A very high deductible will certainly reduce premiums substantially, but how many of us can sustain a rather high up front cost.

Another possibility is catastrophic coverage whereby the insurance company, after you pay a deductible, will cover costs for just hospital and surgical expenses, with very limited coverage outside of the hospital. This solution will also reduce premium costs but will not provide coverage for doctors office visits or prescriptions. And many of the illnesses we are prone to may not require hospitalization, but can run up substantial costs.

There is a new type of medical coverage available today which offers the insured person a choice of benefits as well as deductibles.

Option 1 is the choice of a doctor and/or hospital from a list of "Preferred Providers". Option 2 permits you to go to any doctor or hospital.

If you select option 1, the Preferred Provider, there are enhanced benefits, such as coverage for routine physicals and a more advantageous co-insurance percentage.

Once you have made your

decision, it may not be wise to keep changing companies every six months when you get a premium increase. You may have to go through a new period of contestability when a claim may be held up for a long and very thorough investigation so the company can be certain that your illness does not pre-exist your policy.

At the bottom line, the final decision is up to you. You must decide on the benefit structure which suits you best, allocate the dollars necessary to provide the protection you need and above all, investigate the insurance company to be certain that they are reliable, solvent and will be there when you need them.

If anyone should attempt to advise you to change policies, be sure to get all the information necessary for an accurate comparison — in writing — so that you may make an informed decision.

Look to future issues for articles on what type of life insurance is best for you. We'll also cover Major Medical Health Coverage and Disability Income Insurance.

Saving On INSURANCE

MORTGAGE LIFE INSURANCE — WHAT A RIP!

A friend of mine in the F.I.N.L. program was complementing me on the *Personal Financial Success* Basic Course, and he casually said, "I think I'll cancel my mortgage life insurance."

I told him to do it the moment we got off the phone.

What most people don't realize, when a sales person subtly asks if you want the insurance — whether that insurance is an extended warranty or credit life insurance — is that THIS IS ONE OF THEIR BIGGEST PROFIT CENTERS. The salesperson may seem nonchalant about it, but they (particularly their boss) really hope you'll just say, "Sure."

You can take this to the bank — ANYONE WHO SELLS YOU ANY TYPE OF CREDIT LIFE INSURANCE IS MUCH MORE LIKELY TO MAKE A PROFIT ON YOU THAN YOU ARE TO DIE AND GET ANY BENEFIT FROM THE POLICY.

Besides the pathetic fact that you're actually betting you'll die, betting against yourself, you are also buying a lousy insurance deal. Here's why:

Mortgage Life Insurance is Incredibly Expensive Decreasing Term Insurance

Decreasing term insurance is just a type of insurance where the premium stays the same each month, but the death benefit decreases (in this case monthly). You see, you are NOT insuring the value of the house like with homeowner's insurance. You are insuring the payoff principal balance on your mortgage. And that payoff balance is continually shrinking — BUT YOUR MORTGAGE LIFE PREMI-UMS AREN'T.

So, as you approach the end of your mortgage, you are paying astronomical premiums for a relatively small potential death benefit. But mortgage life premiums are high even at the beginning of a mortgage.

The way the insurance is sold to you by the mortgage loan officer is subtle, and the payment is hidden in your monthly house payment, so you're lulled into ignoring the paltry value of the coverage your getting for your money.

How To Properly Use Insurance To Protect Your Home Against your Death

Death is certainly a possibility for a homeowner — but only to the same extent as with renters or anyone else of your age, health and lifestyle. So, what you need is the best buy in a term life insurance policy that will protect the asset value of your home for your heirs.

Most folks would just guess that this means you should go get a term policy with a death benefit amount equal to your loan balance. But there's another, better way to accomplish your goal, while expanding the overall benefit to your heirs.

Instead of just trying to pay off the mortgage if you die, think about buying a term policy amount that — when the death benefit would be invested by your heirs into a mutual fund paying say 12% interest — that the monthly interest could make your mortgage payments.

This way, when the mortgage is finally paid off (by the mutual fund monthly interest checks) your heirs would still have the full amount of your insurance death benefit in the mutual fund. They can either leave it in there and continue to enjoy the monthly income, or they can cash out and have one heck of a mortgage burning party... in your honor, of course.

So there you have it. Check your mortgage papers and see if you were sucked into buying mortgage life. If you were, just follow the instructions (or call the mortgage company for directions) and cancel it — AFTER YOU HAVE PURCHASED AND QUALIFIED FOR A TERM LIFE POLICY TO REPLACE IT.

If you wish to follow our suggested plan for having the insurance proceeds invested, so the monthly interest will make the house payments, see your lawyer about creating an insurance trust for you. The trust will actually receive the proceeds from your insurance and automatically invest them according to your wishes.

Of course, the best revenge is to outlive your mortgage and enjoy the burning party yourself!

Saving On INSURANCE

HOW TO PICK AN INSURANCE COMPANY

Let's break the insurance company choosing process into two major stages: picking the right TYPE of insurance company, and choosing the BEST BUY among the companies that make it through stage one.

Picking the Right Type of Insurance Company

Their are two major categories for life insurance companies: stock companies and mutual companies. You only want to consider stock companies in your search for the best term life insurance policy.

Beware of mutual type companies, and especially of their sales tactics. While your agent may protest the follow description vigorously, check the rates of several stock and mutual insurance policies and I'm sure you'll see that what I'll tell you here is true.

Mutual companies try to convince you that "Mutual" means that you and the other policy-holders are actually "Owners" of the company, and that you will receive periodic "Dividends" from the company's profits. This is simply NOT TRUE.

What actually happens is that the insurance company overcharges you for your premiums, then periodically gives you back the overcharges... calling them dividends. If your agent tells you that I'm wrong about this, ask him or her if these dividends are taxable as income or capital gains. If they are TRUE dividends, the IRS would consider them to be taxable income. But they don't, because they know (like you do now) that these so-called dividends are just a refund of your own money.

Over-paying insurance premiums just to get your own money back is as senseless as over-paying your income taxes just to let the government have a free loan of your money until you get your refund. Don't do it. If your agent disagrees that you are over-paying on a mutual company policy, make a comparison of premiums for comparable policies offered by mutual-type and stock-type companies. You'll find that the mutual companies' premiums are slightly higher — by about the amount that they usually pay back in "Dividends."

Choose only "Stock" type insurance companies. These companies have stock traded on open stock exchanges, and...when they make a profit...they pay REAL dividends to their stock-holders. They only charge you the real premium cost for a policy.

Choose Only "A" or Higher Rated Insurance Companies

How in the world do you find out how an insurance company is rated? The Reference area of your local library should be able to direct you to two large publications, both from the same company. They are the *A.M. Best* financial stability ratings for both Life/Health insurance companies and Property/Casualty insurance companies.

The ratings you're interested in are "A, A- and A+." So take the companies that made it through your first screening (as described above) and find the ones that are highest rated. Investing premiums with one of these companies will let you sleep better, because you'll be relatively sure that your heirs will actually get paid...should you cross over to the tax-free zone. *(Ed. he means when you die)*

Most libraries will also carry *Best's* monthly reviews as well. These give you the most up-to-date information. The *Best Reviews* and Books can also give you the information you need to select insurance companies for review in the first place. Your agent —especially if he or she works for a specific company—will not likely have information on all the companies you'll want to consider. And the largest, best-known insurance companies are not always the best investments.

You pay life insurance premiums for nearly all your life. Slightly better premium rates can add up to a lot of savings over those years. Savings that can help you pay off your debt faster, then build wealth faster. It's YOUR money, and I believe that you deserve it more than any insurance company does. □

Notes

Key Points	Details

Appendix B
Phase 2 — Operating 100% On Cash

The information in this appendix is comprised of Stage 2 articles from the *Debt-FREE & Prosperous Living* monthly newsletter. They are reprinted here to give you additional tips and tactics to more successfully operate in Phase 2 of the *Financial Freedom Strategy*. The authors include: John Cummuta, Tom Passaro, Steve Homberg, Dick Kroll and Michael DiFrisco.

Any references to the *Personal Financial Success* Basic Course refer to editions of this course book prior to the third printing.

Notes

Key Points	Details

▶ Buying & Maintaining
YOUR AUTOMOBILE

Hupmobile
4 cylinders
20 H. P.
Sliding gears
Bosch magneto
$750

YOU CAN'T BEAT THE SYSTEM IF YOU DON'T KNOW HOW IT WORKS

Consider these numbers: the average American couple will spend over $100,000 dollars on cars during their lives, less than 10% of the public know what they're doing when buying a car, the other 90% will lose an estimated $4 billion annually — simply because of ignorance!

This ignorance is mainly a lack of knowledge of the car selling "System." There is a planned pathway that the dealer and their sales people want to take you down that maximizes their profit. In this column we'll be unveiling that "System" for you, and we'll also be exposing the tactics of the person you believe to be your number-one adversary — the car salesperson.

This business of buying a car is truly one area where knowledge is power, but it's also one where a little knowledge is dangerous. Assumptions can also be a serious problem, whether those assumptions are good or bad.

For example, assuming that all car sales people are crooks is not only a false assumption, but it colors the way you will interact with a salesperson in a showroom. And, like in all human interactions, the way you treat a person goes a long way in determining how they'll treat you. In other words, you treat people how you see them — and people treat you the way you treat them.

Sounds like the "Golden Rule" doesn't it? Well it is.

Automobile sales profes-

sionals are like people in any other line of work. They range from gruff, foul-mouthed Neanderthals to considerate, moral intellectuals — in approximately the same proportions as most other mid-level professions. In most cases they are products of the way they're treated. But they do have an agenda, and the more you understand it the better your car-buying experiences will be.

Make no mistake about it — whether they're good guys or bad, men or women, gruff or well-mannered — they are taught to follow a selling system that involves a lot more than just the price of the car. That system is designed to maximize their profit on both the car you buy AND any car you trade in.

It is an understanding of this "System" that will arm you to work your best deal, avoid getting caught in any of the after-market or paperwork traps that come after the basic price deal is struck, and do all this without any major confrontations with sales people or dealership managers.

In following issues we'll give you a fundamental understanding of how an automobile dealership works, how sales people are trained to sell you a car, and how you can use that knowledge to be a stronger consumer. This knowledge will translate into hundreds maybe thousands of dollars left in your pocket, next time you buy or trade in a car.

▶ Buying & Maintaining
YOUR AUTOMOBILE

CAR BUYING — WHO IS THE ENEMY?

The dictionary says attitude is, "a manner of acting, feeling or thinking that shows one's disposition or opinion...one's disposition, opinion or mental set..."

During the initial stages of learning how to buy a car at a maximum savings, in complete confidence, you must set an attitude (mental set) of a student who knows very little about a complex subject. This is even more important if you have bought many cars and *think* you know what you're doing.

Two Enemies

There are two people who will get you into serious trouble when learning the correct way to buy a car. One is The Attorney and the other is sales professionals.

The Attorney as defined in my book, *Save $100's/ $1,000 Buying Your New Car*, as a know-it-all when it comes to car buying. Usually a friend, neighbor or relative. This individual thinks he's smarter than you, the salesperson, the dealer or anyone else. He's the guy that can get you "The deal of a lifetime." But his advice will usually end up costing you a lot of money. Don't listen to The Attorney.

The Attorney thinks he is doing you a big favor but actually he's only a dupe of the car sales trade. He's the guy who listened and believed the bull that the car salesman told him when he got "put away" buying his last over-priced land boat.

Then There's the Salesman.

When I sold cars I made the customers from whom I made the most obscene profits believed they were the most shrewd car buyers that ever did a deal on the car lot. I fed the person's ego and made him believe that he really knew what he was doing... "Boy, I've got to hand it to you Mr. Farkwarts. My boss said that I screwed up on my last quote. He says you got us over a barrel. We have to give you the car at your price. Boy, you're good. Did you ever sell cars for a living?"

These suckers then drove home in their over-priced pieces thinking they were car buying experts because of the line I gave them. They in fact became "Attorneys" and sent me their friends as customers — who I promptly, but sadly, ripped off. I say sadly because I was selling cars to gather information for my book. The other salespeople were happily ripping off the customers.

We were formally trained to pump up and make the customer think he was an astute consumer. 99% of the customers believed us without question. The other 1% were in or had been in the care sales trade or sought wise counsel from a qualified teacher.

The only person qualified to teach you how to buy a car is someone who has been inside the car sales trade.

THE TWO PRICES IN CAR BUYING

There it sits on the car lot. The car of your dreams. Before we look at the window sticker of this high-tech marvel, let me define an important law that is going to be applied to you by the car dealer, it is called **The Law of Legitimacy.** I define The Law of Legitimacy as, "the more official you make a document, sign, price-tag, procedure, custom, tradition, dog & pony show, speech, etc. appear, the greater the probability is that it will be accepted without question by the person(s) to whom it is presented."

An example of this law is the "12 o'clock Noon Check-out," sign in the hotel. The astute consumer should be aware of The Law of Legitimacy and should question it when it is to his/her advantage.

Once, on a business trip, I called the hotel front desk and told them I would like a waiver to their 12 o'clock check-out time since my transportation to the airport wasn't coming until four. They granted my request telling me that the sign was for the majority of their guests (the other guy) but they would be happy to let me remain in my room until four without additional charge. The group I was traveling with was stiffly sitting in the lobby. They sat there from 11:30 with all there baggage while I spent that time in the comfort of my room. They accepted the official looking 12 o'clock Noon Check-out," sign without question. This is the Law of Legitimacy in action.

This law can be seen vividly applied to the window stickers of most new cars. One sticker is the Factory Retail Sticker and the other is the dealer added Addendum Sticker. This Addendum sTicker usually looks more official than the Factory Retail Sticker. The Addendum Sticker includes such items as: "Dealer Protection package," "Fabric Guard," "Vinyl Guard," "Kar Kop," "Market Adjustment," etc... The money added to the car's price by the Addendum Sticker is almost pure profit to the dealer.

One of the Addendum Sticker's line items may be something called "Market Adjustment," "Dealer Adjustment," "Trade Adjustment," or whatever other term that can be thought up to sound official. This item on the Addendum it was a figure used by his dealer "for negotiations." The smart car buyer will try to negotiate a lower, better, price than what is typeset on the sticker. (You would be surprised how many people are afraid to negotiate and plop down full price and lose thousands.) In order to effectively do this negotiation, the car buyer has to know about, "The two prices in car buying..."

The two prices in car buying are: (1) What the dealer wants for the car (2) What the dealer will eventually sell you the car for after negotiations.

In (1) the dealer wants what he paid for the car (Factory Cost) plus maximum profit. He gets this maximum profit by selling; at full Factory Retail Price, maximum Market Adjustment, all the add-ons he can put on (i.e. Protection Package, Super Blaster Disc Player, Never Steal Alarm System, Extra Heavy Duty Fan Belt Protector, etc. etc. (These add-ons are called, "The Front End Pack" and are in the Addendum Sticker). The dealer will also try to maximize his profits with, "The Sticker is a figure ($500-$2,500+) added by the dealer to the Factory Retail Sticker. One salesman told me, when I questioned about the "Market Adjustment, line on the Addendum Sticker, that Back End Pack." This includes: dealer financing (at maximum interest), credit life and other insurance, extended warranties, special maintenance programs, etc. etc.) The dealer also wants to give you minimum market value for your trade and sell it at top dollar for a large profit ($2,000+ for newer trades). (Later I'll go into how to sell your old car yourself and save you this money.)

The dealer will always sell you the car for his cost plus maximum profit. What we will do in determining our offer to the dealer is find out what they paid for the car and offer him this figure plus minimum profit, no profit, or negative profit. And we will only buy the add-ons that we want on the car — negotiate at dealer cost. The dealer is always going to make money, in the long, run even if he sells you the car below factory cost. He has secret factory incentives and downstream commissions called "Hold Back," that only the dealer and his comptroller ever really know about.

There are many factors/ variables that enter into the car buying equation. When these factors/variables are analyzed in a non-urgent environment — and a logical plan of action paced with realistic milestones is developed, we can than zero in on the lowest possible figure. We will offer this number, as a bid, to the dealer. The dealer will then sell us the car we really need and desire on our terms and not his.

DEVELOP A NEW CAR PLAN OF ACTION

PART ONE

When I fly from point A to B in bad weather I make up, file and fly an Instrument Flight Plan. This is a plan of my flight with a series of check points that I will follow. These check points will be flown over at certain times leading me to my destination at a designated time. It is an orderly series of calculated events that keeps me "in control" along the route of flight. Likewise the prudent car buyer—not the dealer—needs to be "in control" during the route to a new car purchase. This "control" is achieved with a plan — the New Car Plan of Action and Milestones.

Whenever you make a major expenditure such as buying a car, you should develop a plan of action. This plan of action should contain milestones to mark the various events that lead up to the car's purchase. The plan should be written out so that you will become methodical and deliberate throughout the buying process. Writing out the plan will force you to become analytical and emotionally detached from the car you eventually decide to buy. The one sure way of losing money when car buying is to get emotionally involved with the car and buy it in a hurried, rushed atmosphere. That is exactly what the salesman wants you to do.

The best Plan of Action with Milestones (POA&M) should span a time frame of about three months. The best time to start a POA&M is at "Showtime." Showtime is when the new models appear, usually in the Fall. The example of a POA&M I use in my book, *$AVE $100's/$1,000's BUYING YOUR NEW CAR*, starts in September with the actual acceptance of the car taking place during late December or early January.

The POA&M begins with the filling out the "NEEDS CHECK LIST." This Check List is designed to determine your needs for a new vehicle purchase. The car salesperson is delighted to have someone "drift" onto the car lot who doesn't have any idea of what he or she needs or wants. To buy a new car or truck and not have it fulfill your needs is wasting your money. You, and not the car salesperson, should determine your needs and your new car.

This check list is a series of questions to ask yourself at the onset of a new vehicle purchase plan of action. The answers to these questions will help you determine what type of vehicle you need.

Needs Checklist

1. What will this vehicle be primarily used for? Personal use (Pleasure)? Business? Combination business and pleasure? Other?
2. Who will use this vehicle the majority of the time? Myself? My spouse? My children? My business associates? Other?
3. How many miles a year will this vehicle be driven?
4. Is gas mileage an important factor? Desired MPG rating?
5. Is ease and cost of maintenance an important factor?
6. Do I need a car? 4 door sedan? 2 door? Hatchback? compact? Mid-size? Large? Luxury? Sports car? Convertible? Other?
7. Do I need a station wagon?
8. Do I need a van? Mini? Regular? conversion? 4-Wheel Drive? Other?
9. Do I need a truck? Light pickup? Regular pickup? Large pickup? King cab? Panel truck? 4-Wheel Drive? Other?
10. Do I need a combination car/truck? Jeep? Scout? Bronco? Blazer? 4-Wheel Drive? Etc.?
11. Do I need an off-road vehicle?
12. Do I need a Recreational Vehicle (RV)?
13. Do I need a specially designed vehicle? For handicapped driver? To transport handicapped people?

Once you have determined the type of vehicle you need, then you can create a "PRESENT/PAST CAR EVALUATION LIST". This list will draw on your past vehicle likes and dislikes so that you can effectively build the new vehicle you have determined that you need.

The "PRESENT/PAST CAR EVALUATION LIST," is a list of various features found on cars and trucks. What you do is, determine what you liked and/or disliked on vehicles you owned or observed in the past. From this check-list, you come up with the features that you want or definitely do not want on your new vehicle. Give yourself two weeks to complete the "NEEDS CHECK LIST," and the "PRESENT/PAST CAR EVALUATION LIST."

The next step in your POA&M is to Gather new Car Information.

YOUR NEW CAR PLAN OF ACTION

PART TWO

The next step in your Plan of Action and Milestones is to gather new car information from sources such as: car shows, magazines, newspapers, TV, and dealer visits. During the visits to the dealers, pick up brochures and begin your test drives.

I recommend test driving and rating at least six vehicles. One of the things a salesperson is required to do by the system is to "demo" you in the cars he is trying to sell. Be nice to the salesperson. Tell him that all you want to do is test drive a "(One of the cars you have selected that fits your needs and budget.)"

Be up front with him. Tell him what you are doing. Do not lie! Tell him you are looking for a car to buy, but first you must determine the correct one. Part of this evaluation is driving various cars. Tell him that if the type of car

he demonstrates to you is the type of car you decide to buy, you will see to it he gets the opportunity to sell it to you when you custom order the car.

Before you go onto a new car dealer's lot, remember this and remember it well. The car salesperson that comes up to you is going to try to sell you a car right then and there! He is going to sell you a car that he has on the lot. He is going to try to sell you the car that will put the most money in his pocket! The car he is going to try to sell you is the one the New Car Manager has on a "spiff." This is defined in my Dictionary of Car Salesperson's Jargon as, "Tax free cash bonuses paid car salespersons for selling various slow moving units." His objective is to put you down "the Path" and sell you the car with the biggest spiff at full retail with a protection package, and a market adjustment. He is going to try to sell you full dealer financing, credit life and health insurance, and an extended warranty. This is the objective of the car salesperson when he comes out

to you and shakes your hand and gives you his card.

Test Drive at Least 20 Minutes!

You have the advantage over the salesperson. You know what his objectives are. Ninety-nine percent of the car buyers that meet the car salesperson do not know his objectives, and not knowing them ends up costing the unsuspecting car buyer money. But you do. So be fair to him. Tell him all you want to do is test drive today. If he doesn't go along with your test driving, tell the salesperson that you are going to see his New Car Manager and ask him to assign you a salesperson who will serve your needs. This will strike terror into his heart and he will demo you in every car on the lot.

When you test drive, really test drive the car. Take it out for at least twenty to thirty minutes. Drive it over as many different roads as possible. In city traffic. On the interstate. Country roads. Everywhere that you can. Remember, even though you told the salesperson that all you wanted to do is test drive a car, he is going to do his best to sell you one right then and there. Usually the one you have just test driven. So, be strong and resist. Stick to your plan. Do not let him lead you down "The Path."

Gathering New Car Information and the Select Cars & Test Drive portion of you POA&M should take

about four weeks and runs concurrently with and works together with your Needs Check List and Present/Past Car Evaluation List.

If you'd like the new car buying forms and checklist package mentioned in this article, send $5.00 to RMK & Associates, Ltd., 2025 Fox's Lair Trail, Norfolk, VA 23518-4440.

[Editor's Note: Remember, the *Personal Financial Success* Financial Freedom Strategy recommends that you not buy new cars, but rather 2-3 year-old cars. However, if you can afford to buy a new one cash...follow Dick's Plan. And the plan works equally well for buying a pre-owned car.]

YOUR NEW CAR PLAN OF ACTION

PART THREE

During the first phase of developing your New Car Plan of action with Milestones, you determined the type of car you really need based on the Present/Past Car Evaluation Form and your Needs Check List. Then you went out to the various dealerships and test drove at least six cars. Now you have narrowed down your selection to the make and model of the car that you intend to get serious about and buy.

As a side note, I would like to point out that usually the best deal you can get on a new car, is to custom factory/order a new domestically (U.S.) built car whose options you choose to meet your specific needs and wants. However, the procedures I am going through will work for other cars as well. But you may not have the flexibility getting exactly what you want. You may have to compromise on certain options.

When you have selected the make and model, ask the salesman for the latest brochure that applies to your final selection. Sometimes the most up-to date literature on a certain vehicle is still unpacked in a bundle in a back room somewhere. These brochures cost a lot of money and the dealers like to use up the old ones first.

For our purposes you need the Latest information available about your car in order to properly select your options and build it.

Request a Bid

This all comes together when you fill out the New Car Specifications Sheet. The New Car Specifications Sheet is really a request for a bid from the dealer. You put the make and model, color, optional equipment and any other preferences that you want on your new car on this specification sheet. Then you send it out, under a cover letter, with a self-addressed stamped envelope, to as many dealers as possible. The more you send out the better. The sending out of the bids by letter is a very important step in buying your new car. Do not omit this step! It announces to the dealer/salesman that you are an exceptional consumer and that you know what you are doing. You will not be pressured into being worked by the system —The Track, The Path. You will be treated with the dignity and courtesy that befits an intelligent car buyer who has not been placed into a state of urgency by The Track.

The letter should be sent to the "General Manager" or the "New Car Sales Manager" of a particular dealership. Call the dealership and get the name of this person and the person who owns the dealership (the dealer himself). Address the letter to the manager by name. If, after about ten days, the manager doesn't reply to your letter and New Car Specifications Sheet with his offer, write a letter to the dealer and enclose a copy of your letter and the New Car Specifications Sheet to the manager. Tell the dealer you don't think his manager really wants to sell cars for him or something to that effect. You will usually get immediate and very kind attention from the manager or the dealer himself.

The first response to your letter and New Car Specifications Sheet will usually be a phone call from a salesman who wants you to come in right away for "The deal of a lifetime." Do not respond to his sales pitch. Tell him you are a very busy person and this purchase is the first of a multiple purchase and you cannot take the time to come in. Tell him if he wants your business, to fill out the New Car Specifications Sheet and send it back to you in the self addressed stamped envelope that you have included with your bid.

Gathering the Prices

Within a few days you will start receiving your replies. They will be one of two types: one will be the total retail price of the car with a dealer discount added, the other will be the factory invoice price with a dealer profit added to It. It you have a computer, take the results of your bids and put then on a spreadsheet for comparison. If you don't have a computer, list out the replies next to one another so you can view them all at a glance.

The next thing you do is to price out your car. I highly recommend you use H. M. Gousha's, "Automotive Invoice Service - New Car Cost Guide." This Publication is updated continually and new books are sent out as the new prices are published. You can order your own yearly subscription for a bout $70 a year.

Write to:
Automotive Invoice
Service
H. M. Gousha
2001 The Alameda,
PO Box 49006
San Jose, CA 95161-9006
(408) 296-1060, ext. 253

You can also get wholesale /retail car prices at your local bookstore. Look for "Edmund's Car Prices Buyer's Guide" or the "Kelly's Blue Book." After you get the wholesale and retail prices of the car you want, make up a NEW CAR SPEC/ PRICING SHEET. Then, select the dealer and negotiate a final price. This is called "doing the deal." Finally, draft your CONDITIONAL SALES AGREEMENT and you and the dealer sign the agreement. Put down your deposit and in about six weeks, pick up your new car.

Meanwhile, sell your old car yourself. When your car comes in, go through a final acceptance check-off. When you are fully satisfied with your new car, pay for it.

Buying & Maintaining YOUR AUTOMOBILE

YOUR NEW CAR PLAN OF ACTION

PART FOUR

The heart of your *New Car Plan of Action* is the NEW CAR PRICE/SPEC SHEET. This document enables you to be "in control" and not the dealer. It is central to the negotiations that follow. The NEW CAR PRICE/SPEC SHEET helps you to "do the deal" correctly because it contains all of the data necessary to make logical observations and decisions.

To put together the NEW CAR PRICE/SPEC SHEET, take your NEW CAR SPECIFICATIONS SHEET (that you sent to the dealers) and transfer all the information concerning the make, model, optional equipment and other preferences to a piece of paper and run it down the left side of the sheet. Then set up two columns to the right of the data. Title the first one "Dealer Invoice," and the second, "Suggested Retail."

Get a New Car Cost Guide

for that vehicle and fill in the two columns with the figures that apply to your vehicle. You can order a New Car Price Guide from:
Automotive Invoice Service
H.M. Gousha
2001 The Alameda
PO Box 49006
San Jose, CA 95161-9006

F.I.N.L. Subscribers can call 1-800-457-7283 and get unlimited price guides for $25.00 per year. See your F.I.N.L. Subscriber's Manual for details. For computer buffs who have access to CompuServe, another convenient pricing source is AutoVantage OnLine. Connect via "GO ATV."

After you've filled in the numbers under "Dealer Invoice" and "Suggested Retail," total out the columns. You then add the "destination charges" under both columns.

The total "Suggested Retail" column is now complete. This is the total retail price for the car. This is the "window sticker" price. To this price the dealer will usually add his "Addendum Sticker" to boost his profits. This

"Window Sticker" price is what the car salesman will refer to as the "fair price the federal government allows us to sell this vehicle for." Don't believe this!

Total up the "Dealer Invoice" column and add the "Dealer Group Funds" and what you determine to be a fair profit. This is the "Bottom Line Total." This is what you are going to pay for the vehicle, plus the cost of tags, title and taxes.

"Dealer Group Funds" (Chrysler) are called different things by different manufacturers. What they include are items on the factory invoice that are passed onto you directly. These charges do not appear on the window sticker. These legitimate charges include such items as: factory gasoline (8 gallons or less), fee for the vehicle's certificate of origin, national advertising, etc. You can determine these charges by asking the salesman what they are over the phone. Better yet, ask him to mail you a copy of the factory invoice. Tell him you need it for your price out. Believe it or not, most dealers will give you a copy of the factory invoice if you ask for it.

The "fair profit" figure depends on many variables—primarily the make and model of your vehicle. If it's a high demand, hot selling, turbo charged, low-slung piece, your fair profit should be about 1% to 2% over factory invoice. Otherwise, use a figure of about $100 to start, unless

the dealer is offering the vehicle at or below factory invoice. If this is the case, put in a zero or the appropriate negative figure.

Now, just add any local excise tax and state sales tax. Don't forget the cost of title and tags (you can get those figures from the dealer or the Department of Motor Vehicles). Add all these figures together to give you the "bottom line total." This is the maximum price you will pay for the vehicle.

Call the salesman and confirm what he sent you on the NEW CAR SPECIFICATIONS SHEET. Tell him you are coming in to "do the deal" and what you're prepared to offer. If he doesn't have a positive response, tell him you are going to his competitor. That usually gets results.

Don't allow the dealer to sneak in any line items on the final papers that you do not understand or agree with. If there's an item on the dealer's paper you do not want to pay for, simply line out that item and subtract it from the total. I once had a client who lined out "Administrative Fee = $100" and "DVF=$125." When pressed, the dealership said the administrative fee was for the office preparation and the DVF was a local fee that everybody paid. He refused to pay and the dealer finally agreed. Those two strokes of the pen saved $225. By the way, DVF stood for Dealer's Vacation Fund! How's that for nerve?!?

SELLING YOUR OLD CAR YOURSELF

PART ONE

One of the most lucrative profit centers for most car dealers is used car sales. The majority of these used car sales come from trades on the new cars the dealer sells. The average car buyer will trade in his old car and will unknowingly give the dealer a quick $1,000 to $3,000 profit (depending on the trade).

If your trade is a couple of years old, it is the same as if you said to the dealer, "I've got an extra $2,000 in my pocket that I want to give you to sell my car...your slick advertising has me convinced...it's much easier to trade it in than sell it myself...I'm not smart enough to sell it myself...so here, please take my hard-earned money..."

In order to be consistent in the advice I give you in selling your own car, I'm going to quote a section from my book, *$ave $100's/$1,000's Buying Your New Car*. This technique is described in chapter 6, Selling Your Old Car Yourself and *Consumer Reports* really liked it. You'll appreciate it too:

Sell Your Old Car Yourself

It's too hard to sell your car yourself! It's not worth the trouble! NOT TRUE! It's easy. It's easy when you are taking your time and not in a state of urgency. Only when you are rushed, and need the money from your old car for an immediate purchase of another car, does selling your car yourself seem difficult. When you take your time, all you have to do is follow these simple steps to sell your old car successfully.

What's It Worth?

First you have to determine what your old car is worth—it's value. You have to determine both the wholesale and retail prices of your car. Then advertise that the car is for sale. Sell it to someone who responds to the advertisement for a fair price, then transfer the title. That's all there is to it.

The wholesale value of your car is the price that someone who intends to resell your car will pay for it.

The Blue Book

How do you determine the wholesale value of your car? Most people who think they know something about selling cars will tell you to look up the wholesale cost in the "Blue Book." The so-called "Blue Book" does list the wholesale and retail prices of various old cars, but these prices are just representative of the market. Most lending institutions will have copies of the "Blue Book" available for you to look at. However, your car's wholesale price may be worth much more or much less than what's listed in the book. It's all relative. If there is a high demand for your old car in your part of the country, your car will bring in more wholesale dollars than are listed in the book.

A Clean Car = $$$

Before you show your new car to anyone, clean it up. Clean all of the junk out of the trunk. Take the car to a good car wash, or wash it yourself. Consider a thorough wax job. The idea is to give the car the eye appeal to attract the prospective buyer. Cleaning up will probably increase your car's selling potential many times. This one point is overlooked by most sellers, but the car dealers know the potential in a good cleaning. The first, and often the only thing a dealer does to a used car is wash and clean it up. This insures a faster sale at a higher price.

Once your car is looking its best, you are ready to take it around and show it. We want to show it to determine its wholesale value. The best way to determine wholesale value in not by looking it up in the "Blue Book," but by going to various used car lots around town and trying to sell your car to them.

The best negotiated price that you determine these used car dealers will pay for your car is the wholesale price for your car in the locale where you are trying to sell it.

Your Sale Price

The retail value of your car is the wholesale value plus the profit that someone intends to make from the sale of your old car. In order to determine the retail price, all you have to do is look in the classified section of your newspaper and see what prices are being requested for cars like yours. Look at the different "Auto Trader" type classified papers that you see throughout town—the ones you find at most supermarket check-out counters. After some investigation, you will have a pretty good idea of what the retail figure is for your old car.

Also, go look at the vehicles at used car dealers. Locate a car like yours and see what the retail price is on the sticker. Remember though that some dealers will put unrealistically high prices on their cars. There are some people who will pay these prices and the dealers just love them. However, astute buyers will negotiate the inflated price down to a more realistic figure.

Do not ask too little. If you ask too much you can always come down a bit. If you ask too little...well, you will give away dollars that should have ended up in your pocket.

SELLING YOUR OLD CAR YOURSELF

PART TWO

Advertise Your Sale

Sit down and write an ad. Use the ads you see in the newspapers and the auto traders as samples. Just fill in your particular figures. Use a little ingenuity. Tell the truth. Let your ad sit awhile. Revise it a couple of times and then you're ready for the next step.

Pick up the phone and call your ad into the newspaper or auto trader. The newspaper will send you a bill or they may ask for a payment with your ad. It depends on the paper. Some auto traders offer free ads. You pay only if you make the sale through their organization.

Once your ad is run, all you do is sit and wait for the phone to ring. Be aware that some car salespeople may respond to your ad inquiring about your car. Decline their offers to help you sell your car. Tell them you're doing it yourself and you do not require their assistance. Be nice. Say a prayer. Soon someone will respond and you will make a fair and equitable sale. Just be honest. Demand a fair price. Do not be greedy. You'll make out.

Other good places to advertise are through civic league newsletters, on bulletin boards around your neighborhood, on bulletin boards at work. Copy your ad with a bunch of those little tear-offs on the bottom with your phone number on them. Also, don't forget to put a sign in the car itself. Make it a good one. People will respond.

What if you still owe money on your car? What do you do to get the title and sell it to a prospective buyer? Call the lending institution who holds the note on your car and ask them for "the payoff on your car." They will tell you how much you still owe. When you make the sale, have your buyer give you a certified check for the sale amount. Then you and the buyer go to your lending institution together. The lending institution will take the buyer's check, payoff what you owe on the loan and give you the cash difference. The lending institution will then release the title to the new owner. The new owner goes to the Department of Motor Vehicles and gets a new title. It is here, at the Department of Motor Vehicles, where the new owner will pay the state sales tax on the car if a sales tax is levied in the state in which the car was sold.

Your Sales Contract

In order to keep everything in order and professional, you should make up a simple sales contract. I have included an example of a Car Sales Contract in Appendix A of my book. You can tailor it to your own requirements. There is no need to go to a lawyer for this simple buy-sell transaction.

There's one problem that may arise in selling your old car yourself. This problem is one of timing. What if you need the money from the old car to help pay for the new one? What you can do is sell the car before ordering your new one. You know that the new one is going to take about six weeks to arrive from the time you order it. So if you get a buyer, sell your old car to him but ask him if he would hold off until your new car arrives. Tell the buyer that if he will allow you a grace period until your new car arrives you will give him a discount. *Ask and ye shall receive*. You will be surprised at the cooperation people will give you if they feel you are honest and being fair with them.

There you have it. Simple? Sure is. Just follow the steps. You will save a lot of money when compared to the alternative—trading in at the dealer. So save your money and sell your old car yourself.

HOME ADDITION OR HOME IMPROVEMENTS?

When is a home improvement really an IMPROVEMENT? To some people, decorating, furniture, and landscaping mean home improvement, but to most it's adding a garage, room, bathroom or a basement.

As a realtor I'm often asked, "Should we move or improve?" The question requires more data to be answered properly. Will the improvement make your home the most expensive in the neighborhood? If the answer is yes, serious thought should be given to proceeding. If the answer is no, proceed with caution. Why?

People traffic

I'm sure you've been in homes that had a bedroom that only has access through another bedroom. Possibly a garage was converted into a bedroom, but it is located at the other end of the house, or a bathroom that you cannot walk in standing up straight, or even a kitchen where you cannot open the oven door all the way. These mistakes can be easily avoided or minimized by hiring a good architect. Major improvements requiring exterior changes will necessitate an architect because your municipality will insist on a blueprint drawn by a professional before they will issue a building permit.

The next question is cost

Can I do this cheaper than finding another home? The architect will give you a cost estimate so you will know the approximate cost, but the only way to make an accurate assessment is to know the value of your home, add the cost of the improvement, minus the cost of moving. Armed with this information, it's time to see what this will buy you. Your Realtor will be happy to supply you with a list of homes, and possibly give you a tour of the area with specific homes that include your improvements.

Improvement value

Let's list some things you can do and give you some idea about value. A roof , furnace, windows, skylights, kitchen, baths and insulation are all items that were originally included in the house and are expected when you purchase a house. Replacing or upgrading them maintains your home or increases its energy efficiency, or in the case of a new roof, protects your home from damage. But as far as those items increasing its value depends on what your neighbors are doing.

For instance, if everybody on the block is putting on a new roof, but you're not, your property value is *decreasing* because you are not "keeping up with the Jones." You will reap a percentage of this type of maintenance but certainly not all of it. It could possibly reduce your selling time however, and if you ever tried selling a home, you know how important this can be.

Fireplaces, central air conditioning, family rooms, sun rooms, screened porches, decks, additional bedrooms or baths, luxury baths and finished basements will all add value to your property anywhere between 50% and 150% of their cost. A good example might be finishing a walk-out basement (ground level) which could be added as above ground living space and easily get 150% of cost.

Swimming pools, hot tubs and saunas have a value from -50% to +100% depending on climate and acceptance in your area. A swimming pool in the Chicago area can only be used approximately 90 days a year, so most people consider them a liability instead of an asset. And unfortunately for pool owners in the Chicago area, the real estate appraisers agree. I have been known to tell pool owners to fill them with dirt and turn them into a flower garden. The cement deck gives it a nice border. I really recommend consulting your Realtor before embarking on your home improvement venture. You may be surprised at their evaluation of your project.

One thing left to consider

If you really like your home, your neighbors, the schools your children attend, or the trees in your backyard that are just the perfect distance apart for your favorite hammock, or you just hate moving, here's something else to think about. Let's consider what the cost to move includes: either a moving company or truck rental and six cases of beer for your friend, title charges, survey, real estate fees, attorney fees, service charge and points on new loan for your new home, and on and on. I am going to give a combined cost of ten percent of value for these services, i.e., a $100,000 home would be $10,000. If you can change your $100,000 home and not spend over $10,000 and do not get a penny back in added value, you can make the change in your home for FREE.

SELLING YOUR HOME

Why do you want to sell your home?" Your motive and time schedule are going to be the most important factors in determining how to proceed.

Are you taking a new job and have to start in 30 days; is your wife pregnant and due in 60 days; does your oldest child start first grade in 90 days; or are you retiring to a vacation home which you have modernized and upgraded over the years?

What kind of market is it?

How many homes are already for sale in you price RANGE? How many homes were sold in that price range last year during the time you will be selling this year? Has anything changed to influence the marketplace positively or negatively, to change that anticipated market? The most significant change would be interest rates. Next, economic conditions, not just nationally, but local changes i.e. a major employer relocating, laying off or closing like Boeing in Seattle or GM in Detroit.

Environmental issues such as land fills or toxic waste disposal could be a concern. Possible relocation or opening of a major highway near or behind your home can cause uneasiness.

Remember anticipation of a change is sometimes worse than the reality. So if you can wait until a problem passes or a highway opens, WAIT. If not, gather as much information on it as possible. Knowledge is power. If all conditions have remained the same, you can reasonably expect that the same number of homes should sell.

If you determine that you are in a seller's market — less homes for sale than sold in the same time period last year — you have the opportunity to get top dollar for your home. To find out what top dollar is, you can hire an independent fee appraiser or call several Realtors and get what they call a CMA (Competitive Market Analysis). This consists of number of homes for sale in your price range, expired listings and listings under contract or sold and closed. The fee appraiser uses only sold and closed properties which tend to lag behind the market so in a seller's market you could be shorting yourself depending on how hot the marketplace.

Remember, the buyers don't see sold homes, only what is for sale. In a seller' market you have two choices, sell it yourself FSBO (for sale by owner) or use a Realtor.

Why pay a Realtor?

To find out how effective Realtors are in your area, talk to your local township tax assessor. He should be able to tell you what percentage of homes are sold by Realtors versus those sold by owner. A lot depends on the type of community you live in and where the buyers come from.

If you live in a large metropolitan area where business transfers supply a large number of buyers and you want access to them, a Realtor is your best bet. Most of these folks have two house hunting trips; one to see if they like the area and can afford to take the job in the first place and then a trip with their family to locate a home and arrange financing. These people don't have time to look at the newspaper, drive around looking for signs and then wait for you to get home to show it to them. They have to be as efficient as possible in their home search, so they'll work with a realtor.

Local people also use Realtors for some of the same reasons. In this drive in, drive up and "my time is limited" era, the Realtor offers the most efficient source of merchandise, viewing, financing, community and school information, etc. So a seller can only access these buyers through a Realtor.

FOR SALE

However, if you decide you have the time and want to save the Realtor's commission, remember two things: First, the buyer knows you are saving the money too and will think they can save a least half if not all the commission. Second, you have to perform all the tasks a Realtor does; in essence, do his job to earn his wages; i.e. advertise, buy a yard sign, show the house, wait for people who call (and not show up), show the home to those who do show up, and try to qualify the buyer for ability to purchase your home. So get a contract from your attorney so you can lock in the buyer and don't forget to get earnest money from the buyer. Find out what financing is available and pray the buyer is qualified to purchase your home.

The truth is that a good Realtor can make you money. For example: on listings where an agent has a buyer who has seen a home for sale and has asked if any offers have come in, because they can't quite get their customer to make a decision. If the customer believes someone else is going to take it way from them, they'll make an offer to purchase. In this situation the seller now has two customers for his home and has the opportunity not just to pick the best qualified buyer, but in my experience, usually gets 2-5% more for his home.

Buying & Selling
REAL ESTATE

CHOOSING THE RIGHT REAL ESTATE AGENT TO MARKET YOUR HOME

Many homeowners choose an agent to sell their largest and most expensive personal possession, their home, with less care than they choose their wardrobe. They may select a relative or a friend they met at the community swimming pool or the golf course. My suggestion is to pick a good LISTING agent.

The key word here is *listing*. Many times sellers call our office asking for our top sales agent, the agent that sells the most buyers. This is off the mark by a mile. Very few good selling agents are good listing agents. Those that are, are few and far between.

What are the credentials of a good listing agent?

Real estate people should be excited to show you the designations they have earned i.e. CRS (National Association of Realtors' Certified Residential Specialist or some large organizations have their own designation such as Century 21's RS, Residential Specialist) or GRI (Illinois Association of Realtors' Graduate Realtors Institute.) This indicates the agent has an interest in maintaining not only a certain skill level, but also considers Real Estate their profession.

It's important for you to know the person you are "hiring". Ask questions. Is Real Estate the primary source of income for this agent's family? Can you communicate well with this person, understand their explanation of services and programs? Consider this an interview process — you are the "Chief Executive Officer, C.E.O." of your corporation. The agent should be knowledgeable of the marketplace i.e. school rating, utility rates, park district informa-

tion, tax and community information. The agent should pay close attention to details making sure to display items that will help sell your home. Checking with the agents that have shown your home to get their customers' reaction to your home is also an important element. Sometimes a negative feature can be corrected by a minor change resulting in a quicker sale with more money in your pocket. It is extremely important that your agent has a good reputation in the Real Estate community because cooperation and feedback from other Realtors is critical to the sale of our home. In our area over 70% of the homes are sold by the Multiple Listing Service (MLS) cooperation.

The firm of the agent you select is also of great importance. How does the firm stack up in your marketplace? The one with the most listings may not be the best. You are interested in the attention you are going to receive. Being one of hundreds does not make you special or very important to the firm you are about to choose. They have to be big enough to supply all the services you expect but small enough to give your home the attention you're paying for.

National recognition helps to attract transferees to their office. People as a rule like to do business with people they recognize from eating establishments to lodging franchises, and yes, even their real estate needs. We

know the consistency of service to expect from well-known national organizations.

The agent should prepare a Competitive Market Analysis (CMA) and Marketing Plan. A CMA is a detailed comparison of your home with other homes in the same general area. They are of the same style for sale in competition with your home.

These are the homes that buyers will see along with your property. A good listing agent will go look at your competition and make comparisons so your home will compete with them. The second part of the CMA is properties that have sold that are similar to your home. This is particularly important because even if you find a buyer that will pay top dollar for your home, if the buyer requires financing (that is, not a cash transaction) the lender will be sending an appraiser to verify that your property is worth what their customer has agreed to pay. These days with the lenders coming under fire for bad loans, the appraisers are very cautious to be as accurate with their information as possible. This is where a good agent can help, by supplying information to the appraiser - the same information he gave you to help price your home correctly in the first place.

continued next page

The Marketing Plan

The marketing plan is just as important. It is basically the process the agent goes through to market your home, and the reports that will be provided to you. This process will be discussed in great detail in a future article.

I would now ask the agent for two lists:
1. The names and phone numbers of the last two or three of their listings that have sold, these could be under contract or already closed.
2. Copies of the listings they currently have on the market with the materials and reports they have provided those sellers to date.

Call the people on the list and ask them if they would list their home with this agent again, and if not, why not? Please keep in mind most sold sellers are more likely to be happier than the sellers who are currently for sale. This will accomplish two things. It will demonstrate the agent's actual work and give you an opportunity to find out if the agent lives up to his/her promises.

The agent plays a key role in the sale of your property. Skill, knowledge and patience can have a great influence not only on the price you will receive, but how long it will take for your home to sell. Hire you Real Estate Agent wisely.

TAKING ADVANTAGE OF LOWER INTEREST RATES

Now is an excellent time to consider benefitting from the new low interest rates. According to recent newspaper articles, interest rates have fallen to the lowest level in nearly four years. The Chicago-area average on a 30 year fixed rate has slipped to 8.25%. This is the lowest interest rates have been since December 2, 1986. As a residential property owner, this could translate to huge savings for you.

If the interest rate on your current mortgage is between 10.5% and 12.5%, you should give serious consideration to refinancing. Paying off the existing mortgage with funds secured from a new mortgage, you could save substantial dollars by refinancing at today's interest rates. Home equity loan borrowers may also benefit from the new lower interest rates. For example, say you had a prior 30 year fixed mortgage with an interest rate of 12% with a principal amount of $150,000. The payment from that loan would be $1,542.92. If you were to refinance that same loan today, at a 9% fixed payment, the monthly payment would drop to $1,206.94. That would be a savings of $221.55 per month. This translates to an incredible savings of $120,952.80 over the entire life of the loan.

Even after taking into consideration the closing costs associated with your refinance, most mortgagees are finding that this makes sense. Closing costs typically include attorney's fees, closing points and title insurance costs. By shopping around, you might be able to find a lender who will waive the closing points. We will be pleased to assist you in evaluating whether this would be an appropriate time to refinance.

ying & Selling REAL ESTATE

HOW TO GET THE BEST PRICE FOR YOUR HOUSE

The best price at which to sell your home is always determined by how you stack up against your competition. If your property looks better than the next guy's the customers will buy yours.

So, let's make it look great!

Any real estate professional will tell you that the hardest thing to get across to most sellers is that simple changes they can make to fix up their home will yield at least a 2 to 1 dividend, not to mention that it can reduce the selling time. The seller's response is usually, "Why should I do it, the buyers will want to pick their own colors, style or quality."

I'm sure this is true, but here's what the buyers say:

1. This house needs too much work.
2. It's going to cost money

I need for my buying costs.
3. It's going to cost a lot of money to make these changes.

This is what they mean:

1. I have to undo all that the sellers have done before I can live there.
2. It costs me less out-of-pocket cash if these improvements go in my mortgage.
3. When the buyer picks things out for the house they pick out higher quality items than the seller would i.e. if $12.00/yard carpet would be the proper replacement cost for worn out, outdated or wrong color carpet, the buyer would choose $18.00 to $22.00/yard carpet or about 50 to 75% more than an adequate replacement carpet would cost.

I hope you get the picture that *you* should do it, and the sooner the better.

The new term for this process is called "Staging" the house.

Staging is taking what you have, and making sure it shows at its best. This is accomplished with minor repairs, some decorating and a lot of elbow grease. It's no different than a used car dealer shining up the cars inside and out, putting them under bright lights with the red and white ones in the front. You systematically go through your home, inside and out, room by room, and improve it — not for living but for selling.

This is how it works

Start with the outside: paint it, wash it and clip it. First impressions are lasting, and you don't get a second chance to make a good first impression. Make sure it sparkles. Look at your home from the street. If you can't see it through the trees, trim the lower branches off and trim bushes so windows are completely exposed. Make sure your approach to the house is clear of overhanging foliage. Wash the exterior windows. If shutters would be a nice touch, install them. If you have a blacktop drive, put a fresh coat of sealer on it.

The inside: We arrange furniture in a room to accommodate our lifestyles rather than considering whether the room looks its best that way. This is particularly true with rooms in which we spend a great deal of time. We all know that a family room should function as a "room for the family." However, when you're selling your home, because the family room is such an important

room, it's crucial that it be inviting and show well. If all the furniture is arranged without regard for how the room looks, but rather so that watching TV is easy, and if the floor is littered with toys because that's where the children play, the family room may look like a cluttered mess, leaving the buyer with a feeling that it's small, or worse still, that there's something "wrong" with it.

Form Follows Function

The function of a room should essentially be exhibited in that room. For example, a formal dining room can look quite spectacular if the table is set with beautiful linen, fine bone china, silver and crystal. This immediately creates a formal dinner party atmosphere and the buyers can visualize themselves entertaining in this room. On the other hand, if there are file cabinets next to the buffet, a computer and printer on the dining table, and spread sheets strewn everywhere, this can destroy the atmosphere of a formal dining room. Later in the day, the buyer may remember the house "with the ugly dining room," or because it wasn't used as a dining room, the buyer may remember the house, but think it didn't have a dining room at all!

Empty rooms can very often make a home "feel" cold. Not all buyers can visualize how a room will

(continued next page)

look furnished. Sometimes we have an excess of furniture throughout the house. There may be an extra love seat in one of the bedrooms, a rocking chair and miscellaneous tables here and there. Taking a little from here and there, hanging a few pictures on the walls, and filling a huge empty corner with a wonderful big plant can make a room look furnished and warm. Renting the appropriate furniture is also an option.

Next, the closets — the less in them, the larger they look. If the master bedroom is short on closet space, you should check into closet organizers. And while you have the closets empty, why not give them a coat of paint. White, please.

Then the wallpaper. If it is out of date, take it off and paint the walls white. If you have dark, wood panelled walls, consider painting them white. The same with kitchens. The brighter the better, and "busy" is what you want the cook to be, not the floor. If it needs replacing, remember the carpet example. That goes for the kitchen floor too. Kitchen counters should be cleared — just the basic items you have to have.

Bathrooms: make sure faucets shine but not drip. Toilets should flush property and not keep running. Make sure the tile is in good shape and the grout is clean, remove any mildew. Repair or replace chipped sinks and bathtubs. There are a number of companies that perform this service and give you a warrantee. Keep them neat and free of clutter.

Basements should be neat and orderly. The furnace and hot water heater should be dusted and accessible. As a matter of fact, getting them serviced for winter or air conditioners checked for summer would be a good idea. Remember, Murphy's Law! If you have cracks in the basement walls that you've patched, which don't leak, paint the walls. If they're not a problem, don't draw attention to them.

The hardest thing to get across to most sellers is that the changes they can make to fix up their home will yield at least a 2 to 1 dividend.

Staging a home is not necessarily expensive. Sometimes a room can look twice the size if the furniture is rearranged - sometimes rearranging furniture and pictures, purchasing some decorative pillows in the latest colors and adding a few plants can totally transform a room. (Silk plants are perfect for this purpose because you don't have to worry about them dying during the move!)

If the home is over ten years old, you should consider a home warrantee program. Most cover the seller during the time their home is offered for sale and the buyer for one year after closing. Remember to get top price. You have to be better than your competition.

It's critical to consider the impact the newer homes have on buyers. These new homes have all the bells and whistles — skylights, larger windows, Jacuzzi tubs, etc. It's important then if you own a home that has small windows and no skylights that drapes are drawn and blinds opened to let in as much light as possible. This is a good time to see if your windows need washing. In rooms that are dark, leave the lights on.

These are just a few of the things that you, as a seller, can do to insure getting the best price for your home. Always seek the advice of your real estate professional before making any changes. Your agent may even have a video tape on the subject for your viewing. Your agent is as anxious for your property to sell as you are, because their success is dependent upon the sale of your property. If your property doesn't sell, they don't get paid.

WHAT SHOULD BE IN A REALTOR'S MARKETING PLAN TO SELL YOUR HOME?

Here's a list of the items a good realtor will have in his or her marketing bag of tricks while preparing to sell your home:

1. Sign
2. Keybox
3. Information to MLS
4. Write ads and extra photos taken
5. Information to neighbors
6. Special features
7. Target market group
8. Homeowner help
9. Price reduction

Let's take them one at a time.

1. Sign. Over 30% of the inquiries to a Realtor's office come from signs. This doesn't mean that every person that calls is a buyer for your home, but it is a customer for the Realtor. Most people who call in have better taste than they can afford. They underestimate the value of your home but are still a good customer for the Realtor's other properties. That's why having a variety of product prices is why the Realtors can say "If this isn't in your budget, I have others."

2. Keys or Keybox. Access to the property is imperative. If the buyers can't see it, they won't buy it. I recommend the keybox because it's easy access for the agents and gives you an edge on the competition. If they're not used in your area, then make sure your agent has many copies of your key. Agents are known to keep a key until they're finished showing all the properties they've picked out for a customer before they bring the key back. make sure everyone who wants access can have it.

It always brings a smile to my face to see "Owner always home" on the listing sheet. They are never there when I call. Believe me, no one is "ALWAYS" home. It just doesn't mean home - it means able to answer the phone when in the garage, bathtub, backyard, basement etc. A telephone answering machine will take the message of when the agent is coming if you want advance notice. People worry about their valuables, so when your home is open to the public small easy to remove items should be put in a safe deposit box or a relatively safe place not left in the open. The same thing goes for breakables, put them out of harms way. You have a family home, it's likely a family will look at it; many times the children accompany the parents when they view properties.

3. MLS. The details of your home that your realtor provides to the Multiple Listing Service should be prompt, complete and accurate. This is your access to the Real Estate Community and is the largest single factor in the sale of your home.

4. Ads written and extra photos taken. These will be used for not just newspapers, but for other advertisements on your home. These should be seasonal and changed as the seasons change. If your home looks better in a different season,

> ### Marketing a home is really a "TEAM" effort and anything you can do to help the agent will not only reduce selling time, but probably increase the dollars you receive.

put your pictures displaying its beauty in a conspicuous place.

5. Information to neighbors. Your neighbors already like the neighborhood and can be a great help in supplying customers. Their friends, business associates and relatives are common purchasers.

6. Special features can have attention brought to them, both in and outside the home. Energy efficient qualities can be mentioned in literature, but the best way is to enumerate the benefits. Make a list of the utility bills by month for the last 12 months and give an average monthly amount for each as the benefit. If you don't have bills, your local utility bill gives you the averages. Riders telling of special features can be attached to the Realtor's sign in front of your home.

7. Target market group. If your home has a unique feature your agent can get a list of people who might be interested: for example, your on or near a golf course — you would mail information on your home

continued next page

to all the members or frequent players of that course. If you have a swimming pool, your agent would send information to all the swim teams and exercise facilities with pools or medical rehabilitation facilities for distribution to the members or patients or for placement on there respective bulletin boards. If your home is one that would appeal to a first time home buyer, then your agent would target rental complexes where the rent is roughly equivalent to what a buyer's after-tax payment would be. Let me give you an example: I once had an agent who lived in an area where an airstrip for small planes was the feature of the neighborhood. She asked her husband to fly her to all nearby airstrips. She then posted a list of the properties she had for sale on the bulletin boards. Within a few weeks she had sold all the available properties to the specialty audience she knew small plane owners were the target market group most likely to purchase those properties. Who else would want planes taking off and landing in their back yards.

8. The homeowner can help. If you work where your co-workers are potential customers for your home, many companies have bulletin boards or computer mail systems that allow employees to inform co-workers about things they have for sale. These are only available to employees so the agent would not ordinarily have access to this market. If you produce a buyer for your home, I'm sure the agent has a program worked out to offer some discount or bonus to reward you for your effort. I'm sure your thinking if you come up with the buyer you don't need the agent, but actually just the opposite is true. If the buyer is a co-worker, a professional "go-between" is invaluable and can not only get you a higher price, but preserve the co-worker relationship.

9. Price reduction. This is the one no seller wants to hear. The best advice is to start at the right price. If a home is overpriced no amount of marketing is going to sell it. Buyers today are quite knowledgeable. It would be rare for them to look at one home and buy it. They always want selection; a choice, a chance to make comparisons so unless all your competition is overpriced, it's unlikely they're going to choose your home over them. But even if you start out with what seems to be the right price, if market conditions change or the buyers don't agree, you have two choices: make the house worth more, improve it, or reduce the price, if you have a lot of customer showings, but no offers. Sellers generally say bring me an offer and I'll consider it, but the Real Estate professionals (sub agents of the listing agent) try to get the seller as close to asking price as possible. It would be unusual for them to bring in a low offer. Sellers also say, no one has seen my house so how can it be overpriced? But if the agent has exposed it as we've described above, the John W. Public and the Real Estate Public have decided you're not realistic and have ruled you out. So you must reduce the price to be more competitive.

Marketing a home is really a "TEAM" effort and anything you can do to help the agent will not only reduce selling time, but probably increase the dollars you receive.

MARKETING CHECK LIST

WOULD YOU LIKE A NEW HOUSE OR JUST CASH BACK?

Let me tell you a true story. When I asked one of my past customers what his interest rate was he said, "Gee, I'm not sure, but I think it's 12 or 13%." I asked if he thought about re-financing and he said no — we've been here 8 years and I don't want to start over on a 30 year loan." I then asked, "If you could reduce your loan term to 15 years and reduce your payment by $75.00 a month, would you be happy?" His response was something like, if it sounds too good to be true — it usually is. Or, I bet you sell "bridges" too.

Many of us are so busy making enough just to pay the bills, we forget to look at them and think if there is a less expensive way to live.

Here is the above situation described numerically: Original Loan $60,000 at 12.5% for 30 years = $640.35 P/I Balance after 8 years, $57,500 at 8.5% for 15 years = 566.11 P/I Savings of $74.24 or you can keep paying $640.35 each month and borrow $65,000, pay off the 57,500 balance and end up with $7,500. No wonder he thought I was trying to sell him a bridge.

Just so you don't think it's too good, there are a few expenses, i.e. Loan origination, Appraisal fee, Survey, Credit report, Title charges,

Recording fees, etc., all which in this case won't exceed $1,000.00. So to recap, he can have $6,500 to pay his Christmas bills and pay his loan off 7 years early. HAPPY NEW YEAR!

Not all situations are that rewarding. To determine your benefits, you have to first decide how long you plan to stay in your home, then calculate the benefits per month, then see how many months it takes to make up for the expenses to get the new loan. For example, your present loan of $100,000 at 10% for 30 years is $878.10/mo. and now you can get a 9% loan for $805/mo. This is a savings of $73.00. If your expenses for the new loan equal $845.00, it will take you approximately 1 year to make up those expenses so your savings don't start until after the year ends.

So far I've only talked about fixed rate loans and there are other alternatives such as special 5 or 7 year balloon loans. These aren't true balloons, where the loan is due at the end of 5 or 7 year period; these loans are adjusted at the end of those periods to a fixed amount over a predetermined index such as the Fannie Mae rate plus 1%. The benefit of this loan to you is a lower initial rate, the benefit to the lender is it's an adjustable loan

after 5 or 7 years. Again how long you plan to stay in your home will be the critical questions in your selection of the new loan or even if a new loan is worthwhile.

Upgrading Homes

This is a great time to upgrade to your next home. If we use the same example of a $640.35 P/I payment on the original mortgage of $60,000 at 12.5% and a 9% loan for 30 yeats would equal $79,600 that's almost $20,000 more for the same P/I payment just because the interest rate dropped. Now let's consider this advantage and a flat or down market which could create a wonderful opportunity for someone who is confident in their own job security. Most people feel if their home was once worth $110,000 and now worth $100,000 that it's time to dig in, not upgrade, but lets analyze this, if your house is worth 10% less so is the one you'd like to buy.

If it is worth $165,000 and now it's worth $150,000...

YOURS	THE ONE YOU WANT
was $110,000	was $165,000
now $100,000	now $150,000
dif. $ 10,000	dif. $ 15,000

You actually gained $5,000 or a 50% benefit over buying the house in a good market. Now let's finance it.

YOUR HOUSE	THE HOUSE YOU WANT
$100,000	$150,000
40,000 Equity	40,000 Equity
Now $60,000 at 12.5%	$110,000 at 9% for 30 years
Present $640.35 /mo. P/I	$885.08/mo. P/I

If you wait for a normal market to sell and purchase, this is what happens:

	Normal Market
$110,000	$165,000
60,000 Loan amount	50,000 Equity from old house
50,000 Equity	$115,000 Loan at 9% for 30 years
	$925.32/mo. P/I

Even though you have more equity from your present home in an up market, you can see your loan amount and resulting payment is higher.

An added bonus of lower prices is most expenses for sale and purchase are based on sale prices and loan amounts. Since the price is lower, so are the expenses.

With lower interest rates and many areas of the country experiencing lower prices a GOLDEN opportunity could be awaiting you. What are you waiting for? Call your Realtor NOW!

Buying & Selling
REAL ESTATE

THE FIRST STEP IS ALWAYS THE HARDEST

Buying Your First Home

When is the right time to buy your first home? To answer this question the following must be asked:

1. Are you going to stay in the same area for 3 to 5 more years?
2. Are you confident your going to be employed for that time period?

If you answered "yes" to these questions right now is the time to buy.

I'm sure you're thinking, "that's great, but doesn't it cost a lot of money to buy a home?" Yes, it costs money, but money can come from many sources. Number one is mom and dad. Some young folks are uncomfortable asking because they want to try it on their own. Let's face it, since most moms and dads are homeowners, we know that they believe home ownership is a good thing and they will generally help if they can.

Number 2 is to take the down payment out of your savings, which most young folks don't have. That is why option 1 seems so attractive.

Number 3 is to sell your toys, motorcyles, boats, baseball cards, stamps, coin collections, etc

Number 4 is to borrow from your life insurance policy.

What you need from these sources is about 5% of the value of the property you'd like to buy. The other 95% will be provided by the Lender, Savings and Loan, Bank, Mortgage Company, Credit Union, etc. The only other dollars needed are for closing expenses and that sometimes, can come from the seller (see sidebar next page).

What should I buy?

Two things determine this: your income, and the location of employment.

Depending on the area where you live, costs will vary, but generally incomes match the area or employers wouldn't have employees. Here are your options: Single family, town house or condominium depending on your needs and the price you're able to pay.

Here's an example to help determine your price range		
$50,000 @ 9% for 30 yrs	=	$402 50/mo P&I
If taxes are $750/yr 1/12	=	$62 .50/mo
If insur. is $120/yr 1/12	=	$10.00/mo
If assocation dues	=	$50.00/mo
Total	**=**	**$525.00/mo**

To qualify for the payment in the above example, you need to make about $19,000 gross income per year. With two incomes that shouldn't be too difficult. You can multiply or divide all these numbers by 1.5, 2, 3, etc. if your income and the prices in your area are different.

You don't have to be married to combine incomes for the purchase of a home. It can be a friend, brother, sister, father or mother. You do need to have an agreement as to what to do if one of you has to move or if they aren't going to live with you. What happens if they need their equity? And when you sell, who gets what? Consult your attorney for more on this matter.

Let's assume you're not going to get the home of your dreams the first time out. After all, we all have unrealistic expectations when we start out. That's why when you go to an open house it always costs more than you think. But here's how you can speed up the process and get closer to your dream.

Sweat Equity

The Real Estate term is "Sweat Equity" and it means exactly what is says — you get paid for your labor so you can buy something in a good location for a lower price and fix it up. "Fixing it up" can mean many things. I'm referring to minor remodeling, updating and decorating. It could mean buying an unfinished home or putting on an addition (if you're qualified to do it and the home and area warrant it). There's a local builder that finishes homes to various levels of completion giving the buyer the opportunity to do work for "Sweat Equity." It's so successful, he's one of the 10 largest builders in Illinois. Do-it-yourself books and videos are great. Experienced relatives and friends are even better. Do you remember hearing about our ancestors having "Barn Raisings"?

Finding Your Dream Home?

Consult your local Realtor

(continued next page)

and ask if they do "Buyer Brokerage." This is a relatively new concept for most residential real estate agents even though it's been around in commercial real estate for years. Here's what it means in a traditional real estate office: the seller lists his property and pays the fee to the agents so the agents have a legal responsibility to the seller — even the agent that's helping you. This means the agent works for the seller not for you, the buyer.

With Buyer Brokerage *you* hire the agent and sign a contract with him or her. Their allegiance is now to you. They'll supply you with information regarding value, location and conditions. They now can also show you "For Sale By Owner" property as well as listed properties and new homes not listed. This gives you an even a wider selection than before. The dollars to pay your agent comes from the seller in your behalf. Since you'll be signing a contract with the agent, make sure you're comfortable with not just the agent's personality but their ability, knowledge of the market and financing. You want them to help you obtain the best home for the best price with the best terms You may also hire more than one agent but not in the same area. The real estate contract should have a time period, define the specific area in

which they will be looking for you and any other special terms you require.

A good Real Estate agent can not only help you purchase your first home, but also helps you maximize your purchasing power by allowing you to purchase a larger or fancier home now and eliminate the need to move in 3 to 5 years. This is especially true since interest rates are at the lowest level in over a decade. Choose your agent wisely. Use recommendations from parents friends and relatives. If you happen to be lucky enough to know a real estate agent — even if they don't service the area you would like to live — they can often refer you to someone that serves your area of choice.

Remember, if you continue to rent you'll buy the place you live in for your landlord, not for yourself.

A HORROR CLASSIC: "THE LOAN PRINCIPAL THAT WOULDN'T GO AWAY"

WARNING: The following information is not for the squeamish. If you're faint of heart, please turn the page.

Look at the chart below to determine how much of your principal is remaining on your home mortgage. You'll see that, in most cases, you're well past the half-life of your mortgage before your payments begin to whittle away appreciably at the principal amount. Almost all of your payments for the first half of your mortgage term goes toward paying interest (profit) to the wealth-sucking lending institutions.

Loan Remaining After

Interest rate	5 years	10 years	15 years	20 years	25 years	30 years
Life of mortgage—30 years						
7%	94%	86%	74%	57%	33%	0%
7.5%	95%	87%	75%	59%	34%	0%
8%	95%	88%	77%	60%	36%	0%
9%	96%	89%	79%	63%	39%	0%
10%	97%	91%	82%	66%	41%	0%
Life of mortgage—25 years						
7%	91%	79%	61%	36%	0%	
7.5%	92%	80%	62%	37%	0%	
8%	92%	81%	64%	38%	0%	
9%	93%	83%	66%	40%	0%	
10%	94%	85%	69%	43%	0%	
Life of mortgage—20 years						
7%	86%	67%	39%	0%		
7.5%	87%	68%	40%	0%		
8%	87%	79%	41%	0%		
9%	89%	71%	43%	0%		
10%	90%	73%	45%	0%		

Buying & Selling
REAL ESTATE

HOW TO SELL YOUR OWN HOME IN TODAY'S MARKET

The editor of this newsletter has asked me to guide you through selling your own home without using a real estate broker. This is a new perspective for me since my whole real estate career has been spent believing a real estate broker generally gets more money for a seller with a lot less trouble and aggravation. The truth is, it's a matter of paying yourself instead of the real estate broker. The steps to sell a home are as follows:

I. Pricing
II. Marketing
III. Negotiating
IV. Closing

Pricing

This is the one most critical element in selling your home. Price compensates for location, condition, financing etc. To establish the correct price, I suggest you hire an appraiser. One that has an SRA designa-

tion. The appraiser will find three similar properties that have sold within the last 3-6 months. These comparable properties will then be used as a basis to determine the value of your home.

A reconstructive approach will also be used. This means the appraiser will figure out what it would cost to reproduce your home as a new home, then depreciate it for the effective age of yours.

A less common approach is the income approach, and it's rarely used in the valuation of residential property.

Whichever method is used, your appraisal will give you the probable sale price of your home. An appraisal usually costs from $300 to $500 depending on the size of your home and the amount of detail in the appraisal. You can get the needed information from the township assessor's office, but their information is generally 60-120 days old. This could give you an inaccurate

reading, either too high or too low. Timely information is critical.

Now that you have the price, go out and buy your local and regional newspapers. Pick up homes magazines and look for "For Sale" signs in your neighborhood. This information is used to determine the list price for your home (it should be from 3% to 6% above the appraised value you received from the fee appraiser). Do not use the appraisal you get from a home equity loan. These can be less accurate because they don't go into the detail you'll need for a true value. A buyer is going to be much more critical than your bank's appraiser. A buyer may want a 95% loan to value, i.e. $95,000 loan on a $100,000 purchase. Most equity loans only go to 75% loan to value or $75,000 on a $100,000 property so, if the home equity bank appraiser is off $5,000 or even $10,000, there's little risk to the bank, but if your asking price is off $5,000 or $10,000 your buyer won'tget their loan approved.

Marketing

The first step—and this should be done before you have your property appraised—is to re-read my article of a few issues ago on how to get the best price for your house.

The second step is to put up a For Sale sign. About 30% of our inquiries come from signs. If a buyer calls on the sign, he already likes your

neighborhood and the looks of your home from the outside.

The third step is to place a carefully written ad in the regional and local papers. This ad should NOT answer all the questions about your house i.e. lot size, number of bedrooms, baths or whether it has a basement or not, etc. because, if you answer all the questions, there's no reason to call. I find most potential buyers try to eliminate listings, not find them. You want them to call so you can get them out to look at your home. Get an answering machine to take messages when you're not home. No one is home all the time.

The fourth step is a property brochure. This should have room sizes, lot size, personal property to be included or excluded and mention some feature that you believe to be of interest, maybe something that madeYOU buy the house.

The fifth step is to show the home objectively. During the tour, stay in the background and let the buyer discover your home. Don't talk too much. Be careful not to become defensive if buyers point out flaws or shortcomings. This is difficult because you are emotionally attached to your home. Even if they want to change something you are proud of and worked hours planning and completing, keep your cool.

(continued next page)

The sixth step is to hold a weekend open house.

Negotiating

Always remain calm. Logic will prevail. If the buyer's offer is low and you would be happy with the appraised value, show him the appraisal. If he won't pay that, you have to decide how badly you want to sell. It's your motive to sell that will determine what the right price really is. All of this is assuming the buyer is financially able to purchase your home.

Before you sign anything I would ask the buyer to talk to a local lender that you know to be pre-qualified. The buyer will be more likely to give the banker his financial information than he will you, and even if he gave it to you, you still may not know if he is qualified or not. Another thought is to ask the buyer to bring a pre-qualification letter from his lender stating he is qualified to buy a home in your price range. I suggest you center your negotiations around price, possession and personal property. Once you have both agreed, then ask your attorney to draw up the sales contract. The buyer can then sign it or bring it to his attorney for some adjustments, then you bring it to your attorney and so on and so forth.

Closing or Escrow

Your attorney will handle the rest of the details such as title, insurance, survey, deed, closing statement, etc. The sole purpose in "For Sale By Owner" is to save the Realtor's commission. Don't forget though, <u>the buyers who look for "For Sale By Owners" know you're saving the expense of a commission and expect you to discount your home at least one half if not all of that cost.</u>

However, if you are not successful in selling your home and you really have to sell, you will be forced to use the services of a broker to help you. Don't beat it to death. Give it a try for a few weeks and then start interviewing brokers so you don't let the best selling time, usually the spring, pass you by.

It's your decision. But think carefully about all that's involved in terms of time, skill and money. Good Luck!

Buying & Selling REAL ESTATE

CHOOSING YOUR FIRST INVESTMENT PROPERTY

Buying a rental property is a step toward financial independence. No other investment combines the advantages real estate offers: current income, tax shelter and appreciation potential, whether you buy a condo, single family house, apartment building, office building or retail shopping center.

Before you start looking at properties, set your investment goals and discuss them with your real estate broker, and a banker, since you will probably have to borrow money to make up the balance of the purchase price. Remember you'll be tying up your funds for a while. You need to decide how much cash you can afford to invest, what type of property is best for you and whether you will manage the property yourself or hire a managing agent.

Selecting the Right Property

Consider the following criteria:

1. Location: It's best to start around where you live. You know the area and the growth patterns of your own community. Your goals are good appreciation potential and attracting quality tenants.

2. Economics: Your goal is to structure the purchase so you get a pre-tax cash on cash return. This means getting an annual return on all the money you've put into the transaction. Sometimes in the case of apartment buildings it's a matter of increasing income. If you have a plan to make improvements to the building which will increase the willingness of tenants to pay higher rents you can predict and expect income. This will make the building increase in value since you're increasing the income. In choosing investment proper-

ty you must resist the temptation to purchase properties we like vs. properties that show good value. Homes are purchased with the heart, investments MUST be purchased with your head. Investments in residential dwellings can be made two ways: a.) Rent them and keep them. b.) Live in them, fix them up and sell them. When you have selected a property you believe will be suitable check the numbers with your accountant and legalities with your attorney. If you plan to be an investor you need this advise for both tax reasons and peace of mind.

3. Finance: Don't expect to buy a good rental property with the much publicized "no money—down" techniques. These are high risk strategies that usually create large negative cash flows; that means expenses exceed the income. You have to reach into your pocket each month to come up with the difference. Remember, the return on "nothing" is just that—NOTHING

Because of their poor choices on large real estate investments, financial institutions are now applying their new, tougher rules to everyone who has an interest in being a real estate investor. This means large down payments from you so their risk is lower, it also means shorter term loans and in most cases adjustable interest rates. They want to put all the risk on you.
On the other hand, the owner of the property is

stuck selling in a market where this problem with finding willing lenders at a reasonable rates exists. This means he either has to take less for his property to make it a good investment for the buyer, or he has to provide financing himself to make his property a good investment for the buyer.

4. Type of property: Condo, single family house, apartment building office building, retail shopping center. Obviously the amount of money you have to invest will determine how many of these possibilities are available to you. If you're like most of us you'll start small. The time you have to manage, maintain or improve the property will also greatly influence what type of property is best for you.

Buying & Selling
REAL ESTATE

YOUR FIRST REAL ESTATE INVESTMENT

The Process, Step by Step

Goal: Let's say you are going to invest to build money for a college education for a grandchild. The length of the investment should be 10-20 years. This will assure you ample time to reach your goal.

I. Determine a budget.

This is two fold.
A. How much you have to invest now?
B. How much do you have monthly to support the investment?
Positive cash flow (this is the trade term for more rent taken in than your mortgage payment out) can always be achieved if you have enough down payment. But if you don't have a large amount to put down, you may have to supplement the monthly expenses until the income increases sufficiently to yield the profits you desire.

II. What should I buy?

If you're handy with tools you have more flexibility because you can buy something in poor shape and pick up additional equity by fixing it up. Be careful not to over estimate your talent or your time available to complete the project. The time an investment remains unrented is lost revenue. You can expect anything you purchase to need a fresh coat of paint, the better it looks the faster it rents. Time is money!

Let's say you aren't real handy but you can use a paint roller and brush, and you have limited free time. I'd suggest you start with a condo, townhouse or half a duplex. These generally have an association fee to cover exterior building maintenance, snow removal, lawn and shrub care, insurance on the main structure and a reserve fund for replacement of roofs, siding, painting, elevator repairs, furnace replacement, etc. When you purchase, don't forget to make sure they "HAVE THESE RESERVES" and that they don't do them by special assessment. Also check when

these items were last replaced, unless it's a newer building. Make sure the association allows owners to rent their units, some only allow rentals on a case by case basis or hardship situation.

Now that you've made sure you can rent it out, you have to make sure not too many are already being rented. This is important for two reasons: 1. If more than a certain % are rented, financing by Fannie Mae lenders is not possible; and 2. You don't want too much competition for tenants—the less competition the more potential for higher rent.

III. Homework.

Check the papers for similar rentals, then go visit your competition. That's what your tenants are going to do. They're going to go from complex to complex until they find the features they are looking for, i.e., a garage or covered parking, well cared for grounds and units, basements, washers and dryers in the unit, nice recreational facilities, etc. If what you can buy doesn't compete, don't buy it, keep looking. Shop till you drop. This will prevent expensive mistakes.

IV. Financing.

FHA approved units are always a plus because you can find an assumable loan already in place, which will give you an advantage when you sell, if interest rates are high at that time. Since 1986 the FHA has made assumption of these loans subject to

their approval and the buyer's credit worthiness.

The owner must have lived there from 12 to 14 months before you can assume. Please investigate this carefully so you don't get excited about a loan that's unavailable to investors. FHA approval also increases the number of buyers for the future because they will be allowed to purchase with a low down payment when conventional lenders may require 10% or more down. Remember, the more buyers you have, the better chance for a higher price and quicker sale. As an investor you are going to be required to have at least 30% down unless you can assume one of these loans or find a local lender who will portfolio instead of sell your loan.

V. Insurance.

The purchase of insurance for a condo unit is less expensive because you're not covering contents, just the fixtures and appliances that are part of the unit. Don't forget to ask for a "loss of rents" clause, because if the building is rendered uninhabitable by fire or some disaster, your lender is going to be looking for his payments even though your tenant is gone and you're not receiving any rent.

VI. The Lease.

This is a key factor in being a successful investor. I'd check around and find a

(continued next page)

local attorney who does a lot of real estate work and has expertise in leases. His counsel will prove helpful and can save you a great deal of trouble and money in the future. Once he prepares a lease, you can use it over and over again, and since you'll be a client of his, you will have his future guidance in case you have a question or a problem tenant. A letter from an attorney seems to have more impact than one from the landlord. I would suggest you use an attorney for the purchase anyway and I'm sure you could work out a complete package rate.

VII. Finding a tenant.

Use any means possible. In the case of a condo or townhouse, ask the management association, use bulletin boards in the complex clubhouse, or your place of employment, place newspaper ads, etc. If you use a Realtor to help locate your property, ask them to list your unit as a rental in return for you purchasing the unit through them. Remember, when you're successful you'll want to buy more properties and this means more sales for the Realtor. I'm sure this will be of interest to him or her and worth their time and effort.

VIII. Choosing a tenant.

This is the time to be fussy. There's an old saying "a dead dog" is worse than "no dog at all." If you have an

empty unit you are better off than an occupied unit and no rent. Check them out. Use a rental application provided by a credit bureau, it should be filled out completely and be accompanied by the cost of running the check in CASH. Remember, if their credit is not good, neither is their check. This rental check-up should include not just how they pay their bills, but their income and length of employment, as well as their past rental history particularly the landlord before the last. If their present landlord wants to get rid of them, he may tell you false information, but the previous landlord has no stake in this. Patience, patience, patience—it's as important as location, location, location to an investor.

IX. Record Keeping.

You should keep every receipt for any expense connected with your investment. These receipts along with interest, taxes and depreciation will offset the income received for income tax purposes. Depreciation will be the other tax advantage, along with the benefits of appreciation and loan principal reduction. Please see your accountant or tax preparer for further information and explanation.

X. Education Experience.

At the beginning of this article I said to assume the goal of a college education for a grandchild. If this is interesting to you, consider this: Make the child a partner. As the child grows involve him in

the management of the unit. When you visit the unit, introduce him to the tenant as their landlord. Have the child help with maintenance and upkeep of the unit. Have him help clean and paint between tenants. Have him make deposits and show the unit to tenants, etc. This can be quite a powerful lesson and great experience. Who knows, it may lead to the development of another Donald Trump or Ted Turner. ☐

Buying & Selling
REAL ESTATE

THE ADVANTAGE OF HOME OWNERSHIP

Our editor, John Cummuta, has introduced me to some thought provoking concepts in his recent article advocating renting instead of buying a home. Buying a piece of property is a goal that almost every culture covets and most Americans take for granted. Let me present a different perspective.

Why should you buy?

1.) Personal Freedom.
You no longer have a landlord who dictates what you can or cannot do to "your home". If you like unstrippable wallpaper, put it up, if it will take two coats of paint to paint over the color you'd like to paint, paint it "your" favorite color, if you want to make improvements not only don't you have to get permission, but you'll reap the benefits of the improvements. Privacy and freedom of expression are all yours.

2.) No rent increases.
John mentioned that taxes go up regularly. Of course, he's correct, but how much do they go up? If your taxes are $1,200/year and they go up 5% that's $5/ month. I'll bet that's a drop in the bucket compared to most rent increases. Let's also remember what the taxes pay for. In our area almost 65% goes for schools. Take a look at what else it pays for: municipal services, parks, libraries, county roads and services, etc. Even if you rent, believe me, these same services are needed and end up in your landlord's tax bill which he promptly includes in your rent increases.

3.) Better credit risk.
This is not what our editor wants to hear, but there are times when it's unavoidable. When you're a homeowner, home-equity loans are readily available at far better rates than credit cards or auto loans and the interest on home-equity loans is tax deductible.

4.) Pride of Ownership.
Perhaps the most intangible yet the most powerful advantage is the pride of ownership. A home gives you and your family a feeling of stability and commitment. A special sense of security and satisfaction comes as you put roots in a neighborhood and community. We recently watched vivid pictures of Los Angeles riots and burnings. If the people in those neighborhoods *owned* their homes, the demonstrations would have been peaceful. People do not destroy what they work so hard to achieve.

5.) NOT ONLY NO RENT, NO PAYMENT, BUT $ BACK.
At the end of your loan, you will be 100% owner of your home. Whether it's straw, stick or brick, it will be all yours and a source of wealth for the future. Recently a retired lady asked me about selling her home so she could rent. I asked her why she wanted to rent and she said she couldn't maintain the property and needed the money. She didn't want to move, she was being forced out because her income wasn't sufficient. This could happen to any of us, particularly if social security does fail. But since she is a homeowner there's a solution—it's called a "reverse mortgage".

Here's how it works.

You use your home like an annuity. You work out a schedule of payments you'd like to receive from a lender—giving the lender an equity position in your home, i.e. if your home is worth $100,000, you could take up to $75,000 in monthly payments spread over 5, 10, 15 or 20 years. When you sell or die your heirs or estate get the balance equity. An additional bonus is that the home will probably be worth more than the $100,000 it was when the loan was originally set up. Great isn't it? Try *that* with rent receipts Mr. Cummuta.

There is no doubt that there are times when renting is temporarily the right thing to do, but I repeat "temporarily". Here's a list that might support renting.

Why should you rent?

• You will be relocating to another area within two years. Real estate is not a liquid asset so selling costs could eat up or exceed any gains you could enjoy, over that short a time.

• You don't qualify for a loan because of poor credit or job history.

• The economic conditions in your area are causing real estate values to decline. This could be a blessing for you in disguise if you can determine it's only temporary and you have rock solid employment.

To say I'm pro home ownership is an understatement. I don't believe it's a right, I believe it's an obligation. The example of the care, pride and respect we show our homes provides our children with a basis which will shape their opinions.

Homeowners are not just better credit risks, they're better citizens.

SECURING A HOME LOAN STEP-BY-STEP

PART ONE

Obtaining a home loan can be one of the most challenging, important and long lasting decisions you will make. Even though the time people live in the same home averages less than 7 years, many of us have the same home for the duration of a 30 year loan and then some. Initially, if you choose a loan that does not meet your needs, you can always get another one later, but the time, planning and care you take choosing the correct loan can not only save you money but also the aggravation of doing it all over again.

I. Prequalifying

This free service is provided by many lenders as an inducement for you to do business with them when you find a property. This will give you the approximate amount you can borrow based on your income and debt structure.

The financial industry uses basic guidelines to determine your maximum mortgage loan. The most common for conventional loans is a 28/36 percent ratio, to compare your gross income before taxes to your expenses. The first number (28) is the maximum allowable percentage of gross income for Principal, Interest, Taxes, and Insurance (PITI. The second number (36) is the maximum percent of gross income that can be allocated for housing expenses (PITI, car loans, child support, alimony, school loan, furniture payments, credit cards, etc. FHA ratios are 29/41, some adjustable loans are 30/40 and so on.

The exact amount can't be determined until you have a specific home with the exact amount of taxes and insurance coverage with the current interest rates available.

Most lenders will "LOCK IN" an interest rate for 60 to 90 days when you apply for the loan after you have a signed purchase contract.

Loan Types

	BENEFITS	DRAWBACKS
Fixed-Rate, Fixed-Payment		
A. Conventional 30-year mortgage	Fixed monthly payments for 30 years provide absolute certainty on housing costs.	Higher initial rates than adjustables.
B. Conventional 15-year mortgage	Lower rate than 30-year fixed; faster equity buildup and quicker payoff of loan.	Higher monthly payments.
C. FHA/VA fixed-rate mortgages (30-year and 15-year)	Low down payment requirements and fully assumable with no pre-payment penalties.	May require substantial points; may have application red tape and delays.
D. "Balloon" loans (3-10 year terms)	May carry discount rates and other favorable terms, particularly when the loan is provided by the homeseller.	At the end of the 3–10-year term, the entire remaining balance is due in a lump-sum or "balloon" payment, forcing the borrower to find new financing.
E. Bi-Monthly Mortgage	Buyer makes 13 payments each year instead of 12. This results in quicker payoff of the loan.	Higher monthly payments.
F. Two/one Buy Down 30-year fixed rate mortgage.	Lower initial rates qualifying is on first year's rate. Points can be paid by seller.	The cost of the points.
Adjustable-Rate, Variable Payment		
A. Adjustable-rate mortgage (ARM)— payment changes on 1-year, 3-year, and 5-year schedules	Lower initial rates than fixed-rate loans, particularly on the 1-year adjustables. Generally assumable by new buyers. Offers possibility of future rate and payment decreases. Loans with rate "caps" may protect borrowers against increases in rates. May be convertible to fixed-rate plans after three years.	Shifts far greater interest-rate risk onto borrowers than fixed-rate loans. Without "caps," may also sharply push up monthly payments in future years.
B. Graduated payment mortgage (GPM)— payment increases by prearranged increments during first 5-7 years, then level off	Allows buyers with marginal incomes to qualify. Higher incomes over next 5–7 years expected to cover gradual payment increases. May be combined with adjustable-rate mortgage to further lower initial rate and payment.	May have higher annual percentage rate (APR) than standard fixed-rate or adjustable-rate loans. May involve negative amortization—increasing debt owed by lender.
C. Growing equity mortgage (GEM)— contributes rising portions of monthly payments to payoff of principal debt. Typically pays off in 15-18 years, rather than 30.	Lower up-front payments, quicker loan payoff than conventional fixed-rate or adjustable.	May have higher effective rates and higher down payments than other loans in the marketplace. Tax deductions for interest payments decrease over time.

PART TWO

II. Choosing the loan for you

First answer:
1. How long will I live in this home?
2. How much down payment do I have?
3. Can I count on my income to increase each year?

If you have a plan it's easier for a mortgage expert to help choose the right loan for you. With all the loans available it's not surprising that all lenders don't make all types of loans. That's why I usually suggest a mortgage broker. They generally have every type of loan because they have many lenders to choose from. When lenders don't want to make loans, they raise their rates or cut the programs they offer. Mortgage brokers always have lenders looking for loans thus they can offer more programs and better rates.

These brokers earn their fees by originating and packaging loans for lenders. The lenders gladly pay their fee because it reduces the lenders need to have employees perform these services. Remember the lenders usually come in and out of the market. This way they can keep their payroll expenses down, yet originate loans as their needs arise.

III. Should I Pay Points?

This question depends on several factors, like how long are you going to live in this home? And o I need a tax deduction this year?

Either way, to calculate the benefits, take the interest rate with "0" points and then calculate the lower rate with 1 to 5 points and divide the difference into the dollar amount of the points to see how many months/years it would take to break even.

$100,000 @ 9% = $805.00 P/I Mo.

$100,000 @ $8^{1/2}\%$ = $796.00 P/I Mo. 3 points.

The difference is $36/mo.— to get this lower payment we'll say you paid $3,000 or 3 points on the $100,000 loan.
$3,000 divided by 36 = 83.33 months or about 7 years to recoup your original outlay, after this point you are gaining $36/mo. because of the lower interest rate.

IV. Applying for the Loan.

This is a grueling process because of so many S & L failures. The underwriting procedure has become very detailed and exacting. The underwriters are the people who actually approve your loan. They want to know everything that affects your ability to repay this loan, I mean "EVERYTHING." "The Mortgage Application Checklist" should give you a head start.

Everything you provide them must be verified, and if you have been late with any payments you better have good reasons— and have rectified your late paying ways. The lender will call you regularly during the approval process for more information about this or that. Expect it, you're not special— they do it to everyone, even the most qualified borrowers.

They will order an appraisal of the property to verify that it's worth what you're paying and the amount they're lending, as well as its qualification for Private Mortgage Insurance (PMI). If you don't have 20% down payment, most lenders require PMI. This insurance insures the lender for the dollar amount between your down payment and the 20% they would like you to have. PMI underwriters now get to approve you too. Expect more calls!

After all this you are approved. By this time you are worn out but elated that you are worthy of using their money and are allowed to pay it back with interest.

V. Closing or Escrow.

This is when you finally get title to your new home. A time is scheduled and the big day arrives. But you need to bring a few things with you.

1. Homeowners insurance. This must be for at least the amount of the loan and a receipt that you've paid the premium for the first year.

2. A cashiers or certified check for your part of the purchase price and expenses. The amount will be figured at the 11th hour barely leaving you enough time to get the check. No personal checks. I know they know everything about you already, but cashiers or certified checks only. I suggest you make it out to yourself and endorse it at closing.

3. If you sold a home to buy this one, they will want to see the RESPA HUD 1 closing statement. You must bring this to show you are no longer obligated to pay for that house.

Financial
DOLLARS & SENSE

"QUIT PROCRASTINATING"

In January's newsletter I discussed organizing your financial records. It is now July. Do you know where your records are? If you do, Congratulations! If you don't, what can I say, except,..."QUIT PROCRASTINATING".

Organizing your records is the first step to having accurate records. Accurate records is the way to be sure that you don't forget any expenses.

Remembering all your expenses reduces you net taxable income. Reduced net taxable income decreases your tax liability. And a decreased tax liability increases the amount of money you get to keep. In other words "organized records" = $ dollars $. You can't afford to wait any longer. Lets get started.

The first thing to do is to purchase an expandable tickler file. Then list your categories of expenses (i.e., advertising, office supplies, postage, etc.) on the tabs of the file. This listing should either be in alphabetical order or account number order if you want to assign account numbers to the categories. This is where you file all your receipts throughout the year that document your business deductions. When you pur-

> "Organizing your records is the first step to having accurate records. "

chase something or pay a bill, write on your copy the word "PAID", the date paid, the check number used or the word "CASH", and file it in the proper category of your expandable. If there is no receipt or bill, document the transaction on paper, with an explanation of the transaction, the date, the amount paid, the check number used or the word"CASH", and your signature. Now file your receipts from the first six and half months of this year.

The next thing to do is to purchase a record-keeping book or system. You will list all your business transactions for the year here. Having one book helps you keep the details of all your transactions in one place. You can use a check writing system, a ledger, or an accounts journal. Create two separate sections, one for "Cash Receipts" and one for "Cash Disbursements". Next subdivided these sections into your specific income and expense categories.

When entering a transaction be sure to date and label it, and add it to the running year-to-date total. This will save you time at tax deadlines, and will enable you to see your financial situation at the end of each month. Go back and summarize the first six and half months of this year.

I would recommend that you purchase a "One-Write" Check writing system starter kit. A starter kit includes a check writing board, checks, journal sheets, and window envelopes. McBee Systems and Safeguard Business Systems are two of the companies that sell these systems.

The beauty about this system is that you write the check information just once, hence "One-Write". Rather than first writing in the check journal or on the check stub and then writing the check itself, this system carbon or NCR copies the information on to the journal sheet as you write the check. After writing a check you then carry the check amount over to the appro-

priate column of the journal sheet, which is headed with your specific expense category. At the bottom of each column are current and year-to-date income and expense amounts and you are ready to begin the new month. You ring bind the old sheet to store it. What could be simpler? And all your information is in one place.

Be smart, start now! Why take a chance on losing deductions because you forgot or because you lack documentation? Don't give "Uncle Sam" one more dollar of your money than you are obligated by law to do. "QUIT PROCRASTINATING" and put your financial records in order now.

$Financial
DOLLARS & SENSE

MAKING ECONOMIC DECISIONS

Last month I gave you a reason to organize your records. Money. This month I will give you another reason to organize your records that is even more important...ECONOMIC DECISION MAKING.

Every individual makes numerous economic decisions daily. Most of these decisions are made without much conscious thought and seem trivial, such as where to eat lunch, where to buy gasoline, or which brand of product to buy at the grocery store. Other decisions individuals make are significant and can involve substantial dollar commitments, such as purchasing a new car or a new home or investing in a business. And in reality there are no trivial economic decisions, because even trivial amounts add up to noticeable sums over time.

O.K., sure, everyone does make daily economic decisions; but what does that have to do with organized records? The answer to this is that having accurate financial information is essential to making informed, wise economic decisions.

Have you or anyone you know ever gotten a mortgage without providing the lender with all your financial information? Have you ever been issued a credit card without providing at least basic financial information? Probably not.

The lender uses your financial information to make an economic decision on

"...decisions individuals make are significant and can involve substantial dollar commitments."

whether to lend you money. Major credit card companies and department stores use financial information to make economic decisions on whether to extend you credit. So why don't you do the same? Can you make an informed, wise economic decision without projecting and understanding the financial results of your decision? Absolutely not. You must learn how to use your financial information in your decision making process. It's a necessity to financial survival.

We will discuss the decision-making process and the role financial information plays in this process in future articles. Be ready for the discussion...organize your financial records now.

Financial
DOLLARS & SENSE

TO BE OR NOT TO BE: MAKING DECISIONS

"To be or not to be, that is the question..." But what is the answer? The answer is not so simple. To answer this question you must go through a process of thought and deliberation that leads to a choice between two or more alternatives. This process is called "decision making" and the choice made is called a decision.

We all make numerous decisions every day. But how did we arrive at those decisions? Are they good decisions? Could we have made better ones? The answers to these questions are determined by the process we went through to make these decisions. Let's look at the decision-making process.

The decision-making process involves five steps: 1) Setting goals, 2) considering alternatives, 3) making the decision, 4) taking action, 5) evaluating the results. For this process to be effective each process requires that we ask and answer a question. Let's explore these steps and questions.

Step 1:
What goal do we want to achieve? A goal is a an objective that we seek to achieve. Effective goals must be measurable, attainable and reasonable given the current circumstances.

Step 2:
What different ways are available to reach our goal? This is the stage where we search and gather all the verbal, written and financial information available to us. Once gathered, we then digest and assess this information as it applies to our goal. Based on this assessment we organize the information into all the possible alternatives available in achieving our goal.

Step 3:
Which alternative best achieves our goal? Here is where we must choose one out of our alternatives from Step 2. We make the decision using one of four decision modes; 1) maximizing — choosing the alternative that maximizes our advantage or gain; 2) elimination — eliminating all alternatives that cannot achieve our most important objective until only one alternative is left. ; 3) satisfying — choosing the first alternative that satisfies the objective, whether best or not; and 4) intuition — choosing the alternative based on hunches or gut feelings. The decision mode used and the decision made are affected by several factors; significance of the decision, time pressure, level of certainty, level of risk and your personality. Because of these factors, the decision made is not always the best.

Step 4:
What action should be taken? This is the step where we choose how to implement our decision. We choose our course of action. We then communicate our decision, organize support for it and assign resources to implement it.

Step 5:
Was the original goal achieved? This is he stage where we receive feedback from our decision. We use this feedback to to evaluate whether or not we made the right decision and whether or not we have achieved our goal.

Every day we make many decisions. The process we use to make these decisions is complex. Yet by learning this process we avoid the embarrasement and potential financial troubles that could arise from bad decision making.

FINANCIAL INFORMATION IN DECISION-MAKING

Last month we explored the decision-making process. This month we will discuss the role that financial information plays in that process. Financial information is essential when the decision you're making involves economic questions. It provides the basis for such decisions. It provides quantitative information for the three functions of planning (steps 1-3), control (step 4), and evaluation (step 5).

Planning is the process of formulating a course of action. This is the stage where you need to know the financial alternatives available to you. Each financial alternative includes a projection of cash receipts and a budget of cash requirements. Cash receipts are dollars received from sales, commissions, salaries, borrowings, reimbursements, tax savings, etc. Cash requirements are dollars spent on capital expenditures, oper-ating expenses, loan payments, taxes, etc. You must analyze and compare these alternatives. The alternative that best fits your needs and abilities will generally determine the course of action that you choose.

Control is the process of implementing the course of action and seeing that the plans are carried out. This is the stage where financial information is used to monitor the progress of our decision. We compile actual receipts, costs, and cash flows and compare this information with the projections and budgets used to make our decision. This comparison allows us to react and change (i.e., control) our course of action in order to optimize our results.

Evaluation is the process of studying our decision to see if we achieved our original goal. This is the stage where we receive feedback to our decision. This financial information feedback can be cash position, asset accumulation, debt reduction, profit/loss, net worth, etc. Using this information we ask the question, Was our original goal met? If not, we must then determine the reason why not. Was the reason poor planning or control? Or maybe the wrong goal was chosen. By determining the reason, we are able to learn from our error and improve both our decision-making process and our goal achievement.

A simplified example of this would be living within a household budget. First, you begin by "planning" your year. You project your cash receipts and expected cash requirements. Using these you then develop your budget for the year. Second, you "control" your budget by keeping track of your actual cash receipts and cash expenditures each month. This allows you to change your spending habits, if needed, to stay within your budget. Third, you "evaluate" you overall performance as well as each major category of expenditure to determine whether or not you achieved your goal of staying within your budget. You then attempt to determine in which areas you could save money and in which areas you should spend more. Last, you use your evaluation to develop a budget for the next year.

Financial information should provide the basis for all economic decisions you make. Don't guess at the best course of action. It could cost you more than you think. Why take chances with your financial future? The only "guess" that you should pay for are jeans.

Financial
DOLLARS & SENSE

HOME OFFICE DEDUCTIONS

The home office deduction is a deduction for the business use of your home. This deduction may be taken only if the business portion of your home is used *regularly* and **exclusively** for business and is:

- The principal place you conduct your trade or business, or
- The place where you meet or deal with your customers/clients in the normal course of your business, or
- A separate structure that is not attached to your residence and is used in your trade or business.

Some factors to consider when deciding if you qualify for the home office deduction are:

- The reason for having a home office
- The amount of time you spend working there
- The activities performed there are necessary for business
- The home office is furnished in a manner that is suitable for the business
- The home office is necessary for managing your business.

You may deduct a home office used in a sideline business even if you have another full-time job. But remember, it must be used exclusively for business. Don't use it as a TV room or a school homework room or anything else room when you're not using for work.

Once you determine that you qualify for the home office deduction, you calculate the deduction as follows:

1. Figure the business use percentage by dividing the amount of square feet used for business by the total amount of square feet in the home.
2. Identify expenses that relate only to the business part of your home. These are considered direct expenses and are fully deductible.
3. Identify the expenses that relate to the running and upkeep of the entire home. These expenses benefit both the business and personal parts of your home. They are considered indirect expenses and are allocated between business and personal use.
4. Allocate the indirect expenses by multiplying these expenses by the business use percentage calculated in Step 1.
5. Calculate the depreciation expense on the business portion of the home.
6. Add the direct expenses in Step 2 and the indirect expenses allocated to business in Step 4 and the depreciation calculated in Step 5.

The answer to Step 6 is your potential deduction for the year. There is a limit however. The home office deduction cannot be used to create a deductible business loss. In other words, it cannot exceed gross income. Therefore, it it possible that you could only get a portion of the deduction this year and would have to carryover the deduction next year.

The IRS has created a new form this year to be used when claiming a home office deduction. It is form 8829. This form will allow the IRS to more easily identify those taxpayers taking a home office deduction and to eliminate illegitimate claims. The deduction is available for legitimate claims by Independent Marketers of F.I.N.L., as long as you meet the exclusive points outlined above. Consult with your own tax professional to find out if you qualify.

Financial
$DOLLARS & SENSE

AUTO EXPENSES AND TAX DEDUCTIONS

In our continuing effort to help you reduce your tax bill, this month we'll look at the automobile.

Automobile expenses incurred in connection with a business, trade or income producing activity are deductible for tax purposes. There are two methods for deducting expenses; the actual expense method and the mileage allowance method.

The Actual Expense Method

The actual expense method is just that. All actual expenses from operating your auto (gas, oil, tires, maintenance, repairs, insurance, licenses, etc.), and interest on financing or lease costs, are compiled, the business portion being deductible. The business portions determined by the ratio of business miles to total miles driven in the year. Additionally, a depreciation deduction is allowed if you bought your auto. This deduction is determined by the depreciation method you are allowed to use, the write-off period and the dollar caps that restrict the amount of depreciation deduction for what the tax code considers to be "luxury autos."

The Mileage Allowance Method

The mileage allowance method uses a standard mileage rate for an unlimited number of business miles instead of figuring actual expenses. The standard mileage rate for 1991 is 27.5 cents per business mile. Of this amount, 11 cents represents depreciation allowance, which reduces the basis of the auto, and 16.5 cents is the allowance for all operating expenses. Individuals who use this method can also claim a separate deduction for business related parking fees and tolls and the business portion of interest on financing the auto.

You can only use the mileage allowance method if you meet the following conditions:
1) you own (or are paying for) your own auto
2) you don't use two or more autos simultaneously
3) the auto is not used for hire (i.e., limo or taxi), and
4) you choose to use the mileage allowance method in the first year you place the auto in service — or — if you deducted actual expenses, you claimed straight-line depreciation only.

Regardless of the method you choose, you do not get any deduction for the business use of your auto unless you keep a written record made "at or near" the time of use. This log should contain the date, time, place, business purpose, mileage, and any tolls or parking expenses of each trip. It should also contain the total mileage for the year. You can do this by simply recording the odometer readings at the beginning and end of the year. You should also track commuting mileage, if applicable. Additionally, if you use the actual expense method, you must keep records and receipts of all your out-of-pocket expenses.

The method you choose should be the one that gives you the bigger tax deduction. If your mileage is low and you use your auto almost exclusively for business, or your out-of-pocket expenses are high, the actual expense method might yield the bigger deduction. If your auto gets high mileage per gallon of gas, and you log high business mileage, the mileage allowance method may give you the bigger deduction. The only way to know for sure which one gives the the tax advantage is to figure your deduction both ways. Doing so will get you the highest possible deduction dollars out of your auto.

Financial
DOLLARS & SENSE

TURNING A VACATION INTO A BUSINESS TRIP

Wouldn't it be nice if you could get the government to subsidize at least a part of your trip? It is possible. By turning your trip into a business trip you can get the government to share your costs through a business write-off for part of your trip.

Getting a business write-off for your trip takes a little bit of planning and ingenuity. If you're pursuing the F.I.N.L. business opportunity, you can visit people and present the F.I.N.L. program to them—or travel to meet or train some of the down-liners you've signed through the mail—and also get in a little golfing, boating, fishing, sightseeing, or whatever it is you like to do.

The "Primary Purpose" of the trip must be business. This means that you intend to spend more days on business than you do on vacation. That doesn't mean that you have to spend 8 hours or from 9 to 5 in meetings or classes. If a day's schedule only calls for a partial day of classes or meetings, that's all right, you're not compelled to fill the rest of the day with a business purpose to preserve the day as business related. Also, if the business purpose of your trip straddles a weekend, the weekend is not counted as personal time if there is a bona fide business reason for staying over the weekend.

If you meet the primary purpose test, the round trip cost of the trip is deductible even if you extend your stay for a few days of vacation. So, in effect you're getting a subsidy for your vacation. In addition, you are entitled to deduct your lodging expense and 80% of the meals for the days you do have a business purpose. Travel expenses for family members or other traveling companions are not deductible unless you can substantiate a bona fide business purpose for their presence. Performance of incidental services by them does not qualify their travel expenses for a deduction.

Travel & Entertainment deductions are a favorite target of IRS Auditors. Therefore, be sure you can substantiate the "Primary Purpose" of your trip and keep meticulous records. You should keep a written record of the time, place, and expense of your business trip and keep the receipts for all of your out-of-pocket expenditures.

Getting a business write-off for part of your summer vacation is possible. All you need to do is plan, record, and enjoy your government backed trip. ☐

FINANCING HOME IMPROVEMENT

In June's "Buying & Selling Real Estate" article, Tom Passaro wrote that there are times when it's unavoidable to borrow to finance home improvement. This may be because you have an unplanned repair to make. It may be, in today's economy, that you have decided to improve or expand your current home rather than sell it and purchase a new one. If you don't have the cash available, you may need to finance these improvements. What is the most beneficial way for you to arrange this financing?

Two Basic Choices

The choices are to either refinance your first mortgage or to get a second mortgage (called a home equity loan). To decide which is best for you, you must first consider a number of economic factors and their inherent tax liabilities.

The most important factor to consider is whether or not you can afford the monthly home equity loan payment in addition to your current mortgage payment. If you cannot, refinancing is the only way for you to go. If you can afford the monthly payment, you'll need to consider:
1.) the time left on your existing mortgage — generally you would not want to refinance an existing mortgage if it is short term;
2.) potential prepayment penalty on your existing mortgage;
3.) interest you will pay on a refinanced loan versus a home equity loan — generally you will want to choose the loan that generates the least amount of interest due;
4.) closing costs — generally the closing costs will be higher refinancing an existing mortgage because the principal amount of the loan is higher.

The Tax Effects

1.) Interest is in most cases fully deductible, regardless if you refinance or take a home equity loan;
2.) Points paid at closing are currently deductible to the extent the loan proceeds are used to buy, build, or improve your primary residence, but must be amortized to the extent the proceeds are used to refinance existing debt;
3.) To be currently deductible points must be paid in cash, not financed as part of the loan transaction, otherwise they must be amortized over the life of the loan, even if the entire loan is used for home improvement;
4.) Any unamortized points from the existing mortgage are currently deductible when it is refinanced.

Strictly from a tax standpoint there is no contest if you can afford to do so, you should use the home equity loan to finance your home improvement. However, never look at just the tax standpoint. You must consider the economic factors involved and choose the overall best option for you and your financial independence. ☐

Financial
DOLLARS & SENSE

TAX CONSEQUENCES OF SELLING A HOME

"If I sell my home, will I owe any taxes?"

I received this question from a F.I.N.L. member this past month. I felt that if one member had this question, others probably also wondered the same thing.

A Sale With a Gain

When you sell your primary residence you realize either a gain or a loss from that sale. If you realize a gain, you will owe taxes on that gain. However, the tax code allows you to defer the entire amount of your gain and consequently the taxes due if you meet two requirements. First you must purchase or build another primary residence and move into it within two years prior to two years after the sale of your old primary residence. Second, the purchase price of your new primary residence has to equal or exceed the sales price of your old primary residence. If the purchase price on your new residence is less than the sales price of your old residence, you are only entitled to a proportionate deferral of the gain and taxes due.

The deferred gain becomes taxable when you sell the second primary residence unless you again reinvest the proceeds into another home. The one exception to the reinvest-ment rules is the once-in-a-lifetime election to perma-nently escape taxes on up to $125,000 of gain. This elec-tion applies even if you pur-chase a less costly residence or do not purchase one at all. To be able to make this elec-tion, you or your spouse must have attained age 55 before you sell and you must have used the sale property as your primary residence for at least three out of the five years pre-ceding on the sales date.

A married couple only gets one once-in-a-lifetime elec-tion. If they make this elec-tion, both individuals have used their once-in-a-lifetime election. If after making this election either spouse were to enter into a new marriage, the new marriage will be consid-ered to have used their elec-tion, even if the new spouse has not used his or her elec-tion. You are taxed on the gain at your effective tax rate, with a cap of 28% maximum.

A Sale With a Loss

A loss realized from the sale of your primary residence is not deductible and consequent-ly does not reduce your income taxes. If you are in this unfortunate situation, you might consider con-verting your residence to rental property for at least two years. This will allow you to deduct all expenses relating to the property from the rents you receive and to take a depreciation deduction on the property. After two years as rental property, a loss realized from selling the property would be deductible.

It's been said that without a sound tax plan — or a competent and trustworthy accountant — taxes can eat up 50% of your income! That's why beating the high cost of taxes can be such an important strategy in your Debt-FREE and Prosperous Living plan. Look how deeply taxes cut into your wealth-building capacity.

Federal Income Tax	28%
Social Security Tax	7%
State Income Tax	7%
Sales Tax	7%
Property Tax	3%
Total:	**52%**

In addition to that astonishing total, here's some other taxes you may be paying: real estate transfer tax, license tax, gift tax, customs fees, excise tax, personal property tax, recording fees, inheritance tax, airport departure tax, entertainment tax, and more!

Saving On
TRAVEL & LEISURE
GO SHOPPING FOR A CRUISE

Who can resist the concept of a vacation where you're pampered beyond belief, dine on incredible culinary wonders and are surrounded by all manners of popular entertainment? Where else but on a cruise ship can you experience this variety of hedonistic delights.

The first rule in shopping for a cruise is *don't believe the prices quoted in a cruise line's brochures.* All the color coding of decks and berth options are just wishful thinking on the part of the cruise operator. Dozens of travel agencies and cruise specialists are prepared to find you the best rates when you're ready to investigate a cruise vacation. You can save 20% or more by just shopping around.

Other Factors to Consider

Of course price is an important concern, but before you get too wrapped up in discount hunting, make sure you've found the right cruise for you.

Since there is no way to know the character of a ship by the brochure alone, you'll have to depend on the wisdom of an experienced travel agent or someone who has recently cruised on that same line. Some cruise lines cater to a sedate crowd, while others, like Carnival for instance, appeal to younger travels (or those younger at heart). A good agent will know the unpublished intangibles: maintenance, character, level of service, etc.

Look at the deck plan with a cruise pro. They'll steer you clear of staterooms prone to engine noise or heavy traffic flows. Also, think about how you'll be spending your cruise vacation. If you have visions of your time being spent on the deck and around the ship, you can save tons of money by booking an inside cabin with no windows. If, however, you know you'll be spending a lot of time in your room, the extra money for a window looking out over the slowly passing ocean may be worth it.

Now That You've Decided...

Once you know what you want, it's time to go shopping. You'll quickly find that cruise prices are similar to airline rates—they change from day to day and from one phone call to the next. You may find out the person in the stateroom next door paid much more than you for identical accommodations, food and airfare. And not all cruises are discounted. Taking a warm-weather sail during the popular Christmas season will yield full rates. Likewise, a summer cruise to the wilds off Alaska's coast will cost you plenty.

So shop around. And don't only look to the agencies advertising discounted cruises, but even small-town agencies that may just land you the perfect cruise/price package. Be flexible. A cruise line might be packed for one sailing and the very next week be hurting for passengers. Remember that the discounts are typically attached to the cruises with the most openings. Off season travel can also yield huge savings. Consider cruising when other vacationers are busy with spring cleaning. Another way to ensure a bigger discount is to book early. 10% to 20% discounts are typical of many cruise lines if you book well in advance of your trip.

Most cruises tout an "all-inclusive vacation experience." But you should be aware and compare what defines "all-inclusive." Most lines charge extra for alcohol, phone calls, dry cleaning, port taxes and the like. And tipping can really add up (although several cruise lines have a no tipping policy).

Finally, if you think you can find a better deal on airfare to the port city than the cruise line can offer, purchase a "cruise only" option. Maybe you have some frequent flyer mileage to redeem or feel like you're getting a discount cruise only to be raked over the coals by the airfare. Once again, be prepared to shop around and be flexible, and you can save big on your next cruise. Bon voyage!

TRAVEL & LEISURE

TRAVEL RESERVATIONS AND THE LOWEST RATES

When preparing to take a trip, either for business or pleasure, we typically phone around—probably using a toll-free number—to get reservations for air travel, hotels and rental cars. Believe it or not, this may not be your best bet toward budget travel. So, should you call your travel agent for the best prices or would a direct call to the front desk of the air carrier of hotel is a better choice? That depends...

The travel industry is a volatile market. Supply and demand cause great fluctuations in the perceived and actual value of travel-related services. Another reason a simple phone call may not yield the best price is that the uneven and changing pricing information may not be distributed at the same time to the travel agent's central computer, the front desk or the toll-free reservation service. And because some travel bargains and special rates may only be available for a limited time, an agent may not have the same information that the chain's central computer system has.

A recent study by Conde Nast Traveler magazine revealed some interesting results: When they called and asked an operator at Marriott's national reservations center for the least expensive double room at the Philadelphia Marriott, they were quoted a rate of $147 a night. The same question asked of a travel agent was answered with a rate of $122 per night. But a direct call to the hotel itself came up the winner—$84 a night—a savings of 43% over the first quote.

But this isn't always the case. A direct call to the hotel desk of the Philadelphia Airport Hilton yielded a quote of $119 per night, while the central toll-free reservations operator dug up a "Bounce Back" special promotion of only $85. So it would seem that the best answer is to just "call around." That can be time-consuming though, so Conde Nast suggests finding a travel agent who is "equal parts computer wizard, frequent flier-mileage juggler, telephone jockey and newspaper scanner." But above all, find a travel agent you can trust and one you feel is giving you their time and effort to find the best travel bargains.

Here's some other guidelines from Conde Nast:

Hotels

Calls to Comfort Inn, Holiday Inn, Hyatt, Marriott and Hilton all revealed inconsistencies between the hotel's pricing and the central reservations systems. Once again, a resourceful travel agent tapped into the computer system is probably your best bet to root out the lowest rates.

Airlines

The airlines also rely on a centralized reservation system, but once again, a little investigation finds the unwary traveler faced with differing rates. The key word in airline reservations is "availability." The computer looks at two fares when searching for a rate: the lowest fare for the route and the lowest fare available. Between the time you call the central reservations desk and your travel agent does the same, the availability of a given fare may have changed. The solution: When you come across a low fare, use the 24-hour courtesy reservation and hold that fare while you search out other, possibly lower rates.

Car Rentals

The results are similar to the queried hotels; vast and unpredictable differences between the central reservation system and a call to a travel agent. Best bet: call around yourself or use a travel agent you feel is doing their best to find you the lowest rate.

Since travel services are an ever-changing, fluctuating business, don't settle for the first rate or fare that presents itself. A little extra time spent investigating options or working with a reputable travel agent can yield substantial travel savings.

On TRAVEL & LEISURE

BUDGET-STRETCHING SECRETS FOR SUMMER TRAVEL

School bells across the country are about to sound their restless clang for the last time for three months. Summer is approaching head on. This is the time of year when most families plan and take their vacations. A time when the roadways fill with packed autos, stocked campers and anxious kids, all ready to wring the best out of their short week at a specially-chosen destination.

It's easy to make expensive mistakes when traveling—especially with a family—during these hectic summer months, so here are a few secrets that will get you on your way with less worries about how fast money will leave your wallet.

• A great way to start your vacation is early—a planning session with the kids included. They'll not only feel like they had a part in planning your vacation, but you'll be able to decide on some key issues, including how much money they'll be allowed to spend on your vacation.

• If you're strapped for cash, consider a vacation to one of America's beautiful national parks. You'll find reasonable accommodations typically surrounded by many free activities.

• If you're travelling to a resort area, consider staying in a villa or condo instead of a hotel room. Rates are competitive and you'll save hundreds by preparing your own meals instead of eating at restaurants. If the place you are renting is big enough for more than one family, consider vacationing with others whose company you enjoy. Splitting the costs is a real $-saver—and you'll wind up with some great vacation memories.

• Limit the kid's spending money. My wife and I give each kid a roll of quarters ($10.00). It's usually enough for small souvenirs and treats on the road. The second benefit of the quarter roll is if they don't behave themselves, we take a quarter away. The incentive for the kids is to keep as many quarters as they can. It works!

• Do some research ahead of time on your travel destination. This will give you an idea of what types of activities you can do once you arrive. Make a list of the free activities in one column and the ones requiring admission in another column. Plan your day with your budget in mind and select from the appropriate lists.

• If you need more sleeping space in your hotel room, ask for a roll-away bed or let the kid's "camp out" on the floor. They'll think it's cool.

• <u>Don't charge anything on your vacation.</u> Spend cash only. Bring traveler's checks as a safeguard against lost or stolen cash.

• Keep this simple rule in mind when you travel: THINGS AT HOME ARE CHEAPER THAN THINGS ON THE ROAD. So...

—Get your car serviced before you strike out. Have all your hoses, belts and fluid levels checked. Make sure your spare tire is in good condition and that you have tools and an emergency roadside kit. Take along plenty of cash for gas and other necessary services. In accordance with the F.I.N.L. Financial Freedom Strategy, you shouldn't charge gasoline on revolving credit accounts unless you've set aside money to completely pay the charges when the bill comes in. The amount you spend on interest will far outstrip any vacation savings.

—Bring your own soft drinks and snacks in a convenient cooler. You'll save over buying the equivalent on the road.

—When vacationing near water, bring your own floatation devices, rafts and water toys. Renting them once you're there can make for an expensive day.

—Make all your purchases of insect repellent, sun screen, sun glasses, film, batteries, etc. before you leave home.

—Pack a picnic lunch or a simple breakfast. Stop at a roadside park or rest area. It will give the kids a chance to stretch their legs and get rid of nervous energy. When I was a kid, it was tradition to have a box of donuts and a half-gallon of milk in the car for a simple and painless breakfast. And it probably saved my dad hundreds of dollars over the years because he didn't have to pay for bacon, eggs and hash browns at a restaurant.

—Have a meal prepared and put in the freezer before you leave. When you arrive home, you'll avoid one more meal out because there's no food in the house.

Finally, have a safe and relaxing summer vacation. You can do it without spending a lot of money. □

On TRAVEL & LEISURE

UNDERSTAND THE TRAVEL & LEISURE INDUSTRY AND SAVE

The products of the travel industry are perishable. Airlines, hotels, cruise lines, car rental companies and tour operators each sell a product that, by virtue of its time sensitivity, cannot be sold like day-old bread. Once the airplane has left the ground, there's no way for the empty seats to be filled the next day.

This forces the travel industry, with its inherently high overhead costs, to sell those empty seats and vacant staterooms at almost any cost—*as long as they don't go empty*. This is one reason why there is often confusion tracking down wildly gyrating prices or rates from vendor to vendor. Have you ever sat fuming next to smug traveler who just paid $129 for seat 6A when you paid $438 for seat 6B!?!

It's almost impossible to be sure that you are actually getting the best rate. Recently, the New York City Department of Consumer Affairs conducted a study whereby they called almost 50 different travel agents and asked them to locate the best rates for specific destinations. The results were incredible. Prices fluctuated from 20 percent to over 100 percent for the exact same tickets depending on the destination.

Your first reaction might be that some travel agents were just lazier than others and didn't do as much leg work. This is only partially true. Keep in mind when working with a travel agent that it's often much more difficult than their agency commission is worth to track down every possible fare. Travel agents sometimes give you the first good fare that scrolls past on their computer screen.

Get a good travel agent

So first, establish a relationship with an agent you trust. It easier to get an agent to work hard for you when they also get some commissions from your travel requirements that *don't* require a lot of work. They'll be more apt to work hard for you later if they've been rewarded in the past. Also, if you are planning on using an agent, do some of the work beforehand. No agent likes a client who constantly makes last-minute changes and cancels reservations. You'll get better service if you treat your travel agent like the professional they are.

Having said that, you may find that by becoming your own travel agent, you can explore *all* the different possibilities and options for yourself. Sure, you'll spend a lot of time on the phone, but it could be worth it. If you have a personal computer and access to an on-line computer service like Prodigy, it can make this chore even easier.

Comparison Shop

Comparison shopping isn't just for groceries and clothing, but travel as well. Be prepared to make a lot of phone calls and discuss the options available: red eye flights, coach seating, connecting flights, budget hotels, cashing in your frequent flyer mileage, using discount coupons, etc.

Don't Be Afraid to Ask

Discounting is the norm for the travel industry. So don't be shy. ASK for a deal. Look under the rugs for hidden specials. This isn't the time to be bashful. Prod them for information on the best rates. Ask about discounts for seniors (if you're eligible). Ask about special kids' rates and fares. Find out if there are any free meal coupons, free tickets to local attractions or any other gimmicky money-savers attached to the deal.

Knowing when and how to take advantage of the travel industry's sometimes drastic price reductions can save the business or leisure traveler big bucks. □

AIRFARE SIMPLIFICATION?

You may have recently heard about the new fare "simplification" that is being initiated among the major air carriers. It's a little more hype than actual benefits for the air traveler. Here's some of *Consumer Reports'* key findings:

• Coach excursion fares will stay about the same. Although with this year's lower fares it may be difficult to find seats.

• Non-refundable tickets are now exchangeable. If you have to switch, the most you'll lose is $25 to swap tickets.

• Senior Coupons are "under review." If you can use them this year, buy 'em and use 'em.

• Nested excursions and hidden-city tickets—two fare-cutting ploys—will probably lose some appeal.

Appendix C
Phase 3 — Building Retirement Wealth

The information in this appendix is comprised of Stage 3 articles from the *Debt-FREE & Prosperous Living* monthly newsletter. They are reprinted here to give you additional tips and tactics to more successfully operate in Phase 3 of the *Financial Freedom Strategy*. There are fewer Phase 3 articles in this publication than those from the first two stages, because Stage 3 information tends to be more volatile — meaning it pertains only to the time-frame in which it was written, and might not remain relevant for as long as you will own this book. The authors include: John Cummuta and Darlene Todd.

Any references to the *Personal Financial Success* Basic Course refer to editions of this course book prior to the third printing.

Notes

Key Points	Details

Living *Your* AMERICAN DREAM

INVESTING FOR GROWTH

Before you consider investing in growth investments you should establish a fund that can be used in case of emergencies. I usually suggest that six months of expenses be allocated to a money market fund. Be sure and check around for the best rate. Sunday's business section lists the top money market funds and shows the average yield for the last thirty days.

You can open up a money market account with most companies for $1,000. You can add to the account whenever you desire and you can write checks against your account. However, most money market funds require that the checks be written for at least $500.00. Keep in mind that this account should not be used like your checking account. It was designed to be used as an emergency account or as a place to park money until you decide where to invest. Once you have accumulated the equivalent of six months of expenses in your money market account you can start investing into a growth investment to help you accomplish your financial goals.

Growth investments fluctuate in value. Establishing an emergency account before you start a serious investment program will allow you to ride out market swings. I have seen too many cases where the roof leaks or the car needs repair and growth investments have had to be sold when the market is down.

The best place to get started investing for growth is in a good mutual fund family. Most mutual funds can be started for as little as $1,000.00. Some funds can be opened for as little as $100.00.

Mutual funds fall into five main groups and are classified according to their objectives; Cash Reserve, Income, Balanced-Growth - Income, and Growth. Cash reserve funds, as I mentioned before, should be used as an accumulation vehicle or a parking place for money waiting to be invested. Income funds seek high income from dividends or interest; growth in the funds is not the main concern of the investor. Balance funds allocate their assets to spe-

cific proportions of stock and bonds. They are similar to growth and income funds. The prospectus describes how they apportion their assets between stocks and bonds. Growth and income funds seek a combination of growth and income. They tend to favor common stocks that pay dividends. They may hold preferred stocks or bonds but are not required to hold these assets unless specified in the prospectus.

Growth funds seek appreciation rather than income. They tend to keep the majority of assets in common stocks. Growth funds tend to vary in levels of risk. Stock that invest in new companies tend to be more risky than stocks that invest in companies that have been around for some time.

Mutual funds as a family vary a great deal in objectives and performance. Next month I will tell you how to go about choosing the right fund for you.

Living *Your* AMERICAN DREAM

HOW TO CHOOSE THE RIGHT MUTUAL FUND

Last month I gave you a broad overview of the different categories of mutual funds available for your consideration. Mutual funds are the best investment vehicle that has been developed in the twentieth century. When properly chosen, these vehicles combine professional management, ease of purchase and redemption, ease of record keeping, risk reduction through diversification, and excellent performance, all with one investment.

The advantages of investing in mutual funds as you can see are numerous, and once you determine the type of investment that best suits your investment goals, there are several funds available from which to choose. The track record of these funds can be easily obtained, and you can check the performance of all funds in your local business paper.

Each fund has an investment objective, described in the fund's prospectus. The fund's manager must use this as a guide when choosing investments for the funds portfolio. You can use this information to help you select the fund that best suits your needs. Starting with this issue, I will cover in more detail each category of funds, their objectives, and how you can use them in your portfolio. Keep in mind, the younger your age the more risk you can assume and the more growth you can expect to earn.

In this issue we will concentrate on the Aggressive Growth Area. These funds focus strictly on appreciation, with no concern for generating income. These funds strive for maximum capital growth, after using trading strategies such as leverage and options. Most of the portfolio will be comprised of new companies with considerable growth potential. These funds tend to appreciate quickly when favorable market conditions exist. They tend to outperform the market in bull cycles and under perform the market when the bears lead the way. For the past fifteen years, small stocks have outperformed the market by a margin of over two to one.

If you had invested $10,000 fifteen years ago in small stocks, it would have grown to $230,000; that same $10,000 invested in the S & P 500 would have grown to $100,000.

The small stock index, made up from the smallest 20% of companies listed on the S & P 500, outperformed the S & P 500 in all but one ten year period since 1956. Long term small stocks (aggressive growth funds) can be very attractive, even though short-term, small stocks are generally more volatile than other investments, and therefore can rise (and fall) more dramatically.

I recommend you stay clear of these if you are a conservative investor or in your retirement years with few assets. For the moderate risk taker, allocate 10% of your portfolio to this area, and for the aggressive and younger investor, you can risk 20% to this position.

MONEY WATCH

THE GROWTH OF BALANCE FUNDS

Last month's article concentrated on aggressive growth mutual funds. These types of funds tend to outperform the market when we are in a growth period and underperform during a declining market. This issue we will concentrate on balance funds, sometimes referred to as total return funds. Their objective is to provide both growth and income.

The portfolio consists of mostly U.S. stocks, bonds, and convertible securities. The portfolio manager has the ability to weigh the portfolio in favor of stocks or bonds, depending on his perception of the stock market, interest rates, and risk levels.

These funds tend to outperform the market during bull cycles, but suffer greater declines in bear cycles. They will decline less than a pure bond fund when interest rates are climbing, and often outperform bond funds when rates are declining, if the stock market is also doing well. this is an ideal fund for someone who cannot decide between stocks and bonds in which to invest.

In order for a fund to be considered a "Balance Fund," the SEC requires the fund to maintain at least 25% of its assets in fixed income senior securities. for the past three years, balance funds have an average compound return of 6% per year; the five year total return has been 13% and 15% over the last decade. This type of fund has experienced less volatility than any other stock fund category.

HOW MUCH WILL YOU NEED?

This chart will show you how to estimate the effect of inflation on your retirement spending power. If you think you will need $2,000/mo. (in current dollars) to cover your living expenses when you retire in 20 years, and you estimate inflation will be 8 percent a year, multiply $2,000 by 4.7 to give you $9,400. That's the monthly income you will need in 20 years to cover your living expenses.

YEARS TO RETIREMENT	INFLATION RATE PER YEAR				
	4.0%	5.0%	6.0%	7.0%	8.0%
5	1.2	1.3	1.3	1.4	1.5
10	1.5	1.6	1.8	2.0	2.2
15	1.8	2.1	2.4	2.8	3.2
20	2.2	2.7	3.2	3.9	4.7
25	2.7	3.4	4.3	5.4	6.8
30	3.2	4.3	5.7	7.6	10.1

Your F.I.N.L.
MONEY WATCH

INTEREST RATE SHOCK.
WHAT YOU CAN DO.

Are you an investor experiencing interest rate shock? Have you just looked at your latest Money Market statement to see its earnings drop to 4%? Is that 9% CD that's coming due renewing at 5%?

Prices have doubled in the last ten years and your investment income has been cut in half. While you don't want to take a lot of risk, you do have to earn more on your investments.

For the past several months, I have been researching various investment options that offer a higher yield with moderate risk. If you are experiencing interest rate shock, you may want to consider one of these options:

Government Bonds

Government Bonds differ in their structure from company to company. The old variety was comprised mostly of Ginnie Maes. These tended to go down in yield when interest rates declined, and down in share value when interest rates were on the rise. The new variety has a combination of thirty years fixed rate mortgages and variable rate mortgages. This combination has tended to keep the share values stable and a consistent yield of around 8 1/2%. These are backed by government agencies. The share values can fluctuate but to date have been very stable.

Another option you may want to consider if you are in a high tax bracket is a Municipal Bond Fund. Current yields with a high quality fund are in the 6% to 7% tax-free range. You would have to earn over 9% to achieve an equivalent return in a taxable investment.

Going International

For really outstanding returns, you have to look overseas. Europe is experiencing much of the same inflation environment we went through in the early 1980's. You can achieve a 10% yield by investing in CD's and T-Bills of foreign governments such as Germany and England. There are a handful of Mutual Fund companies that have packaged these investments into a single fund. This makes it possible for a person to invest as little as $1,000 and achieve excellent results.

When investing outside the U.S., you should be aware of certain risks.

The first risk is credit risk. You should only invest in funds that invest in creditworthy countries. Let your friends invest in Iraq; you send your money to Germany or Canada.

The second risk associated with these funds is interest rate risk. This risk can be greatly reduced by investing in funds with maturities of three years or less.

The third risk is currency risk. When you convert foreign currency into U.S. currency you could experience a decline in the share value of your funds if our dollar is very strong. To date, the fund managers have been very successful in hedging against this risk. The average share price of these funds has been between $9.80 and $9.97 per share. The yields have averaged between 9% and 11%.

The last investment you may want to consider is Utility Funds. There are quality funds that are paying in excess of 5% in dividends, and you have the up-side potential of appreciation in the growth of funds.

Long range prospects for U.S. interest rates are down, with expected 30 year Treasuries to bottom at 6%. Inflation is expected to average in the 2% range. Investors will have to look for other investment opportunities than our old, familiar CD's.

Your F.I.N.L.

Your F.I.N.L.
MONEY WATCH

MAKING DIVERSIFICATION WORK FOR YOU

Diversification is a simple concept, and a proven way for investors to manage their money. Spreading your dollars across a wide range of investments balances your risk and provides opportunities for gains over time. A well-diversified portfolio puts the law of averages to work for you, increasing your chance for financial success.

To be effective, your portfolio should include several different types of investments which respond differently to economic conditions. While there are risks in virtually any investment strategy, this may lessen the effect of shifting markets on your entire portfolio.

Although it's possible for investors to diversify their assets by choosing individual stocks and bonds, most people don't have the time or expertise to create a well-diversified portfolio, or to make the periodic adjustments required to keep them in balance. Mutual funds are a convenient solution, since they are managed by professionals who constantly monitor and evaluate market trends and adjust portfolios in line with their views of the economy.

Most investors should own both stock and bond mutual funds or a growth and income fund. Stock funds offer potential growth and protection from inflation, while bond funds offer the income many people require. Growth and income funds have the flexibility of increasing or decreasing the percentage of stocks and bonds in their portfolios, depending on market conditions. They can provide the opportunity to participate in stock market advances and provide current income that can offer a cushion against market declines.

Finally, some international diversification of stocks and bonds is a good idea, since nearly 70% of all securities are now issued outside of the United States.

The ideal investment portfolio should be diversified to reflect both your financial goals and your stage of life. As a general rule, you can usually afford to be more aggressive during the early part of your career, and should strive to preserve capital as you approach retirement.

The following is a suggested model portfolio for different stages of life.

Early Career

10% Liquid Assets
50% Growth Stocks
40% Blue Chip Stocks

Mid-Career

20% Liquid Assets
35% Blue Chip Stocks
45% Growth Stocks

Late Career

20% Liquid Assets
20% Bonds
40% Blue Chip Stocks
20% Growth Stocks

Early Retirement

10% Commodity-type Investments
20% Liquid Assets
30% Bonds
20% Blue Chip Stocks
20% Growth Stocks

Late Retirement

10% Commodity-type Investments
20% Liquid Assets
40% Bonds
20% Blue Chip Stocks
10% Growth Stocks

Money Tidbits &
LOOSE CHANGE

A SHOT IN THE "ARM" FOR SMALL INVESTORS

What investment offers a higher yield than most Money Market accounts or CDs but without the inherent risks associated with long-term funds?

An Adjustable Rate Mortgage—or ARM—fund is the answer. An ARM fund invests about 65 percent of its assets in adjustable-rate mortgages. These are typically issued by the Government National Mortgage Association (Ginnie Mae). These agencies buy mortgages from banks and Savings & Loans and package them into securities which are bought by the funds.

A 1.5 to 2 percent higher yield than a Money Market fund is common with an ARM fund, however, unlike a Money Market, ARMs are subject to fluctuations in the interest rate or mortgage caps setting upward or downward limits.

If you are considering stepping up from Money Market funds into something less volatile than a Ginnie Mae, consider an ARM fund, but understand them first.

Don Phillips, publisher of the Chicago-based *Mutual Fund Sourcebook* warns, "One disadvantage occurs when underlying interest rates move down and ARMs must reset at a lower rate, and, in addition there's risk of greater prepayment of mortgages in a low-rate environment. However, these funds have an advantage over Ginnie Mae funds because there's a limit on how much interest can move down.

However there are also limits when the rates begin to move up. A more aggressive move to fixed-rate mortgages has also been taking its toll on the ARM market, which may bring ARM rates closer to yields experienced with Money Markets in the future.

STILL DENYING YOU'RE IN DEBT? TAKE THIS QUICK QUIZ.

The first step in the Financial Freedom Strategy is to get out of debt. Whether you've recently subscribed to the *Debt-FREE and Prosperous Living* ranks, and don't yet realize the danger in your economic situation, or you are a seasoned reader and have yet to get started on your road to financial freedom, take this ten-question quiz to see if you're in — or headed for — certain financial disaster.

1. **Do you owe more than 20 percent of your annual after-tax income (excluding rent or mortgage and car loan)?**

2. **Do you take cash advances on your credit card to pay daily expenses? (NOTE: Many lenders compute the interest starting from the day you take the advance.)**

3. **Do you extend repayment schedules on your bills?**

4. **Do you get loans to pay off other loans?**

5. **Do you make minimum payments on revolving charges?**

6. **Do you use credit for products and services you used to pay for with cash?**

7. **Do you work overtime or a second job just to stay ahead of the bill collector?**

8. **Do you find yourself worrying a lot about bills?**

9. **Do you regularly pay your bills late?**

10. **Is the subject of money the most frequent cause of arguments with your spouse?**

If you answered "yes" to even one of these questions, you need to keep working on your Financial Freedom Strategy. If you answered "yes" to five of these questions, re-read your *Debt-FREE and Prosperous Living* Basic Course and re-commit yourself to achieving financial independence through our comprehensive plan. If you answered "yes" to more than five of these questions, you're either a member of Congress or you need to pour through back issues of this newsletter, re-read your *Debt-FREE and Prosperous Living* Basic Course, and start today to make a difference is the way you manage your finances.

Building Your WEALTH

HOW TO FIND THE BEST MUTUAL FUND

You can't!

Because there is no such thing as the "Best" Mutual Fund. There's no way you can gaze into a crystal ball and find the fund that will out perform all the others over the next 5 or 10 years. But cheer up, because you don't need the best fund. You just need one, two or three funds that are suited to your investment needs, and that have proven their ability to produce good long-term results over the last 5 or 10 years.

While that may seem like a tall order in itself, it's a lot more doable than trying to find that elusive "Perfect Mutual Fund."

The first thing you want to do is decide what type of mutual fund is best aligned with your current investment goals. This is usually related to your "stage of life." In other words, are you young, with a long time before you plan to retire and you want maximum growth, even if it comes with a bit of risk? Or are you closer to retirement and more concerned about risk?

Generally speaking, Stock funds are used for growing your money but are not usually income-generating funds (they are sensitive to the ups and downs of the stock market), Bond funds are income-generating but not usually growth-producing (their value is highly sensitive to interest rates), and money funds are usually low-growth/moderate-income places to hide your money when the market is in a down-turn.

Let's Talk About Risk

When the term "Risk" is used, most people immediately think of losing their money. But, in the world of mainline mutual funds — those that are investing in 100 or more securities, are NOT borrowing money to do that investing, and are NOT investing in highly speculative commodities or precious metals — your risks are relatively low.

Buying shares in a mutual fund that meets the above criteria is much safer than investing in any of the individual stocks or securities that the fund holds. If you were to buy stock in a company that goes out of business, you lose ALL your money. But, if you own shares in a mutual fund that owns stock in that same company, only one-one-hundredth or 1% of your investment has been lost — and it's probable that other securities the mutual fund holds will experience gains that more than override the one loss.

When you invest in mutual funds, there are really only four risks you face.
1. Failing to choose a fund that will out-pace inflation. Choosing an under-performing fund will actually cause your real-dollar assets to shrink.

2. Trying to time the market. If you gain confidence in your investing knowledge, and you begin to feel like trying to pick when to be in stocks, when to be in bonds, and when to be in money funds, move into this strategy cautiously. Don't commit a major portion of your funds until you have proven — over several years — that your strategy works.

3. Trying to do too much too quickly. Remember, the higher the potential growth, the higher the potential risk. When you're young and have plenty of time to recoup losses, you can afford to handle more risk. When you're older, going for high-stakes growth funds may interfere with your sleep.

4. The greatest risk is the risk that you won't plan and execute your wealth-building program. Piecemeal investing gets you nowhere. If you spend all or most of your money in the here-and-now, you'll be a pauper in the there-and-then. The beauty of the F.I.N.L. Financial Freedom Strategy is that you know exactly how much to invest each month. It's 100% of the monthly money you used to be wasting on bills. When your debt is all paid off, just switch the money over to the investment stage of your plan and start socking it away with dedication. It will make you RICH! □

Building Your WEALTH

"NET ASSET VALUE" HOW MUTUAL FUND SHARES ARE PRICED

When you buy shares in a mutual fund, you are essentially buying part ownership in a company whose business is investing in other companies, governments or currencies. Your shares are priced based on what is known as their Net Asset Value or NAV, and that value varies from day to day, depending on the value of the securities your fund has invested in and the number of outstanding shares.

To be precise, the Net Asset Value is calculated by adding the total daily value of a fund's portfolio, plus its cash reserves, minus any liabilities. That sum is then divided by the total number of shares outstanding on that day. The formula looks like this:

$$NAV = \frac{M + C - L}{N}$$

M = the market value of all shares in the fund's holdings at the end of the trading day. In other words, how much all your fund's investments are worth that day.

C = the fund's cash or cash-equivalent positions. The fund's liquid assets.

L = the fund's liabilities.

N = the number of outstanding shares issued by the fund.

Open–End vs. Closed-End Funds

When you buy shares in an open-end fund (the most common kind) each of your shares are worth the fund's Net Asset Value amount. You are buying new, previously unissued stock. The money you invest increases the size of the fund's asset pool, and a small percentage pays management fees and other charges the fund owes. Open-end funds can issue shares to the public as long as there is demand for them. Continually selling new shares like this is called Primary Distribution.

When you go to sell shares in an open-end fund, you are selling them back to the fund rather than to another investor. You will be paid the Net Asset Value of the shares as calculated on the day you sell them. There may also be a small fee for redeeming your shares.

Closed-end funds, on the other hand can trade for more or less than their Net Asset Value. Those that trade above their NAV are said to sell at a "Premium."

The reason that closed-end fund share prices vary is that, unlike open-end funds, closed-end funds only issue a specific number of shares. These shares trade on exchanges just like individual stocks, and their prices are determined by marketplace supply and demand. If demand is strong, prices will be high, and if demand is weak, prices will be low.

Also unlike open-end funds, cash proceeds from the sale of closed-end fund shares flow between buyers and sellers, not to and from the fund itself. That means that, once a closed-end fund has sold all its shares, no additional shareholder capital enters the asset pool.

In many cases the shares in a closed-end fund sell for less than their NAV. This is called selling at a discount. Let's say you buy shares in a given fund at a 20% discount, then demand for the fund's shares grows to the point where the discount shrinks to 10%. Even though the shares are still trading below the fund's NAV, you can sell and make a 10% profit.

Closed-end funds are neither better or worse than open-end funds, just riskier and more difficult to sell. Your broker and the fund's prospectus should both tell you whether a fund is open- or closed-end. And if you're tempted to invest in closed-end funds, be wary of big discounts. While they may appear to be fabulous deals, there are probably good reasons why other investors are staying away.

And don't pay more than a closed-end fund's NAV unless you have specific reasons to believe that demand for the fund's shares will increase after you buy them. You could be buying at the top of demand, only to experience the slide back to lower prices. □

CDs—THEY AIN'T WHAT THEY USED TO BE

You'll note that the *Personal Financial Success* investment strategy is almost exclusively built around mutual funds. That philosophy is neither overly clever nor particularly sophisticated. It just makes plain horse-sense that an investment company (that's what a mutual fund is), headed by a recognized investment expert who specializes in the types of investments the fund focusses on, supported by a staff of researchers and other professionals, will just pick better investments more consistently than you or I likely will.

Now, that's not to say that as investors we shouldn't bother to understand anything about what's going on. It's still important to know how and why to pick the right mutual funds at the right time, and that's usually the main focus of our instruction in this column.

However, people are crea-tures of habit and inertia, and there are a lot of folks who got into Certificates of Deposit (CD) investing a few years back when interest rates were a lot higher — and I thought it might take a little prodding to motivate them to move that money into investments that would serve them better.

What's Wrong With CDs?

Almost everything.

First of all, we invest to GROW our money. Today's CDs are generating around 3.5% to 4%. That's LESS than inflation! Keeping your money in a CD is just barely better than the return you'd get from sticking the money in your mattress. And even if you're at a point where you think that getting more important than capital is bet-ter than growth, how much income can you get from 3.5%?

When you add in the fact that YOU HAVE TO PAY TAXES ON THAT MEASLY 3.5%, you're getting NOTHING for your investment.

But What About the Safety of FDIC Insurance?

When a bank goes insolvent, many people think that FDIC stands for "Fixes Damage In Cash," but that's not really the case. A recent government report indicated that the FDIC only has about 45 cents for every $100 on deposit in accounts it is protecting! And the Government Accounting Office predicts that another 300 banks and S&Ls will go belly-up in the next twelve months.

Another thing you should know: the FDIC doesn't neces-sarily pay you right away, even if it does have the cash on hand. If your money is in a bank that fails, you could wait two weeks to two years to get your deposits covered by the government. Did your banker ever tell you that when he or she was selling you the CD — and earning a commission on it?

And If Those Two Problems Aren't Enough...

You get penalized if you take your money out of these won-derful investments before their maturity date. Imagine the gall of the banker offering you a return on your invest-ment that's less than inflation — and then threatening to penalize you if you try to get any of your money back.

So...What Can You Do?

First of all, when your CDs come due, grab the money and run. Don't roll it over. Look for sound mutual fund investments with solid track records.

Next, if you're looking for something that has the look, smell and secure feel of a CD, consider good old U.S. Treasury Bills. These bills are REALLY covered by the full faith and promise of the United States Government — just like the green paper you sometimes get to carry in your wallet.

And you can invest in T-bills with the convenience and un-complication of mutual funds, by putting your money into Treasury-only money market funds. They're safer than CDs, in almost all states at least a portion of your interest is exempt from state and local taxes, and most funds pay a lot more interest than CDs.

□

Notes

Key Points	Details

Appendix D
Selected Newsletter Editorials

This appendix is comprised of selected editorials and other information of a general or philosophical nature from the *Debt-FREE & Prosperous Living* monthly newsletter. They are reprinted here to give you a sense of the urgency and importance we put on your following our *Financial Freedom Strategy*. We believe that unless you commit to our plan, or one equally as focused on getting you debt-free and secure, you will certainly be one of the victims when the day of reckoning comes for the American economy. The author is John Cummuta.

Any references to the *Personal Financial Success* Basic Course refer to editions of this course book prior to the third printing.

Notes

Key Points	Details

IS LIVING THE AMERICAN DREAM POSSIBLE?

Do you ever feel like you're working harder and harder, yet you have little or nothing to show for it? Does it seem like living the American Dream always takes just a little more money than you bring in?

Well, your problem may not be insufficient income. It's more likely to be unrealistic expectations, and brainwashing!

Financial researchers have determined that, in 1991, it takes about $60,000 a year to live the American Dream. But when they interviewed people who make $60,000 a year, these folks said that they felt it would take about $75,000 to "Really" live it. And people making $75,000 thought it would take about $100,000. Of course, the people making $100,000 felt they would need around $150,000 a year to finally achieve the American Dream. And on it went up the scale.

The truth is that most of us already have enough. We just need to manage it better. We need to understand what we're trying to accomplish with the money that flows into our lives, and then craft a spending/saving/investing plan to get us to our goals. That takes a bit of self-analysis and a lot of discipline. But it DOES NOT necessarily require a ton of self-denial. It just takes a realistic appraisal of our true needs and our reasonable wants.

And it takes a concentrated effort to take control of our minds back from TV advertisers. We are all being brainwashed every day by commercials that tell us that we won't be happy unless our car has more valves, our gym shoes have air pumps, our dog eats a scientific diet, and our clothes come with a proper name on the tag. We are continually being taught to spend, spend, spend. And we obey—much more than we can afford to.

The Biggest Mistake Made by Most Americans

Thinking that, "Things will just sort of work out," is the trap that catches most Americans who are running on the Madison Avenue financial treadmill. They go through life literally burning their income as fast as it comes through the door, naively leaning on the dream that something will come along to bail them out before they have to pay for their lack of control.

This is a serious problem. According to federal government statistics, 96% of Americans DO NOT achieve financial independence. And the evidence shows that the 4% who escape this fate are not just the people who finally figure out how to make more money than their family can spend. The indisputable facts show that these are simply people — from all income levels — that formulate financial goals for their lives, create workable plans to achieve those goals, and then STICK TO THOSE PLANS.

The Importance of Goals and Plans

In 1953 the graduating class of Yale University was surveyed, and it turned out that only 3% of the graduates had formulated financial goals for their lives and written detailed plans to achieve those goals. In 1973, twenty years later, those same people were found and re-surveyed. It turned out that the 3% who left college with goals, and plans to reach those goals, were worth more financially than the other 97% of their classmates COMBINED!

What to Do

1. Act Now. Just like changes in your diet can change your appearance and your health risks over the remainder of your life, changing your spending/saving/investing habits now can change the shape of your financial future.

2. Set Goals. Your family's goals should be tied to your values. Seek help from your financial planner, accountant or the professionals who write in this newsletter, if you feel you need it. Just set those financial goals.

3. Analyze Your Spending. This is the culprit. If your family is like most in America, you dribble enough money through the cracks during your lifetime to have built a very comfortable retirement. Establish the major categories of your spending and put ceilings on each. This should include EVERY area where you spend money, including those impulse trips to the pizza place and the impromptu gift for your favorite uncle (the one with the will).

4. Decide What You REALLY Need. A good measure of the worthiness of an expenditure is its "Lifetime Value." In other words, a year from now how much is it worth to you? Watch how much you're spending on "Experiences" rather than "Things". And be brutally honest about the value of both kinds of expenses.

5. Save At Least 10% Of Your Income. If you had started saving just $100 a month at age 25, at say 7% interest, by the time you reached 65 it would be worth $262,481.34. That's over a quarter million dollars! And all it took was a hundred bucks a month. Ask yourself, what's more important in

(continued next page)

the long run — a couple dinners out each month, or a quarter million dollars at retirement?

6. Maximize Your Pretax Savings. Use IRA's, 401(k) plans and Keoghs. The effective yields are greater than taxable interest in other investments, and your tax calculations will be much simpler.

7. Vary Your Investments As You Age. Forty-year-olds should have 40% of their money in fixed-income investments — 60% in stocks. Sixty-year-olds should reverse that distribution.

8. Dollar-cost Average. Investing the same amount of money each month in stocks will likely more than overcome any ups and downs in the individual values of stocks in your portfolio.

9. Increase Your Savings Percentage As Often As Possible. Every time you get a raise, increase your savings/investment percentage. The 10% mentioned above is a minimum. If you want to retire early or more comfortably, it will take more. If you feel like you're depriving yourself too much, split income increases with your savings plan. Save half and allow yourself to spend the other half.

As un-fun as it might be to read this stuff, THIS IS WHAT IT TAKES TO GAIN TRUE FINANCIAL INDE-PENDENCE. If you think you have a better way, please write in and share it with us all. But in the mean time, please don't fall prey to those false prophets who tell you that, "Making more money is all it takes to achieve financial free-dom." In your heart of hearts you know that's not enough. You have to know what to do with that addi-tional money.

Besides, the F.I.N.L. pro-gram offers one of the most powerful and straight-forward money-making business opportu-nities available anywhere, so we've got the best of both worlds — more money...and the knowl-edge to multiply the value of that money in our lives.

ARE YOU ON CREDIT... LIKE A DRUG?

Personal bankruptcies are up by leaps and bounds in America, and we can't use the crutch that it's all caused by the sluggish economy. It's projected that next year will see over a million personal bankruptcies, and the overwhelming cause is the INABILITY TO MANAGE CONSUMER CREDIT.

The headline of this article asks if you're using credit like a drug. Well if you are, it's at least in part the fault of businesses and even our government — because they've been the pushers.

Here's Why

The economy slows down. So what do you hear business and political leaders asking for? They're asking for the Federal Reserve to put more money into circulation, so it will lower interest rates.

Why do they want lower interest rates? Because they know that it will motivate more Americans to run out and charge more purchases, that's why. Why do you think the car manufacturers offer low-interest-rate promotions? Because it stimulates purchases, that's why. And if purchases increase, the economy appears to be in better shape. The problem is that it's all done with smoke and mirrors.

Most Americans are now just like their government —

paying today for things they bought weeks, months and years ago. In many cases they're still paying for things they've already thrown away.

The staggering truth is that average Americans are now spending 83% of their monthly disposable income on debt payments.

That leaves only 17% to pay "Cash" for something. And what makes it even worse is that only a portion of the 83% is really paying off the debt. With credit card interest rates around 20% (and higher), you end up paying a tremendous price for the short-term pleasure of having something RIGHT NOW instead of saving up to buy it a little further down the road.

For example: if you were to buy a $500 TV with a 20% interest-rate credit card, you could pay as little as $15.22 per month if you take 48 months to pay the purchase off. It's all too easy to say yes to a deal like that — a $500 TV...RIGHT NOW...for only $15.22 a month. But the reality is that you will pay more than $730 for that $500 TV. In other words you'll pay for a TV and a half, for one TV — just so you can have it now.

Think of what else you could do with that $230. And if you're in the 28% tax bracket, you'll have to

earn $319.44 to net the $230 necessary to pay the interest over the following four years.

But the tragic loss is to your future. If you took that $230 and invested it in something that paid an average interest of 10% (we tell you about many investments in *Personal Financial Success* that earn that much), it would increase to $1,685.46 over 20 years. If you're around 45 right now, that's when you'd be needing the money — and the TV set would be a rusted junk in a land-fill.

Are You a Credit Addict?

Maybe you're not spending 83% on credit bills each month, but are you spending a significant portion of your income on debt? Isn't it like a drug? Aren't you doing the same thing a drug addict does each time you take a hit on one of your credit cards? You get the momentary rush of buying something, but then it fades. And next month, when you feel depressed because you have even less money left after paying your credit card bills — do you go out and buy something else on credit...to make yourself feel better?

The only way to break the credit habit is the exact way junkies do it — make a decision. Start immediately to swear off consumer credit. I'm not talking about home loans. Very few people can buy a

home cash, and the interest on mortgages is still tax deductible (at least for now). But I am talking about disciplining yourself to resist impulse buying. If something is really important to own, SAVE UP FOR IT!

You can even do it with cars. I got rid of one "Vette" and got another — cash! The "Vette" I got rid of was a Corvette, and the one I bought cash was a Chevette. And you know what? That Chevette got me to all the same places in the same amount of time. Maybe I didn't feel quite as "Cool," but take my word for it, "Cool" is NOT worth $543 a month. Since then I've saved more and traded up (with cash each time) for better cars, but the bottom lines is that I HAVE NO CAR PAYMENTS!

Do I invest every penny of that $543 I'm saving? No. I save most of it, but I take my wife out to the movies once in a while. It buys a pizza or two. And we occasionally do one of those hotel "Getaway" weekends. The point is that I'm not saying you need to live like a monk. But you have to get control of your money flow so it's making YOU financially free, instead of just enriching the stockholders of Mastercard or Visa.

THIS IS NO DRILL!

I woke up this morning to hear that General Motors, the biggest company in America, is laying off between 70,000 and 75,000 workers. Just a couple weeks ago the newscasters told us that IBM, another of the largest companies in the world, was laying off 4,000 people.

Also on the news this morning was the announcement that the Soviet Union would cease to exist at the end of the year, and by the time you read this it will be history. The untold story there is that all the countries that used to be the Soviet Union are in terrible economic shape, and could disintegrate into civil war because of the dramatic money problems they face.

Here at home there is a growing number of public officials, at the highest levels of our federal government, who are beginning to say that our economy, as we know it, could collapse by the year 2,000. The surplus in the Social Security Trust Fund — the money that's supposed to be there when you and I retire — is being sucked out and used by congress for general funds. And, by the end of this decade, it is expected to take over a third of the entire federal budget just to pay interest payments on the deficit.

It's a New World

—Not Necessarily a Better One

Things are changing. And because of the way they're changing, and the speed with which they're changing, we can no longer think about the future in the same terms as we used to. The old methods and time-tested rules no longer apply.

The bottom line is that — if you're going to survive the new future, you're going to have to start playing by a new gameplan. In fact, changing to this gameplan could make you one of the few people who can actually thrive and prosper in the coming financial decline in America.

The Old Rules

Over the decades since World War II, we were taught to borrow our way to prosperity. Credit was used to super-accelerate the economy, to make things appear to be even better than they really were. And they really were good. During those decades — essentially the forties through the eighties — our domestic economy and our exports were growing at such a rate that we could afford to pay all the interest payments and still prosper.

But by the turn of this century — indeed even now — THERE IS NOT ENOUGH ECONOMIC GROWTH TO SUPPORT THE DEBT. And I'm talking about both government debt and personal debt.

Think about those people being laid off by General Motors and IBM. Most of them probably have credit cards, car payments and mortgage payments that they will not be able to pay without their job. The moment their income stops, their whole personal economy will implode. Their "House of Debt" will collapse around them, because they were playing a balancing game of income verses debt payments. Now their employer comes along and upsets the balance and their lives will crash and burn.

Their main problem — THEY ARE VULNERABLE!

They're vulnerable because they're playing by the old rules. The rules that only apply when you can be sure that NOTHING WILL GO WRONG. But we are now in a time when many things can go wrong. YOU CAN NO LONGER COUNT ON A CONTINUING STREAM OF INCOME.

So You Must Become "Un-Vulnerable"

The entire F.I.N.L. program is based around the *Personal Financial Success* system, where we help you follow a straight-line strategy to pay-

ing off ALL your debt — including your mortgage — in about 5 years. Then we show you how to operate 100% on CASH and never need credit again. Finally, through the pages of this newsletter and the *Personal Financial Success* Basic Course, we give you simple but effect investment advice to use the money that you used to be wasting on debt payments to build your wealth in the shortest period of time.

Reaching that position is the only hope you have for a really secure financial future. You need to get to a point where you are insulated from economic ups and downs. You need to know that if someone takes your job away, you WON'T lose your house, your car, your security.

And you cannot rely on finding some incredible "Get Rich Quick" scheme to bail you out at the last minute. Even though the F.I.N.L. business opportunity can earn you thousands of dollars a month, you should not bet on the income side alone to pull you out of the fire.

Please...if you haven't faced this problem yet...stop ignoring it. Deal with it. Take the steps we teach you in your *Personal Financial Success Basic Course*, and be one of the few people who will really be ready to enjoy the next millennium.

RECESSION OR DEPRESSION?

Some people moan that we're in a recession, others assert that this is really a depression. Economist Milton Friedman put it in perspective when he said that, "A recession is when your neighbor loses his job. A depression is when you lose YOUR job."

So the state of the economy is not just a national thing, it's really more of an individual and personal thing.

Financial advisor Charles Givens says that, "A real recession is having more cash outgo than inflow." The truth is, 90% of American families have been in a recession for most of their lives — living from paycheck to paycheck — even during the period that the media now incorrectly refers to as the greed era of the '80s."

WHO'S RESPONSIBLE?

If a recession is a personal condition, experienced differently by different people, then who is responsible for each of their situations?

To some extent it is the "Economy," but more directly and accurately, your personal economic situation is the result of how you use family income. Pretty unglamorous definition, but precise nonetheless. Every American brings in a certain amount of money, and they then commit to spend that money on various products and services. If they can't restrain their desire for something, yet don't have enough money to actually buy it, they will use someone else's money, and thereby commit to pay them a fee each month for the use of that money.

Little by little they will develop a fixed pattern for the disposition of each month's income, and — in most cases — that pattern will use every penny expected to come in each month.

So the short answer is that YOU ARE RESPONSIBLE for your financial situation, and I AM RESPONSIBLE for my financial situation. Even if we've lost our job and are facing bankruptcy, WE are responsible for being in that desperate a situation. We could have used our money in a more effective way, and then if we lost our job, we would have a financial safety net to fall back on.

TAKE CONTROL

Bankruptcies in Chicago were up 15% in 1991, for the highest jump in 11 years. Why did so many people have to bail out? Because they had been walking on the financial edge for many years before 1991, and when something in the economy knocked them slightly off balance, they had no alternative but to jump. They were NOT PREPARED for anything but a continuance of perfect circumstances, so in essence — they were asking for it.

That may sound brutal, but financial collapse is a brutal thing. I'm trying to help people avoid it. To do that, I need to help them wake up from the coma our culture puts people in. You watch TV, and with the exception of a few news stories about the homeless, it looks like "Business as Usual." The same commercials are motivating you to take advantage of the, "Low monthly payments," and the economy marches on — pushing more and more Americans off balance.

Your only defense is to TAKE CONTROL of your personal economy. In the pages of the *Personal Financial Success* Basic Course and this monthly newsletter you'll find us recommending some pretty drastic actions to help you get a hold of your personal finances. Please don't disregard them as too harsh or radical. Consider how radical it is to go bankrupt. Think about how radical it is to hit retirement and have your income drop 80%. Then think about how radical it could be to have all the money you need, for emergencies now and for retirement in the future.

The people who are stealing your wealth are very sophisticated, and they have powerful money-sucking systems arrayed against you. It will take dramatic and definitive action by you to beat them. Commit yourself to doing whatever is necessary. Your quality of life literally depends on it.

IT'S DOWNRIGHT SCARY OUT THERE

This morning's newscas announced General Motors' plant closings for 1992, and the termination of tens of thousands of jobs. It's not just the 15,000 to 20,000 GM employees who are losing their paychecks, but also the workers in uncounted parts factories across the country. When you factor in the drop in business for the store owners and employees in the towns around all these manufacturing plants, you begin to see the scope of our nation's economic situation.

The cause of these problems will affect more than just one company or one industry. According to *American Demographics* magazine, "The U.S. consumer market — that is, our population — is growing at less than 1 percent per year, and even that modest growth is slowing each year. The Census Bureau predicts that this decade will see the slowest rate of growth in American history."

What this means is that there is NO MAGIC BULLET to shoot us out of this recession. Yes, we will come out of it gradually, but there is no market growth to fuel a large scale bounce-back. In fact, what we are seeing is a major restructuring of our economy, similar to the effects of the Baby Boom — only in the opposite direction. As the number of buyers out there in the population decline, so will the need

to manufacture products — and therefore the need to employ manufacturing workers. And, as these people lose their incomes, all the employees who work in businesses where these unemployed manufacturing workers used to spend their money will also find their jobs in jeopardy.

The good old days of always being able to count on your one paycheck away from bankruptcy.

That's exactly why we created the F.I.N.L. program. Because people in this country are JUST TOO FINANCIALLY VULNERABLE. They are living too close to the edge. But it's not really their fault. They've simply been following the American Consumer Gameplan, buying things on credit, financing everything from cars to lunch — and this strategy has put them on a financial tightwire, juggling bills and paychecks.

But there's a new light at the end of the tunnel. People following the F.I.N.L. Financial Freedom Strategy are reporting rapid financial turnarounds. We've had subscribers telling us that the *Personal Financial Success* Basic Course is their "financial Bible." Others call to tell us that they're cutting up their credit cards and cancelling accounts. One man recent-

ly called to say, "I'm going to pay my mortgage off on Friday!" These people are moving swiftly away from financial vulnerability, towards what we call "Unvulnerability."

Our program is designed so that — if everything remains relatively stable in your life — you'll be able to get completely out of debt and retire in the shortest possible time. However, the program's other purpose is to get you "Un-vulnerable" to ups and downs in your personal economy, as fast as possible. That means that, if your employer goes out of business, you won't be one of the unfortunate people declaring bankruptcy, selling your home, losing your lifestyle.

Instead, you'll already be out of debt, so the loss of an income source won't put you in immediate peril. You'll also have emergency cash reserves to draw on — but because you're expenses will be next to nothing — you won't have to use these reserves. And you'll be able to take your time looking for a new employment situation that suits you. Or you could even spend the time building an F.I.N.L. business of your own, so you could live off that income and never have to work for someone else again.

See how much different an economic downturn can be for someone who follows our Financial Freedom Strategy — compared to how it would impact most Americans, who are typically loaded down with debt and monthly payments that use up almost all their income?

Our Financial Freedom Strategy is SIMPLE! I subscribe to all the big financial newsletters and educational programs, and let me tell you — they could complicate a one-man parade. They make every financial decision sound like planning a space shuttle mission. I'm sorry, but it's just not that complex. The real, short-line principles to financial freedom are simple to understand and simple to implement.

The reason I started this program and wrote the *Personal Financial Success* Basic Course is that I proved out in my own life the incredible power of these financial principles. I am now completely debt-free except for my house (which will be paid for in 4 years or less), and I'm buying everything CASH. We are using NO credit, so every step is moving us forward instead of backwards. And all this is being done with an average income. I am not taking zillions of dollars out of the company.

I have felt and enjoyed the unburdening relief that this financial freedom brings, and I want you to experience it too. Please don't just give these principles lip service. Start following the plan today, and you'll be able to project exactly when you too will be "Un-vulnerable" to America's increasingly unpredictable economy.

SETTING THE CAPTIVES FREE

As each day goes by at F.I.N.L., I see our business changing from just a Financial Freedom Strategy to a CAUSE. People who call and write in are emotional and intense in their commitment to what we're doing. Quite frankly, it's beyond what I had hoped.

I and the great people working with me at F.I.N.L. are sincerely committed to helping our readers and subscribers achieve true financial "Un-vulnerability," and we're gratified by the many wonderful comments we're receiving from people all across America. People who have put our system to work for themselves and are seeing dramatic results.

And we couldn't have timed our program better. America is ripe for the *Personal Financial Success* system of eliminating debt, operating on cash and building wealth safely and quickly. Let me share an excerpt from a Special Report published by the *NEW PARADIGM DIGEST*, a social trend newsletter.

The Simple Life: Rejecting the Rat Race

In the April 8 Time [magazine] cover story, people are saying goodbye to having it all. They are tired of trendiness and materialism and are rediscovering the joys of home life, basic values, and things that last.

Out with the Rolex in with the Timex, out with credit cards in with savings accounts, out with big government in with local activism, out with disposables in with cloth diapers, out with riding lawn mowers and in with push-it-yourself mowers.

After 10 years of gaudy dreams and godless consumerism, Americans are starting to trade down. They want to reduce their attachments to status symbols, fast-track careers and great expectations of having it all. Upscale is out; downscale is in. Yuppies are an ancient civilization. Flaunting money is considered gauche: if you've got it, please keep it to yourself or give some away!

In place of materialism, many Americans are embracing simpler pleasures and homier values. They've been thinking hard about what really matters in their lives, and they've decided to make some changes. What matters is having time for family, friends, rest and recreation, good deeds and spirituality. For some people that means a radical step: changing one's career, living on less, or packing up and moving to a quieter place.

The Evidence is Clear

"This is a rapid and extremely powerful movement," says Ross Goldstein, a San Francisco psychologist and market researcher. "I'm impressed by how deep it goes into the fabric of the country." Many have dubbed the 90's as the "We decade."

In a TIME/CNN survey of 500 adults, 69% said they would like to "slow down and live a more relaxed life," in contrast to only 19% who said they would like to "live a more exciting, faster-paced life."

According to the *PARADIGM* article again, *"Penny pinching is back in vogue, some describe it as thrifty chic even among the rich. Jacki O. shops at the Gap. Christie Brinkley wears plain white mens' T shirts. Outside B.J.'s Wholesale Club in Medford, Mass., a white stretch limo waits at the curb while its passengers roam the cavernous discount warehouse. Lawyers and executives sit next to truckers and shipyard workers at Tom's Barber shop in Jacksonville for a $6 trim."*

We're at the Crest of the Wave

You've heard it said that one of the keys to success is — You have to be at the right place at the right time. Well, I believe that we've positioned F.I.N.L. at the right place with the right message at the right time for America. People are clearly ready for the strong medicine in our Financial Freedom Strategy.

Getting out of debt is a hot topic today. In fact, that's why it has taken so long for the economy to bottom out — because Americans refused to get into more debt to fuel the recovery, and in fact, they are paying off credit debt at a record rate.

And Feedback From You Proves We're Right

We're not only hearing from our readers and subscribers that our message is "Right On," but we're beginning to get calls and letters from referrals. The typical call goes something like, "My uncle gave me these cassettes...and they're great. So I want to find out how to get more of this stuff, and get into your program."

We're grateful that our information is helping. That's why we're publishing it. And if you have any ideas that can make it more valuable or meaningful to you, please let us know.

— EDITORIAL —

BACK TO BASICS

According to recent articles in *Time, Forbes, American Demographics* and other leading news and research magazines, Americans are chucking the Get-Rich-and-Show-It 80's and are moving into the 90's with a rush to simplify and stabilize their lives.

This trend includes a dramatic move to pay off credit debt. Credit cards are being cut up at a rate that registers on the Richter scale, and the people who used to be called "Yuppies" are moving from the fast lane to the slow lane...and even to the exit ramp. The greed that characterized the 80's is being replaced by a new awareness of what really matters in life. And there's an unprecedented move to slow down and enjoy life, instead of blazing through it like a comet burning itself to ash.

Another characteristic of this shift in values is the move away from traditional symbols of success, as defined over the last decade. Yupsters are trading in their BMW's for Chevies and Fords, and they're leaving their downtown condos and upscale suburban homes for the country.

I have to admit that I was already a part of this wave before I realized it was a wave. In the past year Lois and I have paid off ALL debt except our mortgage, and we'll have that paid off in about 4 years. We've cut up all our credit cards, and now use only American Express and a VISA debit card if we are in a situation that requires plastic. I got rid of my Corvette and our Oldsmobile 98 Regency (and their $1,000+ monthly lease payments), and have since purchased (CASH) a Pontiac Bonneville and a Ford Tempo. And we just finished moving from an upscale Chicago suburb to the country (reducing our mortgage balance by $50,000).

I not only lost a few pounds carrying boxes during the move, but I lost several tons of stress from no longer having to support an artificial and expensive lifestyle. I now enjoy my life more than I ever did with the big house and all the toys. In fact, we now have more cash to enjoy life with, because we're not dribbling it all away on big bills.

Returning to Family Values

The most encouraging trend to me is the indication that the fast-trackers of recent years are turning back to their families to find meaning in their lives. They're spending more time with their children, instead of just buying them toys to fill empty hours with. They're spending more time with their spouses, instead of trading them in for this year's newest model. They're finding the peace and joy in making and keeping commitments, both to their families and their communities.

Instead of always taking, it seems that we're becoming a generation of givers.

These very significant changes are reducing stress levels in a big way. People who jump off the "More, bigger, higher, more expensive" band wagon lighten their loads, reduce tension in their lives and create an instantly brighter future. I believe we will see improvements in general health, reductions in divorce and drug usage, and eventually other beneficial manifestations of a less frenetic society — IF WE CAN HELP PEOPLE REALLY ACHIEVE THIS TURN BACK TO THE BASICS.

I'm convinced that the key place to begin is by helping them become LESS VULNERABLE to the financial pressures of life. Then their minds and hearts can be clear and open to seeing the value of other changes in their lifestyles.

F.I.N.L. Is Leading the Way

I have found that most of life's complex situations are usually resolved by implementing simple solutions, and that's the philosophy behind the F.I.N.L. program. The *Personal Financial Success* Basic Course and monthly newsletter offer step-by-step procedures for getting to financial "unvulnerability" — but these steps are only components of a simple, three-part system for (1) Getting completely debt-free, (2) Operating completely on cash, and (3) Building wealth.

This straight-forward process will take you from being crushed by never-ending debt obligations, to complete financial freedom, in an relatively short period of time — and it can all be done with the income you already make. Of course, we do have an opportunity for you to share our unique program with others and add substantially to your monthly income, but that's not necessary to achieving financial freedom through our program.

Once you are on your way to taking the heat off yourself financially, you can begin deciding what other facets of your life you'd like to back down a notch or two. Maybe you'd like to say good-bye to the hustle bustle of the city and move out to where the loudest thing you hear is the robin outside your window. Maybe you'd like to trade arguments with your spouse or children for calm and enjoyable conversations.

It's amazing how many of the conflicts in our relationships — and our life in general — are all just symptoms of the fact that we're living in a pressure-cooker. We're being squeezed financially, professionally, in traffic, by neighbors, by keeping up with the Joneses, and a hundred other points of aggravation. We can't vent our frustrations in most of these situations, so we do it in the only place where we can pretty much do what we want — at home. That means that our families pay for all the pressures we endure throughout the day.

The only way to change these scenarios in your life is to change the parts of your life that are causing the pressures. Then the rest of your

(continued next page)

life will automatically come into balance. And the first key is usually lessening financial pressure.

Step one in this quest is to reject the gospel that teaches that you have to have the best and newest of everything to be "Really" happy. Following that faulty course, you'll likely end up chasing all the things that money CAN buy, while sacrificing those beautiful things in your life that money CAN'T buy. Read my lips — YOU DON'T HAVE TO GET RICH OR MAKE A TON OF MONEY TO BE HAPPY. YOU JUST HAVE TO HAVE ENOUGH TO LIVE COMFORTABLY WITH THOSE YOU LOVE.

My goal is to help you determine what kind of lifestyle would realistically be comfortable for you, and then help you get to a financial point where you can live that lifestyle completely off the interest on your investments, so that work will be optional for you.

So watch for *Personal Financial Success* newsletter to grow in ways that will help you leave the rat race and discover the wonderful life you But even more importantly, it puts YOU in control of your current finances and future financial condition. And being in control is a wonderful feeling.

THE LIVING TRUST: CAN YOU DO IT YOURSELF?

Why would you want a living trust? To transfer an inheritance to your heirs without the expense and delay of probate action, that's why. Probate is where your state government gets into distributing your wealth after you die, so they can see how much of they (and the lawyers) can steal. Even if you have a will, you might want to consider creating a living trust, because even clear and precise wills are subject to probate.

It doesn't require a lot of "Lawyer-ese" to write a living trust. You just want to be sure that your situation is right for this kind of instrument. The conditions that are best for a living trust are:

1. Your estate must be worth LESS than $600,000. This is based on the fact that up to $600,000 is exempted from federal estate taxes, so you need to keep an eye on whether congress changes that limit. If your (or yours and your spouse's) combined estate exceeds $600,000, you'd better find a lawyer who is experienced with estate planning to help minimize you heirs' tax burdens.

2. Do your own living trust only if your situation is uncomplicated. What this means is that you cannot impose controls on the transfer of property in a simple living trust. If you want to have conditions like, "I'll leave the money to my daughter ONLY if she marries a sea captain who has completed at least seven voyages around the world, they live in the town where I grew up, and name their first child Horatio — regardless of gender," you'd better use an attorney to put it together for you.

3. You should use reliable self-help materials to help you prepare your living trust. You need to understand what the living trust really is and how it works, at least in conceptual terms, so you can best adapt it to your needs. You also want to make sure that the document you create will be acceptable to banks, title companies and other financial institutions that may eventually become involved in the transfer of your property to your heirs. Plus you'll need to know the steps necessary to transfer your property into the trust. It's not too complicated by it must be done right.

A good book on this subject is *Plan Your Estate With a Living Trustt*, written by attorney Denis Clifford and published by Nolo Press in 1990. Or check your local library for other titles.

TAKE THE HEAT OFF YOURSELF

"**75** to 90 percent of people visiting doctors suffer from stress-related problems," according to comments made by Michael L. Silverman, Ed.D., a stress-management consultant, in the June issue of *Men's Health* magazine.

Silverman explains, "A lot of people who once felt their companies would take care of them are instead seeing cutbacks and layoffs. Couples used to feel they had a choice about whether there were two wage-earners in the family but don't feel that way today. People aren't living relaxed lives."

Brad Edmondson, the Editor of *American Demographics* magazine put some numbers to the "feelings" people are having in his June editorial. He asks the question, "But what happens when incomes stop growing? Per capita income grew 7 percent a year in the late 1980's. But it grew only 5 percent in 1990 and just 2 percent in 1991. Adjusted for inflation, that means per capita income actually declined last year. The last time it happened was 1982. Before that, it was in the 1930's."

The major difference between today and 1982 is that we don't have a cold war to artificially fuel the economy with massive military spending (borrowed federal deficit money). And the big difference between now and the 1930's is that today we are much more clearly a sub-market in a much larger global market, so we have less leverage over our own economy. Plus, we were brought out of the slumping economy of the 1930's by the massive military spending leading up to and throughout World War II. In other words, it's a new day — and we MUST begin a new way of looking at how money works in today's world, if we are to prosper...indeed, if we are to survive.

I must admit that this program has evolved out of my own personal journey towards sanity and peace of mind. I've made a lot of money in the past, and have seen the bulk of it frittered away on the "Toys" of life. But, in the past there always seemed to be a euphoric feeling that, "We can do it again. This marvelous economy is so powerful that there will always be a way to make up lost financial ground."

Then two things struck me that completely changed my financial course, strategy and goals.
1. I saw nearly all the people in my life (family and friends) who were ahead of me in years failing to achieve any desirable kind of retirement. Most of them had to keep working...in some cases until they dropped dead. The others are scratching out meager existences.
2. A few years ago I realized (hitting 40 I think) that I was getting tired of keeping pace with the fast lane. I came to understand that I did not want to burn myself out always chasing the elusive brass ring. I wanted to enjoy life, have real relationships with my wife and kids, and maybe even give something back to my fellow man. Just making money, buying Corvettes and airplanes, and chasing some "Rich Man's" lifestyle became hollow to me...and definitely not worth what I would have to sacrifice to achieve it.

From that point on I became a fanatic about finding the reasons for most people's failures — and about finding a system that could get the average citizen to the later-years lifestyle they really wanted. This journey (which is not over) has been remarkable.

The first important thing I discovered was that I'm not the "Lone Ranger." Millions of Americans are becoming disenchanted with the consumptive life we led in the 80's, and they're turning back to more meaningful lifestyles and values. I also discovered a strong movement of people away from the stress and uncertainties of depending on an employer in today's economy.

People are beginning to realize how incredibly destructive the stress of carrying credit debt and therefore being slavishly dependent on their employer really is. They feel threatened by every new rumor and newscast that has anything to do with their industry, because they know that their personal economies are houses of cards. The slightest ill breeze could disintegrate them.

These People Are VULNERABLE!

According to a recent CNBC report, "Many Americans used credit cards to help them through the recession. But more than half of them are now worried about being able to make the payments." Credit, just like drugs, feels good when you use it...then KILLS you later.

I am committed to helping you, and all else who will listen, to break free from the crushing financial pressure of trying to succeed in today's economy by yesterday's rules. Please listen to me: THIS IS NO DRILL. There are NO more magic methods, shortcuts or "Hot Programs" for getting yourself to financial freedom — or as we call it: financial "UNVULNERABILITY."

You must begin immediately to follow the concepts taught in the *Personal Financial Success* Basic Course. This will set you on a course that will free you from the financial web in the shortest period of time. It will get you to a place where you are operating on CASH, building wealth... and more importantly...shedding the stress of knowing how vulnerable you are to economic downturns.

Imagine...

Imagine having NO BILLS, NO MORTGAGE PAYMENTS, and even the same income you have now. Don't you think you could be pounding away a pretty good chunk of it into interest-multiplying investments?

— E D I T O R I A L —
IS AMERICA DOOMED?

Jap-Bashing has been fashionable of late, and I have to admit that I have been one of the chief cheerleaders whenever I witnessed it. I was angry that we won the battle (World War II), but lost the war (post-war prosperity). I was also upset by what have been characterized as "Unfair" competitive trade policies, reportedly used by the Japanese government to beat up on us "good guys" over here in the Land of the Free and Home of the Brave.

However, I recently read an article that made me rethink my position...and that rethinking has helped me realize that my frustrations with Japan were really misplaced frustrations with America.

When you think about what this country (America) is supposed to stand for — the Land of Opportunity, the place where anyone can rise from rags to riches — we should be cheering for the Japanese. Talk about a rise from rags to riches, it's more like the mythological Phoenix rising from the ashes.

We should be rallying behind the Japanese, because they did it "Our" way — pulling themselves up by their bootstraps, from utter destruction. They should be held right up there with our greatest entrepreneurial heroes. But they're not. You know why?

Because, in the time since World War II the Japanese have focused on accomplishing exactly what they have accomplished. They knew that it would take several generations of risk-taking entrepreneurs to dig themselves out of the rubble of defeat, so they created government regulations and tax codes that favored individual contribution and individual reward. They made it attractive to step out, take chances, and build a profitable business.

America, on the other hand, has grown fat and lazy. We no longer ask for an opportunity to take risks for great potential rewards. Instead we ask our government to take away all risks and just assure us enough to stay alive.

To quote the article by Robert Posch in DIRECT MARKETING/April 1992, *"Once we sought freedom to pursue our individual and family goals. Today we seek dependance on a 'fair state.' When fairness replaces freedom all of our liberties are in danger."*

"While the Japanese poured money into capital formation," Posch continues, *"we poured a greater percentage into welfare dependency (i.e., human capital depreciation). Counseling ever more dependence to the dependent, we created a growing underclass of family breakup and every known and innovative social problem."*

Iacocca Was Wrong

I remember Lee Iacocca coming back from the Japanese trip with President Bush, whining about how his Japanese competitors could borrow money to expand for a lot lower interest rate than he could. He said it was "Unfair," but the truth is that it's totally fair.

The Japanese government maintains low capital gains taxes...so the result is that more people invest money, because they won't have to pay big taxes on the gains they earn...so there's more cash flowing into Japanese businesses. And because more people invest and save, money is more plentiful, so the law of supply-and-demand drops the interest rates where it's cheaper for Japanese companies to borrow money from Japanese investors than it is for American companies to borrow from American investors.

That's not the Japanese playing dirty pool. That's the counter-productive American government taxing people's investments to the hilt, so they can fund their bloated welfare state.

Americans with any extra money are less inclined to invest — because the government just takes the growth away in capital gains taxes — so American businesses can't afford to expand and compete — so American workers are laid off and the jobs go overseas where they have more intelligent leadership.

What Does This Have to Do With F.I.N.L.?

F.I.N.L. exists to help people find a path to financial self-dependency. Everything we do is focused on helping you become totally Debt-FREE and Prosperous. We want you to get back to the American values that built this country to pre-World War II greatness, and have built Japan to the economic power it is today. Those values do not include sitting back and counting on a government handout to keep us alive when we retire, but rather they involve standing tall as successful, contributing and independent citizens.

A society built on eliminating risk and "taking care of everyone's every need" is a society doomed to decline and eventual destruction. If we remove the incentives for the pioneers, entrepreneurs and other risk-takers to break new ground, they will eventually stop trying. And if they stop trying, this country will not only stop growing, it will begin a rapid fall into second or third world status.

A welfare state (where the government takes care of everyone's welfare) is a doomed state, because no one is motivated to achieve above average accomplishments in their life. And an "Average" society will not be able to compete internationally.

If you have forgotten what our government is supposed to be doing, just read the preamble to the Constitution. It says that the federal government is supposed to "Promote," not "Provide" the general welfare. In other words, the government should just create an atmosphere within which its citizens can thrive — then get the heck out of the way. □

Notes

Key Points	Details

Appendix E
Financial Freedom Strategy
Forms and Tables

This appendix contains the forms and numerical
tables referenced in the text of this book.

Notes

Key Points	Details

Calculating Bill Pay-Off Order

Write down each debt in column 1, it's total balance in column 2, the bill's monthly payment in 3, then divide the total balance by the monthly payment, putting the answer in 4. Prioritize pay-off starting with lowest division answer as the first bill to pay off and so on.

Name of Debt	Total Balance	Monthly Payment	Division Answer	Pay-Off Priority	Pay-Off Date
1	2	3	4	5	6

Debt-Elimination Time Calculator

Total Debt Amount	1 yr.	2 yrs.	3 yrs.	4 yrs.	5 yrs.	6yrs	7 yrs.
1,000	88	46	32	25	21	19	17
3,000	264	138	97	76	64	56	50
5,000	440	231	161	127	106	93	83
7,000	615	323	226	178	149	130	116
10,000	879	461	323	254	212	185	166
15,000	1319	692	484	380	319	278	249
20,000	1758	923	645	507	425	371	332
30,000	2637	1384	968	761	637	556	498
40,000	3517	1846	1291	1015	850	741	664
50,000	4396	2307	1613	1268	1062	926	830
75,000	6594	3461	2420	1902	1594	1389	1245
100,000	8792	4614	3227	2536	2125	1853	1660
125,000	10989	5768	4033	3170	2656	2316	2075
150,000	13187	6922	4840	3804	3187	2779	2490
200,000	17583	9229	6453	5073	4249	3705	3320
250,000	21979	11536	8067	6341	5312	4631	4150
300,000	26375	13843	9680	7609	6374	5558	4980

—————————————— Total Monthly Payment Amount ——————————————

Wealth-Building/Retirement Calculator

Monthly Investment Amount	5 yrs.	10 yrs.	15 yrs.
500	39,041 — 312/mo	103,276 — 826/mo	208,962 — 1,672/mo
1,000	78,082 — 625/mo	206,552 — 1,652/mo	417,924 — 3,343/mo
2,000	156,165 — 1,249/mo	413,104 — 3,305/mo	835,849 — 6,687/mo
3,000	234,247 — 1,874/mo	619,656 — 4,957/mo	1,253,772 — 10,030/mo
5,000	390,412 —3,123/mo	1,032,760 — 8,262/mo	2,089,621 —16,717/mo
7,500	585,618 — 4,685/mo	1,549,140 — 12,393/mo	3,134,431 — 25,075/mo

Example: If you invest 7,500 each month, for 15 years, you'll have $3,134,431 in total principal — and you'll be able to retire at an income of $25,075 per month for the rest of your life without putting another penny in. Based on average 10% Return On Investment.

Your Retirement Lifestyle To-Do List

This is NOT a "To-Do" list in the traditional sense. You are NOT trying to think of all the things you HAVE to do. But rather, you want to create a list of all the things you've always WANTED to do, but never had the time. When you retire through following the F.I.N.L. *Financial Freedom Strategy*, you <u>will</u> have more time than you've ever had before. Some people go crazy when they retire, because they've never bothered to think through what they would like to do with their new-found time. But you'll be ready, because you'll be able to refer to this list any time you start feeling bored. And you can refer to it any time you start losing your resolve to follow your financial plan.

If I had all the time in the world, and sufficient resources, I would...

1. _____
2. _____
3. _____
4. _____
5. _____
6. _____
7. _____
8. _____
9. _____
10. _____
11. _____
12. _____
13. _____
14. _____
15. _____
16. _____
17. _____
18. _____

NOTE: use blank paper to make this list as long as possible. After all, it's a WISH list.

Your Wealth-Building Plan

1. Monthly Amount needed (before taxes):

[ ]

2. Total Investment Amount Required:
Go to the *Wealth-Building/Retirement Calculator* chart   First, in the *Monthly Investment Amount* column, find the amount you'll be investing each month — after you've eliminated all your debt. Then go across that row — making sure that you're looking at the second amounts with the "/mo" after them — and find the approximate amount that you put in the answer box of #1 above. Then write the larger amount that appears to the left of this monthly amount in the box across from question #2 above.

[ ]

3. Number of Years to Achieve Retirement:
Go to top of the column where you found the answer for #2 above. Put the number of years in the answer box for this question.

[ ]

4. Date of Retirement:
Add the number of years in the answer to #3 above to the *Bill Payoff Date* from the last bill on the *Calculating Bill Pay-Off Order* form

[ ]

Additional Resources

Newsletters That Rate Mutual fund Performance:

Donohgue's Moneyletter
290 Eliot Street
P.O. Box 9104
Ashland, MA 01721-9104
508-881-2800

Mutual Fund Forecaster
3471 North Federal
Fort Lauderdale, FL 33306
800-442-9000

Mutual Fund Investing
7811 Montrose Rd.
Potomac, MD 20854
301-424-3700

FUND PROFIT ALERT
1259 Kemper Meadow Drive
Suite 100
Cincinnati, OH 45240
800-327-8833

The Mutual Fund Letter
680 North Lake Shore Drive
Suite 2038
Chicago, IL 60611
800-326-6941

ALL-STAR Mutual Fund Selector
800-832-2330

Asset Management Accounts That Offer Visa Debit Cards:

Company	Account Name	Initial Deposit	Phone #
Schwab	Schwab One	$5,000	800-435-4000
Kemper	Money Plus	$5,000	800-621-1048
Edward D. Jones	Full Service	$1,000	314-851-7221

Your IRA — It Pays to Start Early

This table shows the incredible power of compound interest over time. It also shows the dramatic effect of letting interest compound WITHOUT TAXES BEING TAKEN OUT. All the example investors enjoy the advantage of tax-deferred compounding, but the table also shows how much difference it makes to start your tax-deferred investing early in life.

Age	INVESTOR A Contribution	INVESTOR A Year-End Value	INVESTOR B Contribution	INVESTOR B Year-End Value	INVESTOR C Contribution	INVESTOR C Year-End Value	INVESTOR D Contribution	INVESTOR D Year-End Value	INVESTOR E Contribution	INVESTOR E Year-End Value
8	-0-	-0-	-0-	-0-	-0-	-0-	500	550	500	550
9	-0-	-0-	-0-	-0-	-0-	-0-	750	1,430	750	1,430
10	-0-	-0-	-0-	-0-	-0-	-0-	1,000	2,673	1,000	2,673
11	-0-	-0-	-0-	-0-	-0-	-0-	1,250	4,315	1,250	4,315
12	-0-	-0-	-0-	-0-	-0-	-0-	1,500	6,397	1,500	6,397
13	-0-	-0-	-0-	-0-	-0-	-0-	1,750	8,962	1,750	8,962
14	-0-	-0-	-0-	-0-	2,000	2,200	-0-	9,858	2,000	12,058
15	-0-	-0-	-0-	-0-	2,000	4,620	-0-	10,843	2,000	15,463
16	-0-	-0-	-0-	-0-	2,000	7,282	-0-	11,928	2,000	19,210
17	-0-	-0-	-0-	-0-	2,000	10,210	-0-	13,121	2,000	23,331
18	-0-	-0-	-0-	-0-	2,000	13,431	-0-	14,433	2,000	27,864
19	-0-	-0-	2,000	2,200	-0-	14,774	-0-	15,876	2,000	32,850
20	-0-	-0-	2,000	4,620	-0-	16,252	-0-	17,463	2,000	38,335
21	-0-	-0-	2,000	7,282	-0-	17,877	-0-	19,210	2,000	44,369
22	-0-	-0-	2,000	10,210	-0-	19,665	-0-	21,131	2,000	51,006
23	-0-	-0-	2,000	13,431	-0-	21,631	-0-	23,244	2,000	58,306
24	-0-	-0-	2,000	16,974	-0-	23,794	-0-	25,568	2,000	66,337
25	-0-	-0-	2,000	20,872	-0-	26,174	-0-	28,125	2,000	75,170
26	2,000	2,200	-0-	22,959	-0-	28,791	-0-	30,938	2,000	84,888
27	2,000	4,620	-0-	25,255	-0-	31,670	-0-	34,031	2,000	95,576
28	2,000	7,282	-0-	27,780	-0-	34,837	-0-	37,434	2,000	107,334
29	2,000	10,210	-0-	30,558	-0-	38,321	-0-	41,178	2,000	120,267
30	2,000	13,431	-0-	33,614	-0-	42,153	-0-	45,296	2,000	134,494
31	2,000	16,974	-0-	36,976	-0-	46,368	-0-	49,825	2,000	150,143
32	2,000	20,872	-0-	40,673	-0-	51,005	-0-	54,808	2,000	167,358
33	2,000	25,159	-0-	44,741	-0-	56,106	-0-	60,289	2,000	186,294
34	2,000	29,875	-0-	49,215	-0-	61,716	-0-	66,317	2,000	207,123
35	2,000	35,062	-0-	54,136	-0-	67,888	-0-	72,949	2,000	230,035
36	2,000	40,769	-0-	59,550	-0-	74,676	-0-	80,244	2,000	255,239
37	2,000	47,045	-0-	65,505	-0-	82,144	-0-	88,269	2,000	282,963
38	2,000	53,950	-0-	72,055	-0-	90,359	-0-	97,095	2,000	313,459
39	2,000	61,545	-0-	79,261	-0-	99,394	-0-	106,805	2,000	347,005
40	2,000	69,899	-0-	87,187	-0-	109,334	-0-	117,485	2,000	383,905
41	2,000	79,089	-0-	95,905	-0-	120,267	-0-	129,234	2,000	424,496
42	2,000	89,198	-0-	105,496	-0-	132,294	-0-	142,157	2,000	469,145
43	2,000	100,318	-0-	116,045	-0-	145,523	-0-	156,373	2,000	518,269
44	2,000	112,550	-0-	127,650	-0-	160,076	-0-	172,010	2,000	572,286
45	2,000	126,005	-0-	140,415	-0-	176,083	-0-	189,211	2,000	631,714
46	2,000	140,805	-0-	154,456	-0-	193,692	-0-	208,133	2,000	697,086
47	2,000	157,086	-0-	169,902	-0-	213,061	-0-	228,946	2,000	768,995
48	2,000	174,995	-0-	186,892	-0-	234,367	-0-	251,840	2,000	848,094
49	2,000	194,694	-0-	205,581	-0-	257,803	-0-	277,024	2,000	935,103
50	2,000	216,364	-0-	226,140	-0-	283,358	-0-	304,727	2,000	1,030,814
51	2,000	240,200	-0-	248,754	-0-	311,942	-0-	335,209	2,000	1,136,095
52	2,000	266,420	-0-	273,629	-0-	343,136	-0-	368,719	2,000	1,251,905
53	2,000	295,262	-0-	300,992	-0-	377,450	-0-	405,591	2,000	1,379,295
54	2,000	326,988	-0-	331,091	-0-	415,195	-0-	446,150	2,000	1,519,425
55	2,000	361,887	-0-	364,200	-0-	456,715	-0-	490,766	2,000	1,673,567
56	2,000	400,276	-0-	400,620	-0-	502,386	-0-	539,842	2,000	1,843,124
57	2,000	442,503	-0-	440,682	-0-	552,625	-0-	593,826	2,000	2,029,636
58	2,000	488,953	-0-	484,750	-0-	607,887	-0-	653,209	2,000	2,234,800
59	2,000	540,049	-0-	533,225	-0-	668,676	-0-	718,530	2,000	2,460,480
60	2,000	596,254	-0-	586,548	-0-	735,543	-0-	790,383	2,000	2,708,728
61	2,000	658,079	-0-	645,203	-0-	809,098	-0-	869,421	2,000	2,981,800
62	2,000	726,087	-0-	709,723	-0-	890,007	-0-	956,363	2,000	3,282,180
63	2,000	800,896	-0-	780,695	-0-	979,008	-0-	1,052,000	2,000	3,612,598
64	2,000	883,185	-0-	858,765	-0-	1,076,909	-0-	1,157,200	2,000	3,976,058
65	2,000	973,704	-0-	944,641	-0-	1,184,600	-0-	1,272,930	2,000	4,375,864
Less Total Invested:	(80,000)		(14,000)		(10,000)		(6,750)		(110,750)	
Equals Net Earnings:	893,704		930,641		1,174,600		1,266,170		4,265,114	
Money Grew:	11-fold		66-fold		117-fold		188-fold		38-fold	

Use these coupons to make the *Accelerator Margin* prepayments on your home mortgage loan. WRITE TWO CHECKS: one for the regular mortgage payment and one for this extra amount. Staple the regular payment check to your regular payment coupon. Staple the Accelerator Margin check to a copy of one of these coupons, with the appropriate information filled in. Send them in the same envelope in which you normally make your payment.

NOTE: Your mortgage lender may already have a system for you to follow in making prepayments. Check your normal payment coupon to see if there is a location on it for an extra amount to prepay principal. Also call your lender to find out if there are any specific guidelines they want you to follow in making prepayments.

Apply this amount: [   ]   Check #:_____

To prepay the principal balance of loan number: [   ]

Name(s) on loan:_____

Address:_____

City:_____ State:_____ Zip:_____

If you have questions, call me at:_____

Apply this amount: [   ]   Check #:_____

To prepay the principal balance of loan number: [   ]

Name(s) on loan:_____

Address:_____

City:_____ State:_____ Zip:_____

If you have questions, call me at:_____

Apply this amount: [   ]   Check #:_____

To prepay the principal balance of loan number: [   ]

Name(s) on loan:_____

Address:_____

City:_____ State:_____ Zip:_____

If you have questions, call me at:_____

Apply this amount: [   ]   Check #:_____

To prepay the principal balance of loan number: [   ]

Name(s) on loan:_____

Address:_____

City:_____ State:_____ Zip:_____

If you have questions, call me at:_____

Notes

Key Points	Details

Index

Notes

Key Points	Details

Buy a Copy For a Family Member.

Help Them Get Financially FREE Too!

❑ Absolutely! I'm enclosing $59 + $5 s&h for my copy of **The** *Debt-FREE &* *Prosperous Living* **Basic Course.** (WI residents add $3.20 tax for $67.20 total)
FREE Bonuses: • *Secrets, Myths & Realities of Financial Independence*
• **Complete information on the income opportunity**

Enclosed is my $64: ❑ Check or Money order — *Make payable to FINL*
Credit Card Type: ❑ VISA ❑ Mastercard ❑ Amex

Card #_____ Exp. Date_____

Signature _____

Ship to: Name _____

Office Use Only	Address _____
	City_____ State _____ Zip_____
BKGFT	Day Phone_____ Eve Phone _____

Or mail to: FINL • 310 Second St. • Boscobel, WI 53805

Buy a Copy For a Friend.

Help Them Get Financially FREE Too!

❑ Absolutely! I'm enclosing $59 + $5 s&h for my copy of **The** *Debt-FREE &* *Prosperous Living* **Basic Course.** (WI residents add $3.20 tax for $67.20 total)
FREE Bonuses: • *Secrets, Myths & Realities of Financial Independence*
• **Complete information on the income opportunity**

Enclosed is my $64: ❑ Check or Money order — *Make payable to FINL*
Credit Card Type: ❑ VISA ❑ Mastercard ❑ Amex

Card #_____ Exp. Date_____

Signature _____

Ship to: Name _____

Office Use Only	Address _____
	City_____ State _____ Zip_____
BKGFT	Day Phone_____ Eve Phone _____

Or mail to: FINL • 310 Second St. • Boscobel, WI 53805

Pass This Order Form on to a Friend.

Help Them Get Financially FREE Too!

❑ Absolutely! I'm enclosing $59 + $5 s&h for my copy of **The** *Debt-FREE &* *Prosperous Living* **Basic Course.** (WI residents add $3.20 tax for $67.20 total)
FREE Bonuses: • *Secrets, Myths & Realities of Financial Independence*
• **Complete information on the income opportunity**

Enclosed is my $64: ❑ Check or Money order — *Make payable to FINL*
Credit Card Type: ❑ VISA ❑ Mastercard ❑ Amex

Card #_____ Exp. Date_____

Signature _____

Ship to: Name _____

Office Use Only	Address _____
	City_____ State _____ Zip_____
BKFND	Day Phone_____ Eve Phone _____

Or mail to: FINL • 310 Second St. • Boscobel, WI 53805

Notes

Key Points	Details

Notes

Key Points

Details

Notes

Key Points	Details

Notes

Key Points	Details

Notes

Key Points	Details

Notes

Key Points	Details

Notes

Key Points	Details

Notes

Key Points	Details

Notes

Key Points	Details

Notes

Key Points	Details

Notes

Key Points	Details

Notes

Key Points	Details

Notes

Key Points	Details

Strategic Management Process

Business Ethics, Social Responsibility, and Environmental Sustainability

SIMPLE AND STRAIGHTFORWARD APPROACH TO STRATEGIC PLANNING

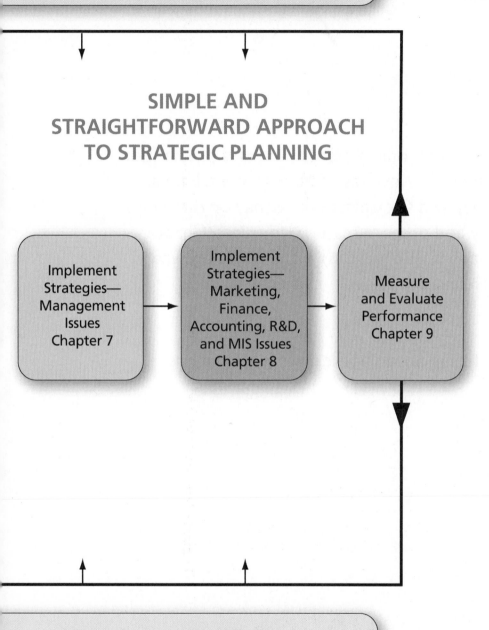

Implement Strategies— Management Issues Chapter 7

Implement Strategies— Marketing, Finance, Accounting, R&D, and MIS Issues Chapter 8

Measure and Evaluate Performance Chapter 9

Global/International Issues

Strategy Implementation | Strategy Evaluation

USED TO INTEGRATE AND ORGANIZE ALL CHAPTERS IN THIS TEXT

MyManagementLab®

MyManagementLab is an online assessment and preparation solution for courses in Principles of Management, Human Resources, Strategy, and Organizational Behavior that helps you actively study and prepare material for class. Chapter-by-chapter activities, including study plans, focus on what you need to learn and to review in order to succeed.

Visit **www.mymanagementlab.com** to learn more.

Strategic Management Concepts
A Competitive Advantage Approach

FOURTEENTH EDITION

Fred R. David

Francis Marion University

Florence, South Carolina

PEARSON

Boston   Columbus   Indianapolis   New York   San Francisco   Upper Saddle River
Amsterdam   Cape Town   Dubai   London   Madrid   Milan   Munich Paris   Montreal   Toronto
Delhi   Mexico City   Sao Paulo   Sydney   Hong Kong   Seoul   Singapore   Taipei   Tokyo

To Spikes and Aubie David—
for fifteen years of love.

Editorial Director: Sally Yagan
Senior Acquisitions Editor: Kim Norbuta
Director of Editorial Services: Ashley Santora
Editorial Project Manager: Claudia Fernandes
Director of Marketing: Maggie Moylan
Senior Marketing Manager: Nikki Ayana Jones
Marketing Assistant: Ian Gold
Senior Managing Editor: Judy Leale
Production Project Manager: Ilene Kahn
Senior Operations Supervisor: Arnold Vila
Operations Specialist: Cathleen Petersen
Creative Director: Blair Brown
Design Supervisor: Janet Slowik
Senior Art Director: Kenny Beck

Cover Designer: Laura C. Ierardi
Interior Designer: Dina Curro
Cover Illustration: Shutterstock/business people with world/Copyright: newart
Senior Media Project Manager, Editorial: Denise Vaughn
MyLab Product Manager: Joan Waxman
Media Project Manager, Production: Lisa Rinaldi
Full-Service Project Management and Composition: Integra
Printer/Binder: Quad Graphics
Cover Printer: Lehigh-Phoenix Color/Hagerstown
Text Font: 10/12 Times

Credits and acknowledgments borrowed from other sources and reproduced, with permission, in this textbook appear on the appropriate page within text with the exception of the fireworks logo which appears throughout the text and is credited to Dan Bannister/DK Images.

Library of Congress Cataloging-in-Publication Data
David, Fred R.
    Strategic management concepts and cases: a competitive advantage approach / Fred R. David.—14th ed.
    p. cm.
    Previously published under title: Strategic management.
    ISBN-13: 978-0-13-266423-3
    ISBN-10: 0-13-266423-2
1. Strategic planning.   2. Strategic planning—Case studies.   I. Title.
HD30.28.D385 2013
658.4'012—dc23
                                                   2011035610

10 9 8 7 6 5 4 3 2 1

ISBN 10:   0-13-266621-9
ISBN 13: 978-0-13-266621-3

Brief Contents

Contents

Preface

Why the Need for This New Edition?

The world is dramatically different than it was two years ago. The global economic recovery has created a business environment that is quite different and more complex than it was when the previous edition of this text was published. Thousands of businesses are now flourishing and consumers are again buying discretionary products. Tight credit markets remain, as do high unemployment and high food prices, but millions of new entrepreneurs have entered the business world globally. Democracy is taking hold in the Middle East, and China has replaced Japan as the world's second largest in gross domestic product. Business firms today are leaner and meaner than ever, so gaining and sustaining competitive advantage is harder than ever. Intense price competition, rapid technological change, and social networking have altered marketing to its core. Opportunities and threats abound today all over the world, including Africa. This new edition reveals how to conduct effective strategic planning in this new world order.

Since the prior edition, thousands of liquidations, bankruptcies, divestitures, mergers, alliances, and partnerships captured the news. Private equity firms returned to the spotlight by taking hundreds of firms public and acquiring hundreds more. Corporate scandals highlighted the need for improved business ethics and corporate disclosure of financial transactions. Downsizing, rightsizing, and reengineering contributed to a permanently altered corporate landscape. Thousands of firms began doing business globally, and thousands more closed their global operations. Thousands prospered, and yet thousands failed in the last two years as more industries commoditized, making strategic management an even more important factor in being successful. Long-held competitive advantages, such as print media, news, and entertainment, eroded in recent years, and new avenues for competitive advantage formed. This new edition captures the complexity of this new business environment.

There is less room for error today in the formulation and implementation of a strategic plan. This new edition provides an effective approach for developing a clear strategic plan. Changes made in this edition are aimed squarely at illustrating the effect of new business concepts and techniques on strategic-management theory and practice. Due to the magnitude of recent changes affecting companies, cultures, and countries, every page of this edition has been updated. This textbook is one of the most widely read strategic-management books in the world, perhaps the most widely read. This text is now published in 10 languages.

What Is New in This Edition?

This 14th edition is 40 percent different than the prior edition and is positioned to be the leader and best choice globally for teaching strategic management. Here is a summary of what is new in this edition:

- Chapter 11, "Global/International Issues," is expanded 70 percent. There is extensive new coverage of cultural and conceptual strategic-management differences across countries. Doing business globally has become a necessity in most industries because nearly all strategic decisions today are affected by global issues and concerns.
- A brand new Cohesion Case on the Walt Disney Company (2011); this is one of the most successful, well-known, and best managed global companies in the world; students apply strategy concepts to Walt Disney at the end of each chapter through new Assurance of Learning Exercises.
- Sixty percent brand new or improved Assurance of Learning Exercises appear at the end of all chapters to apply chapter concepts; the exercises prepare students for strategic-management case analysis.
- A new "Special Note to Students" paragraph is provided at the end of every chapter to guide students in developing and presenting a case analysis that reveals recommendations for how a firm can best gain and sustain competitive advantage. The

whole notion of how to gain and sustain competitive advantage is strengthened through-out this edition. Note the brand-new subtitle heading for this book: "A Competitive Advantage Approach."

- A brand new boxed insert at the beginning of each chapter showcases a company doing strategic management exceptionally well.
- Nearly all-brand new examples throughout the chapters.
- Extensive new narrative on strategic management theory and concepts in every chapter to illustrate the new business world order.
- On average, 15 brand-new review questions at the end of each chapter.
- Brand-new color photographs bring this new edition to life and illustrate companies and concepts.
- All new current readings at the end of each chapter; new research and theories of semi-nal thinkers in strategy development, such as Ansoff, Chandler, Porter, Hamel, Prahalad, Mintzberg, and Barney, are provided in the chapters; practical aspects of strategic manage-ment, however, are still center stage and the trademark of this text.
- Chapter 10, "Business Ethics/Social Responsibility/Environmental Sustainability," is expanded 40 percent, providing extensive new coverage of ethics and sustainability because this text emphasizes that "good ethics is good business." Unique to strategic-management texts, the sustainability discussion is strengthened to promote and encour-age firms to conduct operations in an environmentally sound manner. Respect for the natural environment has become an important concern for consumers, companies, soci-ety, and AACSB-International.

Chapters: Time-Tested Features

This edition continues to offer many special time-tested features and content that have made this text so successful for over 20 years. Historical trademarks of this text that are strengthened in this edition are described below.

- This text meets AACSB-International guidelines that support a practitioner orientation rather than a theory/research approach. It offers a skills-oriented approach to developing a vision and mission statement; performing an external audit; conducting an internal assess-ment; and formulating, implementing, and evaluating strategies.
- The author's writing style is concise, conversational, interesting, logical, lively, and sup-ported by numerous current examples throughout.
- A simple, integrative strategic-management model appears in all chapters and on the inside front cover of the text. This model is widely used for strategic planning among consultants and companies worldwide. At the start of each chapter, the section of the comprehensive strategy model covered in that chapter is highlighted and enlarged so students can see the focus of each chapter in the basic unifying comprehensive model. One reviewer said, "One thing I have admired about David's text is that he follows the fundamental sequence of strategy formulation, implementation, and evaluation. There is a basic flow from vision/mission to internal/external environmental scanning to strategy development, selection, implementation, and evaluation. This has been, and continues to be, a hallmark of the David text. Many other strategy texts are more dis-jointed in their presentation, and thus confusing to the student, especially at the under-graduate level."
- A Cohesion Case follows Chapter 1 and is revisited at the end of each chapter. This Cohesion Case allows students to apply strategic-management concepts and techniques to a real organization as chapter material is covered, which readies students for case analysis in the course.
- End-of-chapter Assurance of Learning Exercises effectively apply concepts and techniques in a challenging, meaningful, and enjoyable manner. Seventeen exercises apply text mate-rial to the Cohesion Case; eleven exercises apply textual material to a college or university; another nine exercises send students into the business world to explore important strategy topics. The exercises are relevant, interesting, and contemporary.

- There is excellent pedagogy in this text, including notable quotes and objectives to open each chapter, and key terms, current readings, discussion questions, and experiential exercises to close each chapter.
- There is excellent coverage of strategy formulation issues, such as business ethics, global versus domestic operations, vision/mission, matrix analysis, partnering, joint venturing, competitive analysis, governance, and guidelines for conducting an internal/external strategy assessment.
- There is excellent coverage of strategy implementation issues such as corporate culture, organizational structure, outsourcing, marketing concepts, financial analysis, and business ethics.
- A systematic, analytical approach is presented in Chapter 6, including matrices such as the SWOT, BCG, IE, GRAND, SPACE, and QSPM.
- The chapter material is again published in a four-color format.
- A chapters-only paperback version of the text is available.
- Custom-case publishing is available whereby an instructor can combine chapters from this text with cases from a variety of sources or select any number of cases desired from the 27 cases in the full text.

Instructor's Resource Center

At www.pearsonhighered.com/irc, instructors can access a variety of print, digital, and presentation resources available with this text in downloadable format. Registration is simple and gives you immediate access to new titles and new editions. As a registered faculty member, you can download resource files and receive immediate access and instructions for installing course management content on your campus server.

If you ever need assistance, our dedicated technical support team is ready to help with the media supplements that accompany this text. Visit http://247.pearsoned.com/ for answers to frequently asked questions and toll-free user support phone numbers.

The following supplements are available for download to adopting instructors:

- Instructor's Manual
- Test Bank
- TestGen® Computerized Test Bank
- PowerPoints

Videos on DVD

Exciting and high-quality video clips help deliver engaging topics to the classroom to help students better understand the concepts explained in the textbook. Please contact your local representative to receive a copy of the DVD.

CourseSmart

CourseSmart eTextbooks were developed for students looking to save on required or recommended textbooks. Students simply select their eText by title or author and purchase immediate access to the content for the duration of the course using any major credit card. With a CourseSmart eText, students can search for specific keywords or page numbers, take notes online, print out reading assignments that incorporate lecture notes, and bookmark important passages for later review. For more information or to purchase a CourseSmart eTextbook, visit www.coursesmart.com.

Author Website

The Strategic Management Club Online at www.strategyclub.com contains templates and links to help students save time in performing analyses and make presentations look professional.

Acknowledgments

Many persons have contributed time, energy, ideas, and suggestions for improving this text over 14 editions. The strength of this text is largely attributed to the collective wisdom, work, and experiences of strategic-management professors, researchers, students, and practitioners. Names of particular individuals whose published research is referenced in this edition of this text are listed alphabetically in the Name Index. To all individuals involved in making this text so popular and successful, I am indebted and thankful.

Many special persons and reviewers contributed valuable material and suggestions for this edition. I would like to thank my colleagues and friends at Auburn University, Mississippi State University, East Carolina University, and Francis Marion University. I have served on the management faculty at all these universities. Scores of students and professors at these schools helped shape the development of this text. Many thanks go to the following 23 reviewers whose comments shaped this 14th edition:

Moses Acquaah, The University of North Carolina at Greensboro

Charles M. Byles, Virginia Commonwealth University

Charles J. Capps III, Sam Houston State University

Neil Dworkin, Western Connecticut State University

Jacalyn M. Florn, University of Toledo

John Frankenstein, Brooklyn College/City University of New York

Bill W. Godair, Landmark College, Community College of Vermont

Carol Jacobson, Purdue University

Susan M. Jensen, University of Nebraska at Kearney

Dmitry Khanin, California State University at Fullerton

Thomas E. Kulik, Washington University at St. Louis

Jerrold K. Leong, Oklahoma State University

Trina Lynch-Jackson, Indiana University

Elouise Mintz, Saint Louis University

Raza Mir, William Paterson University

Gerry N. Muuka, Murray State University

Lori Radulovich, Baldwin-Wallace College

Thomas W. Sharkey, University of Toledo

Frederick J. Slack, Indiana University of Pennsylvania

Daniel Slater, Union University

Jill Lynn Vihtelic, Saint Mary's College

Michael W. Wakefield, Colorado State University–Pueblo

Don Wicker, Brazosport College

Individuals who develop cases for the North American Case Research Association Meeting, the Midwest Society for Case Research Meeting, the Eastern Case Writers Association Meeting, the European Case Research Association Meeting, and Harvard Case Services are vitally important for continued progress in the field of strategic-management. From a research perspective, writing strategic-management cases represents a valuable scholarly activity among faculty. Extensive research is required to structure strategic-management cases in a way that exposes strategic issues, decisions, and behavior. Pedagogically, strategic-management cases are essential for students in learning how to apply concepts, evaluate situations, formulate a "game plan," and resolve implementation problems. Without a continuous stream of updated business policy cases, the strategic-management course and discipline would lose much of its energy and excitement.

Professors who teach this course supplement lecture with simulations, guest speakers, experiential exercises, class projects, and/or outside readings. Case analysis, however, is typically the backbone of the learning process in most strategic-management courses across the country. Case analysis is almost always an integral part of this course.

Analyzing strategic-management cases gives students the opportunity to work in teams to evaluate the internal operations and external issues facing various organizations and to craft strategies that can lead these firms to success. Working in teams gives students practical experience solving problems as part of a group. In the business world, important decisions are generally made within groups; strategic-management students learn to deal with overly aggressive group members and also timid, noncontributing group members. This experience is valuable as strategic-management students near graduation and soon enter the working world a full time.

Students can improve their oral and written communication skills as well as their analytical and interpersonal skills by proposing and defending particular courses of action for the case companies. Analyzing cases allows students to view a company, its competitors, and its industry concurrently, thus simulating the complex business world. Through case analysis, students learn how to apply concepts, evaluate situations, formulate strategies, and resolve implementation problems. Instructors typically ask students to prepare a three-year strategic plan for the firm. Analyzing a strategic-management case entails students applying concepts learned across their entire business curriculum. Students gain experience dealing with a wide range of organizational problems that impact all the business functions.

I especially appreciate the wonderful work completed by the 14th edition ancillary authors as follows:

Instructor's Manual—Amit J. Shah

Test Bank—Maureen Steddin

PowerPoints—Brad Cox

Scores of Prentice Hall employees and salespersons have worked diligently behind the scenes to make this text a leader in strategic management. I appreciate the continued hard work of all those professionals, such as Sally Yagan, Kim Norbuta, Claudia Fernandes, and Ilene Kahn.

I also want to thank you, the reader, for investing the time and effort to read and study this text. It will help you formulate, implement, and evaluate strategies for any organization with which you become associated. I hope you come to share my enthusiasm for the rich subject area of strategic management and for the systematic learning approach taken in this text.

Finally, I want to welcome and invite your suggestions, ideas, thoughts, comments, and questions regarding any part of this text or the ancillary materials. Please call me at 910-612-5343, e-mail me at freddavid9@gmail.com, or write me at the School of Business, Francis Marion University, Florence, SC 29501. I sincerely appreciate and need your input to continually improve this text in future editions. Your willingness to draw my attention to specific errors or deficiencies in coverage or exposition will especially be appreciated.

Thank you for using this text.

Fred R. David

About the Author

Dr. Fred R. David's February 2011 *Business Horizons* article titled "What Are Business Schools Doing for Business Today?" is changing the way many business schools view their curricula. Dr. David is the sole author of two mainstream strategic-management textbooks: (1) *Strategic Management: Concepts and Cases* and (2) *Strategic-Management Concepts*. These texts have been on a two-year revision cycle since 1986, when the first edition was published. These texts are among the best if not the best-selling strategic-management textbooks in the world and have been used at more than 500 colleges and universities, including Harvard University, Duke University, Carnegie-Mellon University, Johns Hopkins University, the University of Maryland, University of North Carolina, University of Georgia, San Francisco State University, University of South Carolina, and Wake Forest University.

This textbook has been translated and published in Chinese, Japanese, Farsi, Spanish, Indonesian, Indian, Thai, German, and Arabic and is widely used across Asia and South America. It is the best-selling strategic-management textbook in Mexico, China, Peru, Chile, and Japan, and is number two in the United States. Approximately 90,000 students read Dr. David's textbook annually as well as thousands of businesspersons. The book has led the field of strategic management for more than a decade in providing an applications/practitioner approach to the discipline.

A native of Whiteville, North Carolina, Fred David received a BS degree in mathematics and an MBA from Wake Forest University before being employed as a bank manager with United Carolina Bank. He received a PhD in Business Administration from the University of South Carolina, where he majored in General Management with an emphasis in Strategic Management. Currently the TranSouth Professor of Strategic Management at Francis Marion University (FMU) in Florence, South Carolina, Dr. David has also taught at Auburn University, Mississippi State University, East Carolina University, the University of South Carolina, and the University of North Carolina at Pembroke. He is the author of 153 referred publications, including 41 journal articles and 56 proceedings publications. David has articles published in such journals as *Academy of Management Review*, *Academy of Management Executive*, *Journal of Applied Psychology*, *Long Range Planning*, and *Advanced Management Journal*.

Dr. David received a Lifetime Honorary Professorship Award from the Universidad Ricardo Palma in Lima, Peru. He delivered the keynote speech at the 21st Annual Latin American Congress on Strategy hosted by the Centrum School of Business in Peru. He has provided an eight-hour Strategic Planning Workshop to the faculty at Pontificia Universidad Catolica Del in Lima, Peru, and an eight-hour Case Writing/Analyzing Workshop to the faculty at Utah Valley State College in Orem, Utah. He has received numerous awards, including FMU's Board of Trustees Research Scholar Award, the university's Award for Excellence in Research given annually to the best faculty researcher on campus, and the Phil Carroll Advancement of Management Award, given annually by the Society for the Advancement of Management (SAM) to a management scholar for outstanding contributions in management research. Dr. David serves on the Board of Directors of SAM. He has given collegiate graduation commencement addresses several times at Troy University.

"NOTABLE QUOTES"

"If we know where we are and something about how we got there, we might see where we are trending—and if the outcomes which lie naturally in our course are unacceptable, to make timely change."
—*Abraham Lincoln*

"Without a strategy, an organization is like a ship without a rudder, going around in circles. It's like a tramp; it has no place to go."
—*Joel Ross and Michael Kami*

"Plans are less important than planning."
—*Dale McConkey*

"The formulation of strategy can develop competitive advantage only to the extent that the

process can give meaning to workers in the trenches." —*David Hurst*

"Most of us fear change. Even when our minds say change is normal, our stomachs quiver at the prospect. But for strategists and managers today, there is no choice but to change."
—*Robert Waterman Jr.*

"If a man takes no thought about what is distant, he will find sorrow near at hand. He who will not worry about what is far off will soon find something worse than worry."
—*Confucius*

"Integrity = Longevity"
—*Michael Johnson, CEO of Herbalife*

The Nature of Strategic Management

CHAPTER OBJECTIVES

After studying this chapter, you should be able to do the following:

1. Describe the strategic-management process.

2. Explain the need for integrating analysis and intuition in strategic management.

3. Define and give examples of key terms in strategic management.

4. Discuss the nature of strategy formulation, implementation, and evaluation activities.

5. Describe the benefits of good strategic management.

6. Discuss the relevance of Sun Tzu's *The Art of War* to strategic management.

7. Discuss how a firm may achieve sustained competitive advantage.

ASSURANCE OF LEARNING EXERCISES

Assurance of Learning Exercise 1A
Compare Business Strategy With Military Strategy

Assurance of Learning Exercise 1B
Gather Strategy Information

Assurance of Learning Exercise 1C
Update the Walt Disney Cohesion Case

Assurance of Learning Exercise 1D
Strategic Planning for My University

Assurance of Learning Exercise 1E
Strategic Planning at a Local Company

Assurance of Learning Exercise 1F
Get Familiar With SMCO

When CEOs from the big three American automakers, Ford, General Motors (GM), and Chrysler, showed up without a clear strategic plan to ask congressional leaders for bailout monies, they were sent home with instructions to develop a clear strategic plan for the future. Austan Goolsbee, one of President Obama's top economic advisers, said, "Asking for a bailout without a convincing business plan was crazy." Goolsbee also said, "If the three auto CEOs need a bridge, it's got to be a bridge to somewhere, not a bridge to nowhere."[1] This textbook gives the instructions on how to develop a clear strategic plan—a bridge to somewhere rather than nowhere.

This chapter provides an overview of strategic management. It introduces a practical, integrative model of the strategic-management process; it defines basic activities and terms in strategic management.

This chapter also introduces the notion of boxed inserts. A boxed insert at the beginning of each chapter reveals how some firms are doing really well competing in a weak global economy. The firms showcased are prospering as their rivals weaken. Each boxed insert examines the strategies of firms doing great amid high unemployment, rising interest rates, unavailability of credit, rising consumer demand, and intense price competition.

The boxed insert beginning each chapter showcases excellent strategic management. The first company featured for excellent performance is Winnebago Industries Inc.

Excellent Strategic Management Showcased

WINNEBAGO INDUSTRIES INC.

Winnebago was recognized for the tenth consecutive year in 2011 as the nation's top-selling motor home manufacturer. The recreational vehicle (RV) manufacturer has an excellent strategic plan. Winnebago posted an incredible 112 percent increase in revenues in fiscal 2010 and profits of $10.2 million.

Winnebago hired 350 new employees in the last twelve months as dealer inventory for its vehicles increased 21 percent. Winnebago dealers sold more Class A and Class C motor homes combined than any other manufacturer's dealer group in calendar 2010, achieving 18.8 percent market share. The company recently became the top-selling Class A market leader for the first time since 1981, achieving a Class A market share for calendar 2010 of 19.5 percent compared to 16.6 percent the prior year. Winnebago's Class A diesel market share was 15.2 percent in calendar 2010, up from 11.4 percent the prior year, while the company's Class A gas market segment grew to 23.7 percent from 22.9 percent.

Despite high gas prices, shrinking consumer credit, rising raw material costs and stubborn high unemployment, Winnebago is successfully offering new, innovative products and marketing its vehicles and trailers to all comers, but especially to retirees, who purchase an RV mainly to experience traveling and camping with fellow retirees. They enjoy camping with fellow RV-ers, grilling out, and in this way making new friends each day while traveling—rather than staying at a motel and meeting few to no new friends.

Based in Forest City, Iowa, Winnebago's new CEO Randy Potts faces major competitors include Fleetwood, Coachman, and Thor Industries. Winnebago recently received the Quality Circle Award from the Recreation Vehicle Dealers Association—an award that the company has received every year since 1996.

Winnebago's Vice President of Sales and Marketing Roger Martin said in 2011: "We're very pleased that Statistical Surveys once

again report Winnebago to be the number one manufacturer of motor homes in the United States. We congratulate our loyal employees and our strong dealer network in achieving this top selling position for the tenth consecutive year. We work very hard to develop exciting new products and to provide support for our dealers and retail customers in the form of what we believe are industry-leading sales and service programs. We are pleased that these efforts have resulted in continued success in the retail market. We are particularly pleased with our market share performance in the Class A gas and diesel motor home market segments, due in part to the success of our new 2011 lineup featuring many innovative industry-exclusive features and floorplans."

For the three months ending May 28, 2011, Winnebago's revenues rose to $135.6 million from $134.8 million the prior year.

Source: Company documents. Also, Timothy Martin, "Winnebago Logs Another Profit," *Wall Street Journal*, October 15, 2010, p. B6.

Walt Disney is featured as the new Cohesion Case because it is a well-known global firm undergoing strategic change and is very well managed. By working through Walt Disney related Assurance of Learning Exercises at the end of each chapter, you will be well prepared to develop an effective strategic plan for any company assigned to you this semester. The end-of-chapter exercises apply chapter tools and concepts.

What Is Strategic Management?

Once there were two company presidents who competed in the same industry. These two presidents decided to go on a camping trip to discuss a possible merger. They hiked deep into the woods. Suddenly, they came upon a grizzly bear that rose up on its hind legs and snarled. Instantly, the first president took off his knapsack and got out a pair of jogging shoes. The second president said, "Hey, you can't outrun that bear." The first president responded, "Maybe I can't outrun that bear, but I surely can outrun you!" This story captures the notion of strategic management, which is to achieve and maintain competitive advantage.

Defining Strategic Management

Strategic management can be defined as the art and science of formulating, implementing, and evaluating cross-functional decisions that enable an organization to achieve its objectives. As this definition implies, strategic management focuses on integrating management, marketing, finance/accounting, production/operations, research and development, and information systems to achieve organizational success. The term *strategic management* in this text is used synonymously with the term *strategic planning*. The latter term is more often used in the business world, whereas the former is often used in academia. Sometimes the term *strategic management* is used to refer to strategy formulation, implementation, and evaluation, with *strategic planning* referring only to strategy formulation. The purpose of strategic management is to exploit and create new and different opportunities for tomorrow; *long-range planning,* in contrast, tries to optimize for tomorrow the trends of today.

The term *strategic planning* originated in the 1950s and was very popular between the mid-1960s and the mid-1970s. During these years, strategic planning was widely believed to be the answer for all problems. At the time, much of corporate America was "obsessed" with strategic planning. Following that "boom," however, strategic planning was cast aside during the 1980s as various planning models did not yield higher returns. The 1990s, however, brought the revival of strategic planning, and the process is widely practiced today in the business world.

A strategic plan is, in essence, a company's game plan. Just as a football team needs a good game plan to have a chance for success, a company must have a good strategic plan to compete successfully. Profit margins among firms in most industries are so slim that there is little room for error in the overall strategic plan. A strategic plan results from tough managerial choices among numerous good alternatives, and it signals commitment to specific markets, policies, procedures, and operations in lieu of other, "less desirable" courses of action.

The term *strategic management* is used at many colleges and universities as the title for the capstone course in business administration. This course integrates material from all business courses. The Strategic Management Club Online at www.strategyclub.com offers many benefits for strategic management students.

Stages of Strategic Management

The *strategic-management process* consists of three stages: strategy formulation, strategy implementation, and strategy evaluation. *Strategy formulation* includes developing a vision and mission, identifying an organization's external opportunities and threats, determining internal strengths and weaknesses, establishing long-term objectives, generating alternative strategies, and choosing particular strategies to pursue. Strategy-formulation issues include deciding what new businesses to enter, what businesses to abandon, how to allocate resources, whether to expand operations or diversify, whether to enter international markets, whether to merge or form a joint venture, and how to avoid a hostile takeover.

Because no organization has unlimited resources, strategists must decide which alternative strategies will benefit the firm most. Strategy-formulation decisions commit an organization to specific products, markets, resources, and technologies over an extended period of time. Strategies determine long-term competitive advantages. For better or worse, strategic decisions have major multifunctional consequences and enduring effects on an organization. Top managers have the best perspective to understand fully the ramifications of strategy-formulation decisions; they have the authority to commit the resources necessary for implementation.

Strategy implementation requires a firm to establish annual objectives, devise policies, motivate employees, and allocate resources so that formulated strategies can be executed. Strategy implementation includes developing a strategy-supportive culture, creating an effective organizational structure, redirecting marketing efforts, preparing budgets, developing and utilizing information systems, and linking employee compensation to organizational performance.

Strategy implementation often is called the "action stage" of strategic management. Implementing strategy means mobilizing employees and managers to put formulated strategies into action. Often considered to be the most difficult stage in strategic management, strategy implementation requires personal discipline, commitment, and sacrifice. Successful strategy implementation hinges upon managers' ability to motivate employees, which is more an art than a science. Strategies formulated but not implemented serve no useful purpose.

Interpersonal skills are especially critical for successful strategy implementation. Strategy-implementation activities affect all employees and managers in an organization. Every division and department must decide on answers to questions such as "What must we do to implement our part of the organization's strategy?" and "How best can we get the job done?" The challenge of implementation is to stimulate managers and employees throughout an organization to work with pride and enthusiasm toward achieving stated objectives.

Strategy evaluation is the final stage in strategic management. Managers desperately need to know when particular strategies are not working well; strategy evaluation is the primary means for obtaining this information. All strategies are subject to future modification because external and internal factors are constantly changing. Three fundamental strategy-evaluation activities are (1) reviewing external and internal factors that are the bases for current strategies, (2) measuring performance, and (3) taking corrective actions. Strategy evaluation is needed because success today is no guarantee of success tomorrow! Success always creates new and different problems; complacent organizations experience demise.

Strategy formulation, implementation, and evaluation activities occur at three hierarchical levels in a large organization: corporate, divisional or strategic business unit, and functional. By fostering communication and interaction among managers and employees across hierarchical levels, strategic management helps a firm function as a competitive team. Most small businesses and some large businesses do not have divisions or strategic business units; they have only the corporate and functional levels. Nevertheless, managers and employees at these two levels should be actively involved in strategic-management activities.

Peter Drucker says the prime task of strategic management is thinking through the overall mission of a business:

…that is, of asking the question, "What is our business?" This leads to the setting of objectives, the development of strategies, and the making of today's decisions for tomorrow's results. This clearly must be done by a part of the organization that can see the entire business; that can balance objectives and the needs of today against the needs of tomorrow; and that can allocate resources of men and money to key results.[2]

Integrating Intuition and Analysis

Edward Deming once said, *"In God we trust. All others bring data."* The strategic-management process can be described as an objective, logical, systematic approach for making major decisions in an organization. It attempts to organize qualitative and quantitative information in a way that allows effective decisions to be made under conditions of uncertainty. Yet strategic management is not a pure science that lends itself to a nice, neat, one-two-three approach.

Based on past experiences, judgment, and feelings, most people recognize that *intuition* is essential to making good strategic decisions. Intuition is particularly useful for making decisions in situations of great uncertainty or little precedent. It is also helpful when highly interrelated variables exist or when it is necessary to choose from several plausible alternatives. Some managers and owners of businesses profess to have extraordinary abilities for using intuition alone in devising brilliant strategies. For example, Will Durant, who organized GM, was described by Alfred Sloan as "a man who would proceed on a course of action guided solely, as far as I could tell, by some intuitive flash of brilliance. He never felt obliged to make an engineering hunt for the facts. Yet at times, he was astoundingly correct in his judgment."[3] Albert Einstein acknowledged the importance of intuition when he said, "I believe in intuition and inspiration. At times I feel certain that I am right while not knowing the reason. Imagination is more important than knowledge, because knowledge is limited, whereas imagination embraces the entire world."[4]

Although some organizations today may survive and prosper because they have intuitive geniuses managing them, most are not so fortunate. Most organizations can benefit from strategic management, which is based upon integrating intuition and analysis in decision making. Choosing an intuitive or analytic approach to decision making is not an either–or proposition. Managers at all levels in an organization inject their intuition and judgment into strategic-management analyses. Analytical thinking and intuitive thinking complement each other.

Operating from the I've-already-made-up-my-mind-don't-bother-me-with-the-facts mode is not management by intuition; it is management by ignorance.[5] Drucker says, "I believe in intuition only if you discipline it. 'Hunch' artists, who make a diagnosis but don't check it out with the facts, are the ones in medicine who kill people, and in management kill businesses."[6] As Henderson notes:

> The accelerating rate of change today is producing a business world in which customary managerial habits in organizations are increasingly inadequate. Experience alone was an adequate guide when changes could be made in small increments. But intuitive and experience-based management philosophies are grossly inadequate when decisions are strategic and have major, irreversible consequences.[7]

In a sense, the strategic-management process is an attempt both to duplicate what goes on in the mind of a brilliant, intuitive person who knows the business and to couple it with analysis.

Adapting to Change

The strategic-management process is based on the belief that organizations should continually monitor internal and external events and trends so that timely changes can be made as needed. The rate and magnitude of changes that affect organizations are increasing dramatically, as evidenced by how the global economic recession has caught so many firms by surprise. Firms, like organisms, must be "adept at adapting" or they will not survive.

For 30 years, Lowe's Company and Home Depot Inc. have been and remain fierce competitors trying to adapt better than the other to changing consumer needs. Home Depot is the larger firm and is reporting faster growing revenues and profits, but Lowe's CEO Robert Niblock says his company is moving quickly to showcase tools and appliances on the Internet as expertly as in stores. Lowe's revenues are about $49 billion annually compared to Home Depot's $68 billion. Home Depot's CEO Frank Blake has recently added 19 centralized distribution centers so store workers can spend more time waiting on shoppers. Both firms are hiring thousands of part-time workers, transitioning away from full-time employees, to keep labor costs down and create a price competitive advantage.

The second-largest bookstore chain in the United States, Borders Group, declared bankruptcy in 2011 as the firm had not adapted well to changes in book retailing from traditional bookstore shopping to customers buying online, preferring digital books to hard copies, and even renting rather than buying books. Borders is second in number of stores behind Barnes & Noble, which also is struggling to survive in an industry rapidly going digital and moving away from brick-and-mortar stores. Based in Ann Arbor, Michigan, Borders Group operates 676 stores nationwide, but was on the brink of financial collapse before being acquired in July 2011 by Direct Brands, a division of Phoenix, Arizona–based Najafi Companies.

To survive, all organizations must astutely identify and adapt to change. The strategic-management process is aimed at allowing organizations to adapt effectively to change over the long run. As Waterman has noted:

> In today's business environment, more than in any preceding era, the only constant is change. Successful organizations effectively manage change, continuously adapting their bureaucracies, strategies, systems, products, and cultures to survive the shocks and prosper from the forces that decimate the competition.[8]

Online social networking, rising food prices, and high energy prices are external changes that are transforming business and society today. On a political map, the boundaries between countries may be clear, but on a competitive map showing the real flow of financial and industrial activity, the boundaries have largely disappeared. The speedy flow of information has eaten away at national boundaries so that people worldwide readily see for themselves how other people live and work. We have become a borderless world with global citizens, global competitors, global customers, global suppliers, and global distributors! U.S. firms are challenged by large rival companies in many industries. To say U.S. firms are being challenged in the automobile industry is an understatement. But this situation is true in many industries.

The need to adapt to change leads organizations to key strategic-management questions, such as "What kind of business should we become?" "Are we in the right field(s)?" "Should we reshape our business?" "What new competitors are entering our industry?" "What strategies should we pursue?" "How are our customers changing?" "Are new technologies being developed that could put us out of business?"

The Internet has changed the way we organize our lives; inhabit our homes; and relate to and interact with family, friends, neighbors, and even ourselves. The Internet promotes endless comparison shopping, which thus enables consumers worldwide to band together to demand discounts. The Internet has transferred power from businesses to individuals. Buyers used to face big obstacles when attempting to get the best price and service, such as limited time and data to compare, but now consumers can quickly scan hundreds of vendor offerings. Both the number of people shopping online and the average amount they spend is increasing dramatically. Digital communication has become the name of the game in marketing. Consumers today are flocking to blogs, short-post forums such as Twitter, video sites such as YouTube, and social networking sites such as Facebook, Myspace, and LinkedIn instead of television, radio, newspapers, and magazines. Facebook and Myspace recently unveiled features that further marry these social sites to the wider Internet. Users on these social sites now can log on to many business shopping sites with their IDs from their social site so their friends can see what items they have purchased on various shopping sites. Both of these social sites want their members to use their IDs to manage all their online identities. Most traditional retailers have learned that their online sales can boost in-store sales as they utilize their websites to promote in-store promotions.

Key Terms in Strategic Management

Before we further discuss strategic management, we should define nine key terms: competitive advantage, strategists, vision and mission statements, external opportunities and threats, internal strengths and weaknesses, long-term objectives, strategies, annual objectives, and policies.

Competitive Advantage

Strategic management is all about gaining and maintaining *competitive advantage*. This term can be defined as "anything that a firm does especially well compared to rival firms." When a firm can do something that rival firms cannot do, or owns something that rival firms desire, that can represent a competitive advantage. For example, having ample cash on the firm's balance sheet can provide a major competitive advantage. Some cash-rich firms are buying distressed rivals. For example, Dish Network Corp. in mid-2011 acquired (for $1 billion) the satellite company DBSD North America based in Reston, Virginia, which was operating under bankruptcy protection. The acquisition gave Dish Network access to varied broadband spectrums. Dish Network is also trying to acquire bankrupt satellite operator Terrestar Networks, which would allow Dish Network to launch mobile video or satellite Internet services.

Having less fixed assets than rival firms also can provide major competitive advantages in a global recession. For example, Apple has no manufacturing facilities of its own, and rival Sony has 57 electronics factories. Apple relies exclusively on contract manufacturers for production of all of its products, whereas Sony owns its own plants. Less fixed assets has enabled Apple to remain financially lean with virtually no long-term debt. Sony, in contrast, has built up massive debt on its balance sheet.

CEO Paco Underhill of Envirosell says, "Where it used to be a polite war, it's now a 21st-century bar fight, where everybody is competing with everyone else for the customers' money." Shoppers are "trading down," so Nordstrom is taking customers from Neiman Marcus and Saks Fifth Avenue, T.J. Maxx and Marshalls are taking customers from most other stores in the mall, and Family Dollar is taking revenues from Wal-Mart.[9] Getting and keeping competitive advantage is essential for long-term success in an organization. In mass retailing, big-box companies such as Wal-Mart, Best Buy, and Sears are losing competitive advantage to smaller stores, so there is a dramatic shift in mass retailing to becoming smaller. For example, Best Buy opened 150 of its small-format Best Buy Mobile stores in 2011. Home Depot is selling off portions of its parking lots to fast-food chains and auto repair shops. Sears in Greensboro, North Carolina, just leased 34,000 square feet of its space to Whole Foods Market, which is set to open in 2012. As customers shift more to online purchases, less brick and mortar is definitely better for sustaining competitive advantage in retailing. Even Wal-Mart began in mid-2011 to open Wal-Mart Express stores of less than 40,000 square feet each, rather than 185,000-square-foot Supercenters. Office Depot's new 5,000-square-foot stores are dramatically smaller than their traditional stores.

Normally, a firm can sustain a competitive advantage for only a certain period due to rival firms imitating and undermining that advantage. Thus it is not adequate to simply obtain competitive advantage. A firm must strive to achieve *sustained competitive advantage* by (1) continually adapting to changes in external trends and events and internal capabilities, competencies, and resources; and by (2) effectively formulating, implementing, and evaluating strategies that capitalize upon those factors.

An increasing number of companies are gaining a competitive advantage by using the Internet for direct selling and for communication with suppliers, customers, creditors, partners, shareholders, clients, and competitors who may be dispersed globally. E-commerce allows firms to sell products, advertise, purchase supplies, bypass intermediaries, track inventory, eliminate paperwork, and share information. In total, e-commerce is minimizing the expense and cumbersomeness of time, distance, and space in doing business, thus yielding better customer service, greater efficiency, improved products, and higher profitability.

The social network company Myspace was acquired in June 2011 by Specific Media based in Irvine, California. Previously owned by Beverly Hills-based News Corp., Myspace is being battered by the rapid rise of rival Facebook. Myspace's customer base dropped to 80 million at the start of 2011 from well over 100 million a year earlier, while Facebook customers at the same time numbered 500 million, up from about 350 million. Analyst Jeremiah Owyang at market research firm Altimeter Group said: "The end was in sight for Myspace before former CEO Chris DeWolfe left. The company did not innovate for years, while Facebook did. It comes down to culture and leadership. Myspace did not evolve its business model. It stuck with its young demographic, and made minimal changes until it was too late."[10]

Strategists

Strategists are the individuals who are most responsible for the success or failure of an organization. Strategists have various job titles, such as chief executive officer, president, owner, chair of the board, executive director, chancellor, dean, or entrepreneur. Jay Conger, professor of organizational behavior at the London Business School and author of *Building Leaders,* says, "All strategists have to be chief learning officers. We are in an extended period of change. If our leaders aren't highly adaptive and great models during this period, then our companies won't adapt either, because ultimately leadership is about being a role model."

Strategists help an organization gather, analyze, and organize information. They track industry and competitive trends, develop forecasting models and scenario analyses, evaluate corporate and divisional performance, spot emerging market opportunities, identify business threats, and develop creative action plans. Strategic planners usually serve in a support or staff role. Usually found in higher levels of management, they typically have considerable authority for decision making in the firm. The CEO is the most visible and critical strategic manager. Any manager who has responsibility for a unit or division, responsibility for profit and loss outcomes, or direct authority over a major piece of the business is a strategic manager (strategist). In the last five years, the position of chief strategy officer (CSO) has emerged as a new addition to the top management ranks of many organizations, including Sun Microsystems, Network Associates, Clarus, Lante, Marimba, Sapient, Commerce One, BBDO, Cadbury Schweppes, General Motors, Ellie Mae, Cendant, Charles Schwab, Tyco, Campbell Soup, Morgan Stanley, and Reed-Elsevier. This corporate officer title represents recognition of the growing importance of strategic planning in business. Franz Koch, the CSO of German sportswear company Puma AG, was promoted to CEO of Puma in mid-2011. When asked about his plans for the company, Mr. Koch said on a conference call "I plan to just focus on the long-term strategic plan."

Strategists differ as much as organizations themselves, and these differences must be considered in the formulation, implementation, and evaluation of strategies. Some strategists will not consider some types of strategies because of their personal philosophies. Strategists differ in their attitudes, values, ethics, willingness to take risks, concern for social responsibility, concern for profitability, concern for short-run versus long-run aims, and management style. The founder of Hershey Foods, Milton Hershey, built the company to manage an orphanage. From corporate profits, Hershey Foods today cares for over a thousand boys and girls in its School for Orphans.

Vision and Mission Statements

Many organizations today develop a *vision statement* that answers the question "What do we want to become?" Developing a vision statement is often considered the first step in strategic planning, preceding even development of a mission statement. Many vision statements are a single sentence. For example, the vision statement of Stokes Eye Clinic in Florence, South Carolina, is "Our vision is to take care of your vision."

Mission statements are "enduring statements of purpose that distinguish one business from other similar firms. A mission statement identifies the scope of a firm's operations in product and market terms."[11] It addresses the basic question that faces all strategists: "What is our business?" A clear mission statement describes the values and priorities of an organization. Developing a mission statement compels strategists to think about the nature and scope of present operations and to assess the potential attractiveness of future markets and activities. A mission statement broadly charts the future direction of an organization. A mission statement is a constant reminder to its employees of why the organization exists and what the founders envisioned when they put their fame and fortune at risk to breathe life into their dreams.

External Opportunities and Threats

External opportunities and *external threats* refer to economic, social, cultural, demographic, environmental, political, legal, governmental, technological, and competitive trends and events that could significantly benefit or harm an organization in the future. Opportunities and threats are largely beyond the control of a single organization—thus the word *external*. A few opportunities and threats that face many firms are listed here:

- Availability of capital can no longer be taken for granted.
- Consumers expect green operations and products.
- Marketing moving rapidly to the Internet.
- Commodity food prices are increasing.
- Political unrest in the Middle East is raising oil prices.
- Computer hacker problems are increasing.
- Intense price competition is plaguing most firms.
- Unemployment and underemployment rates remain high.
- Interest rates are rising.
- Product life cycles are becoming shorter.
- State and local governments are financially weak.
- Turmoil and violence in Mexico is increasing.
- Winters are colder and summers hotter than usual.
- Home prices remain exceptionally low.
- Global markets offer the highest growth in revenues.

The types of changes mentioned above are creating a different type of consumer and consequently a need for different types of products, services, and strategies. Many companies in many industries face the severe external threat of online sales capturing increasing market share in their industry.

Other opportunities and threats may include the passage of a law, the introduction of a new product by a competitor, a national catastrophe, or the declining value of the dollar. A competitor's strength could be a threat. Unrest in the Middle East, rising energy costs, or social media networking could represent an opportunity or a threat.

A basic tenet of strategic management is that firms need to formulate strategies to take advantage of external opportunities and to avoid or reduce the impact of external threats. For this reason, identifying, monitoring, and evaluating external opportunities and threats are essential for success. This process of conducting research and gathering and assimilating external information is sometimes called *environmental scanning* or industry analysis. Lobbying is one activity that some organizations utilize to influence external opportunities and threats.

Internal Strengths and Weaknesses

Internal strengths and *internal weaknesses* are an organization's controllable activities that are performed especially well or poorly. They arise in the management, marketing, finance/accounting, production/operations, research and development, and management information systems activities of a business. Identifying and evaluating organizational strengths and weaknesses in the functional areas of a business is an essential strategic-management activity. Organizations strive to pursue strategies that capitalize on internal strengths and eliminate internal weaknesses.

Strengths and weaknesses are determined relative to competitors. *Relative deficiency or superiority is important information.* Also, strengths and weaknesses can be determined by elements of being rather than performance. For example, a strength may involve ownership of natural resources or a historic reputation for quality. Strengths and weaknesses may be determined relative to a firm's own objectives. For example, high levels of inventory turnover may not be a strength to a firm that seeks never to stock-out.

Internal factors can be determined in a number of ways, including computing ratios, measuring performance, and comparing to past periods and industry averages. Various types of surveys also can be developed and administered to examine internal factors such as employee morale, production efficiency, advertising effectiveness, and customer loyalty.

Long-Term Objectives

Objectives can be defined as specific results that an organization seeks to achieve in pursuing its basic mission. *Long-term* means more than one year. Objectives are essential for organizational success because they state direction; aid in evaluation; create synergy; reveal priorities; focus coordination; and provide a basis for effective planning, organizing, motivating, and controlling activities. Objectives should be challenging, measurable, consistent, reasonable, and clear. In a multidimensional firm, objectives should be established for the overall company and for each division.

Strategies

Strategies are the means by which long-term objectives will be achieved. Business strategies may include geographic expansion, diversification, acquisition, product development, market penetration, retrenchment, divestiture, liquidation, and joint ventures. Strategies currently being pursued by some companies are described in Table 1-1.

Strategies are potential actions that require top management decisions and large amounts of the firm's resources. In addition, strategies affect an organization's long-term prosperity, typically for at least five years, and thus are future-oriented. Strategies have multifunctional or multidivisional consequences and require consideration of both the external and internal factors facing the firm.

Annual Objectives

Annual objectives are short-term milestones that organizations must achieve to reach long-term objectives. Like long-term objectives, annual objectives should be measurable, quantitative, challenging, realistic, consistent, and prioritized. They should be established at the corporate, divisional, and functional levels in a large organization. Annual objectives should be stated in terms of management, marketing, finance/accounting, production/operations, research and

TABLE 1-1   Sample Strategies in Action in 2011

Skype

Headquartered in Luxembourg and acquired by Microsoft Corporation in 2011, Skype offers software applications that enable users to make voice calls over the Internet as well as video conferencing, instant messaging, and file transfer. Wildly popular among people who regularly make international calls, Skype audio conferences support up to 25 people at a time, including the host. Skype 3.0, recently released for Apple's iOS platform, offers video chat for the iPhone, iPad, and iPod Touch devices. Skype recently acquired Qik, a mobile video streaming and storage company, and partnered with Sony and Panasonic to create Skype-ready Blu-ray players. Skype now accounts for more than 25 percent of all international calls, up from 13 percent in 2009. The mobile-based video call market is expected to exceed $1 billion by 2015.

Sbarro Inc.

The fast-food Italian eatery located in many mall food courts around the world is struggling to survive and swamped in debt. Based in Melville, New York, Sbarro is closing weak stores among its 1,000 total in 40 countries, including Qatar, Egypt, and New Zealand. Sbarro has hired bankruptcy and restructuring lawyers to help the firm survive as many consumers have switched, for various reasons, to other mall fast food choices, such as Chick-fil-A. Sbarro needs a clear strategic plan to survive.

Target Corp.

The Minneapolis-based mass retailer expanded into Canada for the first time in 2012, converting about 150 of its acquired Zellers stores into Target stores. With 1,752 stores in the United States, Target is a latecomer to Canada; Wal-Mart and Sears have been in Canada for years. Most of Target's new Canadian stores will be in highly urban areas such as Vancouver, Montreal, Ottawa, Edmonton, and Calgary. Reportedly about 70 percent of Canadians are already familiar with the Target brand.

Caesars Entertainment

Formerly named Harrah's Entertainment, this gaming company for the first time ever is establishing noncasino hotels in Asia, following in the footsteps of its major competitor MGM Resorts International. Both firms are shut out from gaining gambling licenses to operate in Macau and Singapore. Since the U.S. gaming market remains sluggish, Caesars is anxious to take advantage of high growth in China, India, and Vietnam. Caesars plans initially to "manage rather than own" the hotels that soon will use its brand name across Asia.

development, and management information systems (MIS) accomplishments. A set of annual objectives is needed for each long-term objective. Annual objectives are especially important in strategy implementation, whereas long-term objectives are particularly important in strategy formulation. Annual objectives represent the basis for allocating resources.

Policies

Policies are the means by which annual objectives will be achieved. Policies include guidelines, rules, and procedures established to support efforts to achieve stated objectives. Policies are guides to decision making and address repetitive or recurring situations.

Policies are most often stated in terms of management, marketing, finance/accounting, production/operations, research and development, and MIS activities. Policies can be established at the corporate level and apply to an entire organization at the divisional level and apply to a single division, or they can be established at the functional level and apply to particular operational activities or departments. Policies, like annual objectives, are especially important in strategy implementation because they outline an organization's expectations of its employees and managers. Policies allow consistency and coordination within and between organizational departments.

Substantial research suggests that a healthier workforce can more effectively and efficiently implement strategies. Smoking has become a heavy burden for Europe's state-run social welfare systems, with smoking-related diseases costing well over $100 billion a year. Smoking also is a huge burden on companies worldwide, so firms are continually implementing policies to curtail smoking. Table 1-2 gives a ranking of some countries by percentage of people who smoke.

Hotel/motels in the United States are rapidly going "smoke-free throughout" with more than 13,000 now having this policy. The American Hotel and Lodging Association says there are 50,800

TABLE 1-2 Percentage of People Who Smoke in Selected Countries

Country	Percentage
Greece	50
Russia	High
Austria	
Spain	
U.K.	
France	
Germany	
Italy	
Belgium	
Switzerland	Low
USA	19

Source: Based on Christina Passariello, "Smoking Culture Persists in Europe, Despite Bans," *Wall Street Journal*, January 2, 2009, A5.

hotel/motels in the United States with 15 or more rooms. All Marriotts are now nonsmoking. Almost all car rental companies are exclusively nonsmoking, including Avis, Dollar, Thrifty, and Budget. These four rental car companies charge a $250 cleaning fee if a customer smokes in their rental vehicle.

The Strategic-Management Model

The strategic-management process can best be studied and applied using a model. Every model represents some kind of process. The framework illustrated in Figure 1-1 is a widely accepted, comprehensive model of the strategic-management process.[12] This model does not guarantee success, but it does represent a clear and practical approach for formulating, implementing, and evaluating strategies. Relationships among major components of the strategic-management process are shown in the model, which appears in all subsequent chapters with appropriate areas shaped to show the particular focus of each chapter. These are three important questions to answer in developing a strategic plan:

Where are we now?

Where do we want to go?

How are we going to get there?

Identifying an organization's existing vision, mission, objectives, and strategies is the logical starting point for strategic management because a firm's present situation and condition may preclude certain strategies and may even dictate a particular course of action. Every organization has a vision, mission, objectives, and strategy, even if these elements are not consciously designed, written, or communicated. The answer to where an organization is going can be determined largely by where the organization has been!

The strategic-management process is dynamic and continuous. A change in any one of the major components in the model can necessitate a change in any or all of the other components. For instance, third-world countries coming online could represent a major opportunity and require a change in long-term objectives and strategies; a failure to accomplish annual objectives could require a change in policy; or a major competitor's change in strategy could require a change in the firm's mission. Therefore, strategy formulation, implementation, and evaluation activities should be performed on a continual basis, not just at the end of the year or semiannually. The strategic-management process never really ends.

Note in the *strategic-management model* that business ethics/social responsibility/ environmental sustainability issues impact all activities in the model as described in full in Chapter 10. Also, note in the model that global/international issues also impact virtually all strategic decisions today, as described in detail in Chapter 11.

FIGURE 1-1

A Comprehensive Strategic-Management Model

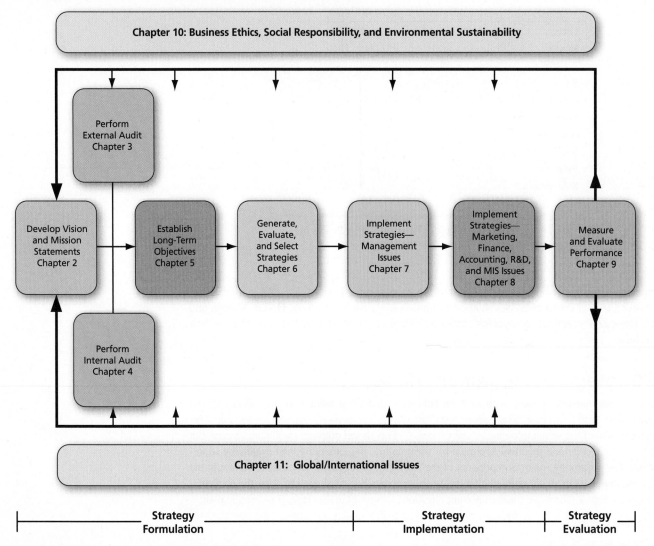

Source: Fred R. David, "How Companies Define Their Mission," *Long Range Planning* 22, no. 3 (June 1988): 40.

The strategic-management process is not as cleanly divided and neatly performed in practice as the strategic-management model suggests. Strategists do not go through the process in lockstep fashion. Generally, there is give-and-take among hierarchical levels of an organization. Many organizations semiannually conduct formal meetings to discuss and update the firm's vision/mission, opportunities/threats, strengths/weaknesses, strategies, objectives, policies, and performance. These meetings are commonly held off-premises and are called *retreats*. The rationale for periodically conducting strategic-management meetings away from the work site is to encourage more creativity and candor from participants. Good communication and feedback are needed throughout the strategic-management process.

Application of the strategic-management process is typically more formal in larger and well-established organizations. Formality refers to the extent that participants, responsibilities, authority, duties, and approach are specified. Smaller businesses tend to be less formal. Firms that compete in complex, rapidly changing environments, such as technology companies, tend to be more formal in strategic planning. Firms that have many divisions, products, markets, and technologies also tend to be more formal in applying strategic-management concepts. Greater formality in applying the strategic-management process is usually positively associated with the cost, comprehensiveness, accuracy, and success of planning across all types and sizes of organizations.[13]

Benefits of Strategic Management

Strategic management allows an organization to be more proactive than reactive in shaping its own future; it allows an organization to initiate and influence (rather than just respond to) activities—and thus to exert control over its own destiny. Small business owners, chief executive officers, presidents, and managers of many for-profit and nonprofit organizations have recognized and realized the benefits of strategic management.

Historically, the principal benefit of strategic management has been to help organizations formulate better strategies through the use of a more systematic, logical, and rational approach to strategic choice. This certainly continues to be a major benefit of strategic management, but research studies now indicate that the process, rather than the decision or document, is the more important contribution of strategic management.[14] *Communication is a key to successful strategic management.* Through involvement in the process, in other words, through dialogue and participation, managers and employees become committed to supporting the organization. Figure 1-2 illustrates this intrinsic benefit of a firm engaging in strategic planning. Note that all firms need all employees on a mission to help the firm succeed.

The manner in which strategic management is carried out is thus exceptionally important. A major aim of the process is to achieve the understanding of and commitment from all managers and employees. Understanding may be the most important benefit of strategic management, followed by commitment. When managers and employees understand what the organization is doing and why, they often feel they are a part of the firm and become committed to assisting it. This is especially true when employees also understand linkages between their own compensation and organizational performance. Managers and employees become surprisingly creative and innovative when they understand and support the firm's mission, objectives, and strategies. A great benefit of strategic management, then, is the opportunity that the process provides to empower individuals. *Empowerment* is the act of strengthening employees' sense of effectiveness by encouraging them to participate in decision making and to exercise initiative and imagination, and rewarding them for doing so.

Strategic planning is a learning, helping, educating, and supporting process, not merely a paper-shuffling activity among top executives. Strategic-management dialogue is more important than a nicely bound strategic-management document.[15] The worst thing strategists can do is develop strategic plans themselves and then present them to operating managers to execute. Through involvement in the process, line managers become "owners" of the strategy. Ownership of strategies by the people who have to execute them is a key to success!

Although making good strategic decisions is the major responsibility of an organization's owner or chief executive officer, both managers and employees must also be involved in strategy formulation, implementation, and evaluation activities. Participation is a key to gaining commitment for needed changes.

An increasing number of corporations and institutions are using strategic management to make effective decisions. But strategic management is not a guarantee for success; it can be dysfunctional if conducted haphazardly.

Financial Benefits

Research indicates that organizations that use strategic-management concepts are more profitable and successful than those that do not.[16] Businesses using strategic-management concepts show significant improvement in sales, profitability, and productivity compared to firms without systematic

FIGURE 1-2

Benefits to a Firm That Does Strategic Planning

planning activities. High-performing firms tend to do systematic planning to prepare for future fluctuations in their external and internal environments. Firms with planning systems more closely resembling strategic-management theory generally exhibit superior long-term financial performance relative to their industry.

High-performing firms seem to make more informed decisions with good anticipation of both short- and long-term consequences. In contrast, firms that perform poorly often engage in activities that are shortsighted and do not reflect good forecasting of future conditions. Strategists of low-performing organizations are often preoccupied with solving internal problems and meeting paperwork deadlines. They typically underestimate their competitors' strengths and overestimate their own firm's strengths. They often attribute weak performance to uncontrollable factors such as a poor economy, technological change, or foreign competition.

More than 100,000 businesses in the United States fail annually. Business failures include bankruptcies, foreclosures, liquidations, and court-mandated receiverships. Although many factors besides a lack of effective strategic management can lead to business failure, the planning concepts and tools described in this text can yield substantial financial benefits for any organization.

Nonfinancial Benefits

Besides helping firms avoid financial demise, strategic management offers other tangible benefits, such as an enhanced awareness of external threats, an improved understanding of competitors' strategies, increased employee productivity, reduced resistance to change, and a clearer understanding of performance–reward relationships. Strategic management enhances the problem-prevention capabilities of organizations because it promotes interaction among managers at all divisional and functional levels. Firms that have nurtured their managers and employees, shared organizational objectives with them, empowered them to help improve the product or service, and recognized their contributions can turn to them for help in a pinch because of this interaction.

In addition to empowering managers and employees, strategic management often brings order and discipline to an otherwise floundering firm. It can be the beginning of an efficient and effective managerial system. Strategic management may renew confidence in the current business strategy or point to the need for corrective actions. The strategic-management process provides a basis for identifying and rationalizing the need for change to all managers and employees of a firm; it helps them view change as an opportunity rather than as a threat.

Greenley stated that strategic management offers the following benefits:

1. It allows for identification, prioritization, and exploitation of opportunities.
2. It provides an objective view of management problems.
3. It represents a framework for improved coordination and control of activities.
4. It minimizes the effects of adverse conditions and changes.
5. It allows major decisions to better support established objectives.
6. It allows more effective allocation of time and resources to identified opportunities.
7. It allows fewer resources and less time to be devoted to correcting erroneous or ad hoc decisions.
8. It creates a framework for internal communication among personnel.
9. It helps integrate the behavior of individuals into a total effort.
10. It provides a basis for clarifying individual responsibilities.
11. It encourages forward thinking.
12. It provides a cooperative, integrated, and enthusiastic approach to tackling problems and opportunities.
13. It encourages a favorable attitude toward change.
14. It gives a degree of discipline and formality to the management of a business.[17]

Why Some Firms Do No Strategic Planning

Some firms do not engage in strategic planning, and some firms do strategic planning but receive no support from managers and employees. Some reasons for poor or no strategic planning are as follows:

- *Lack of knowledge or experience in strategic planning*—No training in strategic planning.
- *Poor reward structures*—When an organization assumes success, it often fails to reward success. When failure occurs, then the firm may punish.

- *Firefighting*—An organization can be so deeply embroiled in resolving crises and fire-fighting that it reserves no time for planning.
- *Waste of time*—Some firms see planning as a waste of time because no marketable product is produced. Time spent on planning is an investment.
- *Too expensive*—Some organizations see planning as too expensive in time and money.
- *Laziness*—People may not want to put forth the effort needed to formulate a plan.
- *Content with success*—Particularly if a firm is successful, individuals may feel there is no need to plan because things are fine as they stand. But success today does not guarantee success tomorrow.
- *Fear of failure*—By not taking action, there is little risk of failure unless a problem is urgent and pressing. Whenever something worthwhile is attempted, there is some risk of failure.
- *Overconfidence*—As managers amass experience, they may rely less on formalized planning. Rarely, however, is this appropriate. Being overconfident or overestimating experience can bring demise. Forethought is rarely wasted and is often the mark of professionalism.
- *Prior bad experience*—People may have had a previous bad experience with planning, that is, cases in which plans have been long, cumbersome, impractical, or inflexible. Planning, like anything else, can be done badly.
- *Self-interest*—When someone has achieved status, privilege, or self-esteem through effectively using an old system, he or she often sees a new plan as a threat.
- *Fear of the unknown*—People may be uncertain of their abilities to learn new skills, of their aptitude with new systems, or of their ability to take on new roles.
- *Honest difference of opinion*—People may sincerely believe the plan is wrong. They may view the situation from a different viewpoint, or they may have aspirations for themselves or the organization that are different from the plan. Different people in different jobs have different perceptions of a situation.
- *Suspicion*—Employees may not trust management.[18]

Pitfalls in Strategic Planning

Strategic planning is an involved, intricate, and complex process that takes an organization into uncharted territory. It does not provide a ready-to-use prescription for success; instead, it takes the organization through a journey and offers a framework for addressing questions and solving problems. Being aware of potential pitfalls and being prepared to address them is essential to success.

Some pitfalls to watch for and avoid in strategic planning are these:

- Using strategic planning to gain control over decisions and resources
- Doing strategic planning only to satisfy accreditation or regulatory requirements
- Too hastily moving from mission development to strategy formulation
- Failing to communicate the plan to employees, who continue working in the dark
- Top managers making many intuitive decisions that conflict with the formal plan
- Top managers not actively supporting the strategic-planning process
- Failing to use plans as a standard for measuring performance
- Delegating planning to a "planner" rather than involving all managers
- Failing to involve key employees in all phases of planning
- Failing to create a collaborative climate supportive of change
- Viewing planning as unnecessary or unimportant
- Becoming so engrossed in current problems that insufficient or no planning is done
- Being so formal in planning that flexibility and creativity are stifled[19]

Guidelines for Effective Strategic Management

Failing to follow certain guidelines in conducting strategic management can foster criticisms of the process and create problems for the organization. Issues such as "Is strategic management in our firm a people process or a paper process?" should be addressed.

Even the most technically perfect strategic plan will serve little purpose if it is not implemented. Many organizations tend to spend an inordinate amount of time, money, and effort on developing the strategic plan, treating the means and circumstances under which it will be implemented as afterthoughts! Change comes through implementation and evaluation, not through the plan. A technically imperfect plan that is implemented well will achieve more than the perfect plan that never gets off the paper on which it is typed.[20]

Strategic management must not become a self-perpetuating bureaucratic mechanism. Rather, it must be a self-reflective learning process that familiarizes managers and employees in the organization with key strategic issues and feasible alternatives for resolving those issues. Strategic management must not become ritualistic, stilted, orchestrated, or too formal, predictable, and rigid. Words supported by numbers, rather than numbers supported by words, should represent the medium for explaining strategic issues and organizational responses. A key role of strategists is to facilitate continuous organizational learning and change.

R. T. Lenz offered some important guidelines for effective strategic management:

Keep the strategic-management process as simple and nonroutine as possible. Eliminate jargon and arcane planning language. Remember, strategic management is a process for fostering learning and action, not merely a formal system for control. To avoid routinized behavior, vary assignments, team membership, meeting formats, and the planning calendar. The process should not be totally predictable, and settings must be changed to stimulate creativity. Emphasize word-oriented plans with numbers as back-up material. If managers cannot express their strategy in a paragraph or so, they either do not have one or do not understand it. Stimulate thinking and action that challenge the assumptions underlying current corporate strategy. Welcome bad news. If strategy is not working, managers desperately need to know it. Further, no pertinent information should be classified as inadmissible merely because it cannot be quantified. Build a corporate culture in which the role of strategic management and its essential purposes are understood. Do not permit "technicians" to co-opt the process. It is ultimately a process for learning and action. Speak of it in these terms. Attend to psychological, social, and political dimensions, as well as the information infrastructure and administrative procedures supporting it.[21]

An important guideline for effective strategic management is open-mindedness. A willingness and eagerness to consider new information, new viewpoints, new ideas, and new possibilities is essential; all organizational members must share a spirit of inquiry and learning. Strategists such as chief executive officers, presidents, owners of small businesses, and heads of government agencies must commit themselves to listen to and understand managers' positions well enough to be able to restate those positions to the managers' satisfaction. In addition, managers and employees throughout the firm should be able to describe the strategists' positions to the satisfaction of the strategists. This degree of discipline will promote understanding and learning.

No organization has unlimited resources. No firm can take on an unlimited amount of debt or issue an unlimited amount of stock to raise capital. Therefore, no organization can pursue all the strategies that potentially could benefit the firm. Strategic decisions thus always have to be made to eliminate some courses of action and to allocate organizational resources among others. Most organizations can afford to pursue only a few corporate-level strategies at any given time. It is a critical mistake for managers to pursue too many strategies at the same time, thereby spreading the firm's resources so thin that all strategies are jeopardized. Joseph Charyk, CEO of the Communication Satellite Corporation (Comsat), said, "We have to face the cold fact that Comsat may not be able to do all it wants. We must make hard choices on which ventures to keep and which to fold."

Strategic decisions require trade-offs such as long-range versus short-range considerations or maximizing profits versus increasing shareholders' wealth. There are ethics issues too. Strategy trade-offs require subjective judgments and preferences. In many cases, a lack of objectivity in formulating strategy results in a loss of competitive posture and profitability. Most organizations today recognize that strategic-management concepts and techniques can enhance the effectiveness of decisions. Subjective factors such as attitudes toward risk, concern for social responsibility, and organizational culture will always affect strategy-formulation decisions, but organizations need to be as objective as possible in considering qualitative factors. Table 1-3 summarizes important guidelines for the strategic-planning process to be effective.

TABLE 1-3   Seventeen Guidelines for the Strategic-Planning Process to Be Effective

1. It should be a people process more than a paper process.
2. It should be a learning process for all managers and employees.
3. It should be words supported by numbers rather than numbers supported by words.
4. It should be simple and nonroutine.
5. It should vary assignments, team memberships, meeting formats, and even the planning calendar.
6. It should challenge the assumptions underlying the current corporate strategy.
7. It should welcome bad news.
8. It should welcome open-mindness and a spirit of inquiry and learning.
9. It should not be a bureaucratic mechanism.
10. It should not become ritualistic, stilted, or orchestrated.
11. It should not be too formal, predictable, or rigid.
12. It should not contain jargon or arcane planning language.
13. It should not be a formal system for control.
14. It should not disregard qualitative information.
15. It should not be controlled by "technicians."
16. Do not pursue too many strategies at once.
17. Continually strengthen the "good ethics is good business" policy.

Comparing Business and Military Strategy

A strong military heritage underlies the study of strategic management. Terms such as *objectives, mission, strengths*, and *weaknesses* first were formulated to address problems on the battlefield. According to *Webster's New World Dictionary,* strategy is "the science of planning and directing large-scale military operations, of maneuvering forces into the most advantageous position prior to actual engagement with the enemy." The word *strategy* comes from the Greek *strategos,* which refers to a military general and combines *stratos* (the army) and *ago* (to lead). The history of strategic planning began in the military. A key aim of both business and military strategy is "to gain competitive advantage." In many respects, business strategy is like military strategy, and military strategists have learned much over the centuries that can benefit business strategists today. Both business and military organizations try to use their own strengths to exploit competitors' weaknesses. If an organization's overall strategy is wrong (ineffective), then all the efficiency in the world may not be enough to allow success. Business or military success is generally not the happy result of accidental strategies. Rather, success is the product of both continuous attention to changing external and internal conditions and the formulation and implementation of insightful adaptations to those conditions. The element of surprise provides great competitive advantages in both military and business strategy; information systems that provide data on opponents' or competitors' strategies and resources are also vitally important.

Of course, a fundamental difference between military and business strategy is that business strategy is formulated, implemented, and evaluated with an assumption of *competition,* whereas military strategy is based on an assumption of *conflict.* Nonetheless, military conflict and business competition are so similar that many strategic-management techniques apply equally to both. Business strategists have access to valuable insights that military thinkers have refined over time. Superior strategy formulation and implementation can overcome an opponent's superiority in numbers and resources.

Both business and military organizations must adapt to change and constantly improve to be successful. Too often, firms do not change their strategies when their environment and competitive conditions dictate the need to change. Gluck offered a classic military example of this:

> When Napoleon won, it was because his opponents were committed to the strategy, tactics, and organization of earlier wars. When he lost—against Wellington, the Russians, and the Spaniards—it was because he, in turn, used tried-and-true strategies against enemies who thought afresh, who were developing the strategies not of the last war but of the next.[22]

Similarities can be construed from Sun Tzu's writings to the practice of formulating and implementing strategies among businesses today. Table 1-4 provides narrative excerpts from *The Art of War*. As you read through the table, consider which of the principles of war apply to business strategy as companies today compete aggressively to survive and grow.

Special Note to Students

In performing strategic management case analysis, emphasize throughout your project, beginning with the first page or slide, where your firm has competitive advantages and disadvantages. More importantly, emphasize throughout how you recommend the firm sustain and grow its competitive advantages and how you recommend the firm overcome its competitive disadvantages. Begin paving the way very early for what you ultimately recommend your firm should do over the next three

TABLE 1-4   Excerpts from Sun Tzu's *The Art of War* Writings

- War is a matter of vital importance to the state: a matter of life or death, the road either to survival or ruin. Hence, it is imperative that it be studied thoroughly.
- Warfare is based on deception. When near the enemy, make it seem that you are far away; when far away, make it seem that you are near. Hold out baits to lure the enemy. Strike the enemy when he is in disorder. Avoid the enemy when he is stronger. If your opponent is of choleric temper, try to irritate him. If he is arrogant, try to encourage his egotism. If enemy troops are well prepared after reorganization, try to wear them down. If they are united, try to sow dissension among them. Attack the enemy where he is unprepared, and appear where you are not expected. These are the keys to victory for a strategist. It is not possible to formulate them in detail beforehand.
- A speedy victory is the main object in war. If this is long in coming, weapons are blunted and morale depressed. When the army engages in protracted campaigns, the resources of the state will fall short. Thus, while we have heard of stupid haste in war, we have not yet seen a clever operation that was prolonged.
- Generally, in war the best policy is to take a state intact; to ruin it is inferior to this. To capture the enemy's entire army is better than to destroy it; to take intact a regiment, a company, or a squad is better than to destroy it. For to win one hundred victories in one hundred battles is not the epitome of skill. To subdue the enemy without fighting is the supreme excellence. Those skilled in war subdue the enemy's army without battle.
- The art of using troops is this: When ten to the enemy's one, surround him. When five times his strength, attack him. If double his strength, divide him. If equally matched, you may engage him with some good plan. If weaker, be capable of withdrawing. And if in all respects unequal, be capable of eluding him.
- Know your enemy and know yourself, and in a hundred battles you will never be defeated. When you are ignorant of the enemy but know yourself, your chances of winning or losing are equal. If ignorant both of your enemy and of yourself, you are sure to be defeated in every battle.
- He who occupies the field of battle first and awaits his enemy is at ease, and he who comes later to the scene and rushes into the fight is weary. And therefore, those skilled in war bring the enemy to the field of battle and are not brought there by him. Thus, when the enemy is at ease, be able to tire him; when well fed, be able to starve him; when at rest, be able to make him move.
- Analyze the enemy's plans so that you will know his shortcomings as well as his strong points. Agitate him to ascertain the pattern of his movement. Lure him out to reveal his dispositions and to ascertain his position. Launch a probing attack to learn where his strength is abundant and where deficient. It is according to the situation that plans are laid for victory, but the multitude does not comprehend this.
- An army may be likened to water, for just as flowing water avoids the heights and hastens to the lowlands, so an army should avoid strength and strike weakness. And as water shapes its flow in accordance with the ground, so an army manages its victory in accordance with the situation of the enemy. And as water has no constant form, there are in warfare no constant conditions. Thus, one able to win the victory by modifying his tactics in accordance with the enemy situation may be said to be divine.
- If you decide to go into battle, do not anounce your intentions or plans. Project "business as usual."
- Unskilled leaders work out their conflicts in courtrooms and battlefields. Brilliant strategists rarely go to battle or to court; they generally achieve their objectives through tactical positioning well in advance of any confrontation.
- When you do decide to challenge another company (or army), much calculating, estimating, analyzing, and positioning bring triumph. Little computation brings defeat.
- Skillful leaders do not let a strategy inhibit creative counter-movement. Nor should commands from those at a distance interfere with spontaneous maneuvering in the immediate situation.
- When a decisive advantage is gained over a rival, skillful leaders do not press on. They hold their position and give their rivals the opportunity to surrender or merge. They do not allow their forces to be damaged by those who have nothing to lose.
- Brillant strategists forge ahead with illusion, obscuring the area(s) of major confrontation, so that opponents divide their forces in an attempt to defend many areas. Create the appearance of confusion, fear, or vulnerability so the opponent is helplessly drawn toward this illusion of advantage.

(Note: Substitute the words *strategy* or *strategic planning* for *war* or *warfare*)

Source: Based on *The Art of War* and from www.ccs.neu.edu/home/thigpen/html/art_of_war.html

years. The notion of competitive advantage should be integral to the discussion of every page or PowerPoint slide. Therefore, avoid being merely *descriptive* in your written or oral analysis; rather, be *prescriptive*, insightful, and forward-looking throughout your project.

Conclusion

All firms have a strategy, even if it is informal, unstructured, and sporadic. All organizations are heading somewhere, but unfortunately some organizations do not know where they are going. The old saying "If you do not know where you are going, then any road will lead you there!" accents the need for organizations to use strategic-management concepts and techniques. The strategic-management process is becoming more widely used by small firms, large companies, nonprofit institutions, governmental organizations, and multinational conglomerates alike. The process of empowering managers and employees has almost limitless benefits.

Organizations should take a proactive rather than a reactive approach in their industry, and they should strive to influence, anticipate, and initiate rather than just respond to events. The strategic-management process embodies this approach to decision making. It represents a logical, systematic, and objective approach for determining an enterprise's future direction. The stakes are generally too high for strategists to use intuition alone in choosing among alternative courses of action. Successful strategists take the time to think about their businesses, where they are with their businesses, and what they want to be as organizations—and then they implement programs and policies to get from where they are to where they want to be in a reasonable period of time.

It is a known and accepted fact that people and organizations that plan ahead are much more likely to become what they want to become than those that do not plan at all. A good strategist plans and controls his or her plans, whereas a bad strategist never plans and then tries to control people! This textbook is devoted to providing you with the tools necessary to be a good strategist.

Key Terms and Concepts

Annual Objectives (p. 11)
Competitive Advantage (p. 8)
Empowerment (p. 15)
Environmental Scanning (p. 11)
External Opportunities (p. 10)
External Threats (p. 10)
Internal Strengths (p. 11)
Internal Weaknesses (p. 11)
Intuition (p. 7)
Long-Range Planning (p. 5)
Long-Term Objectives (p. 11)
Mission Statements (p. 10)
Policies (p. 12)

Retreats (p. 14)
Strategic Management (p. 5)
Strategic-Management Model (p. 13)
Strategic-Management Process (p. 5)
Strategic Planning (p. 5)
Strategies (p. 11)
Strategists (p. 9)
Strategy Evaluation (p. 6)
Strategy Formulation (p. 5)
Strategy Implementation (p. 6)
Sustained Competitive Advantage (p. 9)
Vision Statement (p. 10)

Issues for Review and Discussion

1. Are "strategic management" and "strategic planning" synonymous terms? Explain.
2. What are the three stages in strategic management? Which stage is more analytical? Which relies most on empowerment to be successful? Which relies most on statistics? Justify your answers.
3. Why do many firms move too hastily from vision/mission development to devising alternative strategies?
4. Why are strategic planning retreats often conducted away from the work site? How often should firms have a retreat, and who should participate in them?
5. Distinguish between long-range planning and strategic planning.
6. Compare a company's strategic plan with a football team's game plan.

7. Describe the three activities that comprise strategy evaluation.

8. How important do you feel "being adept at adapting" is for business firms? Explain.

9. Compare the opossum and turtle to the woolly mammoth and saber-toothed tiger in terms of being adept at adapting. What can we learn from the opossum and turtle?

10. As cited in the chapter, Edward Deming, a famous businessman, once said, "*In God we trust. All others bring data.*" What did Deming mean in terms of developing a strategic plan?

11. What strategies do you believe can save newspaper companies from extinction?

12. Distinguish between the concepts of vision and mission.

13. Your university has fierce competitors. List three external opportunities and three external threats that face your university.

14. List three internal strengths and three internal weaknesses that characterize your university.

15. List reasons why objectives are essential for organizational success.

16. List four strategies and a hypothetical example of each.

17. List six characteristics of annual objectives.

18. Why are policies especially important in strategy implementation?

19. What is a "retreat," and why do firms take the time and spend the money to have these?

20. Discuss the notion of strategic planning being more formal versus informal in an organization. On a 1 to 10 scale from formal to informal, what number best represents your view of the most effective approach? Why?

21. List 10 guidelines for making the strategic-planning process effective. Arrange your guidelines in prioritized order of importance in your opinion.

22. List what you feel are the five most important lessons for business that can be garnered from *The Art of War* book.

23. What is the fundamental difference between business strategy and military strategy in terms of basic assumptions?

24. Explain why the strategic management class is often called a "capstone course."

25. What aspect of strategy formulation do you think requires the most time? Why?

26. Why is strategy implementation often considered the most difficult stage in the strategic-management process?

27. Why is it so important to integrate intuition and analysis in strategic management?

28. Explain the importance of a vision and a mission statement.

29. Discuss relationships among objectives, strategies, and policies.

30. Why do you think some chief executive officers fail to use a strategic-management approach to decision making?

31. Discuss the importance of feedback in the strategic-management model.

32. How can strategists best ensure that strategies will be effectively implemented?

33. Give an example of a recent political development that changed the overall strategy of an organization.

34. Who are the major competitors of your college or university? What are their strengths and weaknesses? What are their strategies? How sucessful are these institutions compared to your college?

35. Would strategic-management concepts and techniques benefit foreign businesses as much as domestic firms? Justify your answer.

36. What do you believe are some potential pitfalls or risks in using a strategic-management approach to decision making?

37. In your opinion, what is the single major benefit of using a strategic-management approach to decision making? Justify your answer.

38. Compare business strategy and military strategy.

39. Why is it important for all business majors to study strategic management since most students will never become a chief executive officer nor even a top manager in a large company?

40. Describe the content available on the SMCO website at www.strategyclub.com

41. List four financial and four nonfinancial benefits of a firm engaging in strategic planning.

42. Why is it that a firm can normally sustain a competitive advantage for only a limited period of time?

43. Why it is not adequate to simply obtain competitive advantage?

44. How can a firm best achieve sustained competitive advantage?

Notes

1. Kathy Kiely, "Officials Say Auto CEOs Must Be Specific on Plans," *USA Today*, November 24, 2008, 3B.

2. Peter Drucker, *Management: Tasks, Responsibilities, and Practices* (New York: Harper & Row, 1974), 611.

3. Alfred Sloan, Jr., *Adventures of the White Collar Man* (New York: Doubleday, 1941), 104.

4. Quoted in Eugene Raudsepp, "Can You Trust Your Hunches?" *Management Review* 49, no. 4 (April 1960): 7.

5. Stephen Harper, "Intuition: What Separates Executives from Managers," *Business Horizons* 31, no. 5 (September–October 1988): 16.

6. Ron Nelson, "How to Be a Manager," *Success*, July–August 1985, 69.

7. Bruce Henderson, *Henderson on Corporate Strategy* (Boston: Abt Books, 1979), 6.

8. Robert Waterman, Jr., *The Renewal Factor: How the Best Get and Keep the Competitive Edge* (New York: Bantam, 1987). See also *BusinessWeek*, September 14, 1987, 100. Also, see *Academy of Management Executive* 3, no. 2 (May 1989): 115.

9. Jayne O'Donnell, "Shoppers Flock to Discount Stores," *USA Today*, February 25, 2009, B1.

10. Marc Saltzman, "Many Layoffs at Myspace Could Be Coming Soon," *USA Today*, January 4, 2011, 2B.

11. John Pearce II and Fred David, "The Bottom Line on Corporate Mission Statements," *Academy of Management Executive* 1, no. 2 (May 1987): 109.

12. Fred R. David, "How Companies Define Their Mission," *Long Range Planning* 22, no. 1 (February 1989): 91.

13. Jack Pearce and Richard Robinson, *Strategic Management*, 7th ed. (New York: McGraw-Hill, 2000), 8.

14. Ann Langley, "The Roles of Formal Strategic Planning," *Long Range Planning* 21, no. 3 (June 1988): 40.

15. Bernard Reimann, "Getting Value from Strategic Planning," *Planning Review* 16, no. 3 (May–June 1988): 42.

16. G. L. Schwenk and K. Schrader, "Effects of Formal Strategic Planning in Financial Performance in Small Firms: A Meta-Analysis," *Entrepreneurship and Practice* 3, no. 17 (1993): 53–64. Also, C. C. Miller and L. B. Cardinal, "Strategic Planning and Firm Performance: A Synthesis of More Than Two Decades of Research,"

Academy of Management Journal 6, no. 27 (1994): 1649–1665; Michael Peel and John Bridge, "How Planning and Capital Budgeting Improve SME Performance," *Long Range Planning* 31, no. 6 (October 1998): 848–856; Julia Smith, "Strategies for Start-Ups," *Long Range Planning* 31, no. 6 (October 1998): 857–872.

17. Gordon Greenley, "Does Strategic Planning Improve Company Performance?" *Long Range Planning* 19, no. 2 (April 1986): 106.

18. Adapted from www.mindtools.com/plreschn.html

19. Adapted from www.des.calstate.edu/limitations.html and www.entarga.com/stratplan/purposes.html

20. Dale McConkey, "Planning in a Changing Environment," *Business Horizons*, September–October 1988, 66.

21. R. T. Lenz, "Managing the Evolution of the Strategic Planning Process," *Business Horizons* 30, no. 1 (January–February 1987): 39.

22. Frederick Gluck, "Taking the Mystique out of Planning," *Across the Board*, July–August 1985, 59.

Current Readings

Bach, David, and David Bruce Allen. "What Every CEO Needs to Know About Nonmarket Strategy." *MIT Sloan Management Review* 51, no. 3 (Spring 2010): 41–44.

Bungay, Stephen. "How to Make the Most of Your Company's Strategy." *Harvard Business Review*, January–February 2011, 132–141.

Carmeli, Abraham, and Gideon D. Markman. "Capture, Governance, and Resilience: Strategy Implications from the History of Rome." *Strategic Management Journal* 32, no. 3 (March 2011): 322–341.

Chakravorti, Bhaskar. "Finding Competitive Advantage in Adversity." *Harvard Business Review*, November 2010, 102–109.

Chen, Eric L., Ritta Katila, Rory McDonald, and Kathleen M. Eisenhardt. "Life in the Fast Lane: Origins of Competitive Interaction in New vs. Established Markets." *Strategic Management Journal* 31, no. 13 (December 2010): 1527–1547.

Christensen, H. Kurt. "Defining Customer Value as the Driver of Competitive Advantage." *Strategy & Leadership* 38, no. 5 (2010): 20.

D'Aveni, Richard A., Giovanni Battista Dagnino, and Ken G. Smith. "The Age of Temporary Advantage." *Strategic Management Journal* 31, no. 13 (December 2010): 1371–1385.

Delios, Andrew. "How Can Organizations Be Competitive but Dare to Care?" *The Academy of Management Perspectives* 24, no. 3 (August 2010): 25–36.

Geroski, P. A., Jose Mata, and Pedro Portugal. "Founding Conditions and the Survival of New Firms." *Strategic Management Journal* 31, no. 5 (May 2010): 510–529.

Giesen, Edward, Eric Riddleberger, Richard Christner, and Ragna Bell. "When and How to Innovate Your Business Model." *Strategy & Leadership* 38, no. 4 (2010): 17.

Gilad, Benjamin. "War Gaming: Virtual Reality, Real Lessons." *Strategy & Leadership* 38, no. 6 (2010): 38.

Hansen, Morten T., Herminia Ibarra, and Urs Peyer. "The Best-Performing CEOs in the World." *Harvard Business Review*, January–February 2010, 104–113.

Harris, Jeanne, Elizabeth Craig, and Henry Egan. "How Successful Organizations Strategically Manage Their Analytic Talent." *Strategy & Leadership* 38, no. 3 (2010): 15.

Hitt, Michael A., Katalin Takacs Haynes, and Roy Serpa. "Strategic Leadership for the 21st Century." *Business Horizons* 53, no. 5 (September–October 2010): 437–444.

Jacobides, Michael G. "Strategy Tools for a Shifting Landscape." *Harvard Business Review*, January–February 2010, 76–85.

Marcel, Jeremy J., Pamela S. Barr, and Irene M. Duhaime. "The Influence of Executive Cognition on Competitive Dynamics." *Strategic Management Journal* 32, no. 2 (February 2011): 115–138.

Narayanan, V. K., Lee J. Zane, and Benedict Kemmerer. "The Cognitive Perspective in Strategy: An Integrative Review." *Journal of Management* 37, no. 1 (January 2011): 305–351.

Pfeffer, Jeffrey. "Building Sustainable Organizations: The Human Factor." *The Academy of Management Perspectives* 24, no. 1 (February 2010): 34–45.

Plambeck, Nilis, and Klaus Weber. "When the Glass is Half Full and Half Empty: CEO's Ambivalent Interpretations of Strategic Issues." *Strategic Management Journal* 31, no. 7 (July 2010): 689–710.

Rollinson, Randall. "Should Strategy Professionals Be Certified?" *Strategy & Leadership* 39, no. 1 (March 2011): 39–45.

Wilson, James W., and Soren Eilertsen. "How Did Strategic Planning Help During the Economic Crisis?" *Strategy & Leadership* 38, no. 2 (2010): 5.

Weiss, Jeff, Aram Donigian, and Jonathan Hughes. "Extreme Negotiations." *Harvard Business Review*, November 2010, 66–75.

Zand, Dale E. "Drucker's Strategic Thinking Process: Three Key Techniques." *Strategy & Leadership* 38, no. 3 (2010): 23.

THE COHESION CASE

The Walt Disney Company – 2011

Mernoush Banton

DIS

www.disney.com

Headquartered in Burbank, California, Walt Disney in April 2011 held a groundbreaking ceremony for its new theme park in Shanghai, China—after years of red tape and negotiations with the Chinese government. The new 963-acre park and resort will be 1/26th the size of the 40-square-mile Walt Disney World in Orlando, Florida. But it will be 50 percent larger than Disney Hong Kong, which lost $92.3 million in 2010. Disney will own 43 percent of the new Shanghai Park, a $1.9 billon investment for the company.

For eight decades, Walt Disney has entertained millions of people around the world with its theme parks, resorts, cruises, movies, TV shows, radio programming, and memorabilia. With characters such as Mickey Mouse, Donald Duck, and Goofy, Walt Disney is an American icon noted for wholesome family entertainment, especially through huge theme parks in Orlando, Anaheim, Paris, and Hong Kong.

Disney is the world's largest media conglomerate, owning the ABC television network and 10 broadcast stations, as well as cable networks such as ABC Family, Disney Channel, and ESPN (80%-owned). Walt Disney Studios produces films through the imprints Walt Disney Pictures, Disney Animation, and Pixar, and its Marvel Entertainment is a top comic book publisher and film producer. The company faces very intense competition, especially from NBC Universal and Paramount Pictures. In July 2011, Disney's ESPN acquired television rights to the Wimbledon tennis tournament for 12 years, replacing NBC which previously carried the annual event.

History

Mr. Walt Disney and his brother Roy arrived in California in the summer of 1923 to sell a cartoon called *Alice's Wonderland*. A distributor named M. J. Winkler contracted to distribute the *Alice Comedies* on October 16, 1923, and the Disney Brothers Cartoon Studio was founded. Over the years, the company produced many cartoons, from *Oswald the Lucky Rabbit* (1927) to *Silly Symphonies* (1932), *Snow White and the Seven Dwarfs* (1937), and *Pinocchio* and *Fantasia* (1940). The company name was changed to Walt Disney Studio in 1925. Mickey Mouse emerged in 1928 in the first cartoon with sound. In 1950, Disney completed its first live action film, *Treasure Island*, and in 1954, the company began television with the Disneyland anthology series. In 1955, Disney's most successful series, *The Mickey Mouse Club*, began. Also in 1955, the new Disneyland Park in Anaheim, California opened.

Disney created a series of releases from the 1950s through the 1970s, including *The Shaggy Dog, Zorro, Mary Poppins*, and *The Love Bug*. Mr. Walt Disney died in 1966. In 1969, Disney started its educational films and materials. Another important time in Disney's history was opening Walt Disney World in Orlando, Florida, in 1971. In 1982, the Epcot Center opened as part of Walt Disney World. The following year, Tokyo Disneyland opened.

After leaving network television in 1983, Disney introduced its cable network, The Disney Channel. In 1985, Disney's Touchstone division began the successful *Golden Girls* and *Disney Sunday Movie*. In 1988, Disney opened Grand Floridian Beach and Caribbean Beach Resorts at Walt Disney World along with three new gated attractions: the Disney/MGM Studios Theme Park, Pleasure Island, and Typhoon Lagoon. Filmmaking soon hit new heights as Disney for the first time led Hollywood studios in box-office gross. Some of the successful films were: *Who Framed Roger Rabbit, Good Morning Vietnam, Three Men and a Baby*, and, later, *Honey, I Shrunk the Kids, Dick Tracy, Pretty Woman*, and *Sister Act*. Disney moved into new areas by starting Hollywood Pictures and acquiring the Wrather Corp. (owner of the Disneyland Hotel) and television station KHJ (Los Angeles), which was renamed KCAL. In merchandising, Disney purchased Childcraft and opened numerous highly successful and profitable Disney Stores.

By 1992, Disney's animation reached new heights with *The Little Mermaid*, *Beauty and the Beast*, and *Aladdin*. Hollywood Records was formed to offer a wide selection of recordings ranging from rap to movie soundtracks. New television shows, such as *Live With Regis and Kathy Lee*, *Empty Nest*, *Dinosaurs*, and *Home Improvement*, expanded Disney's television base. For the first time, Disney moved into publishing, forming Hyperion Books, Hyperion Books for Children, and Disney Press, which released books on Disney and non-Disney subjects. In 1991, Disney purchased *Discover* magazine, the leading consumer science monthly. As a totally new venture, Disney was awarded, in 1993, the franchise for a National Hockey League team, the Mighty Ducks of Anaheim.

In 1992, Disneyland Paris opened in France. During the 1990s, Disney introduced Broadway shows, opened 725 Disney Stores, acquired the California Angels baseball team to add to its hockey team, opened Disney's Wide World of Sports in Walt Disney World, and acquired Capital Cities/ABC.

From 2000 to 2007, Disney created new attractions in its theme parks, produced many successful films, opened new hotels, and built Hong Kong Disneyland. More current Disney initiatives include working with Apple on a joint venture to promote the iPad 2 and iTunes, acquiring Marvel for $4.3 billion, and building the new Shanghai Park.

Internal Issues

Organizational Structure

As indicated in Exhibit 1, Walt Disney operates using a strategic business unit (SBU) organizational structure that consists of five diverse, but all family-entertainment, segments: 1) Media Networks, 2) Parks and Resorts, 3) Studio Entertainment, 4) Consumer Products, and 5) Interactive Media. The President, CEO, and director of Walt Disney is Robert Iger.

Six of the 10 highest paid CEOs in the world in 2010 came from the media or entertainment industries, inclnding Leslie Moonves of CBS, $56.9 million; David Zaslav of Discovery Communications, $42.6 million; Brian Roberts of Comcast, $31.1 million; Robert Iger of Walt Disney, $28 million; and Jeff Bewkes of Time Warner, $26.1 million.

The highest-paid CEO in the world in 2010 was Philippe Dauman of Viacom, the entertainment company that owns MTV, Nickelodeon, and Paramount Pictures. He received a pay package valued at $84.5 million, two and a half times what he made the year before. He signed a contract in April 2010 that included stock and options valued by the company at $54.2 million when they were granted.

EXHIBIT 1   Disney's Corporate Structure

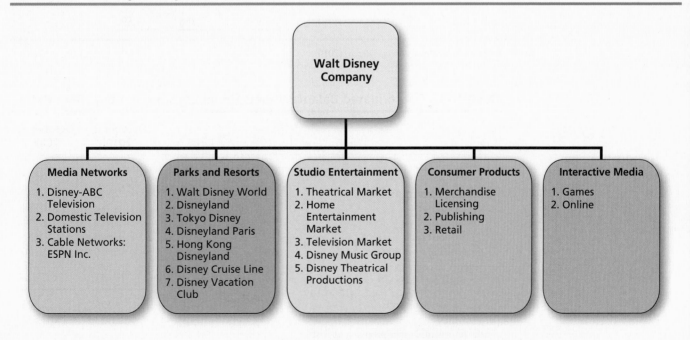

Mission/Vision

Disney does not have a mission statement or vision statement.

Finance

Disney's recent income statements and balance sheets are provided in Exhibits 2 and 3 respectively. Note the 20 percent increase in net income in 2010 and the $24 billion in goodwill. For the six months ended April 2, 2011, Disney's revenues increased 8 percent to $19.793 billion, while the company's net income increased 25 percent to $2.244 billion.

EXHIBIT 2 Consolidated Income Statement (in millions, except per share data)

				% Change Better (Worse)	
	2010	2009	2008	2010 vs. 2009	2009 vs. 2008
Revenues	$ 38,063	$ 36,149	$ 37,843	5 %	(4)%
Costs and expense	(31,337)	(30,452)	(30,400)	(3)%	— %
Restructuring and impairment charges	(270)	(492)	(39)	45 %	— %
Other income (expense)	140	342	(59)	(59)%	— %
Net interest expense	(409)	(466)	(524)	12 %	11 %
Equity in the income of investees	440	577	581	(24)%	(1)%
Income before income taxes	6,627	5,658	7,402	17 %	(24)%
Income taxes	(2,314)	(2,049)	(2,673)	(13)%	23 %
Net income	4,313	3,609	4,729	20 %	(24)%
Less: Net income attributable to noncontrolling interest	(350)	(302)	(302)	(16)%	— %
Net income attributable to The Walt Disney Company (Disney)	$ 3,963	$ 3,307	$ 4,427	20 %	(25)%
Earnings per share attributable to Disney					
Diluted	$ 2.03	$ 1.76	$ 2.28	15 %	(23)%
Basic	$ 2.07	$ 1.78	$ 2.34	16 %	(24)%
Weighted average number of common equivalent shares outstanding:					
Diluted	1,948	1,875	1,948		
Basic	1,915	1,856	1,890		

Source: Walt Disney Company, *Annual Report* (2010).

EXHIBIT 3 Consolidated Balance Sheets (in millions, except per share data)

	October 2, 2010	October 3, 2009
ASSETS		
Current assets		
Cash and cash equivalents	$ 2,722	$ 3,417
Receivables	5,784	4,854
Inventories	1,442	1,271
Television costs	678	631
Deferred income taxes	1,018	1,140
Other current assets	581	576
Total current assets	12,225	11,889
Film and television costs	4,773	5,125
Investments	2,513	2,554
Parks resorts mid other property, at cost		

EXHIBIT 3   **(Continued)**

	October 2, 2010	October 3, 2009
Attractions, buildings and equipment	32,875	32,475
Accumulated depreciation	(18,373)	(17,395)
	14,502	15,080
Projects in progress	2,180	1,350
Land	1,124	1,167
	17,806	17,597
Intangible assets, net	5,081	2,247
Goodwill	24,100	21,683
Other assets	2,708	2,022
Total assets	**$ 69,206**	**$ 63,117**
LIABILITIES		
Current liabilities		
Accounts payable and other accrued liabilities	$ 6,109	$ 5,616
Current portion of borrowings	2,350	1,206
Unearned royalties and other advances	2,541	2,112
Total current liabilities	**11,000**	**8,934**
Borrowings	10,130	11,495
Deferred income taxes	2,630	1,819
Other long-term liabilities	6,104	5,444
Commitments and contingencies	1,823	1,692
Total liabilities	**31,687**	**29,383**
EQUITY		
Preferred stock $.01 par value		
Authorized—100 million shares, Issued—none	—	—
Common stock $.01 par value		
Authorized—4.6 billion shares at October 2, 2010 and 3.6 billion shares at October 3, 2009		
Issued—2.7 billion shares at October 2, 2010 and 2.6 billion shares at October 3 2009	28,736	27,038
Retained earnings	34,327	31,033
Accumulated other comprehensive loss	(1,881)	(1,644)
	61,182	56,427
Treasury stock, at cost, 803.1 million shares at October 2, 2010 and 781.7 million shares at October 3, 2009	(23,663)	(22,693)
Total Shareholders' equity	37,519	33,734
Total liabilities and equity	**$ 69,206**	**$ 63,117**

Source: Walt Disney Company, *Annual Report* (2010).

By-Segment Financials

Exhibit 4 reveals Disney's revenue and operating income by business segment. Note that Disney's Media Networks segment brings in the most revenues and operating income, followed by the Parks & Resorts segment. For the six months ended April 2, 2011, Disney's Studio Entertainment revenues declined 6 percent to $3.272 billion, while that segment's operating income declined 3 percent to $452 million. Also for that six month period, Disney's Interactive Media operating income declined 97 percent to a loss of $128 million. There are obviously some problems in these segments that need to be addressed.

As indicated in Exhibit 5, Disney derives 74 percent of its revenue and 72 percent of its operating income from business in the USA/Canada. All geographic segments had increased revenue and profits in 2010, with Europe being second behind the USA/Canada.

Disney revenues in 2010 were derived from Media Networks (45 percent), Parks & Resorts (28 percent), Studio Entertainment (18 percent), Consumer Products (7 percent), and Interactive Media

EXHIBIT 4   Revenue and Operating Income by Segment

(in millions)	2010	2009	2008	% of change 2010 vs. 2009	% of change 2009 vs. 2008
Revenues					
Media Networks	$17,162	$16,209	15,857	6%	2%
Parks & Resorts	10,761	10,667	11,504	1%	(7)%
Studio Entertainment	6,701	6,136	7,348	9%	(16)%
Consumer Products	2,678	2,425	2,415	10%	–
Interactive Media	761	712	719	7%	(1)%
Total Consolidated Revenues	$38,063	$36,149	$37,843	5%	(4)%
Segment operating income					
Media Networks	$5,132	$4,765	$4,981	8%	(4)%
Parks & Resorts	1,318	1,418	1,897	(7)%	(25)%
Studio Entertainment	693	175	1,086	296%	(84)%
Consumer Products	677	609	778	11%	(22)%
Interactive Media	(234)	(295)	(258)	21%	(14)%
Total segment operating income	$7,586	$6,672	$8,484	14%	(21)%

Source: Walt Disney Company, *Annual Report* (2010).

EXHIBIT 5   Revenue and Operating Income by Region

(in millions)	2010	2009	2008
Revenues			
USA/Canada	$28,279	$27,508	$28,506
Europe	6,550	6,012	6,805
Asia Pacific	2,320	1,860	1,811
Latin America and Other	914	769	721
	$38,063	$36,149	$37,843
Segment operating income			
USA/Canada	$ 5,474	$ 4,923	$ 6,500
Europe	1,275	1,158	1,423
Asia Pacific	620	430	386
Latin America and Other	217	161	175
	$ 7,586	$ 6,672	$ 8,484

Source: Walt Disney Company, *Annual Report* (2010).

(2 percent). Operating income was derived from Media Networks (68 percent), Parks & Resorts (17 percent), Studio Entertainment (9 percent), Consumer Products (9 percent), and Interactive Media (a loss). These percentages reveal weakness in Studio Entertainment, since this segment creates 18 percent of revenues but only 9 percent of operating income. The Interactive Media segment is also a weak part of the company since that division is losing money.

Media Networks

Disney's Media Networks segment includes domestic broadcast television, television production and distribution operations, domestic television stations, international and domestic cable networks, domestic broadcast radio networks and stations, and publishing and digital operations. Disney owns and operates the ABC Television Network, which reaches 99 percent of all U.S. television households.

The Disney-ABC Television Group (Disney-ABC TV) comprises Disney's global entertainment and news television properties, owned television stations group, and radio and publishing businesses. The group's portfolio includes ABC Television Network, ABC Owned Television Stations Group, ABC Studios, Disney Channels Worldwide, ABC Family, SOAPnet, Disney

ABC Domestic Television, Disney Media Distribution, Hyperion, and Radio Disney network. The ABC Television Network operates more than 220 affiliated stations across the United States. ABC Owned Television Stations Group owns 10 television stations in the U.S. that include WABC-TV, KABC-TV, WLS-TV, WPVI-TV, and others. ABC Studios develops, produces, and distributes entertainment content across broadcast and cable television and digital platforms.

Disney Channels Worldwide comprises 94 kid and family entertainment channels available in 169 countries and 33 languages. ABC Family is a mixture of series and movies. SOAPnet owns character-driven soapy drama, from daytime and primetime soaps to reality shows and movies. Disney ABC Domestic Television provides motion pictures and TV programming to U.S.-based media platforms. Disney Media Distribution is an international distributor of branded and nonbranded content to all platforms. Hyperion publishes fiction and nonfiction titles for adults. Radio Disney is available in more than 40 U.S. markets and on satellite radio, mobile apps, and the web. Additionally, Disney-ABC TV holds equity interest in A&E Television Networks.

Within Media Networks, Disney also produces and distributes live action and animated television programming under the ABC Studios, ABC Media Productions, and ABC Family Productions labels. Some of their prime time programming includes the dramas *Army Wives, Brothers & Sisters, Castle, Criminal Minds, Desperate Housewives, Grey's Anatomy,* and *Private Practice;* the returning half-hour comedy *Cougar Town;* new prime-time series that premiered in the fall of 2010, including the one-hour dramas *Body of Proof, Detroit 187, No Ordinary Family, Ugly Betty,* and *Brothers & Sisters*; and *Jimmy Kimmel Live* for late night and a variety of primetime specials for network television and live-action syndicated programming. Syndicated programming includes *Live! with Regis and Kelly,* a daily talk show, and *Who Wants to Be a Millionaire,* a game show.

As listed in Exhibit 6, Disney owns 10 television stations. Note that six are located in the top-10 television markets in the United States.

Disney's cable networks group provides national programming networks and licenses television programming both domestically and internationally. This business derives a majority of its revenue from fees charged to cable, satellite, and telecommunication service providers. Typically, cable networks operate under multi-year agreements. This helps Disney sell time for commercial announcements. Certain programming developed by cable networks is also distributed in (1) DVD format by the home entertainment division in the Studio Entertainment segment, (2) online via Disney's Internet sites such as ESPN.com, and (3) on third party services such as iTunes.

Radio Disney, a 24/7 radio network for kids, teens, and families, also operates under this segment. Radio Disney is available on 37 radio stations, 31 of which the company owns, and on RadioDisney.com, Sirius and XM satellite radio, iTunes Radio Tuner, XM/DIRECTV, and mobile phones. Radio Disney programming can be downloaded via the iTunes Music Store. Radio Disney is also available throughout most of South America via a separate Spanish language terrestrial broadcast.

EXHIBIT 6   Disney-Owned Television Stations

Market	TV Station	Television Market Ranking
New York, NY	WABC-TV	1
Los Angeles, CA	KABC-TV	2
Chicago, IL	WLS-TV	3
Philadelphia, PA	WPVI-TV	4
San Francisco, CA	KGO-TV	6
Houston, TX	KTRK-TV	10
Raleigh-Durham, NC	WTVD-TV	26
Fresno, CA	KFSN-TV	55
Flint, MI	WJRT-TV	68
Toledo, OH	WTVG-TV	73

EXHIBIT 7 Media Networks Segment: Revenue and Operating Income

(in millions)	2010	2009	2008	Change 2010 vs. 2009	2008 vs. 2007
Revenues					
Cable Networks	$ 11,475	$ 10,555	$ 10,041	9%	10%
Broadcasting	5,687	5,654	6,075	1%	2%
	$ 17,162	$ 16,209	$ 16,116	6%	7%
Segment operating income					
Cable Networks	$ 4,473	$ 4,260	$ 4,100	5%	15%
Broadcasting	659	505	655	30%	(6)%
	$ 5,132	$ 4,765	$ 4,755	8%	11%

Source: Walt Disney Company, *Annual Report* (2010).

As indicated in Exhibit 7, Disney's Cable Networks reported a 9 percent increase in revenues in 2010, and the Broadcasting business reported a 30 percent increase in operating income. For the six months ended April 2, 2011, revenues from Cable Networks were $5.894 billion, up 16 percent, while Broadcasting revenues were up 4 percent to $13.073 billion. Note in Exhibit 8 that Disney has 109 million subscribers to its Disney Channel outside the United States versus 100 million domestic subscribers.

Disney's ESPN recently signed a 20-year agreement with The University of Texas (UT) and IMG College to develop and operate a year-round, 24-hour network dedicated to UT. The network will offer a variety of content ranging from sports to academic events. For the first time ever, ESPN offered the NBA finals in 2011 in 3-D.

EXHIBIT 8 Disney's International Cable Satellite Networks and Broadcast Operations

Property	Estimated Domestic Subscribers (in millions)[1]	Estimated International Subscribers (in millions)[2]	Ownership %
ESPN			
ESPN	98	–	80.0
ESPN2	97	–	80.0
ESPN Classic	41	–	80.0
ESPNEWS	74	–	80.0
ESPN Deportes	5	–	80.0
ESPNU	74	–	80.0
Disney Channels Worldwide			
Disney Channel	100	109	100.0
Playhouse Disney	–	45	100.0
Disney XD	78	84	100.0
Disney Cinemagic	–	10	73.3
Hungama	–	7	100.0
ABC Family	99	–	100.0
SOAPnet	76	–	100.0
A&E / Lifetime			
A&E	100	–	42.1
Lifetime Television	100	–	42.1
The History Channel	99	–	42.1
Lifetime Movie Network	79	–	42.1
The Biography Channel	62	–	42.1
History International	61	–	42.1
Lifetime Real Women[2]	16	–	42.1

(1) Estimated U.S. subscriber counts according to Nielsen Media Research as of September 2010.

(2) Subscriber counts are not rated by Nielsen and are based on internal management reports. ESPN and A&E programming are distributed internationally.

Source: Walt Disney Company, *Form 10K* (2010).

EXHIBIT 9   Disney versus News Corp. and Time Warner

	Disney	News Corp.	Time Warner	Industry
$Market Cap:	81.83B	48.88B	39.01B	1.41M
#Employees:	149,000	51,000	31,000	N/A
$Revenue:	39.04B	33.08B	26.89B	79.67M
Gross Margin:	18.58%	36.13%	44.42%	40.88%
$EBITDA:	8.99B	5.76B	6.46B	−7.17M
Operating Margin:	18.58%	13.97%	20.52%	−308.64%
$Net Income:	4.42B	3.13B	2.56B	N/A
EPS:	2.27	1.20	2.25	−5.62
P/E:	19.02	15.53	15.87	N/A

Industry = Entertainment - Diversified

Source: Based on information at finance.yahoo.com (March, 2011)

Competitors in Media Networks

CBS, News Corp., and Time Warner are direct competitors in Disney's Media Networks segment, as indicated in Exhibit 9.

Time Warner is composed of five divisions: AOL, Cable, Filmed Entertainment, Networks, and Publishing. Time Warner owns Time Inc., AOL, Warner Brothers, TBS Networks, and HBO. Time Warner is a media and entertainment company organized in three primary segments: Networks, Filmed Entertainment, and Publishing.

- The Networks segment provides domestic and international networks and premium pay television programming services, which consist of the multichannel HBO and Cinemax pay television programming services.
- The Filmed Entertainment segment produces and distributes theatrical motion pictures, television shows, animation, and other programming; distributes home video products; and licenses rights to its feature films, television programming, and characters. These also compete with Disney.
- The Publishing segment publishes magazines, operates various websites, and is also involved in direct-marketing businesses. It publishes magazines on celebrities; sports; lifestyle, beauty, and fashion; life, home, body, and soul; news and events; economic and business developments.

Exhibit 10 provides Time Warner's 2010 revenue by segment.

News Corp. is a huge, diversified international media and entertainment company with $33 billion in annual revenue, operating in eight industry segments: Filmed Entertainment, Television, Cable Network Programming, Direct Broadcast Satellite Television, Magazines and Inserts, Newspapers, Book Publishing, and Other. The company has been moving aggressively toward digital technologies such as broadband, mobility, storage, and wireless. News Corp. owns MySpace.com, the Internet's popular social networking site, and IGN.com (a gaming and entertainment site).

EXHIBIT 10   Time Warner's Revenue (in millions) by Segment in 2010

Segment	Revenue	Operating Income
Network	$12,480	$4,224
Film Entertainment	11,622	1,107
Publishing	3,675	515

Source: Time Warner Inc., *Form 10K* (2010).

News Corp. owns Fox TV, which has an average audience of 6.7 million every night, followed by CBS with 7.6 million viewers during that prime time, Walt Disney's ABC with 5.4 million viewers per night, and finally NBC (owed by General Electric) with 4.8 million viewers during each prime-time period. News Corp. owns Dow Jones & Co. and the *Wall Street Journal*. News Corp. owns Liberty Media Corp. and a 41 percent interest in the DIRECTV Group, Inc.

Several uncertainties exist in this industry, including splitting up the royalties of DVD distribution fees with screenwriters and competing with lower cable advertising rates and Digital Video Recorder (DVR) devices. In addition, Apple, Inc. is aggressive in forming partnerships with specific media networks. Time Warner Cable Inc. has started a dispute with several large media companies regarding their ability to beam live TV channels to Apple Inc. iPads. This has created tension among major TV-industry players as they each want to offer their own programming over the Internet through hardware companies such as Apple.

Advertising dollars are a major source of income for Walt Disney, which competes with other advertising media such as newspapers, magazines, billboards, and the Internet. This media industry is becoming digitized in almost all areas, and delivery of media is now expanded from traditional TV and radio to handheld devices. The media industry also is benefiting by the introduction of digital television platforms that make it more appealing for companies to develop exclusive programming packages. This should help the companies to sell more advertising time based on the unique customer base.

Parks and Resorts

Disney owns and operates Walt Disney World Resort in Florida, the Disneyland Resort in California, the Disney Vacation Club, the Disney Cruise Line, Tokyo Disney Resort, and Adventures by Disney. Disney has 51 percent ownership in Disneyland Resort Paris and 47 percent ownership in Hong Kong Disneyland. Disney's newest theme park will be in the Pudong district of Shanghai.

The new 4,000-passenger ship *Disney Dream* was christened at Port Canaveral in 2011 and was designed especially for families. *Disney Dream* joins *Disney Magic* and *Disney Wonder*, with another new ship, *Disney Fantasy,* scheduled to join the Disney fleet in 2012. *Disney Dream* will sail to Disney's private island, Castaway Cay. Exhibit 11 summarizes Disney's key park and resort holdings.

Revenue in this segment is generated from the sale of admissions tickets to the theme parks; hotel room charges per night; sales from merchandise, food, and beverages; rentals and sales from vacation club properties; and sales of cruise vacations. Most costs and expenses in this segment are driven from labor; depreciation of assets; costs of merchandise, food, and beverages; marketing and advertising; repairs and maintenance; and entertainment.

Disney revenues from its Parks and Resorts division increased only 1 percent in 2010, or $94 million, to $10.761 billion, due to a decrease of $38 million at domestic resorts and an increase

EXHIBIT 11   Disney's Offerings Under Parks & Resorts

1. Walt Disney World Resorts:	Epcot	Disney-MGM Studios	Magic Kingdom	Disney's Animal Kingdom	Resort & Facilities
2. Disneyland Resort:	Disneyland	Disneyland's California Adventure	Resort & Facilities		
3. Disneyland Resort Paris:	Disneyland Park	Walt Disney Studios Park	Resort & Facilities		
4. Hong Kong Disneyland Resort:	Hong Kong Disneyland	Hotels			
5. Tokyo Disney Resort:	Tokyo Disneyland	Tokyo DisneySea	Hotels & Resort Facilities		
6. Disney Vacation Club:					
7. Disney Cruise Line:					
8. Adventures by Disney:					
9. Walt Disney Imagineering:					

Source: Walt Disney Company, *Form 10K* (2010).

of $132 million at Disney's international resorts. Domestic Parks and Resorts revenues declined due to one fewer week of operations, volume decrease in lower vacation club ownership sales, lower hotel occupancy, and lower passenger cruise ship days. These decreases were partially offset by higher guest spending due to higher average daily hotel room rate and higher average ticket prices. In contrast, the revenue increase in international operations was due to higher guest spending and real estate property sales. Although the impact was nominal, higher attendance and hotel occupancy also helped revenue sales in the international market. Segment operating income decreased by 7 percent, or by $100 million, from 2009 to 2010, mostly due to improvements at international operations.

For the quarter ending April 2, 2011, Parks and Resorts revenues increased 7 percent to $2.6 billion but operating income decreased 3 percent to $145 million. Exhibit 12 provides attendance information for Disney's Parks and Resorts segment.

The Parks and Resorts segment of Disney is growing, having recently added 481 units to its resort in Aulani (an oceanfront resort in Hawaii); two new ships, the *Disney Dream* and *Disney Fantasy;* new personal guide tours; new services and attractions; preferred seating and front-of-line access to rides; as well as new package deals for major corporations and schools.

Disney has plans to offer more stand-alone theme parks and resorts in cities and beach resorts, as well as Disney branded retail and dining districts, and smaller and more sophisticated parks. Disney wants to utilize its brand name to expand in other areas of the travel business. The company has built time-share vacation homes in popular places in the United States. Some of the challenges in this marketing strategy have been tailoring the niche attractions to local markets while keeping the Disney brand reputation. There is also a challenge of avoiding the cannibalization of existing parks and attractions. Food costs increased dramatically in 2010/2011 and negatively impacted Disney's earnings. The United Nations reported that global food costs jumped 25 percent in 2010.

Some additional data for the Disney Parks and Resorts segment is given in Exhibit 13.

Competitors in Parks and Resorts

Disney's theme parks and cruise lines compete worldwide with all other forms of lodging, tourism, and recreational activities. Many uncontrollable factors may influence the profitability of the leisure-time industry such as business cycle and exchange rate fluctuations, travel industry trends, amount of available leisure time, oil and transportation prices, and weather patterns. Seasonality is another concern for this segment as all Disney theme parks and the associated resort facilities are operated on a year-round basis. Peak theme park attendance and resort occupancy generally occur during the summer when school vacations take place and during early-winter and spring-holiday periods.

EXHIBIT 12   Disney Parks and Resorts Data

	Domestic		International[2]		Total	
	2010	2009	2010	2009	2010	2009
Parks						
Increase in Attendance	(1)%	2%	1%	1%	(1)%	2%
Increase in Per Capita Guest	3%	(6)%	3%	(12)%	3%	(7)%
Spending Hotels[1]						
Occupancy	82%	87%	85%	85%	82%	86%
Available Room Nights (in thousands)	9,629	9,549	2,466	2,473	12,095	12,022
Per Room Guest Spending	$ 224	$ 214	$ 273	$ 261	$ 234	$ 223

Source: Walt Disney Company, *Annual Report* (2010).

(1) Per room guest spending consists of the average daily hotel room rate as well as guest spending on food, beverages, and merchandise at the hotels. Hotel statistics include rentals of Disney Vacation Club units.

(2) Per capita guest spending and per room guest spending include the impact of foreign currency translation. Guest spending statistics for Disneyland Paris were converted from euros into U.S. dollars at weighted average exchange rates of 1.36 and 1.35 for fiscal 2010 and 2009, respectively.

EXHIBIT 13 Parks and Resorts: Revenue and Operating Income

(in millions)	2010	2009	% Change
Revenues			
Domestic	$ 8,404	$ 8,442	–
International	2,357	2,225	6%
	$10,761	$10,667	1%
Segment operating income	$ 1,318	$ 1,418	(7)%

Source: Walt Disney Company, *Annual Report* (2010).

According to Datamonitor, the global leisure facilities industry generated a total revenue of $130.7 billion in 2009. Theme parks contributed 18.8 percent or $24.7 billion of that total. Walt Disney is the leader in theme parks with an 8.4 percent share of the market, and Six Flags has 0.8 percent.

Six Flags is based in Oklahoma City, Oklahoma, and owns 20 parks across the United States, Mexico, Canada, and soon in Dubai and Qatar, with more than $1 billion in revenue. Six Flags recently acquired Dick Clark productions, producing television hits such as the *American Music Awards, The Golden Globe Awards, the Academy of Country Music Awards, Dick Clark's New Year's Rockin' Eve* and *So You Think You Can Dance*.

Established in 1977, Ocean Park in Hong Kong aggressively competes with Disney. Ocean Park is a theme park that covers over 870,000 square meters and receives more than five million tourists each year. Ocean Park has two new sightseeing locations in Shanghai aimed at attracting tourists from regions such as the Yangtze River Delta. Ocean Park is increasing the number of travel attractions to 70 from the current 35 and will complete the construction of four themed travel attractions between 2010 and 2013. Residents in Hong Kong are not very impressed with the small park Disney built there, since many have visited Disneyland in Tokyo or Anaheim.

NBC Universal is perhaps the largest threat to Disney in this segment. NBC Universal owns Universal Studios Hollywood and a 50 percent interest in the Universal Orlando Resort. Comcast Corp. owns a controlling 51 percent interest in NBC Universal, with General Electric holding a 49 percent stake. NBC Universal has license agreements with Universal Studios Japan and Universal Studios Singapore. Each year, millions of guests visit Universal's theme parks in Florida, California, and Japan rather than going to Disney parks.

Universal Studios Singapore has over 15 new attractions, and in late 2011 debuted "Transformers," a mega-attraction based on the blockbuster hit movies of the same name. A Universal Studios theme park has been licensed for Dubai, and a Universal Studios theme park in Korea has also been announced. Universal Studios Hollywood is "The Entertainment Capital of L.A." and the only movie and television-based theme park to offer guests the authenticity of a working movie studio. Within its gates, the rich heritage of movies past and the excitement of today's Hollywood come alive. The theme park features the world's largest, most intense 3-D experience: "King Kong 360 3-D Created by Peter Jackson." Other groundbreaking attractions include "Revenge of the Mummy—The Ride," "Shrek 4-D," "Jurassic Park—The Ride," and "The Simpsons Ride," as well as the world-renowned Studio Tour, which takes guests behind the scenes of such landmark TV and movie locations as Steven Spielberg's *War of the Worlds*.

In Orlando, Florida, there are Universal Studios and Islands of Adventure—as well as Universal CityWalk, a 30-acre restaurant, shopping, and nighttime entertainment complex, and three magnificently themed on-site hotels: the Loews Portofino Bay Hotel, Hard Rock Hotel, and the Loews Royal Pacific Resort. Flagship experiences featured in the theme parks include "The Simpsons Ride," "Revenge of the Mummy—The Ride," "The Incredible Hulk Coaster," and "The Amazing Adventures of Spider-Man." On June 18, 2010, Universal Orlando revealed "The Wizarding World of Harry Potter" at Islands of Adventure—an entire land that brings one of the most popular stories of our time to life.

Carnival Corp. is the world's largest cruise operator, owning a dozen cruise lines and about 100 ships with a total passenger capacity of more than 190,000. The company operates in North America primarily through its Princess Cruise Line, Holland America, and Seabourn luxury cruise brands, as well as its flagship Carnival Cruise Lines unit. Brands such as AIDA, P&O Cruises, and Costa Cruises offer services to passengers in Europe, and the Cunard Line runs luxury trans-Atlantic liners. Carnival operates as a dual-listed company with UK-based Carnival plc forming a single enterprise under a unified executive team. Royal Caribbean is another cruise company that competes with Disney's cruise ships.

Studio Entertainment

Disney produces live-action and animated motion pictures, direct-to-video programming, musical recordings, and livestage plays. Disney motion pictures are distributed under the names Theatrical Market, Home Entertainment Market, Television Market, Disney Music Group, and Disney Theatrical Productions. Disney has also licensed the rights to produce and distribute feature films such as *Spider-Man, The Fantastic Four,* and *X-Men* to third party studios. Disney earns a licensing fee on these films, whereas the third-party studio incurs the cost to produce and distribute the films.

In July 2010, Disney sold the majority of the assets of their Miramax Film Corp. for $663 million. Disney distributes live-action motion pictures produced by DreamWorks under the Touchstone Pictures banner. Disney released in 2011 the award winning albums 1) *TRON: Legacy,* 2) *TRON: The Original Classic Special Edition,* and 3) *TRON: Legacy Reconfigured* to Blu-ray 3-D and other platforms. The albums peaked at No. 4 on the Billboard 200. Two weeks after becoming the highest-grossing animated film of all time, *Toy Story 3* exceeded the $1 billion mark at the global box office, joining *Alice in Wonderland* as the second $1 billion film in 2010, and made Disney the first company ever to have two $1 billion films released in one year.

In 2010, Disney's Studio Entertainment segment revenue contributed $6.7 billion to the company's sales, approximately 17.6 percent. While this segment contributed only 9 percent to the total operating income, its percentage change from 2009 to 2010 was an increase of 296 percent, as indicated in Exhibit 14. However, for the quarter that ended April 2, 2011, studio entertainment revenues decreased 13 percent to $1.3 billion while operating income decreased 65 percent to $77 million.

Competitors in Studio Entertainment

The Studio Entertainment segment of Disney competes primarily with 1) NBC Universal (which is owned by General Electric) and 2) Paramount Pictures.

NBC Universal is one of the world's leading media companies in the development, production, and marketing of entertainment, news, and information to a global audience. The new company's assets include some of the most recognized and valuable brands in the industry, such as television networks NBC, Telemundo, USA Network, Sci-Fi Channel, Bravo, Trio, CNBC, and MSNBC (jointly owned with Microsoft); film studio Universal Pictures; television production studios Universal Television and NBC Studios; a stations group comprising 29 NBC and Telemundo television stations; and interests in five theme parks including Universal Studios Hollywood and Universal Orlando. International assets include excellent positions in the sale and distribution of video and DVD titles, television programming, and feature films in more than 200 countries; and distinctive television channels across Europe, Asia, and Latin America.

Universal offers an all-audience family film business with Illumination Entertainment. Its first production, the 3-D CGI blockbuster *Despicable Me*, was one of the highest-grossing and most profitable films of 2010. In addition to filmed entertainment, Universal produces live stage productions, including the cultural phenomenon *Wicked* and the 10-time Tony Award-winning *Billy Elliot the Musical*.

EXHIBIT 14   Studio Entertainment: Revenue and Operating Income

(in millions)	2010	2009	% Change
Revenues			
Theatrical Distribution	$ 2,050	$ 1,325	55%
Home Entertainment	2,666	2,762	(3)%
Television Distribution and Other	1,985	2,049	(3)%
Total Revenues	$ 6,701	$ 6,136	9%
Segment operating income	$ 693	$ 175	296%

Source: Walt Disney Company, *Annual Report* (2010).

Paramount Pictures Corp., a division of Viacom, is a global producer and distributor of filmed entertainment, with robust and multifaceted divisions across all areas including digital, home entertainment, network and cable television distribution, studio operations, and consumer products and recreation. Paramount has many respected brands, including MTV Networks and BET Networks. Paramount consists of several film labels, including the legendary Paramount Pictures; the leading youth brand, MTV Films; the preeminent family entertainment label, Nickelodeon Movies; and specialty film labels Paramount Vantage and Paramount Classics.

Paramount has established distribution deals with iconic comic book creator Marvel Entertainment and renowned animated film producer DreamWorks Animation. The company's global business operations include Paramount Digital Entertainment, Paramount Famous Productions, Paramount Home Entertainment, Paramount Pictures International, Paramount Licensing Inc., Paramount Studio Group, and Worldwide Television Distribution.

As the only major motion picture studio based in Hollywood, Paramount is located on an expansive 64-acre state-of-the-art production and business center. During its nearly 100-year history, the studio's backlot has served as the production site for thousands of notable feature films, television shows, and commercials. Paramount's facilities include 30 sound stages, a newly constructed "Chicago Street," as well as the historic and popular "New York Street," which features 10 distinct city neighborhood backdrops.

Paramount has some of the most respected and talented filmmakers and producers in the business, including J.J. Abrams, Brad Pitt, and Martin Scorsese. Paramount has distributed a host of critically acclaimed and box office hits over the last several years, including *Cloverfield, Transformers, Indiana Jones & The Kingdom of the Crystal Skull, Norbit, Blades of Glory,* and *Disturbia.*

Paramount's library consists of more than 1,000 motion picture titles, some television programming, and varying rights for approximately 2,500 additional motion picture titles. Paramount has numerous Oscar® winning films including 2007's *No Country For Old Men* (co-produced with Miramax Films); 2006's groundbreaking documentary featuring Vice President Al Gore, *An Inconvenient Truth*; the moving historical drama *Braveheart* directed by Mel Gibson in 1995; the worldwide sensation starring Tom Hanks, *Forrest Gump* (1994); and the highest-grossing motion picture of all time, *Titanic* (1997)—as well as enduring classics such as *Breakfast at Tiffany's* (1961), *The Ten Commandments* (1956), and *Sunset Boulevard* (1950), among others.

Consumer Products

Disney's Consumer Products segment includes partners with licenses, manufacturers, publishers, and retailers worldwide who design, promote, and sell a wide variety of products based on new and existing Disney characters. Product offerings are: 1) Character Merchandise and Publications Licensing, 2) Books and Magazines, and 3) the Disney Store. Disney released in mid-2011 a new toy line that captured the fantasy, action, and adventure of *Pirates of the Caribbean: On Stranger Tides*. Disney is perhaps the largest worldwide licensor of character-based merchandise and producer/distributor of children's film-related products based on retail sales.

In 2010, Disney revenues from this segment increased 9 percent to $1.7 billion. Sales growth at the Disney Stores benefited from the acquisition of Marvel and the strong performance of *Toy Story* merchandise. Operating income of this segment increased 11 percent to $677 million, as indicated in Exhibit 15. Disney is on schedule to add more than 25 new and remodeled Disney Store locations in 2011 and plans to transform all of the more than 350 Disney Store locations around the world.

EXHIBIT 15   Consumer Products: Revenue and Operating Income

(in millions)	2010	2009	% Change
Revenues			
Licensing and Publishing	$ 1,725	$ 1,584	9%
Retail and Other	953	841	13%
Total Revenues	$ 2,678	$ 2,425	10%
Segment operating income	$ 677	$ 609	11%

Source: Walt Disney Company, *Annual Report* (2010).

Disney offers licensing of toys, apparel, home décor and furnishings, stationery, accessories, health and beauty products, food, footwear, and consumer electronics. Some of the major brand names licensed and for which royalties are earned include: *Mickey Mouse, Disney Princess, Toy Story, Winnie the Pooh, Cars, Disney Fairies, Hannah Montana*, and the Marvel properties, including *Spider-Man* and *Iron Man*.

Disney Publishing Worldwide (DPW) publishes children's books and magazines in multiple countries and languages. Most titles are related to Disney's cartoon characters such as *Mickey Mouse, Disney Princess, Winnie the Pooh, Cars, Disney Fairies*, and *Toy Story*. For the quarter that ended April 2, 2011, Disney's Consumer Products revenues increased 5 percent to $626 million despite decreases in DPW revenues.

Disney owns and operates many retail stores, both brick and mortar and through Internet sites, under the name of the Disney brand. Actual stores are typically located in large shopping malls and retail complexes and offer a wide range of Disney merchandise. Disney owns 211 stores in North America, 104 stores in Europe, and 48 stores in Japan. Competitors to Disney in this segment are Warner Brothers, Fox, Sony, Marvel, and Nickelodeon.

Interactive Media

Disney's Interactive Media segment creates and delivers Disney-branded entertainment across interactive media platforms, especially in games and online. As indicated in Exhibit 16, games and subscriptions revenue was somewhat flat during 2010; however, advertising dollars received through online enterairment increased 35 percent from the prior year.

Disney's Games business creates, develops, and distributes console, handheld, online, and mobile games worldwide based on properties created by Disney, which includes 2010 titles such as *Toy Story 3, Alice in Wonderland*, and *The Princess and the Frog,* as well as new game properties such as *Split Seconds*. This business also produces online games along with interactive games for social networking websites and games for Smartphone platforms. Disney recently acquired Playdom, Inc., a company that develops and publishes online games for social networking websites.

Disney's Online business develops, publishes, and distributes content of Disney-branded online services intended for family entertainment. The focus here is to create Disney websites such as Disney.com and Disney Family Network. Disney.com promotes the Disney Channel, Disney Parks and Resorts, Walt Disney Pictures, and Disney Consumer Products.

For the quarter that ended April 2, 2011, Disney's Interactive Media revenues increased 3 percent to $159 million, but this segment's operating income decreased by $60 million to a loss of $115 million.

Conclusion

The unifying theme for all of Disney's business segments is family entertainment. In addition to economic conditions, value of the dollar, inflation rates, interest rates, unemployment rates, and GDP variation across countries, Disney's future success depends on the ability to consistently create and distribute movies, films, programs, theme park attractions, resort services, and consumer products. Heavy investment is required to gain and sustain consumer acceptance and attention as preferences change and differ across continents.

EXHIBIT 16   Interactive Media: Revenue and Operating Income

(in millions)	2010	2009	% Change
Revenues			
Games Sales and Subscriptions	$ 563	$ 565	–
Advertising and Other	198	147	35%
Total Revenues	$ 761	$ 712	7%
Segment operating income	$ (234)	$ (295)	21%

Source: Walt Disney Company, *Annual Report* (2010).

Travel and tourism factors impact Disney's business, such as adverse weather conditions, natural disasters, terrorist attacks, health concerns, international concerns, political or military developments, and war. Technological challenges face Disney as consumers are shifting to more on-demand movies and shows.

James Mitchell, a Goldman Sachs media analyst, estimates that 80 percent of Disney's park attendance is from the United States, and that 60 percent of domestic visitors fly to the parks versus 40 percent who drive. Crude oil futures have climbed 19 percent this year in New York. Mitchell has a "buy" rating on Disney and a 12-month share-price forecast of $48. High oil prices are bad for Disney; oil prices dropped 3 percent on May 5, 2011. That was a good day for Disney.

In June 2011, Disney announced plans to layoff 5 percent of the employees or more than 200 people at its film division to reduce costs at the Studio Entertainment segment. Layoffs had been expected as global DVD sales have plunged due to a shift in consumer behavior to on-demand TV services and other digital mediums at home for watching movies. Disney's Studio Entertainment division is also struggling due to sluggish performance of the worldwide home entertainment and theatrical distribution business. Disney's Studio Entertainment revenues came in at $1.34 billion in the second quarter of 2011, a decline of 13 percent versus the year-ago quarter. Operating income plunged 65 percent to $77 million in this segment.

On a positive note for Disney, the state of Florida is moving forward with a $1.3 billion commuter rail system for the Orlando area. Disney had urged the state to build the line, saying it would bring jobs and economic gains to the region where they have operations.

Ultimately, Disney must continue to maintain the image and brand name that Mr. Walt Disney developed while assuring investors and stakeholders that the company will have healthy growth in upcoming years. New competitors like Netflix, Dish Network, and Amazon.com have their eye on taking Disney customers. Prepare a three-year strategic plan for Disney's CEO, Robert Iger.

ASSURANCE OF LEARNING EXERCISES

Assurance of Learning Exercise 1A

Compare Business Strategy with Military Strategy

Purpose

This exercise will enable you to compare and contrast military strategy with business strategy, because in many ways operating a business is similar to conducting a military campaign. Many strategic-management concepts evolved out of the military. Napoleon Bonaparte listed 115 maxims for military strategy. American Civil War General Nathan Bedford Forrest, however, had only one strategic principle: "to git thar furst with the most men" (to get there first with the most men). The strategy concepts given as essential in the United States Army's Field Manual (FM-3-0) of Military Operations (sections 4–32 to 4–39) says there are nine key military strategy maxims:

1. Objective—direct every military operation towards a clearly defined, decisive, and attainable objective
2. Offensive—seize, retain, and exploit the initiative
3. Mass—concentrate combat power at the decisive place and time
4. Economy of Force—allocate minimum essential combat power to secondary efforts
5. Maneuver—place the enemy in a disadvantageous position through the flexible application of combat power
6. Unity of Command—for every objective, ensure unity of effort under one responsible commander

7. Security—never permit the enemy to acquire an unexpected advantage
8. Surprise—strike the enemy at a time, at a place, or in a manner for which he is unprepared
9. Simplicity—prepare clear, uncomplicated plans and clear, concise orders to ensure thorough understanding

Instructions

Step 1	Consider the extent to which each of the nine maxims listed above are applicable in formulating and implementing strategies in a business setting.
Step 2	Rank order the nine maxims above, from 1 = most important to 9 = least important in formulating and implementing strategies in a business setting.
Step 3	Provide a rationale for each of your rankings in Step 2.

Assurance of Learning Exercise 1B

Gather Strategy Information

Purpose

The purpose of this exercise is to get you familiar with strategy terms introduced and defined in Chapter 1. Let's apply these terms to The Walt Disney Company (stock symbol = DIS).

Instructions

Step 1	Go to http://corporate.disney.go.com/ (Walt Disney's website). Along the top of the site, click on Investor Relations. Then scan down one page and click on 2011 *Form 10K* and print that document, which may be 100 pages or more. That *Form 10K* document, however, contains excellent information for developing a list of Walt Disney's internal strengths and weaknesses. You may also want to review Disney's most recent *Annual Report*, which may be found at the website: http://corporate.disney.go.com/investors/annual_reports.html
Step 2	Go to your college library and make a copy of Standard & Poor's Industry Surveys for the entertainment industry. This document will contain excellent information for developing a list of external opportunities and threats facing DIS.
Step 3	Go to the www.finance.yahoo.com website. Enter DIS. Note the wealth of information on DIS that may be obtained by clicking any item along the left column. Click on Competitors down the left column. Then print out the resultant tables and information. Note that DIS's two major competitors are BS, NWS, and TWX.
Step 4	Using the Cohesion Case, the www.finance.yahoo.com information, the 2011 *Form 10K*, and the Industry Survey document, on a separate sheet of paper list what you consider to be DIS's three major strengths, three major weaknesses, three major opportunities, and three major threats. Each factor listed for this exercise must include a %, #, $, or ratio to reveal some quantified fact or trend. These factors provide the underlying basis for a strategic plan because a firm strives to take advantage of strengths, improve weaknesses, avoid threats, and capitalize on opportunities.
Step 5	Through class discussion, compare your lists of external and internal factors to those developed by other students and add to your lists of factors. Keep this information for use in later exercises at the end of other chapters.
Step 6	Whatever case company is assigned to you this semester, update the information on your company by following the steps listed here.

Assurance of Learning Exercise 1C

Update the Walt Disney Cohesion Case

Purpose

Every week Walt Disney updates its website with News Releases of important strategic decisions and information. Since the time this text was published, more than 50 Disney News Releases have been posted. In performing strategic planning and classroom strategic-management case analysis, it is important to have the latest information possible upon which to base decisions and processes.

Instructions

Step 1	Go to the http://corporate.disney.go.com/ website and, down the left column, click on News Releases. Read the most recent Disney News Releases.
Step 2	Type a two-page Executive Summary of Disney's newest strategies being formulated and implemented.
Step 3	Submit your report to your professor.

Assurance of Learning Exercise 1D

Strategic Planning for My University

Purpose

External and internal factors are the underlying bases of strategies formulated and implemented by organizations. Your college or university faces numerous external opportunities/threats and has many internal strengths/weaknesses. The purpose of this exercise is to illustrate the process of identifying critical external and internal factors.

External influences include trends in the following areas: economic, social, cultural, demographic, environmental, technological, political, legal, governmental, and competitive. External factors could include declining numbers of high school graduates; population shifts; community relations; increased competitiveness among colleges and universities; rising numbers of adults returning to college; decreased support from local, state, and federal agencies; increasing numbers of foreign students attending U.S. colleges; and a rising number of Internet courses.

Internal factors of a college or university include faculty, students, staff, alumni, athletic programs, physical plant, grounds and maintenance, student housing, administration, fund-raising, academic programs, food services, parking, placement, clubs, fraternities, sororities, and public relations.

Instructions

Step 1	On a separate sheet of paper, write four headings: External Opportunities, External Threats, Internal Strengths, and Internal Weaknesses.
Step 2	As related to your college or university, list five factors under each of the four headings.
Step 3	Discuss the factors as a class. Write the factors on the board.
Step 4	What new things did you learn about your university from the class discussion? How could this type of discussion benefit an organization?

Assurance of Learning Exercise 1E

Strategic Planning at a Local Company

Purpose

This activity is aimed at giving you practical knowledge about how organizations in your city or town are doing strategic planning. This exercise also will give you experience interacting on a professional basis with local business leaders.

Instructions

Step 1	Use the telephone to contact business owners or top managers. Find an organization that does strategic planning. Make an appointment to visit with the strategist (president, chief executive officer, or owner) of that business.
Step 2	Seek answers to the following questions during the interview:

- How does your firm formally conduct strategic planning? Who is involved in the process? Does the firm hold planning retreats? If yes, how often and where?
- Does your firm have a written mission statement? How was the statement developed? When was the statement last changed?
- What are the benefits of engaging in strategic planning?

- What are the major costs or problems in doing strategic planning in your business?
- Do you anticipate making any changes in the strategic-planning process at your company? If yes, please explain.

Step 3   Report your findings to the class.

Assurance of Learning Exercise 1F

Get Familiar with SMCO

Purpose

This exercise is designed to get you familiar with the Strategic Management Club Online (SMCO), which offers many benefits for the strategy student. The SMCO site also offers templates for doing case analyses in this course.

Instructions

Step 1   Go to the www.strategyclub.com website. Review the various sections of this site.

Step 2   Prepare a critique of the students' oral presentation provided on The Wynn Corporation.

"NOTABLE QUOTES"

"A business is not defined by its name, statutes, or articles of incorporation. It is defined by the business mission. Only a clear definition of the mission and purpose of the organization makes possible clear and realistic business objectives."
—*Peter Drucker*

"A corporate vision can focus, direct, motivate, unify, and even excite a business into superior performance. The job of a strategist is to identify and project a clear vision."
—*John Keane*

"Where there is no vision, the people perish."
—*Proverbs 29:18*

"The last thing IBM needs right now is a vision. (July 1993) What IBM needs most right now is a vision. (March 1996)"
—*Louis V. Gerstner Jr., CEO, IBM Corporation*

"The best laid schemes of mice and men often go awry."
—*Robert Burns (paraphrased)*

"A strategist's job is to see the company not as it is … but as it can become."
—*John W. Teets, Chairman of Greyhound, Inc.*

"That business mission is so rarely given adequate thought is perhaps the most important single cause of business frustration."
—*Peter Drucker*

"The very essence of leadership is that you have to have vision. You can't blow an uncertain trumpet."
—*Theodore Hesburgh*

The Business Vision and Mission

2

CHAPTER OBJECTIVES

After studying this chapter, you should be able to do the following:

1. Describe the nature and role of vision and mission statements in strategic management.

2. Discuss why the process of developing a mission statement is as important as the resulting document.

3. Identify the components of mission statements.

4. Discuss how clear vision and mission statements can benefit other strategic-management activities.

5. Evaluate mission statements of different organizations.

6. Write good vision and mission statements.

ASSURANCE OF LEARNING EXERCISES

Assurance of Learning Exercise 2A
Compare Dollar General's Mission Statement to Family Dollar's Mission Statement

Assurance of Learning Exercise 2B
Evaluate Mission Statements

Assurance of Learning Exercise 2C
Write a Vision and Mission Statement for The Walt Disney Company

Assurance of Learning Exercise 2D
Write a Vision and Mission Statement for My University

Assurance of Learning Exercise 2E
Conduct Mission Statement Research

Assurance of Learning Exercise 2F
Evaluate a Mission Proposal

This chapter focuses on the concepts and tools needed to evaluate and write business vision and mission statements. A practical framework for developing mission statements is provided. Actual mission statements from large and small organizations and for-profit and nonprofit enterprises are presented and critically examined. The process of creating a vision and mission statement is discussed. The recent economic recession resulted in many firms changing direction and thereby altering their entire vision and mission. For example, Microsoft has entered the smartphone business with Nokia, and IBM is focusing more on business analytics.

The boxed insert company examined in this chapter is Dollar General, which has a clear strategic plan. Dollar General is doing great in an improving economy.

We can perhaps best understand vision and mission by focusing on a business when it is first started. In the beginning, a new business is simply a collection of ideas. Starting a new business rests on a set of beliefs that the new organization can offer some product or service to some customers, in some geographic area, using some type of technology, at a profitable price. A new business owner typically believes that the management philosophy of the new enterprise will result in a favorable public image and that this concept of the business can be communicated to, and will be adopted by, important constituencies. When the set of beliefs about a business at its inception is put into writing, the resulting document mirrors the same basic ideas that underlie

Excellent Strategic Management Showcased

DOLLAR GENERAL CORPORATION

Called a statement of purpose, Dollar General's mission statement is as follows: "Serving Others. For Customers A Better Life. For Shareholders A Superior Return. For Employees Respect and Opportunity." In contrast, rival Family Dollar's mission statement reads as follows: "For Our Customers - A compelling place to shop...by providing convenience and low prices. For Our Associates - A compelling place to work...by providing exceptional opportunities and rewards for achievement. For Our Investors - A compelling place to invest...by providing outstanding returns."

While many firms continued to struggle in 2011, Dollar General added 625 new stores and 6,000 new employees in 35 states, boosting its total number of stores and employees to 9,200 and 88,000 respectively. Three new states where Dollar General added stores in 2011 were Connecticut, Nevada, and New Hampshire. Dollar General also remodeled or relocated 550 other stores in 2011. Dollar General's profits increased an incredible 214 percent to $339 million in 2010, while the company's revenues increased 13 percent to $11.8 billion. Dollar General's excellent mass retailing strategy of building small stores in small communities has even mighty Wal-Mart doing the same thing with their new, smaller Wal-Mart Express stores.

Founded in 1939 and headquartered near Nashville, Tennessee, Dollar General operates mainly as stand-alone stores in communities too small for a Wal-Mart. Fierce competitors include Family Dollar and Dollar Tree. Dollar General is the largest of the deep-discount retailers, but Family Dollar is second with $7.8 billion in sales. All heavily discounted variety stores are making significant inroads taking customers away from Wal-Mart, K-mart, and Target. For the first time ever, Wal-Mart's 2010 revenues revealed the second straight year of declining domestic same-store sales—partly due to inroads made by Dollar General "Serving Others."

In addition to selling private label brands, Dollar General sells products from America's most trusted manufacturers, such as Procter & Gamble, Kimberly-Clark, Unilever, Kellogg's, General Mills, Nabisco, Hanes, PepsiCo, and Coca-Cola. More than 25 percent of items for sale in a Dollar General store are $1.00 or less. Two years after being taken private by KKR and Goldman Sachs, Dollar General became a public company in 2009—just as the recession was sending millions of discount shoppers into their stores.

Dollar General recently launched a new promotion whereby shoppers could enter the "Fresh Start Every Day" Sweepstakes for the chance to pay off their bills, including a grand prize $100,000 home payoff. Rick Dreiling, Dollar General's chairman and CEO, says: "In these challenging times, it's exciting for us to give our customers an opportunity to pay off their bills." In addition to the grand prize, the "Fresh Start Every Day" Sweepstakes awards included: 1st Prize $20,000 Car payoff; 2nd Prize $5,000 Credit Card payoff; and 3rd Prize $2,400 Utility Bills payoff.

Source: Based on company documents.

the vision and mission statements. As a business grows, owners or managers find it necessary to revise the founding set of beliefs, but those original ideas usually are reflected in the revised statements of vision and mission.

Vision and mission statements often can be found in the front of annual reports. They often are displayed throughout a firm's premises and are distributed with company information sent to constituencies. The statements are part of numerous internal reports, such as loan requests, supplier agreements, labor relations contracts, business plans, and customer service agreements. In a recent study, researchers concluded that 90 percent of all companies have used a mission statement sometime in the previous five years.[1]

What Do We Want to Become?

It is especially important for managers and executives in any organization to agree on the basic vision that the firm strives to achieve in the long term. A *vision statement* should answer the basic question, "What do we want to become?" A clear vision provides the foundation for developing a comprehensive mission statement. Many organizations have both a vision and mission statement, but the vision statement should be established first and foremost. The vision statement should be short, preferably one sentence, and as many managers as possible should have input into developing the statement.

Several example vision statements are provided in Table 2-1.

What Is Our Business?

Current thought on mission statements is based largely on guidelines set forth in the mid-1970s by Peter Drucker, who is often called "the father of modern management" for his pioneering studies at General Motors Corporation and for his 22 books and hundreds of articles. *Harvard Business Review* has called Drucker "the preeminent management thinker of our time."

Drucker says that asking the question "What is our business?" is synonymous with asking the question "What is our mission?" An enduring statement of purpose that distinguishes one organization from other similar enterprises, the *mission statement* is a declaration of an organization's "reason for being." It answers the pivotal question "What is our business?" A clear mission statement is essential for effectively establishing objectives and formulating strategies.

Sometimes called a *creed statement,* a statement of purpose, a statement of philosophy, a statement of beliefs, a statement of business principles, or a statement "defining our business," a mission statement reveals what an organization wants to be and whom it wants to serve. All organizations

TABLE 2-1   Vision Statement Examples

Tyson Foods' vision is to be the world's first choice for protein solutions while maximizing shareholder value. (*Author comment: Good statement, unless Tyson provides nonprotein products*)

General Motors' vision is to be the world leader in transportation products and related services. (*Author comment: Good statement*)

PepsiCo's responsibility is to continually improve all aspects of the world in which we operate—environment, social, economic—creating a better tomorrow than today. (*Author comment: Statement is too vague; it should reveal beverage and food business*)

Dell's vision is to create a company culture where environmental excellence is second nature. (*Author comment: Statement is too vague; it should reveal computer business in some manner; the word* environmental *is generally used to refer to natural environment so is unclear in its use here*)

The vision of First Reliance Bank is to be recognized as the largest and most profitable bank in South Carolina. (*Author comment: This is a very small new bank headquartered in Florence, South Carolina, so this goal is not achievable in five years; the statement is too futuristic*)

Samsonite's vision is to provide innovative solutions for the traveling world. (*Author comment: Statement needs to be more specific, perhaps mention luggage; statement as is could refer to air carriers or cruise lines, which is not good*)

Royal Caribbean's vision is to empower and enable our employees to deliver the best vacation experience for our guests, thereby generating superior returns for our shareholders and enhancing the well-being of our communities. (*Author comment: Statement is good but could end after the word "guests"*)

Procter & Gamble's vision is to be, and be recognized as, the best consumer products company in the world. (*Author comment: Statement is too vague and readability is not that good*)

have a reason for being, even if strategists have not consciously transformed this reason into writing. As illustrated in Figure 2-1, carefully prepared statements of vision and mission are widely recognized by both practitioners and academicians as the first step in strategic management. Drucker has the following to say about mission statements:

> A business mission is the foundation for priorities, strategies, plans, and work assignments. It is the starting point for the design of managerial jobs and, above all, for the design of managerial structures. Nothing may seem simpler or more obvious than to know what a company's business is. A steel mill makes steel, a railroad runs trains to carry freight and passengers, an insurance company underwrites fire risks, and a bank lends money. Actually, "What is our business?" is almost always a difficult question and the right answer is usually anything but obvious. The answer to this question is the first responsibility of strategists.[2]

Some strategists spend almost every moment of every day on administrative and tactical concerns, and strategists who rush quickly to establish objectives and implement strategies often overlook the development of a vision and mission statement. This problem is widespread even among large organizations. Many corporations in America have not yet

FIGURE 2-1

A Comprehensive Strategic-Management Model

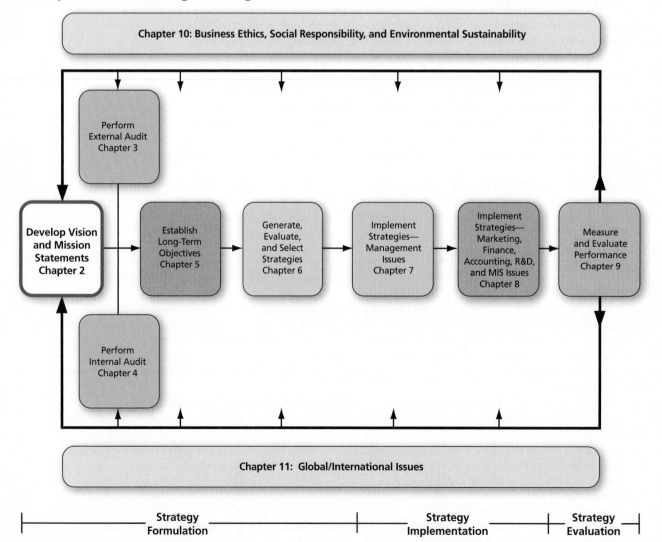

Source: Fred R. David, "How Companies Define Their Mission," *Long Range Planning* 22, no. 3 (June 1988): 40.

developed a formal vision or mission statement.[3] An increasing number of organizations are developing these statements.

Some companies develop mission statements simply because they feel it is fashionable, rather than out of any real commitment. However, as described in this chapter, firms that develop and systematically revisit their vision and mission statements, treat them as living documents, and consider them to be an integral part of the firm's culture realize great benefits. Johnson & Johnson (J&J) is an example firm. J&J managers meet regularly with employees to review, reword, and reaffirm the firm's vision and mission. The entire J&J workforce recognizes the value that top management places on this exercise, and these employees respond accordingly.

Vision versus Mission

Many organizations develop both a mission statement and a vision statement. Whereas the mission statement answers the question "What is our business?" the *vision statement* answers the question "What do we want to become?" Many organizations have both a mission and vision statement.

It can be argued that profit, not mission or vision, is the primary corporate motivator. But profit alone is not enough to motivate people.[4] Profit is perceived negatively by some employees in companies. Employees may see profit as something that they earn and management then uses and even gives away to shareholders. Although this perception is undesired and disturbing to management, it clearly indicates that both profit and vision are needed to motivate a workforce effectively.

When employees and managers together shape or fashion the vision and mission statements for a firm, the resultant documents can reflect the personal visions that managers and employees have in their hearts and minds about their own futures. Shared vision creates a commonality of interests that can lift workers out of the monotony of daily work and put them into a new world of opportunity and challenge.

The Process of Developing Vision and Mission Statements

As indicated in the strategic-management model, clear vision and mission statements are needed before alternative strategies can be formulated and implemented. As many managers as possible should be involved in the process of developing these statements because, through involvement, people become committed to an organization.

A widely used approach to developing a vision and mission statement is first to select several articles about these statements and ask all managers to read these as background information. Then ask managers themselves to prepare a vision and mission statement for the organization. A facilitator or committee of top managers should then merge these statements into a single document and distribute the draft statements to all managers. A request for modifications, additions, and deletions is needed next, along with a meeting to revise the document. To the extent that all managers have input into and support the final documents, organizations can more easily obtain managers' support for other strategy formulation, implementation, and evaluation activities. Thus, the process of developing a vision and mission statement represents a great opportunity for strategists to obtain needed support from all managers in the firm.

During the process of developing vision and mission statements, some organizations use discussion groups of managers to develop and modify existing statements. Some organizations hire an outside consultant or facilitator to manage the process and help draft the language. Sometimes an outside person with expertise in developing such statements, who has unbiased views, can manage the process more effectively than an internal group or committee of managers. Decisions on how best to communicate the vision and mission to all managers, employees, and external constituencies of an organization are needed when the documents are in final form. Some organizations even develop a videotape to explain the statements and how they were developed.

An article by Campbell and Yeung emphasizes that the process of developing a mission statement should create an "emotional bond" and "sense of mission" between the organization and its employees.[5] Commitment to a company's strategy and intellectual agreement on the strategies to be pursued do not necessarily translate into an emotional bond; hence, strategies that have been formulated may not be implemented. These researchers stress that an emotional bond comes when an individual personally identifies with the underlying values and behavior of a firm, thus turning intellectual agreement and commitment to strategy into a sense of mission. Campbell and Yeung also differentiate between the terms *vision* and *mission*, saying that vision is "a possible and desirable future state of an organization" that includes specific goals, whereas mission is more associated with behavior and the present.

Importance (Benefits) of Vision and Mission Statements

The importance (benefits) of vision and mission statements to effective strategic management is well documented in the literature, although research results are mixed. Rarick and Vitton found that firms with a formalized mission statement have twice the average return on shareholders' equity than those firms without a formalized mission statement have; Bart and Baetz found a positive relationship between mission statements and organizational performance; *BusinessWeek* reports that firms using mission statements have a 30 percent higher return on certain financial measures than those without such statements; however, some studies have found that having a mission statement does not directly contribute positively to financial performance.[6] The extent of manager and employee involvement in developing vision and mission statements can make a difference in business success. This chapter provides guidelines for developing these important documents. In actual practice, wide variations exist in the nature, composition, and use of both vision and mission statements. King and Cleland recommend that organizations carefully develop a written mission statement in order to reap the following benefits:

1. To ensure unanimity of purpose within the organization
2. To provide a basis, or standard, for allocating organizational resources
3. To establish a general tone or organizational climate
4. To serve as a focal point for individuals to identify with the organization's purpose and direction, and to deter those who cannot from participating further in the organization's activities
5. To facilitate the translation of objectives into a work structure involving the assignment of tasks to responsible elements within the organization
6. To specify organizational purposes and then to translate these purposes into objectives in such a way that cost, time, and performance parameters can be assessed and controlled.[7]

Reuben Mark, former CEO of Colgate, maintains that a clear mission increasingly must make sense internationally. Mark's thoughts on vision are as follows:

> When it comes to rallying everyone to the corporate banner, it's essential to push one vision globally rather than trying to drive home different messages in different cultures. The trick is to keep the vision simple but elevated: "We make the world's fastest computers" or "Telephone service for everyone." You're never going to get anyone to charge the machine guns only for financial objectives. It's got to be something that makes people feel better, feel a part of something.[8]

A Resolution of Divergent Views

Another benefit of developing a comprehensive mission statement is that divergent views among managers can be revealed and resolved through the process. The question "What is our business?" can create controversy. Raising the question often reveals differences among strategists in the organization. Individuals who have worked together for a long time and who think they know each other suddenly may realize that they are in fundamental disagreement. For example, in a college or university, divergent views regarding the relative importance of teaching, research, and service often are expressed during the mission statement development process. Negotiation, compromise, and eventual agreement on important issues are needed before people can focus on more specific strategy-formulation activities.

Considerable disagreement among an organization's strategists over vision and mission statements can cause trouble if not resolved. For example, unresolved disagreement over the business mission was one of the reasons for W. T. Grant's bankruptcy and eventual liquidation. As one executive reported:

> There was a lot of dissension within the company whether we should go the Kmart route or go after the Montgomery Ward and JCPenney position. Ed Staley and Lou Lustenberger (two top executives) were at loggerheads over the issue, with the upshot being we took a position between the two and that consequently stood for nothing.[9]

Too often, strategists develop vision and business mission statements only when the organization is in trouble. Of course, it is needed then. Developing and communicating a clear mission during troubled times indeed may have spectacular results and even may reverse decline. However, to wait until an organization is in trouble to develop a vision and mission statement is a gamble that characterizes irresponsible management. According to Drucker, the most important time to ask seriously, "What do we want to become?" and "What is our business?" is when a company has been successful:

> Success always obsoletes the very behavior that achieved it, always creates new realities, and always creates new and different problems. Only the fairy tale story ends, "They lived happily ever after." It is never popular to argue with success or to rock the boat. It will not be long before success will turn into failure. Sooner or later, even the most successful answer to the question "What is our business?" becomes obsolete.[10]

In multidivisional organizations, strategists should ensure that divisional units perform strategic-management tasks, including the development of a statement of vision and mission. Each division should involve its own managers and employees in developing a vision and mission statement that is consistent with and supportive of the corporate mission. Ten benefits of having a clear mission and vision are provided in Table 2-2.

An organization that fails to develop a vision statement as well as a comprehensive and inspiring mission statement loses the opportunity to present itself favorably to existing and potential *stakeholders*. All organizations need customers, employees, and managers, and most firms need creditors, suppliers, and distributors. The vision and mission statements are effective vehicles for communicating with important internal and external stakeholders. The principal benefit of these statements as tools of strategic management is derived from their specification of the ultimate aims of a firm:

> They provide managers with a unity of direction that transcends individual, parochial, and transitory needs. They promote a sense of shared expectations among all levels and generations of employees. They consolidate values over time and across individuals and interest groups. They project a sense of worth and intent that can be identified and assimilated by company outsiders. Finally, they affirm the company's commitment to responsible action, which is symbiotic with its need to preserve and protect the essential claims of insiders for sustained survival, growth, and profitability of the firm.[11]

Characteristics of a Mission Statement

A Declaration of Attitude

A mission statement is more than a statement of specific details; it is a declaration of attitude and outlook. It usually is broad in scope for at least two major reasons. First, a good mission

TABLE 2-2 Ten Benefits of Having a Clear Mission and Vision

1. Achieve clarity of purpose among all managers and employees.
2. Provide a basis for all other strategic planning activities, including internal and external assessment, establishing objectives, developing strategies, choosing among alternative strategies, devising policies, establishing organizational structure, allocating resources, and evaluating performance.
3. Provide direction.
4. Provide a focal point for all stakeholders of the firm.
5. Resolve divergent views among managers.
6. Promote a sense of shared expectations among all managers and employees.
7. Project a sense of worth and intent to all stakeholders.
8. Project an organized, motivated organization worthy of support.
9. Achieve higher organizational performance.
10. Achieve synergy among all managers and employees.

statement allows for the generation and consideration of a range of feasible alternative objectives and strategies without unduly stifling management creativity. Excess specificity would limit the potential of creative growth for the organization. However, an overly general statement that does not exclude any strategy alternatives could be dysfunctional. Apple Computer's mission statement, for example, should not open the possibility for diversification into pesticides—or Ford Motor Company's into food processing.

Second, a mission statement needs to be broad to reconcile differences effectively among, and appeal to, an organization's diverse *stakeholders,* the individuals and groups of individuals who have a special stake or claim on the company. Thus a mission statement should be *reconcilatory.* Stakeholders include employees, managers, stockholders, boards of directors, customers, suppliers, distributors, creditors, governments (local, state, federal, and foreign), unions, competitors, environmental groups, and the general public. Stakeholders affect and are affected by an organization's strategies, yet the claims and concerns of diverse constituencies vary and often conflict. For example, the general public is especially interested in social responsibility, whereas stockholders are more interested in profitability. Claims on any business literally may number in the thousands, and they often include clean air, jobs, taxes, investment opportunities, career opportunities, equal employment opportunities, employee benefits, salaries, wages, clean water, and community services. All stakeholders' claims on an organization cannot be pursued with equal emphasis. A good mission statement indicates the relative attention that an organization will devote to meeting the claims of various stakeholders.

The fine balance between specificity and generality is difficult to achieve, but it is well worth the effort. George Steiner offers the following insight on the need for a mission statement to be broad in scope:

Most business statements of mission are expressed at high levels of abstraction. Vagueness nevertheless has its virtues. Mission statements are not designed to express concrete ends, but rather to provide motivation, general direction, an image, a tone, and a philosophy to guide the enterprise. An excess of detail could prove counterproductive since concrete specification could be the base for rallying opposition. Precision might stifle creativity in the formulation of an acceptable mission or purpose. Once an aim is cast in concrete, it creates a rigidity in an organization and resists change. Vagueness leaves room for other managers to fill in the details.[12]

As indicated in Table 2-3, in addition to being broad in scope, an effective mission statement should not be too lengthy; recommended length is less than 250 words. An effective mission statement should arouse positive feelings and emotions about an organization; it should be inspiring in the sense that it motivates readers to action. A mission statement should be enduring.

All of these are desired characteristics of a statement. An effective mission statement generates the impression that a firm is successful, has direction, and is worthy of time, support, and investment—from all socioeconomic groups of people.

It reflects judgments about future growth directions and strategies that are based on forward-looking external and internal analyses. A business mission should provide useful criteria for selecting among alternative strategies. A clear mission statement provides a basis for generating and screening strategic options. The statement of mission should be dynamic in orientation, allowing judgments about the most promising growth directions and those considered less promising.

A Customer Orientation

A good mission statement describes an organization's purpose, customers, products or services, markets, philosophy, and basic technology. According to Vern McGinnis, a mission statement should (1) define what the organization is and what the organization aspires to be, (2) be limited enough to exclude some ventures and broad enough to allow for creative growth, (3) distinguish a given organization from all others, (4) serve as a framework for evaluating both current and prospective activities, and (5) be stated in terms sufficiently clear to be widely understood throughout the organization.[13]

A good mission statement reflects the anticipations of customers. Rather than developing a product and then trying to find a market, the operating philosophy of organizations should be to identify customers' needs and then provide a product or service to fulfill those needs.

Good mission statements identify the utility of a firm's products to its customers. This is why AT&T's mission statement focuses on communication rather than on telephones; it is why ExxonMobil's mission statement focuses on energy rather than on oil and gas; it is why Union Pacific's mission statement focuses on transportation rather than on railroads; it is why Universal Studios' mission statement focuses on entertainment rather than on movies. A major reason for developing a business mission statement is to attract customers who give meaning to an organization.

The following utility statements are relevant in developing a mission statement:

Do not offer me things.

Do not offer me clothes. Offer me attractive looks.

Do not offer me shoes. Offer me comfort for my feet and the pleasure of walking.

Do not offer me a house. Offer me security, comfort, and a place that is clean and happy.

Do not offer me books. Offer me hours of pleasure and the benefit of knowledge.

Do not offer me CDs. Offer me leisure and the sound of music.

Do not offer me tools. Offer me the benefits and the pleasure that come from making beautiful things.

Do not offer me furniture. Offer me comfort and the quietness of a cozy place.

Do not offer me things. Offer me ideas, emotions, ambience, feelings, and benefits.

Please, do not offer me *things*.

Mission Statement Components

Mission statements can and do vary in length, content, format, and specificity. Most practitioners and academicians of strategic management feel that an effective statement should include nine *components*. Because a mission statement is often the most visible and public part of the strategic-management process, it is important that it includes the nine characteristics as summarized in Table 2-3, as well as the following nine components:

1. *Customers*—Who are the firm's customers?
2. *Products or services*—What are the firm's major products or services?
3. *Markets*—Geographically, where does the firm compete?
4. *Technology*—Is the firm technologically current?

TABLE 2-3   Characteristics of a Mission Statement

1. Broad in scope; do not include monetary amounts, numbers, percentages, ratios, or objectives
2. Less than 250 words in length
3. Inspiring
4. Identify the utility of a firm's products
5. Reveal that the firm is socially responsible
6. Reveal that the firm is environmentally responsible
7. Include nine components customers, products or services, markets, technology, concern for survival/growth/profits, philosophy, self-concept, concern for public image, concern for employees
8. Reconciliatory
9. Enduring

5. *Concern for survival, growth, and profitability*—Is the firm committed to growth and financial soundness?
6. *Philosophy*—What are the basic beliefs, values, aspirations, and ethical priorities of the firm?
7. *Self-concept*—What is the firm's distinctive competence or major competitive advantage?
8. *Concern for public image*—Is the firm responsive to social, community, and environmental concerns?
9. *Concern for employees*—Are employees a valuable asset of the firm?[14]

Excerpts from the mission statements of different organizations are provided in Table 2-4 to exemplify the nine essential mission statement components.

Writing and Evaluating Mission Statements

Perhaps the best way to develop a skill for writing and evaluating mission statements is to study actual company missions. Therefore, the mission statements presented in Table 2-5 are evaluated based on the nine desired components. Note in Table 2-5 that numbers provided in each statement reveal what components are included in the respective documents. Among the statements in Table 2-5, note that the Dell mission statement is the best because it lacks only one component, whereas the L'Oreal statement is the worst, lacking six of the nine recommended components.

There is no one best mission statement for a particular organization, so good judgment is required in evaluating mission statements. Realize that some individuals are more demanding than others in assessing mission statements in this manner. For example, if a statement merely includes the word "customers" without specifying who the customers are, is that satisfactory? Ideally a statement would provide more than simply inclusion of a single word such as "products" or "employees" regarding a respective component. Why? Because the statement should be informative, inspiring, enduring, and serve to motivate stakeholders to action. Evaluation of a mission statement regarding inclusion of the nine components is just the beginning of the process to assess a statement's overall effectiveness.

Special Note to Students

Recall that gaining and sustaining competitive advantage is the essence of strategic management, so when presenting your vision/mission analysis for the firm, be sure to address the "self concept" or "distinctive competence" component. Compare your recommended vision/mission statement both with the firm's existing statements and with rival firms' statements in order to clearly reveal how your recommendations or strategic plan enables the firm to gain and sustain competitive advantage. Thus, your proposed mission statement should certainly include the nine components and nine characteristics, but in your vision/mission discussion, focus on competitive advantage. In other words, be prescriptive, forward-looking, and insightful—couching your vision/mission overview in terms of how you believe the firm can

TABLE 2-4 Examples of the Nine Essential Components of a Mission Statement

1. Customers

We believe our first responsibility is to the doctors, nurses, patients, mothers, and all others who use our products and services. (Johnson & Johnson)

To earn our customers' loyalty, we listen to them, anticipate their needs, and act to create value in their eyes. (Lexmark International)

2. Products or Services

AMAX's principal products are molybdenum, coal, iron ore, copper, lead, zinc, petroleum and natural gas, potash, phosphates, nickel, tungsten, silver, gold, and magnesium. (AMAX Engineering Company)

Standard Oil Company (Indiana) is in business to find and produce crude oil, natural gas, and natural gas liquids; to manufacture high-quality products useful to society from these raw materials; and to distribute and market those products and to provide dependable related services to the consuming public at reasonable prices. (Standard Oil Company)

3. Markets

We are dedicated to the total success of Corning Glass Works as a worldwide competitor. (Corning Glass Works)

Our emphasis is on North American markets, although global opportunities will be explored. (Blockway)

4. Technology

Control Data is in the business of applying micro-electronics and computer technology in two general areas: computer-related hardware; and computing-enhancing services, which include computation, information, education, and finance. (Control Data)

We will continually strive to meet the preferences of adult smokers by developing technologies that have the potential to reduce the health risks associated with smoking. (RJ Reynolds)

5. Concern for Survival, Growth, and Profitability

In this respect, the company will conduct its operations prudently and will provide the profits and growth which will assure Hoover's ultimate success. (Hoover Universal)

To serve the worldwide need for knowledge at a fair profit by adhering, evaluating, producing, and distributing valuable information in a way that benefits our customers, employees, other investors, and our society. (McGraw-Hill)

6. Philosophy

Our world-class leadership is dedicated to a management philosophy that holds people above profits. (Kellogg)

It's all part of the Mary Kay philosophy—a philosophy based on the golden rule. A spirit of sharing and caring where people give cheerfully of their time, knowledge, and experience. (Mary Kay Cosmetics)

7. Self-Concept

Crown Zellerbach is committed to leapfrogging ongoing competition within 1,000 days by unleashing the constructive and creative abilities and energies of each of its employees. (Crown Zellerbach)

8. Concern for Public Image

To share the world's obligation for the protection of the environment. (Dow Chemical)

To contribute to the economic strength of society and function as a good corporate citizen on a local, state, and national basis in all countries in which we do business. (Pfizer)

9. Concern for Employees

To recruit, develop, motivate, reward, and retain personnel of exceptional ability, character, and dedication by providing good working conditions, superior leadership, compensation on the basis of performance, an attractive benefit program, opportunity for growth, and a high degree of employment security. (The Wachovia Corporation)

To compensate its employees with remuneration and fringe benefits competitive with other employment opportunities in its geographical area and commensurate with their contributions toward efficient corporate operations. (Public Service Electric & Gas Company)

best gain and sustain competitive advantage. Do not be content with merely showing a nine-component comparison of your proposed statement with rival firms' statements, although that would be nice to include in your analysis.

Conclusion

Every organization has a unique purpose and reason for being. This uniqueness should be reflected in vision and mission statements. The nature of a business vision and mission can represent either a competitive advantage or disadvantage for the firm. An organization achieves a heightened sense of purpose when strategists, managers, and employees develop and communicate a clear business vision and mission. Drucker says that developing a clear business vision and mission is the "first responsibility of strategists."

TABLE 2-5 Example Mission Statements

Fleetwood Enterprises will lead the recreational vehicle and manufactured housing industries (2, 7) in providing quality products, with a passion for customer-driven innovation (1). We will emphasize training, embrace diversity and provide growth opportunities for our associates and our dealers (9). We will lead our industries in the application of appropriate technologies (4). We will operate at the highest levels of ethics and compliance with a focus on exemplary corporate governance (6). We will deliver value to our shareholders, positive operating results and industry-leading earnings (5). *(Author comment: Statement lacks two components: Markets and Concern for Public Image)*

We aspire to make PepsiCo the world's (3) premier consumer products company, focused on convenient foods and beverages (2). We seek to produce healthy financial rewards for investors (5) as we provide opportunities for growth and enrichment to our employees (9), our business partners and the communities (8) in which we operate. And in everything we do, we strive to act with honesty, openness, fairness and integrity (6). *(Author comment: Statement lacks three components: Customers, Technology, and Self-Concept)*

We are loyal to Royal Caribbean and Celebrity and strive for continuous improvement in everything we do. We always provide service with a friendly greeting and a smile (7). We anticipate the needs of our customers and make all efforts to exceed our customers' expectations (1). We take ownership of any problem that is brought to our attention. We engage in conduct that enhances our corporate reputation and employee morale (9). We are committed to act in the highest ethical manner and respect the rights and dignity of others (6). *(Author comment: Statement lacks five components: Products/Services, Markets, Technology, Concern for Survival/Growth/Profits, Concern for Public Image)*

Dell's mission is to be the most successful computer company (2) in the world (3) at delivering the best customer experience in markets we serve (1). In doing so, Dell will meet customer expectations of highest quality; leading technology (4); competitive pricing; individual and company accountability (6); best-in-class service and support (7); flexible customization capability (7); superior corporate citizenship (8); financial stability (5). *(Author comment: Statement lacks only one component: Concern for Employees)*

Procter & Gamble will provide branded products and services of superior quality and value (7) that improve the lives of the world's (3) consumers. As a result, consumers (1) will reward us with industry leadership in sales, profit (5), and value creation, allowing our people (9), our shareholders, and the communities (8) in which we live and work to prosper. *(Author comment: Statement lacks three components: Products/Services, Technology, and Philosophy)*

At L'Oreal, we believe that lasting business success is built upon ethical (6) standards which guide growth and on a genuine sense of responsibility to our employees (9), our consumers, our environment and to the communities in which we operate (8). *(Author comment: Statement lacks six components: Customers, Products/Services, Markets, Technology, Concern for Survival/Growth/Profits, Concern for Public Image)*

Note: The numbers in parentheses correspond to the nine components listed on page 51; author comments also refer to those components.

A good mission statement reveals an organization's customers; products or services; markets; technology; concern for survival, growth, and profitability; philosophy; self-concept; concern for public image; and concern for employees. These nine basic components serve as a practical framework for evaluating and writing mission statements. As the first step in strategic management, the vision and mission statements provide direction for all planning activities.

Well-designed vision and mission statements are essential for formulating, implementing, and evaluating strategy. Developing and communicating a clear business vision and mission are the most commonly overlooked tasks in strategic management. Without clear statements of vision and mission, a firm's short-term actions can be counterproductive to long-term interests. Vision and mission statements always should be subject to revision, but, if carefully prepared, they will require infrequent major changes. Organizations usually reexamine their vision and mission statements annually. Effective mission statements stand the test of time.

Vision and mission statements are essential tools for strategists, a fact illustrated in a short story told by Porsche's former CEO Peter Schultz:

Three people were at work on a construction site. All were doing the same job, but when each was asked what his job was, the answers varied: "Breaking rocks," the first replied; "Earning a living," responded the second; "Helping to build a cathedral," said the third. Few of us can build cathedrals. But to the extent we can see the cathedral in whatever cause we are following, the job seems more worthwhile. Good strategists and a clear mission help us find those cathedrals in what otherwise could be dismal issues and empty causes.[15]

Key Terms and Concepts

Concern for Employees (p. 52)
Concern for Public Image (p. 52)
Concern for Survival, Growth, and Profitability (p. 52)
Creed Statement (p. 45)
Customers (p. 51)
Markets (p. 51)
Mission Statement (p. 45)

Mission Statement Components (p. 51)
Philosophy (p. 52)
Products or Services (p. 51)
Reconciliatory (p. 50)
Self-Concept (p. 52)
Stakeholders (p. 50)
Technology (p. 51)
Vision Statement (p. 45)

Issues for Review and Discussion

1. Some excellent nine-component mission statements consist of just two sentences. Write a two-sentence mission statement for a company of your choice.
2. How do you think an organization can best align company mission with employee mission?
3. What are some different names for "mission statement," and where will you likely find a firm's mission statement?
4. If your company does not have a vision or mission statement, describe a good process for developing these documents.
5. Explain how developing a mission statement can help resolve divergent views among managers in a firm.
6. Drucker says the most important time to seriously reexamine the firm's vision/mission is when the firm is very successful. Why is this?
7. Explain why a mission statement should not include monetary amounts, numbers, percentages, ratios, goals, or objectives.
8. Discuss the meaning of the following statement: "Good mission statements identify the utility of a firm's products to its customers."
9. Distinguish between the "self-concept" and the "philosophy" components in a mission statement. Give an example of each for your university.
10. When someone or some company is "on a mission" to achieve something, many times they cannot be stopped. List three things in prioritized order that you are "on a mission" to achieve in life.
11. Compare and contrast vision statements with mission statements in terms of composition and importance.
12. Do local service stations need to have written vision and mission statements? Why or why not?
13. Why do you think organizations that have a comprehensive mission tend to be high performers? Does having a comprehensive mission cause high performance?
14. Explain why a mission statement should not include strategies and objectives.
15. What is your college or university's self-concept? How would you state that in a mission statement?
16. Explain the principal value of a vision and a mission statement.
17. Why is it important for a mission statement to be reconciliatory?
18. In your opinion, what are the three most important components that should be included when writing a mission statement? Why?
19. How would the mission statements of a for-profit and a nonprofit organization differ?
20. Write a vision and mission statement for an organization of your choice.
21. Conduct a search on the Internet with the keywords *vision statement* and *mission statement*. Find various company vision and mission statements and evaluate the documents. Write a one-page, single-spaced report on your findings.
22. Who are the major stakeholders of the bank that you do business with locally? What are the major claims of those stakeholders?
23. List seven characteristics of a mission statement.
24. List eight benefits of having a clear mission statement.
25. How often do you think a firm's vision and mission statements should be changed?

Notes

1. Barbara Bartkus, Myron Glassman, and Bruce McAfee, "Mission Statements: Are They Smoke and Mirrors?" *Business Horizons*, November–December 2000, 23.
2. Peter Drucker, *Management: Tasks, Responsibilities, and Practices* (New York: Harper & Row, 1974), 61.
3. Fred David, "How Companies Define Their Mission," *Long Range Planning* 22, no. 1 (February 1989): 90–92; John Pearce II and Fred David, "Corporate Mission Statements: The Bottom Line," *Academy of Management Executive* 1, no. 2 (May 1987): 110.

4. Joseph Quigley, "Vision: How Leaders Develop It, Share It and Sustain It," *Business Horizons*, September–October 1994, 39.

5. Andrew Campbell and Sally Yeung, "Creating a Sense of Mission," *Long Range Planning* 24, no. 4 (August 1991): 17.

6. Charles Rarick and John Vitton, "Mission Statements Make Cents," *Journal of Business Strategy* 16 (1995): 11. Also, Christopher Bart and Mark Baetz, "The Relationship Between Mission Statements and Firm Performance: An Exploratory Study," *Journal of Management Studies* 35 (1998): 823; "Mission Possible," *Business Week* (August 1999): F12.

7. W. R. King and D. I. Cleland, *Strategic Planning and Policy* (New York: Van Nostrand Reinhold, 1979), 124.

8. Brian Dumaine, "What the Leaders of Tomorrow See," *Fortune,* July 3, 1989, 50.

9. Drucker, 78, 79.

10. "How W. T. Grant Lost $175 Million Last Year," *Business Week,* February 25, 1975, 75.

11. Drucker, 88.

12. John Pearce II, "The Company Mission as a Strategic Tool," *Sloan Management Review* 23, no. 3 (Spring 1982): 74.

13. George Steiner, *Strategic Planning: What Every Manager Must Know* (New York: The Free Press, 1979), 160.

14. Vern McGinnis, "The Mission Statement: A Key Step in Strategic Planning," *Business* 31, no. 6 (November–December 1981): 41.

15. Drucker, 61.

16. http://ezinearticles.com/?Elements-of-a-Mission-Statement&id=3846671

17. Robert Waterman Jr., *The Renewal Factor: How the Best Get and Keep the Competitive Edge* (New York: Bantam, 1987); *Business Week,* September 14, 1987, 120.

Current Readings

Bartkus, Barbara, Myron Glassman, and R. Bruce McAfee. "Mission Statements: Are They Smoke and Mirrors?" *Business Horizons* 43, no. 6 (November–December 2000): 23.

Church Mission Statements, http://www.missionstatements .com/church_mission_statements.html

Collins, David J., and Michael G. Rukstad. "Can You Say What Your Strategy Is?" *Harvard Business Review*, April 2008, 82.

Company Mission Statements, http://www.missionstatements .com/company_mission_statements.html

Conger, Jay A., and Douglas A. Ready. "Enabling Bold Visions." *MIT Sloan Management Review* 49, no. 2 (Winter 2008): 70.

Day, George S., and Paul Schoemaker. "Peripheral Vision: Sensing and Acting on Weak Signals." *Long Range Planning* 37, no. 2 (April 2004): 117.

Ibarra, Herminia, and Otilia Obodaru. "Women and the Vision Thing." *Harvard Business Review*, January 2009, 62–71.

Lissak, Michael, and Johan Roos. "Be Coherent, Not Visionary." *Long Range Planning* 34, no. 1 (February 2001): 53.

Newsom, Mi Kyong, David A. Collier, and Eric O. Olsen. "Using 'Biztainment' to Gain Competitive Advantage." *Business Horizons*, March–April 2009, 167–166.

Nonprofit Organization Mission Statements, http://www .missionstatements.com/nonprofit_mission_statements .html

Restaurant Mission Statements, http://www.missionstatements .com/restaurant_mission_statements.html

School Mission Statements, http://www.missionstatements .com/school_mission_statements.html

ASSURANCE OF LEARNING EXERCISES

Assurance of Learning Exercise 2A

Compare Dollar General's Mission Statement to Family Dollar's Mission Statement

Purpose

As showcased at the beginning of this chapter, Dollar General goes toe to toe every day competing against Family Dollar. Mission statements of the two companies are provided in the opening boxed insert for this chapter.

Instructions

Step 1	Compare Dollar General and Family Dollar's mission statements in terms of 1) the nine components and 2) the nine characteristics presented in this chapter.
Step 2	Turn your work in for a classwork grade.

Assurance of Learning Exercise 2B

Evaluate Mission Statements

Purpose

A business mission statement is an integral part of strategic management. It provides direction for formulating, implementing, and evaluating strategic activities. This exercise will give you practice evaluating mission statements, a skill that is a prerequisite to writing a good mission statement.

Instructions

Step 1	On a clean sheet of paper, prepare a 9 × 5 matrix. Place the nine mission statement components down the left column and the following five companies across the top of your paper.
Step 2	Write *Yes* or *No* in each cell of your matrix to indicate whether you feel the particular mission statement includes the respective component.
Step 3	Turn your paper in to your instructor for a classwork grade.

Mission Statements

Dole Food Company

Dole Food Company, Inc. is committed to supplying the consumer and our customers with the finest, high-quality products and to leading the industry in nutrition research and education. Dole supports these goals with a corporate philosophy of adhering to the highest ethical conduct in all its business dealings, treatment of its employees, and social and environmental policies.

Mattel, Inc.

Mattel makes a difference in the global community by effectively serving children in need. Partnering with charitable organizations dedicated to directly serving children, Mattel creates joy through the Mattel Children's Foundation, product donations, grant making and the work of employee volunteers. We also enrich the lives of Mattel employees by identifying diverse volunteer opportunities and supporting their personal contributions through the matching gifts program.

Dominos Pizza

To be the leader in delivering off-premise pizza convenience to consumers around the world. As a team united throughout the world, we will accomplish our mission by: 1. Being fanatical about product quality and service consistency; 2. providing product variety to meet all customer needs; 3. placing team member and customer safety and security above all other concerns; 4. creating an environment in which all team members feel valued, because they are; 5. building and maintaining relationships that reward franchisees and other partners for their contributions.

Papa Johns

To deliver the perfect pizza by exceeding the needs and expectations of our customers, franchise family, team members and stockholders.

Pizza Hut

We take pride in making a perfect pizza and providing courteous and helpful service on time all the time. Every customer says, "I'll be back!" We are the employer of choice offering team members opportunities for growth, advancement, and rewarding careers in a fun, safe working environment. We are accountable for profitability in everything we do, providing our shareholders with value growth.

Source: Based on http://www.missionstatements.com/fortune_500_mission_statements.htmlp

Assurance of Learning Exercise 2C

Write a Vision and Mission Statement for The Walt Disney Company

Purpose

There is always room for improvement in regard to an existing vision and mission statement. Currently Disney does not have a vision statement or mission statement, so this exercise asks you to develop one. But first, go to the http://corporate.disney.go.com/ website. Look down the left column and click on Company Overview. Read this material because some of that narrative may be good to include in your proposed a Disney vision and mission statement.

Instructions

Step 1	Refer back to the Cohesion Case and DIS's *Form 10K*.
Step 2	On a clean sheet of paper, write a one-sentence vision statement for The Walt Disney Company.
Step 3	On that same sheet of paper, write a mission statement for The Walt Disney Company.

Assurance of Learning Exercise 2D

Write a Vision and Mission Statement for My University

Purpose

Most universities have a vision and mission statement. The purpose of this exercise is to give you practice writing a vision and mission statement for a nonprofit organization such as your own university.

Instructions

Step 1	Write a vision statement and a mission statement for your university. Your mission statement should include the nine characteristics summarized in Table 2-3, and the nine components in Table 2-4.
Step 2	Read your vision and mission statement to the class.
Step 3	Determine whether your institution has a vision and/or mission statement. Look in the front of the college handbook. If your institution has a written statement, contact an appropriate administrator of the institution to inquire as to how and when the statement was prepared. Share this information with the class. Analyze your college's vision and mission statement in light of the concepts presented in this chapter.

Assurance of Learning Exercise 2E

Conduct Mission Statement Research

Purpose

This exercise gives you the opportunity to study the nature and role of vision and mission statements in strategic management.

Instructions

Step 1	Call various organizations in your city or county to identify firms that have developed a formal vision and/or mission statement. Contact nonprofit organizations and government agencies in addition to small and large businesses. Ask to speak with the director, owner, or chief executive officer of each organization. Explain that you are studying vision and mission statements in class and are conducting research as part of a class activity.
Step 2	Ask several executives the following four questions, and record their answers. 1. When did your organization first develop its vision and/or mission statement? Who was primarily responsible for its development? 2. How long have your current statements existed? When were they last modified? Why were they modified at that time? 3. By what process are your firm's vision and mission statements altered? 4. How are your vision and mission statements used in the firm?
Step 3	Provide an overview of your findings to the class.

Assurance of Learning Exercise 2F

Evaluate a Mission Proposal

Purpose

The Heinz Food Company has a combined vision/mission that is given below. An employee recently proposed to the company that a separate vision statement and mission statement is needed. The employee's proposed new statements are given below the actual company document. This exercise gives you practice evaluating the new employee's proposal.

Instructions

Step 1   Review and analyze the actual and proposed vision/mission statements for Heinz.
Step 2   Respond to the employee's proposal with a one-page written assessment. Turn your analysis in to your professor.

Heinz's Actual Vision/Mission

As a global food company, Heinz is committed to enhancing the nutrition, health and wellness of people and their communities to make the world a better place to live. Heinz aims to manufacture safe, healthy, nutritious, high quality food.

Proposed Vision

To be the world's premier food company, offering affordable, nutritious, superior tasting foods to enhance the quality of life for people everywhere.

Proposed Mission

As a leading global food company, Heinz brand products are recognized for offering high quality, healthy, nutritious food products that enhance the lives of people worldwide. We spot consumer and customer needs and meet them with convenient, creative solutions using the latest innovations in ingredients, processing, packaging, labeling, and storage. Heinz strives to empower all employees to remain attentive and responsive to the ever-changing needs of our customers. Our managers are committed to ensuring the highest return for investors while maintaining the highest levels of integrity and ethical standards.

"NOTABLE QUOTES"

"If you're not faster than your competitor, you're in a tenuous position, and if you're only half as fast, you're terminal."
—George Salk

"The opportunities and threats existing in any situation always exceed the resources needed to exploit the opportunities or avoid the threats. Thus, strategy is essentially a problem of allocating resources. If strategy is to be successful, it must allocate superior resources against a decisive opportunity."
—William Cohen

"Organizations pursue strategies that will disrupt the normal course of industry events and forge new industry conditions to the disadvantage of competitors."
—Ian C. Macmillan

"If everyone is thinking alike, then somebody isn't thinking."
—George Patton

"It is not the strongest of the species that survive, nor the most intelligent, but the one most responsive to change."
—Charles Darwin

"Nothing focuses the mind better than the constant sight of a competitor who wants to wipe you off the map."
—Wayne Calloway

The External Assessment

3

CHAPTER OBJECTIVES

After studying this chapter, you should be able to do the following:

1. Describe how to conduct an external strategic-management audit.

2. Discuss 10 major external forces that affect organizations: economic, social, cultural, demographic, environmental, political, governmental, legal, technological, and competitive.

3. Describe key sources of external information, including the Internet.

4. Discuss important forecasting tools used in strategic management.

5. Discuss the importance of monitoring external trends and events.

6. Explain how to develop an EFE Matrix.

7. Explain how to develop a Competitive Profile Matrix.

8. Discuss the importance of gathering competitive intelligence.

9. Describe the trend toward cooperation among competitors.

10. Discuss market commonality and resource similarity in relation to competitive analysis.

ASSURANCE OF LEARNING EXERCISES

Assurance of Learning Exercise 3A
Competitive Intelligence (CI) Certification

Assurance of Learning Exercise 3B
Develop Divisional Walt Disney EFE Matrices

Assurance of Learning Exercise 3C
Develop an EFE Matrix for Walt Disney

Assurance of Learning Exercise 3D
Perform an External Assessment

Assurance of Learning Exercise 3E
Develop an EFE Matrix for My University

Assurance of Learning Exercise 3F
Develop Divisional Walt Disney CPMs

Assurance of Learning Exercise 3G
Develop a Competitive Profile Matrix for Walt Disney

Assurance of Learning Exercise 3H
Develop a Competitive Profile Matrix for My University

This chapter examines the tools and concepts needed to conduct an external strategic management audit (sometimes called *environmental scanning* or *industry analysis*). An *external audit* focuses on identifying and evaluating trends and events beyond the control of a single firm, such as increased foreign competition, population shifts to the Sunbelt, an aging society, consumer fear of traveling, and stock market volatility. An external audit reveals key opportunities and threats confronting an organization so that managers can formulate strategies to take advantage of the opportunities and avoid or reduce the impact of threats. This chapter presents a practical framework for gathering, assimilating, and analyzing external information. The Industrial Organization (I/O) view of strategic management is introduced.

The Chapter 3 boxed insert company pursuing strategies based on an excellent external strategic analysis is Wells Fargo, the fourth-largest lender by assets in the United States.

The Nature of an External Audit

The purpose of an *external audit* is to develop a finite list of opportunities that could benefit a firm and threats that should be avoided. As the term *finite* suggests, the external audit is not aimed at developing an exhaustive list of every possible factor that could influence the business; rather, it is aimed at identifying key variables that offer actionable responses. Firms should be

Excellent Strategic Management Showcased

WELLS FARGO & COMPANY

Wells Fargo reported $12.4 billion in 2010 net income, placing the company second in profits among all large commercial banks in the United States. Only JPMorgan Chase had more banking profits in 2010 than Wells Fargo. Wells Fargo is the fourth largest bank in the U.S. by assets and the second largest bank in deposits, home mortgage servicing, and debit cards in the United States. Wells Fargo has emerged as the king of consumer banking, rolling out profitable banking products from its "stores." Called cross-selling, Wells Fargo's strategy focuses heavily on selling additional products to existing customers. The company in 2011 sold customers an average of 5.7 different products, up from 5.47 in 2010. An analyst at Rochdale Securities, Richard Bove, recently said "Wells Fargo has a system which every other bank in the world is now emulating. When you go into a Wells Fargo branch, they immediately hit you with some sales pitch."

Headquartered in San Francisco, Wells Fargo originated $386 billion in new home loans in 2010 while its main competitor, Bank of America, spent more time dealing with troubled mortgages and paying $2.8 billion in the month of December alone to end some federal government loan repurchase demands. Wells Fargo has about $90 billion in unpaid principal on portfolio of option—ARMS that it inherited from Wachovia, but the bank is dealing with that problem well.

Through its 187 commercial banking branches across the United States, Wells Fargo is increasing from 2,400 to over 2,700 its number of employees who focus on lending to mid-size businesses. Commercial lending is a growth area of banks even though many companies have increased their cash reserves and may not need loans in the immediate future. D. Anthony Plath, a finance professor at UNC-Charlotte, says, "Wells Fargo can pursue strategic initiatives whereas Bank of America is essentially fighting fires."

A nationwide, diversified, financial services company with $1.3 trillion in assets, Wells Fargo was founded in 1852. The firm provides banking, insurance, investments, mortgage, and consumer and commercial finance through more than 9,000 stores, 12,000 ATMs, the Internet (wellsfargo.com and wachovia.com), and other distribution channels across North America and internationally. With approximately 280,000 employees (called team members), Wells Fargo serves one in three households in America. Wells Fargo is among America's 20 largest corporations. Wells Fargo's vision is "to satisfy all our customers' financial needs and help them succeed financially."

Source: Based on Dakin Campbell, "Wells Fargo Is Ready to Roll," *Bloomberg Business Week*, January 31–February 6, 2011, 43–44. Also, Randall Smith, "In Tribute to Wells, Banks Try Hard Sell," *Wall Street Journal*, February 28, 2011, C1. Also, company documents.

FIGURE 3-1

A Comprehensive Strategic-Management Model

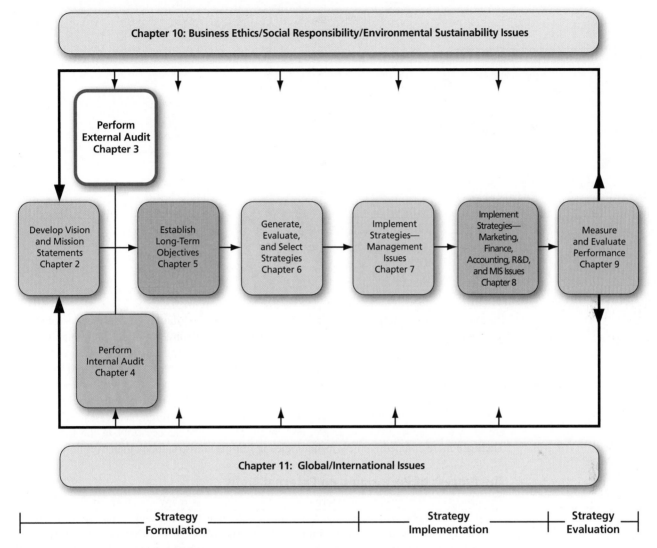

Source: Fred R. David, "How Companies Define Their Mission," *Long Range Planning* 22, no. 3 (June 1988): 40.

able to respond either offensively or defensively to the factors by formulating strategies that take advantage of external opportunities or that minimize the impact of potential threats. Figure 3-1 illustrates how the external audit fits into the strategic-management process.

Key External Forces

External forces can be divided into five broad categories: (1) economic forces; (2) social, cultural, demographic, and natural environment forces; (3) political, governmental, and legal forces; (4) technological forces; and (5) competitive forces. Relationships among these forces and an organization are depicted in Figure 3-2. External trends and events, such as rising food prices and people in African countries coming online, significantly affect products, services, markets, and organizations worldwide. The U.S. unemployment rate is about 10 percent—the most since 1945 when the country downsized from the war effort. All sectors witness high unemployment rates, except for education, health-care services, and government employment. Many Americans still resort to minimum wage jobs to make ends meet.

Changes in external forces translate into changes in consumer demand for both industrial and consumer products and services. External forces affect the types of products developed,

FIGURE 3-2

Relationships Between Key External Forces and an Organization

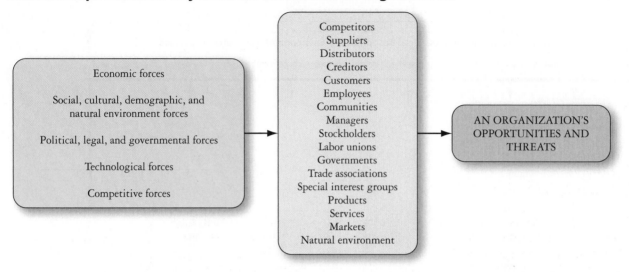

the nature of positioning and market segmentation strategies, the type of services offered, and the choice of businesses to acquire or sell. External forces directly affect both suppliers and distributors. Identifying and evaluating external opportunities and threats enables organizations to develop a clear mission, to design strategies to achieve long-term objectives, and to develop policies to achieve annual objectives.

The increasing complexity of business today is evidenced by more countries developing the capacity and will to compete aggressively in world markets. Foreign businesses and countries are willing to learn, adapt, innovate, and invent to compete successfully in the marketplace. There are more competitive new technologies in Europe and Asia today than ever before.

The Process of Performing an External Audit

The process of performing an external audit must involve as many managers and employees as possible. As emphasized in earlier chapters, involvement in the strategic-management process can lead to understanding and commitment from organizational members. Individuals appreciate having the opportunity to contribute ideas and to gain a better understanding of their firm's industry, competitors, and markets.

To perform an external audit, a company first must gather competitive intelligence and information about economic, social, cultural, demographic, environmental, political, governmental, legal, and technological trends. Individuals can be asked to monitor various sources of information, such as key magazines, trade journals, and newspapers. These persons can submit periodic scanning reports to a committee of managers charged with performing the external audit. This approach provides a continuous stream of timely strategic information and involves many individuals in the external-audit process. The Internet provides another source for gathering strategic information, as do corporate, university, and public libraries. Suppliers, distributors, salespersons, customers, and competitors represent other sources of vital information.

Once information is gathered, it should be assimilated and evaluated. A meeting or series of meetings of managers is needed to collectively identify the most important opportunities and threats facing the firm. These key external factors should be listed on flip charts or a chalkboard. A prioritized list of these factors could be obtained by requesting that all managers rank the factors identified, from 1 for the most important opportunity/threat to 20 for the least important opportunity/threat. These key external factors can vary over time and by industry. Relationships with suppliers or distributors are often a critical success factor. Other variables commonly used include market share, breadth of competing products, world economies, foreign affiliates, proprietary and key account advantages, price competitiveness, technological advancements, population shifts, interest rates, and pollution abatement.

Freund emphasized that these key external factors should be (1) important to achieving long-term and annual objectives, (2) measurable, (3) applicable to all competing firms, and (4) hierarchical in the sense that some will pertain to the overall company and others will be more narrowly focused on functional or divisional areas.[1] A final list of the most important key external factors should be communicated and distributed widely in the organization. Both opportunities and threats can be key external factors.

The Industrial Organization (I/O) View

The *Industrial Organization (I/O)* approach to competitive advantage advocates that external (industry) factors are more important than internal factors in a firm for achieving competitive advantage. Proponents of the I/O view, such as Michael Porter, contend that organizational performance will be primarily determined by industry forces. Porter's Five-Forces Model, presented later in this chapter, is an example of the I/O perspective, which focuses on analyzing external forces and industry variables as a basis for getting and keeping competitive advantage. Competitive advantage is determined largely by competitive positioning within an industry, according to I/O advocates. Managing strategically from the I/O perspective entails firms striving to compete in attractive industries, avoiding weak or faltering industries, and gaining a full understanding of key external factor relationships within that attractive industry. I/O research provides important contributions to our understanding of how to gain competitive advantage.

I/O theorists contend that external factors and the industry in which a firm competes has a stronger influence on the firm's performance than do the internal functional issues in marketing, finance, and the like. Firm performance, they contend, is based more on industry properties such as economies of scale, barriers to market entry, product differentiation, the economy, and level of competitiveness than on internal resources, capabilities, structure, and operations. The recent global economic recession's negative impact on both strong and weak firms added credence to the notion that external forces are more important than internal.

The I/O view has enhanced our understanding of strategic management. However, it is not a question of whether external or internal factors are more important in gaining and maintaining competitive advantage. Effective integration and understanding of *both* external and internal factors is the key to securing and keeping a competitive advantage. In fact, as discussed in Chapter 6, matching key external opportunities/threats with key internal strengths/weaknesses provides the basis for successful strategy formulation.

Economic Forces

The Dow Jones Industrial Average is over 10,500, corporate profits are high, dividend increases are up sharply, and emerging markets are growing in double digits. Yet, job growth is still stymied, home prices remain low, and millions of people work for minimum wages or are either unemployed or underemployed. Strong exports of energy and grains have farm suppliers and railroads hiring, but commodity prices are up sharply, especially food, which is contributing to rising inflation fears. Many firms are switching to the extent possible to part-time rather than full-time employees to avoid having to pay health benefits. Consumer spending rebounded nicely in 2011 from 2010.

Economic factors have a direct impact on the potential attractiveness of various strategies. For example, when interest rates rise, funds needed for capital expansion become more costly or unavailable. Also, as interest rates rise, discretionary income declines, and the demand for discretionary goods falls. When stock prices increase, the desirability of equity as a source of capital for market development increases. Also, when the market rises, consumer and business wealth expands. A summary of economic variables that often represent opportunities and threats for organizations is provided in Table 3-1.

TABLE 3-1 Key Economic Variables to Be Monitored

Shift to a service economy in the United States	Import/export factors
Availability of credit	Demand shifts for different categories of goods and services
Level of disposable income	Income differences by region and consumer groups
Propensity of people to spend	
Interest rates	Price fluctuations
Inflation rates	Export of labor and capital from the United States
Money market rates	
Federal government budget deficits	Monetary policies
Gross domestic product trend	Fiscal policies
Consumption patterns	Tax rates
Unemployment trends	European Economic Community (EEC) policies
Worker productivity levels	
Value of the dollar in world markets	Organization of Petroleum Exporting Countries (OPEC) policies
Stock market trends	
Foreign countries' economic conditions	Coalitions of Lesser Developed Countries (LDC) policies

To take advantage of Canada's robust economy and eager-to-spend people, many firms are aggressively expanding operations into Canada, including TJX opening many Marshalls stores, Target opening 220 stores, Wal-Mart opening 40 supercenters, and Tanger Outlet Factory Centers opening five new stores in 2011. "Canada is one of the most economically prosperous countries in the world," said Howard Davidowitz, chairman of Davidowitz & Associates, a retail consultancy and investment-banking firm. "It has a stable currency, it did not have a banking crisis and it did not spend itself into insanity."

Trends in the dollar's value have significant and unequal effects on companies in different industries and in different locations. For example, the pharmaceutical, tourism, entertainment, motor vehicle, aerospace, and forest products industries benefit greatly when the dollar falls against the yen and euro. Agricultural and petroleum industries are hurt by the dollar's rise against the currencies of Mexico, Brazil, Venezuela, and Australia. Generally, a strong or high dollar makes U.S. goods more expensive in overseas markets. This worsens the U.S. trade deficit. When the value of the dollar falls, tourism-oriented firms benefit because Americans do not travel abroad as much when the value of the dollar is low; rather, foreigners visit and vacation more in the United States.

A low value of the dollar means lower imports and higher exports; it helps U.S. companies' competitiveness in world markets. The dollar has fallen to five-year lows against the euro and yen, which makes U.S. goods cheaper to foreign consumers and combats deflation by pushing up prices of imports. However, European firms such as Volkswagen AG, Nokia Corp., and Michelin complain that the strong euro hurts their financial performance. The low value of the dollar benefits the U.S. economy in many ways. First, it helps stave off the risks of deflation in the United States and also reduces the U.S. trade deficit. In addition, the low value of the dollar raises the foreign sales and profits of domestic firms, thanks to dollar-induced gains, and encourages foreign countries to lower interest rates and loosen fiscal policy, which stimulates worldwide economic expansion. Some sectors, such as consumer staples, energy, materials, technology, and health care, especially benefit from a low value of the dollar. Manufacturers in many domestic industries in fact benefit because of a weak dollar, which forces foreign rivals to raise prices and extinguish discounts. Domestic firms with big overseas sales, such as McDonald's, greatly benefit from a weak dollar. Table 3-2 lists some advantages and disadvantages of a weak U.S. dollar for American firms.

The improving but weak economy worldwide and depressed home prices has dramatically slowed the migration of people from country to country and from the city to the suburbs. Because people are not moving nearly as much as in years past, there is lower and lower demand for new or used houses. Thus the housing market is expected to remain sluggish well into 2012 and 2013.

TABLE 3-2   Advantages and Disadvantages of a Weak Dollar for Domestic Firms

Advantages	Disadvantages
1. Leads to more exports	1. Can lead to inflation
2. Leads to lower imports	2. Can cause rise in oil prices
3. Makes U.S. goods cheaper to foreign consumers	3. Can weaken U.S. government
4. Combats deflation by pushing up prices of imports	4. Makes it unattractive for Americans to travel globally
5. Can contribute to rise in stock prices in short run	5. Can contribute to fall in stock prices in long run
6. Encourages foreign countries to lower interest rates	
7. Raises the revenues and profits of firms that do business outside the United States	
8. Forces foreign firms to raise prices	
9. Reduces the U.S. trade deficit	
10. Encourages firms to globalize	
11. Encourages foreigners to visit the United States	

Social, Cultural, Demographic, and Natural Environment Forces

Social, cultural, demographic, and environmental changes have a major impact on virtually all products, services, markets, and customers. Small, large, for-profit, and nonprofit organizations in all industries are being staggered and challenged by the opportunities and threats arising from changes in social, cultural, demographic, and environmental variables. In every way, the United States is much different today than it was yesterday, and tomorrow promises even greater changes.

The United States is getting older and less white. The oldest members of America's 76 million baby boomers plan to retire soon, and this has lawmakers and younger taxpayers deeply concerned about who will pay their Social Security, Medicare, and Medicaid. Individuals age 65 and older in the United States as a percentage of the population will rise to 18.5 percent by 2025.

By 2075, the United States will have no racial or ethnic majority. This forecast is aggravating tensions over issues such as immigration and affirmative action. Hawaii, California, and New Mexico already have no majority race or ethnic group. For the first time ever, the number of Hispanic people surpassed the number of whites in New Mexico in the recent 2010 census data. New Mexico's population grew 13.2 percent to 2.06 million from 2000 to 2010. Also, people from the West Coast are seeking more affordable living in the Rocky Mountain states. For example, Idaho's population increased 21.1 percent from 2000 to 2010 with 1.7 million people now calling Idaho home. There is a "migration for cheaper life" across the United States.

The population of the world surpassed 7.0 billion in 2011; the United States has just over 310 million people. That leaves billions of people outside the United States who may be interested in the products and services produced through domestic firms. Remaining solely domestic is an increasingly risky strategy, especially as the world population continues to grow to an estimated 8 billion in 2028 and 9 billion in 2054.

Social, cultural, demographic, and environmental trends are shaping the way Americans live, work, produce, and consume. New trends are creating a different type of consumer and, consequently, a need for different products, different services, and different strategies. There are now more American households with people living alone or with unrelated people than there are households consisting of married couples with children. American households are making more and more purchases online.

The trend toward an older America is good news for restaurants, hotels, airlines, cruise lines, tours, resorts, theme parks, luxury products and services, recreational vehicles, home builders, furniture producers, computer manufacturers, travel services, pharmaceutical firms, automakers, and funeral homes. Older Americans are especially interested in health care, financial services, travel, crime prevention, and leisure. The world's longest-living people are the Japanese, with Japanese women living to 86.3 years and men living to 80.1 years on average. By 2050, the Census Bureau projects that the number of Americans age 100 and older will increase to over 834,000 from just under 100,000 centenarians in the United States in 2000. Americans age 65 and over will increase from 12.6 percent of the U.S. population in 2000 to 20.0 percent by the year 2050.

The aging American population affects the strategic orientation of nearly all organizations. Apartment complexes for the elderly, with one meal a day, transportation, and utilities included in the rent, have increased nationwide. Called *lifecare facilities,* these complexes now exceed 2 million. Some well-known companies building these facilities include Avon, Marriott, and Hyatt. Individuals age 65 and older in the United States comprise 13 percent of the total population; Japan's elderly population ratio is 17 percent, and Germany's is 19 percent.

Americans were on the move in a population shift to the South and Rocky Mountain states away from the Northeast and Midwest (Frostbelt), and the expensive West Coast. But the recession and housing bust nationwide has slowed migration throughout the United States. More Americans are staying in place rather than moving. New jobs are the primary reason people move across state lines, so with fewer jobs, there is less need to move. Falling home prices also have prompted people to avoid moving. The historical trend of people moving from the Northeast and Midwest to the Sunbelt and West has dramatically slowed. Hard number data related to this trend can represent key opportunities for many firms and thus can be essential for successful strategy formulation, including where to locate new plants and distribution centers and where to focus marketing efforts.

A summary of important social, cultural, demographic, and environmental variables that represent opportunities or threats for virtually all organizations is given in Table 3-3.

Political, Governmental, and Legal Forces

Federal, state, local, and foreign governments are major regulators, deregulators, subsidizers, employers, and customers of organizations. Political, governmental, and legal factors, therefore, can represent key opportunities or threats for both small and large organizations. Political unrest in the Middle East threatens to raise oil prices globally, which could cause inflation. The political overthrow of monarchies in Egypt, Tunisia, and Libya is spreading to Yemen, Jordan, Syria, and other countries as people in all nations desire liberty and freedom rather than oppression and suppression.

For industries and firms that depend heavily on government contracts or subsidies, political forecasts can be the most important part of an external audit. Changes in patent laws, antitrust legislation, tax rates, and lobbying activities can affect firms significantly. The increasing global interdependence among economies, markets, governments, and organizations makes it imperative that firms consider the possible impact of political variables on the formulation and implementation of competitive strategies.

Many countries worldwide are resorting to protectionism to safeguard their own industries. European Union (EU) nations, for example, have tightened their own trade rules and resumed subsidies for various of their own industries while barring imports from certain other countries. The EU recently restricted imports of U.S. chicken and beef. India is increasing tariffs on foreign steel. Russia perhaps has instituted the most protectionist measures by raising tariffs on most imports and subsidizing its own exports. Russia even imposed a new toll on trucks from the EU, Switzerland, and Turkmenistan. Despite these measures taken by other countries, the United States has largely refrained from "Buy American" policies and protectionist measures, although there are increased tariffs on French cheese and Italian water. Many economists say the current rash of trade constraints will make it harder for global economic growth to recover from the global recession.

TABLE 3-3   Key Social, Cultural, Demographic, and Natural Environment Variables

Childbearing rates	Attitudes toward retirement
Number of special-interest groups	Attitudes toward leisure time
Number of marriages	Attitudes toward product quality
Number of divorces	Attitudes toward customer service
Number of births	Pollution control
Number of deaths	Attitudes toward foreign peoples
Immigration and emigration rates	Energy conservation
Social Security programs	Social programs
Life expectancy rates	Number of churches
Per capita income	Number of church members
Location of retailing, manufacturing, and service businesses	Social responsibility
Attitudes toward business	Attitudes toward careers
Lifestyles	Population changes by race, age, sex, and level of affluence
Traffic congestion	Attitudes toward authority
Inner-city environments	Population changes by city, county, state, region, and country
Average disposable income	
Trust in government	Value placed on leisure time
Attitudes toward government	Regional changes in tastes and preferences
Attitudes toward work	Number of women and minority workers
Buying habits	Number of high school and college graduates by geographic area
Ethical concerns	
Attitudes toward saving	Recycling
Sex roles	Waste management
Attitudes toward investing	Air pollution
Racial equality	Water pollution
Use of birth control	Ozone depletion
Average level of education	Endangered species
Government regulation	

A political debate raging in the United States concerns sales taxes on the Internet. Wal-Mart, Target, and other large retailers are pressuring state governments to collect sales taxes from Amazon.com. Big brick-and-mortar retailers are backing a coalition called the Alliance for Main Street Fairness, which is leading political efforts to change sales-tax laws in more than a dozen states. Wal-Mart's executive Raul Vazquez says, "The rules today don't allow brick-and-mortar retailers to compete evenly with online retailers, and that needs to be addressed."

American Labor Unions

The extent that a state is unionized can be a significant political factor in strategic planning decisions as related to manufacturing plant location and other operational matters. The size of American labor unions has fallen sharply in the last decade due in large part to erosion of the U.S. manufacturing base. The single best example of this is the decline of the United Automobile Workers (UAW) as U.S. automakers and car parts suppliers went through hard times. The number of workers represented by unions in the U.S. fell from 9 percent to 6.9 percent between 2000 and 2010.

Huge declines of late in receipts of federal, state, and municipal governments has contributed to a sharp decline in the membership of public-sector unions. Organized public-sector labor issues are being debated in many state legislatures. State governments seek concessions, the

TABLE 3-4   The Most versus the Least Unionized States

	(% of Workers) Unionized	2000 to 2010 % Change in Union Membership
The Most Unionized States		
1. New York	24.2%	− 5.1%
2. Alaska	22.9%	+ 4.6%
3. Hawaii	21.8%	− 12.1%
4. Washington	19.4%	+ 6.6%
5. California	17.5%	+ 9.4%
6. New Jersey	17.1%	− 17.8%
7. Connecticut	16.7%	+ 2.5%
8. Michigan	16.5%	− 20.7%
9. Rhode Island	16.4%	− 9.9%
10. Oregon	16.2%	+ 0.6%
The Least Unionized States		
1. North Carolina	3.2%	− 11.1%
2. Georgia	4.04%	− 36.5%
3. Arkansas	4.04%	− 31.0%
4. Louisiana	4.3%	− 39.4%
5. Mississippi	4.5%	− 25.0%
6. Virginia	4.62%	− 17.9%
7. South Carolina	4.65%	+ 15.0%
8. Tennessee	4.7%	− 47.2%
9. Texas	5.4%	− 6.9%
10. Oklahoma	5.5%	− 19.1%

Source: Based on: http://247wallst.com/2011/03/10/the-states-with-the-strongest-and-weakest-unions/5/

most drastic of which may be the abolition of collective bargaining rights. Wisconsin recently passed a law eliminating most collective-bargaining rights for the state's public-employee unions. That law sets a precedent that many other states may follow to curb union rights as a way to help state budgets become solvent. Ohio is close to passing a similar bill curbing union rights for 400,000 public workers.

The Republican majority in many state legislatures and governors' offices makes the "declining public unionization" trend likely to continue. Public unions now face the kind of erosion that private unions did in the last decade. Local governments simply do not have sufficient tax receipts to support current union payrolls and benefits. Table 3-4 compares the most unionized states with the least unionized. Note that union membership overall dropped in most states from 2000 to 2010 due to private sector losses, but public sector union employees, on the other hand, have held their own.

Governments worldwide are under pressure to protect jobs at home and maintain the nation's industrial base. For example, in France, Renault SA's factory in Sandouville is one of the most unproductive auto factories in the world. However, Renault has taken $3.9 billion in low-interest loans from the French government, so the company cannot close any French factories for the duration of the loan or resort to mass layoffs in France for a year.

Local, state, and federal laws; regulatory agencies; and special-interest groups can have a major impact on the strategies of small, large, for-profit, and nonprofit organizations. Many companies have altered or abandoned strategies in the past because of political or governmental actions. In the academic world, as state budgets have dropped in recent years, so too has state support for colleges and universities. Due to the decline in monies received from the state, many institutions of higher learning are doing more fund-raising on their own—naming buildings and classrooms, for example, for donors. A summary of political, governmental, and legal variables that can represent key opportunities or threats to organizations is provided in Table 3-5.

TABLE 3-5 Some Political, Governmental, and Legal Variables

Government regulations or deregulations	Sino-American relationships
Changes in tax laws	Russian-American relationships
Special tariffs	European-American relationships
Political action committees	African-American relationships
Voter participation rates	Import–export regulations
Number, severity, and location of government protests	Government fiscal and monetary policy changes
Number of patents	Political conditions in foreign countries
Changes in patent laws	Special local, state, and federal laws
Environmental protection laws	Lobbying activities
Level of defense expenditures	Size of government budgets
Legislation on equal employment	World oil, currency, and labor markets
Level of government subsidies	Location and severity of terrorist activities
Antitrust legislation	Local, state, and national elections

Technological Forces

Papa John's International in 2012 expects to receive 50 percent of all its pizza orders through its website, up from 30 percent in 2011 and far more than the industry average of 10 percent. Technology is a key to Papa John's success as it strives to compete with Domino's Pizza and Pizza Hut. Papa John's new website is interactive, where customers can see a picture of their pizza as they decide upon toppings. Papa John's new loyalty program, called Papa Points, is promoted heavily through its new website.

Lagging behind Netflix and Redbox in technology has been disastrous for Blockbuster, which recently filed for Chapter 11 bankruptcy protection and then barely escaped liquidation before being acquired by Dish Network Corp. for $320 million. Internet streaming giant Netflix and $1 DVD movies offered by Redbox essentially forced Blockbuster to close more than 1,000 of its 3,000 stores while at the same time desperately trying to shift to digital distribution. In virtually every industry, the more technologically astute firms gain overwhelming competitive advantage over less competent rivals.

The *Internet* has changed the very nature of opportunities and threats by altering the life cycles of products, increasing the speed of distribution, creating new products and services, erasing limitations of traditional geographic markets, and changing the historical trade-off between production standardization and flexibility. The Internet is altering economies of scale, changing entry barriers, and redefining the relationship between industries and various suppliers, creditors, customers, and competitors.

Total Internet retail sales the last two months of 2010 jumped 15.4 percent compared to 2009. Purchases online of apparel at specialty stores increased 25 percent, even though people prefer to touch and try on garments.[2] Retail sales over the Internet now account for about 10 percent of all retail sales, excluding purchases of automobiles and gas.

To effectively capitalize on e-commerce, a number of organizations are establishing two new positions in their firms: *chief information officer (CIO)* and *chief technology officer (CTO)*. This trend reflects the growing importance of *information technology (IT)* in strategic management. A CIO and CTO work together to ensure that information needed to formulate, implement, and evaluate strategies is available where and when it is needed. These individuals are responsible for developing, maintaining, and updating a company's information database. The CIO is more a manager, managing the firm's relationship with stakeholders; the CTO is more a technician, focusing on technical issues such as data acquisition, data processing, decision-support systems, and software and hardware acquisition.

Technological forces represent major opportunities and threats that must be considered in formulating strategies. Technological advancements can dramatically affect organizations' products, services, markets, suppliers, distributors, competitors, customers, manufacturing processes, marketing practices, and competitive position. Technological advancements can create new markets, result in a proliferation of new and improved products, change the relative competitive cost positions in an industry, and render existing products and services obsolete. Technological changes can reduce or eliminate cost barriers between businesses, create shorter production runs, create shortages in technical skills, and result in changing values and expectations of employees, managers, and customers. Technological advancements can create new competitive advantages that are more powerful than existing advantages. No company or industry today is insulated against emerging technological developments. In high-tech industries, identification and evaluation of key technological opportunities and threats can be the most important part of the external strategic-management audit.

Organizations that traditionally have limited technology expenditures to what they can fund after meeting marketing and financial requirements urgently need a reversal in thinking. The pace of technological change is increasing and literally wiping out businesses every day. An emerging consensus holds that technology management is one of the key responsibilities of strategists. Firms should pursue strategies that take advantage of technological opportunities to achieve sustainable, competitive advantages in the marketplace.

In practice, critical decisions about technology too often are delegated to lower organizational levels or are made without an understanding of their strategic implications. Many strategists spend countless hours determining market share, positioning products in terms of features and price, forecasting sales and market size, and monitoring distributors; yet too often, technology does not receive the same respect.

Not all sectors of the economy are affected equally by technological developments. The communications, electronics, aeronautics, and pharmaceutical industries are much more volatile than the textile, forestry, and metals industries.

Competitive Forces

An important part of an external audit is identifying rival firms and determining their strengths, weaknesses, capabilities, opportunities, threats, objectives, and strategies.

For example, Tupperware Brands Corp. (TBC) produces and sells household products and beauty items. TBC competes intensely with Avon Products and Newell Rubbermaid. Tupperware parties became synonymous with American suburban life in the 1950s, when independent salespeople organized gatherings to sell their plastic containers. TBC today deploys a sales force of about 2.6 million people in about 100 countries and obtains more than 80 percent of their annual $2.3 billion revenue from outside the United States. Table 3-6 compares Tupperware with its two largest competitors. Note that TBC outperforms Avon and Rubbermaid on most criteria.

Collecting and evaluating information on competitors is essential for successful strategy formulation. Identifying major competitors is not always easy because many firms have divisions that compete in different industries. Many multidivisional firms do not provide sales and profit information on a divisional basis for competitive reasons. Also, privately-held firms do not publish any financial or marketing information. Addressing questions about competitors such as those presented in Table 3-7 is important in performing an external audit.

Competition in virtually all industries can be described as intense—and sometimes as cutthroat. For example, Walgreens and CVS pharmacies are located generally across the street from each other and battle each other every day on price and customer service. Most automobile dealerships also are located close to each other. Dollar General, based in Goodlettsville, Tennessee, and Family Dollar, based in Matthews, North Carolina, compete intensely on price to attract customers away from each other and away from Wal-Mart. Best Buy dropped prices wherever possible to finally put Circuit City totally out of business.

Seven characteristics describe the most competitive companies:

1. Market share matters; the 90th share point isn't as important as the 91st, and nothing is more dangerous than falling to 89.
2. Understand and remember precisely what business you are in.
3. Whether it's broke or not, fix it—make it better; not just products, but the whole company, if necessary.

TABLE 3-6   An Actual CPM for Tupperware

Critical Success Factors	Weight	TUPPERWARE Rating	TUPPERWARE Score	AVON Rating	AVON Score	RUBBERMAID Rating	RUBBERMAID Score
Advertising	0.15	1	0.15	3	0.45	4	0.60
Customer Service	0.03	3	0.09	2	0.06	1	0.03
Price Competitiveness	0.05	2	0.01	3	0.15	4	0.20
Top Management Expertise	0.14	4	0.56	3	0.42	2	0.28
Product Quality	0.08	4	0.32	3	0.24	2	0.16
E-commerce	0.09	1	0.09	3	0.27	2	0.18
Financial Position	0.15	4	0.60	3	0.45	2	0.30
Customer Loyalty	0.04	4	0.16	3	0.12	1	0.04
Global Expansion	0.08	4	0.32	2	0.16	1	0.08
Sales Distribution	0.06	4	0.24	2	0.12	1	0.06
Market Share	0.08	2	0.16	4	0.32	3	0.24
Product Line Offerings	0.05	4	0.20	2	0.10	3	0.15
Total	**1.00**		**2.99**		**2.86**		**2.32**

Source: Based on information provided by Eddie Guzman and David Campbell Jr.

4. Innovate or evaporate; particularly in technology-driven businesses, nothing quite recedes like success.
5. Acquisition is essential to growth; the most successful purchases are in niches that add a technology or a related market.
6. People make a difference; tired of hearing it? Too bad.
7. There is no substitute for quality and no greater threat than failing to be cost-competitive on a global basis.[3]

TABLE 3-7   Key Questions About Competitors

1. What are the major competitors' strengths?
2. What are the major competitors' weaknesses?
3. What are the major competitors' objectives and strategies?
4. How will the major competitors most likely respond to current economic, social, cultural, demographic, environmental, political, governmental, legal, technological, and competitive trends affecting our industry?
5. How vulnerable are the major competitors to our alternative company strategies?
6. How vulnerable are our alternative strategies to successful counterattack by our major competitors?
7. How are our products or services positioned relative to major competitors?
8. To what extent are new firms entering and old firms leaving this industry?
9. What key factors have resulted in our present competitive position in this industry?
10. How have the sales and profit rankings of major competitors in the industry changed over recent years? Why have these rankings changed that way?
11. What is the nature of supplier and distributor relationships in this industry?
12. To what extent could substitute products or services be a threat to competitors in this industry?

Competitive Intelligence Programs

What is competitive intelligence? *Competitive intelligence (CI)*, as formally defined by the Society of Competitive Intelligence Professionals (SCIP), is a systematic and ethical process for gathering and analyzing information about the competition's activities and general business trends to further a business's own goals (SCIP website).

Good competitive intelligence in business, as in the military, is one of the keys to success. The more information and knowledge a firm can obtain about its competitors, the more likely it is that it can formulate and implement effective strategies. Major competitors' weaknesses can represent external opportunities; major competitors' strengths may represent key threats.

Starwood Hotels & Resorts Worldwide recently sued Hilton Hotels Corp. for allegedly stealing more than 100,000 confidential electronic and paper documents containing "Starwood's most competitively sensitive information." The complaint alleges that two Starwood executives, Ross Klein and Amar Lalvani, resigned from Starwood to join Hilton and took this information with them. The legal complaint says, "This is the clearest imaginable case of corporate espionage, theft of trade secrets, unfair competition and computer fraud." In addition to monetary awards, Starwood is seeking to force Hilton to cancel the rollout of the Denizen hotel chain. Hilton is owned by Blackstone Group.

Hiring top executives from rival firms is also a way companies obtain competitive intelligence. Just two days after Facebook's COO, Owen Van Natta, left the company, he accepted the CEO job at Myspace, replacing then CEO and cofounder Chris DeWolfe. Van Natta had previously also been Facebook's COO, chief revenue officer, and vice president of operations. Google Inc. is losing top staff to Facebook, Twitter, and LinkedIn, which are all private companies that can lure top engineers and executives with pre-IPO stock. For example, Facebook's COO, Sheryl Sandberg, was previously Google's vice president of online sales and operations, and Facebook's VP of advertising and global operations, David Fischer, previously held that same position at Google. In 2010 alone, Facebook went from 1,000 employees to 2,000, Twitter went from 100 to 300, and LinkedIn went from 450 to 900.

Many U.S. executives grew up in times when U.S. firms dominated foreign competitors so much that gathering competitive intelligence did not seem worth the effort. Too many of these executives still cling to these attitudes—to the detriment of their organizations today. Even most MBA programs do not offer a course in competitive and business intelligence, thus reinforcing this attitude. As a consequence, three strong misperceptions about business intelligence prevail among U.S. executives today:

1. Running an intelligence program requires lots of people, computers, and other resources.
2. Collecting intelligence about competitors violates antitrust laws; business intelligence equals espionage.
3. Intelligence gathering is an unethical business practice.[4]

Any discussions with a competitor about price, market, or geography intentions could violate antitrust statutes. However, this fact must not lure a firm into underestimating the need for and benefits of systematically collecting information about competitors for strategic planning purposes. The Internet is an excellent medium for gathering competitive intelligence. Information gathering from employees, managers, suppliers, distributors, customers, creditors, and consultants also can make the difference between having superior or just average intelligence and overall competitiveness.

Firms need an effective competitive intelligence (CI) program. The three basic objectives of a CI program are (1) to provide a general understanding of an industry and its competitors, (2) to identify areas in which competitors are vulnerable and to assess the impact strategic actions would have on competitors, and (3) to identify potential moves that a competitor might make that would endanger a firm's position in the market.[5] Competitive information is equally applicable for strategy formulation, implementation, and evaluation decisions. An effective CI program allows all areas of a firm to access consistent and verifiable information in making decisions. All members of an organization—from the chief executive officer to custodians—are valuable intelligence agents and should feel themselves to be a part of the CI process. Special characteristics of a successful CI program include flexibility, usefulness, timeliness, and cross-functional cooperation.

The increasing emphasis on *competitive analysis* in the United States is evidenced by corporations putting this function on their organizational charts under job titles such as Director of Competitive Analysis, Competitive Strategy Manager, Director of Information Services, or Associate Director of Competitive Assessment. The responsibilities of a *director of competitive analysis* include planning, collecting data, analyzing data, facilitating the process of gathering and analyzing data, disseminating intelligence on a timely basis, researching special issues, and recognizing what information is important and who needs to know. Competitive intelligence is not corporate espionage because 95 percent of the information a company needs to make strategic decisions is available and accessible to the public. Sources of competitive information include trade journals, want ads, newspaper articles, and government filings, as well as customers, suppliers, distributors, competitors themselves, and the Internet.

Unethical tactics such as bribery, wiretapping, and computer hacking should never be used to obtain information. Marriott and Motorola—two U.S. companies that do a particularly good job of gathering competitive intelligence—agree that all the information you could wish for can be collected without resorting to unethical tactics.

Hilton Worldwide, Inc. is banned in 2011 and 2012 from creating a luxury "lifestyle" hotel (Denizen) under an agreement to settle a corporate-espionage lawsuit that stemmed from Hilton allegedly stealing confidential documents from rival Starwood Hotels & Resorts regarding their exclusive W Hotel. Also as part of the settlement, Hilton is paying Starwood an undisclosed amount of money.

Market Commonality and Resource Similarity

By definition, competitors are firms that offer similar products and services in the same market. Markets can be geographic or product areas or segments. For example, in the insurance industry the markets are broken down into commercial/consumer, health/life, or Europe/Asia. Researchers use the terms *market commonality* and *resource similarity* to study rivalry among competitors. *Market commonality* can be defined as the number and significance of markets that a firm competes in with rivals.[6] *Resource similarity* is the extent to which the type and amount of a firm's internal resources are comparable to a rival.[7] One way to analyze competitiveness between two or among several firms is to investigate market commonality and resource similarity issues while looking for areas of potential competitive advantage along each firm's value chain.

Competitive Analysis: Porter's Five-Forces Model

As illustrated in Figure 3-3, *Porter's Five-Forces Model* of competitive analysis is a widely used approach for developing strategies in many industries. The intensity of competition among firms varies widely across industries. Table 3-8 reveals the average gross profit margin and earnings per share for firms in different industries. Note the substantial variation among industries. For example, note that gross profit margin ranges from 59.28 percent to 24.50 percent, while EPS ranges from $2.45 to $0.18. Note that brick and mortar bookstores have the lowest EPS, which implies fierce competition in that industry. Intensity of competition is highest in lower-return industries. The collective impact of competitive forces is so brutal in some industries that the market is clearly "unattractive" from a profit-making standpoint. Rivalry among existing firms is severe, new rivals can enter the industry with relative ease, and both suppliers and customers can exercise considerable bargaining leverage. According to Porter, the nature of competitiveness in a given industry can be viewed as a composite of five forces:

1. Rivalry among competing firms
2. Potential entry of new competitors
3. Potential development of substitute products
4. Bargaining power of suppliers
5. Bargaining power of consumers

FIGURE 3-3

The Five-Forces Model of Competition

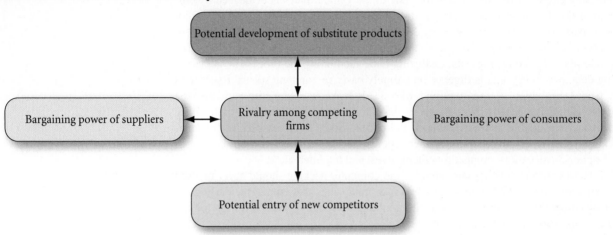

The following three steps for using Porter's Five-Forces Model can indicate whether competition in a given industry is such that the firm can make an acceptable profit:

1. Identify key aspects or elements of each competitive force that impact the firm.
2. Evaluate how strong and important each element is for the firm.
3. Decide whether the collective strength of the elements is worth the firm entering or staying in the industry.

Rivalry Among Competing Firms

Rivalry among competing firms is usually the most powerful of the five competitive forces. The strategies pursued by one firm can be successful only to the extent that they provide competitive advantage over the strategies pursued by rival firms. Changes in strategy by one firm may be met with retaliatory countermoves, such as lowering prices, enhancing quality, adding features, providing services, extending warranties, and increasing advertising.

The Internet, coupled with the common currency in Europe, enables consumers to make price comparisons easily across countries. Just for a moment, consider the implications for car dealers who used to know everything about a new car's pricing, while you, the consumer, knew very little. You could bargain, but being in the dark, you rarely could win. Now you can shop online in a few hours at every dealership within 500 miles to find the best price and terms. So you, the consumer, can win. This is true in many, if not most, business-to-consumer and business-to-business sales transactions today.

TABLE 3-8   Competitiveness Across a Few Industries (year-end 2010 data)

	Gross Profit Margin (%)	EPS ($)
Pharmaceutical	59.28	1.63
Telecommunications	57.37	0.76
Fragrances/Cosmetics	46.12	1.16
Banking	30.78	0.09
Bookstores	35.78	0.18
Food Manufacturers	30.54	0.65
Oil and Gas	32.96	1.68
Airlines	29.59	0.69
Machinery/Construction	27.53	2.45
Paper Products	24.50	1.38

Source: Based on information at www.finance.yahoo.com retrieved on May 10, 2011.

TABLE 3-9   Conditions That Cause High Rivalry Among Competing Firms

1. High number of competing firms
2. Similar size of firms competing
3. Similar capability of firms competing
4. Falling demand for the industry's products
5. Falling product/service prices in the industry
6. When consumers can switch brands easily
7. When barriers to leaving the market are high
8. When barriers to entering the market are low
9. When fixed costs are high among firms competing
10. When the product is perishable
11. When rivals have excess capacity
12. When consumer demand is falling
13. When rivals have excess inventory
14. When rivals sell similar products/services
15. When mergers are common in the industry

The intensity of rivalry among competing firms tends to increase as the number of competitors increases, as competitors become more equal in size and capability, as demand for the industry's products declines, and as price cutting becomes common. Rivalry also increases when consumers can switch brands easily; when barriers to leaving the market are high; when fixed costs are high; when the product is perishable; when consumer demand is growing slowly or declines such that rivals have excess capacity and/or inventory; when the products being sold are commodities (not easily differentiated, such as gasoline); when rival firms are diverse in strategies, origins, and culture; and when mergers and acquisitions are common in the industry. As rivalry among competing firms intensifies, industry profits decline, in some cases to the point where an industry becomes inherently unattractive. When rival firms sense weakness, typically they will intensify both marketing and production efforts to capitalize on the "opportunity." Table 3-9 summarizes conditions that cause high rivalry among competing firms.

Potential Entry of New Competitors

Whenever new firms can easily enter a particular industry, the intensity of competitiveness among firms increases. Barriers to entry, however, can include the need to gain economies of scale quickly, the need to gain technology and specialized know-how, the lack of experience, strong customer loyalty, strong brand preferences, large capital requirements, lack of adequate distribution channels, government regulatory policies, tariffs, lack of access to raw materials, possession of patents, undesirable locations, counterattack by entrenched firms, and potential saturation of the market.

Despite numerous barriers to entry, new firms sometimes enter industries with higher-quality products, lower prices, and substantial marketing resources. The strategist's job, therefore, is to identify potential new firms entering the market, to monitor the new rival firms' strategies, to counterattack as needed, and to capitalize on existing strengths and opportunities. When the threat of new firms entering the market is strong, incumbent firms generally fortify their positions and take actions to deter new entrants, such as lowering prices, extending warranties, adding features, or offering financing specials.

Potential Development of Substitute Products

In many industries, firms are in close competition with producers of substitute products in other industries. Examples are plastic container producers competing with glass, paperboard, and aluminum can producers, and acetaminophen manufacturers competing with other manufacturers of pain and headache remedies. The presence of substitute products puts a ceiling on the price that can be charged before consumers will switch to the substitute product. Price ceilings equate to profit ceilings and more intense competition among rivals. Producers of eyeglasses and contact lenses, for example, face increasing competitive pressures from laser eye surgery. Producers of sugar face similar pressures from artificial sweeteners. Newspapers and magazines face substitute-product competitive pressures from the Internet and 24-hour cable television. The magnitude of competitive pressure derived from the development of substitute products is generally evidenced by rivals' plans for expanding production capacity, as well as by their sales and profit growth numbers.

Competitive pressures arising from substitute products increase as the relative price of substitute products declines and as consumers' costs of switching decrease. The competitive strength of substitute products is best measured by the inroads into the market share those products obtain, as well as those firms' plans for increased capacity and market penetration.

For example, circulation of U.S. newspapers continues to drop drastically, with the exception of the *Wall Street Journal* and a few other bright spots. The growing popularity of free news on the web and more timely news online are two key factors negatively impacting traditional papers such as the *New York Times*, *Los Angeles Times*, and others.

Bargaining Power of Suppliers

The bargaining power of suppliers affects the intensity of competition in an industry, especially when there is a large number of suppliers, when there are only a few good substitute raw materials, or when the cost of switching raw materials is especially high. It is often in the best interest of both suppliers and producers to assist each other with reasonable prices, improved quality, development of new services, just-in-time deliveries, and reduced inventory costs, thus enhancing long-term profitability for all concerned.

Firms may pursue a backward integration strategy to gain control or ownership of suppliers. This strategy is especially effective when suppliers are unreliable, too costly, or not capable of meeting a firm's needs on a consistent basis. Firms generally can negotiate more favorable terms with suppliers when backward integration is a commonly used strategy among rival firms in an industry.

However, in many industries it is more economical to use outside suppliers of component parts than to self-manufacture the items. This is true, for example, in the outdoor power equipment industry, where producers of lawn mowers, rotary tillers, leaf blowers, and edgers such as Murray generally obtain their small engines from outside manufacturers such as Briggs & Stratton that specialize in such engines and have huge economies of scale.

In more and more industries, sellers are forging strategic partnerships with select suppliers in efforts to (1) reduce inventory and logistics costs (e.g., through just-in-time deliveries); (2) speed the availability of next-generation components; (3) enhance the quality of the parts and components being supplied and reduce defect rates; and (4) squeeze out important cost savings for both themselves and their suppliers.[8]

Bargaining Power of Consumers

When customers are concentrated or large in number or buy in volume, their bargaining power represents a major force affecting the intensity of competition in an industry. Rival firms may offer extended warranties or special services to gain customer loyalty whenever the bargaining power of consumers is substantial. Bargaining power of consumers also is higher when the products being purchased are standard or undifferentiated. When this is the case, consumers often can negotiate selling price, warranty coverage, and accessory packages to a greater extent.

The bargaining power of consumers can be the most important force affecting competitive advantage. Consumers gain increasing bargaining power under the following circumstances:

1. If they can inexpensively switch to competing brands or substitutes
2. If they are particularly important to the seller
3. If sellers are struggling in the face of falling consumer demand
4. If they are informed about sellers' products, prices, and costs
5. If they have discretion in whether and when they purchase the product[9]

Sources of External Information

A wealth of strategic information is available to organizations from both published and unpublished sources. Unpublished sources include customer surveys, market research, speeches at professional and shareholders' meetings, television programs, interviews, and conversations with stakeholders. Published sources of strategic information include periodicals, journals, reports, government documents, abstracts, books, directories, newspapers, and manuals. The Internet has made it easier for firms to gather, assimilate, and evaluate information.

There are many excellent websites for gathering strategic information, but six that the author uses routinely are listed here:

1. http://marketwatch.multexinvestor.com
2. http://moneycentral.msn.com
3. http://finance.yahoo.com
4. www.clearstation.com
5. http://us.etrade.com/e/t/invest/markets
6. www.hoovers.com
7. http://globaledge.msu.edu/industries/

An excellent source of industry information is provided by Michigan State University at http://globaledge.msu.edu/industries/ as indicated above. Industry Profiles provided at that site are an excellent source for information, news, events, and statistical data for any industry. In addition to a wealth of indices, risk assessments, and interactive trade information, a wide array of global resources are provided.

Most college libraries subscribe to Standard & Poor's (S&P's) *Industry Surveys*. These documents are exceptionally up-to-date and give valuable information about many different industries. Each report is authored by a Standard & Poor's industry research analyst and includes the following sections:

1. Current Environment
2. Industry Trends
3. How the Industry Operates
4. Key Industry Ratios and Statistics
5. How to Analyze a Company
6. Glossary of Industry Terms
7. Additional Industry Information
8. References
9. Comparative Company Financial Analysis

Forecasting Tools and Techniques

Boeing announced in early 2011 that it forecasts China to need 4,330 new commercial airplanes valued at $480 billion over the next 20 years, making China the world's second-largest airplane market after the United States. Boeing projects that China's airplane market will grow at nearly twice the rate of the rest of the industry globally. Based on these forecasts, Boeing plans to grow its 52 percent airplane market share in China by producing more single-isle jet planes.

Forecasts are educated assumptions about future trends and events. Forecasting is a complex activity because of factors such as technological innovation, cultural changes, new products, improved services, stronger competitors, shifts in government priorities, changing social values, unstable economic conditions, and unforeseen events. Managers often must rely on published forecasts to effectively identify key external opportunities and threats.

A sense of the future permeates all action and underlies every decision a person makes. People eat expecting to be satisfied and nourished in the future. People sleep assuming that in the future they will feel rested. They invest energy, money, and time because they believe their efforts will be rewarded in the future. They build highways assuming that automobiles and trucks will need them in the future. Parents educate children on the basis of forecasts that they will need certain skills, attitudes, and knowledge when they grow up. The truth is we all make implicit forecasts throughout our daily lives. The question, therefore, is not whether we should forecast but rather how we can best forecast to enable us to move beyond our ordinarily unarticulated assumptions about the future. Can we obtain information and then make educated assumptions (forecasts) to better guide our current decisions to achieve a more desirable future state of affairs? We should go into the future with our eyes and our minds open, rather than stumble into the future with our eyes closed.[10]

Sometimes organizations must develop their own projections. Most organizations forecast (project) their own revenues and profits annually. Organizations sometimes forecast market share or customer loyalty in local areas. Because forecasting is so important in strategic management and because the ability to forecast (in contrast to the ability to use a forecast) is essential, selected forecasting tools are examined further here.

Forecasting tools can be broadly categorized into two groups: quantitative techniques and qualitative techniques. Quantitative forecasts are most appropriate when historical data are available and when the relationships among key variables are expected to remain the same in the future. *Linear regression,* for example, is based on the assumption that the future will be just like the past—which, of course, it never is. As historical relationships become less stable, quantitative forecasts become less accurate.

No forecast is perfect, and some forecasts are even wildly inaccurate. This fact accents the need for strategists to devote sufficient time and effort to study the underlying bases for published forecasts and to develop internal forecasts of their own. Key external opportunities and threats can be effectively identified only through good forecasts. Accurate forecasts can provide major competitive advantages for organizations. Forecasts are vital to the strategic-management process and to the success of organizations.

Making Assumptions

Planning would be impossible without assumptions. McConkey defines assumptions as the "best present estimates of the impact of major external factors, over which the manager has little if any control, but which may exert a significant impact on performance or the ability to achieve desired results."[11] Strategists are faced with countless variables and imponderables that can be neither controlled nor predicted with 100 percent accuracy. Wild guesses should never be made in formulating strategies, but reasonable assumptions based on available information must always be made.

By identifying future occurrences that could have a major effect on the firm and by making reasonable assumptions about those factors, strategists can carry the strategic-management process forward. Assumptions are needed only for future trends and events that are most likely to have a significant effect on the company's business. Based on the best information at the time, assumptions serve as checkpoints on the validity of strategies. If future occurrences deviate significantly from assumptions, strategists know that corrective actions may be needed. Without reasonable assumptions, the strategy-formulation process could not proceed effectively. Firms that have the best information generally make the most accurate assumptions, which can lead to major competitive advantages.

Industry Analysis: The External Factor Evaluation (EFE) Matrix

An *External Factor Evaluation (EFE)* Matrix allows strategists to summarize and evaluate economic, social, cultural, demographic, environmental, political, governmental, legal, technological, and competitive information. Illustrated in Table 3-10, the EFE Matrix can be developed in five steps:

1. List key external factors as identified in the external-audit process. Include a total of 15 to 20 factors, including both opportunities and threats, that affect the firm and its industry. List the opportunities first and then the threats. Be as specific as possible, using percentages, ratios, and comparative numbers whenever possible. Recall that Edward Deming said, "In God we trust. Everyone else bring data."
2. Assign to each factor a weight that ranges from 0.0 (not important) to 1.0 (very important). The weight indicates the relative importance of that factor to being successful in

TABLE 3-10   EFE Matrix for a Local Ten-Theater Cinema Complex

Key External Factors	Weight	Rating	Weighted Score
Opportunities			
1. Rowan County is growing 8% annually in population	0.05	3	0.15
2. TDB University is expanding 6% annually	0.08	4	0.32
3. Major competitor across town recently ceased operations	0.08	3	0.24
4. Demand for going to cinema growing 10% annually	0.07	2	0.14
5. Two new neighborhoods being developed within 3 miles	0.09	1	0.09
6. Disposable income among citizens grew 5% in prior year	0.06	3	0.18
7. Unemployment rate in county declined to 3.1%	0.03	2	0.06
Threats			
8. Trend toward healthy eating eroding concession sales	0.12	4	0.48
9. Demand for online movies and DVDs growing 10% annually	0.06	2	0.12
10. Commercial property adjacent to cinemas for sale	0.06	3	0.18
11. TDB University installing an on-campus movie theater	0.04	3	0.12
12. County and city property taxes increasing 25% this year	0.08	2	0.16
13. Local religious groups object to R-rated movies being shown	0.04	3	0.12
14. Movies rented from local Blockbuster store up 12%	0.08	2	0.16
15. Movies rented last quarter from Time Warner up 15%	0.06	1	0.06
Total	**1.00**		**2.58**

the firm's industry. Opportunities often receive higher weights than threats, but threats can receive high weights if they are especially severe or threatening. Appropriate weights can be determined by comparing successful with unsuccessful competitors or by discussing the factor and reaching a group consensus. The sum of all weights assigned to the factors must equal 1.0.

3. Assign a rating between 1 and 4 to each key external factor to indicate how effectively the firm's current strategies respond to the factor, where 4 = *the response is superior*, 3 = *the response is above average*, 2 = *the response is average*, and 1 = *the response is poor.* Ratings are based on effectiveness of the firm's strategies. Ratings are thus company-based, whereas the weights in Step 2 are industry-based. It is important to note that both threats and opportunities can receive a 1, 2, 3, or 4.
4. Multiply each factor's weight by its rating to determine a weighted score.
5. Sum the weighted scores for each variable to determine the total weighted score for the organization.

Regardless of the number of key opportunities and threats included in an EFE Matrix, the highest possible total weighted score for an organization is 4.0 and the lowest possible total weighted score is 1.0. The average total weighted score is 2.5. A total weighted score of 4.0 indicates that an organization is responding in an outstanding way to existing opportunities and threats in its industry. In other words, the firm's strategies effectively take advantage of existing opportunities and minimize the potential adverse effects of external threats. A total score of 1.0 indicates that the firm's strategies are not capitalizing on opportunities or avoiding external threats.

An example of an EFE Matrix is provided in Table 3-10 for a local 10-theater cinema complex. Note that the most important factor to being successful in this business is "Trend toward healthy eating eroding concession sales" as indicated by the 0.12 weight. Also note that the local cinema is doing excellent in regard to handling two factors, "TDB University is expanding 6 percent annually" and "Trend toward healthy eating eroding concession sales." Perhaps the cinema is placing flyers on campus and also adding yogurt and healthy drinks to its concession menu. Note that you may have a 1, 2, 3, or 4 anywhere down the Rating column. Note also that the factors are stated in quantitative terms to the extent possible, rather than being stated in vague terms. Quantify the factors as much as possible in constructing an EFE Matrix. Finally, note that the total weighted score of 2.58 is above the average (midpoint) of 2.5, so this cinema business is doing pretty well, taking advantage of the external opportunities and avoiding the threats facing the firm. There is definitely room for improvement, though, because the highest total weighted score would be 4.0. As indicated by ratings of 1, this business needs to capitalize more on the "two new neighborhoods nearby" opportunity and the "movies rented from Time Warner" threat. Note also that there are many percentage-based factors among the group. Be quantitative to the extent possible! Note also that the ratings range from 1 to 4 on both the opportunities and threats.

An External Factor Evaluation (EFE) Matrix for UPS, Inc. is provided in Table 3-11. Note that "customers outsourcing their supply chain" and "foreign currency obligations" were considered by this researcher to be the most important factors in this industry, as indicated by the 0.10 weight values. UPS does best however on opportunity #1 and #4. Overall, UPS does better internally than externally since the total score of 2.59 is a bit less than the upcoming analogous IFE Matrix in the next chapter.

TABLE 3-11   An Actual External Factor Evaluation Matrix for UPS, Inc.

Opportunities	Weight	Rating	Wt. Score
1. Europe accounts for ~50% of international revenue	0.04	4	0.16
2. Africa is becoming commercially developed	0.03	2	0.06
3. >24 alliances with Asian delivery companies	0.07	2	0.14
4. International market growing 10% faster than U.S.	0.03	4	0.12
5. Customers outsourcing up to 100% of supply chain to lower cost	0.10	3	0.30
6. Increased international usage of wireless access tracking information	0.03	2	0.06
7. Telematics technology in ~12,000 U.S. UPS vehicles	0.03	2	0.06
8. Hybrid vehicles are available to add to the growing UPS alternative fuel vehicle (AFV) fleet	0.06	3	0.18
9. Only 43.2% of employees are not affiliated with a union	0.07	2	0.14
10. Direct-to-consumer business models require delivery services to be 100% effective	0.03	2	0.06
Threats			
11. Incurred $77 million charge on foreign currency obligations	0.10	3	0.30
12. Jet and diesel fuel price variations cause fluctuations in surcharges from a 13% increase to a 21.2% decrease	0.08	3	0.24
13. Adverse currency exchange rate fluctuation (7.2% decline for the year)	0.03	2	0.06
14. FASB guidance requires re-measurement of pension and benefit plans = $44 million reduction to income	0.04	1	0.04
15. 1% change in health care cost trend rates = increase in post-retirement benefit obligation of $83 million	0.06	3	0.18
16. Joint venture partner for Dubai owns 20% put option	0.03	2	0.06
17. Undistributed earnings of non-U.S. subs ~$2.2 billion	0.05	2	0.10
18. Consumers expect "green business operations"	0.04	3	0.12
19. U.S. unemployment rates continue holding near 10%	0.03	2	0.06
20. FedEx has greater international presence (27% compared to UPS 24% of total revenues)	0.05	3	0.15
Totals	**1.00**		**2.59**

The Competitive Profile Matrix (CPM)

The *Competitive Profile Matrix (CPM)* identifies a firm's major competitors and its particular strengths and weaknesses in relation to a sample firm's strategic position. The weights and total weighted scores in both a CPM and an EFE have the same meaning. However, *critical success* factors in a CPM include both internal and external issues; therefore, the ratings refer to strengths and weaknesses, where 4 = major strength, 3 = minor strength, 2 = minor weakness, and 1 = major weakness. The critical success factors in a CPM are not grouped into opportunities and threats as they are in an EFE. In a CPM, the ratings and total weighted scores for rival firms can be compared to the sample firm. This comparative analysis provides important internal strategic information. Avoid assigning the same rating to firms included in your CPM analysis.

A sample Competitive Profile Matrix is provided in Table 3-12. In this example, the two most important factors to being successful in the industry are "advertising" and "global expansion," as indicated by weights of 0.20. If there were no weight column in this analysis, note that each factor then would be equally important. Thus, having a weight column makes for a more robust analysis, because it enables the analyst to assign higher and lower numbers to capture perceived or actual levels of importance. Note in Table 3-12 that Company 1 is strongest on "product quality," as indicated by a rating of 4, whereas Company 2 is strongest on "advertising." Overall, Company 1 is strongest, as indicated by the total weighted score of 3.15 and Company 3 is weakest.

Other than the critical success factors listed in the example CPM, factors often included in this analysis include breadth of product line, effectiveness of sales distribution, proprietary or patent advantages, location of facilities, production capacity and efficiency, experience, union relations, technological advantages, and e-commerce expertise.

A word on interpretation: Just because one firm receives a 3.20 rating and another receives a 2.80 rating in a Competitive Profile Matrix, it does not follow that the first firm is 20 percent better than the second. Numbers reveal the relative strengths of firms, but their implied precision is an illusion. Numbers are not magic. The aim is not to arrive at a single number, but rather to assimilate and evaluate information in a meaningful way that aids in decision making.

Another Competitive Profile Matrix is provided in Table 3-13. Note that Company 2 has the best product quality and management experience; Company 3 has the best market share and inventory system; and Company 1 has the best price as indicated by the ratings. Again, avoid assigning duplicate ratings on any row in a CPM.

TABLE 3-12   An Example Competitive Profile Matrix

Critical Success Factors	Weight	Company 1 Rating	Company 1 Score	Company 2 Rating	Company 2 Score	Company 3 Rating	Company 3 Score
Advertising	0.20	1	0.20	4	0.80	3	0.60
Product Quality	0.10	4	0.40	3	0.30	2	0.20
Price Competitiveness	0.10	3	0.30	2	0.20	1	0.10
Management	0.10	4	0.40	3	0.20	1	0.10
Financial Position	0.15	4	0.60	2	0.30	3	0.45
Customer Loyalty	0.10	4	0.40	3	0.30	2	0.20
Global Expansion	0.20	4	0.80	1	0.20	2	0.40
Market Share	0.05	1	0.05	4	0.20	3	0.15
Total	**1.00**		**3.15**		**2.50**		**2.20**

Note: (1) The ratings values are as follows: 1 = major weakness, 2 = minor weakness, 3 = minor strength, 4 = major strength. (2) As indicated by the total weighted score of 2.50, Competitor 2 is weakest. (3) Only eight critical success factors are included for simplicity; this is too few in actuality.

TABLE 3-13   Another Example Competitive Profile Matrix

Critical Success Factors	Weight	Company 1 Rating	Company 1 Weighted Score	Company 2 Rating	Company 2 Weighted Score	Company 3 Rating	Company 3 Weighted Score
Market Share	0.15	3	0.45	2	0.30	4	0.60
Inventory System	0.08	2	0.16	1	0.08	4	0.32
Financial Position	0.10	2	0.20	3	0.30	4	0.40
Product Quality	0.08	3	0.24	4	0.32	2	.16
Consumer Loyalty	0.02	3	0.06	1	0.02	4	0.08
Sales Distribution	0.10	3	0.30	2	0.20	4	.40
Global Expansion	0.15	3	0.45	2	0.30	4	0.60
Organization Structure	0.05	3	0.15	4	0.20	2	0.10
Production Capacity	0.04	3	0.12	2	0.08	4	0.16
E-commerce	0.10	3	0.30	1	0.10	4	0.40
Customer Service	0.10	3	0.30	2	0.20	4	0.40
Price Competitive	0.02	4	0.08	1	0.02	3	0.06
Management Experience	0.01	2	0.02	4	0.04	3	.03
Total	**1.00**		**2.83**		**2.16**		**3.69**

The Competitive Profile Matrix provided in Table 3-14 was developed for UPS and compares that company to its major rival, Federal Express. Note this analysis reveals UPS to be stronger than FedEx in all areas considered except e-commerce.

Special Note To Students

In developing and presenting your external assessment for the firm, be mindful that gaining and sustaining competitive advantage is the overriding purpose of developing the opportunity/threat lists, value chain, EFEM, and CPM. During this section of your written or oral project, emphasize how and why particular factors can yield competitive advantage for the firm. In other words,

TABLE 3-14   An Actual Competitive Profile Matrix for UPS, Inc.

Critical Success Factors	Weight	UPS Rating	UPS Score	FedEx Rating	FedEx Score
Advertising	0.05	4	0.20	3	0.15
Organization Structure	0.08	2	0.16	1	0.08
Customer Service	0.10	4	0.40	3	0.30
Global Expansion	0.07	4	0.28	3	0.21
Financial Position	0.10	4	0.40	3	0.40
Employee Dedication	0.08	4	0.32	3	0.24
Management Experience	0.10	4	0.40	3	0.30
Customer Loyalty	0.10	4	0.40	3	0.30
Market Share	0.10	4	0.40	3	0.30
Product Quality	0.08	3	0.24	2	0.16
E-commerce	0.06	2	0.12	3	0.18
Price Competitiveness	0.08	4	0.32	2	0.16
Total	**1.00**		**3.64**		**2.78**

instead of robotically going through the weights and ratings (which by the way are critically important), highlight various factors in light of where you are leading the firm. Make it abundantly clear in your discussion how your firm, with your suggestions, can subdue rival firms or at least profitably compete with them. Showcase during this section of your project the key underlying reasons how and why your firm can prosper among rivals. Remember to be *prescriptive*, rather than *descriptive*, in the manner that you present your entire project. If presenting your project orally, be self confident and passionate rather than timid and uninterested. Definitely "bring the data" throughout your project because "vagueness" is the most common downfall of students in case analyses.

Conclusion

Increasing turbulence in markets and industries around the world means the external audit has become an explicit and vital part of the strategic-management process. This chapter provides a framework for collecting and evaluating economic, social, cultural, demographic, environmental, political, governmental, legal, technological, and competitive information. Firms that do not mobilize and empower their managers and employees to identify, monitor, forecast, and evaluate key external forces may fail to anticipate emerging opportunities and threats and, consequently, may pursue ineffective strategies, miss opportunities, and invite organizational demise. Firms not taking advantage of e-commerce and social media networks are technologically falling behind.

A major responsibility of strategists is to ensure development of an effective external-audit system. This includes using information technology to devise a competitive intelligence system that works. The external-audit approach described in this chapter can be used effectively by any size or type of organization. Typically, the external-audit process is more informal in small firms, but the need to understand key trends and events is no less important for these firms. The EFE Matrix and Porter's Five-Forces Model can help strategists evaluate the market and industry, but these tools must be accompanied by good intuitive judgment. Multinational firms especially need a systematic and effective external-audit system because external forces among foreign countries vary so greatly.

Key Terms and Concepts

Chief Information Officer (CIO) (p. 71)
Chief Technology Officer (CTO) (p. 71)
Competitive Analysis (p. 75)
Competitive Intelligence (CI) (p. 74)
Competitive Profile Matrix (CPM) (p. 83)
Director of Competitive Analysis (p. 75)
Environmental Scanning (p. 62)
External Audit (p. 62)
External Factor Evaluation (EFE)
  Matrix (p. 80)

External Forces (p. 63)
Industrial Organization (I/O) (p. 65)
Industry Analysis (p. 62)
Information Technology (IT) (p. 71)
Internet (p. 71)
Lifecare Facilities (p. 68)
Linear Regression (p. 80)
Market Commonality (p. 75)
Porter's Five-Forces Model (p. 75)
Resource Similarity (p. 75)

Issues for Review and Discussion

1. Does McDonald's Corp. benefit from a low or high value of the dollar? Explain why.
2. Explain how Facebook, Twitter, and Myspace can represent a major threat or opportunity for a company.
3. Rate the seven websites provided under the "Sources of External Information" section of the chapter from best to worst for finding current News Releases from a company.
4. If your Competitive Profile Matrix has three firms and they all end up with the same Total Weighted Score, would the analysis still be useful? Why?
5. Describe the "process of performing an external audit" in an organization doing strategic planning for the first time.

6. The global recession forced thousands of firms into bankruptcy. Does this fact alone confirm that "external factors are more important than internal factors" in strategic planning? Discuss.

7. Use a series of two-dimensional (two-variable) graphs to illustrate the historical relationship among the following variables: value of the dollar, oil prices, interest rates, and stock prices. Give one implication of each graph for strategic planning.

8. Do you feel the advantages of a low value of the dollar offset the disadvantages for (1) a firm that derives 60 percent of its revenues from foreign countries and (2) a firm that derives 10 percent of its revenues from foreign countries? Justify your opinion.

9. The migration of people has slowed from (1) region to region across the United States, from (2) city to suburb worldwide, and from (3) country to country across the globe. What are the strategic implications of these trends for companies?

10. Governments worldwide are turning to "nationalization of companies" to cope with economic problems. What are the strategic implications of this trend for firms that compete with these nationalized firms?

11. Governments worldwide are turning to "protectionism" to cope with economic problems, imposing tariffs and subsidies on foreign goods and restrictions/incentives on their own firms to keep jobs at home. What are the strategic implications of this trend for international commerce?

12. Compare and contrast the duties and responsibilities of a CIO with a CTO in a large firm.

13. What are the three basic objectives of a competitive intelligence program?

14. Distinguish between market commonality and resource similarity. Apply these concepts to two rival firms that you are familiar with.

15. Let's say you work for McDonald's and you applied Porter's Five-Forces Model to study the fast-food industry. Would information in your analysis provide factors more readily to an EFE Matrix, a CPM, or to neither matrix? Justify your answer.

16. Explain why it is appropriate for ratings in an EFE Matrix to be 1, 2, 3, or 4 for any opportunity or threat.

17. Why is inclusion of about 20 factors recommended in the EFE Matrix rather than about 10 factors or about 40 factors?

18. In developing an EFE Matrix, would it be advantageous to arrange your opportunities according to the highest weight, and do likewise for your threats? Explain.

19. In developing an EFE Matrix, would it be best to have 10 opportunities and 10 threats, or would 17 opportunities (or threats) be fine with 3 of the other to achieve a total of 20 factors as desired?

20. Could/should critical success factors in a CPM include external factors? Explain.

21. Explain how to conduct an external strategic-management audit.

22. Identify a recent economic, social, political, or technological trend that significantly affects the local Pizza Hut.

23. Discuss the following statement: Major opportunities and threats usually result from an interaction among key environmental trends rather than from a single external event or factor.

24. Identify two industries experiencing rapid technological changes and three industries that are experiencing little technological change. How does the need for technological forecasting differ in these industries? Why?

25. Use Porter's Five-Forces Model to evaluate competitiveness within the U.S. banking industry.

26. How does the external audit affect other components of the strategic-management process?

27. As the owner of a small business, explain how you would organize a strategic-information scanning system. How would you organize such a system in a large organization?

28. Construct an EFE Matrix for an organization of your choice.

29. Give some advantages and disadvantages of cooperative versus competitive strategies.

30. What is your forecast for interest rates and the stock market in the next several months? As the stock market moves up, do interest rates always move down? Why? What are the strategic implications of these trends?

31. Let's say your boss develops an EFE Matrix that includes 62 factors. How would you suggest reducing the number of factors to 20?

32. Discuss the ethics of gathering competitive intelligence.

33. Discuss the ethics of cooperating with rival firms.

34. Do you agree with I/O theorists that external factors are more important than internal factors to a firm's achieving competitive advantage? Explain both your and their position.

35. Define, compare, and contrast the weights versus ratings in an EFE Matrix.

36. Develop a Competitive Profile Matrix for your university. Include six factors.

37. List the 10 external areas that give rise to opportunities and threats.

Notes

1. York Freund, "Critical Success Factors," *Planning Review* 16, no. 4 (July–August 1988): 20.

2. Ann Zimmerman, "Gift Shoppers Flocked to the Web," *Wall Street Journal*, December 24, 2010, B1.

3. Bill Saporito, "Companies That Compete Best," *Fortune*, May 22, 1989, 36.

4. Kenneth Sawka, "Demystifying Business Intelligence," *Management Review*, October 1996, 49.

5. John Prescott and Daniel Smith, "The Largest Survey of 'Leading-Edge' Competitor Intelligence Managers," *Planning Review* 17, no. 3 (May–June 1989): 6–13.

6. M. J. Chen, "Competitor Analysis and Interfirm Rivalry: Toward a Theoretical Integration," *Academy of Management Review* 21 (1996): 106.

7. S. Jayachandran, J. Gimeno, and P. R. Varadarajan, "Theory of Multimarket Competition: A Synthesis and Implications for Marketing Strategy," *Journal of Marketing* 63, 3 (1999): 59; and M. J. Chen. "Competitor Analysis and Interfirm Rivalry: Toward a Theoretical

Integration," *Academy of Management Review* 21 (1996): 107–108.

8. Arthur Thompson, Jr., A. J. Strickland III, and John Gamble, *Crafting and Executing Strategy: Text and Readings* (New York: McGraw-Hill/Irwin, 2005), 63.

9. Michael E. Porter, *Competitive Strategy: Techniques for Analyzing Industries and Competitors* (New York: Free Press, 1980), 24–27.

10. horizon.unc.edu/projects/seminars/futuresresearch/rationale .asp.

11. Dale McConkey, "Planning in a Changing Environment," *Business Horizons* 31, no. 5 (September–October 1988): 67.

Current Readings

Allio, Robert J. "In this Recession's Aftermath, CEO's Face Unique Threats and Opportunities." *Strategy & Leadership* 38, no. 4 (2010): 27.

Denning, Stephen. "Masterclass: Managing the Threats and Opportunities of the Open Corporation." *Strategy & Leadership* 38, no. 6 (2010): 16.

Holburn, Guy L. F., and Bennet A. Zeiner. "Political Capabilities, Policy Risk, and International Investment Strategy: Evidence from the Global Electric Power Generation Industry." *Strategic Management Journal* 31, no. 12 (December 2010): 1290–1315.

Ghemawat, Pankaj. "Finding Your Strategy in the New Landscape." *Harvard Business Review*, March 2010, 54–61.

Gulati, Ranjay, Nitin Nohria, and Franz Wohlgezogen. "Roaring Out of Recession." *Harvard Business Review*, March 2010, 62–69.

Haas, Martine R. "The Double-Edged Swords of Autonomy and External Knowledge: Analyzing Team Effectiveness in a Multinational Organization." *Academy of Management Journal* 53, no. 5 (October 2010): 989.

Kilduff, Gavin J., Hillary Anger Elfenbein, and Barry M. Staw. "The Psychology of Rivalry: A Relationally Dependent Analysis of Competition." *Academy of Management Journal* 53, no. 5 (October 2010): 943–969.

Lam, Shun Yin. "What Kind of Assumptions Need to be Realistic and How to Test Them: A Response to Tsang (2006)." *Strategic Management Journal* 31, no. 6 (June 2010): 679–687.

Makridakis, Spyros, Robin M. Hogarth, and Anil Gaba. "Why Forecasts Fail. What to Do Instead." *MIT Sloan Management Review* 51, no. 2 (Winter 2010): 83–95.

Ofek, Elie, and Luc Wathieu. "Are You Ignoring Trends That Could Shake Up Your Business?" *Harvard Business Review*, July–August 2010, 124–131.

Yang, Hongyan, Corey Phelps, and H. Kevin Steensma. "Learning From What Others Have Learned From You: The Effects of Knowledge Spillovers on Originating Firms." *The Academy of Management Journal* 53, no. 2 (April 2010): 371–389.

ASSURANCE OF LEARNING EXERCISES

Assurance of Learning Exercise 3A

Competitive Intelligence (CI) Certification

Purpose

This exercise will enhance your knowledge of CI, which is the action of defining, gathering, analyzing, and distributing information about products, customers, and competitors as needed to support executives and managers in making strategic decisions for an organization. With the right information, organizations can avoid unpleasant surprises by anticipating competitors' moves and decreasing response time. CI information is available in newspapers and magazines, such as the *Wall Street Journal, Business Week*, and *Fortune*. The Internet has made gathering CI information easier. However, since the Internet is mostly public domain material, information gathered is less likely to be good CI. In fact, there is a risk that information gathered from the Internet may be misinformation and mislead users, so CI researchers are often wary of such information. Many therefore spend their time and budget gathering intelligence using primary research, which includes networking with industry experts, attending trade shows and conferences, gathering information from their own customers and suppliers, and so on. The Internet is primarily used to gather information on what the company says about itself and its online presence (in the form of links to other companies, its strategy regarding search engines and online advertising, mentions in discussion forums and on blogs, etc.). Also important in CI are online subscription databases and news aggregation sources, which have simplified the secondary source collection process. Social media sources also have become important—providing potential interviewee names, as well as opinions and attitudes, and sometimes breaking news.

Instructions

Step 1   Do a Google search for the following five CI topics and write a short overview of each item.

1. Strategic & Competitive Intelligence Professionals
2. *The Journal of Competitive Intelligence and Management*
3. The Institute for Competitive Intelligence
4. The Fuld-Gilad-Herring Academy of Competitive Intelligence
5. *Competitive Intelligence Ethics: Navigating the Gray Zone*

Assurance of Learning Exercise 3B

Develop Divisional Walt Disney EFE Matrices

Purpose

Walt Disney has five major divisions: 1) Media Networks, 2) Parks & Resorts, 3) Studio Entertainment, 4) Consumer Products, and 5) Interactive Media. The company faces fierce but different competitors in each segment as described in the Cohesion Case. The external opportunities and threats that Disney faces are different in each segment, so each division prepares its own list of critical external success factors. This external analysis is critically important in strategic planning because a firm needs to exploit opportunities and avoid or at least mitigate threats.

Instructions

Step 1   Go to http://corporate.disney.go.com/ and review Disney's five major divisions.

Step 2   Conduct research to determine what you believe are the four major threats and the four major opportunities critical to strategic planning within Disney's five business segments. Review the relevant S&P Industry Survey documents for each segment.

Step 3   Based on the information from Step 2, develop divisional EFEMs for Disney. Work within a team of students if your instructor so requests, but you will need an EFEM for each segment.

Step 4   Prioritize the 20 threats and the 20 opportunities developed in the prior step so that corporate Disney top executives can better develop a corporate EFEM.

Assurance of Learning Exercise 3C

Develop an EFE Matrix for Walt Disney

Purpose

This exercise will give you practice developing an EFE Matrix. An EFE Matrix summarizes the results of an external audit. This is an important tool widely used by strategists.

Instructions

Step 1   Join with two other students in class, and jointly prepare an EFE Matrix for Disney. Refer back to the Cohesion Case (p. 24) and to Exercise 1B (p. 39), if necessary, to identify external opportunities and threats. Use the information in the S&P Industry Surveys that you copied as part of Assurance of Learning Exercise 1B. Be sure not to include strategies as opportunities, but do include as many monetary amounts, percentages, numbers, and ratios as possible.

Step 2 All three-person teams participating in this exercise should record their EFE total weighted scores on the board. Put your initials after your score to identify it as your team's.

Step 3 Compare the total weighted scores. Which team's score came closest to the instructor's answer? Discuss reasons for variation in the scores reported on the board.

Assurance of Learning Exercise 3D

Perform an External Assessment

Purpose

This exercise will give you practice doing an external assessment. A key part of preparing an external audit is searching the Internet and examining published sources of information for relevant economic, social, cultural, demographic, environmental, political, governmental, legal, technological, and competitive trends and events. External opportunities and threats must be identified and evaluated before strategies can be formulated effectively.

Instructions

Step 1 Select a company or business where you currently or previously have worked. Conduct an external audit for this company. Find opportunities and threats in recent issues of newspapers and magazines. Search for information using the Internet. Use the following seven websites:

http://marketwatch.multexinvestor.com
www.hoovers.com
http://moneycentral.msn.com
http://finance.yahoo.com
www.clearstation.com
http://us.etrade.com/e/t/invest/markets.
http://globaledge.msu.edu/industries/

Step 2 On a separate sheet of paper, list 10 opportunities and 10 threats that face this company. Be specific in stating each factor.

Step 3 Include a bibliography to reveal where you found the information.

Step 4 Write a three-page summary of your findings, and submit it to your instructor.

Assurance of Learning Exercise 3E

Develop an EFE Matrix for My University

Purpose

Most colleges and universities do strategic planning. Institutions are consciously and systematically identifying and evaluating external opportunities and threats facing higher education in your state, the nation, and the world.

Instructions

Step 1 Join with two other individuals in class and jointly prepare an EFE Matrix for your institution.

Step 2 Go to the board and record your total weighted score in a column that includes the scores of all three-person teams participating. Put your initials after your score to identify it as your team's.

Step 3 Which team viewed your college's strategies most positively? Which team viewed your college's strategies most negatively? Discuss the nature of the differences.

Assurance of Learning Exercise 3F

Develop Divisional Walt Disney CPMs

Purpose

Walt Disney has five major divisions as follows: 1) Media Networks, 2) Parks & Resorts, 3) Studio Entertainment, 4) Consumer Products, and 5) Interactive Media. The company faces fierce but different competitors in each segment. This exercise gives you practice evaluating a firm's diverse competitors across different divisions.

Instructions

Step 1	Go to http://corporate.disney.go.com/ and review Disney's five major divisions.
Step 2	Conduct research to determine Disney's three major competitors in each of the five major divisions.
Step 3	Join with three other students in class to form a group of four.
Step 4	Each team member should select a division of Disney and develop a Competitive Profile Matrix for their selected segment. Include the two most relevant rival firms in each CPM.

Assurance of Learning Exercise 3G

Develop a Competitive Profile Matrix for Walt Disney

Purpose

Monitoring competitors' performance and strategies is a key aspect of an external audit. This exercise is designed to give you practice evaluating the competitive position of organizations in a given industry and assimilating that information in the form of a Competitive Profile Matrix.

Instructions

Step 1	Gather your information from Assurance of Learning Exercise 1B. Also, turn back to the Cohesion Case and review the section on competitors (pages 31–37).
Step 2	On a separate sheet of paper, prepare a Competitive Profile Matrix that includes Disney and CBS.
Step 3	Turn in your Competitive Profile Matrix for a classwork grade.

Assurance of Learning Exercise 3H

Develop a Competitive Profile Matrix for My University

Purpose

Your college or university competes with all other educational institutions in the world, especially those in your own state. State funds, students, faculty, staff, endowments, gifts, and federal funds are areas of competitiveness. Other areas include athletic programs, dorm life, academic reputation, location, and career services. The purpose of this exercise is to give you practice thinking competitively about the business of education in your state.

Instructions

Step 1	Identify two colleges or universities in your state that compete directly with your institution for students. Interview several persons, perhaps classmates, who are aware of particular

strengths and weaknesses of those universities. Record information about the two competing universities.

Step 2   Prepare a Competitive Profile Matrix that includes your institution and the two competing institutions. Include at least the following 10 factors in your analysis:

1. Tuition costs
2. Quality of faculty
3. Academic reputation
4. Average class size
5. Campus landscaping
6. Athletic programs
7. Quality of students
8. Graduate programs
9. Location of campus
10. Campus culture

Step 3   Submit your Competitive Profile Matrix to your instructor for evaluation.

"NOTABLE QUOTES"

"Like a product or service, the planning process itself must be managed and shaped, if it is to serve executives as a vehicle for strategic decision-making."
—*Robert Lenz*

"The difference between now and five years ago is that information systems had limited function. You weren't betting your company on it. Now you are."
—*William Gruber*

"Weak leadership can wreck the soundest strategy."
—*Sun Tzu*

"A firm that continues to employ a previously successful strategy eventually and inevitably falls victim to a competitor."
—*William Cohen*

"Great spirits have always encountered violent opposition from mediocre minds."
—*Albert Einstein*

"The idea is to concentrate our strength against our competitor's relative weakness."
—*Bruce Henderson*

The Internal Assessment

CHAPTER OBJECTIVES

After studying this chapter, you should be able to do the following:

1. Describe how to perform an internal strategic-management audit.

2. Discuss the Resource-Based View (RBV) in strategic management.

3. Discuss key interrelationships among the functional areas of business.

4. Identify the basic functions or activities that make up management, marketing, finance/accounting, production/operations, research and development, and management information systems.

5. Explain how to determine and prioritize a firm's internal strengths and weaknesses.

6. Explain the importance of financial ratio analysis.

7. Discuss the nature and role of management information systems in strategic management.

8. Develop an Internal Factor Evaluation (IFE) Matrix.

9. Explain cost/benefit analysis value chain analysis, and benchmarking as strategic-management tools.

ASSURANCE OF LEARNING EXERCISES

Assurance of Learning Exercise 4A
Apply Breakeven Analysis

Assurance of Learning Exercise 4B
Develop Divisional Disney IFEMs

Assurance of Learning Exercise 4C
Perform a Financial Ratio Analysis For Walt Disney

Assurance of Learning Exercise 4D
Construct an IFE Matrix for Walt Disney

Assurance of Learning Exercise 4E
Construct an IFE Matrix for My University

This chapter focuses on identifying and evaluating a firm's strengths and weaknesses in the functional areas of business, including management, marketing, finance/accounting, production/operations, research and development, and management information systems. Relationships among these areas of business are examined. Strategic implications of important functional area concepts are examined. The process of performing an internal audit is described. The Resource-Based View (RBV) of strategic management is introduced as is the Value Chain Analysis (VCA) concept. Pearson PLC, publisher of this textbook, does an excellent job using its strengths to capitalize upon external opportunities. Pearson is showcased in the opening chapter boxed insert.

The Nature of an Internal Audit

All organizations have strengths and weaknesses in the functional areas of business. No enterprise is equally strong or weak in all areas. Maytag, for example, is known for excellent production and product design, whereas Procter & Gamble is known for superb marketing. Internal strengths/weaknesses, coupled with external opportunities/threats and a clear statement of mission, provide the basis for establishing objectives and strategies. Objectives and strategies are established with the intention of capitalizing upon internal strengths and overcoming weaknesses. The internal-audit part of the strategic-management process is illustrated in Figure 4-1.

Excellent Strategic Management Showcased

PEARSON PLC

Founded in 1844 and headquartered in London, Pearson PLC has 37,000 employees based in more than 60 countries. Pearson is listed on the London and New York stock exchanges (UK: PSON; NYSE: PSO). The company had 2010 sales of over $9.2 billion and a gross profit of $4.98 billion. Pearson's 2010 profit margin was an incredible 22.9 percent and its return on equity was 10.23 percent. With excellent strategic management guidance, Pearson is outperforming all rival firms, which include McGraw-Hill, Thomson Reuters Corporation, Houghton Mifflin Harcourt Publishing, and Gannett Company.

Pearson operates in three strategic business units: 1) Pearson Education, 2) Financial Times, and 3) Penguin. Included in Pearson Education is the Prentice Hall Secondary Education Division (Grades 6–12), a leading publisher of middle school and high school textbooks and technology in the United States, as well as college textbooks. Pearson Education brands include Addison-Wesley, Allyn & Bacon, Benjamin Cummings, Longman, Merrill, and Prentice Hall. This Prentice Hall textbook is available all over the world in several different languages.

Within the Financial Times strategic business unit, Pearson publishes the *Financial Times* newspaper and offers other products such as FT.com, Mergermarket, dealReporter, Wealthmonitor, Pharmawire, Investors Chronicle, Financial Adviser, and The Banker. Pearson's Penguin strategic business unit publishes both fiction and nonfiction books under the names Penguin, Hamish Hamilton, Putnam, Berkley, and Dorling Kindersley.

Over the past five years, Pearson has increased its profit margins and reduced average working capital as a percentage of sales in Pearson Education and Penguin from 30.7 percent to 26.3 percent, freeing up cash for further investment.

Pearson's Chief Executive Marjorie Scardino is "uncomfortable" with the Libyan sovereign wealth fund owning 3 percent of Pearson. Pearson is seeking clarity as to whether the U.K. freeze on Libyan assets covers the stake. This situation reflects an emerging issue for a variety of European companies grappling with the fact that they have the Libyan Investment Authority as a shareholder. "We're in a terrible position," Ms. Scardino said, noting that "Pearson, as a public company, has no control over who invests in its stock." Moammar Gaddafi is presently struggling to remain Libya's dictator.

Source: Based on: Simon Zekaria, "Pearson Raises Its Forecast for 2010," *Wall Street Journal*, January 20, 2011, B5. Also, company documents.

FIGURE 4-1

A Comprehensive Strategic-Management Model

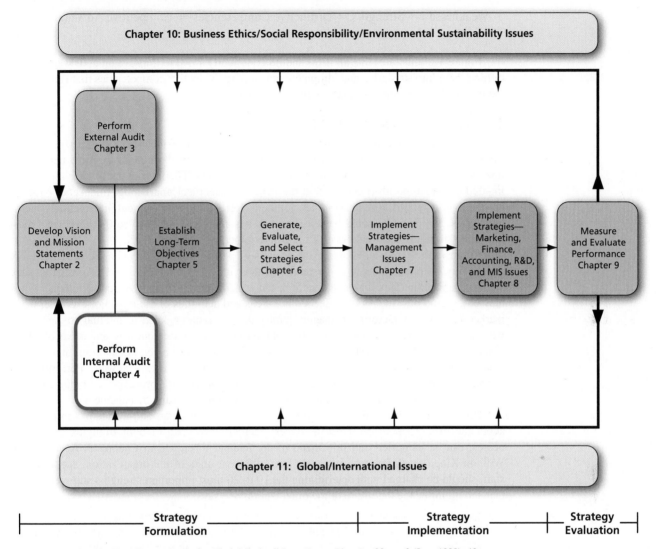

Source: Fred R. David, "How Companies Define Their Mission," *Long Range Planning* 22, no. 3 (June 1988): 40.

Key Internal Forces

It is not possible in a strategic-management text to review in depth all the material presented in courses such as marketing, finance, accounting, management, management information systems, and production/operations; there are many subareas within these functions, such as customer service, warranties, advertising, packaging, and pricing under marketing.

For different types of organizations, such as hospitals, universities, and government agencies, the functional business areas, of course, differ. In a hospital, for example, functional areas may include cardiology, hematology, nursing, maintenance, physician support, and receivables. Functional areas of a university can include athletic programs, placement services, housing, fund-raising, academic research, counseling, and intramural programs. Within large organizations, each division has certain strengths and weaknesses.

A firm's strengths that cannot be easily matched or imitated by competitors are called *distinctive competencies.* Building competitive advantages involves taking advantage of distinctive competencies. For example, the firm Research in Motion (RIM) exploits its distinctive competence in research and development by producing a wide range of innovative products. Strategies are designed in part to improve on a firm's weaknesses, turning them into strengths—and maybe even into distinctive competencies.

FIGURE 4-2

The Process of Gaining Competitive Advantage in a Firm

Weaknesses ⇒ Strengths ⇒ Distinctive Competencies ⇒ Competitive Advantage

Figure 4-2 illustrates that all firms should continually strive to improve on their weaknesses, turning them into strengths, and ultimately developing distinctive competencies that can provide the firm with competitive advantages over rival firms.

The Process of Performing an Internal Audit

The process of performing an *internal audit* closely parallels the process of performing an external audit. Representative managers and employees from throughout the firm need to be involved in determining a firm's strengths and weaknesses. The internal audit requires gathering and assimilating information about the firm's management, marketing, finance/accounting, production/operations, research and development (R&D), and management information systems operations. Key factors should be prioritized as described in Chapter 3 so that the firm's most important strengths and weaknesses can be determined collectively.

Compared to the external audit, the process of performing an internal audit provides more opportunity for participants to understand how their jobs, departments, and divisions fit into the whole organization. This is a great benefit because managers and employees perform better when they understand how their work affects other areas and activities of the firm. For example, when marketing and manufacturing managers jointly discuss issues related to internal strengths and weaknesses, they gain a better appreciation of the issues, problems, concerns, and needs of all the functional areas. In organizations that do not use strategic management, marketing, finance, and manufacturing managers often do not interact with each other in significant ways. Performing an internal audit thus is an excellent vehicle or forum for improving the process of communication in the organization. *Communication* may be the most important word in management.

Performing an internal audit requires gathering, assimilating, and evaluating information about the firm's operations. Critical success factors, consisting of both strengths and weaknesses, can be identified and prioritized in the manner discussed in Chapter 3. According to William King, a task force of managers from different units of the organization, supported by staff, should be charged with determining the 10 to 20 most important strengths and weaknesses that should influence the future of the organization. He says:

> The development of conclusions on the 10 to 20 most important organizational strengths and weaknesses can be, as any experienced manager knows, a difficult task, when it involves managers representing various organizational interests and points of view. Developing a 20-page list of strengths and weaknesses could be accomplished relatively easily, but a list of the 10 to 15 most important ones involves significant analysis and negotiation. This is true because of the judgments that are required and the impact which such a list will inevitably have as it is used in the formulation, implementation, and evaluation of strategies.[1]

Strategic management is a highly interactive process that requires effective coordination among management, marketing, finance/accounting, production/operations, R&D, and management information systems managers. Although the strategic-management process is overseen by strategists, success requires that managers and employees from all functional areas work together to provide ideas and information. Financial managers, for example, may need to restrict the number of feasible options available to operations managers, or R&D managers may develop products for which marketing managers need to set higher objectives. A key to organizational success is effective coordination and understanding among managers from all functional business areas. Through involvement in performing an internal strategic-management audit, managers from different departments and divisions of the firm come to understand the nature and effect of decisions in other functional business areas in their firm. Knowledge of these relationships is critical for effectively establishing objectives and strategies.

A failure to recognize and understand relationships among the functional areas of business can be detrimental to strategic management, and the number of those relationships that must be managed increases dramatically with a firm's size, diversity, geographic dispersion, and the number of products or services offered. Governmental and nonprofit enterprises traditionally have not placed sufficient emphasis on relationships among the business functions. Some firms place too great an emphasis on one function at the expense of others. Ansoff explained:

> During the first fifty years, successful firms focused their energies on optimizing the performance of one of the principal functions: production/operations, R&D, or marketing. Today, due to the growing complexity and dynamism of the environment, success increasingly depends on a judicious combination of several functional influences. This transition from a single function focus to a multifunction focus is essential for successful strategic management.[2]

Financial ratio analysis exemplifies the complexity of relationships among the functional areas of business. A declining return on investment or profit margin ratio could be the result of ineffective marketing, poor management policies, research and development errors, or a weak management information system. The effectiveness of strategy formulation, implementation, and evaluation activities hinges upon a clear understanding of how major business functions affect one another. For strategies to succeed, a coordinated effort among all the functional areas of business is needed. In the case of planning, George wrote:

> We may conceptually separate planning for the purpose of theoretical discussion and analysis, but in practice, neither is it a distinct entity nor is it capable of being separated. The planning function is mixed with all other business functions and, like ink once mixed with water, it cannot be set apart. It is spread throughout and is a part of the whole of managing an organization.[3]

The Resource-Based View (RBV)

Some researchers emphasize the importance of the internal audit part of the strategic-management process by comparing it to the external audit. Robert Grant concluded that the internal audit is more important, saying:

> In a world where customer preferences are volatile, the identity of customers is changing, and the technologies for serving customer requirements are continually evolving, an externally focused orientation does not provide a secure foundation for formulating long-term strategy. When the external environment is in a state of flux, the firm's own resources and capabilities may be a much more stable basis on which to define its identity. Hence, a definition of a business in terms of what it is capable of doing may offer a more durable basis for strategy.[4]

The *Resource-Based View (RBV)* approach to competitive advantage contends that internal resources are more important for a firm than external factors in achieving and sustaining competitive advantage. In contrast to the I/O theory presented in the previous chapter, proponents of the RBV view contend that organizational performance will primarily be determined by internal resources that can be grouped into three all-encompassing categories: physical resources, human resources, and organizational resources.[5] Physical resources include all plant and equipment, location, technology, raw materials, machines; human resources include all employees, training, experience, intelligence, knowledge, skills, abilities; and organizational resources include firm structure, planning processes, information systems, patents, trademarks, copyrights, databases, and so on. RBV theory asserts that resources are actually what helps a firm exploit opportunities and neutralize threats.

The basic premise of the RBV is that the mix, type, amount, and nature of a firm's internal resources should be considered first and foremost in devising strategies that can lead to sustainable competitive advantage. Managing strategically according to the RBV involves developing and exploiting a firm's unique resources and capabilities, and continually maintaining and strengthening those resources. The theory asserts that it is advantageous for a firm to pursue a strategy that is not currently being implemented by any competing firm. When other firms are unable to duplicate a particular strategy, then the focal firm has a sustainable competitive advantage, according to RBV theorists.

For a resource to be valuable, it must be either (1) rare, (2) hard to imitate, or (3) not easily substitutable. Often called *empirical indicators,* these three characteristics of resources enable a firm to implement strategies that improve its efficiency and effectiveness and lead to a sustainable competitive advantage. The more a resource(s) is rare, nonimitable, and nonsubstitutable, the stronger a firm's competitive advantage will be and the longer it will last.

Rare resources are resources that other competing firms do not possess. If many firms have the same resource, then those firms will likely implement similar strategies, thus giving no one firm a sustainable competitive advantage. This is not to say that resources that are common are not valuable; they do indeed aid the firm in its chance for economic prosperity. However, to sustain a competitive advantage, it is more advantageous if the resource(s) is also rare.

It is also important that these same resources be difficult to imitate. If firms cannot easily gain the resources, say RBV theorists, then those resources will lead to a competitive advantage more so than resources easily imitable. Even if a firm employs resources that are rare, a sustainable competitive advantage may be achieved only if other firms cannot easily obtain these resources.

The third empirical indicator that can make resources a source of competitive advantage is substitutability. Borrowing from Porter's Five-Forces Model, to the degree that there are no viable substitutes, a firm will be able to sustain its competitive advantage. However, even if a competing firm cannot perfectly imitate a firm's resource, it can still obtain a sustainable competitive advantage of its own by obtaining resource substitutes.

The RBV has continued to grow in popularity and continues to seek a better understanding of the relationship between resources and sustained competitive advantage in strategic management. However, as alluded to in Chapter 3, one cannot say with any degree of certainty that either external or internal factors will always or even consistently be more important in seeking competitive advantage. Understanding both external and internal factors, and more importantly, understanding the relationships among them, will be the key to effective strategy formulation (discussed in Chapter 6). Because both external and internal factors continually change, strategists seek to identify and take advantage of positive changes and buffer against negative changes in a continuing effort to gain and sustain a firm's competitive advantage. This is the essence and challenge of strategic management, and oftentimes survival of the firm hinges on this work.

Integrating Strategy and Culture

Relationships among a firm's functional business activities perhaps can be exemplified best by focusing on organizational culture, an internal phenomenon that permeates all departments and divisions of an organization. *Organizational culture* can be defined as "a pattern of behavior that has been developed by an organization as it learns to cope with its problem of external adaptation and internal integration, and that has worked well enough to be considered valid and to be taught to new members as the correct way to perceive, think, and feel."[6] This definition emphasizes the importance of matching external with internal factors in making strategic decisions.

Organizational culture captures the subtle, elusive, and largely unconscious forces that shape a workplace. Remarkably resistant to change, culture can represent a major strength or weakness for the firm. It can be an underlying reason for strengths or weaknesses in any of the major business functions.

Defined in Table 4-1, *cultural products* include values, beliefs, rites, rituals, ceremonies, myths, stories, legends, sagas, language, metaphors, symbols, heroes, and heroines. These products or dimensions are levers that strategists can use to influence and direct strategy formulation, implementation, and evaluation activities. An organization's culture compares to an individual's personality in the sense that no two organizations have the same culture and no two individuals have the same personality. Both culture and personality are enduring and can be warm, aggressive, friendly, open, innovative, conservative, liberal, harsh, or likable.

TABLE 4-1   Example Cultural Products Defined

Rites	Planned sets of activities that consolidate various forms of cultural expressions into one event.
Ceremonial	Several rites connected together.
Ritual	A standardized set of behaviors used to manage anxieties.
Myth	A narrative of imagined events, usually not supported by facts.
Saga	A historical narrative describing the unique accomplishments of a group and its leaders.
Legend	A handed-down narrative of some wonderful event, usually not supported by facts.
Story	A narrative usually based on true events.
Folktale	A fictional story.
Symbol	Any object, act, event, quality, or relation used to convey meaning.
Language	The manner in which members of a group communicate.
Metaphors	Shorthand of words used to capture a vision or to reinforce old or new values.
Values	Life-directing attitudes that serve as behavioral guidelines.
Belief	An understanding of a particular phenomenon.
Heroes/Heroines	Individuals greatly respected.

Source: Based on H. M. Trice and J. M. Beyer, "Studying Organizational Cultures through Rites and Ceremonials," *Academy of Management Review* 9, no. 4 (October 1984): 655.

At Google, the culture is very informal. Employees are encouraged to wander the halls on employee-sponsored scooters and brainstorm on public whiteboards provided everywhere. In contrast, the culture at Procter & Gamble (P&G) is so rigid that employees jokingly call themselves "Proctoids." Despite this difference, the two companies are swapping employees and participating in each other's staff training sessions. Why? Because P&G spends more money on advertising than any other company and Google desires more of P&G's $8.7 billion in annual advertising expenses; P&G has come to realize that the next generation of laundry-detergent, toilet-paper, and skin-cream customers now spend more time online than watching TV.

Dimensions of organizational culture permeate all the functional areas of business. It is something of an art to uncover the basic values and beliefs that are deeply buried in an organization's rich collection of stories, language, heroes, and rituals, but cultural products can represent both important strengths and weaknesses. Culture is an aspect of an organization that can no longer be taken for granted in performing an internal strategic-management audit because culture and strategy must work together.

Table 4-2 provides some example (possible) aspects of an organization's culture. Note you could ask employees/managers to rate the degree that the dimension characterizes the firm. When one firm acquires another firm, integrating the two cultures can be important. For example, in Table 4-2, one firm may score mostly 1's (low) and the other firm may score mostly 5's (high), which would present a challenging strategic problem.

The strategic-management process takes place largely within a particular organization's culture. Lorsch found that executives in successful companies are emotionally committed to the firm's culture, but he concluded that culture can inhibit strategic management in two basic ways. First, managers frequently miss the significance of changing external conditions because they are blinded by strongly held beliefs. Second, when a particular culture has been effective in the past, the natural response is to stick with it in the future, even during times of major strategic change.[7] An organization's culture must support the collective commitment of its people to a common purpose. It must foster competence and enthusiasm among managers and employees.

Organizational culture significantly affects business decisions and thus must be evaluated during an internal strategic-management audit. If strategies can capitalize on cultural strengths, such as a strong work ethic or highly ethical beliefs, then management often can swiftly and easily implement changes. However, if the firm's culture is not supportive, strategic changes may be ineffective or even counterproductive. A firm's culture can become antagonistic to new strategies, with the result being confusion and disorientation.

TABLE 4-2 Fifteen Example (Possible) Aspects of an Organization's Culture

Dimension	Low	Degree			High
1. Strong work ethic; arrive early and leave late	1	2	3	4	5
2. High ethical beliefs; clear code of business ethics followed	1	2	3	4	5
3. Formal dress; shirt and tie expected	1	2	3	4	5
4. Informal dress; many casual dress days	1	2	3	4	5
5. Socialize together outside of work	1	2	3	4	5
6. Do not question supervisor's decision	1	2	3	4	5
7. Encourage whistle-blowing	1	2	3	4	5
8. Be health conscious; have a wellness program	1	2	3	4	5
9. Allow substantial "working from home"	1	2	3	4	5
10. Encourage creativity/innovation/openmindness	1	2	3	4	5
11. Support women and minorities; no glass ceiling	1	2	3	4	5
12. Be highly socially responsible; be philanthropic	1	2	3	4	5
13. Have numerous meetings	1	2	3	4	5
14. Have a participative management style	1	2	3	4	5
15. Preserve the natural environment; have a sustainability program	1	2	3	4	5

An organization's culture should infuse individuals with enthusiasm for implementing strategies. Allarie and Firsirotu emphasized the need to understand culture:

> Culture provides an explanation for the insuperable difficulties a firm encounters when it attempts to shift its strategic direction. Not only has the "right" culture become the essence and foundation of corporate excellence, it is also claimed that success or failure of reforms hinges on management's sagacity and ability to change the firm's driving culture in time and in time with required changes in strategies.[8]

The potential value of organizational culture has not been realized fully in the study of strategic management. Ignoring the effect that culture can have on relationships among the functional areas of business can result in barriers to communication, lack of coordination, and an inability to adapt to changing conditions. Some tension between culture and a firm's strategy is inevitable, but the tension should be monitored so that it does not reach a point at which relationships are severed and the culture becomes antagonistic. The resulting disarray among members of the organization would disrupt strategy formulation, implementation, and evaluation. In contrast, a supportive organizational culture can make managing much easier.

Internal strengths and weaknesses associated with a firm's culture sometimes are overlooked because of the interfunctional nature of this phenomenon. It is important, therefore, for strategists to understand their firm as a sociocultural system. Success is often determined by linkages between a firm's culture and strategies. The challenge of strategic management today is to bring about the changes in organizational culture and individual mind-sets that are needed to support the formulation, implementation, and evaluation of strategies.

Management

The *functions of management* consist of five basic activities: planning, organizing, motivating, staffing, and controlling. An overview of these activities is provided in Table 4-3. These activities are important to assess in strategic planning because an organization should continually capitalize on its management strengths and improve on its management weak areas.

Planning

The only thing certain about the future of any organization is change, and *planning* is the essential bridge between the present and the future that increases the likelihood of achieving desired results. Planning is the process by which one determines whether to attempt a task, works out the most effective way of reaching desired objectives, and prepares to overcome unexpected

TABLE 4-3 The Basic Functions of Management

Function	Description	Stage of Strategic-Management Process When Most Important
Planning	Planning consists of all those managerial activities related to preparing for the future. Specific tasks include forecasting, establishing objectives, devising strategies, developing policies, and setting goals.	Strategy Formulation
Organizing	Organizing includes all those managerial activities that result in a structure of task and authority relationships. Specific areas include organizational design, job specialization, job descriptions, job specifications, span of control, unity of command, coordination, job design, and job analysis.	Strategy Implementation
Motivating	Motivating involves efforts directed toward shaping human behavior. Specific topics include leadership, communication, work groups, behavior modification, delegation of authority, job enrichment, job satisfaction, needs fulfillment, organizational change, employee morale, and managerial morale.	Strategy Implementation
Staffing	Staffing activities are centered on personnel or human resource management. Included are wage and salary administration, employee benefits, interviewing, hiring, firing, training, management development, employee safety, affirmative action, equal employment opportunity, union relations, career development, personnel research, discipline policies, grievance procedures, and public relations.	Strategy Implementation
Controlling	Controlling refers to all those managerial activities directed toward ensuring that actual results are consistent with planned results. Key areas of concern include quality control, financial control, sales control, inventory control, expense control, analysis of variances, rewards, and sanctions.	Strategy Evaluation

difficulties with adequate resources. Planning is the start of the process by which an individual or business may turn empty dreams into achievements. Planning enables one to avoid the trap of working extremely hard but achieving little.

Planning is an up-front investment in success. Planning helps a firm achieve maximum effect from a given effort. Planning enables a firm to take into account relevant factors and focus on the critical ones. Planning helps ensure that the firm can be prepared for all reasonable eventualities and for all changes that will be needed. Planning enables a firm to gather the resources needed and carry out tasks in the most efficient way possible. Planning enables a firm to conserve its own resources, avoid wasting ecological resources, make a fair profit, and be seen as an effective, useful firm. Planning enables a firm to identify precisely what is to be achieved and to detail precisely the who, what, when, where, why, and how needed to achieve desired objectives. Planning enables a firm to assess whether the effort, costs, and implications associated with achieving desired objectives are warranted.[9] Planning is the cornerstone of effective strategy formulation. But even though it is considered the foundation of management, it is commonly the task that managers neglect most. Planning is essential for successful strategy implementation and strategy evaluation, largely because organizing, motivating, staffing, and controlling activities depend upon good planning.

The process of planning must involve managers and employees throughout an organization. The time horizon for planning decreases from two to five years for top-level to less than six months for lower-level managers. The important point is that all managers do planning and should involve subordinates in the process to facilitate employee understanding and commitment.

Planning can have a positive impact on organizational and individual performance. Planning allows an organization to identify and take advantage of external opportunities as well as minimize the impact of external threats. Planning is more than extrapolating from the past and present into the future (long range planning). It also includes developing a mission, forecasting future events and trends, establishing objectives, and choosing strategies to pursue (strategic planning).

An organization can develop synergy through planning. *Synergy* exists when everyone pulls together as a team that knows what it wants to achieve; synergy is the 2 + 2 = 5 effect. By establishing and communicating clear objectives, employees and managers can work together toward desired results. Synergy can result in powerful competitive advantages. The strategic-management process itself is aimed at creating synergy in an organization.

Planning allows a firm to adapt to changing markets and thus to shape its own destiny. Strategic management can be viewed as a formal planning process that allows an organization to pursue proactive rather than reactive strategies. Successful organizations strive to control their own futures rather than merely react to external forces and events as they occur. Historically, organisms and organizations that have not adapted to changing conditions have become extinct. Swift adaptation is needed today more than ever because changes in markets, economies, and competitors worldwide are accelerating. Many firms did not adapt to the global recession of late and went out of business.

Organizing

The purpose of *organizing* is to achieve coordinated effort by defining task and authority relationships. Organizing means determining who does what and who reports to whom. There are countless examples in history of well-organized enterprises successfully competing against—and in some cases defeating—much stronger but less-organized firms. A well-organized firm generally has motivated managers and employees who are committed to seeing the organization succeed. Resources are allocated more effectively and used more efficiently in a well-organized firm than in a disorganized firm.

The organizing function of management can be viewed as consisting of three sequential activities: breaking down tasks into jobs (work specialization), combining jobs to form departments (departmentalization), and delegating authority. Breaking down tasks into jobs requires the development of job descriptions and job specifications. These tools clarify for both managers and employees what particular jobs entail. In *The Wealth of Nations,* published in 1776, Adam Smith cited the advantages of work specialization in the manufacture of pins:

> One man draws the wire, another straightens it, a third cuts it, a fourth points it, a fifth grinds it at the top for receiving the head. Ten men working in this manner can produce 48,000 pins in a single day, but if they had all wrought separately and independently, each might at best produce twenty pins in a day.[10]

Combining jobs to form departments results in an organizational structure, span of control, and a chain of command. Changes in strategy often require changes in structure because positions may be created, deleted, or merged. Organizational structure dictates how resources are allocated and how objectives are established in a firm. Allocating resources and establishing objectives geographically, for example, is much different from doing so by product or customer.

The most common forms of departmentalization are functional, divisional, strategic business unit, and matrix. These types of structure are discussed further in Chapter 7.

Delegating authority is an important organizing activity, as evidenced in the old saying "You can tell how good a manager is by observing how his or her department functions when he or she isn't there." Employees today are more educated and more capable of participating in organizational decision making than ever before. In most cases, they expect to be delegated authority and responsibility and to be held accountable for results. Delegation of authority is embedded in the strategic-management process.

Motivating

Motivating can be defined as the process of influencing people to accomplish specific objectives.[11] Motivation explains why some people work hard and others do not. Objectives, strategies, and policies have little chance of succeeding if employees and managers are not motivated to implement strategies once they are formulated. The motivating function of management includes at least four major components: leadership, group dynamics, communication, and organizational change.

When managers and employees of a firm strive to achieve high levels of productivity, this indicates that the firm's strategists are good leaders. Good leaders establish rapport with subordinates, empathize with their needs and concerns, set a good example, and are trustworthy and fair. Leadership includes developing a vision of the firm's future and inspiring people to work hard to achieve that vision. Kirkpatrick and Locke reported that certain traits also characterize effective leaders: knowledge of the business, cognitive ability, self-confidence, honesty, integrity, and drive.[12]

Research suggests that democratic behavior on the part of leaders results in more positive attitudes toward change and higher productivity than does autocratic behavior. Drucker said:

> Leadership is not a magnetic personality. That can just as well be demagoguery. It is not "making friends and influencing people." That is flattery. Leadership is the lifting of a person's vision to higher sights, the raising of a person's performance to a higher standard, the building of a person's personality beyond its normal limitations.[13]

Group dynamics play a major role in employee morale and satisfaction. Informal groups or coalitions form in every organization. The norms of coalitions can range from being very positive to very negative toward management. It is important, therefore, that strategists identify the composition and nature of informal groups in an organization to facilitate strategy formulation, implementation, and evaluation. Leaders of informal groups are especially important in formulating and implementing strategy changes.

Communication, perhaps the most important word in management, is a major component in motivation. An organization's system of communication determines whether strategies can be implemented successfully. Good two-way communication is vital for gaining support for departmental and divisional objectives and policies. Top-down communication can encourage bottom-up communication. The strategic-management process becomes a lot easier when subordinates are encouraged to discuss their concerns, reveal their problems, provide recommendations, and give suggestions. A primary reason for instituting strategic management is to build and support effective communication networks throughout the firm.

> The manager of tomorrow must be able to get his people to commit themselves to the business, whether they are machine operators or junior vice-presidents. The key issue will be empowerment, a term whose strength suggests the need to get beyond merely sharing a little information and a bit of decision making.[14]

Staffing

The management function of *staffing,* also called *personnel management* or *human resource management,* includes activities such as recruiting, interviewing, testing, selecting, orienting, training, developing, caring for, evaluating, rewarding, disciplining, promoting, transferring, demoting, and dismissing employees, as well as managing union relations.

Staffing activities play a major role in strategy-implementation efforts, and for this reason, human resource managers are becoming more actively involved in the strategic-management process. It is important to identify strengths and weaknesses in the staffing area.

The complexity and importance of human resource activities have increased to such a degree that all but the smallest organizations now need a full-time human resource manager. Numerous court cases that directly affect staffing activities are decided each day. Organizations and individuals can be penalized severely for not following federal, state, and local laws and guidelines related to staffing. Line managers simply cannot stay abreast of all the legal developments and requirements regarding staffing. The human resources department coordinates staffing decisions in the firm so that an organization as a whole meets legal requirements. This department also provides needed consistency in administering company rules, wages, policies, and employee benefits as well as collective bargaining with unions.

Human resource management is particularly challenging for international companies. For example, the inability of spouses and children to adapt to new surroundings can be a staffing problem in overseas transfers. The problems include premature returns, job performance slumps, resignations, discharges, low morale, marital discord, and general discontent. Firms such as Ford Motor and ExxonMobil screen and interview spouses and children before assigning persons to overseas positions. 3M Corporation introduces children to peers in the target country and offers spouses educational benefits.

Controlling

The *controlling* function of management includes all of those activities undertaken to ensure that actual operations conform to planned operations. All managers in an organization have controlling responsibilities, such as conducting performance evaluations and taking necessary action to minimize inefficiencies. The controlling function of management is particularly important for effective strategy evaluation. Controlling consists of four basic steps:

1. Establishing performance standards
2. Measuring individual and organizational performance
3. Comparing actual performance to planned performance standards
4. Taking corrective actions

Measuring individual performance is often conducted ineffectively or not at all in organizations. Some reasons for this shortcoming are that evaluations can create confrontations that most managers prefer to avoid, can take more time than most managers are willing to give, and can require skills that many managers lack. No single approach to measuring individual performance is without limitations. For this reason, an organization should examine various methods, such as the graphic rating scale, the behaviorally anchored rating scale, and the critical incident method, and then develop or select a performance-appraisal approach that best suits the firm's needs. Increasingly, firms are striving to link organizational performance with managers' and employees' pay. This topic is discussed further in Chapter 7.

Management Audit Checklist of Questions

The following checklist of questions can help determine specific strengths and weaknesses in the functional area of business. An answer of *no* to any question could indicate a potential weakness, although the strategic significance and implications of negative answers, of course, will vary by organization, industry, and severity of the weakness. Positive or yes answers to the checklist questions suggest potential areas of strength.

1. Does the firm use strategic-management concepts?
2. Are company objectives and goals measurable and well communicated?
3. Do managers at all hierarchical levels plan effectively?
4. Do managers delegate authority well?
5. Is the organization's structure appropriate?
6. Are job descriptions and job specifications clear?
7. Is employee morale high?
8. Are employee turnover and absenteeism low?
9. Are organizational reward and control mechanisms effective?

Marketing

Marketing can be described as the process of defining, anticipating, creating, and fulfilling customers' needs and wants for products and services. There are seven basic *functions of marketing:* (1) customer analysis, (2) selling products/services, (3) product and service planning, (4) pricing, (5) distribution, (6) marketing research, and (7) opportunity analysis.[15] Understanding these functions helps strategists identify and evaluate marketing strengths and weaknesses.

Customer Analysis

Customer analysis—the examination and evaluation of consumer needs, desires, and wants—involves administering customer surveys, analyzing consumer information, evaluating market positioning strategies, developing customer profiles, and determining optimal market segmentation strategies. The information generated by customer analysis can be essential in developing an effective mission statement. Customer profiles can reveal the demographic characteristics of an organization's customers. Buyers, sellers, distributors, salespeople, managers, wholesalers, retailers, suppliers, and creditors can all participate in gathering information to successfully identify customers' needs and wants. Successful organizations continually monitor present and potential customers' buying patterns.

Selling Products/Services

Successful strategy implementation generally rests upon the ability of an organization to sell some product or service. *Selling* includes many marketing activities, such as advertising, sales promotion, publicity, personal selling, sales force management, customer relations, and dealer relations. These activities are especially critical when a firm pursues a market penetration strategy. The effectiveness of various selling tools for consumer and industrial products varies. Personal selling is most important for industrial goods companies, whereas advertising is most important for consumer goods companies.

Internet advertising revenues received from firms such as Google, Amazon, Yahoo, and Facebook reached a record $12.1 billion in the first half of 2010, up more than 11 percent from the first half of the prior year, according to the Interactive Advertising Bureau. In contrast, newspaper advertising in 2010 totaled $7.3 billion, down 4.7 percent from the prior year and the lowest total since 1985.

Total advertising expenditures in the United States in 2011 is expected to be $155.2 billion, up 2.5 percent from the prior year. Global ad spending, however, is forecast to increase 4.2 percent to $470.8 billion. ZenithOptimedia expects the largest ad spending increases in the U.S. in 2011 to flow to the Internet, which is projected to increase 13 percent. One aspect of ads in a recession is that they generally take more direct aim at competitors, and this marketing practice is holding true in our bad economic times. Nick Brien at Mediabrands says, "Ads have to get combative in bad times. It's a dog fight, and it's about getting leaner and meaner." Ads are less lavish and glamorous today and are also more interactive. Table 4-4 lists specific characteristics of ads forthcoming in 2012 in response to the economic hard times many people nationwide and worldwide are facing.

Marketers spent between $2.8 and $3 million per 30-second advertising spot during the 2011 Super Bowl between the Pittsburg Steelers and Green Bay Packers. Advertising can be very expensive, and that is why marketing is a major business function to be studied carefully. Without marketing, even the best products and services have little chance of being successful.

A private company and the world's largest social network, Facebook, may epitomize where the advertising industry is going. Facebook subtly injects the advertiser's brand into the user's consciousness in order to provoke a purchase down the line by getting you to "like" the brand. Companies such as Ford, 7-Eleven, and McDonald's have recently unveiled new products on their Facebook pages. Starbucks offers coupons and free pastries to its 14 million Facebook fans. BP used its Facebook page to release statements and photos during the Gulf Oil Crisis. Anton Vincent, marketing vice president for General Mills' baking products division, says that Facebook allows a company to "leverage the loyalty" of its best customers. If you have recently gotten engaged and updated your Facebook status, you may start seeing ads from local jewelers who have used Facebook's automated ad system to target you. Facebook enables any firm today to very effectively target their exact audience with perfect advertising.[16] In performing a strategic planning analysis, in addition to comparing rival firms' websites, it is important to compare rival firms' Facebook page.

One of the last off-limit advertising outlets has historically been books, but with the proliferation of e-books, marketers are experimenting more and more with advertising to consumers as they read e-books. New ads are being targeted based on the book's content and the demographic profile of the reader. Digital e-book companies such as Wowio and Amazon are trying to

TABLE 4-4 Desirable Characteristics of Ads Today

1. Take direct aim at competitors; so leaner, meaner, and to the point.
2. Be less lavish and glamorous, requiring less production dollars to develop.
3. Be short and sweet, mostly 10- and 15-second ads rather than 30+ seconds.
4. "Make you feel good" or "put you in a good mood" because (a) ads can be more easily avoided than ever and (b) people are experiencing hard times and seek comfort.
5. Be more pervasive such as on buses, elevators, cell phones, and trucks.
6. Appear less on websites as banner ads become the new junk mail.
7. Red will overtake the color orange as the most popular ad color.
8. More than ever emphasize low price and value versus rivals.
9. More than ever emphasize how the product/service will make your life better.

Source: Based on Suzanne Vranica, "Ads to Go Leaner, Meaner in '09," *Wall Street Journal,* January 5, 2009, B8.

insert ads between chapters and along borders of digital pages. Random House says its e-books will soon include ads, but only with author approval. Global advertising expenditures are expected to grow 4.6 percent in 2011 and a bit more in 2012.

Determining organizational strengths and weaknesses in the selling function of marketing is an important part of performing an internal strategic-management audit. With regard to advertising products and services on the Internet, a new trend is to base advertising rates exclusively on sales rates. This new accountability contrasts sharply with traditional broadcast and print advertising, which bases rates on the number of persons expected to see a given advertisement. The new cost-per-sale online advertising rates are possible because any website can monitor which user clicks on which advertisement and then can record whether that consumer actually buys the product. If there are no sales, then the advertisement is free.

Product and Service Planning

Product and service planning includes activities such as test marketing; product and brand positioning; devising warranties; packaging; determining product options, features, style, and quality; deleting old products; and providing for customer service. Product and service planning is particularly important when a company is pursuing product development or diversification.

One of the most effective product and service planning techniques is *test marketing*. Test markets allow an organization to test alternative marketing plans and to forecast future sales of new products. In conducting a test market project, an organization must decide how many cities to include, which cities to include, how long to run the test, what information to collect during the test, and what action to take after the test has been completed. Test marketing is used more frequently by consumer goods companies than by industrial goods companies. Test marketing can allow an organization to avoid substantial losses by revealing weak products and ineffective marketing approaches before large-scale production begins. Starbucks is currently test marketing selling beer and wine in its stores to boost its "after 5 pm" sales.

Pricing

Five major stakeholders affect *pricing* decisions: consumers, governments, suppliers, distributors, and competitors. Sometimes an organization will pursue a forward integration strategy primarily to gain better control over prices charged to consumers. Governments can impose constraints on price fixing, price discrimination, minimum prices, unit pricing, price advertising, and price controls. For example, the Robinson-Patman Act prohibits manufacturers and wholesalers from discriminating in price among channel member purchasers (suppliers and distributors) if competition is injured.

Competing organizations must be careful not to coordinate discounts, credit terms, or condition of sale; not to discuss prices, markups, and costs at trade association meetings; and not to arrange to issue new price lists on the same date, to rotate low bids on contracts, or to uniformly restrict production to maintain high prices. Strategists should view price from both a short-run and a long-run perspective, because competitors can copy price changes with relative ease. Often a dominant firm will aggressively match all price cuts by competitors.

With regard to pricing, as the value of the dollar increases, U.S. multinational companies have a choice. They can raise prices in the local currency of a foreign country or risk losing sales and market share. Alternatively, multinational firms can keep prices steady and face reduced profit when their export revenue is reported in the United States in dollars.

Intense price competition, coupled with Internet price-comparative shopping, has reduced profit margins to bare minimum levels for most companies. For example, airline tickets, rental car prices, hotel room rates, and computer prices are lower today than they have been in many years.

PepsiCo. Inc. recently raised prices for its Tropicana juice line by up to 8 percent after the 2011 harsh winter crushed Florida's citrus crop in many places. Also due to especially cold winters hurting citrus crops, Coca-Cola Co. recently raised prices of their Minute Maid and Simply Juice brands. Fruit and vegetable prices are rising dramatically all over the world as a result not only of harsh winters, but also rising gas prices, which significantly increases the cost of transporting perishable products. The rapid rise in food commodity prices is attributed as one reason why regimes in Tunisia, Egypt, Yemen, and Libya toppled. Global populations are growing, becoming more prosperous and informed, and draining stockpiles of grain and meat.

Corn inventories are used in food, feed, and fuel, and that reserve fell to just 50 days recently, a 37-year low. Soybean stockpiles worldwide are the lowest in two decades. Consumers worldwide are seeing high food prices at supermarkets.

Distribution

Distribution includes warehousing, distribution channels, distribution coverage, retail site locations, sales territories, inventory levels and location, transportation carriers, wholesaling, and retailing. Most producers today do not sell their goods directly to consumers. Various marketing entities act as intermediaries; they bear a variety of names such as wholesalers, retailers, brokers, facilitators, agents, vendors—or simply distributors.

Distribution becomes especially important when a firm is striving to implement a market development or forward integration strategy. Some of the most complex and challenging decisions facing a firm concern product distribution. Intermediaries flourish in our economy because many producers lack the financial resources and expertise to carry out direct marketing. Manufacturers who could afford to sell directly to the public often can gain greater returns by expanding and improving their manufacturing operations.

Successful organizations identify and evaluate alternative ways to reach their ultimate market. Possible approaches vary from direct selling to using just one or many wholesalers and retailers. Strengths and weaknesses of each channel alternative should be determined according to economic, control, and adaptive criteria. Organizations should consider the costs and benefits of various wholesaling and retailing options. They must consider the need to motivate and control channel members and the need to adapt to changes in the future. Once a marketing channel is chosen, an organization usually must adhere to it for an extended period of time.

Marketing Research

Marketing research is the systematic gathering, recording, and analyzing of data about problems relating to the marketing of goods and services. Marketing research can uncover critical strengths and weaknesses, and marketing researchers employ numerous scales, instruments, procedures, concepts, and techniques to gather information. Marketing research activities support all of the major business functions of an organization. Organizations that possess excellent marketing research skills have a definite strength in pursuing generic strategies. The president of PepsiCo said,

> "Looking at the competition is the company's best form of market research. The majority of our strategic successes are ideas that we borrow from the marketplace, usually from a small regional or local competitor. In each case, we spot a promising new idea, improve on it, and then out-execute our competitor."[17]

Cost/Benefit Analysis

The seventh function of marketing is *cost/benefit analysis,* which involves assessing the costs, benefits, and risks associated with marketing decisions. Three steps are required to perform a cost/benefit analysis: (1) compute the total costs associated with a decision, (2) estimate the total benefits from the decision, and (3) compare the total costs with the total benefits. When expected benefits exceed total costs, an opportunity becomes more attractive. Sometimes the variables included in a cost/benefit analysis cannot be quantified or even measured, but usually reasonable estimates can be made to allow the analysis to be performed. One key factor to be considered is risk. Cost/benefit analysis should also be performed when a company is evaluating alternative ways to be socially responsible.

The practice of cost/benefit analysis differs among countries and industries. Some of the main differences include the types of impacts that are included as costs and benefits within appraisals, the extent to which impacts are expressed in monetary terms, and differences in the discount rate. Government agencies across the world rely on a basic set of key cost/benefit indicators, including the following:

1. NPV (net present value)
2. PVB (present value of benefits)

3. PVC (present value of costs)
4. BCR (benefit cost ratio = PVB / PVC)
5. Net benefit (= PVB – PVC)
6. NPV/k (where k is the level of funds available)[18]

Marketing Audit Checklist of Questions

The following questions about marketing must be examined in strategic planning:

1. Are markets segmented effectively?
2. Is the organization positioned well among competitors?
3. Has the firm's market share been increasing?
4. Are present channels of distribution reliable and cost effective?
5. Does the firm have an effective sales organization?
6. Does the firm conduct market research?
7. Are product quality and customer service good?
8. Are the firm's products and services priced appropriately?
9. Does the firm have an effective promotion, advertising, and publicity strategy?
10. Are marketing, planning, and budgeting effective?
11. Do the firm's marketing managers have adequate experience and training?
12. Is the firm's Internet presence excellent as compared to rivals?

Finance/Accounting

Financial condition is often considered the single best measure of a firm's competitive position and overall attractiveness to investors. Determining an organization's financial strengths and weaknesses is essential to effectively formulating strategies. A firm's liquidity, leverage, working capital, profitability, asset utilization, cash flow, and equity can eliminate some strategies as being feasible alternatives. Financial factors often alter existing strategies and change implementation plans.

Especially good websites from which to obtain financial information about firms are provided in Table 4-5.

Finance/Accounting Functions

According to James Van Horne, the *functions of finance/accounting* comprise three decisions: the investment decision, the financing decision, and the dividend decision.[19] Financial ratio analysis is the most widely used method for determining an organization's strengths and weaknesses in the investment, financing, and dividend areas. Because the functional areas of business are so closely related, financial ratios can signal strengths or weaknesses in management, marketing, production, research and development, and management information systems activities. Financial ratios are equally applicable in for-profit and nonprofit organizations. Even though nonprofit organizations obviously would not have return-on-investment or earnings-per-share ratios, they would routinely monitor many other special ratios. For example, a church would

TABLE 4-5 **Excellent Websites to Obtain Information on Companies, Including Financial Ratios**

1. http://marketwatch.multexinvestor.com
2. http://moneycentral.msn.com
3. http://finance.yahoo.com
4. www.clearstation.com
5. http://us.etrade.com/e/t/invest/markets
6. www.hoovers.com
7. http://globaledge.msu.edu/industries/

monitor the ratio of dollar contributions to number of members, while a zoo would monitor dollar food sales to number of visitors. A university would monitor number of students divided by number of professors. Therefore, be creative when performing ratio analysis for nonprofit organizations because they strive to be financially sound just as for-profit firms do.

The *investment decision,* also called *capital budgeting,* is the allocation and reallocation of capital and resources to projects, products, assets, and divisions of an organization. Once strategies are formulated, capital budgeting decisions are required to successfully implement strategies. The *financing decision* determines the best capital structure for the firm and includes examining various methods by which the firm can raise capital (for example, by issuing stock, increasing debt, selling assets, or using a combination of these approaches). The financing decision must consider both short-term and long-term needs for working capital. Two key financial ratios that indicate whether a firm's financing decisions have been effective are the debt-to-equity ratio and the debt-to-total-assets ratio.

Dividend decisions concern issues such as the percentage of earnings paid to stockholders, the stability of dividends paid over time, and the repurchase or issuance of stock. Dividend decisions determine the amount of funds that are retained in a firm compared to the amount paid out to stockholders. Three financial ratios that are helpful in evaluating a firm's dividend decisions are the earnings-per-share ratio, the dividends-per-share ratio, and the price-earnings ratio. The benefits of paying dividends to investors must be balanced against the benefits of internally retaining funds, and there is no set formula on how to balance this trade-off. For the reasons listed here, dividends are sometimes paid out even when funds could be better reinvested in the business or when the firm has to obtain outside sources of capital:

1. Paying cash dividends is customary. Failure to do so could be thought of as a stigma. A dividend change is considered a signal about the future.
2. Dividends represent a sales point for investment bankers. Some institutional investors can buy only dividend-paying stocks.
3. Shareholders often demand dividends, even in companies with great opportunities for reinvesting all available funds.
4. A myth exists that paying dividends will result in a higher stock price.

Most companies have ceased cutting and instead are raising their dividend payout. General Electric raised its quarterly dividend twice in 2010. Honeywell Inc. recently raised its annual dividend 10 percent to $1.33 a share while Germany's Siemens AG raised its dividend 68 percent to $3.57 a share. Siemens strives to pay out 30 to 50 percent of its net income to shareholders. S&P says there were 59 dividend increases in the fourth quarter of 2010 alone, up 25 percent from 2009. S&P expects that more than 50 percent of the S&P 500 firms will raise their dividend payout in 2011.[20]

McDonald's has raised its dividend payout for 35 years in a row, including recent years. Among all S&P 500 companies, 255 increased their dividends in 2010, up from 157 in 2009, and that trend is accelerating as firms' cash reserves grow. In addition to boosting dividend payouts, companies are also buying back their own stock more often and in larger amounts. Investors love dividends and other methods companies use to return capital to shareholders. Other companies recently raising their dividend rate are Tyco International Ltd. (to $0.25 per share per quarter from $0.21), Staples, Inc. (to $0.10 per quarter from $0.09), Prudential PLC (to 23.85 pence from 19.85), Bank of Nova Scotia (to C$0.52 from C$0.49 per share per quarter), Qualcomm Inc. (from $0.19 to $0.215 per share per quarter), and Applied Materials, Inc.(to $0.08 from $0.07 per share per quarter).

Basic Types of Financial Ratios

Financial ratios are computed from an organization's income statement and balance sheet. Computing financial ratios is like taking a picture because the results reflect a situation at just one point in time. Comparing ratios over time and to industry averages is more likely to result in meaningful statistics that can be used to identify and evaluate strengths and weaknesses. Trend analysis, illustrated in Figure 4-3, is a useful technique that incorporates both the time and industry average dimensions of financial ratios. Note that the dotted lines reveal projected ratios. Some websites, such as those provided in Table 4-5, calculate financial ratios and provide data with charts.

FIGURE 4-3

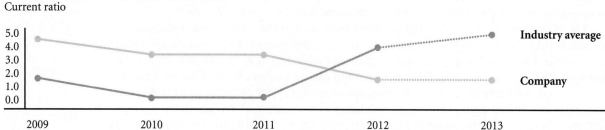

A Financial Ratio Trend Analysis

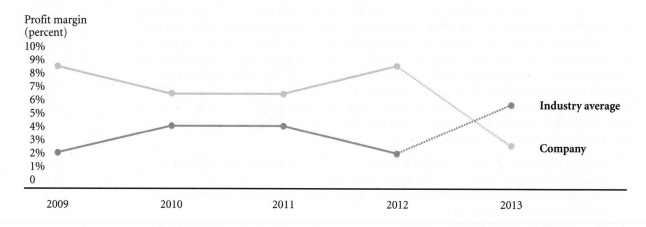

Table 4-6 provides a summary of key financial ratios showing how each ratio is calculated and what each ratio measures. However, all the ratios are not significant for all industries and companies. For example, accounts receivable turnover and average collection period are not very meaningful to a company that primarily does a cash receipts business. Key financial ratios can be classified into the following five types:

1. *Liquidity ratios* measure a firm's ability to meet maturing short-term obligations.
   Current ratio
   Quick (or acid-test) ratio

2. *Leverage ratios* measure the extent to which a firm has been financed by debt.
   Debt-to-total-assets ratio
   Debt-to-equity ratio
   Long-term debt-to-equity ratio
   Times-interest-earned (or coverage) ratio

3. *Activity ratios* measure how effectively a firm is using its resources.
   Inventory turnover
   Fixed assets turnover
   Total assets turnover
   Accounts receivable turnover
   Average collection period

4. *Profitability ratios* measure management's overall effectiveness as shown by the returns generated on sales and investment.
   Gross profit margin
   Operating profit margin
   Net profit margin
   Return on total assets (ROA)
   Return on stockholders' equity (ROE)
   Earnings per share (EPS)
   Price-earnings ratio

TABLE 4-6   A Summary of Key Financial Ratios

Ratio	How Calculated	What It Measures
Liquidity Ratios		
Current Ratio	$\dfrac{\text{Current assets}}{\text{Current liabilities}}$	The extent to which a firm can meet its short-term obligations
Quick Ratio	$\dfrac{\text{Current assets minus inventory}}{\text{Current liabilities}}$	The extent to which a firm can meet its short-term obligations without relying upon the sale of its inventories
Leverage Ratios		
Debt-to-Total-Assets Ratio	$\dfrac{\text{Total debt}}{\text{Total assets}}$	The percentage of total funds that are provided by creditors
Debt-to-Equity Ratio	$\dfrac{\text{Total debt}}{\text{Total stockholders' equity}}$	The percentage of total funds provided by creditors versus by owners
Long-Term Debt-to-Equity Ratio	$\dfrac{\text{Long-term debt}}{\text{Total stockholders' equity}}$	The balance between debt and equity in a firm's long-term capital structure
Times-Interest-Earned Ratio	$\dfrac{\text{Profits before interest and taxes}}{\text{Total interest charges}}$	The extent to which earnings can decline without the firm becoming unable to meet its annual interest costs
Activity Ratios		
Inventory Turnover	$\dfrac{\text{Sales}}{\text{Inventory of finished goods}}$	Whether a firm holds excessive stocks of inventories and whether a firm is slowly selling its inventories compared to the industry average
Fixed Assets Turnover	$\dfrac{\text{Sales}}{\text{Fixed assets}}$	Sales productivity and plant and equipment utilization
Total Assets Turnover	$\dfrac{\text{Sales}}{\text{Total assets}}$	Whether a firm is generating a sufficient volume of business for the size of its asset investment
Accounts Receivable Turnover	$\dfrac{\text{Annual credit sales}}{\text{Accounts receivable}}$	The average length of time it takes a firm to collect credit sales (in percentage terms)
Average Collection Period	$\dfrac{\text{Accounts receivable}}{\text{Total credit sales/365 days}}$	The average length of time it takes a firm to collect on credit sales (in days)
Profitability Ratios		
Gross Profit Margin	$\dfrac{\text{Sales minus cost of goods sold}}{\text{Sales}}$	The total margin available to cover operating expenses and yield a profit
Operating Profit Margin	$\dfrac{\text{Earnings before interest and taxes EBIT}}{\text{Sales}}$	Profitability without concern for taxes and interest
Net Profit Margin	$\dfrac{\text{Net income}}{\text{Sales}}$	After-tax profits per dollar of sales
Return on Total Assets (ROA)	$\dfrac{\text{Net income}}{\text{Total assets}}$	After-tax profits per dollar of assets; this ratio is also called return on investment (ROI)
Return on Stockholders' Equity (ROE)	$\dfrac{\text{Net income}}{\text{Total stockholders' equity}}$	After-tax profits per dollar of stockholders' investment in the firm
Earnings Per Share (EPS)	$\dfrac{\text{Net income}}{\text{Number of shares of common stock outstanding}}$	Earnings available to the owners of common stock
Price-Earnings Ratio	$\dfrac{\text{Market price per share}}{\text{Earnings per share}}$	Attractiveness of firm on equity markets

(continued)

TABLE 4-6   A Summary of Key Financial Ratios—continued

Ratio	How Calculated	What It Measures
Growth Ratios		
Sales	Annual percentage growth in total sales	Firm's growth rate in sales
Net Income	Annual percentage growth in profits	Firm's growth rate in profits
Earnings Per Share	Annual percentage growth in EPS	Firm's growth rate in EPS
Dividends Per Share	Annual percentage growth in dividends per share	Firm's growth rate in dividends per share

5. *Growth ratios* measure the firm's ability to maintain its economic position in the growth of the economy and industry.
   Sales
   Net income
   Earnings per share
   Dividends per share

Financial ratio analysis must go beyond the actual calculation and interpretation of ratios. The analysis should be conducted on three separate fronts:

1. *How has each ratio changed over time?* This information provides a means of evaluating historical trends. It is important to note whether each ratio has been historically increasing, decreasing, or nearly constant. For example, a 10 percent profit margin could be bad if the trend has been down 20 percent each of the last three years. But a 10 percent profit margin could be excellent if the trend has been up, up, up. Therefore, calculate the percentage change in each ratio from one year to the next to assess historical financial performance on that dimension. Identify and examine large percent changes in a financial ratio from one year to the next.

2. *How does each ratio compare to industry norms?* A firm's inventory turnover ratio may appear impressive at first glance but may pale when compared to industry standards or norms. Industries can differ dramatically on certain ratios. For example grocery companies, such as Kroger, have a high inventory turnover whereas automobile dealerships have a lower turnover. Therefore, comparison of a firm's ratios within its particular industry can be essential in determining strength/weakness.

3. *How does each ratio compare with key competitors?* Oftentimes competition is more intense between several competitors in a given industry or location than across all rival firms in the industry. When this is true, financial ratio analysis should include comparison to those key competitors. For example, if a firm's profitability ratio is trending up over time and compares favorably to the industry average, but it is trending down relative to its leading competitor, there may be reason for concern.

Financial ratio analysis is not without some limitations. First of all, financial ratios are based on accounting data, and firms differ in their treatment of such items as depreciation, inventory valuation, research and development expenditures, pension plan costs, mergers, and taxes. Also, seasonal factors can influence comparative ratios. Therefore, conformity to industry composite ratios does not establish with certainty that a firm is performing normally or that it is well managed. Likewise, departures from industry averages do not always indicate that a firm is doing especially well or badly. For example, a high inventory turnover ratio could indicate efficient inventory management and a strong working capital position, but it also could indicate a serious inventory shortage and a weak working capital position.

It is important to recognize that a firm's financial condition depends not only on the functions of finance, but also on many other factors that include (1) management, marketing, management production/operations, research and development, and management information systems decisions; (2) actions by competitors, suppliers, distributors, creditors, customers, and

FIGURE 4-4

A Before and After Breakeven Chart When Prices Are Lowered

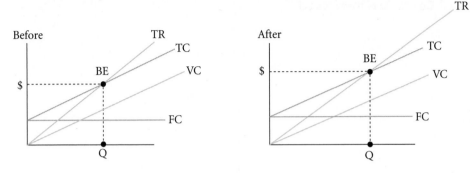

shareholders; and (3) economic, social, cultural, demographic, environmental, political, governmental, legal, and technological trends.

Since consumers remain price sensitive, many firms have lowered prices to compete. As a firm lowers prices, its *breakeven (BE) point* in terms of units sold increases, as illustrated in Figure 4-4. The breakeven point can be defined as the quantity of units that a firm must sell in order for its total revenues (TR) to equal its total costs (TC). Note that the before and after chart in Figure 4-4 reveals that the Total Revenue (TR) line rotates to the right with a decrease in Price, thus increasing the Quantity (Q) that must be sold just to break even. Increasing the breakeven point is thus a huge drawback of lowering prices. Of course when rivals are lowering prices, a firm may have to lower prices anyway to compete. However, the breakeven concept should be kept in mind because it is so important, especially in recessionary times.

Notice in Figure 4-5 that increasing Fixed Costs (FC) also raises a firm's breakeven quantity. Note the before and after chart in Figure 4-5 reveals that adding fixed costs such as more stores, or more plants, or even more advertising as part of a strategic plan raises the Total Cost (TC) line, which makes the intersection of the Total Cost (TC) and Total Revenue (TR) lines at a point farther down the Quantity axis. Increasing a firm's fixed costs (FC) thus significantly raises the quantity of goods that must be sold to break even. This is not just theory for the sake of theory. Firms with less fixed costs, such as Apple and Amazon.com, have lower breakeven points, which give them a decided competitive advantage in harsh economic times. Figure 4-5 reveals that adding *fixed costs (FC),* such as plant, equipment, stores, advertising, and land, may be detrimental whenever there is doubt that significantly more units can be sold to offset those expenditures.

Firms must be cognizant of the fact that lowering prices and adding fixed costs could be a catastrophic double whammy because the firm's breakeven quantity needed to be sold is increased dramatically. Figure 4-6 illustrates this double whammy. Note how far the breakeven

FIGURE 4-5

A Before and After Breakeven Chart When Fixed Costs Are Increased

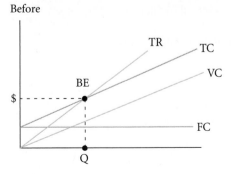
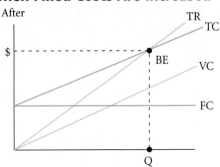

FIGURE 4-6

A Before and After Breakeven Chart When Prices Are Lowered and Fixed Costs Are Increased

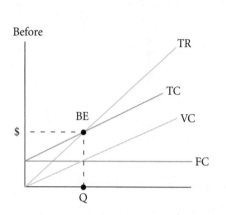

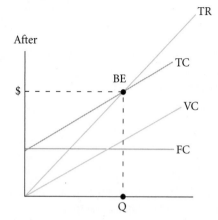

point shifts with both a price decrease and an increase in fixed costs. If a firm does not breakeven, then it will of course incur losses, and losses are not good, especially sustained losses.

Finally, note in Figure 4-4, 4-5, and 4-6 that *Variable Costs (VC)* such as labor and materials, when increased, have the effect of raising the breakeven point, too. Raising Variable Costs is reflected by the Variable Cost line shifting left or becoming steeper. When the Total Revenue (TR) line remains constant, the effect of increasing Variable Costs is to increase Total Costs, which increases the point at which Total Revenue = Total Costs (TC) = Breakeven (BE).

Suffice it to say here that various strategies can have dramatically beneficial or harmful effects on the firm's financial condition due to the concept of breakeven analysis.

There are some limitations of breakeven analysis, including the following points:

1. Breakeven analysis is only a supply side (*i.e.* costs only) analysis, as it tells you nothing about what sales are likely to be for the product at various prices.
2. It assumes that fixed costs (FC) are constant. Although this is true in the short run, an increase in the scale of production will cause fixed costs to rise.
3. It assumes average variable costs are constant per unit of output, at least in the range of likely quantities of sales.
4. It assumes that the quantity of goods produced is equal to the quantity of goods sold (i.e., there is no change in beginning or ending inventory).
5. In multi-product companies, it assumes that the relative proportions of each product sold and produced are constant (*i.e.*, the sales mix is constant).[21]

Finance/Accounting Audit Checklist

The following finance/accounting questions, like the similar questions about marketing and management earlier, should be examined:

1. Where is the firm financially strong and weak as indicated by financial ratio analyses?
2. Can the firm raise needed short-term capital?
3. Can the firm raise needed long-term capital through debt and/or equity?
4. Does the firm have sufficient working capital?
5. Are capital budgeting procedures effective?
6. Are dividend payout policies reasonable?
7. Does the firm have good relations with its investors and stockholders?
8. Are the firm's financial managers experienced and well trained?
9. Is the firm's debt situation excellent?

Production/Operations

The *production/operations function* of a business consists of all those activities that transform inputs into goods and services. Production/operations management deals with inputs, transformations, and outputs that vary across industries and markets. A manufacturing operation transforms or converts inputs such as raw materials, labor, capital, machines, and facilities into finished goods and services. As indicated in Table 4-7, Roger Schroeder suggested that production/operations management comprises five functions or decision areas: process, capacity, inventory, workforce, and quality.

Most automakers require a 30-day notice to build vehicles, but Toyota Motor fills a buyer's new car order in just five days. Honda Motor was considered the industry's fastest producer, filling orders in 15 days. Automakers have for years operated under just-in-time inventory systems, but Toyota's 360 suppliers are linked to the company via computers on a virtual assembly line. The new Toyota production system was developed in the company's Cambridge, Ontario, plant and now applies to its Solara, Camry, Corolla, and Tacoma vehicles.

Production/operations activities often represent the largest part of an organization's human and capital assets. In most industries, the major costs of producing a product or service are incurred within operations, so production/operations can have great value as a competitive weapon in a company's overall strategy. Strengths and weaknesses in the five functions of production can mean the success or failure of an enterprise.

Many production/operations managers are finding that cross-training of employees can help their firms respond faster to changing markets. Cross-training of workers can increase efficiency, quality, productivity, and job satisfaction. For example, at General Motors' Detroit gear and axle plant, costs related to product defects were reduced 400 percent in two years as a result of cross-training workers. As shown in Table 4-8, James Dilworth outlined implications of several types of strategic decisions that a company might make.

Singapore rivals Hong Kong as an attractive site for locating production facilities in Southeast Asia. Singapore is a city-state near Malaysia. An island nation of about 4 million, Singapore is changing from an economy built on trade and services to one built on information technology. A large-scale program in computer education for older (over age 26) residents is very popular. Singapore children receive outstanding computer training in schools. All government services are computerized nicely. Singapore lures multinational businesses with great tax breaks, world-class infrastructure, excellent courts that efficiently handle business disputes, exceptionally low tariffs, large land giveaways, impressive industrial parks, excellent port facilities, and a government very receptive to and cooperative with foreign businesses. Foreign firms now account for 70 percent of manufacturing output in Singapore.

In terms of ship container traffic processed annually, Singapore has the largest and busiest seaport in the world, followed by Hong Kong, Shanghai, Los Angeles, Busan (South Korea), Rotterdam, Hamburg, New York, and Tokyo. The Singapore seaport is five times the size of the New York City seaport.[22]

TABLE 4-7   **The Basic Functions (Decisions) Within Production/Operations**

Decision Areas	Example Decisions
1. Process	These decisions include choice of technology, facility layout, process flow analysis, facility location, line balancing, process control, and transportation analysis. Distances from raw materials to production sites to customers are a major consideration.
2. Capacity	These decisions include forecasting, facilities planning, aggregate planning, scheduling, capacity planning, and queuing analysis. Capacity utilization is a major consideration.
3. Inventory	These decisions involve managing the level of raw materials, work-in-process, and finished goods, especially considering what to order, when to order, how much to order, and materials handling.
4. Workforce	These decisions involve managing the skilled, unskilled, clerical, and managerial employees by caring for job design, work measurement, job enrichment, work standards, and motivation techniques.
5. Quality	These decisions are aimed at ensuring that high-quality goods and services are produced by caring for quality control, sampling, testing, quality assurance, and cost control.

Source: Based on R. Schroeder, *Operations Management* (New York: McGraw-Hill, 1981), 12.

TABLE 4-8 Implications of Various Strategies on Production/Operations

Various Strategies	Implications
1. Low-cost provider	Creates high barriers to entry
	Creates larger market
	Requires longer production runs and fewer product changes
2. A high-quality provider	Requires more quality-assurance efforts
	Requires more expensive equipment
	Requires highly skilled workers and higher wages
3. Provide great customer service	Requires more service people, service parts, and equipment
	Requires rapid response to customer needs or changes in customer tastes
	Requires a higher inventory investment
4. Be the first to introduce new products	Has higher research and development costs
	Has high retraining and tooling costs
5. Become highly automated	Requires high capital investment
	Reduces flexibility
	May affect labor relations
	Makes maintenance more crucial
6. Minimize layoffs	Serves the security needs of employees and may develop employee loyalty
	Helps to attract and retain highly skilled employees

Source: Based on: J. Dilworth, *Production and Operations Management: Manufacturing and Nonmanufacturing,* 2nd ed. Copyright © 1983 by Random House, Inc.

Production/Operations Audit Checklist

Questions such as the following should be examined:

1. Are supplies of raw materials, parts, and subassemblies reliable and reasonable?
2. Are facilities, equipment, machinery, and offices in good condition?
3. Are inventory-control policies and procedures effective?
4. Are quality-control policies and procedures effective?
5. Are facilities, resources, and markets strategically located?
6. Does the firm have technological competencies?

Research and Development

Apple Inc. continues to develop and sell new products such as the iPhone and iPad despite spending less on R&D over the last 10 years than rival Microsoft did even in fiscal 2010 alone.[23] Microsoft routinely spends 14 to 15 percent of its sales on R&D, or $8.7 billion in fiscal 2010, compared to Apple every year spending about 2.5 percent of its annual sales on R&D. The correlation between R&D expenditures and successful product launches is not high. Thus, firms such as Research in Motion (RIM) and Nokia are reducing their R&D expenditures, especially as a percent of sales. RIM is spending $1.35 billion in fiscal 2011 on R&D or about 6 percent of revenues, compared to Nokia spending 13.8 percent of sales in 2010.

The fifth major area of internal operations that should be examined for specific strengths and weaknesses is *research and development (R&D).* Many firms today conduct no R&D, and yet many other companies depend on successful R&D activities for survival. Firms pursuing a product development strategy especially need to have a strong R&D orientation.

Organizations invest in R&D because they believe that such an investment will lead to a superior product or service and will give them competitive advantages. Research and development expenditures are directed at developing new products before competitors do, at improving product quality, or at improving manufacturing processes to reduce costs.

Effective management of the R&D function requires a strategic and operational partnership between R&D and the other vital business functions. A spirit of partnership and mutual trust between general and R&D managers is evident in the best-managed firms today. Managers in these firms jointly explore; assess; and decide the what, when, where, why, and how much of R&D. Priorities, costs, benefits, risks, and rewards associated with R&D activities are discussed openly and shared. The overall mission of R&D thus has become broad-based, including supporting existing businesses, helping launch new businesses, developing new products, improving product quality, improving manufacturing efficiency, and deepening or broadening the company's technological capabilities.[24]

The best-managed firms today seek to organize R&D activities in a way that breaks the isolation of R&D from the rest of the company and promotes a spirit of partnership between R&D managers and other managers in the firm. R&D decisions and plans must be integrated and coordinated across departments and divisions by having the departments share experiences and information. The strategic-management process facilitates this cross-functional approach to managing the R&D function.

R&D spending at major corporations declined in 2009 for the first time in 10 years as the worldwide recession hit most firms hard. Roche Holding AG led all firms in R&D spending at $9.12 billion, followed by Microsoft at $9.01 billion and Nokia at $8.24 billion. Other large spenders were Toyota Motor at $7.82 billion and Pfizer at $7.74 billion. Interestingly absent among the top 10 R&D spenders, Apple spent about 3.1 percent of sales on R&D, roughly half the typical level for computer and electronic companies. Booz and Co. partner Barry Jaruzelski remarked that: "Apple succeeds because it has a deep understanding of consumers, is focused on its projects 'as opposed to trying to spread their bets,' and attracts superior talent."[25]

Internal and External R&D

Cost distributions among R&D activities vary by company and industry, but total R&D costs generally do not exceed manufacturing and marketing start-up costs. Four approaches to determining R&D budget allocations commonly are used: (1) financing as many project proposals as possible, (2) using a percentage-of-sales method, (3) budgeting about the same amount that competitors spend for R&D, or (4) deciding how many successful new products are needed and working backward to estimate the required R&D investment.

R&D in organizations can take two basic forms: (1) internal R&D, in which an organization operates its own R&D department, and/or (2) contract R&D, in which a firm hires independent researchers or independent agencies to develop specific products. Many companies use both approaches to develop new products. A widely used approach for obtaining outside R&D assistance is to pursue a joint venture with another firm. R&D strengths (capabilities) and weaknesses (limitations) play a major role in strategy formulation and strategy implementation.

Most firms have no choice but to continually develop new and improved products because of changing consumer needs and tastes, new technologies, shortened product life cycles, and increased domestic and foreign competition. A shortage of ideas for new products, increased global competition, increased market segmentation, strong special-interest groups, and increased government regulations are several factors making the successful development of new products more and more difficult, costly, and risky. In the pharmaceutical industry, for example, only one out of every few thousand drugs created in the laboratory ends up on pharmacists' shelves. Scarpello, Boulton, and Hofer emphasized that different strategies require different R&D capabilities:

> The focus of R&D efforts can vary greatly depending on a firm's competitive strategy. Some corporations attempt to be market leaders and innovators of new products, while others are satisfied to be market followers and developers of currently available products. The basic skills required to support these strategies will vary, depending on whether R&D becomes the driving force behind competitive strategy. In cases where new product introduction is the driving force for strategy, R&D activities must be extensive.[26]

In an effort to share huge R&D costs associated with developing hybrid and electric cars, Germany's BMW AG and France's PSA Peugeot Citroen in mid-2011 established a 50–50 joint venture to develop fuel-efficient technologies. The joint venture will develop and produce a full range of hybrid car components, such as battery packs and drivetrains, as well as software for hybrid and electric vehicles. Peugeot has a similar R&D partnership with Mitsubishi Motors

Corp., while BMW has a similar alliance with rival Daimler AG. Even fierce rivals Renault SA and Nissan Motor Co have a joint partnership to develop small electric cars—so the days of never working with rival firms is over, especially in regard to defraying heavy R&D expenditures.

Research and Development Audit

Questions such as the following should be asked in performing an R&D audit:

1. Does the firm have R&D facilities? Are they adequate?
2. If outside R&D firms are used, are they cost-effective?
3. Are the organization's R&D personnel well qualified?
4. Are R&D resources allocated effectively?
5. Are management information and computer systems adequate?
6. Is communication between R&D and other organizational units effective?
7. Are present products technologically competitive?

Management Information Systems

Nordstrom Inc. in recent years has tried to stay ahead of competitors by integrating its online and in-store inventory systems, enabling consumers to see what is available in stores near them. Nordstrom has a five-star rating system online to track what people think and say in social media forums. Nordstrom just acquired HauteLook Inc., a fast-growing, online flash sales company that offered luxury clothes at a discount.

Information ties all business functions together and provides the basis for all managerial decisions. It is the cornerstone of all organizations. Information represents a major source of competitive management advantage or disadvantage. Assessing a firm's internal strengths and weaknesses in information systems is a critical dimension of performing an internal audit.

A management information system's purpose is to improve the performance of an enterprise by improving the quality of managerial decisions. An effective information system thus collects, codes, stores, synthesizes, and presents information in such a manner that it answers important operating and strategic questions. The heart of an information system is a database containing the kinds of records and data important to managers.

A *management information system* receives raw material from both the external and internal evaluation of an organization. It gathers data about marketing, finance, production, and personnel matters internally, and social, cultural, demographic, environmental, economic, political, governmental, legal, technological, and competitive factors externally. Data are integrated in ways needed to support managerial decision making.

There is a logical flow of material in a computer information system, whereby data are input to the system and transformed into output. Outputs include computer printouts, written reports, tables, charts, graphs, checks, purchase orders, invoices, inventory records, payroll accounts, and a variety of other documents. Payoffs from alternative strategies can be calculated and estimated. *Data* become *information* only when they are evaluated, filtered, condensed, analyzed, and organized for a specific purpose, problem, individual, or time.

Even Wal-Mart recognizes the immense importance of information technology. In mid-2011 Wal-Mart acquired Kosmix, a social media technology provider that has built a platform that enables users to filter and organize content in social networks in order to connect people with information that matters to them, in realtime. Kosmix powers a site called TweetBeat, essentially a realtime social media filter for live events. Additionally, the technology is used to power RightHealth, a popular health and medical information site. Kosmix is now operating as part of a newly formed group named WalMartLabs, which is creating information technologies and businesses around social and mobile commerce to support Wal-Mart's multichannel strategy. This acquisition blurs the line between offline and online shopping.

Management Information Systems Audit

Questions such as the following should be asked when conducting this audit:

1. Do all managers in the firm use the information system to make decisions?
2. Is there a chief information officer or director of information systems position in the firm?

3. Are data in the information system updated regularly?
4. Do managers from all functional areas of the firm contribute input to the information system?
5. Are there effective passwords for entry into the firm's information system?
6. Are strategists of the firm familiar with the information systems of rival firms?
7. Is the information system user-friendly?
8. Do all users of the information system understand the competitive advantages that information can provide firms?
9. Are computer training workshops provided for users of the information system?
10. Is the firm's information system continually being improved in content and user-friendliness?

Value Chain Analysis (VCA)

According to Porter, the business of a firm can best be described as a *value chain,* in which total revenues minus total costs of all activities undertaken to develop and market a product or service yields value. All firms in a given industry have a similar value chain, which includes activities such as obtaining raw materials, designing products, building manufacturing facilities, developing cooperative agreements, and providing customer service. A firm will be profitable as long as total revenues exceed the total costs incurred in creating and delivering the product or service. Firms should strive to understand not only their own value chain operations but also their competitors', suppliers', and distributors' value chains.

Value chain analysis (VCA) refers to the process whereby a firm determines the costs associated with organizational activities from purchasing raw materials to manufacturing product(s) to marketing those products. VCA aims to identify where low-cost advantages or disadvantages exist anywhere along the value chain from raw material to customer service activities. VCA can enable a firm to better identify its own strengths and weaknesses, especially as compared to competitors' value chain analyses and their own data examined over time.

Substantial judgment may be required in performing a VCA because different items along the value chain may impact other items positively or negatively, so there exist complex interrelationships. For example, exceptional customer service may be especially expensive yet may reduce the costs of returns and increase revenues. Cost and price differences among rival firms can have their origins in activities performed by suppliers, distributors, creditors, or even shareholders. Despite the complexity of VCA, the initial step in implementing this procedure is to divide a firm's operations into specific activities or business processes. Then the analyst attempts to attach a cost to each discrete activity, and the costs could be in terms of both time and money. Finally, the analyst converts the cost data into information by looking for competitive cost strengths and weaknesses that may yield competitive advantage or disadvantage. Conducting a VCA is supportive of the RBV's examination of a firm's assets and capabilities as sources of distinctive competence.

When a major competitor or new market entrant offers products or services at very low prices, this may be because that firm has substantially lower value chain costs or perhaps the rival firm is just waging a desperate attempt to gain sales or market share. Thus value chain analysis can be critically important for a firm in monitoring whether its prices and costs are competitive. An example value chain is illustrated in Figure 4-7. There can be more than a hundred particular value-creating activities associated with the business of producing and marketing a product or service, and each one of the activities can represent a competitive advantage or disadvantage for the firm. The combined costs of all the various activities in a company's value chain define the firm's cost of doing business. Firms should determine where cost advantages and disadvantages in their value chain occur *relative to the value chain of rival firms.*

Value chains differ immensely across industries and firms. Whereas a paper products company, such as Stone Container, would include on its value chain timber farming, logging, pulp mills, and papermaking, a computer company such as Hewlett-Packard would include programming, peripherals, software, hardware, and laptops. A motel would include food, housekeeping, check-in and check-out operations, website, reservations system, and so on. However, all firms should use value chain analysis to develop and nurture a core competence and convert this

FIGURE 4-7

An Example Value Chain for a Typical Manufacturing Firm

Supplier Costs ———— ————
      Raw materials ————
      Fuel ————
      Energy ————
      Transportation ————
      Truck drivers ————
      Truck maintenance ————
      Component parts ————
      Inspection ————
      Storing ————
      Warehouse ————
Production Costs ———— ————
      Inventory system ————
      Receiving ————
      Plant layout ————
      Maintenance ————
      Plant location ————
      Computer ————
      R&D ————
      Cost accounting ————
Distribution Costs ———— ————
      Loading ————
      Shipping ————
      Budgeting ————
      Personnel ————
      Internet ————
      Trucking ————
      Railroads ————
      Fuel · ————
      Maintenance ————
Sales and Marketing Costs ————
      Salespersons ————
      Website ————
      Internet ————
      Publicity ————
      Promotion ————
      Advertising ————
      Transportation ————
      Food and lodging ————
Customer Service Costs ———— ————
      Postage ————
      Phone ————
      Internet ————
      Warranty ———— ————
Management Costs ————
      Human resources ————
      Administration ————
      Employee benefits ————
      Labor relations ————
      Managers ————
      Employees ————
      Finance and legal ————

competence into a distinctive competence. A *core competence* is a value chain activity that a firm performs especially well. When a core competence evolves into a major competitive advantage, then it is called a distinctive competence. Figure 4-8 illustrates this process.

More and more companies are using VCA to gain and sustain competitive advantage by being especially efficient and effective along various parts of the value chain. For example, Wal-Mart has built powerful value advantages by focusing on exceptionally tight inventory control, volume purchasing of products, and offering exemplary customer service. Computer companies in contrast compete aggressively along the distribution end of the value chain. Of course, price competitiveness is a key component of effectiveness among both mass retailers and computer firms.

Benchmarking

Benchmarking is an analytical tool used to determine whether a firm's value chain activities are competitive compared to rivals and thus conducive to winning in the marketplace. Benchmarking entails measuring costs of value chain activities across an industry to determine "best practices" among competing firms for the purpose of duplicating or improving upon those best practices. Benchmarking enables a firm to take action to improve its competitiveness by identifying (and improving upon) value chain activities where rival firms have comparative advantages in cost, service, reputation, or operation.

A comprehensive survey on benchmarking was recently commissioned by the Global Benchmarking Network, a network of benchmarking centers representing 22 countries. Over 450 organizations responded from over 40 countries. The results showed that:

1. Mission and Vision Statements along with Customer (Client) Surveys are the most used (77 percent of organizations) of 20 improvement tools, followed by SWOT analysis (72 percent), and Informal Benchmarking (68 percent). Performance Benchmarking was used by 49 percent and Best Practice Benchmarking by 39 percent.
2. The tools that are likely to increase in popularity the most over the next three years are Performance Benchmarking, Informal Benchmarking, SWOT, and Best Practice Benchmarking. Over 60 percent of organizations not currently using these tools indicated they are likely to use them in the next three years.[27]

The hardest part of benchmarking can be gaining access to other firms' value chain activities with associated costs. Typical sources of benchmarking information, however, include published reports, trade publications, suppliers, distributors, customers, partners, creditors, shareholders, lobbyists, and willing rival firms. Some rival firms share benchmarking data. However, the International Benchmarking Clearinghouse provides guidelines to help ensure that restraint of trade, price fixing, bid rigging, bribery, and other improper business conduct do not arise between participating firms.

Due to the popularity of benchmarking today, numerous consulting firms such as Accenture, AT Kearney, Best Practices Benchmarking & Consulting, as well as the Strategic Planning Institute's Council on Benchmarking, gather benchmarking data, conduct benchmarking studies, and distribute benchmark information without identifying the sources.

FIGURE 4-8

Transforming Value Chain Activities into Sustained Competitive Advantage

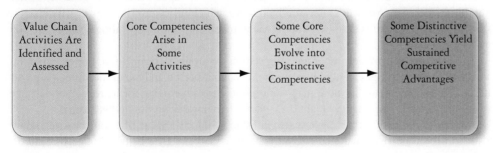

The Internal Factor Evaluation (IFE) Matrix

A summary step in conducting an internal strategic-management audit is to construct an *Internal Factor Evaluation (IFE) Matrix.* This strategy-formulation tool summarizes and evaluates the major strengths and weaknesses in the functional areas of a business, and it also provides a basis for identifying and evaluating relationships among those areas. Intuitive judgments are required in developing an IFE Matrix, so the appearance of a scientific approach should not be interpreted to mean this is an all-powerful technique. A thorough understanding of the factors included is more important than the actual numbers. Similar to the EFE Matrix and Competitive Profile Matrix described in Chapter 3, an IFE Matrix can be developed in five steps:

1. List key internal factors as identified in the internal-audit process. Use a total of from 10 to 20 internal factors, including both strengths and weaknesses. List strengths first and then weaknesses. Be as specific as possible, using percentages, ratios, and comparative numbers. Recall that Edward Deming said, "In God we trust. Everyone else bring data."

2. Assign a weight that ranges from 0.0 (not important) to 1.0 (all-important) to each factor. The weight assigned to a given factor indicates the relative importance of the factor to being successful in the firm's industry. Regardless of whether a key factor is an internal strength or weakness, factors considered to have the greatest effect on organizational performance should be assigned the highest weights. The sum of all weights must equal 1.0.

3. Assign a 1-to-4 rating to each factor to indicate whether that factor represents a major weakness (rating = 1), a minor weakness (rating = 2) a minor strength (rating = 3) or a major strength (rating = 4). Note that strengths must receive a 3 or 4 rating and weaknesses must receive a 1 or 2 rating. Ratings are thus company-based, whereas the weights in step 2 are industry-based.

4. Multiply each factor's weight by its rating to determine a weighted score for each variable.

5. Sum the weighted scores for each variable to determine the total weighted score for the organization.

Regardless of how many factors are included in an IFE Matrix, the total weighted score can range from a low of 1.0 to a high of 4.0, with the average score being 2.5. Total weighted scores well below 2.5 characterize organizations that are weak internally, whereas scores significantly above 2.5 indicate a strong internal position. Like the EFE Matrix, an IFE Matrix should include from 10 to 20 key factors. The number of factors has no effect upon the range of total weighted scores because the weights always sum to 1.0.

When a key internal factor is both a strength and a weakness, the factor should be included twice in the IFE Matrix, and a weight and rating should be assigned to each statement. For example, the Playboy logo both helps and hurts Playboy Enterprises; the logo attracts customers to *Playboy* magazine, but it keeps the Playboy cable channel out of many markets. Be as quantitative as possible when stating factors. Use monetary amounts, percentages, numbers, and ratios to the extent possible.

An example IFE Matrix is provided in Table 4-9 for a retail computer store. Note that the two most important factors to be successful in the retail computer store business are "revenues from repair/service in the store" and "location of the store." Also note that the store is doing best on "average customer purchase amount" and "in-store technical support." The store is having major problems with its carpet, bathroom, paint, and checkout procedures. Note also that the matrix contains substantial quantitative data rather than vague statements; this is excellent. Overall, this store receives a 2.5 total weighted score, which on a 1-to-4 scale is exactly average/halfway, indicating there is definitely room for improvement in store operations, strategies, policies, and procedures.

The IFE Matrix provides important information for strategy formulation. For example, this retail computer store might want to hire another checkout person and repair its carpet, paint, and bathroom problems. Also, the store may want to increase advertising for its repair/services, because that is a really important (weight 0.15) factor to being successful in this business.

Another example IFE Matrix is provided in Table 4-10 for UPS, Inc., the company well known for its brown trucks. Headquartered in Sandy Springs, Georgia, UPS delivers roughly 15 million

TABLE 4-9   A Sample Internal Factor Evaluation Matrix for a Retail Computer Store

Key Internal Factors	Weight	Rating	Weighted Score
Strengths			
1. Inventory turnover increased from 5.8 to 6.7	0.05	3	0.15
2. Average customer purchase increased from $97 to $128	0.07	4	0.28
3. Employee morale is excellent	0.10	3	0.30
4. In-store promotions resulted in 20 percent increase in sales	0.05	3	0.15
5. Newspaper advertising expenditures increased 10 percent	0.02	3	0.06
6. Revenues from repair/service segment of store up 16 percent	0.15	3	0.45
7. In-store technical support personnel have MIS college degrees	0.05	4	0.20
8. Store's debt-to-total assets ratio declined to 34 percent	0.03	3	0.09
9. Revenues per employee up 19 percent	0.02	3	0.06
Weaknesses			
1. Revenues from software segment of store down 12 percent	0.10	2	0.20
2. Location of store negatively impacted by new Highway 34	0.15	2	0.30
3. Carpet and paint in store somewhat in disrepair	0.02	1	0.02
4. Bathroom in store needs refurbishing	0.02	1	0.02
5. Revenues from businesses down 8 percent	0.04	1	0.04
6. Store has no website	0.05	2	0.10
7. Supplier on-time delivery increased to 2.4 days	0.03	1	0.03
8. Often customers have to wait to check out	0.05	1	0.05
Total	**1.00**		**2.50**

packages daily to 220 countries. Note in Table 4-10 that UPS's new Worldport expansion is considered the most important factor to success in the industry as indicated by a weight of 0.09. Also note the use of many $'s, #'s, and %'s in the factor statements. The total weighted score of 2.84 indicates that UPS is doing pretty well, but there definitely is room for improvement.

In multidivisional firms, each autonomous division or strategic business unit should construct an IFE Matrix. Divisional matrices then can be integrated to develop an overall corporate IFE Matrix.

Be as divisional as possible when developing a corporate IFE Matrix. Also, in developing an IFE Matrix, do not allow more than 30 percent of the key factors to be financial ratios, because financial ratios are generally the result of many other factors so it is difficult to know what particular strategies should be considered based on financial ratios. For example, a firm would have no insight on whether to sell in Brazil or South Africa to take advantage of a high ROI ratio.

Special Note to Students

It can be debated whether external or internal factors are more important in strategic planning, but there is no debate regarding the fact that gaining and sustaining competitive advantage is the essence or purpose of strategic planning. In the internal portion of your case analysis, emphasize how and why your internal strengths and weaknesses can be leveraged to both gain competitive advantage and overcome competitive disadvantage, in light of the direction you are taking the firm. Maintain your project's upbeat, insightful, and forward-thinking demeanor during the internal assessment, rather than being mundane, descriptive, and vague. Focus on how your firm's resources, capabilities, structure, and strategies, with your recommended improvements, can lead the firm to prosperity. Although the numbers absolutely must be there, must be accurate, and must be reasonable, do not bore a live audience or class with overreliance on numbers. Periodically throughout your presentation or written analysis, refer to your recommendations, explaining how your plan of action will improve the firm's weaknesses and capitalize on strengths in light of anticipated competitor countermoves. Keep your audience's attention, interest, and suspense, rather than "reading" to them or "defining" ratios for them.

TABLE 4-10 An Actual Internal Factor Evaluation (IFE) Matrix for UPS, Inc.

Key Internal Factors			
Strengths	Weight	Rating	Wt. Score
1. Completed first phase of Worldport expansion, increasing sorting capacity 15 percent growing to 37 percent	0.09	4	0.36
2. First major airline to successfully operate a 100 percent Stage III fleet three years in advance of Federal regulations	0.07	4	0.28
3. Five out of every six UPS drivers come from part-time ranks (promotion within)	0.07	3	0.21
4. Over 4,000 UPS drivers have driven for 25 years or more without an avoidable accident	0.06	3	0.18
5. Dividends of $0.47 per share paid and increasing	0.06	4	0.24
6. Average daily volume for Next-Day Air and Deferred Products increased 2.8 percent and 4.3 percent respectively	0.06	3	0.18
7. Have yielded 1.71 percent cost and production efficiencies, improving operating margin	0.06	4	0.24
8. Owns 80 percent of joint venture headquartered in Dubai with 20 percent option to purchase	0.08	3	0.24
9. Streamlining Domestic Package segment, reducing U.S. regions from five to three and U.S. districts from 46 to 20	0.07	3	0.21
10. Purchased 130 hybrid vehicles, adding to UPS alternative fuel vehicle (AFV) fleet	0.07	4	0.28
Weakness			
11. Approximately 254,000 UPS employees are members of a union	0.03	1	0.03
12. Approximately 2,800 UPS pilots	0.03	1	0.03
13. Approximately 3,400 UPS ground mechanics	0.03	1	0.03
14. Inability to identify sufficient operating cost savings to result in at least 300 furloughs for airline pilots	0.04	1	0.04
15. Top executives diversity percentage is low (25 percent)	0.03	2	0.06
16. Over 4,000 UPS drivers have driven for more than 25 years and are now eligible for retirement	0.04	1	0.04
17. Top executives' tenure in current position five years or less	0.03	2	0.06
18. 80 percent of all UPS U.S. small package delivery services guaranteed	0.02	2	0.04
19. With ~408,000 employees, expenses relating to health and pension benefits are high	0.03	1	0.03
20. 41.7 percent of top UPS executives are cross-trained	0.03	2	0.06
TOTALS	**1.00**		**2.84**

Conclusion

Management, marketing, finance/accounting, production/operations, research and development, and management information systems represent the core operations of most businesses. A strategic-management audit of a firm's internal operations is vital to organizational health. Many companies still prefer to be judged solely on their bottom-line performance. However, an increasing number of successful organizations are using the internal audit to gain competitive advantages over rival firms.

Systematic methodologies for performing strength-weakness assessments are not well developed in the strategic-management literature, but it is clear that strategists must identify and evaluate internal strengths and weaknesses in order to effectively formulate and choose among alternative strategies. The EFE Matrix, Competitive Profile Matrix, IFE Matrix, and clear statements of vision and mission provide the basic information needed to successfully formulate competitive strategies. The process of performing an internal audit represents an opportunity for managers and employees throughout the organization to participate in determining the future of the firm. Involvement in the process can energize and mobilize managers and employees.

Key Terms and Concepts

Activity Ratios (p. 110)
Benchmarking (p. 121)
Breakeven (BE) Point (p. 113)
Capital Budgeting (p. 109)
Communication (p. 96)
Controlling (p. 103)
Core Competence (p. 121)
Cost/Benefit Analysis (p. 107)
Cultural Products (p. 98)
Customer Analysis (p. 104)
Data (p. 118)
Distinctive Competencies (p. 95)
Distribution (p. 107)
Dividend Decisions (p. 109)
Empirical Indicators (p. 98)
Financial Ratio Analysis (p. 97)
Fixed Costs (FC) (p. 113)
Financing Decision (p. 109)
Functions of Finance/Accounting (p. 108)
Functions of Management (p. 100)
Functions of Marketing (p. 104)
Growth Ratios (p. 112)
Human Resource Management (p. 103)
Information (p. 118)
Internal Audit (p. 96)

Internal Factor Evaluation (IFE) Matrix (p. 122)
Investment Decision (p. 109)
Leverage Ratios (p. 110)
Liquidity Ratios (p. 110)
Management Information System (p. 118)
Marketing Research (p. 107)
Motivating (p. 102)
Organizational Culture (p. 98)
Organizing (p. 102)
Personnel Management (p. 103)
Planning (p. 100)
Pricing (p. 106)
Product and Service Planning (p. 106)
Production/Operations Function (p. 115)
Profitability Ratios (p. 110)
Research and Development (R&D) (p. 116)
Resource-Based View (RBV) (p. 97)
Selling (p. 104)
Staffing (p. 103)
Synergy (p. 101)
Test Marketing (p. 106)
Value Chain Analysis (VCA) (p. 119)
Variable Costs (VC) (p. 114)

Issues for Review and Discussion

1. Explain Cost/Benefit analysis.
2. Explain why "communication" may be the most important word in management. What do you think is the most important word in marketing? In finance? In accounting?
3. Discuss how the nature of advertisements have changed in the last few years.
4. Rate the seven websites in Table 4-5 from best to worst for finding comparative financial ratio information about a company.
5. Explain why it is best not to have more than 30 percent of the factors in an IFE Matrix be financial ratios.
6. List three firms you are familiar with and give a distinctive competence for each firm.
7. Give some key reasons why prioritizing strengths and weaknesses is essential.
8. Why may it be easier in performing an internal assessment to develop a list of 80 strengths/weaknesses than to decide on the top 20 to use in formulating strategies?
9. Think of an organization you are very familiar with. List three resources of that entity that are empirical indicators.
10. Think of an organization you are very familiar with. Rate that entity's organizational culture on the 15 example dimensions listed in Table 4-2.
11. If you and a partner were going to visit a foreign country where you have never been before, how much planning would you do ahead of time? What benefit would you expect that planning to provide?
12. Even though planning is considered the foundation of management, why do you think it is commonly the task that managers neglect most?

13. Are you more organized than the person sitting beside you in class? If not, what problems could that present in terms of your performance and rank in the class? How analogous is this situation to rival companies?

14. List the three ways that financial ratios should be compared/utilized. Which of the three comparisons do you feel is most important? Why?

15. Illustrate how value chain activities can become core competencies and eventually distinctive competencies. Give an example for an organization you are familiar with.

16. In an IFEM, would it be advantageous to list your strengths, and then your weaknesses, in order of increasing "weight"? Why?

17. In an IFEM, a critic may say there is no significant difference between a "weight" of 0.08 and 0.06. How would you respond?

18. List six desirable characteristics of advertisements in recessionary times.

19. Why are so many firms cutting their dividend payout amounts?

20. When someone says dividends paid are double taxed, what are they referring to?

21. Draw a breakeven chart to illustrate a drop in labor costs.

22. Draw a breakeven chart to illustrate an increase in advertising expenses.

23. Draw a breakeven chart to illustrate closing stores.

24. Draw a breakeven chart to illustrate lowering price.

25. Explain why prioritizing the relative importance of strengths and weaknesses in an IFE Matrix is an important strategic-management activity.

26. How can delegation of authority contribute to effective strategic management?

27. Diagram a formal organizational chart that reflects the following positions: a president, 2 executive officers, 4 middle managers, and 18 lower-level managers. Now, diagram three overlapping and hypothetical informal group structures. How can this information be helpful to a strategist in formulating and implementing strategy?

28. Which of the three basic functions of finance/accounting do you feel is most important in a small electronics manufacturing concern? Justify your position.

29. Do you think aggregate R&D expenditures for U.S. firms will increase or decrease next year? Why?

30. Explain how you would motivate managers and employees to implement a major new strategy.

31. Why do you think production/operations managers often are not directly involved in strategy-formulation activities? Why can this be a major organizational weakness?

32. Give two examples of staffing strengths and two examples of staffing weaknesses of an organization with which you are familiar.

33. Would you ever pay out dividends when your firm's annual net profit is negative? Why? What effect could this have on a firm's strategies?

34. If a firm has zero debt in its capital structure, is that always an organizational strength? Why or why not?

35. Describe the production/operations system in a police department.

36. After conducting an internal audit, a firm discovers a total of 100 strengths and 100 weaknesses. What procedures then could be used to determine the most important of these? Why is it important to reduce the total number of key factors?

37. Why do you believe cultural products affect all the functions of business?

38. Do you think cultural products affect strategy formulation, implementation, or evaluation the most? Why?

39. Identify cultural products at your college or university. Do these products, viewed collectively or separately, represent a strength or weakness for the organization?

40. Explain the difference between data and information in terms of each being useful to strategists.

41. What are the most important characteristics of an effective management information system?

42. Do you agree or disagree with the RBV theorists that internal resources are more important for a firm than external factors in achieving and sustaining competitive advantage? Explain your and their position.

43. Define and discuss "empirical indicators."

44. Define and discuss the "spam" problem in the United States.

45. Define and explain value chain analysis (VCA).

46. List five financial ratios that may be used by your university to monitor operations.

47. Explain benchmarking.

Notes

1. Reprinted by permission of the publisher from "Integrating Strength–Weakness Analysis into Strategic Planning," by William King, *Journal of Business Research* 2, no. 4: 481. Copyright 1983 by Elsevier Science Publishing Co., Inc.

2. Igor Ansoff, "Strategic Management of Technology" *Journal of Business Strategy* 7, no. 3 (Winter 1987): 38.

3. Claude George Jr., *The History of Management Thought*, 2nd ed. (Upper Saddle River, NJ: Prentice-Hall, 1972), 174.

4. Robert Grant, "The Resource-Based Theory of Competitive Advantage: Implications for Strategy Formulation," *California Management Review*, Spring 1991, 116.

5. J. B. Barney, "Firm Resources and Sustained Competitive Advantage," *Journal of Management* 17 (1991): 99–120; J. B. Barney, "The Resource-Based Theory of the Firm," *Organizational Science* 7 (1996): 469; J. B. Barney, "Is the Resource-Based 'View' a Useful Perspective for Strategic Management Research? Yes." *Academy of Management Review* 26, no. 1 (2001): 41–56.

6. Edgar Schein, *Organizational Culture and Leadership* (San Francisco: Jossey-Bass, 1985), 9.

7. John Lorsch, "Managing Culture: The Invisible Barrier to Strategic Change," *California Management Review* 28, no. 2 (1986): 95–109.

8. Y. Allarie and M. Firsirotu, "How to Implement Radical Strategies in Large Organizations," *Sloan Management Review* (Spring 1985): 19.

9. www.mindtools.com/plfailpl.html

10. Adam Smith, *The Wealth of Nations* (New York: Modern Library, 1937), 3–4.

11. Richard Daft, *Management*, 3rd ed. (Orlando, FL: Dryden Press, 1993), 512.

12. Shelley Kirkpatrick and Edwin Locke, "Leadership: Do Traits Matter?" *Academy of Management Executive* 5, no. 2 (May 1991): 48.

13. Peter Drucker, *Management Tasks, Responsibilities, and Practice* (New York: Harper & Row, 1973), 463.

14. Brian Dumaine, "What the Leaders of Tomorrow See," *Fortune*, July 3, 1989, 51.

15. J. Evans and B. Bergman, *Marketing* (New York: Macmillan, 1982), 17.

16. Brad Stone, "See Your Friends," *Bloomberg Businessweek* (September 27–October 3, 2010): 65–69.

17. Quoted in Robert Waterman, Jr., "The Renewal Factor," *BusinessWeek*, September 14, 1987, 108.

18. http://en.wikipedia.org/wiki/Cost-benefit_analysis

19. J. Van Horne, *Financial Management and Policy* (Upper Saddle River, N.J.: Prentice-Hall, 1974), 10.

20. Bob Sechler and Paul Glader, "GE's Dividend Mends Further," *Wall Street Journal*, December 11–12, 2010, B4.

21. http://en.wikipedia.org/wiki/Break-even_(economics)

22. Kevin Klowden, "The Quiet Revolution in Transportation," *Wall Street Journal*, April 24, 2007, A14.

23. Martin Peers, "RIM: Less Research = More Motion," *Wall Street Journal*, March 30, 2011, C16.

24. Philip Rousebl, Kamal Saad, and Tamara Erickson, "The Evolution of Third Generation R&D," *Planning Review* 19, no. 2 (March–April 1991): 18–26.

25. James Hagerty, "R&D Spending Drops at Major Firms," *Wall Street Journal*, November 3, 2010, B4.

26. Vida Scarpello, William Boulton, and Charles Hofer, "Reintegrating R&D into Business Strategy," *Journal of Business Strategy* 6, no. 4 (Spring 1986): 50–51.

27. http://en.wikipedia.org/wiki/Benchmarking

Current Readings

Bloom, Nick, Tobias Kretschmer, and John Van Reenen. "Are Family-Friendly Workplace Practices a Valuable Firm Resource?" *Strategic Management Journal* 32, no. 4 (April 2011): 343–367.

Boyd, Brian K., Donald D. Bergh, and David J. Ketchen, Jr. "Reconsidering the Reputation-Performance Relationship: A Resource-Based View." *Journal of Management* 36, no. 3 (May 2010): 588.

Connelly, Brian L., Laszlo Tihanyi, S. Trevis Certo, and Michael A. Hitt. "Marching to the Beat of Different Drummers: The Influence of Institutional Owners on Competitive Actions." *The Academy of Management Journal* 53, no. 4 (August 2010): 723–768.

Drayton, Bill, and Valeria Budinich. "A New Alliance for Global Change." *Harvard Business Review*, September 2010, 56–65.

Hoffman, Donna L., and Marek Fodor. "Can You Measure the ROI of Your Social Media Marketing?" *MIT Sloan Management Review* 52, no. 1 (Fall 2010): 41–48.

Hopkins, Michael S. "Collaborate or Race? How to Design the Value Chain You Need." *MIT Sloan Management Review* 51, no. 2 (Winter 2010): 22–24.

Hopkins, Michael S. "The 4 Ways IT Is Revolutionizing Innovation." *MIT Sloan Management Review* 51, no. 3 (Spring 2010): 51–56.

Kraaijenbrink, Jeroen, J. C. Spender, and Aard J. Groen. "The Resource-Based View: A Review and Assessment of Its Critiques." *Journal of Management* 36, no. 1 (January 2010): 349–366.

Kunc, Martin H., and John D. W. Morecroft. "Managerial Decision Making and Firm Performance Under a Resource-Based Paradigm." *Strategic Management Journal* 31, no. 11 (November 2010): 1164–1182.

Lange, Donald, Peggy M. Lee, and Ye Dai. "Organizational Reputation: A Review." *Journal of Management* 37, no. 1 (January 2011): 153–184.

Raes, Anneloes M. L., Marielle G. Heijltjes, Ursula Glunk, and Robert A. Roe. "The Interface of the Top Management Team and Middle Managers: A Process Model." *The Academy of Management Review* 36, no. 1 (January 2011): 102–126.

Sirmon, David G., Michael A. Hitt, Jean-Luc Arregle, and Joanna Tochman Campbell. "The Dynamic Interplay of Capability Strengths and Weaknesses: Investigating the Bases of Temporary Competitive Advantage." *Strategic Management Journal* 31, no. 13 (December 2010): 1386–1409.

Vermeulen, Freek, Phanish Puranam, and Ranjay Gulati. "Change for Change's Sake." *Harvard Business Review* (June 2010): 70–78.

Zhu, Yunxia, and Jianmin Feng. "Does the Relationship Between Job Satisfaction and Job Performance Depend on Culture?" *The Academy of Management Perspectives* 24, no. 1 (February 2010): 86–88.

ASSURANCE OF LEARNING EXERCISES

Assurance of Learning Exercise 4A

Apply Breakeven Analysis

Purpose

Breakeven analysis is one of the simplest yet underused analytical tools in management. It helps to provide a dynamic view of the relationships among sales, costs, and profits. A better understanding of breakeven analysis can enable an organization to formulate and implement strategies more effectively. This exercise will show you how to calculate breakeven points mathematically.

The formula for calculating breakeven point is BE Quantity = TFC/P–VC. In other words, the Quantity (Q) or units of product that need to be sold for a firm to break even is Total Fixed Costs divided by (Price per Unit minus Variable Costs per Unit).

Instructions

Step 1   Lets say an airplane company has Fixed Costs of $100 million and Variable Costs per Unit of $2 million. Planes sell for $3 million each. What is the company's breakeven point in terms of the number of planes that need to be sold just to break even?

Step 2   If the airplane company wants to make a profit of $99 million annually, how many planes will it have to sell?

Step 3   If the company can sell 200 airplanes in a year, how much annual profit will the firm make?

Assurance of Learning Exercise 4B

Develop Divisional Disney IFEMs

Purpose

Walt Disney has five major divisions as follows: 1) Media Networks, 2) Parks & Resorts, 3) Studio Entertainment, 4) Consumer Products, and 5) Interactive media. The company faces fierce but different competitors in each segment. The internal strengths and weaknesses that Disney faces are different in each segment, so each division prepares its own list of critical internal success factors. This exercise gives you practice developing key internal factors for different divisions of a company, so that a firm's overall strategic plan can be developed.

Instructions

Step 1   Go to http://corporate.disney.go.com/ and review Disney's five major divisions.

Step 2   Review Disney's most recent *Annual Report* at http://corporate.disney.go.com/investors/annual_reports.html. Determine what you believe are the four major weaknesses and the four major strengths critical to strategic planning within Disney's five business segments.

Step 3   Armed with the information from Step 2, develop divisional IFEMs for Disney.

Step 4   Prioritize the 20 weaknesses and the 20 strengths developed in the prior step so Disney's top executives can develop an IFEM for the overall company.

Assurance of Learning Exercise 4C

Perform a Financial Ratio Analysis for Walt Disney

Purpose

Financial ratio analysis is one of the best techniques for identifying and evaluating internal strengths and weaknesses. Potential investors and current shareholders look closely at firms' financial ratios, making detailed comparisons to industry averages and to previous periods of time. Financial ratio analyses provide vital input information for developing an IFE Matrix.

Instructions

Step 1	On a separate sheet of paper, number from 1 to 20. Referring to Disney's income statement and balance sheet (pp. 26–27), calculate 20 financial ratios for 2010 for the company. Use Table 4-6 as a reference.
Step 2	In a second column, indicate whether you consider each ratio to be a strength, a weakness, or a neutral factor for Walt Disney.
Step 3	Go to the websites in Table 4-5 that calculate Disney's financial ratios, without your having to pay a subscription (fee) for the service. Make a copy of the ratio information provided and record the source. Report this research to your classmates and your professor.

Assurance of Learning Exercise 4D

Construct an IFE Matrix for Walt Disney

Purpose

This exercise will give you experience in developing an IFE Matrix. Identifying and prioritizing factors to include in an IFE Matrix fosters communication among functional and divisional managers. Preparing an IFE Matrix allows human resource, marketing, production/operations, finance/accounting, R&D, and management information systems managers to articulate their concerns and thoughts regarding the business condition of the firm. This results in an improved collective understanding of the business.

Instructions

Step 1	Join with two other individuals to form a three-person team. Develop a team IFE Matrix for Walt Disney. Use information from Exercise 1B.
Step 2	Compare your team's IFE Matrix to other teams' IFE Matrices. Discuss any major differences.
Step 3	What strategies do you think would allow Disney to capitalize on its major strengths? What strategies would allow Disney to improve upon its major weaknesses?

Assurance of Learning Exercise 4E

Construct an IFE Matrix for My University

Purpose

This exercise gives you the opportunity to evaluate your university's major strengths and weaknesses. As will become clearer in the next chapter, an organization's strategies are largely based upon striving to take advantage of strengths and improving upon weaknesses.

Instructions

Step 1	Join with two other individuals to form a three-person team. Develop a team IFE Matrix for your university. You may use the strengths/weaknesses determined in Assurance of Learning Exercise 1D.
Step 2	Go to the board and diagram your team's IFE Matrix.
Step 3	Compare your team's IFE Matrix to other teams' IFE Matrices. Discuss any major differences.
Step 4	What strategies do you think would allow your university to capitalize on its major strengths? What strategies would allow your university to improve upon its major weaknesses?

"NOTABLE QUOTES"

"Alice said, 'Would you please tell me which way to go from here?' The cat said, 'That depends on where you want to get to.'"
—*Lewis Carroll*

"Tomorrow always arrives. It is always different. And even the mightiest company is in trouble if it has not worked on the future. Being surprised by what happens is a risk that even the largest and richest company cannot afford, and even the smallest business need not run."
—*Peter Drucker*

"Planning. Doing things today to make us better tomorrow. Because the future belongs to those who make the hard decisions today."
—*Eaton Corporation*

"One big problem with American business is that when it gets into trouble, it redoubles its effort. It's like digging for gold. If you dig down twenty feet and haven't found it, one of the strategies you could use is to dig twice as deep. But if the gold is twenty feet to the side, you could dig a long time and not find it."
—*Edward De Bono*

"Even if you're on the right track, you'll get run over if you just sit there."
—*Will Rogers*

"Strategies for taking the hill won't necessarily hold it."
—*Amar Bhide*

"The early bird may get the worm, but the second mouse gets the cheese."
—*Unknown*

Strategies in Action

CHAPTER OBJECTIVES

After studying this chapter, you should be able to do the following:

1. Discuss the value of establishing long-term objectives.
2. Identify 16 types of business strategies.
3. Identify numerous examples of organizations pursuing different types of strategies.
4. Discuss guidelines when particular strategies are most appropriate to pursue.
5. Discuss Porter's five generic strategies.
6. Describe strategic management in nonprofit, governmental, and small organizations.
7. Discuss joint ventures as a way to enter the Russian market.
8. Discuss the Balanced Scorecard.
9. Compare and contrast financial with strategic objectives.
10. Discuss the levels of strategies in large versus small firms.
11. Explain the First Mover Advantages concept.
12. Discuss recent trends in outsourcing.
13. Discuss strategies for competing in turbulent, high-velocity markets.

ASSURANCE OF LEARNING EXERCISES

Assurance of Learning Exercise 5A
Develop Hypothetical Disney Strategies

Assurance of Learning Exercise 5B
Evaluate Disney Divisions in Terms of Porter Strategies

Assurance of Learning Exercise 5C
What Strategies Should Disney Pursue in 2013?

Assurance of Learning Exercise 5D
Examine Strategy Articles

Assurance of Learning Exercise 5E
Classify Some Year 2011 Strategies

Assurance of Learning Exercise 5F
How Risky Are Various Alternative Strategies?

Assurance of Learning Exercise 5G
Develop Alternative Strategies for My University

Assurance of Learning Exercise 5H
Lessons in Doing Business Globally

Hundreds of companies today, including Sears, IBM, Searle, and Hewlett-Packard, have embraced strategic planning fully in their quest for higher revenues and profits. Kent Nelson, former chair of UPS, explains why his company has created a new strategic-planning department: "Because we're making bigger bets on investments in technology, we can't afford to spend a whole lot of money in one direction and then find out five years later it was the wrong direction."[1]

This chapter brings strategic management to life with many contemporary examples. Sixteen types of strategies are defined and exemplified, including Michael Porter's generic strategies: cost leadership, differentiation, and focus. Guidelines are presented for determining when it is most appropriate to pursue different types of strategies. An overview of strategic management in nonprofit organizations, governmental agencies, and small firms is provided. ExxonMobil is an example company that for many years has exemplified excellent strategic management.

Long-Term Objectives

Long-term objectives represent the results expected from pursuing certain strategies. Strategies represent the actions to be taken to accomplish long-term objectives. The time frame for objectives and strategies should be consistent, usually from two to five years.

Excellent Strategic Management Showcased

ExxonMobil CORPORATION

Founded in 1870 and headquartered in Irving, Texas, ExxonMobil engages in the exploration, production, transportation, and sale of crude oil, natural gas, olefins, aromatics, polyethylene, polypropylene plastics, and electric power generation. ExxonMobil is the largest and most profitable publicly traded oil company in the world. Exxon supplies fuel to 28,000 gas stations in 100 countries, is substantially larger than Royal Dutch Shell or BP, has 83,600 employees, and is led by CEO and Chairman of the Board Rex Tillerson. Exxon's 2010 profits increased an incredible 59.7 percent to $30.5 billion, while the company's revenues increased 23 percent to $383 billion.

Exxon earned $10.65 billion in profits in the first quarter of 2011. That compares with $6.3 billion, or 1.33 per share. Revenue increased 26 percent to $114 billion. The quarter was Exxon's best since earning a record-setting $14.83 billion in 2008's third quarter. It comes at a time when some drivers are paying $4 or more for gas. Earnings grew across the company's business segments as profits from its exploration and production business gained 49 percent to $8.7 billion, while the company's downstream business, which includes refineries, posted a huge 30-fold jump to more than $1.1 billion.

As escalating political unrest in the Middle East threatens to disrupt fuel supplies, oil and gas prices could rise further. ExxonMobil produces more oil when prices are high. Protests that started in Tunisia and Egypt have spread to Syria, Yemen, Bahrain, Iran, and Jordan. Protesters in Libya ousted Moammar Gaddafi, the longest-ruling Arab leader, following the ouster of Hosni Mubarak in Egypt.

Exxon's 2010 EPS increased 55 percent to $6.22, while the company's capital and exploration expenditures were $32.2 billion, up 19 percent. Exxon is a gigantic, money-making, money-investing, well oiled, strategic management machine that has been incredibly successful

for more than 14 decades. And, Exxon pays about 35 percent of its net income in federal taxes every year, rather than being intent on avoiding taxes.

A key ingredient of ExxonMobil's strategic plan is the company's bet that natural gas will overtake coal as the world's second-largest source of energy by 2030. That is why Exxon recently purchased XTO Energy for $25 billion. XTO has a patented procedure to extract natural gas from shale in an economical manner. Exxon also recently acquired the shale producer Ellora Inc. for $695 million and purchased the natural-gas shale assets of Petrohawk Energy Corp. for $575 million. Exxon predicts that the world will consume about 35 percent more energy in 2030 than today, and that natural gas will quench 26 percent of the world's demand for energy, up from 21 percent today.

Ukraine's state-run energy firm Naftogaz and ExxonMobil recently signed a memorandum of cooperation to explore for shale gas deposits in Ukraine. That country imports 60 percent of its energy from Russia at arguably too-high import prices. ExxonMobil is also helping Ukraine look for methane gas deposits in coalmines.

Source: Company documents. Also, Angel Gonzalez, "Exxon Predicts Gas Use Will Surpass Coal's," *Wall Street Journal*, January 27, 2011, B3.

The Nature of Long-Term Objectives

Objectives should be quantitative, measurable, realistic, understandable, challenging, hierarchical, obtainable, and congruent among organizational units. Each objective should also be associated with a timeline. Objectives are commonly stated in terms such as growth in assets, growth in sales, profitability, market share, degree and nature of diversification, degree and nature of vertical integration, earnings per share, and social responsibility. Clearly established objectives offer many benefits. They provide direction, allow synergy, aid in evaluation, establish priorities, reduce uncertainty, minimize conflicts, stimulate exertion, and aid in both the allocation of resources and the design of jobs. Objectives provide a basis for consistent decision making by managers whose values and attitudes differ. Objectives serve as standards by which individuals, groups, departments, divisions, and entire organizations can be evaluated.

Long-term objectives are needed at the corporate, divisional, and functional levels of an organization. They are an important measure of managerial performance. Many practitioners and academicians attribute a significant part of U.S. industry's competitive decline to the short-term, rather than long-term, strategy orientation of managers in the United States. Arthur D. Little argues that bonuses or merit pay for managers today must be based to a greater extent on long-term objectives and strategies. A general framework for relating objectives to performance evaluation is provided in Table 5-1. A particular organization could tailor these guidelines to meet its own needs, but incentives should be attached to both long-term and annual objectives.

Without long-term objectives, an organization would drift aimlessly toward some unknown end. It is hard to imagine an organization or individual being successful without clear objectives (see Tables 5-2 and 5-3). Success only rarely occurs by accident; rather, it is the result of hard work directed toward achieving certain objectives.

Financial versus Strategic Objectives

Two types of objectives are especially common in organizations: financial and strategic objectives. *Financial objectives* include those associated with growth in revenues, growth in earnings, higher dividends, larger profit margins, greater return on investment, higher earnings per share, a rising stock price, improved cash flow, and so on; while *strategic objectives* include things such as a larger market share, quicker on-time delivery than rivals, shorter design-to-market times

TABLE 5-1   Varying Performance Measures by Organizational Level

Organizational Level	Basis for Annual Bonus or Merit Pay
Corporate	75% based on long-term objectives
	25% based on annual objectives
Division	50% based on long-term objectives
	50% based on annual objectives
Function	25% based on long-term objectives
	75% based on annual objectives

TABLE 5-2   The Desired Characteristics of Objectives

1. Quantitative
2. Measurable
3. Realistic
4. Understandable
5. Challenging
6. Hierarchical
7. Obtainable
8. Congruent across departments

TABLE 5-3 The Benefits of Having Clear Objectives

1. Provide direction by revealing expectations
2. Allow synergy
3. Aid in evaluation by serving as standards
4. Establish priorities
5. Reduce uncertainty
6. Minimize conflicts
7. Stimulate exertion
8. Aid in allocation of resources
9. Aid in design of jobs
10. Provide basis for consistent decision making

than rivals, lower costs than rivals, higher product quality than rivals, wider geographic coverage than rivals, achieving technological leadership, consistently getting new or improved products to market ahead of rivals, and so on.

Although financial objectives are especially important in firms, oftentimes there is a trade-off between financial and strategic objectives such that crucial decisions have to be made. For example, a firm can do certain things to maximize short-term financial objectives that would harm long-term strategic objectives. To improve financial position in the short run through higher prices may, for example, jeopardize long-term market share. The dangers associated with trading off long-term strategic objectives with near-term bottom-line performance are especially severe if competitors relentlessly pursue increased market share at the expense of short-term profitability. And there are other trade-offs between financial and strategic objectives, related to riskiness of actions, concern for business ethics, need to preserve the natural environment, and social responsibility issues. Both financial and strategic objectives should include both annual and long-term performance targets. Ultimately, the best way to sustain competitive advantage over the long run is to relentlessly pursue strategic objectives that strengthen a firm's business position over rivals. Financial objectives can best be met by focusing first and foremost on achieving on strategic objectives that improve a firm's competitiveness and market strength.

Not Managing by Objectives

An unidentified educator once said, "If you think education is expensive, try ignorance." The idea behind this saying also applies to establishing objectives. Strategists should avoid the following alternative ways of "not managing by objectives."

- *Managing by Extrapolation*—adheres to the principle "If it ain't broke, don't fix it." The idea is to keep on doing the same things in the same ways because things are going well.
- *Managing by Crisis*—based on the belief that the true measure of a really good strategist is the ability to solve problems. Because there are plenty of crises and problems to go around for every person and every organization, strategists ought to bring their time and creative energy to bear on solving the most pressing problems of the day. Managing by crisis is actually a form of reacting rather than acting and of letting events dictate the what and when of management decisions.
- *Managing by Subjectives*—built on the idea that there is no general plan for which way to go and what to do; just do the best you can to accomplish what you think should be done. In short, "Do your own thing, the best way you know how" (sometimes referred to as *the mystery approach to decision making* because subordinates are left to figure out what is happening and why).
- *Managing by Hope*—based on the fact that the future is laden with great uncertainty and that if we try and do not succeed, then we hope our second (or third) attempt will succeed. Decisions are predicated on the hope that they will work and that good times are just around the corner, especially if luck and good fortune are on our side![2]

The Balanced Scorecard

Developed in 1993 by Harvard Business School professors Robert Kaplan and David Norton, and refined continually through today, the Balanced Scorecard is a strategy evaluation and control technique.[3] *Balanced Scorecard* derives its name from the perceived need of firms to "balance" financial measures that are oftentimes used exclusively in strategy evaluation and control with nonfinancial measures such as product quality and customer service. An effective Balanced Scorecard contains a carefully chosen combination of strategic and financial objectives tailored to the company's business.

As a tool to manage and evaluate strategy, the Balanced Scorecard is currently in use at Sears, United Parcel Service, 3M Corporation, Heinz, and hundreds of other firms. For example, 3M Corporation has a financial objective to achieve annual growth in earnings per share of 10 percent or better, as well as a strategic objective to have at least 30 percent of sales come from products introduced in the past four years. The overall aim of the Balanced Scorecard is to "balance" shareholder objectives with customer and operational objectives. Obviously, these sets of objectives interrelate and many even conflict. For example, customers want low price and high service, which may conflict with shareholders' desire for a high return on their investment. The Balanced Scorecard concept is consistent with the notions of continuous improvement in management (CIM) and total quality management (TQM).

Although the Balanced Scorecard concept is covered in more detail in Chapter 9 as it relates to evaluating strategies, firms should establish objectives and evaluate strategies on criteria other than financial measures. Financial measures and ratios are vitally important in strategic planning, but of equal importance are factors such as customer service, employee morale, product quality, pollution abatement, business ethics, social responsibility, community involvement, and other such items. In conjunction with financial measures, these "softer" factors comprise an integral part of both the objective-setting process and the strategy-evaluation process. A Balanced Scorecard for a firm is simply a listing of all key objectives to work toward, along with an associated time dimension of when each objective is to be accomplished, as well as a primary responsibility or contact person, department, or division for each objective.

Types of Strategies

The model illustrated in Figure 5-1 provides a conceptual basis for applying strategic management. Defined and exemplified in Table 5-4, alternative strategies that an enterprise could pursue can be categorized into 11 actions: forward integration, backward integration, horizontal integration, market penetration, market development, product development, related diversification, unrelated diversification, retrenchment, divestiture, and liquidation. Each alternative strategy has countless variations. For example, market penetration can include adding salespersons, increasing advertising expenditures, couponing, and using similar actions to increase market share in a given geographic area.

Many, if not most, organizations simultaneously pursue a combination of two or more strategies, but a *combination strategy* can be exceptionally risky if carried too far. No organization can afford to pursue all the strategies that might benefit the firm. Difficult decisions must be made. Priority must be established. Organizations, like individuals, have limited resources. Both organizations and individuals must choose among alternative strategies and avoid excessive indebtedness.

Hansen and Smith explain that strategic planning involves "choices that risk resources" and "trade-offs that sacrifice opportunity." In other words, if you have a strategy to go north, then you must buy snowshoes and warm jackets (spend resources) and forgo the opportunity of "faster population growth in southern states." You cannot have a strategy to go north and then take a step east, south, or west "just to be on the safe side." Firms spend resources and focus on a finite number of opportunities in pursuing strategies to achieve an uncertain outcome in the future. Strategic planning is much more than a roll of the dice; it is a wager based on predictions and hypotheses that are continually tested and refined by knowledge, research, experience, and learning. Survival of the firm itself may hinge on your strategic plan.[4]

FIGURE 5-1

A Comprehensive Strategic-Management Model

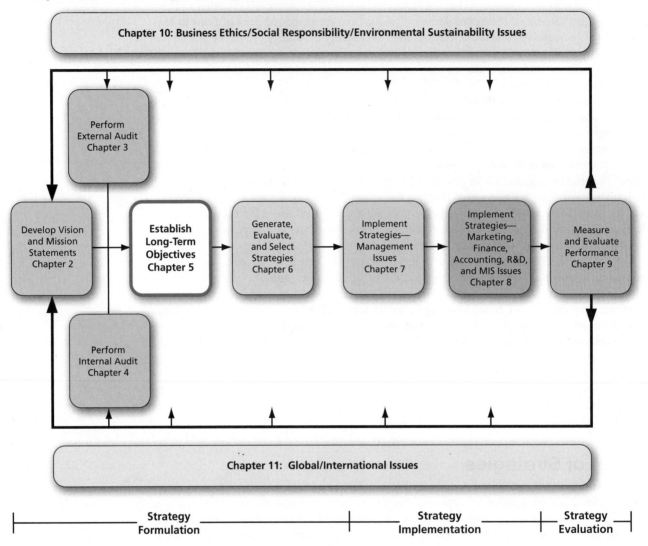

Source: Fred R. David, "How Companies Define Their Mission," *Long Range Planning* 22, no. 3 (June 1988): 40.

Organizations cannot do too many things well because resources and talents get spread thin and competitors gain advantage. In large, diversified companies, a combination strategy is commonly employed when different divisions pursue different strategies. Also, organizations struggling to survive may simultaneously employ a combination of several defensive strategies, such as divestiture, liquidation, and retrenchment.

Levels of Strategies

Strategy making is not just a task for top executives. Middle-and lower-level managers also must be involved in the strategic-planning process to the extent possible. In large firms, there are actually four levels of strategies: corporate, divisional, functional, and operational—as illustrated in Figure 5-2. However, in small firms, there are actually three levels of strategies: company, functional, and operational.

In large firms, the persons primarily responsible for having effective strategies at the various levels include the CEO at the corporate level; the president or executive vice president at the

TABLE 5-4 Alternative Strategies Defined and Exemplified

Strategy	Definition	2011 Examples
Forward Integration	Gaining ownership or increased control over distributors or retailers	Forward Integration—Starbucks reached a deal with Green Mountain Coffee Roasters for that firm to sell packs of Starbucks Tazo-branded coffee and tea in their brewers
Backward Integration	Seeking ownership or increased control of a firm's suppliers	Backward Integration—Dell Inc. acquired network security (virus protection) producer Secure Works Inc.
Horizontal Integration	Seeking ownership or increased control over competitors	Horizontal Integration—French drugmaker SanofiAventis purchased U.S. biotech drugmaker Genzyme for $20.1 billion
Market Penetration	Seeking increased market share for present products or services in present markets through greater marketing efforts	Market Penetration—Neiman Marcus (NM) launched NM Daily to attract less-affluent customers and hired a new "Managing Editor of Social Media" (Jean Scheidnes) to tweet and post for NM
Market Development	Introducing present products or services into new geographic area	Market Development—Hawaiian Airlines began offering flights from Hawaii to Seoul, Korea, and Tokyo, Japan—rather than mostly flying to and from the U.S. mainland
Product Development	Seeking increased sales by improving present products or services or developing new ones	Product Development—Apple introduced the new iPad 2
Related Diversification	Adding new but related products or services	Related Diversification—Amazon.com began allowing users to pay $79 per year for "Amazon Prime," which allows users to stream over 5,000 movies and TV shows
Unrelated Diversification	Adding new, unrelated products or services	Unrelated Diversification—Many banks now own, by default, many properties, putting many banks reluctantly in the real estate and/or property management business
Retrenchment	Regrouping through cost and asset reduction to reverse declining sales and profit	Retrenchment—Borders closed 200 of its 488 superstores and laid off 6,000 of its 19,500 employees
Divestiture	Selling a division or part of an organization	Divestiture—Marriott sold its timeshare business, creating the world's largest autonomous timeshare business, consisting of 71 properties with 33,000 rooms
Liquidation	Selling all of a company's assets, in parts, for their tangible worth	Liquidation—Blockbuster Inc. barely escaped liquidation in March 2011

divisional level; the respective chief finance officer (CFO), chief information officer (CIO), human resource manager (HRM), chief marketing officer (CMO), and so on at the functional level; and the plant manager, regional sales manager, and so on at the operational level. In small firms, the persons primarily responsible for having effective strategies at the various levels include the business owner or president at the company level and then the same range of persons at the lower two levels, as with a large firm.

It is important that all managers at all levels participate and understand the firm's strategic plan to help ensure coordination, facilitation, and commitment while avoiding inconsistency, inefficiency, and miscommunication. Plant managers, for example, need to understand and be supportive of the overall strategic plan (game plan), while the president and the CEO need to be knowledgeable of strategies being employed in various sales territories and manufacturing plants.

FIGURE 5-2

Levels of Strategies With Persons Most Responsible

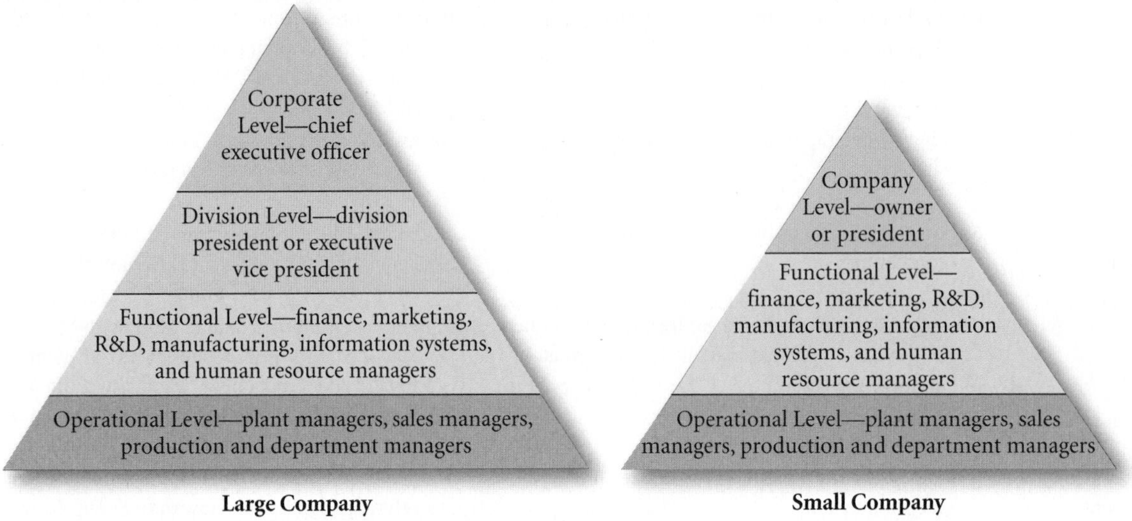

Corporate Level—chief executive officer

Division Level—division president or executive vice president

Functional Level—finance, marketing, R&D, manufacturing, information systems, and human resource managers

Operational Level—plant managers, sales managers, production and department managers

Large Company

Company Level—owner or president

Functional Level—finance, marketing, R&D, manufacturing, information systems, and human resource managers

Operational Level—plant managers, sales managers, production and department managers

Small Company

Integration Strategies

Forward integration, backward integration, and horizontal integration are sometimes collectively referred to as *vertical integration* strategies. Vertical integration strategies allow a firm to gain control over distributors, suppliers, and/or competitors.

Forward Integration

Forward integration involves gaining ownership or increased control over distributors or retailers. Increasing numbers of manufacturers (suppliers) today are pursuing a forward integration strategy by establishing websites to directly sell products to consumers. This strategy is causing turmoil in some industries. For example, Apple Inc. recently began selling its iPad and iPhone through Verizon Wireless's 2,000 stores and AT&T's 2,200 stores. Apple's forward integration strategy aims to capitalize on its lead in tablets before the rival BlackBerry and Motorola versions are released.

Based in Herzogenaurach, Germany, Adidas plans to add 2,500 stores in China between 2011 and 2015 as the company widens its distribution in that country from 500 cities currently to over 1,400. As part of its new forward integration strategy in China, Adidas plans also to boost its presence in basketball, a sport that Adidas emphasizes less than competitors such as Nike and Li Ning Company, China's leading sports-apparel maker. Adidas recently sponsored the Beijing Marathon, the company's first running competition in China.

Chrysler Group LLC in 2011 opened its first company-owned dealership, Motor Village of Los Angeles, a four-level facility in downtown Los Angeles that houses all of Chrysler's brands, including Fiat. This dealership sells and services all Chrysler vehicles and is a test facility for showroom innovations.

Wal-Mart Stores recently began allowing customers to buy merchandise online at www.walmart.com and have it delivered free of charge to urban FedEx Corp. locations. Wal-Mart has never been very successful in large cities, and the company sees this new forward integration strategy as beneficial. Wal-Mart is test marketing this new strategy in Boston and Los Angeles, where the company has no stores.

The Washington Post Co. recently launched a free news-aggregation website called Trove that lets readers build their own news site based on particular topics they choose. Battered by declining revenues, newspaper companies are using forward integration to provide services that tailor the news experience to each individual reader. Trove sifts through more than 10,000 news sources and delivers articles to a personalized customer page.

An effective means of implementing forward integration is *franchising*. Approximately 2,000 companies in about 50 different industries in the United States use franchising to distribute their products or services. Businesses can expand rapidly by franchising because costs and opportunities are spread among many individuals. Total sales by franchises in the United States are annually about $1 trillion.

The International Franchise Association Educational Foundations reports that the number of franchise businesses in the United States is expected to grow 2.5 percent in 2011 to 784,802. However, a growing trend is for franchisees, who for example may operate 10 franchised restaurants, stores, or whatever, to buy out their part of the business from their franchiser (corporate owner). There is a growing rift between franchisees and franchisers as the segment often outperforms the parent. For example, McDonald's today owns only about 20 percent of its 32,800 restaurants. Restaurant chains are increasingly being pressured to own fewer of their locations. Companies such as McDonald's are using proceeds from the sale of company stores/restaurants to franchisees to buy back company stock, pay higher dividends, and make other investments to benefit shareholders.

The following six guidelines indicate when forward integration may be an especially effective strategy:[5]

- When an organization's present distributors are especially expensive, or unreliable, or incapable of meeting the firm's distribution needs.
- When the availability of quality distributors is so limited as to offer a competitive advantage to those firms that integrate forward.
- When an organization competes in an industry that is growing and is expected to continue to grow markedly; this is a factor because forward integration reduces an organization's ability to diversify if its basic industry falters.
- When an organization has both the capital and human resources needed to manage the new business of distributing its own products.
- When the advantages of stable production are particularly high; this is a consideration because an organization can increase the predictability of the demand for its output through forward integration.
- When present distributors or retailers have high profit margins; this situation suggests that a company could profitably distribute its own products and price them more competitively by integrating forward.

Backward Integration

Both manufacturers and retailers purchase needed materials from suppliers. *Backward integration* is a strategy of seeking ownership or increased control of a firm's suppliers. This strategy can be especially appropriate when a firm's current suppliers are unreliable, too costly, or cannot meet the firm's needs.

Wal-Mart recently announced that over the next five years the company will double the amount of food bought from local farmers in the United States. This backward integration strategy complements the company's plan to build hundreds of new, smaller Wal-Mart Express stores in small towns across the U.S. Wal-Mart hopes to reverse the booming business of Family Dollar, Dollar General, and Dollar Tree—which together have caused Wal-Mart's U.S. revenues to decline.

The largest coffee company in the world and, based in Switzerland, Nestle is training thousands of farmers over the next 10 years and providing them with new coffee trees. With this backward integration strategy, Nestle does not own the plantations or bind farmers into long-term contracts, but CEO Paul Bulcke says the relationship the firm develops with farmers will lead them to sell to Nestle. This may be a wise strategy for Nestle because rival firms such as Unilever and Kraft Foods struggle to obtain better control of raw materials. Nestle's coffee strategy comes just after the firm's backward integration strategy of recently spending $106 million to replant cocoa trees in Ivory Coast in West Africa.

Some industries in the United States, such as the automotive and aluminum industries, are reducing their historical pursuit of backward integration. Instead of owning their suppliers, companies negotiate with several outside suppliers. Ford and Chrysler buy over half of their component parts from outside suppliers such as TRW, Eaton, General Electric, and Johnson Controls. *De-integration* makes sense in industries that have global sources of supply. Companies today shop around, play one seller against another, and go with the best deal.

Global competition is also spurring firms to reduce their number of suppliers and to demand higher levels of service and quality from those they keep. Although traditionally relying on many suppliers to ensure uninterrupted supplies and low prices, American firms now are following the lead of Japanese firms, which have far fewer suppliers and closer, long-term relationships with those few. "Keeping track of so many suppliers is onerous," says Mark Shimelonis, formerly of Xerox.

Seven guidelines when backward integration may be an especially effective strategy are:[6]

- When an organization's present suppliers are especially expensive, or unreliable, or incapable of meeting the firm's needs for parts, components, assemblies, or raw materials.
- When the number of suppliers is small and the number of competitors is large.
- When an organization competes in an industry that is growing rapidly; this is a factor because integrative-type strategies (forward, backward, and horizontal) reduce an organization's ability to diversify in a declining industry.
- When an organization has both capital and human resources to manage the new business of supplying its own raw materials.
- When the advantages of stable prices are particularly important; this is a factor because an organization can stabilize the cost of its raw materials and the associated price of its product(s) through backward integration.
- When present supplies have high profit margins, which suggests that the business of supplying products or services in the given industry is a worthwhile venture.
- When an organization needs to quickly acquire a needed resource.

Horizontal Integration

Horizontal integration refers to a strategy of seeking ownership of or increased control over a firm's competitors. One of the most significant trends in strategic management today is the increased use of horizontal integration as a growth strategy. Mergers, acquisitions, and takeovers among competitors allow for increased economies of scale and enhanced transfer of resources and competencies. Kenneth Davidson makes the following observation about horizontal integration:

> The trend towards horizontal integration seems to reflect strategists' misgivings about their ability to operate many unrelated businesses. Mergers between direct competitors are more likely to create efficiencies than mergers between unrelated businesses, both because there is a greater potential for eliminating duplicate facilities and because the management of the acquiring firm is more likely to understand the business of the target.[7]

Consolidation is intensifying weekly in the airline industry. Dallas, Texas-based Southwest Airlines recently paid $1.4 billion in cash and stock to acquire AirTran Holdings based in Orlando, Florida. AirTran also had a hub at the world's largest airport—Atlanta International Airport in Georgia. Fierce rivals United Airlines and Continental Airlines recently combined forces to eclipse Delta as the world's largest airline. Southwest now flies more passengers inside the United States (105 million) annually than any other airline.

Horizontal integration is becoming the strategy of choice in countless industries to achieve economies of scale and efficiencies. Unilever PLC, for example, just acquired the U.S. hair-care firm Alberto Culver, moving into direct competition with Procter & Gamble and L'Oreal SA in shampoo and other personal products. Although known primarily for food products such as Ben & Jerry's ice cream and Lipton tea, Unilever is a huge personal-care products firm having months earlier purchased Sara Lee Corp.'s deodorant and body care products for $1.73 billion.

Canadian banks in general came through the recession in excellent shape and are aggressively looking to acquire U.S. banks. The Bank of Montreal recently purchased Milwaukee-based Marshall & Ilsley Corp. for $4.1 billion and there are many similar examples. Unlike U.S. banks, Canada's banks did not require bailout funds and avoided the subprime-mortgage crisis due to conservative lending practices and tight regulations.

These five guidelines indicate when horizontal integration may be an especially effective strategy:[8]

- When an organization can gain monopolistic characteristics in a particular area or region without being challenged by the federal government for "tending substantially" to reduce competition.
- When an organization competes in a growing industry.
- When increased economies of scale provide major competitive advantages.
- When an organization has both the capital and human talent needed to successfully manage an expanded organization.
- When competitors are faltering due to a lack of managerial expertise or a need for particular resources that an organization possesses; note that horizontal integration would not be appropriate if competitors are doing poorly, because in that case overall industry sales are declining.

Intensive Strategies

Market penetration, market development, and product development are sometimes referred to as *intensive strategies* because they require intensive efforts if a firm's competitive position with existing products is to improve.

Market Penetration

A *market penetration* strategy seeks to increase market share for present products or services in present markets through greater marketing efforts. This strategy is widely used alone and in combination with other strategies. Market penetration includes increasing the number of salespersons, increasing advertising expenditures, offering extensive sales promotion items, or increasing publicity efforts. United Parcel Service (UPS) recently launched its largest marketing campaign ever, replacing its memorable slogan "What can Brown do for you?' with the slogan "We [Heart] Logistics". Advertisements promoting this new slogan are running worldwide on both television and digital-media outlets. The television ads feature a new UPS jingle set to the tune of the Dean Martin classic "That's Amore" sung in Mandarin, Spanish, or English as appropriate.

The maker of Guinness beer recently launched its largest marketing push ever in the United States, including a sports-themed advertising campaign that features ex-footballer Jerome Bettis and ex-NFL coach Bill Cowher. Guinness has long been associated with soccer and rugby, but now wants to be associated with football and basketball.

Starbucks is tripling its number of outlets in China. Dunkin' Brands, which owns both Dunkin' Donuts and Baskin-Robbins, also is opening thousands of new outlets in China.

These five guidelines indicate when market penetration may be an especially effective strategy:[9]

- When current markets are not saturated with a particular product or service.
- When the usage rate of present customers could be increased significantly.
- When the market shares of major competitors have been declining while total industry sales have been increasing.
- When the correlation between dollar sales and dollar marketing expenditures historically has been high.
- When increased economies of scale provide major competitive advantages.

Market Development

Market development involves introducing present products or services into new geographic areas. For example, Ford Motor is introducing eight new vehicles in India between 2011 and 2015 to capitalize on increasing demand in the fast-expanding car market. Ford also has begun exporting its new Figo small car from India to 50 new markets, including Mexico, North Africa, and the Middle East. Ford's new market development strategy is aimed at taking advantage of fast-growing emerging markets while insulating the firm from slow-growing U.S. and European markets.

The oldest American beer brewer, D.G. Yuengling & Son, recently expanded beyond its 13-state footprint in the Eastern U.S. Pronounced ying-ling, the 181-year-old regional beer brewer bought a former Coors brewery in Memphis, Tennessee, more than doubling its overall capacity and enabling an aggressive market development strategy. Yuengling has about 250 employees compared to about 700 at rival firm Samuel Adams.

Based in Sweden, Volvo is building three new assembly plants in China and increasing its number of vehicles in that country from 24,000 to 300,000 in the next three years. Volvo desires to become one of China's largest car manufacturers and is launching 24 new models in that country between 2011 and 2015. Volvo used to be owned by Ford.

Las Vegas Sands Corp. recently built the only casino in Singapore, the famous city-state that has a global reputation for being crime-free and family-friendly. Called the Marina Bay Sands, this casino was a booming success in 2010–2011 and expectations are that as early as 2012, Singapore may take in more gaming revenues than Las Vegas. Another new casino in Singapore is the $4.4 billion Resorts World Sentosa owned by Malaysia's Genting Bhd.

Both Subway and Dunkin' Brands recently opened their first restaurants in Vietnam. Subway also just opened its first outlet in Bahrain. Subway expects its number of international restaurants to surpass its number of U.S. restaurants by 2020. Many customers say it is hard to beat Subway's $5 foot-long sandwiches in terms of value and nutrition. Starbucks expects to open its first restaurants in India within 12 months.

These six guidelines indicate when market development may be an especially effective strategy:[10]

- When new channels of distribution are available that are reliable, inexpensive, and of good quality.
- When an organization is very successful at what it does.
- When new untapped or unsaturated markets exist.
- When an organization has the needed capital and human resources to manage expanded operations.
- When an organization has excess production capacity.
- When an organization's basic industry is rapidly becoming global in scope.

Product Development

Product development is a strategy that seeks increased sales by improving or modifying present products or services. Product development usually entails large research and development expenditures. Google's new Chrome OS operating system illuminates years of monies spent on product development. Google expects Chrome OS to overtake Microsoft Windows by 2015.

Product development is perhaps the most important strategy for high-tech firms such as Acer. To compete with Apple's iPad and tablets, the world's second-largest PC maker by shipments, Acer, released in 2011 a tablet running Microsoft Windows software with a 10.1- inch screen. Acer also released two tablets using Google's Android software. Acer expects to sell about 50 million tablets worldwide in 2011. Historically, Acer had relied on netbooks (tiny, low-priced laptops). Also recently, Acer released a smartphone with a 4.8-inch screen running on Android software.

The world's largest hotel chain, Holiday Inn, recently completed a $1 billion upgrade to all of its 3,400 hotels. The mandatory upgrades includes new bedding, flat-screen TVs, better shower fixtures, and sleeker roadside signs. The product development strategy also includes closing 700 older, outdated hotels and adding 1,100 new, deluxe Holiday Inn hotels so the average age of Holiday Inn hotels is now 15 years.

Hilton Worldwide recently opened its first new hotel brand in 20 years—a Home2 Suites in Fayetteville, North Carolina. Home2 Suites moves Hilton into the mid-tier extended-stay market, although the company already owns Homewood Suites, aimed at the upscale extended-stay segment. Hilton opened about 10 new Home2 Suites in the U.S. in 2011.

In total, there were 40,820 new products introduced in the United States in 2010, up from 38,738 in 2009, and expected to exceed 45,000 in 2011.[11] Social media, especially Facebook, Twitter, and YouTube, is being used extensively by companies to both generate new ideas and market resultant new products, such as Colgate's new foaming toothpaste called Colgate MaxClean SmartFoam.

These five guidelines indicate when product development may be an especially effective strategy to pursue:[12]

- When an organization has successful products that are in the maturity stage of the product life cycle; the idea here is to attract satisfied customers to try new (improved) products as a result of their positive experience with the organization's present products or services.
- When an organization competes in an industry that is characterized by rapid technological developments.
- When major competitors offer better-quality products at comparable prices.
- When an organization competes in a high-growth industry.
- When an organization has especially strong research and development capabilities.

Diversification Strategies

There are two general types of *diversification strategies:* related and unrelated. Businesses are said to be *related* when their value chains possesses competitively valuable cross-business strategic fits; businesses are said to be *unrelated* when their value chains are so dissimilar that no competitively valuable cross-business relationships exist.[13] Most companies favor related diversification strategies in order to capitalize on synergies as follows:

- Transferring competitively valuable expertise, technological know-how, or other capabilities from one business to another.
- Combining the related activities of separate businesses into a single operation to achieve lower costs.
- Exploiting common use of a well-known brand name.
- Cross-business collaboration to create competitively valuable resource strengths and capabilities.[14]

Diversification strategies are becoming less popular as organizations are finding it more difficult to manage diverse business activities. In the 1960s and 1970s, the trend was to diversify to avoid being dependent on any single industry, but the 1980s saw a general reversal of that thinking. Diversification is now on the retreat. Michael Porter, of the Harvard Business School, says, "Management found it couldn't manage the beast." Hence businesses are selling, or closing, less profitable divisions to focus on core businesses.

The greatest risk of being in a single industry is having all of the firm's eggs in one basket. Although many firms are successful operating in a single industry, new technologies, new products, or fast-shifting buyer preferences can decimate a particular business.

Diversification must do more than simply spread business risk across different industries, however, because shareholders could accomplish this by simply purchasing equity in different firms across different industries or by investing in mutual funds. Diversification makes sense only to the extent the strategy adds more to shareholder value than what shareholders could accomplish acting individually. Thus, the chosen industry for diversification must be attractive enough to yield consistently high returns on investment and offer potential across the operating divisions for synergies greater than those entities could achieve alone.

A few companies today, however, pride themselves on being conglomerates, from small firms such as Pentair Inc. and Blount International to huge companies such as Textron, Allied Signal, Emerson Electric, General Electric, Viacom, and Samsung. Conglomerates prove that focus and diversity are not always mutually exclusive.

Many strategists contend that firms should "stick to the knitting" and not stray too far from the firms' basic areas of competence. However, diversification is still sometimes an appropriate strategy, especially when the company is competing in an unattractive industry. Hamish Maxwell, Philip Morris's former CEO, says, "We want to become a consumer-products company." Diversification makes sense for Philip Morris because cigarette consumption is declining, product liability suits are a risk, and some investors reject tobacco stocks on principle.

Related Diversification

In the 2010–2015 era, firms are generally moving away from diversification to focus. That dismantling is a clear trend. For example, ITT Corp. recently divided itself into three separate, specialized companies. ITT once owned everything from Sheraton hotels and Hartford Insurance to the maker of Wonder bread and Hostess Twinkies. About the ITT breakup, analyst Barry Knap said, "Companies generally are not very efficient diversifiers; investors usually can do a better job of that by purchasing stock in a variety of companies."

Bucking the trend however is Berkshire Hathaway, a holding company for diverse companies that include Dairy Queen, Burlington Northern Santa Fe Railroad, and Geico Insurance. Also bucking the trend, Panasonic Corp. recently diversified into hand-held, online video-games with a new product called the Jungle. Panasonic for years had focused on rechargeable batteries for electric cars as well as solar cells for home and industry, but with the Jungle, the firm is re-entering a business that it abandoned more than a decade ago.

PepsiCo in 2011 diversified into the dairy market by acquiring the Russian firm Wimm-Bill-Dann for $5.4 billion. This acquisition establishes PepsiCo as the largest food-and-beverage firm in Russia, and that country becomes PepsiCo's largest revenue generator outside of the United States. This acquisition comes soon after PepsiCo's $2 billion acquisition of the Russian fruit-juice maker OAO Lebedyansky. PepsiCo and Coke are fierce rivals in Russia, and of course around the world.

Electricity producer, NRG Energy Inc., recently entered the car-charging business, creating a network of 150 public charging points in Houston, Texas, and New York City. This is a "first mover" strategy because it signals that car charging may follow a subscription-based business model, rather than the price-per-unit model that has been used for decades to sell gasoline. NRG's customers will have a choice of three subscription plans, each with a three-year contract, beginning with a $49 monthly fee.

Based in Peoria, Illinois, Caterpillar recently diversified beyond its core areas of construction and mining machinery by acquiring a maker of railroad locomotives, Electro-Motive Diesel, and by also acquiring MWM Holding GmbH, a German maker of power-generation equipment. Caterpillar had cash and short-term investments of $2.27 billion and preferred to use those monies "to fund attractive growth initiatives" rather than to repurchase stock or increase dividend payouts.

Intel Corp. recently diversified beyond providing chips for personal computers by acquiring for $7.68 billion the security-software company McAfee, well known for its virus protection software. As part of this diversification strategy away from personal computer chips, Intel also acquired a Texas Instruments division that sells cable-modem chips as well as Infineon Technologies, AG's wireless chip business. Intel is also working with Google to supply chips that enable people to more easily navigate through websites and TV programs.

In a related diversification move, Tyson Foods recently entered the dog food business, selling refrigerated pet food targeted to consumers who give their pets everything from clothes and car seats to cemetery graves. Prior to this move by Tyson, meatpacking companies had been content to sell scraps such as chicken fat and by-products to makers of canned and dry pet food. Scott Morris of Freshpet Company in Secaucus, New Jersey, says this move by Tyson will change the fact that "pet food today looks the same as it did 30 years ago."

Six guidelines for when related diversification may be an effective strategy are as follows.[15]

- When an organization competes in a no-growth or a slow-growth industry.
- When adding new, but related, products would significantly enhance the sales of current products.
- When new, but related, products could be offered at highly competitive prices.
- When new, but related, products have seasonal sales levels that counterbalance an organization's existing peaks and valleys.
- When an organization's products are currently in the declining stage of the product's life cycle.
- When an organization has a strong management team.

Unrelated Diversification

An unrelated diversification strategy favors capitalizing on a portfolio of businesses that are capable of delivering excellent financial performance in their respective industries, rather than striving to capitalize on value chain strategic fits among the businesses. Firms that employ unrelated diversification continually search across different industries for companies that can be acquired for a deal and yet have potential to provide a high return on investment. Pursuing unrelated diversification entails being on the hunt to acquire companies whose assets are undervalued, or companies that are financially distressed, or companies that have high growth prospects but are short on investment capital. An obvious drawback of unrelated diversification is that the parent firm must have an excellent top management team that plans, organizes, motivates, delegates, and controls effectively. It is much more difficult to manage businesses in many industries than in a single industry. However, some firms are successful pursuing unrelated diversification, such as Walt Disney, which owns ABC, and General Electric, which owns NBC Universal. GE also produces locomotives, airplanes, appliances, and MRI machines and offers consumer finance, media, entertainment, oil, gas, and lighting products and services.

Tyson Foods recently launched a new diversification strategy, successfully opening a manufacturing plant that makes diesel and jet fuel from chicken fat, beef tallow, and leftover food grease from the firm's meat-processing plants. Tyson's new Louisiana factory can produce 75 million gallons of fat-based fuel annually. Working with Syntroleum Corp, Tyson is using heat to change the molecular structure of fats and oils so their new product performs like conventional fuels rather than similar biodiesel products.

In early 2011, Deutsche Bank opened a $4 billion, 3,000-room casino called the Cosmopolitan on the Las Vegas Strip. The huge German bank was originally just funding the project, but when developers defaulted on their loans, Deutsche decided to finish the last two years of work on the project and own and operate the new casino themselves. The new Cosmopolitan features a three-story, crystal-strewn bar meant to evoke the inside of a chandelier. Other financial institutions worldwide perhaps should consider unrelated diversification also by taking over some of their gone-bad projects rather than taking huge losses. Many more firms have failed at unrelated diversification than have succeeded due to immense management challenges.

Ten guidelines for when unrelated diversification may be an especially effective strategy are:[16]

- When revenues derived from an organization's current products or services would increase significantly by adding the new, unrelated products.
- When an organization competes in a highly competitive and/or a no-growth industry, as indicated by low industry profit margins and returns.
- When an organization's present channels of distribution can be used to market the new products to current customers.
- When the new products have countercyclical sales patterns compared to an organization's present products.
- When an organization's basic industry is experiencing declining annual sales and profits.
- When an organization has the capital and managerial talent needed to compete successfully in a new industry.
- When an organization has the opportunity to purchase an unrelated business that is an attractive investment opportunity.
- When there exists financial synergy between the acquired and acquiring firm. (Note that a key difference between related and unrelated diversification is that the former should be based on some commonality in markets, products, or technology, whereas the latter is based more on profit considerations.)
- When existing markets for an organization's present products are saturated.
- When antitrust action could be charged against an organization that historically has concentrated on a single industry.

Defensive Strategies

In addition to integrative, intensive, and diversification strategies, organizations also could pursue retrenchment, divestiture, or liquidation.

Retrenchment

Retrenchment occurs when an organization regroups through cost and asset reduction to reverse declining sales and profits. Sometimes called a *turnaround* or *reorganizational strategy,* retrenchment is designed to fortify an organization's basic distinctive competence. During retrenchment, strategists work with limited resources and face pressure from shareholders, employees, and the media. Retrenchment can entail selling off land and buildings to raise needed cash, pruning product lines, closing marginal businesses, closing obsolete factories, automating processes, reducing the number of employees, and instituting expense control systems.

Abbott Laboratories in 2011 cut about 3,000 jobs, or 3 percent of its workforce, as part of a major retrenchment strategy to streamline operations and improve efficiencies. Based in Abbott Park, Illinois, the company says most of the layoffs will be in its European operations. Abbott recently acquired Solvay SA's pharmaceutical division for about $6.1 billion. Abbott restructuring included closure of the Solvay facility in Marietta, Georgia.

A total of 157 banks in the United States ceased operations in 2010 due to financial insolvency. Many more banks followed suit in 2011, such as First Tier Bank in Louisville, Colorado and Enterprise Banking in McDonough, Georgia.

In some cases, *bankruptcy* can be an effective type of retrenchment strategy. Bankruptcy can allow a firm to avoid major debt obligations and to void union contracts. There are five major types of bankruptcy: Chapter 7, Chapter 9, Chapter 11, Chapter 12, and Chapter 13.

Chapter 7 bankruptcy is a liquidation procedure used only when a corporation sees no hope of being able to operate successfully or to obtain the necessary creditor agreement. All the organization's assets are sold in parts for their tangible worth. Chapter 7 is also the bankruptcy provision most frequently used by individuals to wipe out many types of unsecured debt.

Chapter 9 bankruptcy applies to municipalities. Prichard, Alabama (near Mobile), recently declared Chapter 9 bankruptcy when it "simply ran out of money to pay its pension obligations." Five municipalities in the United States filed Chapter 9 bankruptcy in 2010, but this part of the bankruptcy code is largely untested in courts. In fact, 21 states currently do not allow municipalities to file Chapter 9 bankruptcy. More than a dozen towns/cities in California, however, are expected to declare bankruptcy in the next 12 months., including San Diego, San Jose, and San Francisco.

Jefferson County in Alabama is home to Birmingham. The county is on the verge of declaring bankruptcy, as its fiscal soundness has deteriorated way beyond repair. Several Jefferson County former officials have been convicted of corruption charges related to sewer-bond dealings, which, coupled with inept management over many years, has led to the County's predicament. Norfolk, Virginia is in serious financial trouble, as is Reno, New York City, and Detroit.

Chapter 11 bankruptcy allows organizations to reorganize and come back after filing a petition for protection.

Chapter 12 bankruptcy was created by the Family Farmer Bankruptcy Act of 1986. This law became effective in 1987 and provides special relief to family farmers with debt equal to or less than $1.5 million.

Chapter 13 bankruptcy is a reorganization plan similar to Chapter 11, but it is available only to small businesses owned by individuals with unsecured debts of less than $100,000 and secured debts of less than $350,000. The Chapter 13 debtor is allowed to operate the business while a plan is being developed to provide for the successful operation of the business in the future.

Based in Los Angeles, California, Metro-Goldwyn-Mayer (MGM) Inc. recently declared Chapter 11 bankruptcy. MGM owns more than 4,100 movie titles, including the *James Bond* and *Rocky* franchises, but the firm's huge debt situation became too high to service.

Publisher of the *National Enquirer* and the *Star and Men's Fitness* magazines, American Media Inc. recently declared Chapter 11 bankruptcy. Based in Boca Raton, Florida, American Media told its advertisers, employees, customers, and vendors to expect "business as usual" during its restructuring.

Based in Secaucus, New Jersey, Urban Brands recently filed bankruptcy and is closing most of its 210 Ashley Stewart stores in 26 states. The stores primarily provide apparel for plus-size urban women.

The fast-food pizza chain, Sbarro Inc., recently declared Chapter 11 bankruptcy. Founded in the late 1950s by the Sbarro family, the company had grown to operate more than 1,000 stores in 40 countries, becoming a common sight in malls. Based in Melville, New York, Sbarro employs about 5,000 people.

Some of the largest bankruptcies in the United States in 2010 were: Ambac Financial Group, Corus Bankshares, FirstFed Financial, Blockbuster, Great Atlantic & Pacific (A&P) Tea, Mesa Air Group, and Affiliated Media. However, there were only 106 public U.S. companies filing bankruptcy in 2010, less than half the 211 public firms that filed the prior year, according to BankruptcyData.com. Owners of the Viceroy resort on the Caribbean island of Anguilla recently declared Chapter 11 bankruptcy protection in Delaware.

Five guidelines for when retrenchment may be an especially effective strategy to pursue are as follows:[17]

- When an organization has a clearly distinctive competence but has failed consistently to meet its objectives and goals over time.
- When an organization is one of the weaker competitors in a given industry.
- When an organization is plagued by inefficiency, low profitability, poor employee morale, and pressure from stockholders to improve performance.
- When an organization has failed to capitalize on external opportunities, minimize external threats, take advantage of internal strengths, and overcome internal weaknesses over time; that is, when the organization's strategic managers have failed (and possibly will be replaced by more competent individuals).
- When an organization has grown so large so quickly that major internal reorganization is needed.

Divestiture

Selling a division or part of an organization is called *divestiture*. Divestiture often is used to raise capital for further strategic acquisitions or investments. Divestiture can be part of an overall retrenchment strategy to rid an organization of businesses that are unprofitable, that require too much capital, or that do not fit well with the firm's other activities. Divestiture has also become a popular strategy for firms to focus on their core businesses and become less diversified. For example, the New York-based entertainment company, Viacom, recently divested of its Harmonix videogame division, which had produced the popular "Rock Band" line of games. Harmonix's "Rock Band" had been locked in brutal competition with a rival video game, "Guitar Hero," from Activision Blizzard, which is 60 percent owned by Vivendi SA.

Based in Downers Grove, Illinois, Sara Lee Corp. recently divested its North American bread division to Mexican bakery giant Grupo Bimbo for nearly $1 billion. Sara Lee continues to divest nonfood and low-margin units in order to focus on top brands such as Jimmy Dean, Ballpark hot dogs, and Hillshire Farm. Sara Lee is using much of those proceeds to buy back 2.5 million shares of their own stock (because the smaller, more focused company is a candidate for a takeover).

Based in Louisville, Kentucky, the maker of Jack Daniel's whiskey, Brown-Forman Corp., is trying to divest its wine business, which consists of eight wine brands that generated $310 million in sales in fiscal 2011. The company's flagship wines include Fetzer, Boneterra, and Sonoma-Cutrer. The wine business is challenging because it is capital intensive and wine consumers commonly experiment with different brands.

The private-equity fund Cerberus Capital Management LP recently sold its Chrysler Financial Corp. division to Toronto, Canada-based Toronto-Dominion Bank for roughly $80 billion. The acquisition by Canada's second-largest bank makes it one of the five biggest auto lenders in the U.S.

Clorox Company recently divested its auto-care division to private-equity firm Avista Capital Partners for about $780 million. Clorox desires to focus on its health-and-wellness products and desires to buy back some of its own stock. Clorox's auto-care brands that included STP and Armor All generated global sales of about $300 million.

Yum Brands is trying to divest its Long John Silver's and A&W Restaurants chains so the firm can focus on its KFC, Pizza Hut, and Taco Bell international businesses.

Historically firms have divested their unwanted or poorly performing divisions, but the global recession has witnessed firms simply closing such operations. For example, Home Depot is shutting down its Expo home-design stores; defense and aerospace manufacturer Textron Corp is closing groups that financed real estate deals; Pioneer Corp. will soon stop making televisions; Praxair Inc. is closing some of its service-related businesses outside the United States; even Google recently halted efforts to sell advertising on radio stations and in newspapers. Saks, the luxury clothing chain, recently closed 16 of its 18 bridal salons, leaving open only its departments in Manhattan and Beverly Hills.

Six guidelines for when divestiture may be an especially effective strategy to pursue follow:[18]

- When an organization has pursued a retrenchment strategy and failed to accomplish needed improvements.
- When a division needs more resources to be competitive than the company can provide.
- When a division is responsible for an organization's overall poor performance.
- When a division is a misfit with the rest of an organization; this can result from radically different markets, customers, managers, employees, values, or needs.
- When a large amount of cash is needed quickly and cannot be obtained reasonably from other sources.
- When government antitrust action threatens an organization.

Liquidation

Selling all of a company's assets, in parts, for their tangible worth is called *liquidation.* Liquidation is a recognition of defeat and consequently can be an emotionally difficult strategy. However, it may be better to cease operating than to continue losing large sums of money. For example, based in Mayodan, North Carolina, General Tobacco (GT) liquidated in 2011, as the maker of low-priced cigarettes failed to make payments owed to states under a massive industry settlement. Some GT brands were Bronco, Silver, and GT One.

Thousands of small businesses in the United States liquidate annually without ever making the news. It is tough to start and successfully operate a small business. In China and Russia, thousands of government-owned businesses liquidate annually as those countries try to privatize and consolidate industries.

These three guidelines indicate when liquidation may be an especially effective strategy to pursue:[19]

- When an organization has pursued both a retrenchment strategy and a divestitute strategy, and neither has been successful.
- When an organization's only alternative is bankruptcy. Liquidation represents an orderly and planned means of obtaining the greatest possible cash for an organization's assets. A company can legally declare bankruptcy first and then liquidate various divisions to raise needed capital.
- When the stockholders of a firm can minimize their losses by selling the organization's assets.

Michael Porter's Five Generic Strategies

Probably the three most widely read books on competitive analysis in the 1980s were Michael Porter's *Competitive Strategy* (Free Press, 1980), *Competitive Advantage* (Free Press, 1985), and *Competitive Advantage of Nations* (Free Press, 1989). According to Porter, strategies allow organizations to gain competitive advantage from three different bases: cost leadership, differentiation, and focus. Porter calls these bases *generic strategies.*

Cost leadership emphasizes producing standardized products at a very low per-unit cost for consumers who are price-sensitive. Two alternative types of cost leadership strategies can be defined. Type 1 is a *low-cost* strategy that offers products or services to a wide range of customers at the lowest price available on the market. Type 2 is a *best-value* strategy that offers products or services to a wide range of customers at the best price-value available on the market; the best-value strategy aims to offer customers a range of products or services at the lowest price available compared to a rival's products with similar attributes. Both Type 1 and Type 2 strategies target a large market.

Porter's Type 3 generic strategy is *differentiation,* a strategy aimed at producing products and services considered unique industrywide and directed at consumers who are relatively price-insensitive.

Focus means producing products and services that fulfill the needs of small groups of consumers. Two alternative types of focus strategies are Type 4 and Type 5. Type 4 is a *low-cost focus* strategy that offers products or services to a small range (niche group) of customers at the lowest price available on the market. Examples of firms that use the Type 4 strategy include Jiffy Lube International and Pizza Hut, as well as local used car dealers and hot dog restaurants. Type 5 is a *best-value focus* strategy that offers products or services to a small range of customers at the best price-value available on the market. Sometimes called "focused differentiation," the best-value focus strategy aims to offer a niche group of customers products or services that meet their tastes and requirements better than rivals' products do. Both Type 4 and Type 5 focus strategies target a small market. However, the difference is that Type 4 strategies offer products or services to a niche group at the lowest price, whereas Type 5 offers products/services to a niche group at higher prices but loaded with features so the offerings are perceived as the best value. Examples of firms that use the Type 5 strategy include Cannondale (top-of-the-line mountain bikes), Maytag (washing machines), and Lone Star Restaurants (steak house), as well as bed-and-breakfast inns and local retail boutiques.

Porter's five strategies imply different organizational arrangements, control procedures, and incentive systems. Larger firms with greater access to resources typically compete on a cost leadership and/or differentiation basis, whereas smaller firms often compete on a focus basis. Porter's five generic strategies are illustrated in Figure 5-3. Note that a differentiation strategy (Type 3) can be pursued with either a small target market or a large target market. However, it is not effective to pursue a cost leadership strategy in a small market because profits margins are generally too small. Likewise, it is not effective to pursue a focus strategy in a large market because economies of scale would generally favor a low-cost or best-value cost leadership strategy to gain and/or sustain competitive advantage.

Porter stresses the need for strategists to perform cost-benefit analyses to evaluate "sharing opportunities" among a firm's existing and potential business units. Sharing activities and resources enhances competitive advantage by lowering costs or increasing differentiation.

FIGURE 5-3

Porter's Five Generic Strategies

Type 1: Cost Leadership—Low Cost
Type 2: Cost Leadership—Best Value
Type 3: Differentiation
Type 4: Focus—Low Cost
Type 5: Focus—Best Value

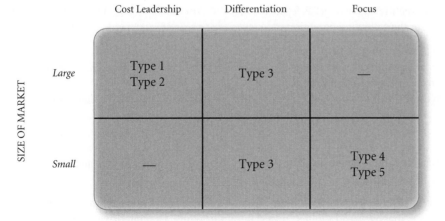

Source: Based on Michael E. Porter, *Competitive Strategy: Techniques for Analyzing Industries and Competitors* (New York: Free Press, 1980), 35–40.

In addition to prompting sharing, Porter stresses the need for firms to effectively "transfer" skills and expertise among autonomous business units to gain competitive advantage. Depending on factors such as type of industry, size of firm, and nature of competition, various strategies could yield advantages in cost leadership, differentiation, and focus.

Cost Leadership Strategies (Type 1 and Type 2)

A primary reason for pursuing forward, backward, and horizontal integration strategies is to gain low-cost or best-value cost leadership benefits. But cost leadership generally must be pursued in conjunction with differentiation. A number of cost elements affect the relative attractiveness of generic strategies, including economies or diseconomies of scale achieved, learning and experience curve effects, the percentage of capacity utilization achieved, and linkages with suppliers and distributors. Other cost elements to consider in choosing among alternative strategies include the potential for sharing costs and knowledge within the organization, R&D costs associated with new product development or modification of existing products, labor costs, tax rates, energy costs, and shipping costs.

Striving to be the low-cost producer in an industry can be especially effective when the market is composed of many price-sensitive buyers, when there are few ways to achieve product differentiation, when buyers do not care much about differences from brand to brand, or when there are a large number of buyers with significant bargaining power. The basic idea is to underprice competitors and thereby gain market share and sales, entirely driving some competitors out of the market. Companies employing a low-cost (Type 1) or best-value (Type 2) cost leadership strategy must achieve their competitive advantage in ways that are difficult for competitors to copy or match. If rivals find it relatively easy or inexpensive to imitate the leader's cost leadership methods, the leaders' advantage will not last long enough to yield a valuable edge in the marketplace. Recall that for a resource to be valuable, it must be either rare, hard to imitate, or not easily substitutable. To employ a cost leadership strategy successfully, a firm must ensure that its total costs across its overall value chain are lower than competitors' total costs. There are two ways to accomplish this:[20]

1. Perform value chain activities more efficiently than rivals and control the factors that drive the costs of value chain activities. Such activities could include altering the plant layout, mastering newly introduced technologies, using common parts or components in different products, simplifying product design, finding ways to operate close to full capacity year-round, and so on.
2. Revamp the firm's overall value chain to eliminate or bypass some cost-producing activities. Such activities could include securing new suppliers or distributors, selling products online, relocating manufacturing facilities, avoiding the use of union labor, and so on.

When employing a cost leadership strategy, a firm must be careful not to use such aggressive price cuts that their own profits are low or nonexistent. Constantly be mindful of cost-saving technological breakthroughs or any other value chain advancements that could erode or destroy the firm's competitive advantage. A Type 1 or Type 2 cost leadership strategy can be especially effective under the following conditions:[21]

1. When price competition among rival sellers is especially vigorous.
2. When the products of rival sellers are essentially identical and supplies are readily available from any of several eager sellers.
3. When there are few ways to achieve product differentiation that have value to buyers.
4. When most buyers use the product in the same ways.
5. When buyers incur low costs in switching their purchases from one seller to another.
6. When buyers are large and have significant power to bargain down prices.
7. When industry newcomers use introductory low prices to attract buyers and build a customer base.

A successful cost leadership strategy usually permeates the entire firm, as evidenced by high efficiency, low overhead, limited perks, intolerance of waste, intensive screening of budget requests, wide spans of control, rewards linked to cost containment, and broad employee participation in cost control efforts. Some risks of pursuing cost leadership are that competitors may imitate the strategy, thus driving overall industry profits down; that technological breakthroughs in the industry may make the strategy ineffective; or that buyer interest may swing to other differentiating features besides price. Several example firms that are well known for their low-cost leadership strategies are Wal-Mart, BIC, McDonald's, Black & Decker, Lincoln Electric, and Briggs & Stratton.

Differentiation Strategies (Type 3)

Different strategies offer different degrees of differentiation. Differentiation does not guarantee competitive advantage, especially if standard products sufficiently meet customer needs or if rapid imitation by competitors is possible. Durable products protected by barriers to quick copying by competitors are best. Successful differentiation can mean greater product flexibility, greater compatibility, lower costs, improved service, less maintenance, greater convenience, or more features. Product development is an example of a strategy that offers the advantages of differentiation.

A differentiation strategy should be pursued only after a careful study of buyers' needs and preferences to determine the feasibility of incorporating one or more differentiating features into a unique product that features the desired attributes. A successful differentiation strategy allows a firm to charge a higher price for its product and to gain customer loyalty because consumers may become strongly attached to the differentiation features. Special features that differentiate one's product can include superior service, spare parts availability, engineering design, product performance, useful life, gas mileage, or ease of use.

A risk of pursuing a differentiation strategy is that the unique product may not be valued highly enough by customers to justify the higher price. When this happens, a cost leadership strategy easily will defeat a differentiation strategy. Another risk of pursuing a differentiation strategy is that competitors may quickly develop ways to copy the differentiating features. Firms thus must find durable sources of uniqueness that cannot be imitated quickly or cheaply by rival firms.

Common organizational requirements for a successful differentiation strategy include strong coordination among the R&D and marketing functions and substantial amenities to attract scientists and creative people. Firms can pursue a differentiation (Type 3) strategy based on many different competitive aspects. For example, Mountain Dew and root beer have a unique taste; Lowe's, Home Depot, and Wal-Mart offer wide selection and one-stop shopping; Dell Computer and FedEx offer superior service; BMW and Porsche offer engineering design and performance; IBM and Hewlett-Packard offer a wide range of products; and E*Trade and Ameritrade offer Internet convenience. Differentiation opportunities exist or can potentially be developed anywhere along the firm's value chain, including supply chain activities, product R&D activities, production and technological activities, manufacturing activities, human resource management activities, distribution activities, or marketing activities.

The most effective differentiation bases are those that are hard or expensive for rivals to duplicate. Competitors are continually trying to imitate, duplicate, and outperform rivals along any differentiation variable that has yielded competitive advantage. For example, when U.S. Airways cut its prices, Delta quickly followed suit. When Caterpillar instituted its quick-delivery-of-spare-parts policy, John Deere soon followed suit. To the extent that differentiating attributes are tough for rivals to copy, a differentiation strategy will be especially effective, but the sources of uniqueness must be time-consuming, cost prohibitive, and simply too burdensome for rivals to match. A firm, therefore, must be careful when employing a differentiation (Type 3) strategy. Buyers will not pay the higher differentiation price unless their perceived value exceeds the price they are paying.[22] Based on such matters as attractive packaging, extensive advertising, quality of sales presentations, quality of website, list of customers, professionalism, size of the firm, and/or profitability of the company, perceived value may be more important to customers than actual value.

A Type 3 differentiation strategy can be especially effective under the following conditions:[23]

1. When there are many ways to differentiate the product or service and many buyers perceive these differences as having value.
2. When buyer needs and uses are diverse.

3. When few rival firms are following a similar differentiation approach.
4. When technological change is fast paced and competition revolves around rapidly evolving product features.

Focus Strategies (Type 4 and Type 5)

A successful focus strategy depends on an industry segment that is of sufficient size, has good growth potential, and is not crucial to the success of other major competitors. Strategies such as market penetration and market development offer substantial focusing advantages. Midsize and large firms can effectively pursue focus-based strategies only in conjunction with differentiation or cost leadership–based strategies. All firms in essence follow a differentiated strategy. Because only one firm can differentiate itself with the lowest cost, the remaining firms in the industry must find other ways to differentiate their products.

Focus strategies are most effective when consumers have distinctive preferences or requirements and when rival firms are not attempting to specialize in the same target segment. Milwaukee, Wisconsin-based Johnson Controls focuses on being a supplier of car interior products. Johnson Controls recently purchased Germany's Keiper Recaro Group's auto-parts business, which added 4,750 employees in seven countries producing devices that recline and adjust automobile seats. Johnson Controls now sells about $18 billion in auto-related products annually, although it also has a heating and ventilation equipment segment of the business.

Risks of pursuing a focus strategy include the possibility that numerous competitors will recognize the successful focus strategy and copy it or that consumer preferences will drift toward the product attributes desired by the market as a whole. An organization using a focus strategy may concentrate on a particular group of customers, geographic markets, or on particular product-line segments to serve a well-defined but narrow market better than competitors who serve a broader market.

A low-cost (Type 4) or best-value (Type 5) focus strategy can be especially attractive under the following conditions:[24]

1. When the target market niche is large, profitable, and growing.
2. When industry leaders do not consider the niche to be crucial to their own success.
3. When industry leaders consider it too costly or difficult to meet the specialized needs of the target market niche while taking care of their mainstream customers.
4. When the industry has many different niches and segments, thereby allowing a focuser to pick a competitively attractive niche suited to its own resources.
5. When few, if any, other rivals are attempting to specialize in the same target segment.

Strategies for Competing in Turbulent, High-Velocity Markets

The world is changing more and more rapidly, and consequently industries and firms themselves are changing faster than ever. Some industries are changing so fast that researchers call them *turbulent, high-velocity markets,* such as telecommunications, medical, biotechnology, pharmaceuticals, computer hardware, software, and virtually all Internet-based industries. High-velocity change is clearly becoming more and more the rule rather than the exception, even in such industries as toys, phones, banking, defense, publishing, and communication.

Meeting the challenge of high-velocity change presents the firm with a choice of whether to react, anticipate, or lead the market in terms of its own strategies. To primarily react to changes in the industry would be a defensive strategy used to counter, for example, unexpected shifts in buyer tastes and technological breakthroughs. The react-to-change strategy would not be as effective as the anticipate-change strategy, which would entail devising and following through with plans for dealing with the expected changes. However, firms ideally strive to be in a position to lead the changes in high-velocity markets, whereby they pioneer new and better technologies and products and set industry standards. Being the leader or pioneer of change in a high-velocity market is an aggressive, offensive strategy that includes rushing next-generation products to market ahead of rivals and being continually proactive in shaping the market to one's own benefit. Although a lead-change strategy is best whenever the firm has the resources to pursue this approach, on occasion even the strongest firms in turbulent industries have to employ the react-to-the-market strategy and the anticipate-the-market strategy.

An example turbulent, high-velocity market is the tablet computer, with more than 100 companies trying to emulate Apple's iPad and tablet products. Sales of tablet computers exceeded 20 million units in 2010 and 60 million units in 2011. A version of Google's Android operating system is now powering tablets, including Google's Honeycomb system. Apple utilizes a lead-change strategy as one of the strongest firms in the turbulent computer tablet industry, with firms such as Samsung and Toshiba aggressively pursuing a react-to-change strategy. The first laptop computers running on Google's Chrome OS were manufactured by Acer Inc. and Samsung Electronics and went on sale in mid-2011. Google is working with Verizon Wireless to ensure that Chrome laptops always stay online.

One strategy to compete in a turbulent industry is to acquire rivals, thus gaining economies of scale and improved efficiencies. For example, AT&T just acquired rival T-Mobile USA for $39 billion, creating the largest U.S. cellphone company, and Charles Schwab Corp. acquired online brokerage services provider OptionsXpress for $1 billion.

Means for Achieving Strategies

Cooperation Among Competitors

Strategies that stress cooperation among competitors are being used more. For collaboration between competitors to succeed, both firms must contribute something distinctive, such as technology, distribution, basic research, or manufacturing capacity. But a major risk is that unintended transfers of important skills or technology may occur at organizational levels below where the deal was signed.[25] Information not covered in the formal agreement often gets traded in the day-to-day interactions and dealings of engineers, marketers, and product developers. Firms often give away too much information to rival firms when operating under cooperative agreements! Tighter formal agreements are needed.

Perhaps the best example of rival firms in an industry forming alliances to compete against each other is the airline industry. Today there are three major alliances: Star, SkyTeam, and Oneworld, but other alliances are forming, such as the new trans-Atlantic joint venture among American Air, British Air, and Iberia Air formed by Oneworld. There is also a new trans-Pacific joint venture among American, Japan Air, United Continental, and All Nippon Air.

The idea of joining forces with a competitor is not easily accepted by Americans, who often view cooperation and partnerships with skepticism and suspicion. Indeed, joint ventures and cooperative arrangements among competitors demand a certain amount of trust if companies are to combat paranoia about whether one firm will injure the other. However, multinational firms are becoming more globally cooperative, and increasing numbers of domestic firms are joining forces with competitive foreign firms to reap mutual benefits. Kathryn Harrigan at Columbia University says, "Within a decade, most companies will be members of teams that compete against each other." Once major rivals, Google's YouTube and Vivendi SA's Universal Music Group have formed a partnership called Vevo to provide a new music-video service. Google provides the technology and Universal Music provides the content, and both firms share the revenues. The two firms now operate the stand-alone site Vevo.com.

U.S. companies often enter alliances primarily to avoid investments, being more interested in reducing the costs and risks of entering new businesses or markets than in acquiring new skills. In contrast, *learning from the partner* is a major reason why Asian and European firms enter into cooperative agreements. U.S. firms, too, should place learning high on the list of reasons to be cooperative with competitors. U.S. companies often form alliances with Asian firms to gain an understanding of their manufacturing excellence, but Asian competence in this area is not easily transferable. Manufacturing excellence is a complex system that includes employee training and involvement, integration with suppliers, statistical process controls, value engineering, and design. In contrast, U.S. know-how in technology and related areas can be imitated more easily. U.S. firms thus need to be careful not to give away more intelligence than they receive in cooperative agreements with rival Asian firms.

Joint Venture/Partnering

Joint venture is a popular strategy that occurs when two or more companies form a temporary partnership or consortium for the purpose of capitalizing on some opportunity. Often, the two or more sponsoring firms form a separate organization and have shared equity ownership in the new entity. Other types of *cooperative arrangements* include research and development partnerships, cross-distribution agreements, cross-licensing agreements, cross-manufacturing agreements, and joint-bidding consortia. Facebook Inc. and Skype SA recently combined their communications services more closely under a new partnership that allows Facebook members to sign into Skype through their Facebook Connect account and then send text messages or set up voice chats and video chats with their Facebook friends from within Skype. The partnership puts pressure on Google because it links Skype's 580 million registered users with Facebook's 500 million members. For the first time ever, U.S. Internet users spent 41.1 billion minutes on Facebook in August 2010, surpassing Google's 39.8 billion minutes.[26]

The world's largest cellphone maker, Nokia Corp., recently formed a partnership with the world's largest software company, Microsoft, whereby the Finnish company will receive billions of dollars from Microsoft to develop and market smartphones using Microsoft's operating system. Nokia still has the largest market share in the handset business but is losing ground. The partnership is designed to compete with Google's Android mobile-phone operating system and with Apple Inc.'s iPhone. Nokia's new smartphones will use Window Phone as their principal operating system, replacing its own Symbian software and Intel's MeeGo operating system. About the Nokia-Microsoft partnership, Google executive Vic Gundrota said, "Two turkeys do not make an eagle."

Joint ventures and cooperative arrangements are being used increasingly because they allow companies to improve communications and networking, to globalize operations, and to minimize risk. Joint ventures and partnerships are often used to pursue an opportunity that is too complex, uneconomical, or risky for a single firm to pursue alone. Such business creations also are used when achieving and sustaining competitive advantage when an industry requires a broader range of competencies and know-how than any one firm can marshal. Kathryn Rudie Harrigan, summarizes the trend toward increased joint venturing:

> In today's global business environment of scarce resources, rapid rates of technological change, and rising capital requirements, the important question is no longer "Shall we form a joint venture?" Now the question is "Which joint ventures and cooperative arrangements are most appropriate for our needs and expectations?" followed by "How do we manage these ventures most effectively?"[27]

In a global market tied together by the Internet, joint ventures, and partnerships, alliances are proving to be a more effective way to enhance corporate growth than mergers and acquisitions.[28] Strategic partnering takes many forms, including outsourcing, information sharing, joint marketing, and joint research and development. Many companies, such as Eli Lilly, now host partnership training classes for their managers and partners. There are today more than 10,000 joint ventures formed annually, more than all mergers and acquisitions. There are countless examples of successful strategic alliances, such as Internet coverage.

A major reason why firms are using partnering as a means to achieve strategies is globalization. Wal-Mart's successful joint venture with Mexico's Cifra is indicative of how a domestic firm can benefit immensely by partnering with a foreign company to gain substantial presence in that new country. Technology also is a major reason behind the need to form strategic alliances, with the Internet linking widely dispersed partners. The Internet paved the way and legitimized the need for alliances to serve as the primary means for corporate growth.

Striving to compete with Google, Microsoft and Facebook recently unveiled a plan to improve the results of Microsoft's Bing search engine by including peoples's social connections on Facebook. The sharing of personal data between Micorsoft and Facebook raises privacy concerns because the partnership gives Bing access to all public information about a Facebook user, including their friends' names and photos. Bing powers both Microsoft searches (11.2 percent) and Yahoo searches (16.7 percent), but Google's share of U.S. searches is 66.1 percent.

Evidence is mounting that firms should use partnering as a means for achieving strategies. However, the sad fact is that most U.S. firms in many industries—such as financial services, forest products, metals, and retailing—still operate in a merger or acquire mode to obtain growth. Partnering is not yet taught at most business schools and is often viewed within companies as a financial issue rather than a strategic issue. However, partnering has become a core competency, a strategic issue of such importance that top management involvement initially and throughout the life of an alliance is vital.[29]

Joint ventures among once rival firms are commonly being used to pursue strategies ranging from retrenchment to market development. Although ventures and partnerships are preferred over mergers as a means for achieving strategies, certainly they are not all successful. The good news is that joint ventures and partnerships are less risky for companies than mergers, but the bad news is that many alliances fail. There are countless examples of failed joint ventures. A few common problems that cause joint ventures to fail are as follows:

1. Managers who must collaborate daily in operating the venture are not involved in forming or shaping the venture.
2. The venture may benefit the partnering companies but may not benefit customers, who then complain about poorer service or criticize the companies in other ways.
3. The venture may not be supported equally by both partners. If supported unequally, problems arise.
4. The venture may begin to compete more with one of the partners than the other.[30]

Six guidelines for when a joint venture may be an especially effective means for pursuing strategies are:[31]

- When a privately owned organization is forming a joint venture with a publicly owned organization; there are some advantages to being privately held, such as closed ownership; there are some advantages of being publicly held, such as access to stock issuances as a source of capital. Sometimes, the unique advantages of being privately and publicly held can be synergistically combined in a joint venture.
- When a domestic organization is forming a joint venture with a foreign company; a joint venture can provide a domestic company with the opportunity for obtaining local management in a foreign country, thereby reducing risks such as expropriation and harassment by host country officials.
- When the distinct competencies of two or more firms complement each other especially well.
- When some project is potentially very profitable but requires overwhelming resources and risks.
- When two or more smaller firms have trouble competing with a large firm.
- When there exists a need to quickly introduce a new technology.

Merger/Acquisition

Google acquired 48 companies in 2010 and is on pace to eclipse that number in 2011, as the firm seeks ways to boost revenue growth and compete more aggressively in social networking. That may be a record annual number of acquisitions for any company ever. Cisco had 23 acquisitions back in 2000, Microsoft had 18 in 2008, and Oracle had 13 in 2005, but 48 is unreal. Despite Google's 48 acquisitions, the company's stock price dropped 4 percent in 2010—even when the stock market was roaring back.

Merger and acquisition are two commonly used ways to pursue strategies. A *merger* occurs when two organizations of about equal size unite to form one enterprise. An *acquisition* occurs when a large organization purchases (acquires) a smaller firm, or vice versa. When a merger or acquisition is not desired by both parties, it can be called a *takeover* or *hostile takeover*. In contrast, if the acquisition is desired by both firms, it is termed a *friendly merger*. Most mergers are friendly. For example, two Japanese steel producers, Nippon Steel Corp. and Sumitomo Metal Industries Ltd., recently merged in friendly fashion to form the world's second largest steel producer behind ArcelorMittal. Canada's Valeant Pharmaceuticals International recently made a hostile takeover bid of $5.7 billion for smaller rival Cephalon, or $73 per share, a 24.5 percent premium to Cephalon's stock price of $58.

There were numerous examples in 2011 of hostile takeover attempts. For example, the French pharmaceutical giant Sanofi-Aventis SA recently launched an $18.5 billion hostile takeover bid for the U.S. biotech company Genzyme Corp. Sanofi has offered $69 per share for Genzyme, but analysts say that bid may have to increase to $85 to seal the deal.

Nasdaq, with help from IntercontinentalExchange (ICE), which operates a global futures exchange and over-the-counter (OTC) markets and derivatives clearing houses, plans to place a hostile takeover bid for the New York Stock Exchange (NYSE) Euronext. Any Nasdaq bid, however, would face significant obstacles, including possible antitrust problems, since nearly every U.S. stock is listed on either the NYSE or Nasdaq. There has been a recent merger frenzy in the stock exchange business. Deutsche Boerse and NYSE Euronext desire to merge to create the world's largest exchange operator in a deal worth $10.2 billion. There is speculation that Nasdaq might even merge with another international exchange, such as the London Stock Exchange (LSE). The LSE is eyeing a takeover of Nasdaq after recently merging with the Canadian TMX Group, which operates the Toronto and Montreal stock exchanges.

With hundreds of companies flush with excess cash, the year 2010 saw a 13 percent increase in mergers and acquisitions in the United States; 2011 is on pace to exceed that percentage as firms increasingly use mergers to quickly tap into new businesses and reach new markets, both top priorities as companies were previously hunkered down during the recession.

General Electric continues to acquire diverse firms, including its recent purchase of oil-and-gas equipment maker Dresser Inc. for $3 billion. Based in Dallas, Texas, about 60 percent of Dresser's revenues come from outside the United States. General Electric desires to scale back its big finance business at GE Capital and beef up its industrial and infrastructure operations.

White knight is a term that refers to a firm that agrees to acquire another firm when that other firm is facing a hostile takeover by some company. For example, recently Palo Alto, California–based CV Thereapeutics Inc., a heart-drug maker, was fighting a hostile takeover bid by Japan's Astellas Pharma. Then CVT struck a friendly deal to be acquired by Forest City, California–based Gilead Sciences at a higher price of $1.4 billion in cash. Gilead is known for its HIV drugs, so its move into the heart-drug business surprised many analysts.

Not all mergers are effective and successful. For example, even 12 months after PulteGroup recently bought rival Centex Corp. for $1.3 billion in stock, creating the largest home builder in the United States, PulteGroup's profits are still negative and the company's stock price is 30 percent lower than the week of the acquisition. PulteGroup's dismal performance is in sharp contrast to rival firms such as Toll Brothers and Lennar Corp., whose stock price is up 22 percent during the same period. Many analysts say that PulteGroup's acquisition of Centex was poorly timed and a mistake. So a merger between two firms can yield great benefits, but the price and reasoning must be right. Some key reasons why many mergers and acquisitions fail are provided in Table 5-5.

Among mergers, acquisitions, and takeovers in recent years, same-industry combinations have predominated. A general market consolidation is occurring in many industries, especially banking, insurance, defense, and health care, but also in pharmaceuticals, food, airlines, accounting, publishing, computers, retailing, financial services, and biotechnology. For example, There are many potential benefits of merging with or acquiring another firm, as indicated in Table 5-6.

TABLE 5-5 Key Reasons Why Many Mergers and Acquisitions Fail

- Integration difficulties
- Inadequate evaluation of target
- Large or extraordinary debt
- Inability to achieve synergy
- Too much diversification
- Managers overly focused on acquisitions
- Too large an acquisition
- Difficult to integrate different organizational cultures
- Reduced employee morale due to layoffs and relocations

TABLE 5-6   Potential Benefits of Merging With or Acquiring Another Firm

- To provide improved capacity utilization
- To make better use of the existing sales force
- To reduce managerial staff
- To gain economies of scale
- To smooth out seasonal trends in sales
- To gain access to new suppliers, distributors, customers, products, and creditors
- To gain new technology
- To reduce tax obligations

The volume of mergers completed annually worldwide is growing dramatically and exceeds $1 trillion. There are annually more than 10,000 mergers in the United States that total more than $700 billion. The proliferation of mergers is fueled by companies' drive for market share, efficiency, and pricing power, as well as by globalization, the need for greater economies of scale, reduced regulation and antitrust concerns, the Internet, and e-commerce.

A *leveraged buyout (LBO)* occurs when a corporation's shareholders are bought (hence *buyout*) by the company's management and other private investors using borrowed funds (hence *leverage*).[32] Besides trying to avoid a hostile takeover, other reasons for initiating an LBO are senior management decisions that particular divisions do not fit into an overall corporate strategy or must be sold to raise cash, or receipt of an attractive offering price. An LBO takes a corporation private.

Private-Equity Acquisitions

As stock prices increased and companies became cash-rich in 2010–2012, private-equity firms such as Kohlberg Kravis Roberts (KKR) jumped aggressively back into the business of acquiring and selling firms. Private-equity firms have unleashed a wave of new initial public offerings (IPO), such as the IPO of Nielsen Holdings BV, the largest private-equity-backed IPO in the United States in five years. Apollo Global Management is a large private-equity firm that owns many companies. Some private-equity owned firms expected to go public soon include BankUnited Inc., Kinder Morgan Inc., and Toys "R" Us Inc.

The intent of virtually all private-equity acquisitions is to buy firms at a low price and sell them later at a high price, arguably just good business. Many if not most acquisitions in 2010–2012 were by large private-investment firms. For example, 3G Capital Management acquired Burger King Holdings for about $3.3 billion. CKE Restaurants, owner of the Carl's Jr. and Hardee's burger chains, was acquired by an affiliate of Apollo Management LLC for almost $700 million. Goldman Sachs's private-equity arm acquired Apple American Group, the largest franchisee (269 restaurants) of Applebee's Neighborhood Grill and Bar based in Independence, Ohio.

First Mover Advantages

First mover advantages refer to the benefits a firm may achieve by entering a new market or developing a new product or service prior to rival firms.[33] As indicated in Table 5-7, some advantages of being a first mover include securing access to rare resources, gaining new

TABLE 5-7   Benefits of a Firm Being the First Mover

1. Secure access and commitments to rare resources
2. Gain new knowledge of critical success factors and issues
3. Gain market share and position in the best locations
4. Establish and secure long-term relationships with customers, suppliers, distributors, and investors
5. Gain customer loyalty and commitments

knowledge of key factors and issues, and carving out market share and a position that is easy to defend and costly for rival firms to overtake. First mover advantages are analogous to taking the high ground first, which puts one in an excellent strategic position to launch aggressive campaigns and to defend territory. Being the first mover can be especially wise when such actions (1) build a firm's image and reputation with buyers, (2) produce cost advantages over rivals in terms of new technologies, new components, new distribution channels, and so on, (3) create strongly loyal customers, and (4) make imitation or duplication by a rival hard or unlikely.[34]

To sustain the competitive advantage gained by being the first mover, a firm needs to be a fast learner. There are, however, risks associated with being the first mover, such as unexpected and unanticipated problems and costs that occur from being the first firm doing business in the new market. Therefore, being a slow mover (also called *fast follower* or *late mover*) can be effective when a firm can easily copy or imitate the lead firm's products or services. If technology is advancing rapidly, slow movers can often leapfrog a first mover's products with improved second-generation products. However, slow movers often are relegated to relying on the first mover being a slow mover and making strategic and tactical mistakes. This situation does not occur often, so first mover advantages clearly offset the first mover disadvantages most of the time. Apple Inc. has always been a good example of a first mover firm.

Nokia, the world's largest mobile phone maker by units, has been a late mover in the smartphone industry, following Apple, by introducing the Nokia N8 smartphone. The N8 is a sleek phone with a 12-megapixel camera and high-definition video recording feature. Also a late mover, Hewlett-Packard (H-P) introduced its first tablet computer and first smartphone in 2011, well behind Apple and Google. Apple sold 14 million iPad computers before the H-P announcement. Sales of iPads are forecasted to reach 24.1 million in 2011 and eclipse 44 million annually by 2015 according to Forrester Research.

Based in Santa Clara, California, Intel is a first mover firm in terms of introducing new production processes sooner than competitors. Intel is investing $7 billion between 2011 and 2014 to upgrade its manufacturing plants in the United States and build a new research facility in Oregon. Intel is moving beyond PCs into chips for smartphones and other products.

First mover advantages tend to be greatest when competitors are roughly the same size and possess similar resources. If competitors are not similar in size, then larger competitors can wait while others make initial investments and mistakes, and then respond with greater effectiveness and resources.

Outsourcing

Business-process outsourcing (BPO) involves companies taking over the functional operations, such as human resources, information systems, payroll, accounting, customer service, and even marketing of other firms. Companies are choosing to outsource their functional operations more and more for several reasons: (1) it is less expensive, (2) it allows the firm to focus on its core businesses, and (3) it enables the firm to provide better services. Other advantages of outsourcing are that the strategy (1) allows the firm to align itself with "best-in-world" suppliers who focus on performing the special task, (2) provides the firm flexibility should customer needs shift unexpectedly, and (3) allows the firm to concentrate on other internal value chain activities critical to sustaining competitive advantage. BPO is a means for achieving strategies that are similar to partnering and joint venturing. The worldwide BPO market exceeds $173 billion.

Many firms, such as Dearborn, Michigan–based Visteon Corp. and J.P. Morgan Chase & Co., outsource their computer operations to IBM, which competes with firms such as Electronic Data Systems and Computer Sciences Corp. in the computer outsourcing business. 3M Corp. is outsourcing all of its manufacturing operations to Flextronics International Ltd. of Singapore or Jabil Circuit in Florida. 3M is also outsourcing all design and manufacturing of low-end standardized volume products by building a new design center in Taiwan.

U.S. and European companies for more than a decade have been outsourcing their manufacturing, tech support, and back-office work, but most insisted on keeping research and development activities in-house. However, an ever-growing number of firms today are outsourcing their product design to Asian developers. China and India are becoming increasingly important suppliers of intellectual property. For companies that include Hewlett-Packard, PalmOne, Dell, Sony, Apple, Kodak, Motorola, Nokia, Ericsson, Lucent, Cisco, and Nortel, the design of personal computers and cameras is mostly outsourced to China and India.

Companies pay about $68 billion annually in outsourcing operations to other firms, but the details of what work to outsource, to whom, where, and for how much can challenge even the biggest, most sophisticated companies.[35] And some outsourcing deals do not work out, such as the J.P. Morgan Chase deal with IBM and Dow Chemical's deal with Electronic Data Systems. Both outsourcing deals were abandoned after several years. Lehman Brothers Holdings and Dell Inc. both recently reversed decisions to move customer call centers to India after a customer rebellion. India has become a booming place for outsourcing. A recent *Wall Street Journal* article reported that roughly 85 percent of all Americans believe "outsourcing of production and manufacturing work to foreign countries is a major reason the U.S. economy is struggling and more people are not being hired."[36] However, organizations that outsource are seeking to realize benefits or address the following issues:[37]

- Cost savings — Access lower wages in foreign countries.
- Focus on core business — Focus resources on developing the core business rather than being distracted by other functions.
- Cost restructuring — Outsourcing changes the balance of fixed costs to variable costs by moving the firm more to variable costs. Outsourcing also makes variable costs more predictable.
- Improve quality — Improve quality by contracting out various business functions to specialists.
- Knowledge — Gain access to intellectual property and wider experience and knowledge.
- Contract — Gain access to services within a legally binding contract with financial penalties and legal redress. This is not the case with services performed internally.
- Operational expertise — Gain access to operational best practice that would be too difficult or time consuming to develop in-house.
- Access to talent — Gain access to a larger talent pool and a sustainable source of skills, especially science and engineering.
- Catalyst for change — Use an outsourcing agreement as a catalyst for major change that cannot be achieved alone.
- Enhance capacity for innovation — Use external knowledge to supplement limited in-house capacity for product innovation.
- Reduce time to market — Accelerate development and/or production of a product through additional capability brought by the supplier.
- Risk management — Manage risk by partnering with an outside firm.
- Tax benefit — Capitalize on tax incentives to locate manufacturing plants to avoid high taxes in various countries.

Strategic Management in Nonprofit and Governmental Organizations

Nonprofit organizations are basically just like for-profit companies except for two major differences: 1) nonprofits do not pay taxes and 2) nonprofits do not have shareholders to provide capital. In virtually all other ways, nonprofits are just like for-profits. Nonprofits have competitors that want to put them out of business. Nonprofits have employees, customers, creditors, suppliers, and distributors as well as financial budgets, income statements, balance sheets, cash flow statements, and so on. Nonprofit organizations embrace strategic planning just as much as for-profit firms, and perhaps even more, since equity capital is not an alternative source of financing.

The strategic-management process is being used effectively by countless nonprofit and governmental organizations, such as the Girl Scouts, Boy Scouts, the Red Cross, chambers of commerce, educational institutions, medical institutions, public utilities, libraries, government agencies, and churches. The nonprofit sector, surprisingly, is by far America's largest employer. Many nonprofit and governmental organizations outperform private firms and corporations on innovativeness, motivation, productivity, and strategic management.

Compared to for-profit firms, nonprofit and governmental organizations may be totally dependent on outside financing. Especially for these organizations, strategic management provides an excellent vehicle for developing and justifying requests for needed financial support.

Religious Facilities

A recent *Wall Street Journal* article reveals that the number of religious facilities having to close their doors is surging as many borrowed too much and built too big during boom times.[38] Chris Macke, a real-estate strategist at CoStar, recently said, "religious organizations may be subject to the laws of God but they are also subject to the laws of economics." Religious denominations of all kinds have suffered in recent years from consumer hardships, including high unemployment and underemployment, which translates into less money in the offering plate and declining attendance.

Six states in particular had 15 or more religious facilities foreclosed upon in the 2006–2010 period: California (29), Michigan (23), Florida (23), Georgia (19), Texas (17), and Ohio (15). Religious facilities are like businesses in many ways, including: 1) they can be foreclosed upon if their finances fall into disarray, and 2) they need effective strategic planning.

Educational Institutions

Educational institutions are more frequently using strategic-management techniques and concepts. Richard Cyert, former president of Carnegie Mellon University, said, "I believe we do a far better job of strategic management than any company I know." Population shifts nationally from the Northeast and Midwest to the Southeast and West are but one factor causing trauma for educational institutions that have not planned for changing enrollments. Ivy League schools in the Northeast are recruiting more heavily in the Southeast and West. This trend represents a significant change in the competitive climate for attracting the best high school graduates each year.

Online college degrees are common place and represent a threat to traditional colleges and universities. "You can put the kids to bed and go to law school," says Andrew Rosen, chief operating officer of Kaplan Education Centers, a subsidiary of the Washington Post Company.

Many American colleges and universities have now established campuses outside the United States. For example, Yale University and the National University of Singapore will establish a joint campus in Singapore in 2013. The institution will be Singapore's first liberal-arts college and Yale's first campus outside the Ivy League institution's New Haven, Connecticut home.

Medical Organizations

The $200 billion U.S. hospital industry is experiencing declining margins, excess capacity, bureaucratic overburdening, poorly planned and executed diversification strategies, soaring health care costs, reduced federal support, and high administrator turnover. The seriousness of this problem is accented by a 20 percent annual decline in use by inpatients nationwide. Declining occupancy rates, deregulation, and accelerating growth of health maintenance organizations, preferred provider organizations, urgent care centers, outpatient surgery centers, diagnostic centers, specialized clinics, and group practices are other major threats facing hospitals today. Many private and state-supported medical institutions are in financial trouble as a result of traditionally taking a reactive rather than a proactive approach in dealing with their industry.

Hospitals—originally intended to be warehouses for people dying of tuberculosis, smallpox, cancer, pneumonia, and infectious diseases—are creating new strategies today as advances in the diagnosis and treatment of chronic diseases are undercutting that earlier mission. Hospitals are beginning to bring services to the patient as much as bringing the patient to the hospital; health care is more and more being concentrated in the home and in the residential community, not on the hospital campus. Chronic care will require day-treatment facilities, electronic monitoring at home, user-friendly ambulatory services, decentralized service networks, and laboratory testing. A successful hospital strategy for the future will require renewed and deepened collaboration with physicians, who are central to hospitals' well-being, and a reallocation of resources from acute to chronic care in home and community settings.

Current strategies being pursued by many hospitals include creating home health services, establishing nursing homes, and forming rehabilitation centers. Backward integration strategies that some hospitals are pursuing include acquiring ambulance services, waste disposal services, and diagnostic services. Millions of persons annually research medical ailments online, which is causing a dramatic shift in the balance of power between doctor, patient, and hospitals. The number of persons using the Internet to obtain medical information is skyrocketing. A motivated patient using the Internet can gain knowledge on a particular subject far beyond his or her doctor's knowledge, because no person can keep up with the results and implications of billions of dollars' worth of medical research reported weekly. Patients today often walk into the doctor's office with a file folder of the latest articles detailing research and treatment options for their ailments.

Governmental Agencies and Departments

Federal, state, county, and municipal agencies and departments, such as police departments, chambers of commerce, forestry associations, and health departments, are responsible for formulating, implementing, and evaluating strategies that use taxpayers' dollars in the most cost-effective way to provide services and programs. Strategic-management concepts are generally required and thus widely used to enable governmental organizations to be more effective and efficient.

Strategists in governmental organizations operate with less strategic autonomy than their counterparts in private firms. Public enterprises generally cannot diversify into unrelated businesses or merge with other firms. Governmental strategists usually enjoy little freedom in altering the organizations' missions or redirecting objectives. Legislators and politicians often have direct or indirect control over major decisions and resources. Strategic issues get discussed and debated in the media and legislatures. Issues become politicized, resulting in fewer strategic choice alternatives. There is now more predictability in the management of public sector enterprises.

Government agencies and departments are finding that their employees get excited about the opportunity to participate in the strategic-management process and thereby have an effect on the organization's mission, objectives, strategies, and policies. In addition, government agencies are using a strategic-management approach to develop and substantiate formal requests for additional funding.

Strategic Management in Small Firms

The reason why "becoming your own boss" has become a national obsession is that entrepreneurs are America's role models. Almost everyone wants to own a business—from teens and college students, who are signing up for entrepreneurial courses in record numbers, to those over age 65, who are forming more companies every year.

As hundreds of thousands of people have been laid off from work in the last two years, many of these individuals have started small businesses. The *Wall Street Journal* recently provided a 10-page article on how to be a successful entrepreneur.[39] Not only laid off employees but also college graduates are seeking more and more to open their own businesses.[40]

Strategic management is vital for large firms' success, but what about small firms? The strategic-management process is just as vital for small companies. From their inception, all organizations have a strategy, even if the strategy just evolves from day-to-day operations. Even if conducted informally or by a single owner/entrepreneur, the strategic-management process can significantly enhance small firms' growth and prosperity. Because an ever-increasing number of men and women in the United States are starting their own businesses, more individuals are becoming strategists. Widespread corporate layoffs have contributed to an explosion in small businesses and new ideas.

Numerous magazine and journal articles have focused on applying strategic-management concepts to small businesses. A major conclusion of these articles is that a lack of strategic-management knowledge is a serious obstacle for many small business owners. Other problems often encountered in applying strategic-management concepts to small businesses are a lack of both sufficient capital to exploit external opportunities and a day-to-day cognitive frame of reference. Research also indicates that strategic management in small firms is more informal than in large firms, but small firms that engage in strategic management outperform those that do not.

Special Note to Students

There are numerous alternative strategies that could benefit any firm, but your strategic management case analysis should result in specific recommendations that you decide will best provide the firm competitive advantages. Since company recommendations with costs comprise the most important pages/slides in your case project, introduce bits of that information early in the presentation as relevant supporting material is presented to justify your expenditures. Your recommendations page(s) itself should therefore be a summary of suggestions mentioned throughout your paper or presentation, rather than being a surprise shock to your reader or audience. You may even want to include with your recommendations insight as to why certain other feasible strategies were not chosen for implementation. That information too should be anchored in the notion of competitive advantage and disadvantage with respect to perceived costs and benefits.

Conclusion

The main appeal of any managerial approach is the expectation that it will enhance organizational performance. This is especially true of strategic management. Through involvement in strategic-management activities, managers and employees achieve a better understanding of an organization's priorities and operations. Strategic management allows organizations to be efficient, but more important, it allows them to be effective. Although strategic management does not guarantee organizational success, the process allows proactive rather than reactive decision making. Strategic management may represent a radical change in philosophy for some organizations, so strategists must be trained to anticipate and constructively respond to questions and issues as they arise. The strategies discussed in this chapter can represent a new beginning for many firms, especially if managers and employees in the organization understand and support the plan for action.

Key Terms and Concepts

Acquisition (p. 155)
Backward Integration (p. 139)
Balanced Scorecard (p. 135)
Bankruptcy (p. 146)
Business-Process Outsourcing (BPO) (p. 158)
Combination Strategy (p. 135)
Cooperative Arrangements (p. 154)
Cost Leadership (p. 148)
De-integration (p. 139)
Differentiation (p. 149)
Diversification Strategies (p. 143)
Divestiture (p. 147)
Financial Objectives (p. 133)
First Mover Advantages (p. 157)
Focus (p. 149)
Forward Integration (p. 138)
Franchising (p. 138)
Friendly Merger (p. 155)
Generic Strategies (p. 148)
Horizontal Integration (p. 140)

Hostile Takeover (p. 155)
Integration Strategies (p. 138)
Intensive Strategies (p. 141)
Joint Venture (p. 153)
Leveraged Buyout (LBO) (p. 157)
Liquidation (p. 148)
Long-Term Objectives (p. 132)
Market Development (p. 141)
Market Penetration (p. 141)
Merger (p. 155)
Product Development (p. 142)
Related Diversification (p. 143)
Retrenchment (p. 146)
Strategic Objectives (p. 133)
Takeover (p. 155)
Turbulent, High-Velocity Markets (p. 152)
Unrelated Diversification (p. 143)
Vertical Integration (p. 138)
White Knight (p. 156)

Issues for Review and Discussion

1. List and describe six major benefits that a firm may reap from outsourcing some of its operations.
2. How are for-profit firms different from nonprofit firms in terms of business? What are the implications for strategic planning?

3. If the CEO of a beverage company such as Dr Pepper/Snapple asked you whether backward or forward integration would be better for the firm, how would you respond?
4. In order of importance, list six "characteristics of objectives."

5. In order of importance, list six "benefits of objectives."

6. Called de-integration, there appears to be a growing trend for firms to become less forward integrated. Discuss why.

7. Called de-integration, there appears to be a growing trend for firms to become less backward integrated. Discuss why.

8. If a company has $1 million to spend on a new strategy and is considering market development versus product development, what determining factors would be most important to consider?

9. What conditions, externally and internally, would be desired/necessary for a firm to diversify?

10. Could a firm simultaneously pursue focus, differentiation, and cost leadership? Should firms do that? Discuss.

11. There is a growing trend of increased collaboration among competitors. List the benefits and drawbacks of this practice.

12. List four major benefits of forming a joint venture to achieve desired objectives.

13. List six major benefits of acquiring another firm to achieve desired objectives.

14. List five reasons why many merger/acquisitions historically have failed.

15. Can you think of any reasons why not-for-profit firms would benefit less from doing strategic planning than for-profit companies?

16. Discuss how important it is for a college football or basketball team to have a good game plan for the big rival game this coming weekend. How much time and effort do you feel the coaching staff puts into developing that game plan? Why is such time and effort essential?

17. Why are more than 60 percent of Fortune 500 firms headquartered in Wilmington, Delaware?

18. Define and give a hypothetical example of a "white knight" in the fast-food industry.

19. How does strategy formulation differ for a small versus a large organization? How does it differ for a for-profit versus a nonprofit organization?

20. Give recent examples of market penetration, market development, and product development.

21. Give recent examples of forward integration, backward integration, and horizontal integration.

22. Give recent examples of related and unrelated diversification.

23. Give recent examples of joint venture, retrenchment, divestiture, and liquidation.

24. Do you think hostile takeovers are unethical? Why or why not?

25. What are the major advantages and disadvantages of diversification?

26. What are the major advantages and disadvantages of an integrative strategy?

27. How does strategic management differ in for-profit and nonprofit organizations?

28. Why is it not advisable to pursue too many strategies at once?

29. Consumers can purchase tennis shoes, food, cars, boats, and insurance on the Internet. Are there any products today than cannot be purchased online? What is the implication for traditional retailers?

30. What are the pros and cons of a firm merging with a rival firm?

31. Compare and contrast financial objectives with strategic objectives. Which type is more important in your opinion? Why?

32. Diagram a two-division organizational chart that includes a CEO, COO, CIO, CSO, CFO, CMO, HRM, R&D, and two division presidents. *Hint:* Division presidents report to the COO.

33. How do the levels of strategy differ in a large firm versus a small firm?

34. List 11 types of strategies. Give a hypothetical example of each strategy listed.

35. Discuss the nature of as well as the pros and cons of a "friendly merger" versus "hostile takeover" in acquiring another firm. Give an example of each.

36. Define and explain "first mover advantages."

37. Define and explain "outsourcing."

38. What strategies are best for turbulent, high-velocity markets?

Notes

1. John Byrne, "Strategic Planning—It's Back," *BusinessWeek*, August 26, 1996, 46.

2. Steven C. Brandt, *Strategic Planning in Emerging Companies* (Reading, MA: Addison-Wesley, 1981). Reprinted with permission of the publisher.

3. R. Kaplan and D. Norton, "Putting the Balanced Scorecard to Work," *Harvard Business Review*, September–October, 1993, 147.

4. F. Hansen and M. Smith, "Crisis in Corporate America: The Role of Strategy," *Business Horizons* (January–February 2003, 9.

5. Adapted from F. R. David, "How Do We Choose Among Alternative Growth Strategies?" *Managerial Planning* 33, no. 4 (January–February 1985): 14–17, 22.

6. Ibid.

7. Kenneth Davidson, "Do Megamergers Make Sense?" *Journal of Business Strategy* 7, no. 3 (Winter 1987): 45.

8. David, "How Do We Choose."

9. Ibid.

10. Ibid.

11. Bruce Horovitz, "Marketing Trends Popping Up in 2011," *USA Today*, January 24, 2011, B1–B2.

12. Bruce Horovitz, "Marketing Trends Popping Up in 2011," *USA Today*, January 24, 2011, B1–B2.

13. David, "How Do we Choose."

14. Arthur Thompson Jr., A. J. Strickland III, and John Gamble, *Crafting and Executing Strategy: Text and Readings* (New York: McGraw-Hill/Irwin, 2005, 241.

15. Michael E. Porter, *Competitive Strategy: Techniques for Analyzing Industries and Competitors* (New York: Free Press, 1980, 53–57, 318–319.

16. Sheila Muto, "Seeing a Boost, Hospitals Turn to Retail Stores," *Wall Street Journal*, November 7, 2001, B1, B8.

17. David, "How Do We Choose."

18. Ibid.

19. Ibid.

20. Ibid.

21. Michael Porter, *Competitive Advantage* (New York: Free Press, 1985), 97. Also, Arthur Thompson Jr., A. J. Strickland III, and John Gamble, *Crafting and Executing Strategy: Text and Readings* (New York: McGraw-Hill/Irwin, 2005), 117.

22. Arthur Thompson Jr., A. J. Strickland III, and John Gamble, *Crafting and Executing Strategy: Text and Readings* (New York: McGraw-Hill/Irwin, 2005), 125–126.

23. Porter, *Competitive Advantage,* 160–162.

24. Thompson, Strickland, and Gamble, 129–130.

25. Ibid., 134.

26. Gary Hamel, Yves Doz, and C. K. Prahalad, "Collaborate with Your Competitors—and Win," *Harvard Business Review* 67, no. 1 (January–February 1989): 133.

27. Scott Morrison, "Facebook, Skype Ponder Alliance," *Wall Street Journal*, September 30, 2010, B4.

28. Kathryn Rudie Harrigan, "Joint Ventures: Linking for a Leap Forward," *Planning Review* 14, no. 4 (July–August 1986): 10.

29. Matthew Schifrin, "Partner or Perish," *Forbes* (May 21, 2001): 26.

30. Ibid., 28.

31. Ibid., 32.

32. Steven Rattner, "Mergers: Windfalls or Pitfalls?" *Wall Street Journal*, October 11, 1999, A22; Nikhil Deogun, "Merger Wave Spurs More Stock Wipeouts," *Wall Street Journal*, November 29, 1999, C1.

33. Joel Millman, "Mexican Mergers/Acquisitions Triple from 2001," *Wall Street Journal*, December 27, 2002, A2.

34. Robert Davis, "Net Empowering Patients," *USA Today*, July 14, 1999, 1A.

35. M. J. Gannon, K. G. Smith, and C. Grimm, "An Organizational Information-Processing Profile of First Movers," *Journal of Business Research* 25 (1992): 231–241; M. B. Lieberman and D. B. Montgomery, "First Mover Advantages," *Strategic Management Journal* 9 (Summer 1988): 41–58.

36. Scott Thurm, "Behind Outsourcing: Promise and Pitfalls," *Wall Street Journal*, February 26, 2007, B3.

37. Louise Radnofsky and Jim Carlton, "Recession-Weary Americans Sour on Free Trade," *Wall Street Journal*, October 4, 2010, A2.

38. http://en.wikipedia.org/wiki/Outsourcing. Also, R. Gareiss, "Analyzing The Outsourcers," *Information Week*, Nov. 18, 2002; D.W. Drezner, "The Outsourcing Bogeyman," 2004, www.foreignaffairs.org; P. Engardio, (2006). "Outsourcing: Job Killer or Innovation Boost?" *Business Week*, 2006; Justin Chakma, Jeff L. Calcagno, Ali Behbahani, and Shawn Moitahedian, "Is it Virtuous to be Virtual? The VC Viewpoint." *Nature Biotechnology* 27, no. 10 (October 2009).

39. Shelly Banjo, "Churches Find End is Nigh," *Wall Street Journal*, January 25, 2011, A3.

40. Kelly Spors, "So, You Want to Be an Entrepreneur," *Wall Street Journal*, February 28, 2009, R1.

Current Readings

Adegbesan, J. Adetunji, and Matthew J. Higgins. "The Intra-Alliance of Value Created Through Collaboration." *Strategic Management Journal* 32, no. 2 (February 2011): 187–211.

Bruton, Garry D., Igor Filatotchev, Salim Chahine, and Mike Wright. "Governance, Ownership Structure, and Performance of IPO Firms: The Impact of Different Types of Private Equity Investors and Institutional Environments." *Strategic Management Journal* 31, no. 5 (May 2010): 491–509.

Cedergren, Stefan, Anders Wall, and Christer Norstrom. "Evaluation of Performance in a Product Development Context." *Business Horizons* 53, no. 4 (July–August 2010): 359–370.

Combs, James G., David J. Ketchen Jr., Christopher L. Shook, and Jeremy C. Short. "Antecedents and Consequences of Franchising: Past Accomplishments and Future Challenges." *Journal of Management* 37, no. 1 (January 2011): 99–126.

Datta, Deepak K., James P. Guthrie, Dynah Basuil, and Alankrita Pandey. "Causes and Effects of Employee Downsizing: A Review and Synthesis." *Journal of Management* 36, no. 1 (January 2010): 281–348.

David, Parthiban, Jonathan P. O'Brien, Toru Yoshikawa, and Andrew Delios. "Do Shareholders or Stakeholders Appropriate the Rents from Corporate Diversification? The Influence of Ownership Structure." *The Academy of Management Journal* 53, no. 3 (June 2010): 636–648.

Graebner, Melissa E., Kathleen M. Eisenhardt, and Philip T. Roundy. "Success and Failure in Technology Acquisitions: Lessons for Buyers and Sellers." *The Academy of Management Perspectives* 24, no. 3 (August 2010): 73–92.

Kaplan, Robert S., David P. Norton, and Bjarne Rugelsjoen. "Managing Alliances with the Balanced Scorecard." *Harvard Business Review*, January–February 2010, 114–124.

Kumar, M. V. Shyam. "Are Joint Ventures Positive Sum Games? The Relative Effects of Cooperative and Noncooperative Behavior." *Strategic Management Journal* 32, no. 1 (January 2011): 32–54.

Lee, Gwendolyn K., and Marvin Lieberman. "Acquisition vs. Internal Development As Modes of Market Entry." *Strategic Management Journal* 31, no. 2 (February 2010): 140–158.

Lansiluoto, Aapo, and Marko Jarvenpaa. "Greening the Balanced Scorecard." *Business Horizons* 53, no. 4 (July–August 2010): 385–396.

Martin, John A., and Kevin J. Davis. "Learning of Hubris? Why CEOs Create Less Value in Successive Acquisitions." *The Academy of Management Perspectives* 24, no. 1 (February 2010): 79.

Rawley, Evan. "Diversification, Coordination Costs, and Organizational Rigidity: Evidence From Microdata." *Strategic Management Journal* 31, no. 8 (August 2010): 873–891.

Reitzig, Markus, and Stefan Wagner. "The Hidden Costs of Outsourcing: Evidence From Patent Data." *Strategic Management Journal* 31, no. 11 (November 2010): 1183–1201.

Salomon, Robert, and Byungchae Jin. "Do Leading or Lagging Firms Learn More From Exporting?" *Strategic Management Journal* 31, no. 10 (October 2010): 1088–1113.

Siegel, Donald S., and Kenneth L. Simons. "Assessing the Effects of Mergers and Acquisitions on Firm Performance, Plant Productivity, and Workers: Evidence From Matched Employer-Employee Data. *Strategic Management Journal* 31, no. 8 (August 2010): 903–916.

Upson, John W., and Annette L. Ranft. "When Strategies Collide: Divergent Multipoint Strategies Within Competitive Triads." *Business Horizons* 53, no. 1 (January–February 2010): 49–58.

Yu, Jifeng, Brett Anitra Gilbert, and Benjamin M. Oviatt. "Effects of Alliances, Time, and Network Cohesion on the Initiation of Foreign Sales by New Ventures." *Strategic Management Journal* 32, no. 4 (April 2011): 424–446.

Wassmer, Ulrich. "Alliance Portfolios: A Review and Research Agenda." *Journal of Management* 36, no. 1 (January 2010): 141–171.

Wassmer, Ulrich, Pierre Dussauge, and Marcel Planellas. "How to Manage Alliances Better Than One at a Time." *MIT Sloan Management Review* 51, no. 3 (Spring 2010): 77–84.

ASSURANCE OF LEARNING EXERCISES

Assurance of Learning Exercise 5A

Develop Hypothetical Disney Strategies

Purpose

Table 5-4 identifies, defines, and exemplifies 11 key types of strategies available to firms. This exercise will give you practice formulating possible strategies within each broad category.

Instructions

Step 1 On a clear sheet of paper, develop an 11 x 2 matrix where two Disney divisions are along the top and the 11 Table 5-4 strategies are along the left side of your paper. In other words, along the top you will have any two of the following five captions: 1) Media Networks, 2) Parks & Resorts, 3) Studio Entertainment, 4) Consumer Products; and 5) Interactive Media, and along the left side of your paper, simply write the basic Table 5-4 strategy types as described in the chapter.

Step 2 Review the text material related to Table 5-4. Also, review the Disney divisional information provided in both the company *Annual Report* and *Form 10K*.

Step 3 In each of the 22 cells within your 11 x 2 matrix, write in a hypothetical strategy for the respective business segment indicated.

Assurance of Learning 5B

Evaluate Disney Divisions in Terms of Porter's Strategies

Purpose

Figure 5-3 and associated narrative describe Porter's five generic strategies. Disney has five business segments. This exercise will give you practice assessing the degree or extent that various segments or divisions of a business utilize or follow Porter's generic strategies.

Instructions

Step 1   On a clear sheet of paper, develop a 5 × 5 matrix where the five Disney divisions are along the top and the five Porter strategies are along the left side of your paper. In other words, along the top you will have the captions 1) Media Networks, 2) Parks & Resorts, 3) Studio Entertainment, 4) Consumer Products; and 5) Interactive Media and along the left side of your paper simply write Type 1, Type 2, Type 3, Type 4, and Type 5 that refer to Porter's basic strategy types as described in the chapter.

Step 2   Review the text material that explains Porter's five strategies. Also, review the Disney divisional information provided in the company *Annual Report* and *Form 10K* as well as in the Cohesion Case.

Step 3   In each of the 25 cells within your 5 × 5 matrix, write the word High, Medium, or Low to indicate the extent or degree that the respective Disney division utilizes or follows the respective Porter strategy.

Step 4   Write a one to two page Executive Summary that reveals your rationale for your assigned High, Medium, and Low assessments, as well as your overall evaluation of the effectiveness of the Disney strategy—particularly in light of the conditions listed in the chapter for each Porter strategy in terms of when it is most attractive.

Step 5   In your 5 × 5 matrix, consider adding a sixth row along the bottom to indicate what grade (A, B, C, D, or F) you would give each Disney segment for their overall strategy formulation and implementation efforts.

Assurance of Learning Exercise 5C

What Strategies Should Disney Pursue in 2013?

Purpose

In performing strategic management case analysis, you can find information about the respective company's actual and planned strategies. Comparing *what is planned* versus *what you recommend* is an important part of case analysis. Do not recommend what the firm actually plans, unless in-depth analysis of the situation reveals those strategies to be best among all feasible alternatives. This exercise gives you experience conducting library and Internet research to determine what Disney is doing in 2012 and should do in 2013.

Instructions

Step 1   Look up DIS using the websites provided in Table 4-5. Find some recent articles about Disney. Also review recent news releases at the DIS website.

Step 2   Summarize your findings in a three-page report entitled "My Thoughts on Strategies Being Pursued by Disney in 2013."

Assurance of Learning Exercise 5D

Examine Strategy Articles

Purpose

Strategy articles can be found weekly in journals, magazines, and newspapers. By reading and studying strategy articles, you can gain a better understanding of the strategic-management process. Several of the best journals in which to find corporate strategy articles are *Advanced Management Journal, Business Horizons, Long Range Planning, Journal of Business Strategy*, and *Strategic Management Journal*. These journals are devoted to reporting the results of empirical research in management. They apply strategic-management concepts to specific organizations and industries. They introduce new strategic-management techniques and provide short case studies on selected firms.

Other good journals in which to find strategic-management articles are *Harvard Business Review, Sloan Management Review, California Management Review, Academy of Management Review, Academy of Management Journal, Academy of Management Executive, Journal of Management*, and *Journal of Small Business Management*.

In addition to journals, many magazines regularly publish articles that focus on business strategies. Several of the best magazines in which to find applied strategy articles are *Dun's Business Month, Fortune, Forbes, BusinessWeek, Inc.,* and *Industry Week.* Newspapers such as *USA Today, Wall Street Journal, New York Times,* and *Barrons* cover strategy events when they occur—for example, a joint venture announcement, a bankruptcy declaration, a new advertising campaign start, acquisition of a company, divestiture of a division, a chief executive officer's hiring or firing, or a hostile takeover attempt.

In combination, journal, magazine, and newspaper articles can make the strategic-management course more exciting. They allow current strategies of for-profit and nonprofit organizations to be identified and studied.

Instructions

Step 1   Go to your college library and find a recent journal article that focuses on a strategic-management topic. Select your article from one of the journals listed previously, not from a magazine. Copy the article and bring it to class.

Step 2   Give a 3-minute oral report summarizing the most important information in your article. Include comments giving your personal reaction to the article. Pass your article around in class.

Assurance of Learning Exercise 5E

Classify Some Year 2011 Strategies

Purpose

This exercise can improve your understanding of various strategies by giving you experience classifying strategies. This skill will help you use the strategy-formulation tools presented later. Consider the following sixteen actual year-2011 strategies by various firms:

1. General Electric sold its NBC Universal division to Comcast for $6.5 billion.
2. Vision Airlines added more than 40 new cities to its flight destination portfolio.
3. J.C. Penney closed many of its stores, outlets, call centers, and its catalog business.
4. Citigroup sold its EMI Group Ltd. music company.
5. Nestle S.A. acquired CM&D Pharma Ltd., the first move by Nestle to sell foods that target diseases.
6. Caterpillar recently acquired Bucyrus International, another mining equipment maker.
7. Limited Brands opened its first Victoria's Secret in Canada.
8. Wal-Mart opened 40 new supercenters in Canada.
9. The top four advertisers (in order) during Super Bowl XLV were Anheuser-Busch (InBev), PepsiCo, General Motors, and Paramount Pictures, each having at least five 30-second ads.
10. Grocery-store chain SuperValu Inc. is closing underperforming stores and laying off employees.
11. General Motors entered the entertainment business by producing the "Inside the Vault" television series.
12. Caesars Entertainment opens its first noncasino hotel in Asia.
13. AOL laid off 20 percent of its work force in mid-2011.
14. Wal-Mart's 40 new Express stores opened at a cost of $1.2 million each; each store has a pharmacy, grocery section, 75 parking spaces, and three or four checkouts.
15. Dell Inc. spent $1 billion to move away from its PC focus to providing cloud-computing services.
16. Siemens sold its Osram lighting unit, which had generated $6.6 billion in 2010.

Instructions

Step 1   On a separate sheet of paper, number from 1 to 16. These numbers correspond to the strategies described.

Step 2   What type of strategy best describes the sixteen actions cited? Indicate your answers.

Step 3   Exchange papers with a classmate, and grade each other's paper as your instructor gives the right answers.

Assurance of Learning Exercise 5F

How Risky Are Various Alternative Strategies?

Purpose

This exercise focuses on how risky various alternative strategies are for organizations to pursue. Different degrees of risk are based largely on varying degrees of *externality*, defined as movement away from present business into new markets and products. In general, the greater the degree of externality, the greater the probability of loss resulting from unexpected events. High-risk strategies generally are less attractive than low-risk strategies.

Instructions

Step 1	On a separate sheet of paper, number vertically from 1 to 10. Think of 1 as "most risky," 2 as "next most risky," and so forth to 10, "least risky."
Step 2	Write the following strategies beside the appropriate number to indicate how risky you believe the strategy is to pursue: horizontal integration, related diversification, liquidation, forward integration, backward integration, product development, market development, market penetration, retrenchment, and unrelated diversification.
Step 3	Grade your paper as your instructor gives you the right answers and supporting rationale. Each correct answer is worth 10 points.

Assurance of Learning Exercise 5G

Develop Alternative Strategies for My University

Purpose

It is important for representatives from all areas of a college or university to identify and discuss alternative strategies that could benefit faculty, students, alumni, staff, and other constituencies. As you complete this exercise, notice the learning and understanding that occurs as people express differences of opinion. Recall that *the process of planning is more important than the document.*

Instructions

Step 1	Recall or locate the external opportunity/threat and internal strength/weakness factors that you identified as part of Exercise 1D. If you did not do that exercise, discuss now as a class important external and internal factors facing your college or university.
Step 2	Identify and put on the chalkboard alternative strategies that you feel could benefit your college or university. Your proposed actions should allow the institution to capitalize on particular strengths, improve upon certain weaknesses, avoid external threats, and/or take advantage of particular external opportunities. List 10 possible strategies on the board. Number the strategies as they are written on the board.
Step 3	On a separate sheet of paper, number from 1 to 10. Everyone in class individually should rate the strategies identified, using a 1 to 3 scale, where 1 = *I do not support implementation*, 2 = *I am neutral about implementation*, and 3 = *I strongly support implementation*. In rating the strategies, recognize that your institution cannot do everything desired or potentially beneficial.
Step 4	Go to the board and record your ratings in a row beside the respective strategies. Everyone in class should do this, going to the board perhaps by rows in the class.
Step 5	Sum the ratings for each strategy so that a prioritized list of recommended strategies is obtained. This prioritized list reflects the collective wisdom of your class. Strategies with the highest score are deemed best.
Step 6	Discuss how this process could enable organizations to achieve understanding and commitment from individuals.
Step 7	Share your class results with a university administrator, and ask for comments regarding the process and top strategies recommended.

Assurance of Learning Exercise 5H

Lessons in Doing Business Globally

Purpose
The purpose of this exercise is to discover some important lessons learned by local businesses that do business internationally.

Instructions
Contact several local business leaders by phone. Find at least three firms that engage in international or export operations. Visit the owner or manager of each business in person. Ask the businessperson to give you several important lessons that his or her firm has learned in globally doing business. Record the lessons on paper, and report your findings to the class.

"NOTABLE QUOTES"

"Strategic management is not a box of tricks or a bundle of techniques. It is analytical thinking and commitment of resources to action. But quantification alone is not planning. Some of the most important issues in strategic management cannot be quantified at all."
—*Peter Drucker*

"Objectives are not commands; they are commitments. They do not determine the future; they are the means to mobilize resources and energies of an organization for the making of the future."
—*Peter Drucker*

"Life is full of lousy options."
—*General P. X. Kelley*

"When a crisis forces choosing among alternatives, most people will choose the worst possible one."
—*Rudin's Law*

"Strategy isn't something you can nail together in slapdash fashion by sitting around a conference table."
—*Terry Haller*

"Planning is often doomed before it ever starts, either because too much is expected of it or because not enough is put into it."
—*T. J. Cartwright*

"Whether it's broke or not, fix it—make it better. Not just products, but the whole company if necessary."
—*Bill Saporito*

Strategy Analysis and Choice

CHAPTER OBJECTIVES

After studying this chapter, you should be able to do the following:

1. Describe a three-stage framework for choosing among alternative strategies.

2. Explain how to develop a SWOT Matrix, SPACE Matrix, BCG Matrix, IE Matrix, and QSPM.

3. Identify important behavioral, political, ethical, and social responsibility considerations in strategy analysis and choice.

4. Discuss the role of intuition in strategic analysis and choice.

5. Discuss the role of organizational culture in strategic analysis and choice.

6. Discuss the role of a board of directors in choosing among alternative strategies.

ASSURANCE OF LEARNING EXERCISES

Assurance of Learning Exercise 6A
Perform a SWOT Analysis for Disney's Parks & Resorts Business Segment

Assurance of Learning Exercise 6B
Develop a SWOT Matrix for Walt Disney

Assurance of Learning Exercise 6C
Develop a SPACE Matrix for Disney's Media Networks Business Segment

Assurance of Learning Exercise 6D
Develop a SPACE Matrix for Walt Disney

Assurance of Learning Exercise 6E
Develop a BCG Matrix for Walt Disney

Assurance of Learning Exercise 6F
Develop a QSPM for Walt Disney

Assurance of Learning Exercise 6G
Formulate Individual Strategies

Assurance of Learning Exercise 6H
The Mach Test

Assurance of Learning Exercise 6I
Develop a BCG Matrix for My University

Assurance of Learning Exercise 6J
The Role of Boards of Directors

Assurance of Learning Exercise 6K
Locate Companies in a Grand Strategy Matrix

Strategy analysis and choice largely involve making subjective decisions based on objective information. This chapter introduces important concepts that can help strategists generate feasible alternatives, evaluate those alternatives, and choose a specific course of action. Behavioral aspects of strategy formulation are described, including politics, culture, ethics, and social responsibility considerations. Modern tools for formulating strategies are described, and the appropriate role of a board of directors is discussed. Netfix Inc. is an example company pursuing an excellent strategic plan.

The Nature of Strategy Analysis and Choice

As indicated by Figure 6-1, this chapter focuses on generating and evaluating alternative strategies, as well as selecting strategies to pursue. Strategy analysis and choice seek to determine alternative courses of action that could best enable the firm to achieve its mission and objectives. The firm's present strategies, objectives, and mission, coupled with the external and internal audit information, provide a basis for generating and evaluating feasible alternative strategies.

Excellent Strategic Management Showcased

NETFLIX, INC.

Based in Los Gatos, California, Netflix posted a 39 percent profit increase and a 29 percent revenue increase for 2010 as the firm dominated the movie-streaming services industry. Netflix profits for the first quarter of 2011 jumped another 83.6 percent as its revenues jumped 46 percent and its number of subscribers jumped 69 percent. Netflix's more than 30 million customers pay as little as $7.99 per month to watch an unlimited number of movies and TV episodes streamed over the Internet to PCs, Macs, and TVs. Netflix is doing much better than rival firms Showtime, Starz owned by Liberty Media, Home Box Office (HBO) owned by Time Warner, Blockbuster, and Red Box. Netflix has excellent strategic planning processes and procedures. Netflix is the world's leading Internet subscription service for enjoying movies and TV shows. Netflix has the second-largest video subscription base of customers, behind Comcast.

Among the large and expanding base of devices streaming Netflix products are Microsoft's Xbox 360, Nintendo's Wii, and Sony's PS3 consoles; an array of Blu-ray disc players, Internet-connected TVs, home theater systems, digital video recorders, and Internet video players; Apple's iPhone, iPad, and iPod touch; as well as Apple TV and Google TV. In all, more than 200 devices that stream from Netflix are available in the United States and a growing number are available in Canada. Netflix's stock price tripled in the last 12 months to a high of $296 per share in July 2011.

Although Amazon is maneuvering into the video streaming business, Netflix may dominate the industry for years since Netflix mailers are in 20 million homes and Netflix is integrated into nearly every new TV, Blu-ray player, game device, and smart phone. Also to Netflix's benefit, DVDs still matter because people like seeing the latest movies that studios won't stream via Netflix or Amazon. People like getting their HBO and other disc-only content for a reasonable cost,

and nearly everyone still has a DVD or Blu-ray player and plays DVDs on their computers.

In addition to Amazon being a rival of concern, Netflix also contends with 1) Comcast, which has 22.8 million customers, and 2) DIRECTV, the satellite television company that has 20 million subscribers in North America. DIRECTV is gaining the ground that Comcast is yielding. DIRECTV has another 5.4 million subscribers in Latin America. Also a rival to Netflix is Sirius XM, the one and only satellite radio company, which currently has 20.2 million subscribers, growing to 21.6 million accounts by the end of 2011. But all in all, Netflix is an excellent company using excellent strategic planning tools and concepts to stay on top of a rapidly changing industry.

Netflix has secured exclusive distribution rights for *House of Cards*, an original series directed by Hollywood hotshot David Fincher of *The Social Network* fame. The rumored deal is for Netflix to pay about $100 million for two full seasons of the political drama based on a BBC show starring Kevin Spacey. Media Rights Capital is producing the show.

Source: Based on Nick Wingfield, "Netflix See's Surge in Subscribers," *Wall Street Journal*, January 27, 2011, B9. Also, company documents.

FIGURE 6-1

A Comprehensive Strategic-Management Model

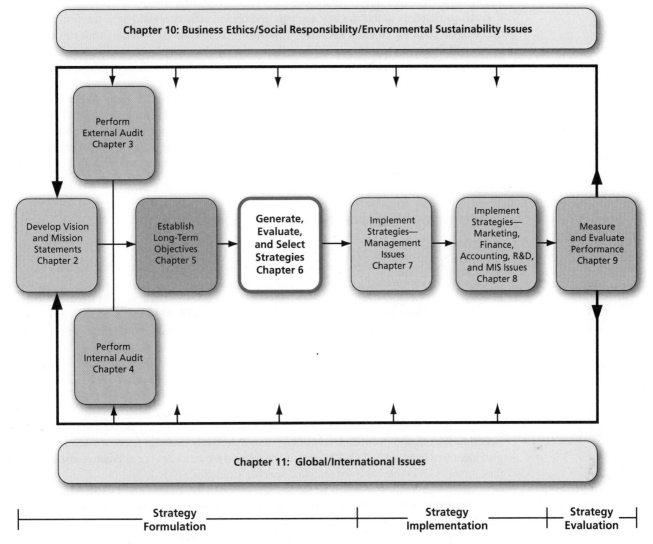

Source: Fred R. David, "How Companies Define Their Mission," *Long Range Planning* 22, no. 3 (June 1988): 40.

Unless a desperate situation confronts the firm, alternative strategies will likely represent incremental steps that move the firm from its present position to a desired future position. Alternative strategies do not come out of the wild blue yonder; they are derived from the firm's vision, mission, objectives, external audit, and internal audit; they are consistent with, or build on, past strategies that have worked well.

The Process of Generating and Selecting Strategies

Strategists never consider all feasible alternatives that could benefit the firm because there are an infinite number of possible actions and an infinite number of ways to implement those actions. Therefore, a manageable set of the most attractive alternative strategies must be developed. The advantages, disadvantages, trade-offs, costs, and benefits of these strategies should be determined. This section discusses the process that many firms use to determine an appropriate set of alternative strategies.

Identifying and evaluating alternative strategies should involve many of the managers and employees who earlier assembled the organizational vision and mission statements, performed the external audit, and conducted the internal audit. Representatives from each department and division of the firm should be included in this process, as was the case in previous strategy-formulation activities. Recall that involvement provides the best opportunity for managers and employees to gain an understanding of what the firm is doing and why and to become committed to helping the firm accomplish its objectives.

All participants in the strategy analysis and choice activity should have the firm's external and internal audit information available. This information, coupled with the firm's mission statement, will help participants crystallize in their own minds particular strategies that they believe could benefit the firm most. Creativity should be encouraged in this thought process.

Alternative strategies proposed by participants should be considered and discussed in a meeting or series of meetings. Proposed strategies should be listed in writing. When all feasible strategies identified by participants are given and understood, the strategies should be ranked in order of attractiveness by all participants, with 1 = should not be implemented, 2 = possibly should be implemented, 3 = probably should be implemented, and 4 = definitely should be implemented. This process will result in a prioritized list of best strategies that reflects the collective wisdom of the group.

A Comprehensive Strategy-Formulation Framework

Important strategy-formulation techniques can be integrated into a three-stage decision-making framework, as shown in Figure 6-2. The tools presented in this framework are applicable to all sizes and types of organizations and can help strategists identify, evaluate, and select strategies.

Stage 1 of the formulation framework consists of the EFE Matrix, the IFE Matrix, and the Competitive Profile Matrix (CPM). Called the *Input Stage,* Stage 1 summarizes the basic input information needed to formulate strategies. Stage 2, called the *Matching Stage,* focuses upon generating feasible alternative strategies by aligning key external and internal factors. Stage 2 techniques include the Strengths-Weaknesses-Opportunities-Threats (SWOT) Matrix, the Strategic Position and Action Evaluation (SPACE) Matrix, the Boston Consulting Group (BCG) Matrix, the Internal-External (IE) Matrix, and the Grand Strategy Matrix. Stage 3, called the *Decision Stage,* involves a single technique, the Quantitative Strategic Planning Matrix (QSPM). A QSPM uses input information from Stage 1 to objectively evaluate feasible alternative strategies identified in Stage 2. A QSPM reveals the relative attractiveness of alternative strategies and thus provides objective basis for selecting specific strategies.

All nine techniques included in the *strategy-formulation framework* require the integration of intuition and analysis. Autonomous divisions in an organization commonly use strategy-formulation techniques to develop strategies and objectives. Divisional analyses provide a basis for identifying, evaluating, and selecting among alternative corporate-level strategies.

FIGURE 6-2

The Strategy-Formulation Analytical Framework

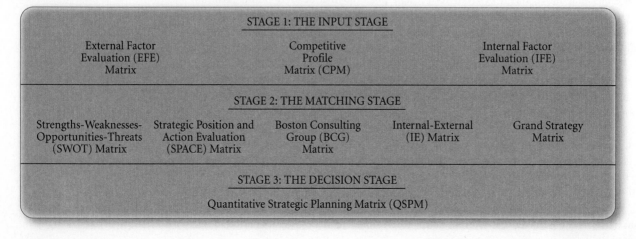

STAGE 1: THE INPUT STAGE		
External Factor Evaluation (EFE) Matrix	Competitive Profile Matrix (CPM)	Internal Factor Evaluation (IFE) Matrix

STAGE 2: THE MATCHING STAGE				
Strengths-Weaknesses-Opportunities-Threats (SWOT) Matrix	Strategic Position and Action Evaluation (SPACE) Matrix	Boston Consulting Group (BCG) Matrix	Internal-External (IE) Matrix	Grand Strategy Matrix

STAGE 3: THE DECISION STAGE
Quantitative Strategic Planning Matrix (QSPM)

Strategists themselves, not analytic tools, are always responsible and accountable for strategic decisions. Lenz emphasized that the shift from a words-oriented to a numbers-oriented planning process can give rise to a false sense of certainty; it can reduce dialogue, discussion, and argument as a means for exploring understandings, testing assumptions, and fostering organizational learning.[1] Strategists, therefore, must be wary of this possibility and use analytical tools to facilitate, rather than to diminish, communication. Without objective information and analysis, personal biases, politics, emotions, personalities, and *halo error* (the tendency to put too much weight on a single factor) unfortunately may play a dominant role in the strategy-formulation process.

The Input Stage

Procedures for developing an EFE Matrix, an IFE Matrix, and a CPM were presented in Chapters 3 and 4. The information derived from these three matrices provides basic input information for the matching and decision stage matrices described later in this chapter.

The input tools require strategists to quantify subjectivity during early stages of the strategy-formulation process. Making small decisions in the input matrices regarding the relative importance of external and internal factors allows strategists to more effectively generate and evaluate alternative strategies. Good intuitive judgment is always needed in determining appropriate weights and ratings.

The Matching Stage

Strategy is sometimes defined as the match an organization makes between its internal resources and skills and the opportunities and risks created by its external factors.[2] The matching stage of the strategy-formulation framework consists of five techniques that can be used in any sequence: the SWOT Matrix, the SPACE Matrix, the BCG Matrix, the IE Matrix, and the Grand Strategy Matrix. These tools rely upon information derived from the input stage to match external opportunities and threats with internal strengths and weaknesses. *Matching* external and internal critical success factors is the key to effectively generating feasible alternative strategies. For example, a firm with excess working capital (an internal strength) could take advantage of the cell phone industry's 20 percent annual growth rate (an external opportunity) by acquiring Cellfone, Inc., a firm in the cell phone industry. This example portrays simple one-to-one matching. In most situations, external and internal relationships are more complex, and the matching requires multiple alignments for each strategy generated. The basic concept of matching is illustrated in Table 6-1.

Any organization, whether military, product-oriented, service-oriented, governmental, or even athletic, must develop and execute good strategies to win. A good offense without a good defense, or vice versa, usually leads to defeat. Developing strategies that use strengths to capitalize on opportunities could be considered an offense, whereas strategies designed to improve upon weaknesses while avoiding threats could be termed defensive. Every organization has some external opportunities and threats and internal strengths and weaknesses that can be aligned to formulate feasible alternative strategies.

TABLE 6-1   Matching Key External and Internal Factors to Formulate Alternative Strategies

Key Internal Factor	Key External Factor	Resultant Strategy
Excess working capital (an internal strength)	+ 20 percent annual growth in the cell phone industry (an external opportunity)	= Acquire Cellfone, Inc.
Insufficient capacity (an internal weakness)	+ Exit of two major foreign competitors from the industry (an external opportunity)	= Pursue horizontal integration by buying competitors' facilities
Strong R&D expertise (an internal strength)	+ Decreasing numbers of younger adults (an external threat)	= Develop new products for older adults
Poor employee morale (an internal weakness)	+ Rising health care costs (an external threat)	= Develop a new wellness program

The *Strengths-Weaknesses-Opportunities-Threats (SWOT) Matrix* is an important matching tool that helps managers develop four types of strategies: SO (strengths-opportunities) Strategies, WO (weaknesses-opportunities) Strategies, ST (strengths-threats) Strategies, and WT (weaknesses-threats) Strategies.[3] Matching key external and internal factors is the most difficult part of developing a SWOT Matrix and requires good judgment—and there is no one best set of matches. Note in Table 6-1 that the first, second, third, and fourth strategies are SO, WO, ST, and WT strategies, respectively.

SO Strategies use a firm's internal strengths to take advantage of external opportunities. All managers would like their organizations to be in a position in which internal strengths can be used to take advantage of external trends and events. Organizations generally will pursue WO, ST, or WT strategies to get into a situation in which they can apply SO Strategies. When a firm has major weaknesses, it will strive to overcome them and make them strengths. When an organization faces major threats, it will seek to avoid them to concentrate on opportunities.

WO Strategies aim at improving internal weaknesses by taking advantage of external opportunities. Sometimes key external opportunities exist, but a firm has internal weaknesses that prevent it from exploiting those opportunities. For example, there may be a high demand for electronic devices to control the amount and timing of fuel injection in automobile engines (opportunity), but a certain auto parts manufacturer may lack the technology required for producing these devices (weakness). One possible WO Strategy would be to acquire this technology by forming a joint venture with a firm having competency in this area. An alternative WO Strategy would be to hire and train people with the required technical capabilities.

ST Strategies use a firm's strengths to avoid or reduce the impact of external threats. This does not mean that a strong organization should always meet threats in the external environment head-on. An example ST Strategy occurred when Texas Instruments used an excellent legal department (a strength) to collect nearly $700 million in damages and royalties from nine Japanese and Korean firms that infringed on patents for semiconductor memory chips (threat). Rival firms that copy ideas, innovations, and patented products are a major threat in many industries. This is still a major problem for U.S. firms selling products in China.

WT Strategies are defensive tactics directed at reducing internal weakness and avoiding external threats. An organization faced with numerous external threats and internal weaknesses may indeed be in a precarious position. In fact, such a firm may have to fight for its survival, merge, retrench, declare bankruptcy, or choose liquidation.

A schematic representation of the SWOT Matrix is provided in Figure 6-3. Note that a SWOT Matrix is composed of nine cells. As shown, there are four key factor cells, four strategy cells, and one cell that is always left blank (the upper-left cell). The four strategy cells, labeled *SO, WO, ST,* and *WT,* are developed after completing four key factor cells, labeled *S, W, O,* and *T.* There are eight steps involved in constructing a SWOT Matrix:

1. List the firm's key external opportunities.
2. List the firm's key external threats.
3. List the firm's key internal strengths.
4. List the firm's key internal weaknesses.
5. Match internal strengths with external opportunities, and record the resultant SO Strategies in the appropriate cell.
6. Match internal weaknesses with external opportunities, and record the resultant WO Strategies.
7. Match internal strengths with external threats, and record the resultant ST Strategies.
8. Match internal weaknesses with external threats, and record the resultant WT Strategies.

Some important aspects of a SWOT Matrix are evidenced in Figure 6-3. For example, note that both the internal/external factors and the SO/ST/WO/WT Strategies are stated in quantitative terms to the extent possible. This is important. For example, regarding the second SO #2 and ST #1 strategies, if the analyst just said, "Add new repair/service persons," the reader might think that 20 new repair/service persons are needed. Actually only two are needed. Always *be specific* to the extent possible in stating factors and strategies.

It is also important to include the "S1, O2" type notation after each strategy in a SWOT Matrix. This notation reveals the rationale for each alternative strategy. Strategies do not rise out of the blue. Note in Figure 6-3 how this notation reveals the internal/external factors that were matched to formulate desirable strategies. For example, note that this retail computer store business may need to "purchase land to build new store" because a new Highway 34 will make its location less desirable. The notation (W2, O2) and (S8, T3) in Figure 6-3 exemplifies this matching process.

FIGURE 6-3

A SWOT Matrix for a Retail Computer Store

	Strengths	Weaknesses
	1. Inventory turnover up 5.8 to 6.7	1. Software revenues in store down 12%
	2. Average customer purchase up $97 to $128	2. Location of store hurt by new Hwy 34
	3. Employee morale is excellent	3. Carpet and paint in store in disrepair
	4. In-store promotions = 20% increase in sales	4. Bathroom in store needs refurbishing
	5. Newspaper advertising expenditures down 10%	5. Total store revenues down 8%
	6. Revenues from repair/service in store up 16%	6. Store has no website
	7. In-store technical support persons have MIS degrees	7. Supplier on-time-delivery up to 2.4 days
	8. Store's debt-to-total-assets ratio down 34%	8. Customer checkout process too slow
		9. Revenues per employee up 19%
Opportunities	**SO Strategies**	**WO Strategies**
1. Population of city growing 10%	1. Add 4 new in-store promotions monthly (S4, O3)	1. Purchase land to build new store (W2, O2)
2. Rival computer store opening 1 mile away	2. Add 2 new repair/service persons (S6, O5)	2. Install new carpet/paint/bath (W3, W4, O1)
3. Vehicle traffic passing store up 12%	3. Send flyer to all seniors over age 55 (S5, O5)	3. Up website services by 50% (W6, O7, O8)
4. Vendors average six new products/yr		4. Launch mailout to all realtors in city (W5, O7)
5. Senior citizen use of computers up 8%		
6. Small business growth in area up 10%		
7. Desire for websites up 18% by realtors		
8. Desire for websites up 12% by small firms		
Threats	**ST Strategies**	**WT Strategies**
1. Best Buy opening new store in 1 yr nearby	1. Hire 2 more repair persons and market these new services (S6, S7, T1)	1. Hire 2 new cashiers (W8, T1, T4)
2. Local university offers computer repair	2. Purchase land to build new store (S8, T3)	2. Install new carpet/paint/bath (W3, W4, T1)
3. New bypass Hwy 34 in 1 yr will divert traffic	3. Raise out-of-store service calls from $60 to $80 (S6, T5)	
4. New mall being built nearby		
5. Gas prices up 14%		
6. Vendors raising prices 8%		

The purpose of each Stage 2 matching tool is to generate feasible alternative strategies, not to select or determine which strategies are best. Not all of the strategies developed in the SWOT Matrix, therefore, will be selected for implementation.

The strategy-formulation guidelines provided in Chapter 5 can enhance the process of matching key external and internal factors. For example, when an organization has both the capital and human resources needed to distribute its own products (internal strength) and distributors are unreliable, costly, or incapable of meeting the firm's needs (external threat), forward integration can be an attractive ST Strategy. When a firm has excess production capacity (internal weakness) and its basic industry is experiencing declining annual sales and profits (external threat), related diversification can be an effective WT Strategy.

Although the SWOT matrix is widely used in strategic planning, the analysis does have some limitations.[4] First, SWOT does not show how to achieve a competitive advantage, so it must not be an end in itself. The matrix should be the starting point for a discussion on how proposed strategies could be implemented as well as cost-benefit considerations that ultimately could lead to competitive advantage. Second, SWOT is a static assessment (or snapshot) in time. A SWOT matrix can be like studying a single frame of a motion picture where you see the lead characters and the setting but have no clue as to the plot. As circumstances, capabilities, threats, and strategies change, the dynamics of a competitive environment may not be revealed in a single matrix. Third, SWOT analysis may lead the firm to overemphasize a single internal or external factor in formulating strategies. There are interrelationships among the key internal and external factors that SWOT does not reveal that may be important in devising strategies.

The Strategic Position and Action Evaluation (SPACE) Matrix

The *Strategic Position and Action Evaluation (SPACE) Matrix,* another important Stage 2 matching tool, is illustrated in Figure 6-4. Its four-quadrant framework indicates whether aggressive, conservative, defensive, or competitive strategies are most appropriate for a given organization. The axes of the SPACE Matrix represent two internal dimensions (*financial position [FP]* and *competitive position [CP]*) and two external dimensions (*stability position [SP]* and *industry position [IP]*). These four factors are perhaps the most important determinants of an organization's overall strategic position.[5]

Depending on the type of organization, numerous variables could make up each of the dimensions represented on the axes of the SPACE Matrix. Factors that were included earlier in the firm's EFE and IFE Matrices should be considered in developing a SPACE Matrix. Other variables commonly included are given in Table 6-2. For example, return on investment, leverage,

FIGURE 6-4

The SPACE Matrix

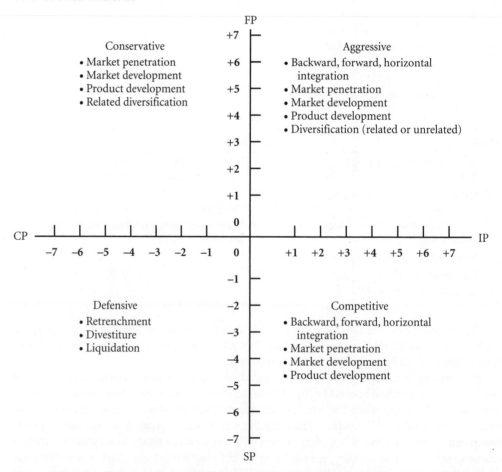

Source: Adapted from H. Rowe, R. Mason, and K. Dickel, *Strategic Management and Business Policy: A Methodological Approach* (Reading, MA: Addison-Wesley Publishing Co. Inc., © 1982), 155.

TABLE 6-2   Example Factors That Make Up the SPACE Matrix Axes

Internal Strategic Position	External Strategic Position
Financial Position (FP)	*Stability Position (SP)*
Return on investment	Technological changes
Leverage	Rate of inflation
Liquidity	Demand variability
Working capital	Price range of competing products
Cash flow	Barriers to entry into market
Inventory turnover	Competitive pressure
Earnings per share	Ease of exit from market
Price earnings ratio	Price elasticity of demand
	Risk involved in business
Competitive Position (CP)	*Industry Position (IP)*
Market share	Growth potential
Product quality	Profit potential
Product life cycle	Financial stability
Customer loyalty	Extent leveraged
Capacity utilization	Resource utilization
Technological know-how	Ease of entry into market
Control over suppliers and distributors	Productivity, capacity utilization

Source: Adapted from H. Rowe, R. Mason, and K. Dickel, *Strategic Management and Business Policy: A Methodological Approach* (Reading, MA: Addison-Wesley Publishing Co. Inc., © 1982), 155–156.

liquidity, working capital, and cash flow are commonly considered to be determining factors of an organization's financial strength. Like the SWOT Matrix, the SPACE Matrix should be both tailored to the particular organization being studied and based on factual information as much as possible.

The steps required to develop a SPACE Matrix are as follows:

1. Select a set of variables to define financial position (FP), competitive position (CP), stability position (SP), and industry position (IP).
2. Assign a numerical value ranging from +1 (worst) to +7 (best) to each of the variables that make up the FP and IP dimensions. Assign a numerical value ranging from –1 (best) to –7 (worst) to each of the variables that make up the SP and CP dimensions. On the FP and CP axes, make comparison to competitors. On the IP and SP axes, make comparison to other industries.
3. Compute an average score for FP, CP, IP, and SP by summing the values given to the variables of each dimension and then by dividing by the number of variables included in the respective dimension.
4. Plot the average scores for FP, IP, SP, and CP on the appropriate axis in the SPACE Matrix.
5. Add the two scores on the *x*-axis and plot the resultant point on *X*. Add the two scores on the *y*-axis and plot the resultant point on *Y*. Plot the intersection of the new *xy* point.
6. Draw a *directional vector* from the origin of the SPACE Matrix through the new intersection point. This vector reveals the type of strategies recommended for the organization: aggressive, competitive, defensive, or conservative.

Some examples of strategy profiles that can emerge from a SPACE analysis are shown in Figure 6-5. The directional vector associated with each profile suggests the type of strategies to pursue: aggressive, conservative, defensive, or competitive. When a firm's directional vector is located in the *aggressive quadrant* (upper-right quadrant) of the SPACE Matrix, an organization is in an excellent position to use its internal strengths to (1) take advantage of external opportunities, (2) overcome internal weaknesses, and (3) avoid external threats. Therefore, market penetration, market development, product development, backward integration, forward integration, horizontal integration, or diversification, can be feasible, depending on the specific circumstances that face the firm.

FIGURE 6-5

Example Strategy Profiles

Aggressive Profiles

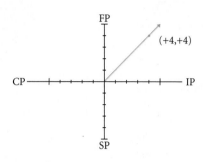

A financially strong firm that has achieved major competitive advantages in a growing and stable industry

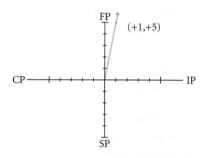

A firm whose financial strength is a dominating factor in the industry

Conservative Profiles

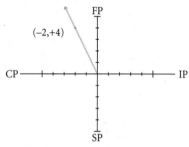

A firm that has achieved financial strength in a stable industry that is not growing; the firm has few competitive advantages

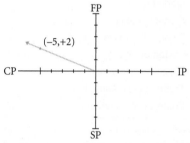

A firm that suffers from major competitive disadvantages in an industry that is technologically stable but declining in sales

Competitive Profiles

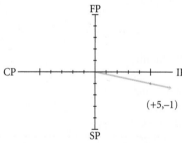

A firm with major competitive advantages in a high-growth industry

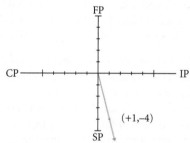

An organization that is competing fairly well in an unstable industry

Defensive Profiles

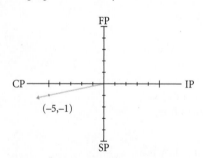

A firm that has a very weak competitive position in a negative growth, stable industry

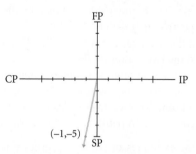

A financially troubled firm in a very unstable industry

Source: Adapted from H. Rowe, R. Mason, and K. Dickel, *Strategic Management and Business Policy: A Methodological Approach* (Reading, MA: Addison-Wesley Publishing Co. Inc., © 1982), 155.

When a particular company is known, the analyst must be much more specific in terms of recommended strategies. For example, instead of saying market penetration is a recommended strategy when your vector goes in the Conservative quadrant, say that adding 34 new stores in India is a recommended strategy. This is a very important point for students doing case analyses because a particular company is generally known, and terms such as *market development* are too vague to use. That term could refer to adding a manufacturing plant in Thailand or Mexico or South Africa—so students—*Be specific to the extent possible regarding implications of all the matrices presented in Chapter 6.*

The directional vector may appear in the *conservative quadrant* (upper-left quadrant) of the SPACE Matrix, which implies staying close to the firm's basic competencies and not taking excessive risks. Conservative strategies most often include market penetration, market development, product development, and related diversification. The directional vector may be located in the lower-left or *defensive quadrant* of the SPACE Matrix, which suggests that the firm should focus on rectifying internal weaknesses and avoiding external threats. Defensive strategies include retrenchment, divestiture, liquidation, and related diversification. Finally, the directional vector may be located in the lower-right or *competitive quadrant* of the SPACE Matrix, indicating competitive strategies. Competitive strategies include backward, forward, and horizontal integration; market penetration; market development; and product development.

A SPACE Matrix analysis for a bank is provided in Table 6-3. Note that competitive type strategies are recommended. Headquartered in Winston-Salem, North Carolina, Krispy

TABLE 6-3   A SPACE Matrix for a Bank

Financial Position (FP)	Ratings
The bank's primary capital ratio is 7.23 percent, which is 1.23 percentage points over the generally required ratio of 6 percent.	1.0
The bank's return on assets is negative 0.77, compared to a bank industry average ratio of positive 0.70.	1.0
The bank's net income was $183 million, down 9 percent from a year earlier.	3.0
The bank's revenues increased 7 percent to $3.46 billion.	4.0
	9.0

Industry Position (IP)	
Deregulation provides geographic and product freedom.	4.0
Deregulation increases competition in the banking industry.	2.0
Pennsylvania's interstate banking law allows the bank to acquire other banks in New Jersey, Ohio, Kentucky, the District of Columbia, and West Virginia.	4.0
	10.0

Stability Position (SP)	
Less-developed countries are experiencing high inflation and political instability.	−4.0
Headquartered in Pittsburgh, the bank historically has been heavily dependent on the steel, oil, and gas industries. These industries are depressed.	−5.0
Banking deregulation has created instability throughout the industry.	−4.0
	−13.0

Competitive Position (CP)	
The bank provides data processing services for more than 450 institutions in 38 states.	−2.0
Superregional banks, international banks, and nonbanks are becoming increasingly competitive.	−5.0
The bank has a large customer base.	−2.0
	−9.0

Conclusion

SP Average is −13.0 ÷ 3 = −4.33   IP Average is +10.0 ÷ 3 = 3.33

CP Average is −9.0 ÷ 3 = −3.00   FP Average is +9.0 ÷ 4 = 2.25

Directional Vector Coordinates: x-axis: −3.00 + (+3.33) = +0.33

y-axis: −4.33 + (+2.25) = −2.08

The bank should pursue Competitive Strategies.

Kreme Doughnut (KKD) Corp. has offered delicious doughnuts and coffee since 1937. Today, Krispy Kreme's "Hot Light" stores can be found in approximately 649 locations in 20 countries, including the United States, Australia, Bahrain, Canada, China, Dominican Republic, Indonesia, Japan, Kuwait, Lebanon, Malaysia, Mexico, the Philippines, Puerto Rico, the Republic of Korea, Qatar, the Kingdom of Saudi Arabia, Thailand, Turkey, the United Arab Emirates, and the United Kingdom. The company's mission statement is "To touch and enhance lives through the joy that is Krispy Kreme," and its vision statement is "To be the worldwide leader in sharing delicious tastes and creating joyful memories." A SPACE Matrix for KKD is given in Table 6-4 followed by the KKD SPACE diagram in Figure 6-6. Note that KKD is in a precarious defensive position, struggling to compete against Dunkin Donuts, Starbucks, and Tim Hortons.

The Boston Consulting Group (BCG) Matrix

Based in Boston and having 1,713 employees, the Boston Consulting Group (BCG) is a large consulting firm that endured the recent economic downturn without laying off any employees and in 2010 hired the most new consultants ever. BCG ranks #2 in *Fortune*'s recent list of the "100 Best Companies To Work For."

Autonomous divisions (or profit centers) of an organization make up what is called a *business portfolio*. When a firm's divisions compete in different industries, a separate strategy often must be developed for each business. The *Boston Consulting Group (BCG) Matrix* and the *Internal-External (IE) Matrix* are designed specifically to enhance a multidivisional firm's efforts to formulate strategies. (BCG is a private management consulting firm based in Boston that currently employs about 4,400 consultants in 40 countries.)

TABLE 6-4   An Actual SPACE Matrix for Krispy Kreme

Internal Analysis		*External Analysis*	
Financial Position (FP)		Stability Position (SP)	
Return on Investment (ROI)	1	Rate of Inflation	−2
Leverage	4	Technological Changes	−6
Liquidity	2	Price Elasticity of Demand	−3
Working Capital	1	Competitive Pressure	−7
Cash Flow	2	Barriers to Entry into Market	−4
Financial Position (FP) Average	**2**	**Stability Position (SP) Average**	**−4.4**
Internal Analysis		*External Analysis*	
Competitive Position (CP)		Industry Position (IP)	
Market Share	−7	Growth Potential	6
Product Quality	−2	Financial Stability	2
Customer Loyalty	−3	Ease of Entry into Market	4
Technological Know-how	−4	Resource Utilization	1
Control over Suppliers/Distributors	−5	Profit Potential	2
Competitive Position (CP) Average	**−4.2**	**Industry Position (IP) Average**	**3.0**

2.0+(−4.4)=−2.4   y-axis

3.0+(−4.2)=−1.2   x-axis

Coordinate (−1.2, −2.4)

Conclusion: Vector points in Defensive Quadrant

FIGURE 6-6

A SPACE Matrix for Krispy Kreme

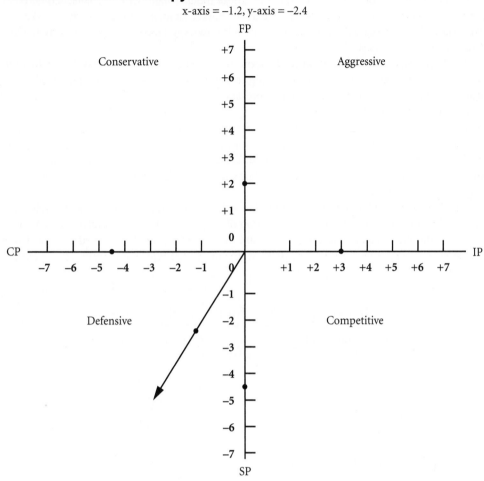

x-axis = −1.2, y-axis = −2.4

In a *Form 10K* or *Annual Report*, some companies do not disclose financial information by segment, so a BCG portfolio analysis is not possible by external entities. Reasons to disclose by-division financial information in the author's view, however, more than offset the reasons not to disclose, as indicated in Table 6-5.

The BCG Matrix graphically portrays differences among divisions in terms of relative market share position and industry growth rate. The BCG Matrix allows a multidivisional organization to manage its portfolio of businesses by examining the relative market share position and the industry growth rate of each division relative to all other divisions in the organization. *Relative market share position* is defined as the ratio of a division's own market share (or revenues) in a particular

TABLE 6-5   Reasons to (or Not to) Disclose Financial Information by Segment (by Division)

Reasons to Disclose	Reasons Not to Disclose
1. Transparency is a good thing in today's world of Sarbanes-Oxley	1. Can become free competitive information for rival firms
2. Investors will better understand the firm, which can lead to greater support	2. Can hide performance failures
3. Managers/employees will better understand the firm, which should lead to greater commitment	3. Can reduce rivalry among segments
4. Disclosure enhances the communication process both within the firm and with outsiders	

industry to the market share (or revenues) held by the largest rival firm in that industry. Note in Table 6-6 that other variables can be in this analysis besides revenues. For example, number of stores, or number of restaurants, or in the airline industry number of airplanes could be used for comparative purposes to determine relative market share position. Relative market share position for Heineken could also be determined by dividing Heineken's revenues by the leader Corona Extra's revenues.

Relative market share position is given on the *x*-axis of the BCG Matrix. The midpoint on the *x*-axis usually is set at .50, corresponding to a division that has half the market share of the leading firm in the industry. The *y*-axis represents the industry growth rate in sales, measured in percentage terms. The growth rate percentages on the *y*-axis could range from −20 to +20 percent, with 0.0 being the midpoint. The average annual increase in revenues for several leading firms in the industry would be a good estimate of the value. Also, various sources such as the S&P Industry Survey would provide this value. These numerical ranges on the *x*- and *y*-axes are often used, but other numerical values could be established as deemed appropriate for particular organizations, such as −10 to +10 percent.

The basic BCG Matrix appears in Figure 6-7. Each circle represents a separate division. The size of the circle corresponds to the proportion of corporate revenue generated by that business unit, and the pie slice indicates the proportion of corporate profits generated by that division. Divisions located in Quadrant I of the BCG Matrix are called "Question Marks," those located in

TABLE 6-6   Marker Share Data for Selected Industries

Business Analytics (using software to mine huge volumes of data to enhance decision-making; *WSJ*, 1/18/11, B4)—Market Share Leaders

Oracle	18.3%
SAP	13.6%
IBM	12.4%
SAS	7.8%
Microsoft	7.5%

Book Sales (*USA Today*, 2/10/11, 2A)

Amazon	22.6%
Barnes & Noble	17.3%
Borders	8.1%
Books-A-Million	3.0%
Independents	6.0%

Ready-to-Drink Beverages (*WSJ*, 2/10/11, B4)

Soft drinks	46.6%
Bottled water	19.9%
Non-refrigerated juice	9.0%
Refrigerated juice	9.0%
Sports drinks	6.2%
Tea	4.2%
Enhanced water	2.5%
Energy drinks	2.4%
Coffee	0.2%

U.S. Carbonated Soft Drinks (*WSJ*, 3/18/11, B5)

BY COMPANY		BY BRAND	
Coca-Cola	42.0%	Coke	17.0%
PepsiCo	29.3%	Diet Coke	9.9%
Dr Pepper/Snapple	16.7%	Pepsi-Cola	9.5%
Cott	4.8%	Mt. Dew	6.8%
National Beverage	2.8%	Dr Pepper	6.3%

Quadrant II are called "Stars," those located in Quadrant III are called "Cash Cows," and those divisions located in Quadrant IV are called "Dogs."

- *Question Marks*—Divisions in Quadrant I have a low relative market share position, yet they compete in a high-growth industry. Generally these firms' cash needs are high and their cash generation is low. These businesses are called *Question Marks* because the organization must decide whether to strengthen them by pursuing an intensive strategy (market penetration, market development, or product development) or to sell them.
- *Stars*—Quadrant II businesses (*Stars*) represent the organization's best long-run opportunities for growth and profitability. Divisions with a high relative market share and a high industry growth rate should receive substantial investment to maintain or strengthen their dominant positions. Forward, backward, and horizontal integration; market penetration; market development; and product development are appropriate strategies for these divisions to consider, as indicated in Figure 6-7.
- *Cash Cows*—Divisions positioned in Quadrant III have a high relative market share position but compete in a low-growth industry. Called *Cash Cows* because they generate cash in excess of their needs, they are often milked. Many of today's Cash Cows were yesterday's Stars. Cash Cow divisions should be managed to maintain their strong position for as long as possible. Product development or diversification may be attractive strategies for strong Cash Cows. However, as a Cash Cow division becomes weak, retrenchment or divestiture can become more appropriate.
- *Dogs*—Quadrant IV divisions of the organization have a low relative market share position and compete in a slow- or no-market-growth industry; they are *Dogs* in the firm's portfolio. Because of their weak internal and external position, these businesses are often liquidated, divested, or trimmed down through retrenchment. When a division first becomes a Dog, retrenchment can be the best strategy to pursue because many Dogs have bounced back, after strenuous asset and cost reduction, to become viable, profitable divisions.

The major benefit of the BCG Matrix is that it draws attention to the cash flow, investment characteristics, and needs of an organization's various divisions. The divisions of many firms evolve over time: Dogs become Question Marks, Question Marks become Stars, Stars become Cash Cows, and Cash Cows become Dogs in an ongoing counterclockwise motion. Less frequently, Stars become Question Marks, Question Marks become Dogs, Dogs become Cash Cows, and Cash Cows become Stars (in a clockwise motion). In some organizations, no cyclical motion is apparent. Over time, organizations should strive to achieve a portfolio of divisions that are Stars.

FIGURE 6-7

The BCG Matrix

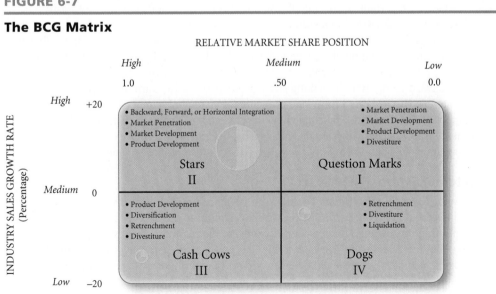

Source: Based on the BCG Portfolio Matrix from the Product Portfolio Matrix, © 1970, The Boston Consulting Group.

FIGURE 6-8

An Example BCG Matrix

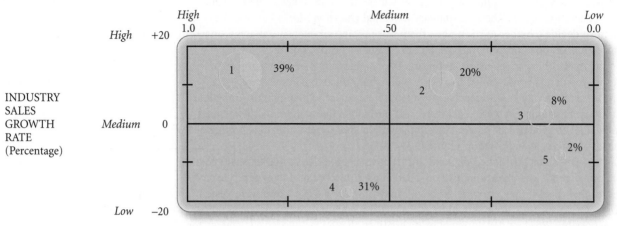

Division	Revenues	Percent Revenues	Profits	Percent Profits	Relative Market Share	Industry Growth Rate (%)
1	$60,000	37	$10,000	39	.80	+15
2	40,000	24	5,000	20	.40	+10
3	40,000	24	2,000	8	.10	+1
4	20,000	12	8,000	31	.60	−20
5	5,000	3	500	2	.05	−10
Total	**$165,000**	**100**	**$25,500**	**100**	—	—

An example BCG Matrix is provided in Figure 6-8, which illustrates an organization composed of five divisions with annual sales ranging from $5,000 to $60,000. Division 1 has the greatest sales volume, so the circle representing that division is the largest one in the matrix. The circle corresponding to Division 5 is the smallest because its sales volume ($5,000) is least among all the divisions. The pie slices within the circles reveal the percent of corporate profits contributed by each division. As shown, Division 1 contributes the highest profit percentage, 39 percent. Notice in the diagram that Division 1 is considered a Star, Division 2 is a Question Mark, Division 3 is also a Question Mark, Division 4 is a Cash Cow, and Division 5 is a Dog.

The BCG Matrix, like all analytical techniques, has some limitations. For example, viewing every business as either a Star, Cash Cow, Dog, or Question Mark is an oversimplification; many businesses fall right in the middle of the BCG Matrix and thus are not easily classified. Furthermore, the BCG Matrix does not reflect whether or not various divisions or their industries are growing over time; that is, the matrix has no temporal qualities, but rather it is a snapshot of an organization at a given point in time. Finally, other variables besides relative market share position and industry growth rate in sales, such as size of the market and competitive advantages, are important in making strategic decisions about various divisions.

An example BCG Matrix is provided in Figure 6-9. Note in Figure 6-9 that Division 5 had an operating loss of $188 million. Take note how the percent profit column is still calculated because oftentimes a firm will have a division that incurs a loss for a year. In terms of the pie slice in circle 5 of the diagram, note that it is a *different color* from the positive profit segments in the other circles.

The Internal-External (IE) Matrix

The *Internal-External (IE) Matrix* positions an organization's various divisions in a nine-cell display, illustrated in Figure 6-10. The IE Matrix is similar to the BCG Matrix in that both tools involve plotting organization divisions in a schematic diagram; this is why they are both called "portfolio matrices." Also, the size of each circle represents the percentage sales contribution of each division, and pie slices reveal the percentage profit contribution of each division in both the BCG and IE Matrix.

But there are some important differences between the BCG Matrix and the IE Matrix. First, the axes are different. Also, the IE Matrix requires more information about the divisions than the

FIGURE 6-9

An Example BCG Matrix

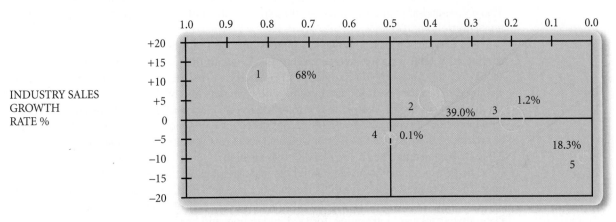

RELATIVE MARKET SHARE POSITION (RMSP)

Division	$ Sales (millions)	% Sales	$ Profits (millions)	% Profits	RMSP	IG Rate %
1.	$5,139	51.5	$799	68.0	0.8	10
2.	2,556	25.6	400	39.0	0.4	05
3.	1,749	17.5	12	1.2	0.2	00
4.	493	4.9	4	0.1	0.5	−05
5.	42	0.5	−188	(18.3)	.02	−10
Total	**$9,979**	**100.0**	**$1,027**	**100.0**		

FIGURE 6-10

The Internal–External (IE) Matrix

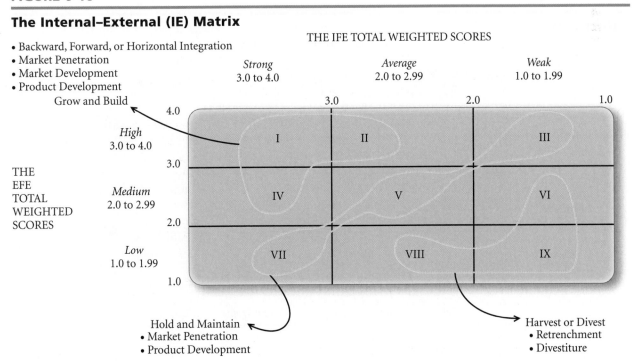

THE IFE TOTAL WEIGHTED SCORES

- Backward, Forward, or Horizontal Integration
- Market Penetration
- Market Development
- Product Development

Grow and Build

Hold and Maintain
- Market Penetration
- Product Development

Harvest or Divest
- Retrenchment
- Divestiture

Source: Adapted. The IE Matrix was developed from the General Electric (GE) Business Screen Matrix. For a description of the GE Matrix see Michael Allen, "Diagramming GE's Planning for What's WATT," in R. Allio and M. Pennington, eds., *Corporate Planning: Techniques and Applications* lpar;New York: AMACOM, 1979).

BCG Matrix. Furthermore, the strategic implications of each matrix are different. For these reasons, strategists in multidivisional firms often develop both the BCG Matrix and the IE Matrix in formulating alternative strategies. A common practice is to develop a BCG Matrix and an IE Matrix for the present and then develop projected matrices to reflect expectations of the future. This before-and-after analysis forecasts the expected effect of strategic decisions on an organization's portfolio of divisions.

The IE Matrix is based on two key dimensions: the IFE total weighted scores on the *x*-axis and the EFE total weighted scores on the *y*-axis. Recall that each division of an organization should construct an IFE Matrix and an EFE Matrix for its part of the organization. The total weighted scores derived from the divisions allow construction of the corporate-level IE Matrix. On the *x*-axis of the IE Matrix, an IFE total weighted score of 1.0 to 1.99 represents a weak internal position; a score of 2.0 to 2.99 is considered average; and a score of 3.0 to 4.0 is strong. Similarly, on the *y*-axis, an EFE total weighted score of 1.0 to 1.99 is considered low; a score of 2.0 to 2.99 is medium; and a score of 3.0 to 4.0 is high.

The IE Matrix can be divided into three major regions that have different strategy implications. First, the prescription for divisions that fall into cells I, II, or IV can be described as *grow and build.* Intensive (market penetration, market development, and product development) or integrative (backward integration, forward integration, and horizontal integration) strategies can be most appropriate for these divisions. Second, divisions that fall into cells III, V, or VII can be managed best with *hold and maintain* strategies; market penetration and product development are two commonly employed strategies for these types of divisions. Third, a common prescription for divisions that fall into cells VI, VIII, or IX is *harvest or divest.* Successful organizations are able to achieve a portfolio of businesses positioned in or around cell I in the IE Matrix.

An example of a completed IE Matrix is given in Figure 6-11, which depicts an organization composed of four divisions. As indicated by the positioning of the circles, *grow and build* strategies are appropriate for Division 1, Division 2, and Division 3. Division 4 is a candidate for *harvest or divest.* Division 2 contributes the greatest percentage of company sales and thus is represented by the largest circle. Division 1 contributes the greatest proportion of total profits; it has the largest-percentage pie slice.

FIGURE 6-11

An Example IE Matrix

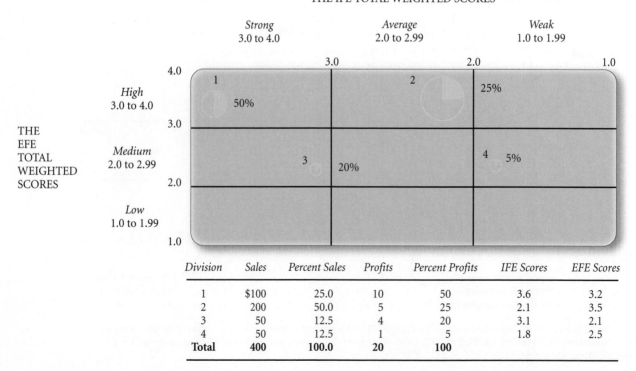

Division	Sales	Percent Sales	Profits	Percent Profits	IFE Scores	EFE Scores
1	$100	25.0	10	50	3.6	3.2
2	200	50.0	5	25	2.1	3.5
3	50	12.5	4	20	3.1	2.1
4	50	12.5	1	5	1.8	2.5
Total	**400**	**100.0**	**20**	**100**		

FIGURE 6-12

The IE Matrix

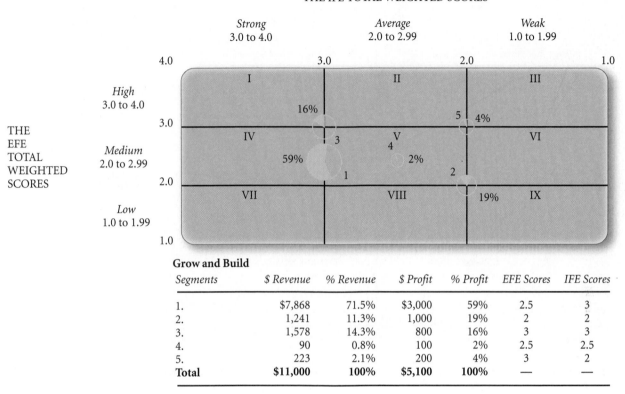

THE IFE TOTAL WEIGHTED SCORES

Grow and Build

Segments	$ Revenue	% Revenue	$ Profit	% Profit	EFE Scores	IFE Scores
1.	$7,868	71.5%	$3,000	59%	2.5	3
2.	1,241	11.3%	1,000	19%	2	2
3.	1,578	14.3%	800	16%	3	3
4.	90	0.8%	100	2%	2.5	2.5
5.	223	2.1%	200	4%	3	2
Total	$11,000	100%	$5,100	100%	—	—

As indicated in Figure 6-12, the IE Matrix has five product segments. Note that Division 1 has the largest revenues (as indicated by the largest circle) and the largest profits (as indicated by the largest pie slice) in the matrix. It is common for organizations to develop both geographic and product-based IE Matrices to more effectively formulate strategies and allocate resources among divisions. In addition, firms often prepare an IE (or BCG) Matrix for competitors. Furthermore, firms will often prepare "before and after" IE (or BCG) Matrices to reveal the situation at present versus the expected situation after one year. This latter idea minimizes the limitation of these matrices being a "snapshot in time." In performing case analysis, feel free to estimate the IFE and EFE scores for the various divisions based upon your research into the company and industry—rather than preparing a separate IE Matrix for each division.

The Grand Strategy Matrix

In addition to the SWOT Matrix, SPACE Matrix, BCG Matrix, and IE Matrix, the *Grand Strategy Matrix* has become a popular tool for formulating alternative strategies. All organizations can be positioned in one of the Grand Strategy Matrix's four strategy quadrants. A firm's divisions likewise could be positioned. As illustrated in Figure 6-13, the Grand Strategy Matrix is based on two evaluative dimensions: competitive position and market (industry) growth. Any industry whose annual growth in sales exceeds 5 percent could be considered to have rapid growth. Appropriate strategies for an organization to consider are listed in sequential order of attractiveness in each quadrant of the matrix.

Firms located in Quadrant I of the Grand Strategy Matrix are in an excellent strategic position. For these firms, continued concentration on current markets (market penetration and market development) and products (product development) is an appropriate strategy. It is unwise for a Quadrant I firm to shift notably from its established competitive advantages. When a Quadrant I organization has excessive resources, then backward, forward, or horizontal integration may be effective strategies. When a Quadrant I firm is too heavily committed to a single product, then related diversification may reduce the risks associated with a narrow product line. Quadrant I firms can afford to take advantage of external opportunities in several areas. They can take risks aggressively when necessary.

FIGURE 6-13

The Grand Strategy Matrix

RAPID MARKET GROWTH

Quadrant II

1. Market development
2. Market penetration
3. Product development
4. Horizontal integration
5. Divestiture
6. Liquidation

Quadrant I

1. Market development
2. Market penetration
3. Product development
4. Forward integration
5. Backward integration
6. Horizontal integration
7. Related diversification

WEAK COMPETITIVE POSITION

STRONG COMPETITIVE POSITION

Quadrant III

1. Retrenchment
2. Related diversification
3. Unrelated diversification
4. Divestiture
5. Liquidation

Quadrant IV

1. Related diversification
2. Unrelated diversification
3. Joint ventures

SLOW MARKET GROWTH

Source: Based on Roland Christensen, Norman Berg, and Malcolm Salter, *Policy Formulation and Administration* (Homewood, IL: Richard D. Irwin, 1976), 16–18.

Firms positioned in Quadrant II need to evaluate their present approach to the marketplace seriously. Although their industry is growing, they are unable to compete effectively, and they need to determine why the firm's current approach is ineffective and how the company can best change to improve its competitiveness. Because Quadrant II firms are in a rapid-market-growth industry, an intensive strategy (as opposed to integrative or diversification) is usually the first option that should be considered. However, if the firm is lacking a distinctive competence or competitive advantage, then horizontal integration is often a desirable alternative. As a last resort, divestiture or liquidation should be considered. Divestiture can provide funds needed to acquire other businesses or buy back shares of stock.

Quadrant III organizations compete in slow-growth industries and have weak competitive positions. These firms must make some drastic changes quickly to avoid further decline and possible liquidation. Extensive cost and asset reduction (retrenchment) should be pursued first. An alternative strategy is to shift resources away from the current business into different areas (diversify). If all else fails, the final options for Quadrant III businesses are divestiture or liquidation.

Finally, Quadrant IV businesses have a strong competitive position but are in a slow-growth industry. These firms have the strength to launch diversified programs into more promising growth areas: Quadrant IV firms have characteristically high cash-flow levels and limited internal growth needs and often can pursue related or unrelated diversification successfully. Quadrant IV firms also may pursue joint ventures.

The Decision Stage

Analysis and intuition provide a basis for making strategy-formulation decisions. The matching techniques just discussed reveal feasible alternative strategies. Many of these strategies will likely have been proposed by managers and employees participating in the strategy analysis and choice activity. Any additional strategies resulting from the matching analyses could be discussed and added to the list of feasible alternative options. As indicated earlier in this chapter, participants could rate these strategies on a 1 to 4 scale so that a prioritized list of the best strategies could be achieved.

The Quantitative Strategic Planning Matrix (QSPM)

Other than ranking strategies to achieve the prioritized list, there is only one analytical technique in the literature designed to determine the relative attractiveness of feasible alternative actions. This technique is the *Quantitative Strategic Planning Matrix (QSPM),* which comprises Stage 3 of the strategy-formulation analytical framework.[6] This technique objectively indicates which alternative strategies are best. The QSPM uses input from Stage 1 analyses and matching results from Stage 2 analyses to decide objectively among alternative strategies. That is, the EFE Matrix, IFE Matrix, and Competitive Profile Matrix that comprise Stage 1, coupled with the SWOT Matrix, SPACE Matrix, BCG Matrix, IE Matrix, and Grand Strategy Matrix that comprise Stage 2, provide the needed information for setting up the QSPM (Stage 3). The QSPM is a tool that allows strategists to evaluate alternative strategies objectively, based on previously identified external and internal critical success factors. Like other strategy-formulation analytical tools, the QSPM requires good intuitive judgment.

The basic format of the QSPM is illustrated in Table 6-7. Note that the left column of a QSPM consists of key external and internal factors (from Stage 1), and the top row consists of feasible alternative strategies (from Stage 2). Specifically, the left column of a QSPM consists of information obtained directly from the EFE Matrix and IFE Matrix. In a column adjacent to the critical success factors, the respective weights received by each factor in the EFE Matrix and the IFE Matrix are recorded.

The top row of a QSPM consists of alternative strategies derived from the SWOT Matrix, SPACE Matrix, BCG Matrix, IE Matrix, and Grand Strategy Matrix. These matching tools usually generate similar feasible alternatives. However, not every strategy suggested by the matching techniques has to be evaluated in a QSPM. Strategists should use good intuitive judgment in selecting strategies to include in a QSPM.

Conceptually, the QSPM determines the relative attractiveness of various strategies based on the extent to which key external and internal critical success factors are capitalized upon or improved. The relative attractiveness of each strategy within a set of alternatives is computed by determining the cumulative impact of each external and internal critical success factor. Any number of sets of alternative strategies can be included in the QSPM, and any number of strategies can make up a given set, but only strategies within a given set are evaluated relative to each other. For example, one set of strategies may include diversification, whereas another set may include issuing stock and selling a division to raise needed capital. These two sets of strategies are totally different, and the QSPM evaluates strategies only within sets. Note in Table 6-7 that three strategies are included, and they make up just one set.

A QSPM for a retail computer store is provided in Table 6-8. This example illustrates all the components of the QSPM: Strategic Alternatives, Key Factors, Weights, Attractiveness Scores (AS), Total Attractiveness Scores (TAS), and the Sum Total Attractiveness Score. The three new

TABLE 6-7 The Quantitative Strategic Planning Matrix—QSPM

Key Factors	Weight	Strategic Alternatives		
		Strategy 1	Strategy 2	Strategy 3
Key External Factors				
Economy				
Political/Legal/Governmental				
Social/Cultural/Demographic/Environmental				
Technological				
Competitive				
Key Internal Factors				
Management				
Marketing				
Finance/Accounting				
Production/Operations				
Research and Development				
Management Information Systems				

TABLE 6-8   A QSPM for a Retail Computer Store

		STRATEGIC ALTERNATIVES			
		1		2	
		Buy New Land and Build New Larger Store		Fully Renovate Existing Store	
Key Factors	Weight	AS	TAS	AS	TAS
Opportunities					
1. Population of city growing 10%	0.10	4	0.40	2	0.20
2. Rival computer store opening 1 mile away	0.10	2	0.20	4	0.40
3. Vehicle traffic passing store up 12%	0.08	1	0.08	4	0.32
4. Vendors average six new products/year	0.05	—		—	
5. Senior citizen use of computers up 8%	0.05	—		—	
6. Small business growth in area up 10%	0.10	—		—	
7. Desire for websites up 18% by Realtors	0.06	—		—	
8. Desire for websites up 12% by small firms	0.06	—		—	
Threats					
1. Best Buy opening new store nearby in 1 year	0.15	4	0.60	3	0.45
2. Local university offers computer repair	0.08	—		—	
3. New bypass for Hwy 34 in 1 year will divert traffic	0.12	4	0.48	1	0.12
4. New mall being built nearby	0.08	2	0.16	4	0.32
5. Gas prices up 14%	0.04	—		—	
6. Vendors raising prices 8%	0.03	—		—	
Total	**1.00**				
Strengths					
1. Inventory turnover increased from 5.8 to 6.7	0.05	—		—	
2. Average customer purchase increased from $97 to $128	0.07	2	0.14	4	0.28
3. Employee morale is excellent	0.10	—		—	
4. In-store promotions resulted in 20% increase in sales	0.05	—		—	
5. Newspaper advertising expenditures increased 10%	0.02	—		—	
6. Revenues from repair/service segment of store up 16%	0.15	4	0.60	3	0.45
7. In-store technical support personnel have MIS college degrees	0.05	—		—	
8. Store's debt-to-total-assets ratio declined to 34%	0.03	4	0.12	2	0.06
9. Revenues per employee up 19%	0.02	—		—	
Weaknesses					
1. Revenues from software segment of store down 12%	0.10	—		—	
2. Location of store negatively impacted by new Hwy 34	0.15	4	0.60	1	0.15
3. Carpet and paint in store somewhat in disrepair	0.02	1	0.02	4	0.08
4. Bathroom in store needs refurbishing	0.02	1	0.02	4	0.08
5. Revenues from businesses down 8%	0.04	3	0.12	4	0.16
6. Store has no website	0.05	—		—	
7. Supplier on-time delivery increased to 2.4 days	0.03	—		—	
8. Often customers have to wait to check out	0.05	2	0.10	4	0.20
Total	**1.00**		**4.36**		**3.27**

terms just introduced—(1) Attractiveness Scores, (2) Total Attractiveness Scores, and (3) the Sum Total Attractiveness Score—are defined and explained as the six steps required to develop a QSPM are discussed:

Step 1 *Make a list of the firm's key external opportunities/threats and internal strengths/ weaknesses in the left column of the QSPM.* This information should be taken directly from the EFE Matrix and IFE Matrix. A minimum of 10 external key success factors and 10 internal key success factors should be included in the QSPM.

Step 2 *Assign weights to each key external and internal factor.* These weights are identical to those in the EFE Matrix and the IFE Matrix. The weights are presented in a straight column just to the right of the external and internal critical success factors.

Step 3 *Examine the Stage 2 (matching) matrices, and identify alternative strategies that the organization should consider implementing.* Record these strategies in the top row of the QSPM. Group the strategies into mutually exclusive sets if possible.

Step 4 *Determine the Attractiveness Scores (AS)* defined as numerical values that indicate the relative attractiveness of each strategy in a given set of alternatives. *Attractiveness Scores (AS)* are determined by examining each key external or internal factor, one at a time, and asking the question "Does this factor affect the choice of strategies being made?" If the answer to this question is yes, then the strategies should be compared relative to that key factor. Specifically, Attractiveness Scores should be assigned to each strategy to indicate the relative attractiveness of one strategy over others, considering the particular factor. The range for Attractiveness Scores is 1 = not attractive, 2 = somewhat attractive, 3 = reasonably attractive, and 4 = highly attractive. By attractive, we mean the extent that one strategy, compared to others, enables the firm to either capitalize on the strength, improve on the weakness, exploit the opportunity, or avoid the threat. Work row by row in developing a QSPM. If the answer to the previous question is *no,* indicating that the respective key factor has no effect upon the specific choice being made, then do not assign Attractiveness Scores to the strategies in that set. Use a dash to indicate that the key factor does not affect the choice being made. *Note:* If you assign an AS score to one strategy, then assign AS score(s) to the other. In other words, if one strategy receives a dash, then all others must receive a dash in a given row.

Step 5 *Compute the Total Attractiveness Scores. Total Attractiveness Scores (TAS)* are defined as the product of multiplying the weights (Step 2) by the Attractiveness Scores (Step 4) in each row. The Total Attractiveness Scores indicate the relative attractiveness of each alternative strategy, considering only the impact of the adjacent external or internal critical success factor. The higher the Total Attractiveness Score, the more attractive the strategic alternative (considering only the adjacent critical success factor).

Step 6 *Compute the Sum Total Attractiveness Score.* Add Total Attractiveness Scores in each strategy column of the QSPM. The *Sum Total Attractiveness Scores (STAS)* reveal which strategy is most attractive in each set of alternatives. Higher scores indicate more attractive strategies, considering all the relevant external and internal factors that could affect the strategic decisions. The magnitude of the difference between the Sum Total Attractiveness Scores in a given set of strategic alternatives indicates the relative desirability of one strategy over another.

In Table 6-8, two alternative strategies—(1) buy new land and build new larger store and (2) fully renovate existing store—are being considered by a computer retail store. Note by sum total attractiveness scores of 4.63 versus 3.27 that the analysis indicates the business should buy new land and build a new larger store. Note the use of dashes to indicate which factors do not affect the strategy choice being considered. If a particular factor affects one strategy but not the other, it affects the choice being made, so attractiveness scores should be recorded for both strategies. Never rate one strategy and not the other. Note also in Table 6-8 that there are no double 1's, 2's, 3's, or 4's in a row. Never duplicate scores in a row. Never work column by column; always prepare a QSPM working row by row. If you have more than one strategy in the QSPM, then let the AS scores range from 1 to "the number of strategies being evaluated." This will enable you to have a different AS score for each strategy. These are all important guidelines to follow in developing a QSPM. In actual practice, the store did purchase the new land and build a new store; the business also did some minor refurbishing until the new store was operational.

There should be a rationale for each AS score assigned. Note in Table 6-8 in the first row that the "city population growing 10 percent annually" opportunity could be capitalized on best by strategy 1, "building the new, larger store," so an AS score of 4 was assigned to Strategy 1. AS scores, therefore, are not mere guesses; they should be rational, defensible, and reasonable.

An example QSPM for UPS is given in Table 6-9. UPS owns its own airline, based in Louisville, Kentucky. Note in the analysis that UPS is considering converting all its trucks to green technology and also is considering extending services deeper into Africa. Note that the "Africa" strategy is most attractive as indicated by the sum total attractiveness score of 3.78 versus 2.37.

Positive Features and Limitations of the QSPM

A positive feature of the QSPM is that sets of strategies can be examined sequentially or simultaneously. For example, corporate-level strategies could be evaluated first, followed by division-level strategies, and then function-level strategies. There is no limit to the number of strategies that can be evaluated or the number of sets of strategies that can be examined at once using the QSPM.

Another positive feature of the QSPM is that it requires strategists to integrate pertinent external and internal factors into the decision process. Developing a QSPM makes it less likely that key factors will be overlooked or weighted inappropriately. A QSPM draws attention to important relationships that affect strategy decisions. Although developing a QSPM requires a number of subjective decisions, making small decisions along the way enhances the probability that the final strategic decisions will be best for the organization. A QSPM can be adapted for use by small and large for-profit and nonprofit organizations so can be applied to virtually any type of organization. A QSPM can especially enhance strategic choice in multinational firms because many key factors and strategies can be considered at once. It also has been applied successfully by a number of small businesses.[7]

The QSPM is not without some limitations. First, it always requires intuitive judgments and educated assumptions. The ratings and attractiveness scores require judgmental decisions, even though they should be based on objective information. Discussion among strategists, managers, and

TABLE 6-9   An Actual QSPM for UPS

	Convert All UPS Trucks to Green Technology			Extend UPS Service in Africa	
	Weight	AS	TAS	AS	TAS
Strengths					0.36
1. Completed first phase of Worldport expansion, increasing sorting capacity by 15%, going to 37%	0.09	1	0.09	4	
2. 1st major airline to successfully operate a 100% Stage III fleet >3 years in advance of Fed regulations	0.07	1	0.07	4	0.28
3. Five out of every 6 UPS drivers come from part-timeranks (promotion within)	0.07	0	0.00	0	0.00
4. Over 4,000 UPS drivers have driven >25 years without an avoidable accident	0.06	0	0.00	0	0.00
5. Dividend of $0.47 per share paid and increasing	0.06	0	0.00	0	0.00
6. Average daily volume for Next Day Air and Deferred Products increased 2.8% and 4.3% respectively	0.06	3	0.18	4	0.24
7. Have yielded 1.71% cost and production efficiencies, improving profits	0.06	0	0.00	0	0.00
8. Owns 80% of joint venture headquartered in Dubai with 20% option to purchase	0.08	2	0.16	4	0.32
9. Streamlining Domestic Package segment, reducing U.S. regions from 5 to 3 and U.S. Districts from 46 to 20	0.07	0	0.00	0	0.00
10. Purchased 130 hybrid vehicles adding to UPS alternative-fuel vehicle (AFV) fleet	0.07	4	0.28	1	0.07

	Convert All UPS Trucks to Green Technology			Extend UPS Service in Africa	
	Weight	AS	TAS	AS	TAS
Weaknesses					
11. Approximately 254,000 UPS employees are members of a union	0.03	0	0.00	0	0.00
12. Approximately 2,800 UPS pilots	0.03	1	0.03	4	0.12
13. Approximately 3,400 UPS truck mechanics	0.03	4	0.12	1	0.03
14. Inability to identify sufficient operating cost savings to result in at least 300 furloughs for airline pilots	0.04	4	0.16	1	0.04
15. Top executives diversity percentage (25%) is low compared to rival firms	0.03	0	0.00	0	0.00
16. Over 4,000 UPS drivers have driven for 25 years or more and are eligible for retirement	0.04	0	0.00	0	0.00
17. Top executives' tenure 5 years or less	0.03	0	0.00	0	0.00
18. 80% of all U.S. small package delivery services guaranteed	0.02	0	0.00	0	0.00
19. With ~408,000 employees, expenses relating to health and pension benefits are high	0.03	0	0.00	0	0.00
20. 41.7% of top UPS executives have more than one role	0.03	0	0.00	0	0.00
Subtotal	**1.00**		**1.09**		**1.46**
	Weight	AS	TAS	AS	TAS
Opportunities					
1. Europe accounts for ~50% of international revenue	0.04	1	0.04	4	0.16
2. Africa is becoming commercially developed	0.03	1	0.03	4	0.12
3. >24 alliances with Asian delivery companies	0.07	1	0.07	4	0.28
4. International market growing 10% faster than U.S.	0.03	1	0.03	4	0.12
5. Customers outsourcing up to 100% of supply chain to lower costs	0.10	0	0.00	0	0.00
6. Increase internationally in use of wireless access tracking information	0.03	1	0.03	4	0.12
7. Telematics technology in ~12,000 U.S. UPS vehicles	0.03	3	0.09	1	0.03
8. Hybrid vehicles are available to add to UPS alternative fuel vehicle (AFV) fleet	0.06	4	0.24	1	0.06
9. Only 43.2% of employees are not union member	0.07	0	0.00	0	0.00
10. Direct-to-consumer business models require delivery services to be 100% effective	0.03	1	0.03	4	0.12
	Weight	AS	TAS	AS	TAS
Threats					
11. Incurred $77 million foreign currency charge	0.10	1	0.10	4	0.40
12. Jet and diesel fuel price variations cause fuel surcharges (13% increase to a 21.2% decrease)	0.08	2	0.16	4	0.32
13. Adverse currency exchange rate fluctuation (7.2% decline for the year)	0.03	4	0.12	1	0.03
14. FASB guidance requires re-measurement of pension plan = $44 million reduction to earnings	0.04	0	0.00	0	0.00
15. 1% change in health care cost trend = increase in post-retirement benefit obligation $83 million	0.06	0	0.00	0	0.00
16. Joint venture partner in Dubai owns 20% put option	0.03	1	0.03	4	0.12
17. Undistributed earnings of non-U.S. subsidiaries ~$2.2 billion	0.05	2	0.10	4	0.20
18. Consumers expect "green business operations"	0.04	4	0.16	1	0.04
19. U.S. unemployment rates holding around 10%	0.03	0	0.00	0	0.00
20. FedEx has greater international presence (27% as compared to UPS 24% of total revenues)	0.05	1	0.05	4	0.20
Subtotal	**1.00**		**1.28**		**2.32**
Grand Total	**2.00**		**2.37**		**3.78**

employees throughout the strategy-formulation process, including development of a QSPM, is constructive and improves strategic decisions. Constructive discussion during strategy analysis and choice may arise because of genuine differences of interpretation of information and varying opinions. Another limitation of the QSPM is that it can be only as good as the prerequisite information and matching analyses upon which it is based.

Cultural Aspects of Strategy Choice

All organizations have a culture. *Culture* includes the set of shared values, beliefs, attitudes, customs, norms, personalities, heroes, and heroines that describe a firm. Culture is the unique way an organization does business. It is the human dimension that creates solidarity and meaning, and it inspires commitment and productivity in an organization when strategy changes are made. All human beings have a basic need to make sense of the world, to feel in control, and to make meaning. When events threaten meaning, individuals react defensively. Managers and employees may even sabotage new strategies in an effort to recapture the status quo.

It is beneficial to view strategic management from a cultural perspective because success often rests upon the degree of support that strategies receive from a firm's culture. If a firm's strategies are supported by cultural products such as values, beliefs, rites, rituals, ceremonies, stories, symbols, language, heroes, and heroines, then managers often can implement changes swiftly and easily. However, if a supportive culture does not exist and is not cultivated, then strategy changes may be ineffective or even counterproductive. A firm's culture can become antagonistic to new strategies, and the result of that antagonism may be confusion and disarray.

Strategies that require fewer cultural changes may be more attractive because extensive changes can take considerable time and effort. Whenever two firms merge, it becomes especially important to evaluate and consider culture-strategy linkages.

Culture provides an explanation for the difficulties a firm encounters when it attempts to shift its strategic direction, as the following statement explains:

> Not only has the "right" corporate culture become the essence and foundation of corporate excellence, but success or failure of needed corporate reforms hinges on management's sagacity and ability to change the firm's driving culture in time and in tune with required changes in strategies.[8]

The Politics of Strategy Choice

All organizations are political. Unless managed, political maneuvering consumes valuable time, subverts organizational objectives, diverts human energy, and results in the loss of some valuable employees. Sometimes political biases and personal preferences get unduly embedded in strategy choice decisions. Internal politics affect the choice of strategies in all organizations. The hierarchy of command in an organization, combined with the career aspirations of different people and the need to allocate scarce resources, guarantees the formation of coalitions of individuals who strive to take care of themselves first and the organization second, third, or fourth. Coalitions of individuals often form around key strategy issues that face an enterprise. A major responsibility of strategists is to guide the development of coalitions, to nurture an overall team concept, and to gain the support of key individuals and groups of individuals.

In the absence of objective analyses, strategy decisions too often are based on the politics of the moment. With development of improved strategy-formation tools, political factors become less important in making strategic decisions. In the absence of objectivity, political factors sometimes dictate strategies, and this is unfortunate. Managing political relationships is an integral part of building enthusiasm and esprit de corps in an organization.

A classic study of strategic management in nine large corporations examined the political tactics of successful and unsuccessful strategists.[9] Successful strategists were found to let weakly supported ideas and proposals die through inaction and to establish additional hurdles or tests for strongly supported ideas considered unacceptable but not openly opposed. Successful strategists kept a low political profile on unacceptable proposals and strived to let most negative decisions come from subordinates or a group consensus, thereby reserving their personal vetoes for big issues and crucial moments. Successful strategists did a lot of chatting and informal questioning to stay abreast of how things were progressing and to know when to intervene. They led strategy but did not dictate it. They gave few orders, announced few decisions, depended heavily on informal questioning, and sought to probe and clarify until a consensus emerged.

Successful strategists generously and visibly rewarded key thrusts that succeeded. They assigned responsibility for major new thrusts to *champions,* the individuals most strongly identified with the idea or product and whose futures were linked to its success. They stayed alert to the symbolic impact of their own actions and statements so as not to send false signals that could stimulate movements in unwanted directions.

Successful strategists ensured that all major power bases within an organization were represented in, or had access to, top management. They interjected new faces and new views into considerations of major changes. This is important because new employees and managers generally have more enthusiasm and drive than employees who have been with the firm a long time. New employees do not see the world the same old way; nor do they act as screens against changes. Successful strategists minimized their own political exposure on highly controversial issues and in circumstances in which major opposition from key power centers was likely. In combination, these findings provide a basis for managing political relationships in an organization.

Because strategies must be effective in the marketplace and capable of gaining internal commitment, the following tactics used by politicians for centuries can aid strategists:

- *Equifinality*—It is often possible to achieve similar results using different means or paths. Strategists should recognize that achieving a successful outcome is more important than imposing the method of achieving it. It may be possible to generate new alternatives that give equal results but with far greater potential for gaining commitment.
- *Satisfying*—Achieving satisfactory results with an acceptable strategy is far better than failing to achieve optimal results with an unpopular strategy.
- *Generalization*—Shifting focus from specific issues to more general ones may increase strategists' options for gaining organizational commitment.
- *Focus on Higher-Order Issues*—By raising an issue to a higher level, many short-term interests can be postponed in favor of long-term interests. For instance, by focusing on issues of survival, the airline and automotive industries were able to persuade unions to make concessions on wage increases.
- *Provide Political Access on Important Issues*—Strategy and policy decisions with significant negative consequences for middle managers will motivate intervention behavior from them. If middle managers do not have an opportunity to take a position on such decisions in appropriate political forums, they are capable of successfully resisting the decisions after they are made. Providing such political access provides strategists with information that otherwise might not be available and that could be useful in managing intervention behavior.[10]

Governance Issues

A "director," according to Webster's Dictionary, is "one of a group of persons entrusted with the overall direction of a corporate enterprise." A *board of directors* is a group of individuals who are elected by the ownership of a corporation to have oversight and guidance over management and who look out for shareholders' interests. The act of oversight and direction is referred to as *governance.* The National Association of Corporate Directors defines governance as "the characteristic of ensuring that long-term strategic objectives and plans are established and that the proper management structure is in place to achieve those objectives, while at the same time making sure that the structure functions to maintain the corporation's integrity, reputation, and responsibility to its various constituencies." This broad scope of responsibility for the board shows how boards are being held accountable for the entire performance of the firm. In the Worldcom, Tyco, and Enron bankruptcies and scandals, the firms' boards of directors were sued by shareholders for mismanaging their interests. New accounting rules in the United States and Europe now enhance corporate-governance codes and require much more extensive financial disclosure among publicly held firms. The roles and duties of a board of directors can be divided into four broad categories, as indicated in Table 6-10.

The recent recession and credit crunch prompted shareholders to become more wary of boards of directors. Shareholders of hundreds of firms are demanding that their boards do a better job of governing corporate America.[11] New compensation policies are needed as well as direct shareholder involvement in some director activities. For example, boards could require CEOs to groom possible replacements from inside the firm because exorbitant compensation is most often paid to new CEOs coming from outside the firm.

Shareholders are also upset at boards for allowing CEOs to receive huge end-of-year bonuses when the firm's stock price drops drastically during the year.[12] For example, Chesapeake Energy Corp. and its board of directors came under fire from shareholders for paying Chairman and CEO Aubrey McClendon $112 million as the firm's stock price plummeted. Investor Jeffrey Bronchick wrote in a letter to the Chesapeake board that the CEO's compensation was a "near perfect illustration of the complete collapse of appropriate corporate governance."

Until recently, boards of directors did most of their work sitting around polished wooden tables. However, Hewlett-Packard's directors, among many others, now log on to their own special board website twice a week and conduct business based on extensive confidential briefing information posted there by the firm's top management team. Then the board members meet face to face and fully informed every two months to discuss the biggest issues facing the firm. Even the decision of whether to locate operations in countries with low corporate tax rates would be reviewed by a board of directors.

Today, boards of directors are composed mostly of outsiders who are becoming more involved in organizations' strategic management. The trend in the United States is toward much

TABLE 6-10   Board of Director Duties and Responsibilities

1. CONTROL AND OVERSIGHT OVER MANAGEMENT
    a. Select the Chief Executive Officer (CEO).
    b. Sanction the CEO's team.
    c. Provide the CEO with a forum.
    d. Ensure managerial competency.
    e. Evaluate management's performance.
    f. Set management's salary levels, including fringe benefits.
    g. Guarantee managerial integrity through continuous auditing.
    h. Chart the corporate course.
    i. Devise and revise policies to be implemented by management.

2. ADHERENCE TO LEGAL PRESCRIPTIONS
    a. Keep abreast of new laws.
    b. Ensure the entire organization fulfills legal prescriptions.
    c. Pass bylaws and related resolutions.
    d. Select new directors.
    e. Approve capital budgets.
    f. Authorize borrowing, new stock issues, bonds, and so on.

3. CONSIDERATION OF STAKEHOLDERS' INTERESTS
    a. Monitor product quality.
    b. Facilitate upward progression in employee quality of work life.
    c. Review labor policies and practices.
    d. Improve the customer climate.
    e. Keep community relations at the highest level.
    f. Use influence to better governmental, professional association, and educational contacts.
    g. Maintain good public image.

4. ADVANCEMENT OF STOCKHOLDERS' RIGHTS
    a. Preserve stockholders' equity.
    b. Stimulate corporate growth so that the firm will survive and flourish.
    c. Guard against equity dilution.
    d. Ensure equitable stockholder representation.
    e. Inform stockholders through letters, reports, and meetings.
    f. Declare proper dividends.
    g. Guarantee corporate survival.

greater board member accountability with smaller boards, now averaging 12 members rather than 18 as they did a few years ago. *BusinessWeek* recently evaluated the boards of most large U.S. companies and provided the following "principles of good governance":

1. No more than two directors are current or former company executives.
2. The audit, compensation, and nominating committees are made up solely of outside directors.
3. Each director owns a large equity stake in the company, excluding stock options.
4. Each director attends at least 75 percent of all meetings.
5. The board meets regularly without management present and evaluates its own performance annually.
6. The CEO is not also the chairperson of the board.
7. Stock options are considered a corporate expense.
8. There are no interlocking directorships (where a director or CEO sits on another director's board).[13]

Being a member of a board of directors today requires much more time, is much more difficult, and requires much more technical knowledge and financial commitment than in the past. Jeff Sonnerfeld, associate dean of the Yale School of Management, says, "Boards of directors are now rolling up their sleeves and becoming much more closely involved with management decision making." Since the Enron and Worldcom scandals, company CEOs and boards are required to personally certify financial statements; company loans to company executives and directors are illegal; and there is faster reporting of insider stock transactions.

Just as directors are beginning to place more emphasis on staying informed about an organization's health and operations, they are also taking a more active role in ensuring that publicly issued documents are accurate representations of a firm's status. It is becoming widely recognized that a board of directors has legal responsibilities to stockholders and society for all company activities, for corporate performance, and for ensuring that a firm has an effective strategy. Failure to accept responsibility for auditing or evaluating a firm's strategy is considered a serious breach of a director's duties. Stockholders, government agencies, and customers are filing legal suits against directors for fraud, omissions, inaccurate disclosures, lack of due diligence, and culpable ignorance about a firm's operations with increasing frequency. Liability insurance for directors has become exceptionally expensive and has caused numerous directors to resign.

The Sarbanes-Oxley Act resulted in scores of boardroom overhauls among publicly traded companies. The jobs of chief executive and chairman are now held by separate persons, and board audit committees must now have at least one financial expert as a member. Board audit committees now meet 10 or more times per year, rather than three or four times as they did prior to the act. The act put an end to the "country club" atmosphere of most boards and has shifted power from CEOs to directors. Although aimed at public companies, the act has also had a similar impact on privately owned companies.[14]

In Sweden, a new law has recently been passed requiring 25 percent female representation in boardrooms. The Norwegian government has passed a similar law that requires 40 percent of corporate director seats to go to women. In the United States, women currently hold about 13 percent of board seats at S&P 500 firms and 10 percent at S&P 1,500 firms. The Investor Responsibility Research Center in Washington, D.C., reports that minorities hold just 8.8 percent of board seats of S&P 1,500 companies. Progressive firms realize that women and minorities ask different questions and make different suggestions in boardrooms than white men, which is helpful because women and minorities comprise much of the consumer base everywhere.

A direct response to increased pressure on directors to stay informed and execute their responsibilities is that audit committees are becoming commonplace. A board of directors should conduct an annual strategy audit in much the same fashion that it reviews the annual financial audit. In performing such an audit, a board could work jointly with operating management and/or seek outside counsel. Boards should play a role beyond that of performing a strategic audit. They should provide greater input and advice in the strategy-formulation process to ensure that strategists are providing for the long-term needs of the firm. This is being done through the formation of three particular board committees: nominating committees to propose candidates for the board and senior officers of the firm; compensation committees to evaluate the performance of top executives and determine the terms and conditions of their employment; and audit committees to give board-level attention to company accounting and financial policies and performance.

Special Note to Students

Your SWOT, SPACE, BCG, IE, GRAND, and QSPM need to be developed accurately, but in covering those matrices in an oral presentation, focus more on the implications of those analyses than the nuts-and-bolts calculations. In other words, as you go through those matrices in a presentation, your goal is not to prove to the class that you did the calculations correctly. They expect accuracy and clarity and certainly you should have that covered. It is the implications of each matrix that your audience will be most interested in, so use these Chapter 6 matrices to pave the way for your recommendations with costs, which generally come just a page or two deeper into the project. A good rule of thumb is to spend at least an equal amount of time on the implications as the actual calculations of each matrix when presented. This approach will improve the delivery aspect of your presentation or paper by maintaining the high interest level of your audience. Focusing on implications rather than calculations will also encourage questions from the audience when you finish. Questions upon completion are a good thing. Silence upon completion is a bad thing, since silence could mean your audience was asleep, disinterested, or did not feel you did a good job.

Conclusion

The essence of strategy formulation is an assessment of whether an organization is doing the right things and how it can be more effective in what it does. Every organization should be wary of becoming a prisoner of its own strategy, because even the best strategies become obsolete sooner or later. Regular reappraisal of strategy helps management avoid complacency. Objectives and strategies should be consciously developed and coordinated and should not merely evolve out of day-to-day operating decisions.

An organization with no sense of direction and no coherent strategy precipitates its own demise. When an organization does not know where it wants to go, it usually ends up some place it does not want to be. Every organization needs to consciously establish and communicate clear objectives and strategies.

Modern strategy-formulation tools and concepts are described in this chapter and integrated into a practical three-stage framework. Tools such as the SWOT Matrix, SPACE Matrix, BCG Matrix, IE Matrix, and QSPM can significantly enhance the quality of strategic decisions, but they should never be used to dictate the choice of strategies. Behavioral, cultural, and political aspects of strategy generation and selection are always important to consider and manage. Because of increased legal pressure from outside groups, boards of directors are assuming a more active role in strategy analysis and choice. This is a positive trend for organizations.

Key Terms and Concepts

Issues for Review and Discussion

1. Rather than developing a QSPM, what is an alternative procedure for prioritizing the relative attractiveness of alternative strategies?

2. Overlay a BCG Matrix with a Grand Strategy Matrix and discuss similarities in terms of format and implications.

3. Walt Disney's Board of Directors consists of eight men and five women. Why should a Board not consist of all men, or all women, or all whites, or all minorities?

4. Many multidivisional firms do not report revenues or profits by division or segment in their *Form 10K* or *Annual Report*. What are the pros and cons of this management practice? Discuss.

5. Define halo error. How can halo error inhibit selecting the best strategies to pursue?

6. List six drawbacks of using only subjective information in formulating strategies.

7. For a firm that you know well, give an example of SO Strategy, showing how an internal strength can be matched with an external opportunity to formulate a strategy.

8. For a firm that you know well, give an example WT Strategy, showing how an internal weakness can be matched with an external threat to formulate a strategy.

9. List three limitations of the SWOT matrix and analysis.

10. For the following three firms using the given factors, calculate a reasonable Stability Position (SP) coordinate to go on their SPACE Matrix axis, given what you know about the nature of those industries.

Factors	Winnebago	Apple	U.S. Postal Service
Barriers to entry into market			
Seasonal nature of business			
Technological changes SP Score			

11. Would the angle or degrees of the vector in a SPACE Matrix be important in generating alternative strategies? Explain.

12. On the Competitive Position (CP) axis of a SPACE Matrix, what level of capacity utilization would be necessary for you to give the firm a negative 1? Negative 7? Why?

13. If a firm has weak financial position and competes in an unstable industry, in which quadrant will the SPACE vector lie?

14. Describe a situation where the SPACE analysis would have no vector. In other words, describe a situation where the SPACE analysis coordinate would be (0,0). What should an analyst do in this situation?

15. Develop a BCG Matrix for your university. Because your college does not generate profits, what would be a good surrogate for the pie slice values? How many circles do you have and how large are they? Explain.

16. In a BCG Matrix, would the Question Mark quadrant or the Cash Cow quadrant be more desirable? Explain.

17. Would a BCG Matrix and analysis be worth performing if you do not know the profits of each segment? Why?

18. What major limitations of the BCG Matrix does the IE Matrix overcome?

19. In an IE Matrix, do you believe it is more advantageous for a division to be located in quadrant II or IV? Why?

20. Develop a $2 \times 2 \times 2$ QSPM for an organization of your choice (i.e., two strengths, two weaknesses, two opportunities, two threats, and two strategies). Follow all the QSPM guidelines presented in the chapter.

21. Give an example of "equifinality" as defined in the chapter.

22. Do you believe the reasons to disclose by-segment financial information offset the reasons not to disclose by-segment financial information? Explain why or why not.

23. How would application of the strategy-formulation framework differ from a small to a large organization?

24. What types of strategies would you recommend for an organization that achieves total weighted scores of 3.6 on the IFE and 1.2 on the EFE Matrix?

25. Given the following information, develop a SPACE Matrix for the XYZ Corporation: FP= + 2; SP = − 6; CP= −2; IP= +4.

26. Given the information in the following table, develop a BCG Matrix and an IE Matrix:

Divisions	1	2	3
Profits	$10	$15	$25
Sales	$100	$50	$100
Relative Market Share	0.2	0.5	0.8
Industry Growth Rate	+.20	+.10	−.10
IFE Total Weighted Scores	1.6	3.1	2.2
EFE Total Weighted Scores	2.5	1.8	3.3

27. Explain the steps involved in developing a QSPM.
28. How would you develop a set of objectives for your school or business?
29. What do you think is the appropriate role of a board of directors in strategic management? Why?
30. Discuss the limitations of various strategy-formulation analytical techniques.
31. Explain why cultural factors should be an important consideration in analyzing and choosing among alternative strategies.
32. How are the SWOT Matrix, SPACE Matrix, BCG Matrix, IE Matrix, and Grand Strategy Matrix similar? How are they different?
33. How would for-profit and nonprofit organizations differ in their applications of the strategy-formulation framework?
34. Develop a SPACE Matrix for a company that is weak financially and is a weak competitor. The industry for this company is pretty stable, but the industry's projected growth in revenues and profits is not good. Label all axes and quadrants.
35. List four limitations of a BCG Matrix.
36. Make up an example to show clearly and completely that you can develop an IE Matrix for a three-division company, where each division has $10, $20, and $40 in revenues and $2, $4, and $1 in profits. State other assumptions needed. Label axes and quadrants.
37. What procedures could be necessary if the SPACE vector falls right on the axis between the Competitive and Defensive quadrants?
38. In a BCG Matrix or the Grand Strategy Matrix, what would you consider to be a rapid market (or industry) growth rate?
39. What are the pros and cons of a company (and country) participating in a Sustainability Report?
40. How did the Sarbanes-Oxley Act of 2002 impact boards of directors?
41. Rank *BusinessWeek*'s "principles of good governance" from 1 to 14 (1 being most important and 14 least important) to reveal your assessment of these new rules.
42. Why is it important to work row by row instead of column by column in preparing a QSPM?
43. Why should one avoid putting double 4s in a row in preparing a QSPM?
44. Envision a QSPM with no weight column. Would that still be a useful analysis? Why or why not? What do you lose by deleting the weight column?
45. Prepare a BCG Matrix for a two-division firm with sales of $5 and $8 versus profits of $3 and $1, respectively. State assumptions for the RMSP and IGR axes to enable you to construct the diagram.
46. Consider developing a before-and-after BCG or IE Matrix to reveal the expected results of your proposed strategies. What limitation of the analysis would this procedure overcome somewhat?
47. If a firm has the leading market share in its industry, where on the BCG Matrix would the circle lie?
48. If a firm competes in a very unstable industry, such as telecommunications, where on the SP axis of the SPACE Matrix would you plot the appropriate point?
49. Why do you think the SWOT Matrix is the most widely used of all strategy matrices?

Notes

1. R. T. Lenz, "Managing the Evolution of the Strategic Planning Process," *Business Horizons* 30, no. 1 (January–February 1987): 37.
2. Robert Grant, "The Resource-Based Theory of Competitive Advantage: Implications for Strategy Formulation," *California Management Review*, Spring 1991, 114.
3. Heinz Weihrich, "The TOWS Matrix: A Tool for Situational Analysis," *Long Range Planning* 15, no. 2 (April 1982): 61. Note: Although Dr. Weihrich first modified SWOT analysis to form the TOWS matrix, the acronym SWOT is much more widely used than TOWS in practice.
4. Greg Dess, G. T. Lumpkin, and Alan Eisner, *Strategic Management: Text and Cases* (New York: McGraw-Hill/Irwin, 2006), 72.
5. Adapted from H. Rowe, R. Mason, and K. Dickel, *Strategic Management and Business Policy: A Methodological Approach* (Reading, MA: Addison-Wesley, 1982), 155–156.
6. Fred David, "The Strategic Planning Matrix—A Quantitative Approach," *Long Range Planning* 19, no. 5 (October 1986): 102; Andre Gib and Robert Margulies, "Making Competitive Intelligence Relevant to the User," *Planning Review* 19, no. 3 (May–June 1991): 21.
7. Fred David, "Computer-Assisted Strategic Planning in Small Businesses," *Journal of Systems Management* 36, no. 7 (July 1985): 24–34.
8. Y. Allarie and M. Firsirotu, "How to Implement Radical Strategies in Large Organizations," *Sloan Management Review* 26, no. 3 (Spring 1985): 19. Another excellent article is P. Shrivastava, "Integrating Strategy Formulation with Organizational Culture," *Journal of Business Strategy* 5, no. 3 (Winter 1985): 103–111.
9. James Brian Quinn, *Strategies for Changes: Logical Incrementalism* (Homewood, IL: Richard D. Irwin, 1980), 128–145. These political tactics are listed in A. Thompson and A. Strickland, *Strategic Management: Concepts and Cases* (Plano, TX: Business Publications, 1984), 261.
10. William Guth and Ian MacMillan, "Strategy Implementation Versus Middle Management Self-Interest," *Strategic Management Journal* 7, no. 4 (July–August 1986): 321.

11. Joann Lublin, "Corporate Directors' Group Gives Repair Plan to Boards," *Wall Street Journal*, March 24, 2009, B4.
12. Phred Dvorak, "Poor Year Doesn't Stop CEO Bonuses," *Wall Street Journal*, March 18, 2009, B1.
13. Louis Lavelle, "The Best and Worst Boards," *BusinessWeek*, October 7, 2002, 104–110.
14. Matt Murray, "Private Companies Also Feel Pressure to Clean Up Acts," *Wall Street Journal*, July 22, 2003, B1.

Current Readings

Buytendijk, Toby Hatch, and Pietro Micheli. "Scenario-Based Strategy Maps." *Business Horizons 53*, no. 4 (July–August 2010): 335–348.

Cooper, Tim, Mark Purdy, and Mark Foster. "A Portfolio Strategy for Locating Operations in the New 'Multi-Polar World.' *Strategy & Leadership* 38, no. 4 (2010): 42.

Dalton, Dan R., and Catherine M. Dalton. "Women and Corporate Boards of Directors: The Promise of Increased, and Substantive, Participation in the Post Sarbanes-Oxley Era." *Business Horizons* 53, no. 3 (May–June 2010): 257–268.

Deutsch, Yuval, Thomas Keil, and Tomi Laamanen. "A Dual Agency View of Board Compensation: The Joint Effects of Outside Director and CEO Stock Options on Firm Risk." *Strategic Management Journal* 32, no. 2 (February 2011): 212–227.

Fong, Eric A., Vilmos F. Misangyi, and Henry L. Tosi. "The Effect of CEO Pay Deviations on CEO Withdrawal, Firm Size, and Firm Profits." *Strategic Management Journal* 31,

no. 6 (June 2010): 629–651.

McDonald, Michael L., and James D. Westphal. "A Little Help Here? Board Control, CEO Identification with the Corporate Elite, and Strategic Help Provided to CEOs at Other Firms." *The Academy of Management Journal* 53, no. 2 (April 2010): 343–370.

Pozen, Robert C. "The Case for Professional Boards." *Harvard Business Review*, December 2010, 50.

"Succeeding at Succession." *Harvard Business Review*, November 2010, 29–35.

Tuggle, Christopher S., Karen Schnatterly, and Richard A. Johnson. "Attention Patterns in the Boardroom: How Board Composition and Processes Affect Discussion of Entrepreneurial Issues." *The Academy of Management Journal* 53, no. 3 (June 2010): 550–571.

Walters, Bruce A., Mark Kroll, and Peter Wright. "The Impact of TMT Board Member Control and Environment on Post-IPO Performance." *The Academy of Management Journal* 53, no. 3 (June 2010): 572–595.

ASSURANCE OF LEARNING EXERCISES

Assurance of Learning Exercise 6A

Perform a SWOT Analysis for Disney's Parks & Resorts Business Segment

Purpose

Each Disney business segment could be required annually to submit a SWOT analysis to corporate top executives who merge divisional analyses into an overall corporate analysis. This exercise will give you practice performing a SWOT analysis. Disney's Parks & Resorts business segment has grown to encompass the world-class Disney Cruise Line, eight Disney Vacation Club resorts (with more than 100,000 members), Adventures by Disney (immersive Disney-guided travel around the world), and five resort locations (encompassing 11 theme parks, including some owned or co-owned by independent entities) on three continents: Disneyland Resort, Anaheim, California; Walt Disney World Resort, Lake Buena Vista, Florida; Tokyo Disney Resort, Urayasu, Chiba; Disneyland Resort Paris, Marne La Valle, France; and Hong Kong Disneyland, Penny's Bay, Lantau Island.

Instructions

Step 1   Review Disney's Parks & Resorts business segment as described in the Cohesion Case and the company's most recent *Annual Report* and *Form 10K*.

Step 2   Review industry and competitive information pertaining to the Parks & Resorts Disney business segment, including competitors such as Royal Caribbean and Carnival and rival theme parks such as Sea World, Busch Gardens, and Six Flags.

Step 3   Join with two other students in class. Together, develop a SWOT Matrix for Disney's Parks & Resorts business segment. Follow all the SWOT guidelines provided in the chapter, including (S4,T3)-type notation at the end of each strategy. Include three strategies in each of the four (SO, ST, WT, WO) quadrants. Be specific regarding your strategies, avoiding generic terms such as Forward Integration.

Step 4   Turn in your team-developed SWOT Matrix to your professor for a classwork grade.

Assurance of Learning Exercise 6B

Develop a SWOT Matrix for Walt Disney

Purpose
The most widely used strategy-formulation technique among U.S. firms is the SWOT Matrix. This exercise requires the development of a SWOT Matrix for Disney. Matching key external and internal factors in a SWOT Matrix requires good intuitive and conceptual skills. You will improve with practice in developing a SWOT Matrix.

Instructions
Recall from Assurance of Learning Exercise 1A that you already may have determined Disney's external opportunities/threats and internal strengths/weaknesses. This information could be used to complete this exercise. Follow the steps outlined as follows:

Step 1   On a separate sheet of paper, construct a large nine-cell diagram that will represent your SWOT Matrix. Appropriately label the cells.

Step 2   Appropriately record Disney's opportunities/threats and strengths/weaknesses in your diagram.

Step 3   Match external and internal factors to generate feasible alternative strategies for Disney. Record SO, WO, ST, and WT strategies in the appropriate cells of the SWOT Matrix. Use the proper notation to indicate the rationale for the strategies. You do not necessarily have to have strategies in all four strategy cells.

Step 4   Compare your SWOT Matrix to another student's SWOT Matrix. Discuss any major differences.

Assurance of Learning Exercise 6C

Develop a SPACE Matrix for Disney's Media Networks Business Segment

Purpose
Each Disney business segment could be required annually to submit a SPACE analysis to corporate top executives who merge divisional analyses into an overall corporate analysis. This exercise will give you practice performing a SPACE analysis.

A division of Walt Disney is Media Networks, comprising a vast array of broadcast, cable, radio, publishing, and Internet businesses, including: Disney-ABC Television Group, ESPN Inc., Walt Disney Internet Group, ABC-owned television stations, ABC Television Network, ABC Daytime, ABC Entertainment Group, ABC News, the Disney Channel Worldwide, ABC Family and SOAPnet, Disney-ABC Domestic Television and Disney-ABC ESPN Television, Radio Disney Network, and the nonfiction book imprint Hyperion. ESPN is a worldwide leader in sports entertainment.

Instructions

Step 1   Review Disney's Media Networks business segment as described in the Cohesion Case as well as the company's most recent *Annual Report* and *Form 10K*. Review the division's financial summary information.

Step 2   Review industry and competitive information pertaining to the Media Networks Disney business segment. A major rival firm is CBS Broadcasting, Inc.

Step 3   Develop a SPACE Matrix for Disney's Media Networks business segment. Write a one-page Executive Overview summarizing strategies that you recommend for this business segment, given your SPACE analysis. Avoid generic, vague terms such as market development.

Assurance of Learning Exercise 6D

Develop a SPACE Matrix for Walt Disney

Purpose

Should Disney pursue aggressive, conservative, competitive, or defensive strategies? Develop a SPACE Matrix for Disney to answer this question. Elaborate on the strategic implications of your directional vector. Be specific in terms of strategies that could benefit Disney.

Instructions

Step 1   Join with two other people in class and develop a joint SPACE Matrix for Disney.
Step 2   Diagram your SPACE Matrix on the board. Compare your matrix with other team's matrices.
Step 3   Discuss the implications of your SPACE Matrix.

Assurance of Learning Exercise 6E

Develop a BCG Matrix for Walt Disney

Purpose

Portfolio matrices are widely used by multidivisional organizations to help identify and select strategies to pursue. A BCG analysis identifies particular divisions that should receive fewer resources than others. It may identify some divisions that need to be divested. This exercise can give you practice developing a BCG Matrix.

Instructions

Step 1   Place the following five column headings at the top of a separate sheet of paper: Divisions, Revenues, Profits, Relative Market Share Position, Industry Growth Rate. Down the far left of your page, list Disney's geographic divisions. Now turn back to the Cohesion Case and find information to fill in all the cells in your data table from page 28.
Step 2   Complete a BCG Matrix for Disney.
Step 3   Compare your BCG Matrix to other students' matrices. Discuss any major differences.

Assurance of Learning Exercise 6F

Develop a QSPM for Walt Disney

Purpose

This exercise can give you practice developing a Quantitative Strategic Planning Matrix to determine the relative attractiveness of various strategic alternatives.

Instructions

Step 1   Join with two other students in class to develop a joint QSPM for Disney.
Step 2   Go to the blackboard and record your strategies and their Sum Total Attractiveness Score. Compare your team's strategies and Sum Total Attractiveness Score to those of other teams. Be sure not to assign the same AS score in a given row. Recall that dashes should be inserted all the way across a given row when used.
Step 3   Discuss any major differences.

Assurance of Learning Exercise 6G

Formulate Individual Strategies

Purpose

Individuals and organizations are alike in many ways. Each has competitors, and each should plan for the future. Every individual and organization faces some external opportunities and threats and has some internal strengths and weaknesses. Both individuals and organizations establish objectives and allocate resources. These and other similarities make it possible for individuals to use many strategic-management concepts and tools. This exercise is designed to demonstrate how the SWOT Matrix can be used by individuals to plan their futures. As one nears completion of a college degree and begins interviewing for jobs, planning can be particularly important.

Instructions

On a separate sheet of paper, construct a SWOT Matrix. Include what you consider to be your major external opportunities, your major external threats, your major strengths, and your major weaknesses. An internal weakness may be a low grade point average. An external opportunity may be that your university offers a graduate program that interests you. Match key external and internal factors by recording in the appropriate cell of the matrix alternative strategies or actions that would allow you to capitalize upon your strengths, overcome your weaknesses, take advantage of your external opportunities, and minimize the impact of external threats. Be sure to use the appropriate matching notation in the strategy cells of the matrix. Because every individual (and organization) is unique, there is no one right answer to this exercise.

Assurance of Learning Exercise 6H

The Mach Test

Purpose

The purpose of this exercise is to enhance your understanding and awareness of the impact that behavioral and political factors can have on strategy analysis and choice.

Instructions

Step 1   On a separate sheet of paper, number from 1 to 10. For each of the 10 statements given as follows, record a *1, 2, 3, 4,* or *5* to indicate your attitude,

where
   1 = I disagree a lot.
   2 = I disagree a little.
   3 = My attitude is neutral.
   4 = I agree a little.
   5 = I agree a lot.

1. The best way to handle people is to tell them what they want to hear.
2. When you ask someone to do something for you, it is best to give the real reason for wanting it, rather than a reason that might carry more weight.
3. Anyone who completely trusts anyone else is asking for trouble.
4. It is hard to get ahead without cutting corners here and there.
5. It is safest to assume that all people have a vicious streak, and it will come out when they are given a chance.
6. One should take action only when it is morally right.
7. Most people are basically good and kind.
8. There is no excuse for lying to someone else.
9. Most people forget more easily the death of their father than the loss of their property.
10. Generally speaking, people won't work hard unless they're forced to do so.

Step 2   Add up the numbers you recorded beside statements 1, 3, 4, 5, 9, and 10. This sum is Subtotal One. For the other four statements, reverse the numbers you recorded, so a *5* becomes a *1, 4* becomes *2, 2* becomes *4, 1* becomes *5,* and *3* remains *3.* Then add those four numbers to get Subtotal Two. Finally, add Subtotal One and Subtotal Two to get your Final Score.

Your Final Score

Your Final Score is your Machiavellian Score. Machiavellian principles are defined in a dictionary as "manipulative, dishonest, deceiving, and favoring political expediency over morality." These tactics are not desirable, are not ethical, and are not recommended in the strategic-management process! You may, however, encounter some highly Machiavellian individuals in your career, so beware. It is important for strategists not to manipulate others in the pursuit of organizational objectives. Individuals today recognize and resent manipulative tactics more than ever before. J. R. Ewing (on *Dallas,* a television show in the 1980s) was a good example of someone who was a high Mach (score over 30). The National Opinion Research Center used this short quiz in a random sample of U.S. adults and found the national average Final Score to be 25.[1] The higher your score, the more Machiavellian (manipulative) you tend to be. The following scale is descriptive of individual scores on this test:

- Below 16: Never uses manipulation as a tool.
- 16 to 20: Rarely uses manipulation as a tool.
- 21 to 25: Sometimes uses manipulation as a tool.
- 26 to 30: Often uses manipulation as a tool.
- Over 30: Always uses manipulation as a tool.

Test Development

The Mach (Machiavellian) test was developed by Dr. Richard Christie, whose research suggests the following tendencies:

1. Men generally are more Machiavellian than women.
2. There is no significant difference between high Machs and low Machs on measures of intelligence or ability.
3. Although high Machs are detached from others, they are detached in a pathological sense.
4. Machiavellian scores are not statistically related to authoritarian values.
5. High Machs tend to be in professions that emphasize the control and manipulation of individuals—for example, law, psychiatry, and behavioral science.
6. Machiavellianism is not significantly related to major demographic characteristics such as educational level or marital status.
7. High Machs tend to come from a city or have urban backgrounds.
8. Older adults tend to have lower Mach scores than younger adults.[2]

A classic book on power relationships, *The Prince,* was written by Niccolo Machiavelli. Several excerpts from *The Prince* follow:

Men must either be cajoled or crushed, for they will revenge themselves for slight wrongs, while for grave ones they cannot. The injury therefore that you do to a man should be such that you need not fear his revenge.

We must bear in mind ... that there is nothing more difficult and dangerous, or more doubtful of success, than an attempt to introduce a new order of things in any state. The innovator has for enemies all those who derived advantages from the old order of things, while those who expect to be benefitted by the new institution will be but lukewarm defenders.

A wise prince, therefore, will steadily pursue such a course that the citizens of his state will always and under all circumstances feel the need for his authority, and will therefore always prove faithful to him.

A prince should seem to be merciful, faithful, humane, religious, and upright, and should even be so in reality, but he should have his mind so trained that, when occasion requires it, he may know how to change to the opposite.[3]

Notes
1. Richard Christie and Florence Geis, *Studies in Machiavellianism* (Orlando, FL: Academic Press, 1970). Material in this exercise adapted with permission of the authors and the Academic Press.
2. Ibid., 82–83.
3. Niccolo Machiavelli, *The Prince* (New York: The Washington Press, 1963).

Assurance of Learning Exercise 6I

Develop a BCG Matrix for My University

Purpose

Developing a BCG Matrix for many nonprofit organizations, including colleges and universities, is a useful exercise. Of course, there are no profits for each division or department—and in some cases no revenues. However, you can be creative in performing a BCG Matrix. For example, the pie slice in the circles can represent the number of majors receiving jobs upon graduation, the number of faculty teaching in that area, or some other variable that you believe is important to consider. The size of the circles can represent the number of students majoring in particular departments or areas.

Instructions

Step 1	On a separate sheet of paper, develop a BCG Matrix for your university. Include all academic schools, departments, or colleges.
Step 2	Diagram your BCG Matrix on the blackboard.
Step 3	Discuss differences among the BCG Matrices on the board.

Assurance of Learning Exercise 6J

The Role of Boards of Directors

Purpose

This exercise will give you a better understanding of the role of boards of directors in formulating, implementing, and evaluating strategies.

Instructions

Identify a person in your community who serves on a board of directors. Make an appointment to interview that person, and seek answers to the following questions. Summarize your findings in a five-minute oral report to the class.

- On what board are you a member?
- How often does the board meet?
- How long have you served on the board?
- What role does the board play in this company?
- How has the role of the board changed in recent years?
- What changes would you like to see in the role of the board?
- To what extent do you prepare for the board meeting?
- To what extent are you involved in strategic management of the firm?

Assurance of Learning Exercise 6K

Locate Companies in a Grand Strategy Matrix

Purpose

The Grand Strategy Matrix is a popular tool for formulating alternative strategies. All organizations can be positioned in one of the Grand Strategy Matrix's four strategy quadrants. The divisions of a firm likewise could be positioned. The Grand Strategy Matrix is based on two evaluative dimensions: competitive position and market growth. Appropriate strategies for an organization to consider are listed in sequential order of attractiveness in each quadrant of the matrix. This exercise gives you experience using a Grand Strategy Matrix.

Instructions

Using the year-end 2010 financial information provided, prepare a Grand Strategy Matrix on a separate sheet of paper. Write the respective company names in the appropriate quadrant of the matrix. Based on this analysis, what strategies are recommended for each company?

Company	Company Revenue Growth % Operating Margin %	Industry	Industry Revenue Growth % Operating Margin %
Lockheed Martin	2.90	Aerospace/Defense	19.30
	8.50		10.66
Caterpillar	57.20	Form & Construction	12.20
	11.21	Equipment	8.57
Hershey	11.10	Confectioners	0.10
	17.79		12.91
Merck	1.40	Drug Manufacturers	10.50
	21.01		11.96
Barnes & Noble	4.10	Specialty Retailing	5.90
	−0.89		4.32

Source: Based on information at www.finance.yahoo.com on 7-15-11.

"NOTABLE QUOTES"

"You want your people to run the business as if it were their own."
—*William Fulmer*

"Poor Ike; when he was a general, he gave an order and it was carried out. Now, he's going to sit in that office and give an order and not a damn thing is going to happen."
—*Harry Truman*

"Changing your pay plan is a big risk, but not changing it could be a bigger one."
—*Nancy Perry*

"Objectives can be compared to a compass bearing by which a ship navigates. A compass bearing is firm, but "in actual navigation, a ship may veer off its course for many miles. Without a compass bearing, a ship would neither find its port nor be able to estimate the time required to get there."
—*Peter Drucker*

"The best game plan in the world never blocked or tackled anybody."
—*Vince Lombardi*

"Pretend that every single person you meet has a sign around his or her neck that says, 'Make me feel important.'"
—*Mary Kay Ash*

Implementing Strategies: Management and Operations Issues

CHAPTER OBJECTIVES

After studying this chapter, you should be able to do the following:

1. Explain why strategy implementation is more difficult than strategy formulation.

2. Discuss the importance of annual objectives and policies in achieving organizational commitment for strategies to be implemented.

3. Explain why organizational structure is so important in strategy implementation.

4. Compare and contrast restructuring and reengineering.

5. Describe the relationships between production/operations and strategy implementation.

6. Explain how a firm can effectively link performance and pay to strategies.

7. Discuss employee stock ownership plans (ESOPs) as a strategic-management concept.

8. Describe how to modify an organizational culture to support new strategies.

ASSURANCE OF LEARNING EXERCISES

Assurance of Learning Exercise 7A
Hershey Company Needs Your Help

Assurance of Learning Exercise 7B
Draw an Organizational Chart Using a Free, Online Template

Assurance of Learning Exercise 7C
Revise Walt Disney's Organizational Chart

Assurance of Learning Exercise 7D
Do Organizations Really Establish Objectives?

Assurance of Learning Exercise 7E
Understanding My University's Culture

The strategic-management process does not end upon deciding what strategy or strategies to pursue. There must be a translation of strategic thought into strategic action. This translation is much easier if managers and employees of the firm understand the business, feel a part of the company, and through involvement in strategy-formulation activities have become committed to helping the organization succeed. Without understanding and commitment, strategy-implementation efforts face major problems.

Implementing strategy affects an organization from top to bottom, including all the functional and divisional areas of a business. It is beyond the purpose and scope of this text to examine all of the business administration concepts and tools important in strategy implementation. This chapter focuses on management issues most central to implementing strategies in 2012–2013 and Chapter 8 focuses on marketing, finance/accounting, R&D, and management information systems issues. Halliburton Company is an example firm with excellent management practices.

> Even the most technically perfect strategic plan will serve little purpose if it is not implemented. Many organizations tend to spend an inordinate amount of time, money, and effort on developing the strategic plan, treating the means and circumstances under which it will be implemented as afterthoughts! Change comes through implementation and evaluation, not through the plan. A technically imperfect plan that is implemented well will achieve more than the perfect plan that never gets off the paper on which it is typed.[1]

Excellent Strategic Management Showcased

HALLIBURTON COMPANY

Headquartered in Houston, Texas, Halliburton is an $18 billion oil-field services firm that is implementing strategies exceptionally well and generating record profit and revenue increases. Halliburton operates from an excellent Strategic Business Unit (SBU) organizational structure with two segments: 1) Drilling and Evaluation, and 2) Completion and Production. The firm's SBU organizational chart is illustrated later in this chapter. Note that CEO Lesar also carries the titles President and Chairman of the Board—violating two guidelines in this chapter.

Halliburton's 2010 revenues increased 22.4 percent to $17.97 billion, while the company's profits increased an incredible 59.5 percent to $1.84 billion. Company profits for the first three months of 2011 doubled to $511 million from $201 million the prior year, as revenue rose 40 percent to $5.3 billion.

Halliburton's CEO David Lesar says increasing oil prices are driving up demand for drilling around the world and his firm is investing heavily in new technology for both onshore and offshore drilling. Halliburton's North American revenue is soaring despite losses from its Gulf of Mexico operations. The company's revenues and profits from operations in Norway, Algeria, West Africa, Iraq, Brazil, Colombia, and Mexico are increasing nicely. Halliburton emerged from the Gulf of Mexico oil disaster unscathed, even though many experts say the firm was responsible for the failed cement seal that allowed explosive gas to flow into the well and reach the doomed rig.

Founded in 1919, Halliburton is one of the world's largest providers of products and services to the energy industry, with 58,000 employees in approximately 70 countries. The company serves the upstream oil and gas industry throughout the lifecycle of the reservoir—from locating hydrocarbons and managing geological data, to drilling and formation evaluation, well construction and completion, and optimizing production through the life of the field.

To strengthen its presence in the Eastern Hemisphere, Halliburton recently established a second headquarters in Dubai, United Arab Emirates. A primary reason for this move is that Halliburton's oil and gas customers are moving their focus from the increasingly difficult reserves of the Western Hemisphere to the bounty of the Eastern Hemisphere. This move puts Halliburton closer to key markets and reduces the costs of moving materials, products, tools, and people.

Source: Based on Ryan Dezember, "Halliburton Doubles Net and Plans New Investments," *Wall Street Journal*, January 25, 2011, B4. Also, Ben Casselman, "Halliburton Emerges from Gulf Disaster Unscathed," *Wall Street Journal*, April 19, 2011, B1. Also, www.halliburton.com.

The Nature of Strategy Implementation

The strategy-implementation stage of strategic management is revealed in Figure 7-1. Successful strategy formulation does not guarantee successful strategy implementation. It is always more difficult to do something (strategy implementation) than to say you are going to do it (strategy formulation)! Although inextricably linked, strategy implementation is fundamentally different from strategy formulation. Strategy formulation and implementation can be contrasted in the following ways:

- Strategy formulation is positioning forces before the action.
- Strategy implementation is managing forces during the action.
- Strategy formulation focuses on effectiveness.
- Strategy implementation focuses on efficiency.
- Strategy formulation is primarily an intellectual process.
- Strategy implementation is primarily an operational process.
- Strategy formulation requires good intuitive and analytical skills.
- Strategy implementation requires special motivation and leadership skills.
- Strategy formulation requires coordination among a few individuals.
- Strategy implementation requires coordination among many individuals.

FIGURE 7-1

Comprehensive Strategic-Management Model

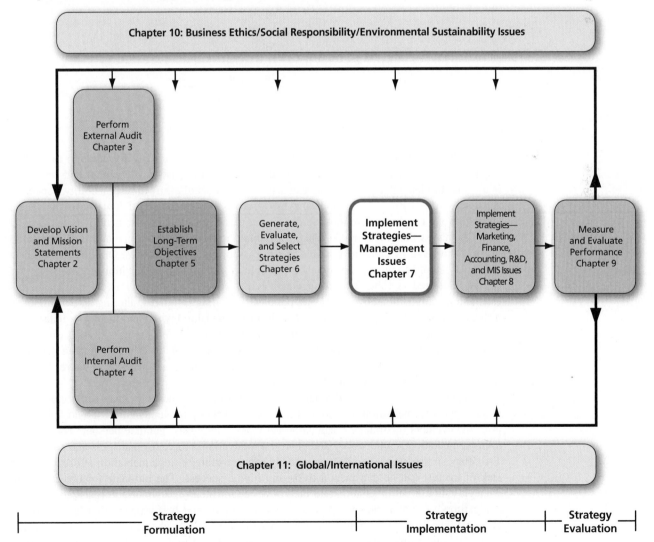

Source: Fred R. David, "How Companies Define Their Mission," *Long Range Planning* 22, no. 3 (June 1988): 40.

Strategy-formulation concepts and tools do not differ greatly for small, large, for-profit, or nonprofit organizations. However, strategy implementation varies substantially among different types and sizes of organizations. Implementing strategies requires such actions as altering sales territories, adding new departments, closing facilities, hiring new employees, changing an organization's pricing strategy, developing financial budgets, developing new employee benefits, establishing cost-control procedures, changing advertising strategies, building new facilities, training new employees, transferring managers among divisions, and building a better management information system. These types of activities obviously differ greatly among manufacturing, service, and governmental organizations.

Management Perspectives

In terms of "Quality of Management," *Fortune* in 2011 ranked the following companies as best in the world:

Rank	Company
1	McDonald's
2	ExxonMobil
3*	W.W. Grainger
3*	Walt Disney
5	U.S. Bancorp
6	Amazon.com
7	Apple
8	Nestlé
9	Nike
10	Occidental Petroleum

Source: Based on: http://money.cnn.com/ magazines/fortune/mostadmired/2011/best_ worst/best5.html

In all but the smallest organizations, the transition from strategy formulation to strategy implementation requires a shift in responsibility from strategists to divisional and functional managers. Implementation problems can arise because of this shift in responsibility, especially if strategy-formulation decisions come as a surprise to middle- and lower-level managers. Managers and employees are motivated more by perceived self-interests than by organizational interests, unless the two coincide. This is a primary reason why divisional and functional managers be involved as much as possible in strategy-formulation activities. Of equal importance, strategists should be involved as much as possible in strategy-implementation activities.

As indicated in Table 7-1, management issues central to strategy implementation include establishing annual objectives, devising policies, allocating resources, altering an existing organizational structure, restructuring and reengineering, revising reward and incentive plans, minimizing resistance to change, matching managers with strategy, developing a strategy-supportive culture, adapting production/operations processes, developing an effective human resources function, and, if necessary, downsizing. Management changes are necessarily more extensive when strategies to be implemented move a firm in a major new direction.

Managers and employees throughout an organization should participate early and directly in strategy-implementation decisions. Their role in strategy implementation should build upon prior involvement in strategy-formulation activities. Strategists' genuine personal commitment to implementation is a necessary and powerful motivational force for managers and employees. Too often, strategists are too busy to actively support strategy-implementation efforts, and their lack of interest can be detrimental to organizational success. The rationale for objectives and strategies should be understood and clearly communicated throughout an organization. Major competitors' accomplishments, products, plans, actions, and performance should be apparent to all organizational members. Major external opportunities and threats should be clear, and managers' and employees' questions should be answered. Top-down flow of communication is essential for developing bottom-up support.

TABLE 7-1   Some Management Issues Central to Strategy Implementation

Establish annual objectives

Devise policies

Allocate resources

Alter an existing organizational structure

Restructure and reengineer

Revise reward and incentive plans

Minimize resistance to change

Match managers with strategy

Develop a strategy-supportive culture

Adapt production/operations processes

Develop an effective human resources function

Downsize and furlough as needed

Link performance and pay to strategies

Firms need to develop a competitor focus at all hierarchical levels by gathering and widely distributing competitive intelligence; every employee should be able to benchmark her or his efforts against best-in-class competitors so that the challenge becomes personal. For example, Starbucks Corp. recently instituted "lean production/operations" at its 11,000 U.S. stores. This system eliminates idle employee time and unnecessary employee motions, such as walking, reaching, and bending. Starbucks says 30 percent of employees' time is motion and the company wants to reduce that. They say "motion and work are two different things."

Annual Objectives

Establishing annual objectives is a decentralized activity that directly involves all managers in an organization. Active participation in establishing annual objectives can lead to acceptance and commitment. *Annual objectives* are essential for strategy implementation because they (1) represent the basis for allocating resources; (2) are a primary mechanism for evaluating managers; (3) are the major instrument for monitoring progress toward achieving long-term objectives; and (4) establish organizational, divisional, and departmental priorities. Considerable time and effort should be devoted to ensuring that annual objectives are well conceived, consistent with long-term objectives, and supportive of strategies to be implemented. Approving, revising, or rejecting annual objectives is much more than a rubber-stamp activity. The purpose of annual objectives can be summarized as follows:

> Annual objectives serve as guidelines for action, directing and channeling efforts and activities of organization members. They provide a source of legitimacy in an enterprise by justifying activities to stakeholders. They serve as standards of performance. They serve as an important source of employee motivation and identification. They give incentives for managers and employees to perform. They provide a basis for organizational design.[2]

Clearly stated and communicated objectives are critical to success in all types and sizes of firms. Annual objectives, stated in terms of profitability, growth, and market share by business segment, geographic area, customer groups, and product, are common in organizations. Figure 7-2 illustrates how the Stamus Company could establish annual objectives based on long-term objectives. Table 7-2 reveals associated revenue figures that correspond to the objectives outlined in Figure 7-2. Note that, according to plan, the Stamus Company will slightly exceed its long-term objective of doubling company revenues between 2012 and 2014.

FIGURE 7-2

The Stamus Company's Hierarchy of Aims

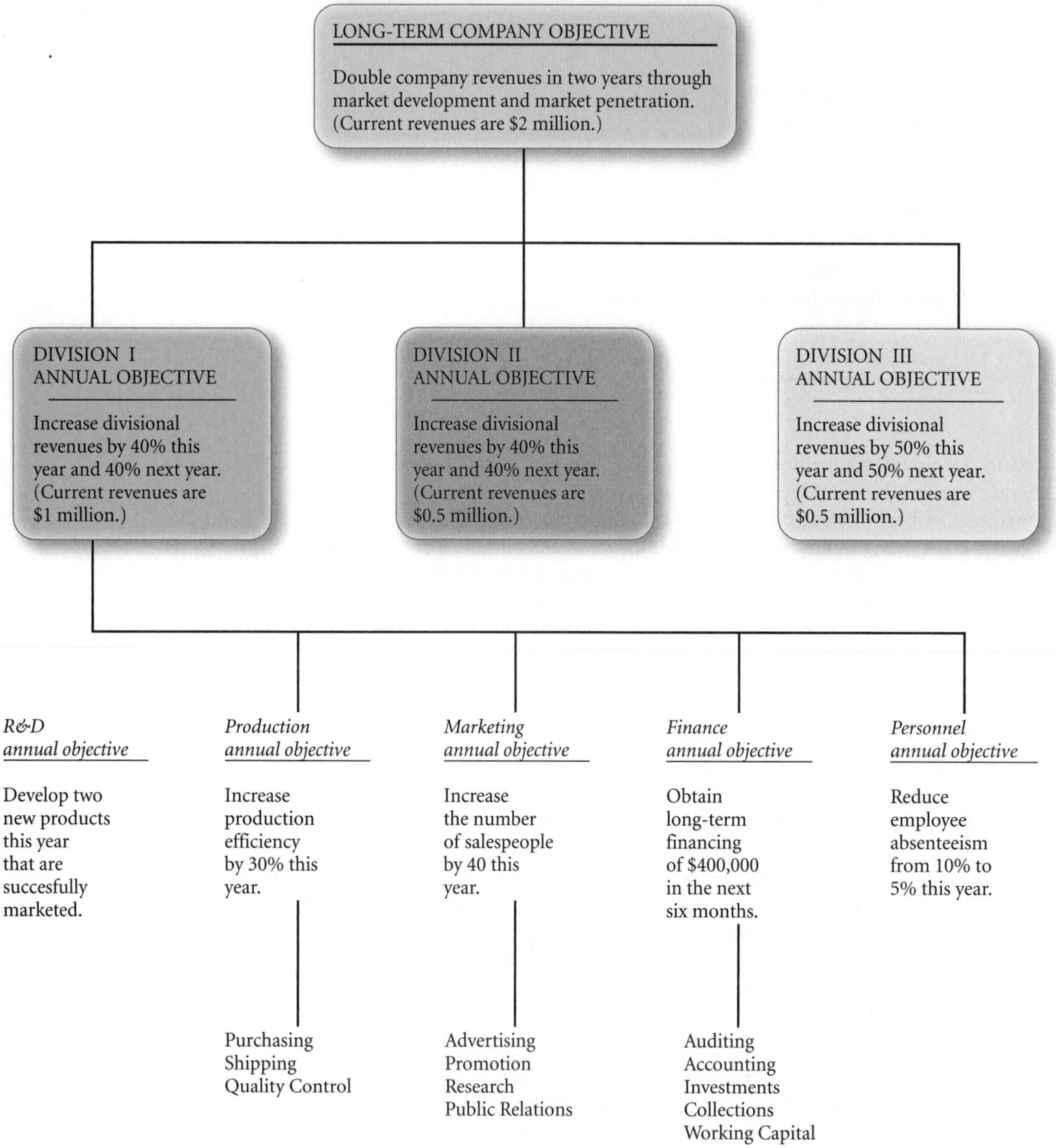

LONG-TERM COMPANY OBJECTIVE

Double company revenues in two years through market development and market penetration. (Current revenues are $2 million.)

DIVISION I
ANNUAL OBJECTIVE

Increase divisional revenues by 40% this year and 40% next year. (Current revenues are $1 million.)

DIVISION II
ANNUAL OBJECTIVE

Increase divisional revenues by 40% this year and 40% next year. (Current revenues are $0.5 million.)

DIVISION III
ANNUAL OBJECTIVE

Increase divisional revenues by 50% this year and 50% next year. (Current revenues are $0.5 million.)

R&D
annual objective

Develop two new products this year that are succesfully marketed.

Production
annual objective

Increase production efficiency by 30% this year.

Marketing
annual objective

Increase the number of salespeople by 40 this year.

Finance
annual objective

Obtain long-term financing of $400,000 in the next six months.

Personnel
annual objective

Reduce employee absenteeism from 10% to 5% this year.

Purchasing
Shipping
Quality Control

Advertising
Promotion
Research
Public Relations

Auditing
Accounting
Investments
Collections
Working Capital

Figure 7-2 also reflects how a hierarchy of annual objectives can be established based on an organization's structure. Objectives should be consistent across hierarchical levels and form a network of supportive aims. *Horizontal consistency of objectives* is as important as *vertical consistency of objectives.* For instance, it would not be effective for manufacturing to achieve more than its annual objective of units produced if marketing could not sell the additional units.

Annual objectives should be measurable, consistent, reasonable, challenging, clear, communicated throughout the organization, characterized by an appropriate time dimension, and accompanied by commensurate rewards and sanctions. Too often, objectives are stated in generalities, with little operational usefulness. Annual objectives, such as "to

TABLE 7-2   The Stamus Company's Revenue Expectations (in $millions)

	2012	2013	2014
Division I Revenues	1.0	1.400	1.960
Division II Revenues	0.5	0.700	0.980
Division III Revenues	0.5	0.750	1.125
Total Company Revenues	**2.0**	**2.850**	**4.065**

improve communication" or "to improve performance," are not clear, specific, or measurable. Objectives should state quantity, quality, cost, and time—and also be verifiable. Terms and phrases such as *maximize, minimize, as soon as possible*, and *adequate* should be avoided.

Annual objectives should be compatible with employees' and managers' values and supported by clearly stated policies. More of something is not always better. Improved quality or reduced cost may, for example, be more important than quantity. It is important to tie rewards and sanctions to annual objectives so that employees and managers understand that achieving objectives is critical to successful strategy implementation. Clear annual objectives do not guarantee successful strategy implementation, but they do increase the likelihood that personal and organizational aims can be accomplished. Overemphasis on achieving objectives can result in undesirable conduct, such as faking the numbers, distorting the records, and letting objectives become ends in themselves. Managers must be alert to these potential problems.

Policies

Changes in a firm's strategic direction do not occur automatically. On a day-to-day basis, policies are needed to make a strategy work. Policies facilitate solving recurring problems and guide the implementation of strategy. Broadly defined, *policy* refers to specific guidelines, methods, procedures, rules, forms, and administrative practices established to support and encourage work toward stated goals. Policies are instruments for strategy implementation. Policies set boundaries, constraints, and limits on the kinds of administrative actions that can be taken to reward and sanction behavior; they clarify what can and cannot be done in pursuit of an organization's objectives. For example, Carnival's *Paradise* ship has a no smoking policy anywhere, anytime aboard ship. It was the first cruise ship to ban smoking comprehensively. Another example of corporate policy relates to surfing the web while at work. About 40 percent of companies today do not have a formal policy preventing employees from surfing the Internet, but software is being marketed now that allows firms to monitor how, when, where, and how long various employees use the Internet at work.

Policies let both employees and managers know what is expected of them, thereby increasing the likelihood that strategies will be implemented successfully. They provide a basis for management control, allow coordination across organizational units, and reduce the amount of time managers spend making decisions. Policies also clarify what work is to be done and by whom. They promote delegation of decision making to appropriate managerial levels where various problems usually arise. Many organizations have a policy manual that serves to guide and direct behavior. Wal-Mart has a policy that it calls the "10 Foot" Rule, whereby customers can find assistance within 10 feet of anywhere in the store. This is a welcomed policy in Japan, where Wal-Mart is trying to gain a foothold; 58 percent of all retailers in Japan are mom-and-pop stores and consumers historically have had to pay "top yen" rather than "discounted prices" for merchandise.

Policies can apply to all divisions and departments (for example, "We are an equal opportunity employer"). Some policies apply to a single department ("Employees in this department must take at least one training and development course each year"). Whatever their scope and form, policies serve as a mechanism for implementing strategies and obtaining objectives. Policies should be stated in writing whenever possible. They represent the means for carrying out strategic decisions. Examples of policies that support a company strategy, a divisional objective, and a departmental objective are given in Table 7-3.

Some example issues that may require a management policy are provided in Table 7-4.

TABLE 7-3   A Hierarchy of Policies

Company Strategy

Acquire a chain of retail stores to meet our sales growth and profitability objectives.

Supporting Policies

1. "All stores will be open from 8 a.m. to 8 p.m. Monday through Saturday." (This policy could increase retail sales if stores currently are open only 40 hours a week.)
2. "All stores must submit a Monthly Control Data Report." (This policy could reduce expense-to-sales ratios.)
3. "All stores must support company advertising by contributing 5 percent of their total monthly revenues for this purpose." (This policy could allow the company to establish a national reputation.)
4. "All stores must adhere to the uniform pricing guidelines set forth in the Company Handbook." (This policy could help assure customers that the company offers a consistent product in terms of price and quality in all its stores.)

Divisional Objective

Increase the division's revenues from $10 million in 2012 to $15 million in 2013.

Supporting Policies

1. "Beginning in January 2012, each one of this division's salespersons must file a weekly activity report that includes the number of calls made, the number of miles traveled, the number of units sold, the dollar volume sold, and the number of new accounts opened." (This policy could ensure that salespersons do not place too great an emphasis in certain areas.)
2. "Beginning in January 2012, this division will return to its employees 5 percent of its gross revenues in the form of a Christmas bonus." (This policy could increase employee productivity.)
3. "Beginning in January 2012, inventory levels carried in warehouses will be decreased by 30 percent in accordance with a just-in-time (JIT) manufacturing approach." (This policy could reduce production expenses and thus free funds for increased marketing efforts.)

Production Department Objective

Increase production from 20,000 units in 2012 to 30,000 units in 2013.

Supporting Policies

1. "Beginning in January 2012, employees will have the option of working up to 20 hours of overtime per week." (This policy could minimize the need to hire additional employees.)
2. "Beginning in January 2012, perfect attendance awards in the amount of $100 will be given to all employees who do not miss a workday in a given year." (This policy could decrease absenteeism and increase productivity.)
3. "Beginning in January 2012, new equipment must be leased rather than purchased." (This policy could reduce tax liabilities and thus allow more funds to be invested in modernizing production processes.)

TABLE 7-4   Some Issues That May Require a Management Policy

- To offer extensive or limited management development workshops and seminars
- To centralize or decentralize employee-training activities
- To recruit through employment agencies, college campuses, and/or newspapers
- To promote from within or to hire from the outside
- To promote on the basis of merit or on the basis of seniority
- To tie executive compensation to long-term and/or annual objectives
- To offer numerous or few employee benefits
- To negotiate directly or indirectly with labor unions
- To delegate authority for large expenditures or to centrally retain this authority
- To allow much, some, or no overtime work
- To establish a high- or low-safety stock of inventory
- To use one or more suppliers
- To buy, lease, or rent new production equipment
- To greatly or somewhat stress quality control
- To establish many or only a few production standards
- To operate one, two, or three shifts
- To discourage using insider information for personal gain
- To discourage sexual harassment
- To discourage smoking at work
- To discourage insider trading
- To discourage moonlighting

Resource Allocation

Resource allocation is a central management activity that allows for strategy execution. In organizations that do not use a strategic-management approach to decision making, resource allocation is often based on political or personal factors. Strategic management enables resources to be allocated according to priorities established by annual objectives.

Nothing could be more detrimental to strategic management and to organizational success than for resources to be allocated in ways not consistent with priorities indicated by approved annual objectives.

All organizations have at least four types of resources that can be used to achieve desired objectives: financial resources, physical resources, human resources, and technological resources. Allocating resources to particular divisions and departments does not mean that strategies will be successfully implemented. A number of factors commonly prohibit effective resource allocation, including an overprotection of resources, too great an emphasis on short-run financial criteria, organizational politics, vague strategy targets, a reluctance to take risks, and a lack of sufficient knowledge.

Below the corporate level, there often exists an absence of systematic thinking about resources allocated and strategies of the firm. Yavitz and Newman explain why:

> Managers normally have many more tasks than they can do. Managers must allocate time and resources among these tasks. Pressure builds up. Expenses are too high. The CEO wants a good financial report for the third quarter. Strategy formulation and implementation activities often get deferred. Today's problems soak up available energies and resources. Scrambled accounts and budgets fail to reveal the shift in allocation away from strategic needs to currently squeaking wheels.[3]

The real value of any resource allocation program lies in the resulting accomplishment of an organization's objectives. Effective resource allocation does not guarantee successful strategy implementation because programs, personnel, controls, and commitment must breathe life into the resources provided. Strategic management itself is sometimes referred to as a "resource allocation process."

Managing Conflict

Interdependency of objectives and competition for limited resources often leads to conflict. *Conflict* can be defined as a disagreement between two or more parties on one or more issues. Establishing annual objectives can lead to conflict because individuals have different expectations and perceptions, schedules create pressure, personalities are incompatible, and misunderstandings between line managers (such as production supervisors) and staff managers (such as human resource specialists) occur. For example, a collection manager's objective of reducing bad debts by 50 percent in a given year may conflict with a divisional objective to increase sales by 20 percent.

Establishing objectives can lead to conflict because managers and strategists must make trade-offs, such as whether to emphasize short-term profits or long-term growth, profit margin or market share, market penetration or market development, growth or stability, high risk or low risk, and social responsiveness or profit maximization. Trade-offs are necessary because no firm has sufficient resources to pursue all strategies that would benefit the firm. Table 7-5 reveals some important management trade-off decisions required in strategy implementation.

Conflict is unavoidable in organizations, so it is important that conflict be managed and resolved before dysfunctional consequences affect organizational performance. Conflict is not always bad. An absence of conflict can signal indifference and apathy. Conflict can serve to energize opposing groups into action and may help managers identify problems.

Various approaches for managing and resolving conflict can be classified into three categories: avoidance, defusion, and confrontation. *Avoidance* includes such actions as ignoring the problem in hopes that the conflict will resolve itself or physically separating the conflicting individuals (or groups). *Defusion* can include playing down differences between conflicting parties while accentuating similarities and common interests, compromising so that there is neither a clear winner nor loser, resorting to majority rule, appealing to a higher authority, or redesigning

TABLE 7-5 Some Management Trade-Off Decisions Required in Strategy Implementation

To emphasize short-term profits or long-term growth

To emphasize profit margin or market share

To emphasize market development or market penetration

To lay off or furlough

To seek growth or stability

To take high risk or low risk

To be more socially responsible or more profitable

To outsource jobs or pay more to keep jobs at home

To acquire externally or to build internally

To restructure or reengineer

To use leverage or equity to raise funds

To use part-time or full-time employees

present positions. *Confrontation* is exemplified by exchanging members of conflicting parties so that each can gain an appreciation of the other's point of view or holding a meeting at which conflicting parties present their views and work through their differences.

Matching Structure with Strategy

Changes in strategy often require changes in the way an organization is structured for two major reasons. First, structure largely dictates how objectives and policies will be established. For example, objectives and policies established under a geographic organizational structure are couched in geographic terms. Objectives and policies are stated largely in terms of products in an organization whose structure is based on product groups. The structural format for developing objectives and policies can significantly impact all other strategy-implementation activities.

The second major reason why changes in strategy often require changes in structure is that structure dictates how resources will be allocated. If an organization's structure is based on customer groups, then resources will be allocated in that manner. Similarly, if an organization's structure is set up along functional business lines, then resources are allocated by functional areas. Unless new or revised strategies place emphasis in the same areas as old strategies, structural reorientation commonly becomes a part of strategy implementation.

Changes in strategy lead to changes in organizational structure. Structure should be designed to facilitate the strategic pursuit of a firm and, therefore, follow strategy. Without a strategy or reasons for being (mission), companies find it difficult to design an effective structure. Chandler found a particular structure sequence to be repeated often as organizations grow and change strategy over time.

There is no one optimal organizational design or structure for a given strategy or type of organization. What is appropriate for one organization may not be appropriate for a similar firm, although successful firms in a given industry do tend to organize themselves in a similar way. For example, consumer goods companies tend to emulate the divisional structure-by-product form of organization. Small firms tend to be functionally structured (centralized). Medium-sized firms tend to be divisionally structured (decentralized). Large firms tend to use a strategic business unit (SBU) or matrix structure. As organizations grow, their structures generally change from simple to complex as a result of concatenation, or the linking together of several basic strategies.

Numerous external and internal forces affect an organization; no firm could change its structure in response to every one of these forces, because to do so would lead to chaos. However, when a firm changes its strategy, the existing organizational structure may become ineffective. As indicated in Table 7-6, symptoms of an ineffective organizational structure include too many levels of management, too many meetings attended by too many people, too much attention being directed toward solving interdepartmental conflicts, too large a span of control, and too many unachieved objectives. Changes in structure can facilitate strategy-implementation efforts, but changes in structure should not be expected to make a bad strategy good, to make bad managers good, or to make bad products sell.

TABLE 7-6   Symptoms of an Ineffective Organizational Structure

1. Too many levels of management
2. Too many meetings attended by too many people
3. Too much attention being directed toward solving interdepartmental conflicts
4. Too large a span of control
5. Too many unachieved objectives
6. Declining corporate or business performance
7. Losing ground to rival firms
8. Revenue and/or earnings divided by number of employees and/or number of managers is low compared to rival firms

Structure undeniably can and does influence strategy. Strategies formulated must be workable, so if a certain new strategy required massive structural changes it would not be an attractive choice. In this way, structure can shape the choice of strategies. But a more important concern is determining what types of structural changes are needed to implement new strategies and how these changes can best be accomplished. We examine this issue by focusing on seven basic types of organizational structure: functional, divisional by geographic area, divisional by product, divisional by customer, divisional process, strategic business unit (SBU), and matrix.

The Functional Structure

The most widely used structure is the functional or centralized type because this structure is the simplest and least expensive of the seven alternatives. A *functional structure* groups tasks and activities by business function, such as production/operations, marketing, finance/accounting, research and development, and management information systems. A university may structure its activities by major functions that include academic affairs, student services, alumni relations, athletics, maintenance, and accounting. Besides being simple and inexpensive, a functional structure also promotes specialization of labor, encourages efficient use of managerial and technical talent, minimizes the need for an elaborate control system, and allows rapid decision making.

Some disadvantages of a functional structure are that it forces accountability to the top, minimizes career development opportunities, and is sometimes characterized by low employee morale, line/staff conflicts, poor delegation of authority, and inadequate planning for products and markets.

A functional structure often leads to short-term and narrow thinking that may undermine what is best for the firm as a whole. For example, the research and development department may strive to overdesign products and components to achieve technical elegance, while manufacturing may argue for low-frills products that can be mass produced more easily. Thus, communication is often not as good in a functional structure. Schein gives an example of a communication problem in a functional structure:

> The word "marketing" will mean product development to the engineer, studying customers through market research to the product manager, merchandising to the salesperson, and constant change in design to the manufacturing manager. Then when these managers try to work together, they often attribute disagreements to personalities and fail to notice the deeper, shared assumptions that vary and dictate how each function thinks.[4]

Most large companies have abandoned the functional structure in favor of decentralization and improved accountability. However, a large firm that still successfully uses a functional structure is Nucor Steel, based in Charlotte, North Carolina. Netflix, the company showcased for excellent strategic management in the prior chapter, also operates from a functional structure—as illustrated in Figure 7-3.

Table 7-7 summarizes the advantages and disadvantages of a functional organizational structure.

FIGURE 7-3

Netflix's Organizational Structure

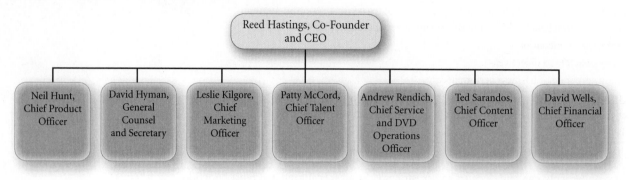

The Divisional Structure

The *divisional* or *decentralized structure* is the second most common type used by U.S. businesses. As a small organization grows, it has more difficulty managing different products and services in different markets. Some form of divisional structure generally becomes necessary to motivate employees, control operations, and compete successfully in diverse locations. The divisional structure can be organized in one of four ways: *by geographic area, by product or service, by customer,* or *by process*. With a divisional structure, functional activities are performed both centrally and in each separate division.

Cisco Systems recently discarded its divisional structure by customer and reorganized into a functional structure. CEO John Chambers replaced the three-customer structure based on big businesses, small businesses, and telecoms, and now the company has five functional executive vice presidents (EVPs). Chambers says the goal was to eliminate duplication, but the change should not be viewed as a shift in strategy. Chambers's span of control in the new structure is reduced from 15 to 12 managers reporting directly to him.

Sun Microsystems recently reduced the number of its business units from seven to four. Kodak recently reduced its number of business units from seven by-customer divisions to five by-product divisions. As consumption patterns become increasingly similar worldwide, a by-product structure is becoming more effective than a by-customer or a by-geographic type divisional structure. In the restructuring, Kodak eliminated its global operations division and distributed those responsibilities across the new by-product divisions.

A divisional structure has some clear advantages. First and perhaps foremost, accountability is clear. That is, divisional managers can be held responsible for sales and profit levels. Because a divisional structure is based on extensive delegation of authority, managers and employees can easily see the results of their good or bad performances. As a result, employee morale is generally higher in a divisional structure than it is in a centralized structure. Other advantages of

TABLE 7-7 Advantages and Disadvantages of a Functional Organizational Structure

Advantages	Disadvantages
1. Simple and inexpensive	1. Accountability forced to the top
2. Capitalizes on specialization of business activities such as marketing and finance	2. Delegation of authority and responsibility not encouraged
3. Minimizes need for elaborate control system	3. Minimizes career development
4. Allows for rapid decision making	4. Low employee/manager morale
	5. Inadequate planning for products and markets
	6. Leads to short-term, narrow thinking
	7. Leads to communication problems

TABLE 7-8   Advantages and Disadvantages of a Divisional Organizational Structure

Advantages	Disadvantages
1. Accountability is clear	1. Can be costly
2. Allows local control of local situations	2. Duplication of functional activities
3. Creates career development chances	3. Requires a skilled management force
4. Promotes delegation of authority	4. Requires an elaborate control system
5. Leads to competitive climate internally	5. Competition among divisions can become so intense as to be dysfunctional
6. Allows easy adding of new products or regions	6. Can lead to limited sharing of ideas and resources
7. Allows strict control and attention to products, customers, and/or regions	7. Some regions/products/customers may receive special treatment

the divisional design are that it creates career development opportunities for managers, allows local control of situations, leads to a competitive climate within an organization, and allows new businesses and products to be added easily.

The divisional design is not without some limitations, however. Perhaps the most important limitation is that a divisional structure is costly, for a number of reasons. First, each division requires functional specialists who must be paid. Second, there exists some duplication of staff services, facilities, and personnel; for instance, functional specialists are also needed centrally (at headquarters) to coordinate divisional activities. Third, managers must be well qualified because the divisional design forces delegation of authority; better-qualified individuals require higher salaries. A divisional structure can also be costly because it requires an elaborate, head-quarters-driven control system. Fourth, competition between divisions may become so intense that it is dysfunctional and leads to limited sharing of ideas and resources for the common good of the firm. Table 7-8 summarizes the advantages and disadvantages of divisional organizational structure.

Ghoshal and Bartlett, two leading scholars in strategic management, note the following:

As their label clearly warns, divisions divide. The divisional model fragments companies' resources; it creates vertical communication channels that insulate business units and prevents them from sharing their strengths with one another. Consequently, the whole of the corporation is often less than the sum of its parts. A final limitation of the divisional design is that certain regions, products, or customers may sometimes receive special treatment, and it may be difficult to maintain consistent, companywide practices. Nonetheless, for most large organizations and many small firms, the advantages of a divisional structure more than offset the potential limitations.[5]

A *divisional structure by geographic area* is appropriate for organizations whose strategies need to be tailored to fit the particular needs and characteristics of customers in different geographic areas. This type of structure can be most appropriate for organizations that have similar branch facilities located in widely dispersed areas. A divisional structure by geographic area allows local participation in decision making and improved coordination within a region. Hershey Foods is an example company organized using the divisional-by geographic region type of structure. Hershey's divisions are United States, Canada, Mexico, Brazil, and Other. Analysts contend that this type of structure may not be best for Hershey because consumption patterns for candy are quite similar worldwide. An alternative—and perhaps better—type of structure for Hershey would be divisional by product because the company produces, and sells three types of products worldwide: (1) chocolate, (2) nonchocolate, and (3) grocery.

Coca-Cola Company operates from a divisional-by-geographic region type organizational structure, as illustrated in Figure 7-4.

FIGURE 7-4

Coca-Cola Company Executive Officers

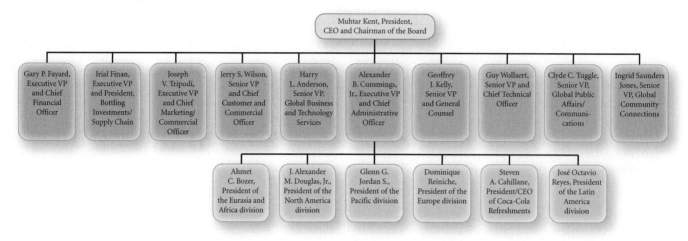

Source: Coke's 2010 *Annual Report.*

The *divisional structure by product (or services)* is most effective for implementing strategies when specific products or services need special emphasis. Also, this type of structure is widely used when an organization offers only a few products or services or when an organization's products or services differ substantially. The divisional structure allows strict control over and attention to product lines, but it may also require a more skilled management force and reduced top management control. General Motors, DuPont, and Procter & Gamble use a divisional structure by product to implement strategies. Huffy, the largest bicycle company in the world, is another firm that is highly decentralized based on a divisional-by-product structure. Based in Ohio, Huffy's divisions are the Bicycle division, the Gerry Baby Products division, the Huffy Sports division, YLC Enterprises, and Washington Inventory Service. Harry Shaw, Huffy's chairman, believes decentralization is one of the keys to Huffy's success.

Eastman Chemical established a new by-product divisional organizational structure. The company's two new divisions, Eastman Company and Voridian Company, focus on chemicals and polymers, respectively. The Eastman division focuses on coatings, adhesives, inks, and plastics, whereas the Voridian division focuses on fibers, polyethylene, and other polymers. Microsoft recently reorganized the whole corporation into three large divisions-by-product. Headed by a president, the new divisions are (1) platform products and services, (2) business, and (3) entertainment and devices. The Swiss electrical-engineering company ABB Ltd. recently scrapped its two core divisions, (1) power technologies and (2) automation technologies, and replaced them with five new divisions: (1) power products, (2) power systems, (3) automation products, (4) process automation, and (5) robotics.

When a few major customers are of paramount importance and many different services are provided to these customers, then a *divisional structure by customer* can be the most effective way to implement strategies. This structure allows an organization to cater effectively to the requirements of clearly defined customer groups. For example, book publishing companies often organize their activities around customer groups, such as colleges, secondary schools, and private commercial schools. Some airline companies have two major customer divisions: passengers and freight or cargo services. Utility companies often use (1) commercial, (2) residential, and (3) industrial as their divisions-by-customer.

Merrill Lynch is organized into separate divisions that cater to different groups of customers, including wealthy individuals, institutional investors, and small corporations. Motorola's semiconductor chip division is also organized divisionally by customer, having three separate segments that sell to (1) the automotive and industrial market, (2) the mobile phone market, and (3) the data-networking market. The automotive and industrial segment is doing well, but the other two segments are faltering, which is a reason why Motorola is trying to divest its semiconductor operations.

A *divisional structure by process* is similar to a functional structure, because activities are organized according to the way work is actually performed. However, a key difference between these two designs is that functional departments are not accountable for profits or revenues, whereas divisional process departments are evaluated on these criteria. An example of a divisional structure by process is a manufacturing business organized into six divisions: electrical work, glass cutting, welding, grinding, painting, and foundry work. In this case, all operations related to these specific processes would be grouped under the separate divisions. Each process (division) would be responsible for generating revenues and profits. The divisional structure by process can be particularly effective in achieving objectives when distinct production processes represent the thrust of competitiveness in an industry. Halliburton's organizational chart illustrated on the next page features aspects of the division-by-process design.

The Strategic Business Unit (SBU) Structure

As the number, size, and diversity of divisions in an organization increase, controlling and evaluating divisional operations become increasingly difficult for strategists. Increases in sales often are not accompanied by similar increases in profitability. The span of control becomes too large at top levels of the firm. For example, in a large conglomerate organization composed of 90 divisions, such as ConAgra, the chief executive officer could have difficulty even remembering the first names of divisional presidents. In multidivisional organizations, an SBU structure can greatly facilitate strategy-implementation efforts. ConAgra has put its many divisions into three primary SBUs: (1) food service (restaurants), (2) retail (grocery stores), and (3) agricultural products.

The SBU structure groups similar divisions into strategic business units and delegates authority and responsibility for each unit to a senior executive who reports directly to the chief executive officer. This change in structure can facilitate strategy implementation by improving coordination between similar divisions and channeling accountability to distinct business units. In a 100-division conglomerate, the divisions could perhaps be regrouped into 10 SBUs according to certain common characteristics, such as competing in the same industry, being located in the same area, or having the same customers.

Two disadvantages of an SBU structure are that it requires an additional layer of management, which increases salary expenses. Also, the role of the group vice president is often ambiguous. However, these limitations often do not outweigh the advantages of improved coordination and accountability. Another advantage of the SBU structure is that it makes the tasks of planning and control by the corporate office more manageable.

Citigroup recently reorganized the whole company into two SBUs: (1) Citigroup, which includes the retail bank, the corporate and investment bank, the private bank, and global transaction services; and (2) Citi Holdings, which includes Citi's asset management and consumer finance segments, CitiMortgage, CitiFinancial, and the joint brokerage operations with Morgan Stanley. Citigroup's CEO, Vikram Pandit, says the restructuring will allow the company to reduce operating costs and to divest (spin off) Citi Holdings.

The huge computer firm Dell Inc. recently reorganized into two SBUs. One SBU is Consumer Products and the other is Commercial. As part of its reorganization, Dell deleted the geographic divisions within its Consumer Products segment. However within its Commercial segment, there are now three worldwide units: (1) large enterprise, (2) public sector, and (3) small and midsize businesses. Dell is also closing a manufacturing facility in Austin, Texas, and laying off more employees as the company struggles to compete. Computer prices and demand are falling as competition increases. Atlantic Richfield Fairchild Industries, and Honeywell International are examples of firms that successfully use an SBU-type structure.

As illustrated in Figure 7-5, Sonoco Products Corporation, based in Hartsville, South Carolina, utilizes an SBU organizational structure. Note that Sonoco's SBUs—Industrial Products and Consumer Products—each have four autonomous divisions that have their own sales, manufacturing, R&D, finance, HRM, and MIS functions.

An excellent example of an SBU organizational chart is the one posted at the Halliburton Company website and shown in Figure 7-6. Note that six division executives report to the Drilling and Evaluation top executive, while four division heads report to the Completion and Production top executive. It is interesting and somewhat unusual that the 10 Halliburton divisions are organized by process rather than by geographic region or product.

FIGURE 7-5

Sonoco Products' SBU Organizational Chart

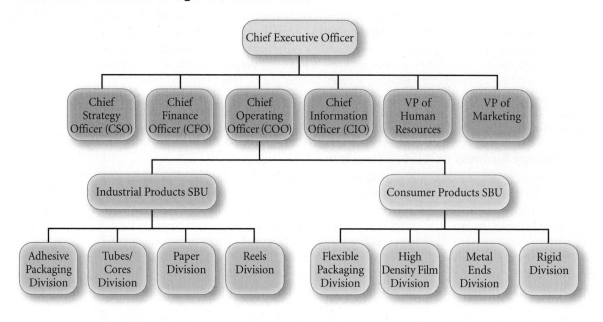

FIGURE 7-6

Halliburton Company's SBU Organizational Chart

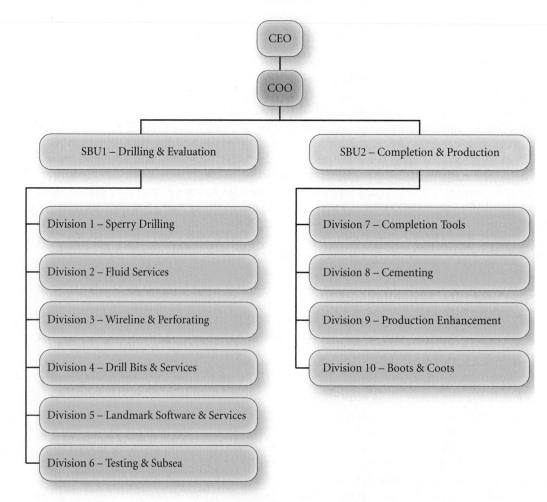

Source: Based on http://www.halliburton.com/AboutUs/default.aspx?pageid=2458&navid=966

The Matrix Structure

A *matrix structure* is the most complex of all designs because it depends upon both vertical and horizontal flows of authority and communication (hence the term *matrix*). In contrast, functional and divisional structures depend primarily on vertical flows of authority and communication. A matrix structure can result in higher overhead because it creates more management positions. Other disadvantages of a matrix structure that contribute to overall complexity include dual lines of budget authority (a violation of the unity-of-command principle), dual sources of reward and punishment, shared authority, dual reporting channels, and a need for an extensive and effective communication system.

Despite its complexity, the matrix structure is widely used in many industries, including construction, health care, research, and defense. As indicated in Table 7-9, some advantages of a matrix structure are that project objectives are clear, there are many channels of communication, workers can see the visible results of their work, and shutting down a project can be accomplished relatively easily. Another advantage of a matrix structure is that it facilitates the use of specialized personnel, equipment, and facilities. Functional resources are shared in a matrix structure, rather than duplicated as in a divisional structure. Individuals with a high degree of expertise can divide their time as needed among projects, and they in turn develop their own skills and competencies more than in other structures.

A typical matrix structure is illustrated in Figure 7-7. Note that the letters (A through Z4) refer to managers. For example, if you were manager A, you would be responsible for financial aspects of Project 1, and you would have two bosses: the Project 1 Manager onsite and the CFO off site.

For a matrix structure to be effective, organizations need participative planning, training, clear mutual understanding of roles and responsibilities, excellent internal communication, and mutual trust and confidence. The matrix structure is being used more frequently by U.S. businesses because firms are pursuing strategies that add new products, customer groups, and technology to their range of activities. Out of these changes are coming product managers, functional managers, and geographic-area managers, all of whom have important strategic responsibilities. When several variables, such as product, customer, technology, geography, functional area, and line of business, have roughly equal strategic priorities, a matrix organization can be an effective structural form.

Some Do's and Don'ts in Developing Organizational Charts

Students analyzing strategic-management cases are often asked to revise and develop a firm's organizational structure. This section provides some basic guidelines for this endeavor. There are some basic do's and don'ts in regard to devising or constructing organizational charts, especially for midsize to large firms. First of all, reserve the title CEO for the top executive of the firm. Don't use the title "president" for the top person; use it for the division top managers if there are divisions within the firm. Also, do not use the title "president" for functional business executives. They should have the title "chief," or "vice president," or "manager," or "officer," such as "Chief Information Officer," or "VP of Human Resources." Further, do not recommend a dual

---

TABLE 7-9 Advantages and Disadvantages of a Matrix Structure

Advantages	Disadvantages
1. Project objectives are clear	1. Requires excellent vertical and horizontal flows of communication
2. Employees can clearly see results of their work	2. Costly because creates more manager positions
3. Shutting down a project is easily accomplished	3. Violates unity of command principle
4. Facilitates uses of special equipment/personnel/facilities	4. Creates dual lines of budget authority
5. Functional resources are shared instead of duplicated as in a divisional structure	5. Creates dual sources of reward/punishment
	6. Creates shared authority and reporting
	7. Requires mutual trust and understanding

FIGURE 7-7

An Example Matrix Structure

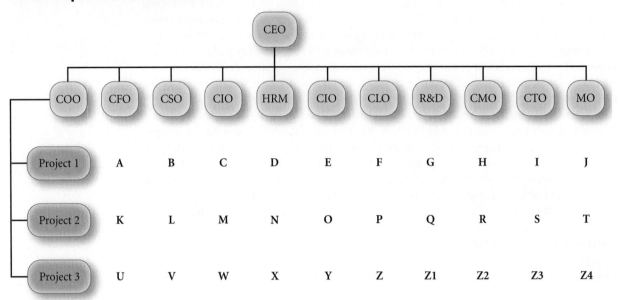

Note: Titles spelled out as follows.

Chief Executive Officer (CEO)
Chief Finance Officer (CFO)
Chief Strategy Officer (CSO)
Chief Information Officer (CIO)
Human Resources Manager (HRM)
Chief Operating Officer (COO)
Chief Legal Officer (CLO)
Research & Development Officer (R&D)
Chief Marketing Officer (CMO)
Chief Technology Officer (CTO)
Competitive Intelligence Officer (CIO)
Maintenance Officer (MO)

title (such as "CEO and president") for just one executive. The chairman of the board and CEO of Bristol-Myers Squibb, Peter Dolan, recently gave up his title as chairman. However, Pfizer's CEO, Jeffrey Kindler, recently added chairman of the board to his title when he succeeded Hank McKinnell as chairman of Pfizer's board. And Comverse Technology recently named Andre Dahan as its president, chief executive officer, and board director. Actually, "chairperson" is much better than "chairman" for this title.

A significant movement began among corporate America in mid-2009 to split the chairperson of the board and the CEO positions in publicly-held companies.[6] The movement includes asking the New York Stock Exchange and Nasdaq to adopt listing rules that would require separate positions. About 37 percent of companies in the S&P 500 stock index have separate positions, up from 22 percent in 2002, but this still leaves plenty of room for improvement. Among European and Asian companies, the split in these two positions is much more common. For example, 79 percent of British companies split the positions, and all German and Dutch companies split the position.

Directly below the CEO, it is best to have a COO (chief operating officer) with any division presidents reporting directly to the COO. On the same level as the COO and also reporting to the CEO, draw in your functional business executives, such as a CFO (chief financial officer), VP of human resources, a CSO (chief strategy officer), a CIO (chief information officer), a CMO (chief marketing officer), a VP of R&D, a VP of legal affairs, an investment relations officer, maintenance officer, and so on. Note in Figure 7-8 that these positions are labeled and placed appropriately. Note that a controller and/or treasurer would normally report to the CFO.

FIGURE 7-8

Typical Top Managers of a Large Firm

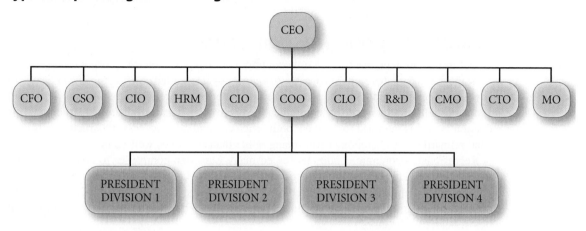

Note: Titles spelled out as follows.

Chief Executive Officer (CEO)
Chief Finance Officer (CFO)
Chief Strategy Officer (CSO)
Chief Information Officer (CIO)
Human Resources Manager (HRM)
Chief Operating Officer (COO)
Chief Legal Officer (CLO)
Research & Development Officer (R&D)
Chief Marketing Officer (CMO)
Chief Technology Officer (CTO)
Competitive Intelligence Officer (CIO)
Maintenance Officer (MO)

In developing an organizational chart, avoid having a particular person reporting to more than one person in the chain of command. This would violate the unity-of-command principle of management that "every employee should have just one boss." Also, do not have the CFO, CIO, CSO, human resource officer, or other functional positions report to the COO. All these positions report directly to the CEO.

A key consideration in devising an organizational structure concerns the divisions. Note whether the divisions (if any) of a firm presently are established based upon geography, customer, product, or process. If the firm's organizational chart is not available, you often can devise a chart based on the titles of executives. An important case analysis activity is for you to decide how the divisions of a firm should be organized for maximum effectiveness. Even if the firm presently has no divisions, determine whether the firm would operate better with divisions. In other words, which type of divisional breakdown do you (or your group or team) feel would be best for the firm in allocating resources, establishing objectives, and devising compensation incentives? This important strategic decision faces many midsize and large firms (and teams of students analyzing a strategic-management case).

As consumption patterns become more and more similar worldwide, the divisional-by-product form of structure is increasingly the most effective. Be mindful that all firms have functional staff below their top executive and often readily provide this information, so be wary of concluding prematurely that a particular firm utilizes a functional structure. If you see the word "president" in the titles of executives, coupled with financial-reporting segments, such as by product or geographic region, then the firm is divisionally structured.

If the firm is large with numerous divisions, decide whether an SBU type of structure would be more appropriate to reduce the span of control reporting to the COO. Note in Figure 7-5 that the Sonoco Products' strategic business units (SBUs) are based on product groupings. An alternative SBU structure would have been to base the division groupings on location. One never knows for sure if a proposed or actual structure is indeed most effective for a particular firm. According to Alfred Chandler, declining financial performance signals a need for altering the structure.

Restructuring and Reengineering

Restructuring and reengineering are becoming commonplace on the corporate landscape across the United States and Europe. *Restructuring*—also called *downsizing, rightsizing,* or *delayering*—involves reducing the size of the firm in terms of number of employees, number of divisions or units, and number of hierarchical levels in the firm's organizational structure. This reduction in size is intended to improve both efficiency and effectiveness. Restructuring is concerned primarily with shareholder well-being rather than employee well-being.

Recessionary economic conditions forced many European companies to downsize, laying off managers and employees. This practice has historically been rare in Europe. because labor unions and laws required lengthy negotiations or huge severance checks before workers could be terminated. In contrast to the United States, labor union executives of large European firms sit on most boards of directors.

Job security in European companies is slowly moving toward a U.S. scenario, in which firms lay off almost at will. From banks in Milan to factories in Mannheim, European employers are starting to show people the door in an effort to streamline operations, increase efficiency, and compete against already slim and trim U.S. firms. Massive U.S.-style layoffs are still rare in Europe, but unemployment rates throughout the continent are rising quite rapidly. European firms still prefer to downsize by attrition and retirement rather than by blanket layoffs because of culture, laws, and unions.

In contrast, *reengineering* is concerned more with employee and customer well-being than shareholder well-being. Reengineering—also called process management, process innovation, or process redesign—involves reconfiguring or redesigning work, jobs, and processes for the purpose of improving cost, quality, service, and speed. Reengineering does not usually affect the organizational structure or chart, nor does it imply job loss or employee layoffs. Whereas restructuring is concerned with eliminating or establishing, shrinking or enlarging, and moving organizational departments and divisions, the focus of reengineering is changing the way work is actually carried out. Reengineering is characterized by many tactical (short-term, business-function-specific) decisions, whereas restructuring is characterized by strategic (long-term, affecting all business functions) decisions.

Developed by Motorola in 1986 and made famous by CEO Jack Welch at General Electric and more recently by Robert Nardelli, former CEO of Home Depot, *Six Sigma* is a quality-boosting process improvement technique that entails training several key persons in the firm in the techniques to monitor, measure, and improve processes and eliminate defects. Six Sigma has been widely applied across industries from retailing to financial services. CEO Dave Cote at Honeywell and CEO Jeff Immelt at General Electric spurred acceptance of Six Sigma, which aims to improve work processes and eliminate waste by training "select" employees who are given judo titles such as Master Black Belts, Black Belts, and Green Belts.

Six Sigma was criticized in a *Wall Street Journal* article that cited many example firms whose stock price fell for a number of years after adoption of Six Sigma. The technique's reliance on the special group of trained employees is problematic and its use within retail firms such as Home Depot has not been as successful as in manufacturing firms.[7]

Restructuring

Firms often employ restructuring when various ratios appear out of line with competitors as determined through benchmarking exercises. Recall that *benchmarking* simply involves comparing a firm against the best firms in the industry on a wide variety of performance-related criteria. Some benchmarking ratios commonly used in rationalizing the need for restructuring are head-count-to-sales-volume, or corporate-staff-to-operating-employees, or span-of-control figures.

The primary benefit sought from restructuring is cost reduction. For some highly bureaucratic firms, restructuring can actually rescue the firm from global competition and demise. But the downside of restructuring can be reduced employee commitment, creativity, and innovation that accompanies the uncertainty and trauma associated with pending and actual employee layoffs. Avon Products restructured in 2011 partly due to corruption investigations in its Russia and Brazil operations. The company reduced its six commercial business units down to two—(1) Developed Markets and (2) Developing Markets—in essence going to a divisional by geographic region type structure. Avon has been reporting lower sales and profits amid missteps in key markets. CEO Andrea Jung is installing five new regional heads and new presidents in Avon's U.S. and Russia markets.

Another downside of restructuring is that many people today do not aspire to become managers, and many present-day managers are trying to get off the management track.[8] Sentiment against joining management ranks is higher today than ever. About 80 percent of employees say they want nothing to do with management, a major shift from just a decade ago when 60 to 70 percent hoped to become managers. Managing others historically led to enhanced career mobility, financial rewards, and executive perks; but in today's global, more competitive, restructured arena, managerial jobs demand more hours and headaches with fewer financial rewards. Managers today manage more people spread over different locations, travel more, manage diverse functions, and are change agents even when they have nothing to do with the creation of the plan or disagree with its approach. *Employers today are looking for people who can do things, not for people who make other people do things.* Restructuring in many firms has made a manager's job an invisible, thankless role. More workers today are self-managed, entrepreneurs, interpreneurs, or team-managed. Managers today need to be counselors, motivators, financial advisors, and psychologists. They also run the risk of becoming technologically behind in their areas of expertise. "Dilbert" cartoons commonly portray managers as enemies or as morons.

Reengineering

The argument for a firm engaging in reengineering usually goes as follows: Many companies historically have been organized vertically by business function. This arrangement has led over time to managers' and employees' mind-sets being defined by their particular functions rather than by overall customer service, product quality, or corporate performance. The logic is that all firms tend to bureaucratize over time. As routines become entrenched, turf becomes delineated and defended, and politics takes precedence over performance. Walls that exist in the physical workplace can be reflections of "mental" walls.

In reengineering, a firm uses information technology to break down functional barriers and create a work system based on business processes, products, or outputs rather than on functions or inputs. Cornerstones of reengineering are decentralization, reciprocal interdependence, and information sharing. A firm that exemplifies complete information sharing is Springfield Remanufacturing Corporation, which provides to all employees a weekly income statement of the firm, as well as extensive information on other companies' performances.

The *Wall Street Journal* noted that reengineering today must go beyond knocking down internal walls that keep parts of a company from cooperating effectively; it must also knock down the external walls that prohibit or discourage cooperation with other firms—even rival firms.[9] A maker of disposable diapers echoes this need differently when it says that to be successful "cooperation at the firm must stretch from stump to rump."

Hewlett-Packard is a good example of a company that has knocked down the external barriers to cooperation and practices modern reengineering. The HP of today shares its forecasts with all of its supply-chain partners and shares other critical information with its distributors and other stakeholders. HP does all the buying of resin for its many manufacturers, giving it a volume discount of up to 5 percent. HP has established many alliances and cooperative agreements of the kind discussed in Chapter 5.

A benefit of reengineering is that it offers employees the opportunity to see more clearly how their particular jobs affect the final product or service being marketed by the firm. However, reengineering can also raise manager and employee anxiety, which, unless calmed, can lead to corporate trauma.

Linking Performance and Pay to Strategies

With so many people out of work and executive salaries so large, politicians are more and more giving shareholders greater control over executive pay. The new Dodd-Frank Wall Street Reform and Consumer Protection Act grants shareholders advisory votes on compensation. A recent

Bloomberg Businessweek article says companies should install five policies to improve their compensation practices:

1. Provide full transparency to all stakeholders. Novartis does an excellent job on this.
2. Reward long-term performance with long-term pay, rather than annual incentives. ExxonMobil does an excellent job on this.
3. Base executive compensation on actual company performance, rather than on stock price. Target, for example, bases executive pay on same-store sales growth rather than stock price.
4. Extend the time-horizon for bonuses. Replace short-term with long-term incentives. Goldman Sachs does an excellent job on this.
5. Increase equity between workers and executives. Delete many special perks and benefits for executives. Be more consistent across levels, although employees with greater responsibility must receive greater compensation.[10]

CEOs at Japanese companies with more than $10 billion in annual revenues are paid about $1.3 million annually, including bonuses and stock options.[11] This compares to an average CEO pay among European firms of $6 million and an average among U.S. firms of $12 million. As firms acquire other firms in other countries, these pay differences can cause resentment and even turmoil. Larger pay packages of American CEOs are socially less acceptable in many other countries. For example, in Japan, seniority rather than performance has been the key factor in determining pay, and harmony among managers is emphasized over individual excellence.

How can an organization's reward system be more closely linked to strategic performance? How can decisions on salary increases, promotions, merit pay, and bonuses be more closely aligned to support the long-term strategic objectives of the organization? There are no widely accepted answers to these questions, but a dual bonus system based on both annual objectives and long-term objectives is becoming common. The percentage of a manager's annual bonus attributable to short-term versus long-term results should vary by hierarchical level in the organization. A chief executive officer's annual bonus could, for example, be determined on a 75 percent short-term and 25 percent long-term basis. It is important that bonuses not be based solely on short-term results because such a system ignores long-term company strategies and objectives.

One result of the global recession was that companies instituted policies to allow their shareholders to vote on executive compensation policies. Aflac was the first U.S. corporation to voluntarily give shareholders an advisory vote on executive compensation. Aflac did this back in 2007. Apple did this in 2008, as did H&R Block. Several companies that instituted say-on-pay policies more recently were Ingersoll-Rand, Verizon, Motorola, Occidental Petroleum, and Hewlett-Packard. These new policies underscore how the financial crisis and shareholder outrage about top executive pay has affected compensation practice. None of the shareholder votes are binding on the companies, however, at least not so far. The U.S. House of Representatives recently passed a bill to formalize this shareholder tactic, which is gaining steam across the country as a means to combat exorbitant executive pay.

In an effort to cut costs and increase productivity, more and more Japanese companies are switching from seniority-based pay to performance-based approaches. Toyota has switched to a full merit system for 20,000 of its 70,000 white-collar workers. Fujitsu, Sony, Matsushita Electric Industrial, and Kao also have switched to merit pay systems. This switching is hurting morale at some Japanese companies, which have trained workers for decades to cooperate rather than to compete and to work in groups rather than individually.

Richard Brown, CEO of Electronic Data Systems (EDS), once said,

> You have to start with an appraisal system that gives genuine feedback and differentiates performance. Some call it ranking people. That seems a little harsh. But you can't have a manager checking a box that says you're either stupendous, magnificent, very good, good, or average. Concise, constructive feedback is the fuel workers use to get better. A company that doesn't differentiate performance risks losing its best people.[12]

Profit sharing is another widely used form of incentive compensation. More than 30 percent of U.S. companies have profit sharing plans, but critics emphasize that too many factors affect profits for this to be a good criterion. Taxes, pricing, or an acquisition would wipe out profits, for example. Also, firms try to minimize profits in a sense to reduce taxes.

General Motors paid its 45,000 hourly workers in the United States $3,000 each in profit-sharing payouts in 2011, the largest amount ever for the company. In comparison, Ford Motor paid its U.S. hourly workers $5,000 in profit sharing, more than the company was required to pay under the profit-sharing formula in its United Auto Workers contract. Unlike GM and Ford, Chrysler Group LLC did not make money in 2010 but in early 2011 still paid its hourly workers a $750 bonus in recognition of their contribution to the firm's progress toward recovery.

Still another criterion widely used to link performance and pay to strategies is gain sharing. *Gain sharing* requires employees or departments to establish performance targets; if actual results exceed objectives, all members get bonuses. More than 26 percent of U.S. companies use some form of gain sharing; about 75 percent of gain sharing plans have been adopted since 1980. Carrier, a subsidiary of United Technologies, has had excellent success with gain sharing in its six plants in Syracuse, New York; Firestone's tire plant in Wilson, North Carolina, has experienced similar success with gain sharing.

Criteria such as sales, profit, production efficiency, quality, and safety could also serve as bases for an effective *bonus system.* If an organization meets certain understood, agreed-upon profit objectives, every member of the enterprise should share in the harvest. A bonus system can be an effective tool for motivating individuals to support strategy-implementation efforts. BankAmerica, for example, recently overhauled its incentive system to link pay to sales of the bank's most profitable products and services. Branch managers receive a base salary plus a bonus based both on the number of new customers and on sales of bank products. Every employee in each branch is also eligible for a bonus if the branch exceeds its goals. Thomas Peterson, a top BankAmerica executive, says, "We want to make people responsible for meeting their goals, so we pay incentives on sales, not on controlling costs or on being sure the parking lot is swept."

Five tests are often used to determine whether a performance-pay plan will benefit an organization:

1. *Does the plan capture attention?* Are people talking more about their activities and taking pride in early successes under the plan?
2. *Do employees understand the plan?* Can participants explain how it works and what they need to do to earn the incentive?
3. *Is the plan improving communication?* Do employees know more than they used to about the company's mission, plans, and objectives?
4. *Does the plan pay out when it should?* Are incentives being paid for desired results—and being withheld when objectives are not met?
5. *Is the company or unit performing better?* Are profits up? Has market share grown? Have gains resulted in part from the incentives?[13]

In addition to a dual bonus system, a combination of reward strategy incentives, such as salary raises, stock options, fringe benefits, promotions, praise, recognition, criticism, fear, increased job autonomy, and awards, can be used to encourage managers and employees to push hard for successful strategic implementation. The range of options for getting people, departments, and divisions to actively support strategy-implementation activities in a particular organization is almost limitless. Merck, for example, recently gave each of its 37,000 employees a 10-year option to buy 100 shares of Merck stock at a set price of $127. Steven Darien, Merck's vice president of human resources, says, "We needed to find ways to get everyone in the workforce on board in terms of our goals and objectives. Company executives will begin meeting with all Merck workers to explore ways in which employees can contribute more."

There is rising public resentment over executive pay. The Associated Press (AP), using data provided by Equilar, recently revealed that the average pay package for CEOs in the United States in 2010 was 24 percent higher than a year earlier, reversing two years of declines. In contrast, employees' pay only grew 3 percent in 2010, to an average of about $40,500. CEOs received more pay of all types—salaries, bonuses, stock options, and perks. The biggest gains came in cash bonuses, typically based on corporate profits, which rose 41 percent last year.

The highest-paid CEO in 2010 was Philippe Dauman of Viacom, the entertainment company that owns MTV, Nickelodeon, and Paramount Pictures. He received a 2010 pay package valued at $84.5 million, two and a half times what he made the year before. Besides

Dauman, other top paid CEOs included Leslie Moonves of CBS, $56.9 million; David Zaslav of Discovery Communications, $42.6 million; Brian Roberts of Comcast, $31.1 million; Robert Iger of Walt Disney, $28 million; and Jeff Bewkes of Time Warner, $26.1 million. The 10 highest-paid CEOs made $440 million in 2010, a third more than the top 10 made in 2009.

To calculate CEO pay, the AP adds an executive's salary, bonuses, perks, any interest on deferred pay that's above market interest rates, and the value a company places on stock and stock options awarded during the year. The median pay value of $9 million, calculated by Equilar, is the midpoint of the companies used in the AP analysis; half of the CEOs made more and half made less. In 2007, the median pay was $8.4 million. In 2008 it was $7.6 million, and in 2009 it was $7.2 million. The $9 million median for 2010 is the highest since the AP began the analysis in 2006.

The *Wall Street Journal's* late 2010 CEO pay survey revealed that annual bonuses rose 11 percent to a median of $1.67 million in 2010, compared with a 3.4 percent rise the previous year.[14] The top paid U.S. CEOs in that survey were Gregory Maffei at Liberty Media with $87.1 million, followed by Larry Ellison at Oracle ($68.6 million), Ray Irani at Occidental Petroleum ($52.2 million), and Carol Bartz at Yahoo ($44.6 million).

Managing Resistance to Change

No organization or individual can escape change. But the thought of change raises anxieties because people fear economic loss, inconvenience, uncertainty, and a break in normal social patterns. Almost any change in structure, technology, people, or strategies has the potential to disrupt comfortable interaction patterns. For this reason, people resist change. The strategic-management process itself can impose major changes on individuals and processes. Reorienting an organization to get people to think and act strategically is not an easy task.

Resistance to change can be considered the single greatest threat to successful strategy implementation. Resistance regularly occurs in organizations in the form of sabotaging production machines, absenteeism, filing unfounded grievances, and an unwillingness to cooperate. People often resist strategy implementation because they do not understand what is happening or why changes are taking place. In that case, employees may simply need accurate information. Successful strategy implementation hinges upon managers' ability to develop an organizational climate conducive to change. Change must be viewed as an opportunity rather than as a threat by managers and employees.

Resistance to change can emerge at any stage or level of the strategy-implementation process. Although there are various approaches for implementing changes, three commonly used strategies are a force change strategy, an educative change strategy, and a rational or self-interest change strategy. A *force change strategy* involves giving orders and enforcing those orders; this strategy has the advantage of being fast, but it is plagued by low commitment and high resistance. The *educative change strategy* is one that presents information to convince people of the need for change; the disadvantage of an educative change strategy is that implementation becomes slow and difficult. However, this type of strategy evokes greater commitment and less resistance than does the force change strategy. Finally, a *rational* or *self-interest change strategy* is one that attempts to convince individuals that the change is to their personal advantage. When this appeal is successful, strategy implementation can be relatively easy. However, implementation changes are seldom to everyone's advantage.

The rational change strategy is the most desirable, so this approach is examined a bit further. Managers can improve the likelihood of successfully implementing change by carefully designing change efforts. Jack Duncan described a rational or self-interest change strategy as consisting of four steps. First, employees are invited to participate in the process of change and in the details of transition; participation allows everyone to give opinions, to feel a part of the change process, and to identify their own self-interests regarding the recommended change. Second, some motivation or incentive to change is required; self-interest can be the most important motivator. Third, communication is needed so that people can understand the purpose for the changes. Giving and receiving feedback is the fourth step: everyone enjoys knowing how things are going and how much progress is being made.[15]

Because of diverse external and internal forces, change is a fact of life in organizations. The rate, speed, magnitude, and direction of changes vary over time by industry and organization. Strategists should strive to create a work environment in which change is recognized as necessary and beneficial so that individuals can more easily adapt to change. Adopting a strategic-management approach to decision making can itself require major changes in the philosophy and operations of a firm.

Strategists can take a number of positive actions to minimize managers' and employees' resistance to change. For example, individuals who will be affected by a change should be involved in the decision to make the change and in decisions about how to implement the change. Strategists should anticipate changes and develop and offer training and development workshops so that managers and employees can adapt to those changes. They also need to effectively communicate the need for changes. The strategic-management process can be described as a process of managing change.

Organizational change should be viewed today as a continuous process rather than as a project or event. The most successful organizations today continuously adapt to changes in the competitive environment, which themselves continue to change at an accelerating rate. It is not sufficient today to simply react to change. Managers need to anticipate change and ideally be the creator of change. Viewing change as a continuous process is in stark contrast to an old management doctrine regarding change, which was to unfreeze behavior, change the behavior, and then refreeze the new behavior. The new "continuous organizational change" philosophy should mirror the popular "continuous quality improvement philosophy."

Creating a Strategy-Supportive Culture

Strategists should strive to preserve, emphasize, and build upon aspects of an existing *culture* that support proposed new strategies. Aspects of an existing culture that are antagonistic to a proposed strategy should be identified and changed. Substantial research indicates that new strategies are often market-driven and dictated by competitive forces. For this reason, changing a firm's culture to fit a new strategy is usually more effective than changing a strategy to fit an existing culture. As indicated in Table 7-10, numerous techniques are available to alter an organization's culture, including recruitment, training, transfer, promotion, restructure of an organization's design, role modeling, positive reinforcement, and mentoring.

Schein indicated that the following elements are most useful in linking culture to strategy:

1. Formal statements of organizational philosophy, charters, creeds, materials used for recruitment and selection, and socialization
2. Designing of physical spaces, facades, buildings
3. Deliberate role modeling, teaching, and coaching by leaders
4. Explicit reward and status system, promotion criteria

TABLE 7-10 Ways and Means for Altering an Organization's Culture

1. Recruitment
2. Training
3. Transfer
4. Promotion
5. Restructuring
6. Reengineering
7. Role modeling
8. Positive reinforcement
9. Mentoring
10. Revising vision and/or mission
11. Redesigning physical spaces/facades
12. Altering reward system
13. Altering organizational policies/procedures/practices

5. Stories, legends, myths, and parables about key people and events
6. What leaders pay attention to, measure, and control
7. Leader reactions to critical incidents and organizational crises
8. How the organization is designed and structured
9. Organizational systems and procedures
10. Criteria used for recruitment, selection, promotion, leveling off, retirement, and "excommunication" of people[16]

In the personal and religious side of life, the impact of loss and change is easy to see.[17] Memories of loss and change often haunt individuals and organizations for years. Ibsen wrote, "Rob the average man of his life illusion and you rob him of his happiness at the same stroke."[18] When attachments to a culture are severed in an organization's attempt to change direction, employees and managers often experience deep feelings of grief. This phenomenon commonly occurs when external conditions dictate the need for a new strategy. Managers and employees often struggle to find meaning in a situation that changed many years before. Some people find comfort in memories; others find solace in the present. Weak linkages between strategic management and organizational culture can jeopardize performance and success. Deal and Kennedy emphasized that making strategic changes in an organization always threatens a culture:

> People form strong attachments to heroes, legends, the rituals of daily life, the hoopla of extravaganza and ceremonies, and all the symbols of the workplace. Change strips relationships and leaves employees confused, insecure, and often angry. Unless something can be done to provide support for transitions from old to new, the force of a culture can neutralize and emasculate strategy changes.[19]

Production/Operations Concerns When Implementing Strategies

Production/operations capabilities, limitations, and policies can significantly enhance or inhibit the attainment of objectives. Production processes typically constitute more than 70 percent of a firm's total assets. A major part of the strategy-implementation process takes place at the production site. Production-related decisions on plant size, plant location, product design, choice of equipment, kind of tooling, size of inventory, inventory control, quality control, cost control, use of standards, job specialization, employee training, equipment and resource utilization, shipping and packaging, and technological innovation can have a dramatic impact on the success or failure of strategy-implementation efforts.

Examples of adjustments in production systems that could be required to implement various strategies are provided in Table 7-11 for both for-profit and nonprofit organizations. For instance, note that when a bank formulates and selects a strategy to add 10 new branches, a production-related implementation concern is site location. The largest bicycle company in the

TABLE 7-11   Production Management and Strategy Implementation

Type of Organization	Strategy Being Implemented	Production System Adjustments
Hospital	Adding a cancer center (Product Development)	Purchase specialized equipment and add specialized people.
Bank	Adding 10 new branches (Market Development)	Perform site location analysis.
Beer brewery	Purchasing a barley farm operation (Backward Integration)	Revise the inventory control system.
Steel manufacturer	Acquiring a fast-food chain (Unrelated Diversification)	Improve the quality control system.
Computer company	Purchasing a retail distribution chain (Forward Integration)	Alter the shipping, packaging, and transportation systems.

United States, Huffy, recently ended its own production of bikes and now contracts out those services to Asian and Mexican manufacturers. Huffy focuses instead on the design, marketing, and distribution of bikes, but it no longer produces bikes itself. The Dayton, Ohio, company closed its plants in Ohio, Missouri, and Mississippi.

Just-in-time (JIT) production approaches have withstood the test of time. JIT significantly reduces the costs of implementing strategies. With JIT, parts and materials are delivered to a production site just as they are needed, rather than being stockpiled as a hedge against later deliveries. Harley-Davidson reports that at one plant alone, JIT freed $22 million previously tied up in inventory and greatly reduced reorder lead time.

Factors that should be studied before locating production facilities include the availability of major resources, the prevailing wage rates in the area, transportation costs related to shipping and receiving, the location of major markets, political risks in the area or country, and the availability of trainable employees.

For high-technology companies, production costs may not be as important as production flexibility because major product changes can be needed often. Industries such as biogenetics and plastics rely on production systems that must be flexible enough to allow frequent changes and the rapid introduction of new products. An article in the *Harvard Business Review* explained why some organizations get into trouble:

> They too slowly realize that a change in product strategy alters the tasks of a production system. These tasks, which can be stated in terms of requirements for cost, product flexibility, volume flexibility, product performance, and product consistency, determine which manufacturing policies are appropriate. As strategies shift over time, so must production policies covering the location and scale of manufacturing facilities, the choice of manufacturing process, the degree of vertical integration of each manufacturing facility, the use of R&D units, the control of the production system, and the licensing of technology.[20]

A common management practice, cross-training of employees, can facilitate strategy implementation and can yield many benefits. Employees gain a better understanding of the whole business and can contribute better ideas in planning sessions. Cross-training employees can, however, thrust managers into roles that emphasize counseling and coaching over directing and enforcing and can necessitate substantial investments in training and incentives.

Human Resource Concerns When Implementing Strategies

In terms of Human Resource or "People Management," *Fortune* in 2011 ranked the following companies as best in the world:

Rank	Company
1	Goldman Sachs Group
2	Apple
3	Walt Disney
4	Google
5	Nike
6	Royal Dutch Shell
7	Nestlé
8	Amazon.com
9	Accenture
9	Procter & Gamble

Source: Based on: http://money.cnn.com/magazines/fortune/mostadmired/2011/best_worst/best2.html

More and more companies are instituting furloughs to cut costs as an alternative to laying off employees. *Furloughs* are temporary layoffs and even white-collar managers are being given furloughs, once confined to blue-collar workers. A few organizations furloughing professional workers include Gulfstream Aerospace, Media General, Gannett, the University of Maryland, Clemson University, and Spansion. Most companies are still using temporary and part-time workers rather than hiring full-time employees, which suggests that high unemployment rates may be a long-term trend. More and more companies may follow Harley-Davidson's lead when that firm signed a new union contract in late 2010 that creates a tier of "casual workers" with no benefits and no minimum number of hours, allowing Harley to call up workers only as needed.[21] Table 7-12 lists ways that companies today are reducing labor costs to stay financially sound.

The job of human resource manager is changing rapidly as companies continue to downsize and reorganize. Strategic responsibilities of the human resource manager include assessing the staffing needs and costs for alternative strategies proposed during strategy formulation and developing a staffing plan for effectively implementing strategies. This plan must consider how best to manage spiraling health care insurance costs. Employers' health coverage expenses consume an average 26 percent of firms' net profits, even though most companies now require employees to pay part of their health insurance premiums. The plan must also include how to motivate employees and managers during a time when layoffs are common and workloads are high.

The human resource department must develop performance incentives that clearly link performance and pay to strategies. The process of empowering managers and employees through their involvement in strategic-management activities yields the greatest benefits when all organizational members understand clearly how they will benefit personally if the firm does well. Linking company and personal benefits is a major new strategic responsibility of human resource managers. Other new responsibilities for human resource managers may include establishing and administering an *employee stock ownership plan (ESOP),* instituting an effective child-care policy, and providing leadership for managers and employees in a way that allows them to balance work and family.

A well-designed strategic-management system can fail if insufficient attention is given to the human resource dimension. Human resource problems that arise when businesses implement strategies can usually be traced to one of three causes: (1) disruption of social and political structures, (2) failure to match individuals' aptitudes with implementation tasks, and (3) inadequate top management support for implementation activities.[22]

TABLE 7-12   Labor Cost-Saving Tactics

Salary freeze

Hiring freeze

Salary reductions

Reduce employee benefits

Raise employee contribution to health-care premiums

Reduce employee 401(k)/403(b) match

Reduce employee workweek

Mandatory furlough

Voluntary furlough

Hire temporary instead of full-time employees

Hire contract employees instead of full-time employees

Volunteer buyouts (Walt Disney is doing this)

Halt production for 3 days a week (Toyota Motor is doing this)

Layoffs

Early retirement

Reducing/eliminating bonuses

Source: Based on Dana Mattioli, "Employers Make Cuts Despite Belief Upturn Is Near," *Wall Street Journal,* April 23, 2009, B4.

Strategy implementation poses a threat to many managers and employees in an organization. New power and status relationships are anticipated and realized. New formal and informal groups' values, beliefs, and priorities may be largely unknown. Managers and employees may become engaged in resistance behavior as their roles, prerogatives, and power in the firm change. Disruption of social and political structures that accompany strategy execution must be anticipated and considered during strategy formulation and managed during strategy implementation.

A concern in matching managers with strategy is that jobs have specific and relatively static responsibilities, although people are dynamic in their personal development. Commonly used methods that match managers with strategies to be implemented include transferring managers, developing leadership workshops, offering career development activities, promotions, job enlargement, and job enrichment.

A number of other guidelines can help ensure that human relationships facilitate rather than disrupt strategy-implementation efforts. Specifically, managers should do a lot of chatting and informal questioning to stay abreast of how things are progressing and to know when to intervene. Managers can build support for strategy-implementation efforts by giving few orders, announcing few decisions, depending heavily on informal questioning, and seeking to probe and clarify until a consensus emerges. Key thrusts that succeed should be rewarded generously and visibly.

It is surprising that so often during strategy formulation, individual values, skills, and abilities needed for successful strategy implementation are not considered. It is rare that a firm selecting new strategies or significantly altering existing strategies possesses the right line and staff personnel in the right positions for successful strategy implementation. The need to match individual aptitudes with strategy-implementation tasks should be considered in strategy choice.

Inadequate support from strategists for implementation activities often undermines organizational success. Chief executive officers, small business owners, and government agency heads must be personally committed to strategy implementation and express this commitment in highly visible ways. Strategists' formal statements about the importance of strategic management must be consistent with actual support and rewards given for activities completed and objectives reached. Otherwise, stress created by inconsistency can cause uncertainty among managers and employees at all levels.

Perhaps the best method for preventing and overcoming human resource problems in strategic management is to actively involve as many managers and employees as possible in the process. Although time consuming, this approach builds understanding, trust, commitment, and ownership and reduces resentment and hostility. The true potential of strategy formulation and implementation resides in people.

Employee Stock Ownership Plans (ESOPs)

An *ESOP* is a tax-qualified, defined-contribution, employee-benefit plan whereby employees purchase stock of the company through borrowed money or cash contributions. ESOPs empower employees to work as owners; this is a primary reason why the number of ESOPs have grown dramatically to more than 10,000 firms covering more than 14 million employees. ESOPs now control more than $600 billion in corporate stock in the United States.

Some ESOP companies include:

- W. L. Gore & Associates—maker of medical and industrial products as well as Gore-Tex
- Herman Miller—famous for making innovative office furniture
- KCI—a civil engineering firm
- HCSS—a software manufacturer for the heavy construction industry

Besides reducing worker alienation and stimulating productivity, ESOPs allow firms other benefits, such as substantial tax savings. Principal, interest, and dividend payments on ESOP-funded debt are tax deductible. Banks lend money to ESOPs at interest rates below prime. This money can be repaid in pretax dollars, lowering the debt service as much as 30 percent in some cases. "The ownership culture really makes a difference, when management is a facilitator, not a dictator," says Corey Rosen, executive director of the National Center for Employee Ownership. Fifteen employee-owned companies are listed in Table 7-13.

TABLE 7-13   Fifteen Example ESOP Firms

Firm	Headquarters Location
Publix Supermarkets	Florida
Tribune Company	Illinois
Lifetouch	Minnesota
John Lewis Partnership	United Kingdom
Mondragon Cooperative	Spain
Houchens Industries	Kentucky
Amsted Industries	Illinois
Mast General Store	North Carolina
HDR, Inc.	Nebraska
Yoke's Fresh Market	Washington
SPARTA, Inc.	California
Hy-Vee	Iowa
Bi-Mart	Washington
Ferrellgas Partners	Kansas

Source: Based on Edward Iwata, "ESOPs Can Offer Both Upsides, Drawbacks," *USA Today*, April 3, 2007, 2B.

If an ESOP owns more than 50 percent of the firm, those who lend money to the ESOP are taxed on only 50 percent of the income received on the loans. ESOPs are not for every firm, however, because the initial legal, accounting, actuarial, and appraisal fees to set up an ESOP are about $50,000 for a small or midsized firm, with annual administration expenses of about $15,000. Analysts say ESOPs also do not work well in firms that have fluctuating payrolls and profits. Human resource managers in many firms conduct preliminary research to determine the desirability of an ESOP, and then they facilitate its establishment and administration if benefits outweigh the costs.

Wyatt Cafeterias, a southwestern United States operator of 120 cafeterias, also adopted the ESOP concept to prevent a hostile takeover. Employee productivity at Wyatt greatly increased since the ESOP began, as illustrated in the following quote:

> The key employee in our entire organization is the person serving the customer on the cafeteria line. We now tell the tea cart server, "Don't wait for the manager to tell you how to do your job better or how to provide better service. You take care of it." Sure, we're looking for productivity increases, but since we began pushing decisions down to the level of people who deal directly with customers, we've discovered an awesome side effect—suddenly the work crews have this "happy to be here" attitude that the customers really love.[23]

Balancing Work Life and Home Life

More women earn both undergraduate and graduate degrees in the United States than men, but a wage disparity still persists between men and women at all education levels.[24] Women on average make 25 percent less than men. The average age today for women to get married in the United States is 30 for those with a college degree, and 26 for those with just a high school degree. About 29 percent of both men and women in the United States today have a college degree, whereas in 1970 only 8 percent of women and 14 percent of men had college degrees.

Work/family strategies have become so popular among companies today that the strategies now represent a competitive advantage for those firms that offer such benefits as elder care assistance, flexible scheduling, job sharing, adoption benefits, an on-site summer camp, employee help lines, pet care, and even lawn service referrals. New corporate titles such as work/life coordinator and director of diversity are becoming common.

Working Mother magazine annually published its listing of "The 100 Best Companies for Working Mothers" (www.workingmother.com). Three especially important variables used in the ranking were availability of flextime, advancement opportunities, and equitable distribution of benefits among companies. Other important criteria are compressed weeks, telecommuting, job sharing, childcare facilities, maternity leave for both parents, mentoring, career development, and promotion for women. *Working Mother's* top 10 best companies for working women in 2011 are provided in Table 7-14. *Working Mother* also conducts extensive research to determine the best U.S. firms for women of color.

Human resource managers need to foster a more effective balancing of professional and private lives because nearly 60 million people in the United States are now part of two-career families. A corporate objective to become more lean and mean must today include consideration for the fact that a good home life contributes immensely to a good work life.

The work/family issue is no longer just a women's issue. Some specific measures that firms are taking to address this issue are providing spouse relocation assistance as an employee benefit; providing company resources for family recreational and educational use; establishing employee country clubs, such as those at IBM and Bethlehem Steel; and creating family/work interaction opportunities. A study by Joseph Pleck of Wheaton College found that in companies that do not offer paternity leave for fathers as a benefit, most men take short, informal paternity leaves anyway by combining vacation time and sick days.

Some organizations have developed family days, when family members are invited into the workplace, taken on plant or office tours, dined by management, and given a chance to see exactly what other family members do each day. Family days are inexpensive and increase the employee's pride in working for the organization. Flexible working hours during the week are another human resource response to the need for individuals to balance work life and home life. The work/family topic is being made part of the agenda at meetings and thus is being discussed in many organizations.

There is great room for improvement in removing the *glass ceiling* domestically, especially considering that women make up 47 percent of the U.S. labor force. *Glass ceiling* refers to the invisible barrier in many firms that bars women and minorities from top-level management positions. The United States leads the world in promoting women and minorities into mid- and top-level managerial positions in business. Only 2.6 percent of Fortune 500 firms have a woman CEO. Table 7-15 gives the 18 Fortune 500 Women CEOs in 2012.

Boeing's firing of CEO Harry Stonecipher for having an extramarital affair raised public awareness of office romance. However, just 12 percent of 391 companies surveyed by the American Management Association have written guidelines on office dating.[25] The fact of the matter is that most employers in the United States turn a blind eye to marital cheating. Some employers, such as Southwest Airlines, which employs more than 1,000 married couples, explicitly allow consensual office relationships. Research suggests that more men than women engage in extramarital affairs at work, roughly 22 percent to 15 percent; however, the percentage of women having extramarital affairs is increasing steadily, whereas the percentage of men having

TABLE 7-14   Top Ten Companies for Working Women

1. Bank of America—allows employees to define how they work
2. Deloitte—grants employees four unpaid weeks off annually
3. Discovery Communications—maternity leave is with full pay and consists of nine weeks for moms and three weeks for dads
4. Ernst & Young—up to 75 percent of its employees work outside E&Y offices
5. General Mills—women head five of the seven US. retail divisions
6. IBM—offers outstanding assistance to children of employees through its Special Care for Children program
7. KPMG—employees may take 26 (job guaranteed, partially paid) weeks off following the birth or adoption of a child
8. PricewaterhouseCoopers—many female partners go through the Breakthrough Leadership Development Program and achieve top executive positions
9. University of Wisconsin Hospital and Clinics—spends about $1.6 million annually on tuition to help employees further their education
10. WellStar Health System—has an in-house concierge service to help moms get things done

Source: Based on 2011: http://www.workingmother.com/BestCompanies/node/7818/list/4767

TABLE 7-15   Fortune 500 Women CEOs in 2012

CEO	Company
Angela Braly	WellPoint
Patricia Woertz	Archer Daniels Midland
Lynn Elsenhans	Sunoco
Indra Nooyi	PepsiCo
Irene Rosenfeld	Kraft Foods
Carol Meyrowitz	TJX
Mary Sammons	Rite Aid
Anne Mulcahy	Xerox
Brenda Barnes	Sara Lee
Andrea Jung	Avon Products
Susan Ivey	Reynolds American
Christina Gold	Western Union
Cathie Lesjak	Hewlett-Packard
Susan Ivey	Reynolds American
Carol Meyrowitz	TJX Cos.
Oprah Winfrey	Harpo and Own
Ellen Kullman	DuPont
Ursula Burns	Xerox

affairs with co-workers is holding steady.[26] If an affair is disrupting your work, then "the first step is to go to the offending person privately and try to resolve the matter. If that fails, then go to the human-resources manager seeking assistance."[27] Filing a discrimination lawsuit based on the affair is recommended only as a last resort because courts generally rule that co-workers' injuries are not pervasive enough to warrant any damages.

Benefits of a Diverse Workforce

Advertising agencies are an example industry transitioning from being specialist Hispanic, African American, and Asian agencies to becoming multicultural, generalist agencies. Leading executives of culturally specialized agencies are defecting in large numbers to generalist agencies as companies increasingly embrace multicultural marketing using multicultural ad agencies. Companies such as Burger King are shifting their Hispanic and African American ad agencies to generalist firms such as Crispin. Church's Chicken says pooling everything at a generalist agency helps reinforce the multicultural component of its overall market strategy.[28]

In Latin and South America, the number of women in high office has increased dramatically in recent years. Brazil recently elected its first woman president, Dilma Rouseff. Both Argentina and Chile already have a woman president, Cristina Kirchner and Michelle Bachelet respectively. Regarding the percent of national congressional seats held by women, Argentina has 38.3 percent followed by Honduras with 23.4 percent, as compared to Europe with 20.0 percent, Nordic countries at 41.6 percent, and Arab states at 11.1 percent.[29] Women now make up 53 percent of the work force in Latin and South America.

An organization can perhaps be most effective when its workforce mirrors the diversity of its customers. For global companies, this goal can be optimistic, but it is a worthwhile goal.

Corporate Wellness Programs

A recent *Harvard Business Review* article details how companies such as Johnson & Johnson (J&J), Lowe's Home-Improvement, the supermarket chain H-E-B, and Healthwise report impressive returns on investment of comprehensive, well-run employee wellness programs, sometimes as high as six to one.[30] J&J estimates that wellness programs have cumulatively saved the company $250 million on health care costs over the past decade. All J&J facilities around the world are tobacco free. At the software firm SAS Institute headquartered in Cary, North Carolina, voluntary turnover of employees has dropped to just 4 percent, largely, the firm says, due to its effective wellness program. On the SAS main campus, 70 percent of employees use the recreation center at least twice a week. SAS has maintained its #1 ranking in recent years among *Fortune*'s "100 Best Companies to Work For." At Healthwise, CEO Don Kemper's personal commitment to wellness permeates the entire culture of the firm, from monthly staff meetings to an annual Wellness Day. Starting in January 2011, Lowe's offered employees a monthly $50 discount on medical insurance if they pledge that they and covered dependents will not use any tobacco products.

Chevron is also a model corporate wellness company that sponsors many internal and external wellness activities. Chevron and other companies such as Biltmore that provide exemplary wellness programs think beyond diet and exercise and focus also on stress management by assisting employees with such issues as divorce, serious illness, death and grief recovery, child rearing, and care of aging parents. Biltmore's two-day health fairs twice a year focus on physical, financial, and spiritual wellness. At Lowe's headquarters, an impressive spiral staircase in the lobby makes climbing the stairs more appealing than riding the elevator. Such practices as "providing abundant bicycle racks," "conducting walking meetings," and "offering five minute stress breaks" are becoming common at companies to promote a corporate wellness culture.

Whole Foods Market headquartered in Austin, Texas, is another outstanding corporate wellness company with their employees receiving a 30 percent discount card on all products sold in their stores "if they maintain and document a healthy lifestyle." In addition, Wegman's Food Markets, headquartered in Rochester, New York, is another supermarket chain with an excellent corporate wellness program. More than 11,000 of Wegman's 39,000 employees recently took part in a challenge to eat five cups of fruit and vegetables and walk up to 10,000 steps a day for eight weeks. Wegman recently ranked #2 among *Fortune*'s "100 Best Companies to Work For."

Firms are striving to lower the accelerating costs of employees' health-care insurance premiums. Many firms such as Scotts Miracle-Gro Company (based in Marysville, Ohio), IBM, and Microsoft are implementing wellness programs, requiring employees to get healthier or pay higher insurance premiums. Employees that do get healthier win bonuses, free trips, and pay lower premiums; nonconforming employees pay higher premiums and receive no "healthy" benefits. Wellness of employees has become a strategic issue for many firms. Most firms require a health examination as a part of an employment application, and healthiness is more and more becoming a hiring factor. Michael Porter, coauthor of *Redefining Health Care*, says, "We have this notion that you can gorge on hot dogs, be in a pie-eating contest, and drink every day, and society will take care of you. We can't afford to let individuals drive up company costs because they're not willing to address their own health problems."

Wellness programs provide counseling to employees and seek lifestyle changes to achieve healthier living. For example, trans fats are a major cause of heart disease. Near elimination of trans fats in one's diet will reduce one's risk for heart attack by as much as 19 percent, according to a recent article.

Saturated fats are also bad, so one should avoid eating too much red meat and dairy products, which are high in saturated fats. Seven key lifestyle habits listed in Table 7-16 may significantly improve health and longevity.

TABLE 7-16   The Key to Staying Healthy, Living to 100, and Being a "Well" Employee

1. Eat nutritiously—eat a variety of fruits and vegetables daily because they have ingredients that the body uses to repair and strengthen itself.
2. Stay hydrated—drink plenty of water to aid the body in eliminating toxins and to enable body organs to function efficiently; the body is mostly water.
3. Get plenty of rest—the body repairs itself during rest, so get at least seven hours of sleep nightly, preferably eight hours.
4. Get plenty of exercise—exercise vigorously at least 30 minutes daily so the body can release toxins and strengthen vital organs.
5. Reduce stress—the body's immune system is weakened when one is under stress, making the body vulnerable to many ailments, so keep stress to a minimum.
6. Do not smoke—smoking kills, no doubt about it anymore.
7. Take vitamin supplements—consult your physician, but because it is difficult for diet alone to supply all the nutrients and vitamins needed, supplements can be helpful in achieving good health and longevity.

Source: Based on Lauren Etter, "Trans Fats: Will They Get Shelved?" *Wall Street Journal*, December 8, 2006, A6; Joel Fuhrman, MD, *Eat to Live* (Boston: Little, Brown, 2003).

Special Note to Students

An integral part of managing a firm is continually and systematically seeking to gain and sustain competitive advantage through effective planning, organizing, motivating, staffing, and controlling. Rival firms engage in these same activities, so emphasize in your strategic-management case analysis how your firm implementing your recommendations will outperform rival firms. Remember to be prescriptive rather than descriptive on every page or slide in your project, meaning to be insightful, forward-looking, and analytical rather than just describing operations. It is easy to *describe* a company but is difficult to *analyze* a company. Strategic-management case analysis is about *analyzing* a company and its industry, uncovering ways and means for the firm to best gain and sustain competitive advantage. So communicate throughout your project how your firm, and especially your recommendations, will lead to improved growth and profitability versus rival firms. Avoid vagueness and generalities throughout your project, as your audience or reader seeks great ideas backed up by great analyses. Use an analytical rather than descriptive approach in highlighting every slide you show an audience.

Conclusion

Successful strategy formulation does not at all guarantee successful strategy implementation. Although inextricably interdependent, strategy formulation and strategy implementation are characteristically different. In a single word, strategy implementation means *change*. It is widely agreed that "the real work begins after strategies are formulated." Successful strategy implementation requires the support of, as well as discipline and hard work from, motivated managers and employees. It is sometimes frightening to think that a single individual can irreparably sabotage strategy-implementation efforts.

Formulating the right strategies is not enough, because managers and employees must be motivated to implement those strategies. Management issues considered central to strategy implementation include matching organizational structure with strategy, linking performance and pay to strategies, creating an organizational climate conducive to change, managing political relationships, creating a strategy-supportive culture, adapting production/ operations processes, and managing human resources. Establishing annual objectives, devising policies, and allocating resources are central strategy-implementation activities common to all organizations. Depending on the size and type of the organization, other management issues could be equally important to successful strategy implementation.

Key Terms and Concepts

Annual Objectives (p. 215)
Avoidance (p. 219)
Benchmarking (p. 230)
Bonus System (p. 233)
Conflict (p. 219)
Confrontation (p. 220)
Culture (p. 235)
Decentralized Structure (p. 222)
Defusion (p. 219)
Delayering (p. 230)
Divisional Structure by Geographic Area, Product, Customer, or Process (p. 223)
Downsizing (p. 230)
Educative Change Strategy (p. 234)
Employee Stock Ownership Plans (ESOP) (p. 238)
Establishing Annual Objectives (p. 215)
Force Change Strategy (p. 234)
Functional Structure (p. 221)

Furloughs (p. 238)
Gain Sharing (p. 233)
Glass Ceiling (p. 241)
Horizontal Consistency of Objectives (p. 216)
Just-in-Time (JIT) (p. 237)
Matrix Structure (p. 227)
Policy (p. 217)
Profit Sharing (p. 232)
Rational Change Strategy (p. 234)
Reengineering (p. 230)
Resistance to Change (p. 234)
Resource Allocation (p. 219)
Restructuring (p. 230)
Rightsizing (p. 230)
Self-Interest Change Strategy (p. 234)
Six Sigma (p. 230)
Strategic Business Unit (SBU) Structure (p. 225)
Vertical Consistency of Objectives (p. 216)

Issues for Review and Discussion

1. *Businessweek* says firms should "base executive compensation on actual company performance, rather than on the company's stock price." For example, Target Corp. bases executive pay on same-store sales growth rather than stock price. Discuss.

2. What do you especially like and dislike about Halliburton's organizational chart shown in the chapter? What would you change if anything? Why?

3. List four corporate wellness practices that could be especially effective for a company.

4. Women now make up 53 percent of the work force in Latin and South America. Do some research to determine how that percentage compares with other parts of the world. What are the implications for a business in doing business globally?

5. Advertising agencies are an example industry transitioning from specialist Hispanic, African American, and Asian firms to multicultural, generalist agencies. Why is this occurring? What other industries or institutions may follow suit? Why?

6. Describe three conflict situations in which to resolve the problems you would use (1) Avoidance, (2) Defusion, and (3) Confrontation respectively.

7. List the five labor cost-saving activities that you believe would be most effective for (1) Best Buy, (2) your university, and (3) the U.S. Postal Service. Give a rationale for each company.

8. The chapter says strategy formulation focuses on effectiveness, whereas strategy implementation focuses on efficiency. Which is more important, effectiveness or efficiency? Give an example of each concept.

9. In stating objectives, why should terms such as *increase, minimize, maximize, as soon as possible, adequate,* and *decrease* be avoided?

10. What are four types of resources that all organizations have? List them in order of importance for your university or business school.

11. Considering avoidance, defusion, and confrontation, which method of conflict resolution do you prefer most? Why? Which do you prefer least? Why?

12. Explain why Alfred Chandler's strategy-structure relationship commonly exists among firms.

13. If you owned and opened three restaurants after you graduated, would you operate from a functional or divisional structure? Why?

14. Explain how to choose between a divisional-by-product and a divisional-by-region organizational structure.

15. Think of a company that would operate best in your opinion by a division-by-services organizational structure. Explain your reasoning.

16. What are the two major disadvantages of an SBU-type organizational structure? What are the two major advantages? At what point in a firm's growth do you feel the advantages offset the disadvantages? Explain.

17. In order of importance in your opinion, list six advantages of a matrix organizational structure.

18. Why should division head persons have the title president rather than vice president?

19. Compare and contrast profit sharing with gain sharing as employee performance incentives.

20. List three resistance to change strategies. Give an example when you would use each method or approach.

21. In order of importance in your opinion, list six techniques or activities widely used to alter an organization's culture.

22. What are the benefits of establishing an ESOP in a company?

23. List reasons why is it important for an organization not to have a "glass ceiling."

24. Allocating resources can be a political and an ad hoc activity in firms that do not use strategic management. Why is this true? Does adopting strategic management ensure easy resource allocation? Why?

25. Compare strategy formulation with strategy implementation in terms of each being an art or a science.

26. Describe the relationship between annual objectives and policies.

27. Identify a long-term objective and two supporting annual objectives for a familiar organization.

28. Identify and discuss three policies that apply to your present strategic-management class.

29. Explain the following statement: Horizontal consistency of goals is as important as vertical consistency.

30. Describe several reasons why conflict may occur during objective-setting activities.

31. In your opinion, what approaches to conflict resolution would be best for resolving a disagreement between a personnel manager and a sales manager over the firing of a particular salesperson? Why?

32. Describe the organizational culture of your college or university.

33. Explain why organizational structure is so important in strategy implementation.

34. In your opinion, how many separate divisions could an organization reasonably have without using an SBU-type organizational structure? Why?

35. Would you recommend a divisional structure by geographic area, product, customer, or process for a medium-sized bank in your local area? Why?

36. What are the advantages and disadvantages of decentralizing the wage and salary functions of an organization? How could this be accomplished?

37. Do you believe expenditures for child care or fitness facilities are warranted from a cost-benefit perspective? Why or why not?

38. Explain why successful strategy implementation often hinges on whether the strategy-formulation process empowers managers and employees.

39. Discuss the glass ceiling in the United States, giving your ideas and suggestions.
40. Discuss three ways discussed in this book for linking performance and pay to strategies.
41. List the different types of organizational structure. Diagram what you think is the most complex of these structures and label your chart clearly.

42. List the advantages and disadvantages of a functional versus a divisional organizational structure.
43. Discuss recent trends in women and minorities becoming top executives in the United States.
44. Discuss recent trends in firms downsizing family-friendly programs.
45. List seven guidelines to follow in developing an organizational chart.

Notes

1. Dale McConkey, "Planning in a Changing Environment," *Business Horizons*, September–October 1988, 66.
2. A. G. Bedeian and W. F. Glueck, *Management,* 3rd ed. (Chicago: The Dryden Press, 1983), 212.
3. Boris Yavitz and William Newman, *Strategy in Action: The Execution, Politics, and Payoff of Business Planning* (New York: The Free Press, 1982), 195.
4. E. H. Schein, "Three Cultures of Management: The Key to Organizational Learning," *Sloan Management Review* 38, 1 (1996): 9–20.
5. S. Ghoshal and C. A. Bartlett, "Changing the Role of Management: Beyond Structure to Processes." *Harvard Business Review* 73, 1 (1995): 88.
6. Joann Lublin, "Chairman-CEO Split Gains Allies," *Wall Street Journal*, March 30, 2009, B4.
7. Karen Richardson, "The 'Six Sigma' Factor for Home Depot," *Wall Street Journal*, January 4, 2007, C3.
8. "Want to Be a Manager? Many People Say No, Calling Job Miserable," *Wall Street Journal*, April 4, 1997, 1; Stephanie Armour, "Management Loses Its Allure," *USA Today*, October 10, 1997, 1B.
9. Paul Carroll, "No More Business as Usual, Please. Time to Try Something Different," *Wall Street Journal*, October 23, 2001, A24.
10. Bill George, "Executive Pay: Rebuilding Trust in an Era of Rage," *Bloomberg Businessweek*, September 13–19, 2010, 56.
11. Yuka Hayashi and Phred Dvorak, "Japanese Wrestle with CEO Pay as They Go Global," *Wall Street Journal*, November 28, 2008, B1.
12. Richard Brown, "Outsider CEO: Inspiring Change with Force and Grace," *USA Today* (July 19, 1999): 3B.
13. Yavitz and Newman, 58.
14. Joann Lublin, "Pay Survey Shuffles Top CEOs," *Wall Street Journal*, November 15, 2010, B1.
15. Jack Duncan, *Management* (New York: Random House, 1983): 381–390.
16. E. H. Schein, "The Role of the Founder in Creating Organizational Culture," *Organizational Dynamics* (Summer 1983): 13–28.
17. T. Deal and A. Kennedy, "Culture: A New Look Through Old Lenses," *Journal of Applied Behavioral Science* 19, no. 4 (1983): 498–504.
18. H. Ibsen, "The Wild Duck," in O. G. Brochett and L. Brochett (eds.), *Plays for the Theater* (New York: Holt, Rinehart & Winston, 1967); R. Pascale, "The Paradox of 'Corporate Culture': Reconciling Ourselves to Socialization," *California Management Review* 28, no. 2 (1985): 26, 37–40.
19. T. Deal and A. Kennedy, *Corporate Cultures: The Rites and Rituals of Corporate Life* (Reading, MA: Addison-Wesley, 1982): 256.
20. Robert Stobaugh and Piero Telesio, "Match Manufacturing Policies and Product Strategy," *Harvard Business Review* 61, no. 2 (March–April 1983): 113.
21. Sudeep Reddy, "Employers Increasingly Rely on Temps, Part-Timers," *Wall Street Journal*, October 11, 2010, A4.
22. R. T. Lenz and Marjorie Lyles, "Managing Human Resource Problems in Strategy Planning Systems," *Journal of Business Strategy* 60, no. 4 (Spring 1986): 58.
23. J. Warren Henry, "ESOPs with Productivity Payoffs," *Journal of Business Strategy* (July–August 1989): 33.
24. Conor Dougherty, "Strides by Women, Still a Wage Gap," *Wall Street Journal*, March 1, 2011, A3. Also, David Jackson and Mimi Hall, "Women Gain in Education and Longevity," *USA Today*, March 2, 2011, 5A.
25. Sue Shellenbarger, "Employers Often Ignore Office Affairs, Leaving Co-workers in Difficult Spot," *Wall Street Journal* (March 10, 2005): D1.
26. Ibid.
27. Ibid.
28. Suzanne Vranica, "Ad Firms Heed Diversity," *Wall Street Journal*, November 29, 2010, B7.
29. Paulo Prada, "Women Ascend in Latin America," *Wall Street Journal*, December 24, 2010, A10.
30. Berry, Leonard L,, Ann Mirabito, and William Baun, "What's The Hard Return On Employee Wellness Programs?" *Harvard Business Review*, December 2010, 104–112.

Current Readings

Kulich, Clara, Grzegors Trojanowski, Michelle K. Ryan, S. Alexander Haslam, and Luc D. R. Renneboog. "Who Gets the Carrot and Who Gets the Stick? Evidence of Gender Disparities in Executive Remuneration." *Strategic Management Journal* 32, no. 3 (March 2011): 301–321.

Berry, Leonard L., Ann M. Mirabito, and William B. Baun. "What's the Hard Return On Employee Wellness

Programs?" *Harvard Business Review*, December 2010, 104–114.

Blenko, Marcia W., Michael C. Mankins, and Paul Rogers. "The Decision-Driven Organization." *Harvard Business Review*, June 2010, 54–63.

Core, John E., and Wayne R. Guay. "Is CEO Pay Too High and Are Incentives Too Low? A Wealth-Based Contracting Framework." *The Academy of Management Perspectives* 24, no. 1 (February 2010): 5–19.

Davenport, Thomas H., Jeanne Harris, and Jeremy Shapiro. "Competing on Talent Analytics," *Harvard Business Review*, October 2010, 52–89.

Filatotchev, Igor, and Deborah Allcock. "Corporate Governance and Executive Remuneration: A Contingency Framework." *The Academy of Management Perspectives* 24, no. 1 (February 2010): 20–33.

Fredrickson, James W., Alison Davis-Blake, and Gerard Sanders. "Sharing the Wealth: Social Comparisons and Pay Dispersion in the CEO's Top Team." *Strategic Management Journal* 31, no. 10 (October 2010): 1031– 1053.

Gaines-Ross, Leslie. "Reputation Warfare." *Harvard Business Review*, December 2010, 70–77.

Moschieri, Caterina. "The Implementation and Structuring of Divestitures: The Unit's Perspective." *Strategic Management Journal* 32, no. 4 (April 2011): 368–401.

Mossholder, Kevin W., Hettie A. Richardson, and Randall

P. Settoon. "Human Resource Systems and Helping in Organizations: A Relational Perspective." *The Academy of Management Review* 36, no. 1 (January 2011): 33–52.

Pearce, John A. II. "What Execs Don't Get About Office Romance." *MIT Sloan Management Review* 51, no. 3 (Spring 2010): 39–40.

Santora, Joseph C., and Mark Esposito. "Do Competitive Work Environments Help or Hurt Employees?" *The Academy of Management Perspectives* 24, no. 1 (February 2010): 81.

Shook, John. "How to Change a Culture: Lessons From NUMMI." *MIT Sloan Management Review* 51, no. 2 (Winter 2010): 63–68.

Sonenshein, Scott. "We're Changning—Or Are We? Untangling the Role of Progressive, Regressive, and Stability Narratives During Strategic Change Implementation." *The Academy of Management Journal* 53, no. 3 (June 2010): 477–512.

"Women in Management: Delusions of Progress" *Harvard Business Review*, March 2010, 19–27.

Wowak, Adam J., and Donald C. Hambrick. "A Model of Person-Pay Interaction: How Executives Vary in Their Responses to Compensation Arrangements." *Strategic Management Journal* 31, no. 8 (August 2010): 803–821.

Yuan, Feirong, and Richard W. Woodman. "Innovative Behavior in the Workplace: The Role of Performance and Image Outcome Expectations." *The Academy of Management Journal* 53, no. 2 (April 2010): 323–342.

ASSURANCE OF LEARNING EXERCISES

Assurance of Learning Exercise 7A

The Hershey Company Needs Your Help

Purpose

Hershey needs your assistance in developing a clear organizational chart. Some of its top executives believe the company needs a divisional by product type structure, and others believe the firm needs a divisional by geographic type structure. Hershey makes such well-known chocolate and candy brands as Hershey's Kisses, Reese's peanut butter cups, Twizzlers licorice, Mounds, and York Peppermint Patty. Hershey also makes grocery goods such as baking chocolate, ice cream toppings, chocolate syrup, cocoa mix, cookies, snack nuts, hard candies, and lollipops. Its products are sold throughout North America and exported overseas. Currently, Hershey's top executives have the following titles:

CEO and President of North American Commercial Group

EVP and COO

SVP and CFO

SVP and President of Hershey International

SVP for Strategy and Business Development

SVP of Global Operations

SVP, General Counsel, and Secretary

VP of Global R&D

VP of Investor Relations

VP of Global Innovation

VP of Corporation Communication

Instructions

Step 1 Based on the executive titles given above, construct an organizational chart for Hershey, following all the guidelines provided in Chapter 7.

Step 2 Review some information about Hershey on the Internet. Decide whether you believe Hershey would benefit most from a divisional-by-product or a divisional-by-geographic region design.

Step 3 Diagram your recommended chart.

Step 4 Write a one to two page Executive Summary of your organizational chart analysis and recommendations for Hershey.

Assurance of Learning Exercise 7B

Draw an Organizational Chart Using a Free, Online Template

Purpose

Strategic management students and business executives are oftentimes asked to construct an organizational chart. This exercise will make you aware of various online websites that provide free software for developing an organizational chart. Some websites in particular are as follows:

www.vertex42.com

http://office.microsoft.com/en-us/templates/business-organizational-chart-TC006088976.aspx

www.edrawsoft.com

www.smartdraw.com/specials/orgchart.asp

www.orgchart.net

Instructions

Do a Google search for "organizational charts" and examine various free templates for constructing a chart. Decide which template you think is most user friendly and effective. List some reasons why you decided on that particular template. Develop a sample organizational chart using the template you selected. Include 12 positions in your chart. Follow all guidelines provided in the chapter. In addition, use your template to develop an organizational chart for Hershey Foods as described in the previous exercise. Present your "reasons and charts" to your professor.

Assurance of Learning Exercise 7C

Revise Walt Disney's Organizational Chart

Purpose

Developing and altering organizational charts is an important skill for strategists to possess. This exercise can improve your skill in altering an organization's hierarchical structure in response to new strategies being formulated.

Instructions

Step 1 Turn to the Disney's Cohesion Case (p. 24) and review the organizational chart. On a separate sheet of paper, answer the following questions:

1. What type of organizational chart is illustrated for Disney?

Strategy implementation directly affects the lives of plant managers, division managers, department managers, sales managers, product managers, project managers, personnel managers, staff managers, supervisors, and all employees. In some situations, individuals may not have participated in the strategy-formulation process at all and may not appreciate, understand, or even accept the work and thought that went into strategy formulation. There may even be foot dragging or resistance on their part. Managers and employees who do not understand the business and are not committed to the business may attempt to sabotage strategy-implementation efforts in hopes that the organization will return to its old ways. The strategy-implementation stage of the strategic-management process is highlighted in Figure 8-1.

Current Marketing Issues

Countless marketing variables affect the success or failure of strategy implementation, and the scope of this text does not allow us to address all those issues. Some examples of marketing decisions that may require policies are as follows:

1. How to make advertisements more interactive to be more effective.
2. How to best take advantage of Facebook and Twitter conservations about the company and industry.

FIGURE 8-1

A Comprehensive Strategic-Management Model

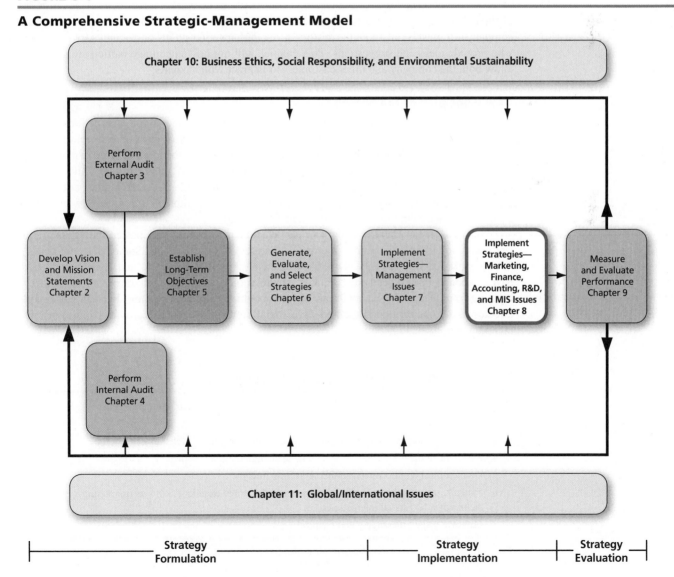

Source: Fred R. David, "How Companies Define Their Mission," *Long Range Planning* 22, no. 3 (June 1988): 40.

3. To use exclusive dealerships or multiple channels of distribution
4. To use heavy, light, or no TV advertising versus online advertising
5. To limit (or not) the share of business done with a single customer
6. To be a price leader or a price follower
7. To offer a complete or limited warranty
8. To reward salespeople based on straight salary, straight commission, or a combination salary/commission

Marketing of late has become more about building a two-way relationship with consumers than just informing consumers about a product or service. Marketers today must get their customers involved in their company website and solicit suggestions from customers in terms of product development, customer service, and ideas. The online community is much quicker, cheaper, and effective than traditional focus groups and surveys.

Companies and organizations should encourage their employees to create *wikis*—websites that allows users to add, delete, and edit content regarding frequently asked questions and information across the firm's whole value chain of activities. The most common wiki is Wikipedia, but think of wikis as user-generated content. Know that anyone can change the content in a wiki but the group and other editors can change the content or changes that you submit.

Firms should provide incentives to consumers to share their thoughts, opinions, and experiences on the company website. Encourage consumers to network among themselves on topics of their choosing on the company website. So the company website must not be all about the company—it must be all about the customer too. Perhaps offer points or discounts for customers who provide ideas and suggestions. This practice will not only encourage participation but will allow both the company and other customers to interact with "experts."

New Principles of Marketing

Today a business or organization's website must provide clear and simple instructions for customers to set up a blog and/or contribute to a wiki. Customers trust each others' opinions more than a company's marketing pitch, and the more they talk freely, the more the firm can learn how to improve its product, service, and marketing. Marketers today monitor blogs daily to determine, evaluate, and influence opinions being formed by customers. Customers must not feel like they are a captive audience for advertising at a firm's website. Table 8-1 provides new principles of marketing according to Parise, Guinan, and Weinberg.[1]

Wells Fargo and Bank of America *tweet* customers, meaning they posted messages of 140 characters or less on Twitter.com to describe features of bank products. Some banks are placing marketing videos on YouTube. Discover Financial, American Express, and Citigroup all now have Facebook or Myspace pages. UMB Financial of Kansas City, Missouri, tweets about everything from the bank's financial stability to the industry's prospects. Steve Furman, Discover's director of e-commerce, says the appeal of social networking is that it provides "pure, instant" communication with customers.[2]

TABLE 8-1 The New Principles of Marketing

1. Don't just talk at consumers—work with them throughout the marketing process.
2. Give consumers a reason to participate.
3. Listen to—and join—the conversation outside your company's website.
4. Resist the temptation to sell, sell, sell. Instead attract, attract, attract.
5. Don't control online conversations; let it flow freely.
6. Find a "marketing technologist," a person who has three excellent skill sets (marketing, technology, and social interaction).
7. Embrace instant messaging and chatting.

Source: Based on Salvatore Parise, Patricia Guinan, and Bruce Weinberg, "The Secrets of Marketing in a Web 2.0 World," *Wall Street Journal*, December 15, 2008, R1.

PepsiCo recently established a "Mission Control" staffed with social marketing employees promoting the company's long-time product Gatorade, which had been on a three-year sales slide. PepsiCo employees staff Mission Control 24/7 to tweet encouragement to high-school athletes and respond to Facebook questions.[3] Whenever anybody uses Twitter or Facebook to comment on Gatorade, that message pops up on a screen in Mission Control and a PepsiCo employee joins that person's social circle. PepsiCo is a leading company that tracks social media, tracks online-ad traffic, heads off potential crises, builds support for products, and monitors consumer behavior in depth. Gatorade is under intense pressure from Coca-Cola's Powerade, whose sales increased 16.8 percent in the first half of 2010 compared to Gatorade's 2.4 percent increase.

Although the exponential increase in social networking and business online has created huge opportunities for marketers, it also has produced some severe threats. Perhaps the greatest threat is that any kind of negative publicity travels fast online. For example, Dr Pepper recently suffered immensely when an attorney for the rock band Guns N' Roses accused the company of not following through on giving every American a soft drink if they released their album *Chinese Democracy*. Other examples abound, such as Motrin ads that lightheartedly talked about Mom's back pain from holding babies in slings, and Burger King's Whopper Virgin campaign, which featured a taste test of a Whopper versus a McDonald's Big Mac in remote areas of the world. Even Taco Bell suffered from its ads that featured asking 50 Cent (aka Curtis Jackson) if he would change his name to 79 Cent or 89 Cent for a day in exchange for a $10,000 donation to charity. Seemingly minor ethical and questionable actions can catapult these days into huge public relations problems for companies as a result of the monumental online social and business communications.

In increasing numbers, people living in underdeveloped and poor nations around the world have cell phones but no computers, so the Internet is rapidly moving to cell phone platforms. This is opening up even larger markets to online marketing. People in remote parts of Indonesia, Egypt, and Africa represent the fastest growing customer base for Opera Software ASA, a Norwegian maker of Internet browsers for mobile devices. Actually, persons who cannot afford computers live everywhere in every country, and many of these persons will soon be on the Internet on their cell phones. Cell phones are rapidly becoming used for data transfer, not just for phone calls. Companies such as Nokia, AT&T, Purple Labs SA of France, Japan's Access, Vodafone Group PLC, Siemens AG, Research in Motion, and Apple are spurring this transition by developing new and improved web-capable mobile products every day.[4]

Advertising Media

Recent research by Forrester Research reveals that people ages 18 to 27 spend more time weekly on the Internet than watching television, listening to the radio, or watching DVDs or VHS tapes. Companies are rapidly coming to the realization that social networking sites and video sites are better means of reaching their customers than spending so many marketing dollars on traditional yellow pages or television, magazine, radio, or newspaper ads. People spend time on the Internet. And it is not just the time. Television viewers are passive viewers of ads, whereas Internet users take an active role in choosing what to look at—so customers on the Internet are tougher for marketers to reach.[5]

According to analysts at Corporate Eye, advertising investments are expected to decrease or stay fairly even through 2013 with one exception—Internet advertising is expected to increase 27.9 percent between 2010 and 2013, as indicated in the table found at http://www .corporate-eye.com/blog/2010/12/ad-spending-forecasts-highlight-china-and-the-internet/. That website also notes that television advertising is by far the most commonly relied upon medium and is expected to slightly increase its share of total dollars spent. When it comes to regional investments, Corporate Eye says the Asia Pacific region will see advertising expenditures increase by 31.0 percent between 2009 and 2013. That's not as high, however, as increases in Latin America (43.3%), Central Europe (39.8%), or Africa and the Middle East (32.2%). Considering that China accounts for 20 percent of the world's population, the return on advertising investments in the Asia Pacific region could be exponentially higher than in any other area of the world.[6]

New companies such as Autonet Mobile based in San Francisco are selling new technology equipment for cars so the front passenger may conduct an iChat video conference while persons in the back each have a laptop and watch a YouTube video or download music or wirelessly transfer pictures from a digital camera. Everyone in the vehicle can be online except, of course, the driver. This technology is now available for installation in nearly all cars and is accelerating the movement from hard media to web-based media. With this technology also, when the vehicle drives into a new location, you may instantly download information on shows, museums, hotels, and other attractions around you.

Internet advertising is growing so rapidly that marketers are more and more allowed to create bigger, more intrusive ads that take up more space on the web page. Web sites are allowing lengthier ads to run before short video clips play. And blogs are creating more content that doubles also as an ad. Companies are also waiving minimum ad purchases. Companies are redesigning their websites to be much more interactive and are building new sponsorship programs and other enticements on their sites. Editorial content and advertising content are increasingly being mixed on blogs.

J.C. Penney CEO Myron Ullman says, "Consumers now shop for what they 'need' and less for what they 'want.' And they don't need much." Essentials, such as food, health-care products, and beauty aids are selling, but even in those industries, consumers are shifting to less costly brands and stores. There is a need for marketers to convince consumers that their brand will make life easier or better. Consumers now often wait until prices are slashed 75 percent or more to buy. Consumers today are very cautious about how they spend their money. Gone are the days when retailers could convince consumers to buy something they do not need.

J.C. Penney is among many firms that today have revamped their marketing to be more digital related. Penney's is segmenting its e-mail databases according to customers' shopping behaviors and then sending out relevant messages. Penney's corporate director of brand communications recently said, "Tailoring the e-mail insures that our customers are receiving timely, relevant information."

Purpose-Based Marketing

The former global marketing chief at Procter & Gamble, Jim Stengel, recently started his own LLC business to try to persuade companies that the best way to sell in a weak economy is to "show customers how they can improve their lives" with your product or service. Stengel calls this "*purpose-based marketing*," and hundreds of firms have now adopted this approach successfully. He says there is need in an ad to build trust and an emotional connection to the customer in order to differentiate your product or service.[7]

In a weak economy when consumers are more interested in buying cheaper brands, Stengel acknowledges that ads must promote price, but he says ads must also show the intrinsic value of the product or service to be cost effective. Stengel contends that ads should do both: promote low price and build emotional equity through "purpose-based appeal."

As an example of purpose-based marketing, the second-largest department-store chain in the United States, Macy's, introduced 2,200 local-themed tree ornaments in late 2010 as part of its "My Macy's" program, to better customize merchandise to local shoppers. You can buy Chicago Blackhawk ornaments in Illinois or Elvis ornaments in Memphis. Sales at Macy's 810 stores were up 5 percent in 2010.

The Coca-Cola Company is leading the way to another new kind of selling in a weak economy. CEO Muhtar Kent at Coke says marketing today must "employ optimism." That is why Coca-Cola recently launched a new global ad campaign appealing to consumers' longing for comfort and optimism. The new campaign features the new slogan "Open Happiness," which replaced Coke's prior popular slogan of three years, "The Coke Side of Life." The Coke CEO says marketers must use feel-good messages to counter the fallout from the economic crisis. Firms must today project to customers that their products or services offer a beacon of comfort and optimism.

Market Segmentation

Two variables are of central importance to strategy implementation: *market segmentation* and *product positioning*. Market segmentation and product positioning rank as marketing's most important contributions to strategic management.

TABLE 8-2   The Marketing Mix Component Variables

Product	Place	Promotion	Price
Quality	Distribution channels	Advertising	Level
Features and options	Distribution coverage	Personal selling	Discounts and allowances
Style	Outlet location	Sales promotion	Payment terms
Brand name	Sales territories	Publicity	
Packaging	Inventory levels and locations		
Product line	Transportation carriers		
Warranty			
Service level			
Other services			

Source: Based on E. Jerome McCarthy, *Basic Marketing: A Managerial Approach,* 9th ed. (Homewood, IL: Richard D. Irwin, Inc., 1987), 37–44. Used with permission.

Market segmentation is widely used in implementing strategies, especially for small and specialized firms. Market segmentation can be defined as the subdividing of a market into distinct subsets of customers according to needs and buying habits.

Market segmentation is an important variable in strategy implementation for at least three major reasons. First, strategies such as market development, product development, market penetration, and diversification require increased sales through new markets and products. To implement these strategies successfully, new or improved market-segmentation approaches are required. Second, market segmentation allows a firm to operate with limited resources because mass production, mass distribution, and mass advertising are not required. Market segmentation enables a small firm to compete successfully with a large firm by maximizing per-unit profits and per-segment sales. Finally, market segmentation decisions directly affect *marketing mix variables:* product, place, promotion, and price, as indicated in Table 8-2.

Perhaps the most dramatic new market-segmentation strategy is the targeting of regional tastes. Firms from Pizza Hut to Honda Motors are increasingly modifying their products to meet different regional preferences of customers around the world. Campbell's has a spicier version of its nacho cheese soup for the Southwest, and Burger King offers breakfast burritos in New Mexico but not in South Carolina. Geographic and demographic bases for segmenting markets are the most commonly employed, as illustrated in Table 8-3.

Evaluating potential market segments requires strategists to determine the characteristics and needs of consumers, to analyze consumer similarities and differences, and to develop consumer group profiles. Segmenting consumer markets is generally much simpler and easier than segmenting industrial markets, because industrial products, such as electronic circuits and forklifts, have multiple applications and appeal to diverse customer groups.

Segmentation is a key to matching supply and demand, which is one of the thorniest problems in customer service. Segmentation often reveals that large, random fluctuations in demand actually consist of several small, predictable, and manageable patterns. Matching supply and demand allows factories to produce desirable levels without extra shifts, overtime, and subcontracting. Matching supply and demand also minimizes the number and severity of stock-outs. The demand for hotel rooms, for example, can be dependent on foreign tourists, businesspersons, and vacationers. Focusing separately on these three market segments, however, can allow hotel firms to more effectively predict overall supply and demand.

Banks now are segmenting markets to increase effectiveness. "You're dead in the water if you aren't segmenting the market," says Anne Moore, president of a bank consulting firm in Atlanta. The Internet makes market segmentation easier today because consumers naturally form "communities" on the web.

Retention-Based Segmentation

To aid in more effective and efficient deployment of marketing resources, companies commonly tag each of their active customers with three values:

TABLE 8-3   Alternative Bases for Market Segmentation

Variable	Typical Breakdowns
Geographic	
Region	Pacific, Mountain, West North Central, West South Central, East North Central, East South Central, South Atlantic, Middle Atlantic, New England
County Size	A, B, C, D
City Size	Under 5,000; 5,000–20,000; 20,001–50,000; 50,001–100,000; 100,001–250,000; 250,001–500,000; 500,001–1,000,000; 1,000,001–4,000,000; 4,000,001 or over
Density	Urban, suburban, rural
Climate	Northern, southern
Demographic	
Age	Under 6, 6–11, 12–19, 20–34, 35–49, 50–64, 65+
Gender	Male, female
Family Size	1–2, 3–4, 5+
Family Life Cycle	Young, single; young, married, no children; young, married, youngest child under 6; young, married, youngest child 6 or over; older, married, with children; older, married, no children under 18; older, single; other
Income	Under $10,000; $10,001–$15,000; $15,001–$20,000; $20,001–$30,000; $30,001–$50,000; $50,001–$70,000; $70,001–$100,000; over $100,000
Occupation	Professional and technical; managers, officials, and proprietors; clerical and sales; craftspeople; foremen; operatives; farmers; retirees; students; housewives; unemployed
Education	Grade school or less; some high school; high school graduate; some college; college graduate
Religion	Catholic, Protestant, Jewish, Islamic, other
Race	White, Asian, Hispanic, African American
Nationality	American, British, French, German, Scandinavian, Italian, Latin American, Middle Eastern, Japanese
Psychographic	
Social Class	Lower lowers, upper lowers, lower middles, upper middles, lower uppers, upper uppers
Personality	Compulsive, gregarious, authoritarian, ambitious
Behavioral	
Use Occasion	Regular occasion, special occasion
Benefits Sought	Quality, service, economy
User Status	Nonuser, ex-user, potential user, first-time user, regular user
Usage Rate	Light user, medium user, heavy user
Loyalty Status	None, medium, strong, absolute
Readiness Stage	Unaware, aware, informed, interested, desirous, intending to buy
Attitude Toward Product	Enthusiastic, positive, indifferent, negative, hostile

Source: Adapted from Philip Kotler, *Marketing Management: Analysis, Planning and Control,* © 1984: 256. Adapted by permission of Prentice-Hall, Inc., Upper Saddle River, New Jersey.

Tag #1: Is this customer at high risk of canceling the company's service? One of the most common indicators of high-risk customers is a drop off in usage of the company's service. For example, in the credit card industry this could be signaled through a customer's decline in spending on his or her card.

Tag #2: Is this customer worth retaining? This determination boils down to whether the post-retention profit generated from the customer is predicted to be greater than the cost incurred to retain the customer. Customers need to be managed as investments.

Tag #3: What retention tactics should be used to retain this customer? For customers who are deemed "save-worthy," it's essential for the company to know which save tactics are most likely to be successful. Tactics commonly used range from providing "special" customer discounts to sending customers communications that reinforce the value proposition of the given service.[8]

The basic approach to tagging customers is to utilize historical retention data to make predictions about active customers regarding:

- Whether they are at high risk of canceling their service
- Whether they are profitable to retain
- What retention tactics are likely to be most effective

The idea with retention-based segmentation is to match up active customers with customers from historic retention data who share similar attributes. Using the theory that "birds of a feather flock together," the approach is based on the assumption that active customers will have similar retention outcomes as those of their comparable predecessor. This whole process is possible through business analytics or data mining (discussed later in this chapter).

Does the Internet Make Market Segmentation Easier?

Yes. The segments of people whom marketers want to reach online are much more precisely defined than the segments of people reached through traditional forms of media, such as television, radio, and magazines. For example, Quepasa.com is widely visited by Hispanics. Marketers aiming to reach college students, who are notoriously difficult to reach via traditional media, focus on sites such as collegeclub.com and studentadvantage.com. The gay and lesbian population, which is estimated to comprise about 5 percent of the population worldwide, has always been difficult to reach via traditional media but now can be focused on at sites such as gay.com. Marketers can reach persons interested in specific topics, such as travel or fishing, by placing banners on related websites.

People all over the world are congregating into virtual communities on the web by becoming members/customers/visitors of websites that focus on an endless range of topics. People in essence segment themselves by nature of the websites that comprise their "favorite places," and many of these websites sell information regarding their "visitors." Businesses and groups of individuals all over the world pool their purchasing power in websites to get volume discounts.

Product Positioning

After markets have been segmented so that the firm can target particular customer groups, the next step is to find out what customers want and expect. This takes analysis and research. A severe mistake is to assume the firm knows what customers want and expect. Countless research studies reveal large differences between how customers define service and rank the importance of different service activities and how producers view services. Many firms have become successful by filling the gap between what customers and producers see as good service. What the customer believes is good service is paramount, not what the producer believes service should be.

Identifying target customers to focus marketing efforts on sets the stage for deciding how to meet the needs and wants of particular consumer groups. Product positioning is widely used for this purpose. Positioning entails developing schematic representations that reflect how your products or services compare to competitors' on dimensions most important to success in the industry. The following steps are required in product positioning:

1. Select key criteria that effectively differentiate products or services in the industry.
2. Diagram a two-dimensional product-positioning map with specified criteria on each axis.
3. Plot major competitors' products or services in the resultant four-quadrant matrix.
4. Identify areas in the positioning map where the company's products or services could be most competitive in the given target market. Look for vacant areas (niches).
5. Develop a marketing plan to position the company's products or services appropriately.

Because just two criteria can be examined on a single product-positioning map, multiple maps are often developed to assess various approaches to strategy implementation. *Multidimensional scaling* could be used to examine three or more criteria simultaneously, but this technique requires computer assistance and is beyond the scope of this text. Some examples of product-positioning maps are illustrated in Figure 8-2.

Some rules for using product positioning as a strategy-implementation tool are the following:

1. Look for the hole or *vacant niche*. The best strategic opportunity might be an unserved segment.
2. Don't serve two segments with the same strategy. Usually, a strategy successful with one segment cannot be directly transferred to another segment.
3. Don't position yourself in the middle of the map. The middle usually means a strategy that is not clearly perceived to have any distinguishing characteristics. This rule can vary with the number of competitors. For example, when there are only two competitors, as in U.S. presidential elections, the middle becomes the preferred strategic position.[9]

An effective product-positioning strategy meets two criteria: (1) it uniquely distinguishes a company from the competition, and (2) it leads customers to expect slightly less service than a company can deliver. Firms should not create expectations that exceed the service the firm

FIGURE 8-2

Examples of Product-Positioning Maps

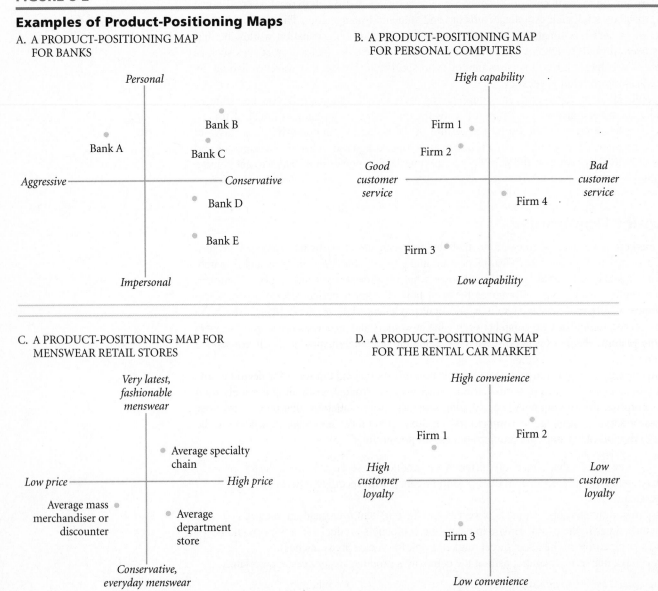

A. A PRODUCT-POSITIONING MAP FOR BANKS

B. A PRODUCT-POSITIONING MAP FOR PERSONAL COMPUTERS

C. A PRODUCT-POSITIONING MAP FOR MENSWEAR RETAIL STORES

D. A PRODUCT-POSITIONING MAP FOR THE RENTAL CAR MARKET

can or will deliver. Network Equipment Technology is an example of a company that keeps customer expectations slightly below perceived performance. This is a constant challenge for marketers. Firms need to inform customers about what to expect and then exceed the promise. Underpromise and then overdeliver is the key!

Finance/Accounting Issues

In terms of "Financial Soundness," *Fortune* in 2011 ranked the following companies as best in the world:

Rank	Company
1	Google
2	Apple
3	McDonald's
4	Occidental Petroleum
5	W.W. Grainger
6	Nestlé
7	Amazon.com
8	Wal-Mart Stores
9	Microsoft
10	Walt Disney

Source: Based on http://money.cnn.com/magazines/fortune/mostad-mired/2011/best_worst/best6.html

In this section, we examine several finance/accounting concepts considered to be central to strategy implementation: acquiring needed capital, developing projected financial statements, preparing financial budgets, and evaluating the worth of a business. Some examples of decisions that may require finance/accounting policies are these:

1. To raise capital with short-term debt, long-term debt, preferred stock, or common stock
2. To lease or buy fixed assets
3. To determine an appropriate dividend payout ratio
4. To use LIFO (Last-in, First-out), FIFO (First-in, First-out), or a market-value accounting approach
5. To extend the time of accounts receivable
6. To establish a certain percentage discount on accounts within a specified period of time
7. To determine the amount of cash that should be kept on hand

Acquiring Capital to Implement Strategies

When students complete their Recommendations Page as part of a case analysis, or in actual company practice when a firm decides what strategies to pursue, it is necessary to address the question: Where should the company obtain needed capital?

Successful strategy implementation often requires additional capital. Besides net profit from operations and the sale of assets, two basic sources of capital for an organization are debt and equity. Determining an appropriate mix of debt and equity in a firm's capital structure can be vital to successful strategy implementation. An *Earnings Per Share/Earnings Before Interest and Taxes (EPS/EBIT) analysis* is the most widely used technique for determining whether debt, stock, or a combination of debt and stock is the best alternative for raising capital to implement strategies. This technique involves an examination of the impact that debt versus stock financing has on earnings per share under various assumptions as to EBIT.

Theoretically, an enterprise should have enough debt in its capital structure to boost its return on investment by applying debt to products and projects earning more than the cost of the debt. In low earning periods, too much debt in the capital structure of an organization can endanger stockholders' returns and jeopardize company survival. Fixed debt obligations generally must be met, regardless of circumstances. This does not mean that stock issuances are always better than debt for raising capital. Some special concerns with stock issuances are dilution of ownership, effect on stock price, and the need to share future earnings with all new shareholders.

Before explaining EPS/EBIT analysis, it is important to know that EPS = Earnings per Share, which is Net Income divided by # of Shares Outstanding. Another term for Shares Outstanding is Shares Issued. Also know that EBIT = Earnings Before Interest and Taxes. Another name for EBIT is Operating Income. EBT = Earnings Before Tax. EAT = Earnings After Tax.

The purpose of EPS/EBIT analysis is to determine whether All Debt, or All Stock, or some combination of debt and stock yields the highest EPS values for the firm. EPS is perhaps the best measure of success of a company, so it is widely used in making the capital acquisition decision. EPS reflects the common "maximizing shareholders' wealth" overarching corporate objective. By chance if profit maximization is the company's goal, then in performing an EPS/EBIT analysis, you may focus more on the EAT row more than the EPS row. Large companies may have millions of shares outstanding, so even small differences in EPS across different financing options can equate to large sums of money saved by using that highest EPS value alternative. Any number of combination debt/stock scenarios, such as 70/30 D/S or 30/70 D/S, may be examined in an EPS/EBIT analysis.

EPS/EBIT analysis may best be explained by working through an example for the XYZ Company, as provided in Table 8-4. Note that 100% Stock is the best financing alternative as indicated by the EPS values of 0.279 and 0.056. An EPS/EBIT chart can be constructed to determine the break-even point, where one financing alternative becomes more attractive than another. Figure 8-3 reveals that issuing common stock is the best financing alternative for the XYZ Company. As noted in Figure 8-3, you simply graph the top row (EBIT) on the x-axis with the bottom row (EPS) on the y-axis and the highest plotted line reveals the best method. Sometimes the plotted lines will interact, so a graph is especially helpful in making the capital acquisition decision, rather than solely relying on a table of numbers.

TABLE 8-4   EPS/EBIT Analysis for the XYZ Company

Input Data	The Number	How Determined
$Amount of Capital Needed	$100 million	Estimated $cost of recommendations
EBIT Range	$20 to $40 million	Estimate based on prior year EBIT and recommendations for the coming year(s)
Interest Rate	5 percent	Estimate based on cost of capital
Tax Rate	30 percent	Use prior year %: taxes divided by income before taxes, as given on income statement
Stock Price	$50	Use most recent stock price
#Shares Outstanding	500 million	For the debt columns, enter the existing #shares outstanding. For stock columns, use the existing #shares outstanding + the #new shares that must be issued to raise the needed capital, i.e., based on stock price. So divide the stock price into the $amount of capital needed.

	100% Debt		100% Stock		50/50 Debt/Stock Combo	
$ EBIT	20,000,000	40,000,000	20,000,000	40,000,000	20,000,000	40,000,000
$ Interest	5,000,000	5,000,000	0	0	2,500,000	2,500,000
$ EBT	15,000,000	35,000,000	20,000,000	40,000,000	17,500,000	37,500,000
$ Taxes	4,500,000	10,500,000	6,000,000	12,000,000	5,250,000	11,250,000
$ EAT	10,500,000	24,500,000	14,000,000	28,000,000	12,250,000	26,250,000
# Shares	500,000,000	500,000,000	502,000,000	502,000,000	501,000,000	501,000,000
$ EPS	0.210	0.049	0.279	0.056	0.245	0.0523

Conclusion—the best financing alternative is 100% Stock since the EPS values are largest; the worst financing alternative is 100% Debt since the EPS values are lowest.

FIGURE 8-3

An EPS/EBIT Chart for the XYZ Company

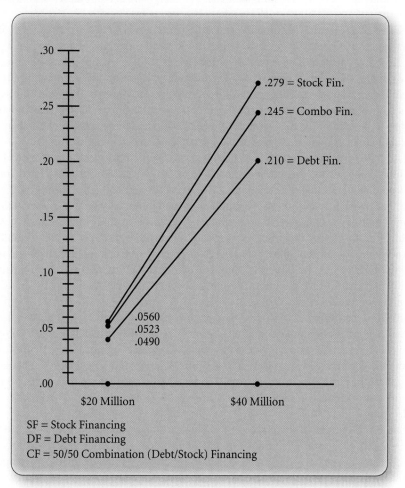

SF = Stock Financing
DF = Debt Financing
CF = 50/50 Combination (Debt/Stock) Financing

A consideration when using EPS/EBIT analysis is flexibility. As an organization's capital structure changes, so does its flexibility for considering future capital needs. Using all debt or all stock to raise capital in the present may impose fixed obligations, restrictive covenants, or other constraints that could severely reduce a firm's ability to raise additional capital in the future. Control is also a concern. When additional stock is issued to finance strategy implementation, ownership and control of the enterprise are diluted. This can be a serious concern in today's business environment of hostile takeovers, mergers, and acquisitions.

IBM has in fact bought back on average $10 billion worth of its own stock per year during the 2009 to 2012 years, dropping its number of outstanding shares from a high of 1.72 billion in 2003 to less than 1.0 billion in 2012. IBM is buying back its stock because it believes the stock price is going up and thus it is a better investment of company monies than some other strategic alternatives.

For all of 2010, companies bought back $299 billion of their own stock, up a record 117 percent from the prior year. However, that total was roughly half of the record total in 2007. Many analysts say buyouts reflect optimism among companies and say it is a good sign. However, other analysts argue that buybacks eat cash that a firm could better utilize to grow the firm.

Dilution of ownership can be an overriding concern in closely held corporations in which stock issuances affect the decision-making power of majority stockholders. For example, the Smucker family owns 30 percent of the stock in Smucker's, a well-known jam and jelly company. When Smucker's acquired Dickson Family, Inc., the company used mostly debt rather than stock in order not to dilute the family ownership.

When using EPS/EBIT analysis, timing in relation to movements of stock prices, interest rates, and bond prices becomes important. In times of depressed stock prices, debt may prove to be the most suitable alternative from both a cost and a demand standpoint. However, when cost of capital (interest rates) is high, stock issuances become more attractive.

The United States has $9.7 trillion in outstanding debt, equal to 63 percent of GDP. Based on that percentage, S&P recently lowered the USA's AAA credit rating. It is interesting, however, that 147 of the S&P 500 companies have total debt that is 63 percent or greater than the company's revenue. For example, GE, Lennar, and Harley-Davidson have debt that is 300, 131, and 116 percent greater than their revenues, respectively. A key difference of course is that companies generate money while governments consume money. The U.S. government pays $210 billion in interest annually, about 10 percent of the $2.1 trillion it collects annually in taxes. Only 24 companies in the S&P 500 however incur interest payments that total at least 10 percent of their revenue.

Tables 8-5 and 8-6 provide EPS/EBIT analyses for two companies—Gateway and Boeing. Notice in those analyses that the combination stock/debt options vary from 30/70 to 70/30. Any number of combinations could be explored. However, sometimes in preparing the EPS/EBIT graphs, the lines will intersect, thus revealing break-even points at which one financing alternative becomes more or less attractive than another. The slope of these lines will be determined by a combination of factors including stock price, interest rate, number of shares, and amount of capital needed. Also, it should be noted here that the best financing alternatives are indicated by the highest EPS values. In Tables 8-5 and 8-6, note that the tax rates for the companies vary considerably and should be computed from the respective income statements by dividing taxes paid by income before taxes.

In Table 8-5, the higher EPS values indicate that Gateway should use stock to raise capital in recession or normal economic conditions but should use debt financing under boom conditions. Stock is the best alternative for Gateway under all three conditions if EAT (profit maximization) were the decision criteria, but EPS (maximize shareholders' wealth) is the better ratio to make this decision. Firms can do many things in the short run to maximize profits, so investors and creditors consider maximizing shareholders' wealth to be the better criteria for making financing decisions.

In Table 8-6, note that Boeing should use stock to raise capital in recession (see 0.92) or normal (see 2.29) economic conditions but should use debt financing under boom conditions (see 5.07). Let's calculate here the number of shares figure of 1014.68 given under Boeing's stock alternative. Divide $10,000 M funds needed by the stock price of $53 = 188.68 M new shares to be issued + the 826 M shares outstanding already = 1014.68 M shares under the stock scenario. Along the final row, EPS is the number of shares outstanding divided by EAT in all columns.

Note in Table 8-5 and Table 8-6 that a dividends row is absent from both the Gateway and Boeing analyses. The more shares outstanding, the more dividends to be paid (if the firm indeed pays dividends). To consider dividends in an EPS/EBIT analysis, simply insert another row for "Dividends" right below the "EAT" row and then insert an "Earnings After Taxes and Dividends" row. Considering dividends would make the analysis more robust.

Note in both the Gateway and Boeing graphs, there is a break-even point between the normal and boom range of EBIT where the debt option overtakes the 70% Debt/30% Stock option as the best financing alternative. A break-even point is where two lines cross each other. A break-even point is the EBIT level where various financing alternative represented by lines crossing are equally attractive in terms of EPS. Both the Gateway and Boeing graphs indicate that EPS values are highest for the 100 percent debt option at high EBIT levels. The two graphs also reveal that the EPS values for 100 percent debt increase faster than the other financing options as EBIT levels increase beyond the break-even point. At low levels of EBIT however, both the Gateway and Boeing graphs indicate that 100 percent stock is the best financing alternative because the EPS values are highest.

Projected Financial Statements

Projected financial statement analysis is a central strategy-implementation technique because it allows an organization to examine the expected results of various actions and approaches. This type of analysis can be used to forecast the impact of various implementation decisions (for example, to increase promotion expenditures by 50 percent to support a market-development strategy, to increase salaries by 25 percent to support a market-penetration strategy, to increase

TABLE 8-5 EPS/EBIT Analysis for Gateway (M = in millions)

Amount Needed: $1,000 M

EBIT Range: – $500 M to + $100 M to + $500 M

Interest Rate: 5%

Tax Rate: 0% (because the firm has been incurring a loss annually)

Stock Price: $6.00

# of Shares Outstanding: 371 M

	Common Stock Financing			Debt Financing		
	Recession	*Normal*	*Boom*	*Recession*	*Normal*	*Boom*
EBIT	(500.00)	100.00	500.00	(500.00)	100.00	500.00
Interest	0.00	0.00	0.00	50.00	50.00	50.00
EBT	(500.00)	100.00	500.00	(550.00)	50.00	450.00
Taxes	0.00	0.00	0.00	0.00	0.00	0.00
EAT	(500.00)	100.00	500.00	(550.00)	50.00	450.00
#Shares	537.67	537.67	537.67	371.00	371.00	371.00
EPS	**(0.93)**	**0.19**	**0.93**	**(1.48)**	**0.13**	**1.21**

	70 Percent Stock—30 Percent Debt			70 Percent Debt—30 Percent Stock		
	Recession	*Normal*	*Boom*	*Recession*	*Normal*	*Boom*
EBIT	(500.00)	100.00	500.00	(500.00)	100.00	500.00
Interest	15.00	15.00	15.00	35.00	35.00	35.00
EBT	(515.00)	85.00	485.00	(535.00)	65.00	465.00
Taxes	0.00	0.00	0.00	0.00	0.00	0.00
EAT	(515.00)	85.00	485.00	(535.00)	65.00	465.00
#Shares	487.67	487.67	487.67	421.00	421.00	421.00
EPS	**(1.06)**	**0.17**	**0.99**	**(1.27)**	**0.15**	**1.10**

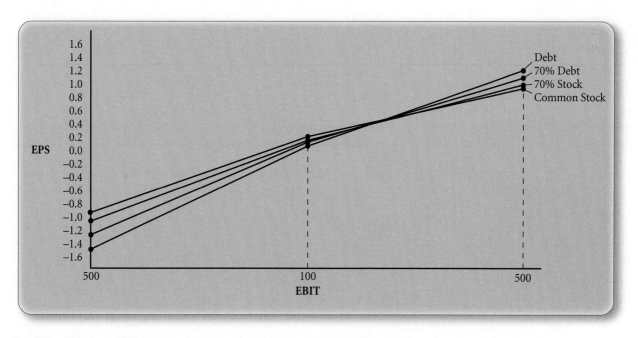

Conclusion: Gateway should use common stock to raise capital in recession or normal economic conditions but should use debt financing under boom conditions. Note that stock is the best alternative under all three conditions according to EAT (profit maximization), but EPS (maximize shareholders' wealth) is the better ratio to make this decision.

TABLE 8-6   EPS/EBIT Analysis for Boeing (M = in millions)

Amount Needed: $10,000 M

Interest Rate: 5%

Tax Rate: 7%

Stock Price: $53.00

# of Shares Outstanding: 826 M

	Common Stock Financing			Debt Financing		
	Recession	*Normal*	*Boom*	*Recession*	*Normal*	*Boom*
EBIT	1,000.00	2,500.00	5,000.00	1,000.00	2,500.00	5,000.00
Interest	0.00	0.00	0.00	500.00	500.00	500.00
EBT	1,000.00	2,500.00	5,000.00	500.00	2,000.00	4,500.00
Taxes	70.00	175.00	350.00	35.00	140.00	315.00
EAT	930.00	2,325.00	4,650.00	465.00	1,860.00	4,185.00
# Shares	1,014.68	1,014.68	1,014.68	826.00	826.00	826.00
EPS	**0.92**	**2.2 9**	**4.58**	**0.56**	**2.25**	**5.07**

	70% Stock—30% Debt			70% Debt—30% Stock		
	Recession	*Normal*	*Boom*	*Recession*	*Normal*	*Boom*
EBIT	1,000.00	2,500.00	5,000.00	1,000.00	2,500.00	5,000.00
Interest	150.00	150.00	150.00	350.00	350.00	350.00
EBT	850.00	2,350.00	4,850.00	650.00	2,150.00	4,650.00
Taxes	59.50	164.50	339.50	45.50	150.50	325.50
EAT	790.50	2,185.50	4,510.50	604.50	1,999.50	4,324.50
# Shares	958.08	958.08	958.08	882.60	882.60	882.60
EPS	**0.83**	**2.28**	**4.71**	**0.68**	**2.27**	**4.90**

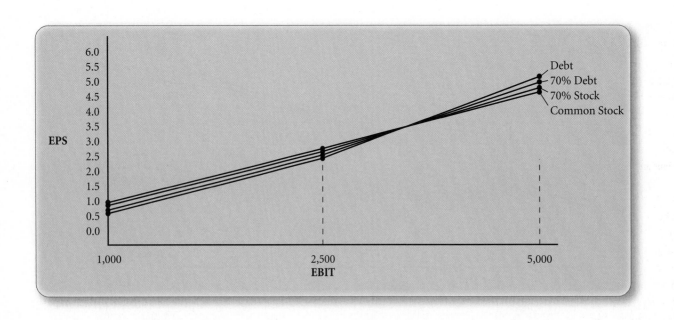

Conclusion: Boeing should use common stock to raise capital in recession (see 0.92) or normal (see 2.29) economic conditions but should use debt financing under boom conditions (see 5.07). Note that a dividends row is absent from this analysis. The more shares outstanding, the more dividends to be paid (if the firm pays dividends), which would lower the common stock EPS values.

research and development expenditures by 70 percent to support product development, or to sell $1 million of common stock to raise capital for diversification). Nearly all financial institutions require at least three years of projected financial statements whenever a business seeks capital. A projected income statement and balance sheet allow an organization to compute projected financial ratios under various strategy-implementation scenarios. When compared to prior years and to industry averages, financial ratios provide valuable insights into the feasibility of various strategy-implementation approaches.

Primarily as a result of the Sarbanes-Oxley Act, companies today are being much more diligent in preparing projected financial statements to "reasonably rather than too optimistically" project future expenses and earnings. There is much more care not to mislead shareholders and other constituencies.

A 2013 projected income statement and a balance sheet for the Litten Company are provided in Table 8-7. The projected statements for Litten are based on five assumptions: (1) The company needs to raise $45 million to finance expansion into foreign markets; (2) $30 million of

TABLE 8-7   A Projected Income Statement and Balance Sheet for the Litten Company (in millions)

	Prior Year 2012	Projected Year 2013	Remarks
PROJECTED INCOME STATEMENT			
Sales	$100	$150.00	50% increase
Cost of Goods Sold	70	105.00	70% of sales
Gross Margin	30	45.00	
Selling Expense	10	15.00	10% of sales
Administrative Expense	5	7.50	5% of sales
Earnings Before Interest and Taxes	15	22.50	
Interest	3	3.00	
Earnings Before Taxes	12	19.50	
Taxes	6	9.75	50% rate
Net Income	**6**	**9.75**	
Dividends	2	5.00	
Retained Earnings	4	4.75	
PROJECTED BALANCE SHEET			
Assets			
Cash	5	7.75	Plug figure
Accounts Receivable	2	4.00	100% increase
Inventory	20	45.00	
Total Current Assets	27	56.75	
Land	15	15.00	
Plant and Equipment	50	80.00	Add three new plants at $10 million each
Less Depreciation	10	20.00	
Net Plant and Equipment	40	60.00	
Total Fixed Assets	55	75.00	
Total Assets	**82**	**131.75**	
Liabilities			
Accounts Payable	10	10.00	
Notes Payable	10	10.00	
Total Current Liabilities	20	20.00	
Long-term Debt	40	70.00	Borrowed $30 million
Additional Paid-in-Capital	20	35.00	Issued 100,000 shares at $150 each
Retained Earnings	2	6.75	$2 + $4.75
Total Liabilities and Net Worth	**82**	**131.75**	

this total will be raised through increased debt and $15 million through common stock; (3) sales are expected to increase 50 percent; (4) three new facilities, costing a total of $30 million, will be constructed in foreign markets; and (5) land for the new facilities is already owned by the company. Note in Table 8-7 that Litten's strategies and their implementation are expected to result in a sales increase from $100 million to $150 million and in a net increase in income from $6 million to $9.75 million in the forecasted year.

There are six steps in performing projected financial analysis:

1. Prepare the projected income statement before the balance sheet. Start by forecasting sales as accurately as possible. Be careful not to blindly push historical percentages into the future with regard to revenue (sales) increases. Be mindful of what the firm did to achieve those past sales increases, which may not be appropriate for the future unless the firm takes similar or analogous actions (such as opening a similar number of stores, for example). If dealing with a manufacturing firm, also be mindful that if the firm is operating at 100 percent capacity running three eight-hour shifts per day, then probably new manufacturing facilities (land, plant, and equipment) will be needed to increase sales further.

2. Use the percentage-of-sales method to project cost of goods sold (CGS) and the expense items in the income statement. For example, if CGS is 70 percent of sales in the prior year (as it is in Table 8-7), then use that same percentage to calculate CGS in the future year—unless there is a reason to use a different percentage. Items such as interest, dividends, and taxes must be treated independently and cannot be forecasted using the percentage-of-sales method.

3. Calculate the projected net income.

4. Subtract from the net income any dividends to be paid for that year. This remaining net income is retained earnings (RE). Bring this retained earnings amount for that year (NI - DIV = RE) over to the balance sheet by adding it to the prior year's RE shown on the balance sheet. In other words, every year a firm adds its RE for that particular year (from the income statement) to its historical RE total on the balance sheet. Therefore, the RE amount on the balance sheet is a cumulative number rather than money available for strategy implementation! Note that RE is the first projected balance sheet item to be entered. Due to this accounting procedure in developing projected financial statements, the RE amount on the balance sheet is usually a large number. However, it also can be a low or even negative number if the firm has been incurring losses. The only way for RE to decrease from one year to the next on the balance sheet is (1) if the firm incurred an earnings loss that year or (2) the firm had positive net income for the year but paid out dividends more than the net income. Be mindful that RE is the key link between a projected income statement and balance sheet, so be careful to make this calculation correctly.

5. Project the balance sheet items, beginning with retained earnings and then forecasting stockholders' equity, long-term liabilities, current liabilities, total liabilities, total assets, fixed assets, and current assets (in that order). Use the cash account as the plug figure—that is, use the cash account to make the assets total the liabilities and net worth. Then make appropriate adjustments. For example, if the cash needed to balance the statements is too small (or too large), make appropriate changes to borrow more (or less) money than planned.

6. List comments (remarks) on the projected statements. Any time a significant change is made in an item from a prior year to the projected year, an explanation (remark) should be provided. Remarks are essential because otherwise pro formas are meaningless.

Projected Financial Statement Analysis for Whole Foods Market

Because so many strategic management students have limited experience developing projected financial statements, let's apply the steps outlined on the previous pages to Whole Foods Market, the company showcased at the beginning of this chapter for excellent strategic management.

Whole Foods Market opened 16 stores in fiscal 2010. The projected statements given on the next page(s) are based on the following recommendations:

1. WFMI opens 40 new stores in 2011 and 60 new stores in 2012.
2. WFMI uses a 50/50 debt/stock combination to finance the 100 new stores.
3. After paying almost no dividends in 2010, WFMI starts paying dividends at $1.00 per share in 2011 and 2012.
4. WFMI boosts its advertising expenses by $20 million per year.
5. WFMI installs a new inventory control system that increases the company's low gross margin from 34.8 percent to 40.0 percent.
6. WFMI's per store revenues will increase 10 percent annually in 2011–2013 due to the new ad campaign and the improving economy.
7. Total cost of recommendations for two years are $800 million = $200 million per year to be raised through both debt and equity.

Whole Food's actual consolidated income statements and balance sheets are provided in Table 8-8 and Table 8-9 respectively. The projected statements, based on the above recommendations, are provided in Table 8-10 and 8-11 respectively. Read carefully the notes (a through f), which reveal the rationale for various changes and exemplify the pro forma process. Note in Table 8-10 that Whole Foods' operating margin with the proposed strategic plan increases from 4.9 percent in 2010 to 16.9 percent in 2012. Note in Table 8-11 that Whole Foods' current ratio would be $3,580.3/$400 = 8.95, which is high. Thus in 2012 the company could better use that money to perhaps pay down some of its $908 million in long-term debt.

The projected financial statements were prepared using the six steps outlined on prior pages and the above seven strategy statements. Note the cash account is used as the plug figure, and it is too high, so WFMI could reduce this number and concurrently reduce a liability and/or equity account the same amount to keep the statement in balance. Rarely is the cash account perfect on the first pass through, so adjustments are needed and made. However, these adjustments are *not* made on the projected statements given in Tables 8-10 and 8-11, so that the five strategy statements above can be more readily seen on respective rows. Note the author's comments on Tables 8-10 and 8-11 that help explain changes in the numbers.

TABLE 8-8 Actual Whole Foods Market Income Statements (in millions)

	2010	2009
Revenue (a)	$9,005.8	$8,031.6
Cost of Goods Sold	5,870.4	5,277.3
Gross Profit	3,135.4	2,754.3
Gross Profit Margin	34.8%	34.3%
SG&A Expense	2,697.4	2,470.0
Depreciation & Amortization	275.6	266.7
Operating Income	438.0	284.3
Operating Margin	4.9%	3.5%
Nonoperating Income	6.9	3.4
Nonoperating Expenses	(33.0)	(36.9)
Income Before Taxes	411.8	250.9
Income Taxes (b)	165.9	104.1
Net Income After Taxes	245.8	146.8
Net Income	$245.8	$146.8

(a) – Note that the 16 news stores in 2010 resulted in ($9,005.8 – 8,031.6 = 974.2 revenue increase = an average of $974.2 / 16 = $60.89) $60.89 million as the average revenue per new store.

(b) – Note WFMI's effective tax rate is $165.9 / 411.8 = 40.3%.

TABLE 8-9 Actual Whole Foods Market Balance Sheets (in millions)

	2010	2009
Assets		
Current Assets		
Cash	$132.0	$430.1
Net Receivables	133.3	104.7
Inventories	323.5	310.6
Other Current Assets	572.7	209.9
Total Current Assets	1,161.5	1,055.4
Net Fixed Assets (a)	1,886.1	1,897.9
Other Noncurrent Assets	938.9	830.2
Total Assets	**3,986.5**	**3,783.4**
Liabilities		
Current Liabilities		
Accounts Payable	213.2	189.6
Short-Term Debt	0.4	0.4
Other Current Liabilities	534.3	494.0
Total Current Liabilities	747.9	684.0
Long-Term Debt	508.3	738.8
Other Noncurrent Liabilities	357.0	732.6
Total Liabilities	**1,613.2**	**2,155.5**
Shareholders' Equity		
Common Stock	500	400
Additional-paid-in-capital	1,274.7	869.7
Retained Earnings (b)	598.6	358.2
Total Shareholders' Equity	2,373.3	1,627.9
Total Liabilities and SE	**$3,986.5**	**$3,783.4**
Shares Outstanding (thou.)	172,033	140,542

(a) – Since WFMI operated 300 stores in 2010, we can estimate cost per store = $1,886 / 300 = $6.3 million and use that cost # for each new store to be built.

(b) – Note that WFMI reinvested back into the company $240.4 million of its total $245.8 million in net income, so in 2010 the company paid out only $5.4 million in dividends. We know that because $598.6 – $358.2 = $240.4.

The U.S. Securities and Exchange Commission (SEC) conducts fraud investigations if projected numbers are misleading or if they omit information that's important to investors. Projected statements must conform with generally accepted accounting principles (GAAP) and must not be designed to hide poor expected results. The Sarbanes-Oxley Act requires CEOs and CFOs of corporations to personally sign their firms' financial statements attesting to their accuracy. These executives could thus be held personally liable for misleading or inaccurate statements. The collapse of the Arthur Andersen accounting firm, along with its client Enron, fostered a "zero tolerance" policy among auditors and shareholders with regard to a firm's financial statements. But plenty of firms still "inflate" their financial projections and call them "pro formas," so investors, shareholders, and other stakeholders must still be wary of different companies' financial projections.[10]

On financial statements, different companies use different terms for various items, such as *revenues* or *sales* used for the same item by different companies. For net income, many firms use the term *earnings*, and many others use the term *profits*.

Financial Budgets

A *financial budget* is a document that details how funds will be obtained and spent for a specified period of time. Annual budgets are most common, although the period of time for a budget

TABLE 8-10   Projected Whole Foods Market Income Statements (in millions)

	2010	2011	2012
Revenue (a)	$9,005.8	12,584.0	17,860.0
Cost of Goods Sold	5,870.4	7,550.0	10,716.0
Gross Profit	3,135.4	5,034.0	7,144.0
Gross Profit Margin (b)	34.8%	40%	40%
SG&A Expense (c)	2,697.4	3,782.0	4,109.0
Depreciation & Amortization	275.6	290	310.0
Operating Income	438.0	1,252.0	3,035.0
Operating Margin	4.9%	9.9%	16.9%
Nonoperating Income	6.9	0	0
Nonoperating Expenses	(33.0)	0	0
Income Before Taxes	411.8	1,252.0	3,035.0
Income Taxes (d)	165.9	504.0	1,223.0
Net Income After Taxes	245.8	748.0	1,812.0
Net Income	$245.8	748.0	1,812.0
Dividends	5.4	175.0	180.0
Retained Earnings	$240.4	573.0	1,632.0

(a) - $60.89 million per new store + 10% increase for all stores, so in 2011 we have $60.89 x 40 = $2,435 + 9,005 = $11,440 + 10% = $12,584. In 2012 we have $60.89 x 60 = 3,653 + 12,584 = $16,237 + 10% = $17,860.

(b) increases to 40% due to better inventory control; note that 5,034/12,584 = 40% and 7,144/17,860 = 40%.

(c) same 29.9% of revenue + $20 million per year, new ad campaign; note that $12,584 × .299 + $20 = $3,782.

(d) same 40.3% rate as in 2010.

can range from one day to more than 10 years. Fundamentally, financial budgeting is a method for specifying what must be done to complete strategy implementation successfully. Financial budgeting should not be thought of as a tool for limiting expenditures but rather as a method for obtaining the most productive and profitable use of an organization's resources. Financial budgets can be viewed as the planned allocation of a firm's resources based on forecasts of the future.

There are almost as many different types of financial budgets as there are types of organizations. Some common types of budgets include cash budgets, operating budgets, sales budgets, profit budgets, factory budgets, capital budgets, expense budgets, divisional budgets, variable budgets, flexible budgets, and fixed budgets. When an organization is experiencing financial difficulties, budgets are especially important in guiding strategy implementation.

Perhaps the most common type of financial budget is the *cash budget*. The Financial Accounting Standards Board (FASB) has mandated that every publicly-held company in the United States must issue an annual cash-flow statement in addition to the usual financial reports. The statement includes all receipts and disbursements of cash in operations, investments, and financing. It supplements the Statement on Changes in Financial Position formerly included in the annual reports of all publicly held companies. A cash budget for the year 2013 for the Toddler Toy Company is provided in Table 8-12. Note that Toddler is not expecting to have surplus cash until November 2013.

Financial budgets have some limitations. First, budgetary programs can become so detailed that they are cumbersome and overly expensive. Overbudgeting or underbudgeting can cause problems. Second, financial budgets can become a substitute for objectives. A budget is a tool and not an end in itself. Third, budgets can hide inefficiencies if based solely on precedent rather than on periodic evaluation of circumstances and standards. Finally, budgets are sometimes used as instruments of tyranny that result in frustration, resentment, absenteeism, and high turnover. To minimize the effect of this last concern, managers should increase the participation of subordinates in preparing budgets.

TABLE 8-11   Projected Whole Foods Market Balance Sheets (in millions)

	2010	2011	2012
Assets			
Current Assets			
Cash	$132.0	$1,55.3	$3,260.3
Net Receivables	133.3	140.0	160.0
Inventories	323.5	330.0	360.0
Other Current Assets	572.7	0	0
Total Current Assets	1,161.5	2,020.3	3,580.3
Net Fixed Assets (a)	1,886.1	2,138.0	2,516.0
Other Noncurrent Assets	938.9	0	0
Total Assets	**$3,986.5**	**$4,159.3**	**$6,296.3**
Liabilities			
Current Liabilities			
Accounts Payable	213.2	300.0	400.0
Short-Term Debt	0.4	0	0
Other Current Liabilities	534.3	0	0
Total Current Liabilities	747.9	300.0	400.0
Long-Term Debt (b)	508.3	708.0	908.0
Other Noncurrent Liabilities	357.0	0	0
Total Liabilities	1,613.2	1,008.0	1,308.0
Shareholders' Equity			
Common Stock (c)	500.0	505.0	510.0
Additional-paid-in-capital (d)	1,247.7	1,474.7	1,674.7
Retained Earnings (e)	598.6	1,171.6	2,803.6
Total Shareholders' Equity	2,373.3	3151.3	4,988.3
Total Liabilities and SE	**$3,986.5**	**$4,159.3**	**$6,296.3**
Shares Outstanding (in thousands) (f)	172,033	177,033	182,033

(a) $6.3 M per store × 40 stores = 252 + 1,886 = 2,138; 6.3 × 60 = 378 + 2,139 = 2,516

(b) $200 M to be raised by debt annually

(c) add 5 M new shares annually since $40 per share and need $200 M to be raised by equity annually

(d) add $200 M annually thru stock issuance

(e) $ 598.6 + $ 573.0 = $1,171.6 + 1,632.0 = $2,803.6

(f) stock price = $40, $200 M needed per year thru equity, so 5 M new shares to be issued annually; thus 172,033 + 5 M = 177,033

Evaluating the Worth of a Business

Evaluating the worth of a business is central to strategy implementation because integrative, intensive, and diversification strategies are often implemented by acquiring other firms. Other strategies, such as retrenchment and divestiture, may result in the sale of a division of an organization or of the firm itself. Thousands of transactions occur each year in which businesses are bought or sold in the United States. In all these cases, it is necessary to establish the financial worth or cash value of a business to successfully implement strategies.

All the various methods for determining a business's worth can be grouped into three main approaches: what a firm owns, what a firm earns, or what a firm will bring in the market. But it is important to realize that valuation is not an exact science. The valuation of a firm's worth is based on financial facts, but common sense and intuitive judgment must enter into the process. It is difficult to assign a monetary value to some factors—such as a loyal customer base,

TABLE 8-12   Six-Month Cash Budget for the Toddler Toy Company in 2013

Cash Budget (in thousands)	July	Aug.	Sept.	Oct.	Nov.	Dec.	Jan.
Receipts							
Collections	$12,000	$21,000	$31,000	$35,000	$22,000	$18,000	$11,000
Payments							
Purchases	14,000	21,000	28,000	14,000	14,000	7,000	
Wages and Salaries	1,500	2,000	2,500	1,500	1,500	1,000	
Rent	500	500	500	500	500	500	
Other Expenses	200	300	400	200	—	100	
Taxes	—	8,000	—	—	—	—	
Payment on Machine	—	—	10,000	—	—	—	
Total Payments	$16,200	$31,800	$41,400	$16,200	$16,000	$8,600	
Net Cash Gain (Loss) During Month	–4,200	–10,800	–10,400	18,800	6,000	9,400	
Cash at Start of Month if No Borrowing Is Done	6,000	1,800	–9,000	–19,400	-600	5,400	
Cumulative Cash (Cash at start plus gains or minus losses)	1,800	–9,000	–19,400	–600	5,400	14,800	
Less Desired Level of Cash	–5,000	–5,000	–5,000	–5,000	–5,000	–5,000	
Total Loans Outstanding to Maintain $5,000 Cash Balance	$3,200	$14,000	$24,400	$5,600	—	—	
Surplus Cash	—	—	—	—	400	9,800	

a history of growth, legal suits pending, dedicated employees, a favorable lease, a bad credit rating, or good patents—that may not be reflected in a firm's financial statements. Also, different valuation methods will yield different totals for a firm's worth, and no prescribed approach is best for a certain situation. Evaluating the worth of a business truly requires both qualitative and quantitative skills.

The first approach in evaluating the worth of a business is determining its net worth or stockholders' equity. Net worth represents the sum of common stock, additional paid-in capital, and retained earnings. After calculating net worth, subtract an appropriate amount for goodwill and intangibles. Whereas intangibles include copyrights, patents, and trademarks, goodwill arises only if a firm acquires another firm and pays more than the book value for that firm.

It should be noted that Financial Accounting Standards Board (FASB) Rule 142 requires companies to admit once a year if the premiums they paid for acquisitions, called goodwill, were a waste of money. Goodwill is not a good thing to have on a balance sheet. Note in Table 8-13 that Merck is worth almost eight times the value of Hershey. Note also that Home Depot's $Goodwill to $Total Assets ratio (2.86%) is significantly better (lower) than either Hershey or Merck.

The second approach to measuring the value of a firm grows out of the belief that the worth of any business should be based largely on the future benefits its owners may derive through net profits. A conservative rule of thumb is to establish a business's worth as five times the firm's current annual profit. A five-year average profit level could also be used. When using this approach, remember that firms normally suppress earnings in their financial statements to minimize taxes.

The third approach is called the *price-earnings ratio method.* To use this method, divide the market price of the firm's common stock by the annual earnings per share and multiply this number by the firm's average net income for the past five years.

The fourth method can be called the *outstanding shares method.* To use this method, simply multiply the number of shares outstanding by the market price per share. If the purchase price is more than this amount, the additional dollars are called a *premium.* The outstanding

TABLE 8-13   **Company Worth Analysis for Hershey Co., Home Depot, and Merck (year-end 2010, in millions, except stock price and EPS)**

Input Data	Hershey Co.	Home Depot	Merck
$ Shareholders' Equity (SE)	902	19,393	54,376
$ Net Income (NI)	509	2,661	861
$ Stock Price (SP)	50	35	32
$ EPS	2.21	2.30	0.28
# of Shares Outstanding	227	1,610	3,080
$ Goodwill	524	1,171	12,378
$ Intangibles	123	0.0	39,456
$ Total Assets	4,270	40,877	105,781
Company Worth Analyses			
1. SE – Goodwill – Intangibles	$255	$18,222	$2,542
2. Net Income x 5	2,545	13,305	4,305
3. (SP / EPS) x NI	11,510	40,493	98,399
4. # of Shares Out x Stock Price	11,350	56,350	98,560
5. Four Method Average	$6,415	$32,092	$50,951
$ Goodwill / $ Total Assets	12.27%	2.86%	11.7%

shares method may be called the book value of the firm. The premium is a per-share dollar amount that a person or firm is willing to pay beyond the book value of the firmal to control (acquire) the other company.

When Chevron Corp. acquired Atlas Energy in 2011 for $3.2 billion, that price represented a 37 percent premium over and above Atlas's closing stock price. Based in Moon Township, Pennsylvania, Atlas was a leading producer of natural gas, whereas the much larger Chevron, based in San Ramon, California, was weak in natural gas reserves. Similarly, J. Crew Group Inc. was acquired recently by two private-equity firms for $43.50 a share in cash, or about $3 billion. That price represented a 16 percent premium to the stock's closing price, but J. Crew's shares jumped 17 percent the next business day. When Danaher Corp. purchased Beckman Coulter in 2011 for $5.87 billion, that was a 45 percent premium over Beckman's $83.50 stock price.

If the purchase price is less than the stock price times # of shares outstanding, rather than more, that difference is called a *discount*. For example, when Clayton Doubilier & Rice LLC recently acquired Emergency Medical Services (EMS) Corp. for $2.9 billion, that was a 9.4 percent discount below EMS's stock price of $64.00.

Business evaluations are becoming routine in many situations. Businesses have many strategy-implementation reasons for determining their worth in addition to preparing to be sold or to buy other companies. Employee plans, taxes, retirement packages, mergers, acquisitions, expansion plans, banking relationships, death of a principal, divorce, partnership agreements, and IRS audits are other reasons for a periodic valuation. It is just good business to have a reasonable understanding of what your firm is worth. This knowledge protects the interests of all parties involved.

Table 8-13 provides the cash value analyses for three companies—Hershey, Home Depot, and Merck—for year-end 2010. Notice that there is significant variation among the four methods used to determine cash value. For example, the worth of Hershey ranged from $255 million to $11.5 billion. Obviously, if you were selling your company, you would seek the larger values, while if purchasing a company you would seek the lower values. In practice, substantial negotiation takes place in reaching a final compromise (or averaged) amount. Also recognize that if a firm's net income is negative, theoretically the approaches involving that figure would result in a negative number, implying that the firm would pay you to acquire them. Of course, you obtain all of the firm's debt and liabilities in an acquisition, so theoretically this would be possible.

Deciding Whether to Go Public

Hundreds of companies in 2011 held *initial public offerings* (IPOs) to move from being private to being public. These firms took advantage of high stock market prices. For example, the Internet phone company Skype Ltd. was set to hold its IPO in 2011 in what would have been one of the biggest initial public offerings in the technology sector since Google went public in 2004 raising $1.67 billion. Having over 600 million registered users, Skype expected to raise close to $1 billion through its IPO.

Going public means selling off a percentage of your company to others in order to raise capital; consequently, it dilutes the owners' control of the firm. Going public is not recommended for companies with less than $10 million in sales because the initial costs can be too high for the firm to generate sufficient cash flow to make going public worthwhile. One dollar in four is the average total cost paid to lawyers, accountants, and underwriters when an initial stock issuance is under $1 million; 1 dollar in 20 will go to cover these costs for issuances over $20 million.

In addition to initial costs involved with a stock offering, there are costs and obligations associated with reporting and management in a publicly held firm. For firms with more than $10 million in sales, going public can provide major advantages. It can allow the firm to raise capital to develop new products, build plants, expand, grow, and market products and services more effectively.

Research and Development (R&D) Issues

In terms of "Innovation," *Fortune* in 2011 ranked the following companies as best in the world. Note that Whole Foods Market was # 10 in the world.

Rank	Company
1	Apple
2	Google
3	Nike
4	Amazon.com
5	Charles Schwab
6	3M
7	Statoil
8	ExxonMobil
9	Walt Disney
10	Whole Foods Market

Source: Based on http://money.cnn.com/magazines/fortune/mostadmired/2011/best_worst/best1.html

Research and development (R&D) personnel can play an integral part in strategy implementation. These individuals are generally charged with developing new products and improving old products in a way that will allow effective strategy implementation. R&D employees and managers perform tasks that include transferring complex technology, adjusting processes to local raw materials, adapting processes to local markets, and altering products to particular tastes and specifications. Strategies such as product development, market penetration, and related diversification require that new products be successfully developed and that old products be significantly improved. But the level of management support for R&D is often constrained by resource availability.

Technological improvements that affect consumer and industrial products and services shorten product life cycles. Companies in virtually every industry are relying on the development of new products and services to fuel profitability and growth.[11] Surveys suggest that the most successful organizations use an R&D strategy that ties external opportunities to internal strengths and is linked with objectives. Well-formulated R&D policies match market opportunities with internal capabilities. R&D policies can enhance strategy implementation efforts to:

1. Emphasize product or process improvements.
2. Stress basic or applied research.

3. Be leaders or followers in R&D.
4. Develop robotics or manual-type processes.
5. Spend a high, average, or low amount of money on R&D.
6. Perform R&D within the firm or to contract R&D to outside firms.
7. Use university researchers or private-sector researchers.

R&D policy among rival firms often varies dramatically. For example, Pfizer spent $9.4 billion on R&D in 2010 but slashed that to $5.0 billion in 2011. In contrast, rival Merck spent $11 billion on R&D in 2010 and increased that amount further in 2011. Underlying this difference in strategy between the two pharmaceutical giants is a philosophical dispute over the merits of heavy investment to discover new drugs versus waiting for others to spend the money and discover and then follow up with similar products. Pfizer and Merck "are going in different directions," said Les Funtleyder, portfolio manager of the Miller Tabak Health Care Transformation mutual fund.

There must be effective interactions between R&D departments and other functional departments in implementing different types of generic business strategies. Conflicts between marketing, finance/accounting, R&D, and information systems departments can be minimized with clear policies and objectives. Table 8-14 gives some examples of R&D activities that could be required for successful implementation of various strategies. Many U.S. utility, energy, and automotive companies are employing their research and development departments to determine how the firm can effectively reduce its gas emissions.

Many firms wrestle with the decision to acquire R&D expertise from external firms or to develop R&D expertise internally. The following guidelines can be used to help make this decision:

1. If the rate of technical progress is slow, the rate of market growth is moderate, and there are significant barriers to possible new entrants, then in-house R&D is the preferred solution. The reason is that R&D, if successful, will result in a temporary product or process monopoly that the company can exploit.
2. If technology is changing rapidly and the market is growing slowly, then a major effort in R&D may be very risky, because it may lead to the development of an ultimately obsolete technology or one for which there is no market.
3. If technology is changing slowly but the market is growing quickly, there generally is not enough time for in-house development. The prescribed approach is to obtain R&D expertise on an exclusive or nonexclusive basis from an outside firm.
4. If both technical progress and market growth are fast, R&D expertise should be obtained through acquisition of a well-established firm in the industry.[12]

There are at least three major R&D approaches for implementing strategies. The first strategy is to be the first firm to market new technological products. This is a glamorous and exciting strategy but also a dangerous one. Firms such as 3M and General Electric have been successful with this approach, but many other pioneering firms have fallen, with rival firms seizing the initiative.

A second R&D approach is to be an innovative imitator of successful products, thus minimizing the risks and costs of start-up. This approach entails allowing a pioneer firm to develop the first version of the new product and to demonstrate that a market exists. Then, laggard firms develop a similar product. This strategy requires excellent R&D personnel and an excellent marketing department.

TABLE 8-14   Research and Development Involvement in Selected Strategy-Implementation Situations

Type of Organization	Strategy Being Implemented	R&D Activity
Pharmaceutical company	Product development	Test the effects of a new drug on different subgroups.
Boat manufacturer	Related diversification	Test the performance of various keel designs under various conditions.
Plastic container manufacturer	Market penetration	Develop a biodegradable container.
Electronics company	Market development	Develop a telecommunications system in a foreign country.

A third R&D strategy is to be a low-cost producer by mass-producing products similar to but less expensive than products recently introduced. As a new product is accepted by customers, price becomes increasingly important in the buying decision. Also, mass marketing replaces personal selling as the dominant selling strategy. This R&D strategy, requires substantial investment in plant and equipment but fewer expenditures in R&D than the two approaches described previously.

R&D activities among U.S. firms need to be more closely aligned to business objectives. There needs to be expanded communication between R&D managers and strategists. Corporations are experimenting with various methods to achieve this improved communication climate, including different roles and reporting arrangements for managers and new methods to reduce the time it takes research ideas to become reality.

Perhaps the most current trend in R&D management has been lifting the veil of secrecy whereby firms, even major competitors, are joining forces to develop new products. Collaboration is on the rise due to new competitive pressures, rising research costs, increasing regulatory issues, and accelerated product development schedules. Companies not only are working more closely with each other on R&D, but they are also turning to consortia at universities for their R&D needs. More than 600 research consortia are now in operation in the United States. Lifting of R&D secrecy among many firms through collaboration has allowed the marketing of new technologies and products even before they are available for sale. For example, some firms are collaborating on the efficient design of solar panels to power homes and businesses.

Management Information Systems (MIS) Issues

Firms that gather, assimilate, and evaluate external and internal information most effectively are gaining competitive advantages over other firms. Having an effective *management information system (MIS)* may be the most important factor in differentiating successful from unsuccessful firms. The process of strategic management is facilitated immensely in firms that have an effective information system.

Information collection, retrieval, and storage can be used to create competitive advantages in ways such as cross-selling to customers, monitoring suppliers, keeping managers and employees informed, coordinating activities among divisions, and managing funds. Like inventory and human resources, information is now recognized as a valuable organizational asset that can be controlled and managed. Firms that implement strategies using the best information will reap competitive advantages in the twenty-first century.

A good information system can allow a firm to reduce costs. For example, online orders from salespersons to production facilities can shorten materials ordering time and reduce inventory costs. Direct communications between suppliers, manufacturers, marketers, and customers can link together elements of the value chain as though they were one organization. Improved quality and service often result from an improved information system.

Firms must increasingly be concerned about computer hackers and take specific measures to secure and safeguard corporate communications, files, orders, and business conducted over the Internet. Thousands of companies today are plagued by computer hackers who include disgruntled employees, competitors, bored teens, sociopaths, thieves, spies, and hired agents. Computer vulnerability is a giant, expensive headache.

Dun & Bradstreet is an example company that has an excellent information system. Every D&B customer and client in the world has a separate nine-digit number. The database of information associated with each number has become so widely used that it is like a business Social Security number. D&B reaps great competitive advantages from its information system.

In many firms, information technology is doing away with the workplace and allowing employees to work at home or anywhere, anytime. The mobile concept of work allows employees to work the traditional 9-to-5 workday across any of the 24 time zones around the globe. Affordable desktop videoconferencing software allows employees to "beam in" whenever needed. Any manager or employee who travels a lot away from the office is a good candidate for working at home rather than in an office provided by the firm. Salespersons or consultants are good examples, but any person whose job largely involves talking to others or handling information could easily operate at home with the proper computer system and software.

Many people see the officeless office trend as leading to a resurgence of family togetherness in U.S. society. Even the design of homes may change from having large open areas to having more private small areas conducive to getting work done.[13]

Business Analytics

Business analytics is a management information systems technique that involves using software to mine huge volumes of data to help executives make decisions. Sometimes called predictive analytics, machine learning, or data mining, this software enables a researcher to assess and utilize the aggregate experience of an organization, a priceless strategic asset for a firm. The history of a firm's interaction with its customers, suppliers, distributors, employees, rival firms, and more can all be tapped with *data mining* to generate predictive models. Business analytics is very similar to the actuarial methods used by insurance companies to rate customers by the chance of positive or negative outcomes. Every business is basically a risk management endeavor! Therefore, like insurance companies, all businesses can benefit from measuring, tracking, and computing the risk associated with hundreds of strategic and tactical decisions made everyday. Business analytics enables a company to benefit from measuring and managing risk.

As more and more products become commoditized (so similar as to be indistinguishable), competitive advantage more and more hinges on improvements to business processes. Business analytics can provide a firm with proprietary business intelligence regarding, for example, which segment(s) of customers choose your firm versus those who defer, delay, or defect to a competitor and why. Business analytics can reveal where your competitors are weak so that marketing and sales activities can be directly targeted to take advantage of resultant opportunities (knowledge). In addition to understanding consumer behavior better, which yields more effective and efficient marketing, business analytics also is being used to slash expenses by, for example, withholding retention offers from customers who are going to stay with the firm anyway, or managing fraudulent transactions involving invoices, credit care purchases, tax returns insurance claims, mobile phone calls, online ad clicks, and more.

A key distinguishing feature of business analytics is that it is predictive rather than retrospective, in that it enables a firm to learn from experience and make current and future decisions based on prior information. Deriving robust predictive models from data mining to support hundreds of commonly occurring business decisions is the essence of learning from experience. The mathematical models associated with business analytics can dramatically enhance decision-making at all organizational levels and all stages of strategic management. In a sense, art becomes science with business analytics due to the mathematical generalization of thousands, millions, or even billions of prior data points to discover patterns of behavior for optimizing the deployment of resources.

IBM's CEO Samuel Palmisano recently announced that IBM is moving aggressively into business analytics, trying to overtake Oracle's market share lead.[14] IBM's annual business analytics revenues of about $40 billion are growing about 15 percent every quarter compared to the industry growing about 15 percent annually. IBM's acquisition of SPSS for $1.2 billion, among other recent acquisitions, launched the firm heavily into the business analytics consulting business. Microsoft currently has a software program called PowerPivot that offers data-mining capability in a spreadsheet-like way, but this is not nearly as powerful as business analytics software. IBM recently completed a business analytics project for the New York City Fire Department whereby buildings in the city were assessed for risk.

Special Note to Students

Regardless of your business major, be sure to capitalize on that special knowledge in delivering your strategic management case analysis. Whenever the opportunity arises in your oral or written project, reveal how your firm can gain and sustain competitive advantage using your marketing, finance/accounting, and/or MIS recommendations. Continuously compare your firm to rivals and draw insights and conclusions so that your recommendations come across as well conceived. Never shy away from the EPS/EBIT or projected financial statement analyses because your audience must be convinced that what you recommend is financially feasible and worth the dollars to be spent. Spend sufficient time on the nuts-and-bolts of those analyses, so fellow students (and your professor) will be assured that you did them correctly and reasonably. Too often, when students rush at the end, it means their financial statements are overly optimistic or incorrectly developed—so avoid that issue. The marketing, finance/accounting, and MIS aspects of your recommended strategies must ultimately work together to gain and sustain competitive advantage for the firm—so point that out frequently.

Conclusion

Successful strategy implementation depends on cooperation among all functional and divisional managers in an organization. Marketing departments are commonly charged with implementing strategies that require significant increases in sales revenues in new areas and with new or improved products. Finance and accounting managers must devise effective strategy-implementation approaches at low cost and minimum risk to that firm. R&D managers have to transfer complex technologies or develop new technologies to successfully implement strategies. Information systems managers are being called upon more and more to provide leadership and training for all individuals in the firm. The nature and role of marketing, finance/accounting, R&D, and management information systems activities, coupled with the management activities described in Chapter 7, largely determine organizational success.

Key Terms and Concepts

Business Analytics (p. 278)
Cash Budget (p. 271)
Data mining (p. 278)
EPS/EBIT Analysis (p. 261)
Financial Budget (p. 270)
Initial Public Offering (p. 275)
Management Information System (MIS) (p. 277)
Market Segmentation (p. 256)
Marketing Mix Variables (p. 257)
Multidimensional Scaling (p. 260)

Outstanding Shares Method (p. 273)
Premium (p. 273)
Price-Earnings Ratio Method (p. 273)
Product Positioning (p. 256)
Projected Financial Statement Analysis (p. 264)
Purpose-Based Marketing (p. 256)
Research and Development (R&D) (p. 275)
Tweet (p. 254)
Vacant Niche (p. 260)
Wikis (p. 254)

Issues for Review and Discussion

1. Define and give an example of *business analytics*. Why is this technique becoming so widely used in organizations today?
2. Give a hypothetical example where Company A buys Company B for a 15.0% premium.
3. Give a hypothetical example where Company A buys Company B for a 15.0% discount.
4. What is Treasury Stock? When should a company purchase Treasury Stock?
5. What is an initial public offering (IPO)? When is an IPO good for a company? Why did Dunkin' Donuts recently utilize an IPO? Was that a wise strategic move? Why?
6. Discuss the new principles of marketing according to Parise, Guinan, and Weinberg.
7. For companies in general, identify and discuss three opportunities and three threats associated with social networking activities on the Internet.
8. Do you agree or disagree with the following statement? "Television viewers are passive viewers of ads, whereas Internet users take an active role in choosing what to look at—so customers on the Internet are tougher for marketers to reach." Explain your reasoning.
9. How important or relevant do you believe "purpose-based marketing" is for organizations today?

10. Why is it essential for organizations to segment markets and target particular groups of consumers?
11. Explain how and why the Internet makes market segmentation easier.
12. A product-positioning rule given in the chapter is that "When there are only two competitors, the middle becomes the preferred strategic position." Illustrate this for the cruise ship industry, where two firms, Carnival and Royal Caribbean, dominate. Illustrate this for the commercial airliner building industry, where Boeing and Airbus dominate.
13. How could/would dividends affect an EPS/EBIT analysis? Would it be correct to refer to "earnings after taxes, interest, and dividends" as retained earnings for a given year?
14. In performing an EPS/EBIT analysis, where does the first row (EBIT) numbers come from?
15. In performing an EPS/EBIT analysis, where does the tax rate percentage come from?
16. For the Litten Company in Table 8-7, what would the Retained Earnings value have to have been in 2011 on the balance sheet, given that the 2012 NI-DIV value was $4?
17. Show algebraically that the price earnings ratio formula is identical to the number of shares outstanding times stock price formula. Why are the values obtained from these two methods sometimes different?

18. In accounting terms, distinguish between intangibles and goodwill on a balance sheet. Why do these two items generally stay the same on projected financial statements?

19. Explain how you would estimate the total worth of a business.

20. Diagram and label clearly a product-positioning map that includes six fast-food restaurant chains.

21. Explain why EPS/EBIT analysis is a central strategy-implementation technique.

22. Discuss the limitations of EPS/EBIT analysis.

23. Explain how marketing, finance/accounting, R&D, and management information systems managers' involvement in strategy formulation can enhance strategy implementation.

24. Consider the following statement: "Retained earnings on the balance sheet are not monies available to finance strategy implementation." Is it true or false? Explain.

25. Explain why projected financial statement analysis is considered both a strategy-formulation and a strategy-implementation tool.

26. Describe some marketing, finance/accounting, R&D, and management information systems activities that a small restaurant chain might undertake to expand into a neighboring state.

27. What effect is e-commerce having on firms' efforts to segment markets?

28. How has the Sarbanes-Oxley Act of 2002 changed CEOs' and CFOs' handling of financial statements?

29. To what extent have you been exposed to natural environment issues in your business courses? Which course has provided the most coverage? What percentage of your business courses provided no coverage? Comment.

30. Complete the following EPS/EBIT analysis for a company whose stock price is $20, interest rate on funds is 5 percent, tax rate is 20 percent, number of shares outstanding is 500 million, and EBIT range is $100 million to $300 million. The firm needs to raise $200 million in capital. Use the accompanying table (to the right) to complete the work.

31. Under what conditions would retained earnings on the balance sheet decrease from one year to the next?

32. In your own words, list all the steps in developing projected financial statements.

33. Based on the financial statements provided for Disney (pp. 26–27), how much dividends in dollars did Disney pay in 2009? In 2010?

34. Based on the financial statements provided in this chapter for the Litten Company, calculate the value of this company if you know that its stock price is $20 and it has 1 million shares outstanding. Calculate four different ways and average.

35. Why should you be careful not to use historical percentages blindly in developing projected financial statements?

36. In developing projected financial statements, what should you do if the $ amount you must put in the cash account (to make the statement balance) is far more (or less) than desired?

37. Why is it both important and necessary to segment markets and target groups of customers, rather than market to all possible consumers?

38. In full detail, explain the following EPS/EBIT chart.

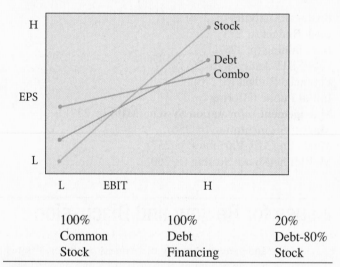

EBIT	100% Common Stock	100% Debt Financing	20% Debt-80% Stock
Interest			
EBT			
Taxes			
EAT			
#Shares			
EPS			

Notes

1. Salvatore Parise, Patricia Guinan, and Bruce Weinberg, "The Secrets of Marketing in a Web 2.0 World," *Wall Street Journal*, December 15, 2008, R1.

2. Kathy Chu and Kim Thai, "Banks Jump on Twitter Wagon," *USA Today*, May 12, 2009, B1.

3. Valerie Bauerlein, "Gatorade's Mission: Sell More Drinks," *Wall Street Journal*, September 14, 2010, B6.

4. Tom Wright, "Poor Nations Go Online on Cell Phones," *Wall Street Journal*, December 5, 2008, B8.

5. http://www.corporate-eye.com/blog/2010/12/ad-spending-forecasts-highlight-china-and-the-internet/

6. Ellen Byron, "A New Odd Couple: Google, P&G Swap Workers to Spur Innovation," *Wall Street Journal*, November 19, 2008, A1.

7. Susanne Vranica, "Veteran Marketer Promotes a New Kind of Selling," *Wall Street Journal*, October 31, 2008, B4.

8. Gupta, Sunil, and Donald R. Lehmann, *Managing Customers as Investments: The Strategic Value of*

Customers in the Long Run ("Customer Retention" section) (Upper Saddle River, NJ: Pearson Education/Wharton School Publishing, 2005).

9. Ralph Biggadike, "The Contributions of Marketing to Strategic Management," *Academy of Management Review* 6, no. 4 (October 1981): 627.

10. Michael Rapoport, "Pro Forma Is a Hard Habit to Break," *Wall Street Journal*, September 18, 2003, B3A.

11. Amy Merrick, "U.S. Research Spending to Rise Only 3.2 Percent," *Wall Street Journal*, December 28, 2001, A2.

12. Pier Abetti, "Technology: A Key Strategic Resource," *Management Review* 78, no. 2 (February 1989): 38.

13. Adapted from Edward Baig, "Welcome to the Officeless Office," *BusinessWeek*, June 26, 1995.

14. Spencer Ante, "IBM Ready for Close-Up," *Wall Street Journal*, January 18, 2011, B4.

Current Readings

Bertini, Marco, and Luc Wathieu. "How to Stop Customers from Fixating on Price." *Harvard Business Review*, May 2010, 84–91.

Comstock, Beth, Ranjay Culati, and Stephen Liguori. "Unleashing the Power of Marketing." *Harvard Business Review*, October 2010, 90–99.

Cuervo-Cazurra, Alvaro, and C. Annique Un. "Why Some Firms Never Invest in Formal R&D." *Strategic Management Journal* 31, no. 7 (July 2010): 759–779.

Dixon, Matthew, Karen Freeman, and Nicholas Toman. "Stop Trying to Delight Your Customers." *Harvard Business Review*, July–August 2010, 116–123.

Dunn, Brian J. "Best Buy's CEO on Learning To Love Social Media." *Harvard Business Review*, December 2010, 43–50.

Hayashi, Alden M. "How Not to Market On the Web." *MIT Sloan Management Review* 51, no. 2 (Winter 2010): 14–16.

Hey, Tony. "The Next Scientific Revolutions." *Harvard Business Review*, November 2010, 56–91.

Hopkins, Michael S., and Leslie Brokaw. "Matchmaking With Math: How Analytics Beats Intuition to Win Customers." *MIT Sloan Management Review* 52, no. 2 (Winter 2011): 35–42.

Kaplan, Andreas M., and Michael Haenlein. "Users of the World, Unite! The Challenges and Opportunities of Social Media." *Business Horizons* 53, no. 1 (January–February 2010): 59–68.

Kruschwitz, Nina, and Rebecca Shockley. "10 Data Points: Information and Analytics at Work." *MIT Sloan Management Review* 52, no. 1 (Fall 2010): 28–32.

Lavalle, Steve, Eric Lesser, Rebecca Shockley, Michael S. Hopkins, and Nina Kruschwitz. "Big Data, Analytics and the Path From Insights to Value." *MIT Sloan Management Review* 52, no. 2 (Winter 2011): 21–34.

Roy, Abhijit, and Satya P. Chattopadhyay. "Stealth Marketing as a Strategy." *Business Horizons* 53, no. 1 (January–February 2010): 69–77.

Rust, Roland T., Christine Moorman, and Gaurav Bhalla. "Rethinking Marketing." *Harvard Business Review*, January–February 2010, 94–101.

Slater, Stanley F., Eric M. Olson, and G. Thomas M. Hult. "Worried About Strategy Implementation? Don't Overlook Marketing's Role." *Business Horizons* 53, no. 5 (September–October 2010): 469–480.

Yujuico, Emmanuel, and Betsy D. Gelb. "Better Marketing to Developing Countries: Why and How." *Business Horizons* 53, no. 5 (September–October 2010): 501–510.

ASSURANCE OF LEARNING EXERCISES

Assurance of Learning Exercise 8A

Develop Divisional Product Positioning Maps for Walt Disney

Purpose

Organizations continually monitor how their products and services are positioned relative to competitors. Walt Disney has five major divisions as follows: 1) Media Networks, 2) Parks & Resorts, 3) Studio Entertainment, 4) Consumer Products, and 5) Interactive Media. The company faces fierce but different competitors in each segment. Product positioning maps provide useful strategic information for marketing managers as well as corporate executives responsible for strategic planning.

Instructions

Step 1	Go to http://corporate.disney.go.com/ and review Disney's five major divisions.
Step 2	Conduct research to determine Disney's three major competitors in each of the five major divisions. Use the Cohesion Case as needed.
Step 3	Develop five product-positioning maps for Disney—one map for each of its five major divisions. Include two major competitors in each map.

Assurance of Learning Exercise 8B

Gain Practice Developing Product Positioning Maps

Purpose

In product (or market) positioning, a key is to utilize what dimensions of a product are most important to consumers. A positioning map with price and quality is obvious, but other dimensions may be more important. Think strategically. Some possible positioning dimensions for beer and shampoo are given below:

> **Beer**—high or low calorie, dark or light, domestic or imported, brand name or store brand

> **Shampoo**—dandruff control, harsh or light, perfume level, conditioner included or not

Instructions

For 1) beer and 2) shampoo products that you are familiar with, develop positioning maps that reflect your knowledge of particular products in these categories. Include four products in both your beer map and your shampoo map. Below each map give a rationale as per your favorite brand.

Assurance of Learning Exercise 8C

Perform an EPS/EBIT Analysis for Walt Disney

Purpose

An EPS/EBIT analysis is one of the most widely used techniques for determining the extent that debt and/or stock should be used to finance strategies to be implemented. This exercise can give you practice performing EPS/EBIT analysis.

Instructions (4-1-11 Data)

Let's say Walt Disney's needs to raise $1.2 billion in 2012 to build a new theme park in Africa. Determine whether Walt Disney should use all debt, all stock, or a 50-50 combination of debt and stock to finance this market-development strategy. Assume a 29 percent tax rate, 5 percent interest rate. Walt Disney stock price of per share, and an annual dividend of $0.40 per share of common stock. The EBIT range for 2012 is between $6 billion and $9 billion. A total of 1.9 billion shares of common stock are outstanding. Develop an EPS/EBIT chart to reflect your analysis.

Assurance of Learning Exercise 8D

Prepare Projected Financial Statements for Walt Disney

Purpose

This exercise is designed to give you experience preparing projected financial statements. Pro forma analysis is a central strategy-implementation technique because it allows managers to anticipate and evaluate the expected results of various strategy-implementation approaches.

Instructions

Step 1	Work with a classmate. Develop a 2012 projected income statement and balance sheet for Disney. Assume that Disney plans to raise $900 million in 2012 to build a new theme park in Africa, and plans to obtain 50 percent financing from a bank and 50 percent financing from a stock issuance. Make other assumptions as needed, and state them clearly in written form.

Step 2   Compute Disney's current ratio, debt-to-equity ratio, and return-on-investment ratio for 2012. How do your 2012 ratios compare to the 2010 and 2011 ratios? Why is it important to make this comparison? Use http://finance.yahoo.com to obtain actual 2011 financial statements.

Step 3   Bring your projected statements to class, and discuss any problems or questions you encountered.

Step 4   Compare your projected statements to the statements of other students. What major differences exist between your analysis and the work of other students?

Assurance of Learning Exercise 8E

Determine the Cash Value of Walt Disney

Purpose
It is simply good business to periodically determine the financial worth or cash value of your company. This exercise gives you practice determining the total worth of a company using several methods. Use year-end 2010 data as given in the Cohesion Case on pages 26–27.

Instructions

Step 1   Calculate the financial worth of Walt Disney based on four methods: (1) the net worth or stockholders' equity, (2) the future value of Disney's earnings, (3) the price-earnings ratio, and (4) the outstanding shares method.

Step 2   In a dollar amount, how much is Disney worth?

Step 3   Compare your analyses and conclusions with those of other students.

Assurance of Learning Exercise 8F

Develop a Product-Positioning Map for My University

Purpose
The purpose of this exercise is to give you practice developing product-positioning maps. Nonprofit organizations, such as universities, are increasingly using product-positioning maps to determine effective ways to implement strategies.

Instructions

Step 1   Join with two other people in class to form a group of three.

Step 2   Jointly prepare a product-positioning map that includes your institution and four other colleges or universities in your state.

Step 3   At the chalkboard, diagram your product-positioning map.

Step 4   Discuss differences among the maps diagrammed on the board.

Assurance of Learning Exercise 8G

Do Banks Require Projected Financial Statements?

Purpose
The purpose of this exercise is to explore the practical importance and use of projected financial statements in the banking business.

Instructions
Contact two local bankers by phone and seek answers to the questions that follow. Record the answers you receive, and report your findings to the class.

1. Does your bank require projected financial statements as part of a business loan application?
2. How does your bank use projected financial statements when they are part of a business loan application?
3. What special advice do you give potential business borrowers in preparing projected financial statements?

"NOTABLE QUOTES"

"Complicated controls do not work. They confuse. They misdirect attention from what is to be controlled to the mechanics and methodology of the control." —*Seymour Tilles*

"Although Plan A may be selected as the most realistic ... the other major alternatives should not be forgotten. They may well serve as contingency plans." —*Dale McConkey*

"Organizations are most vulnerable when they are at the peak of their success." —*R. T. Lenz*

"Strategy evaluation must make it as easy as possible for managers to revise their plans and reach quick agreement on the changes." —*Dale McConkey*

"While strategy is a word that is usually associated with the future, its link to the past is no less central. Life is lived forward but understood backward. Managers may live strategy in the future, but they understand it through the past." —*Henry Mintzberg*

"Unless strategy evaluation is performed seriously and systematically, and unless strategists are willing to act on the results, energy will be used up defending yesterday. No one will have the time, resources, or will to work on exploiting today, let alone to work on making tomorrow." —*Peter Drucker*

"Executives, consultants, and B-school professors all agree that strategic planning is now the single most important management issue and will remain so for the next five years. Strategy has become a part of the main agenda at lots of organizations today. Strategic planning is back with a vengeance." —*John Byrne*

"Planners should not plan, but serve as facilitators, catalysts, inquirers, educators, and synthesizers to guide the planning process effectively." —*A. Hax and N. Majluf*

9

Strategy Review, Evaluation, and Control

CHAPTER OBJECTIVES

After studying this chapter, you should be able to do the following:

1. Describe a practical framework for evaluating strategies.

2. Explain why strategy evaluation is complex, sensitive, and yet essential for organizational success.

3. Discuss the importance of contingency planning in strategy evaluation.

4. Discuss the role of auditing in strategy evaluation.

5. Discuss the Balanced Scorecard.

6. Discuss three twenty-first-century challenges in strategic management.

ASSURANCE OF LEARNING EXERCISES

Assurance of Learning Exercise 9A
Examine 100 Balanced Scorecards

Assurance of Learning Exercise 9B
Prepare A Strategy-Evaluation Report for Walt Disney

Assurance of Learning Exercise 9C
Evaluate My University's Strategies

The best formulated and best implemented strategies become obsolete as a firm's external and internal environments change. It is essential, therefore, that strategists systematically review, evaluate, and control the execution of strategies. This chapter presents a framework that can guide managers' efforts to evaluate strategic-management activities, to make sure they are working, and to make timely changes. Management information systems being used to evaluate strategies are discussed. Guidelines are presented for formulating, implementing, and evaluating strategies. McDonald's Corp. evaluates strategies really well and takes corrective actions promptly as needed.

The Nature of Strategy Evaluation

The strategic-management process results in decisions that can have significant, long-lasting consequences. Erroneous strategic decisions can inflict severe penalties and can be exceedingly difficult, if not impossible, to reverse. Most strategists agree, therefore, that strategy evaluation is vital to an organization's well-being; timely evaluations can alert management to problems

Excellent Strategic Management Showcased

MCDONALD'S CORPORATION

Headquartered in Oak Brook, Illinois, McDonald's for decades has done an outstanding job evaluating strategies and making timely adjustments to generate rising revenues and earnings every quarter in recent memory. Even the severe 2011 winter and high commodity prices did not slow down McDonald's from easily outpacing rivals, such as Burger King and Wendy's. McDonald's provides an increasingly diverse menu, such as the new McRib sandwich and the new caramel mocha McCafé drink. Almost everybody likes McDonald's Quarter Pounders, Chicken McNuggets, and Big Macs.

McDonald's recently put its longtime mascot, Ronald McDonald, back on television as the company tries to re-focus on kids after a recent focus on targeting adults with specialty coffee drinks and smoothies. New TV ads aimed directly at kids rather than through their parents encourage kids to go to HappyMeal.com and play games and create photos with Ronald.

About 40 percent of McDonald's total debt is in foreign currencies, primarily the euro, British pound, Australian dollar, and Canadian dollar—so the company benefits immensely from a low value of the dollar. The company receives about two thirds of its revenues from outside the United States, as it has restaurants in 118 countries. There are more than 14,000 "Golden Arch" restaurants in the United States alone, with another 21,000+ outside the U.S. The company has over 400,000 employees, led by CEO and Vice Chairman James Skinner. McDonald's 32,737 restaurants at year-end 2010 was surpassed for the first time ever by Subway, which had 33,749 restaurants worldwide. Subway surpassed the number of McDonald's in the U.S. back in 2002, but even today McDonald's has greater revenues than Subway.

McDonald's opened 1,100 new restaurants in 2011 and closed about 350 for a net of 750 new restaurants, compared to a net of 541 new restaurants opened in 2010. McDonald's net capital expenditures for 2011 were about $2.5 billion as the company continued expansion around the world to take advantage of rising demand for its varied menu of products. McDonald's feeds about 62 million customers every day and operates Hamburger University in suburban Chicago.

Nearly 80 percent of McDonald's restaurants are operated by franchisees (or affiliates) rather than being company owned.

McDonald's competes directly with Wendy's, Arby's Group, Burger King Holdings, Yum Brands, and Hardees, but also with Kentucky Fried Chicken, Chic-Filet, Sonic, and thousands of mom-and-pop fast food restaurants. McDonald's 2010 revenues increased 5.8 percent to $24 billion, while profits increased 8.7 percent to $4.9 billion. McDonald's continues to expertly tailor its product offerings to particular locations. For example, you can order a McLobster sandwich in Maine and Canada, a product that may soon be rolled out across the United States.

Who are the most loyal coffee drinkers—Dunkin' Donuts, Tim Horton's, Starbucks, or McDonald's? A recent huge study says the answer is McDonald's, because McDonald's coffee lovers do not "roam" as much. According to the study of 15,000 coffee drinkers, only 29 percent of McDonald's loyalists will go elsewhere in a month, compared to 53 percent of Starbucks and Dunkin' Donuts aficionados. Calling out this behavior as key to the quick-serve breakfast wars, CustomersDNA co-founder Dave Jenkins told Dow Jones: "Getting that customer to come one more time to their restaurant and one less time to their competitor's is how the battle will be won or lost."

Source: Based on Anne Gasparro and Tess Stynes, "McDonald's Profit Edges Up," *Wall Street Journal*, January 25, 2011, B4. Also, Annie Gasparro, "McDonald's Brings Back Ronald," *Wall Street Journal*, April 7, 2011, B5. Also, http://chicagobreakingbusiness.com/2011/04/study-mcdonalds-winning-coffee-loyalty-battle.html.

or potential problems before a situation becomes critical. Strategy evaluation includes three basic activities: (1) examining the underlying bases of a firm's strategy, (2) comparing expected results with actual results, and (3) taking corrective actions to ensure that performance conforms to plans. The strategy-evaluation stage of the strategic-management process is illustrated in Figure 9-1.

Adequate and timely feedback is the cornerstone of effective strategy evaluation. Strategy evaluation can be no better than the information on which it is based. Too much pressure from top managers may result in lower managers contriving numbers they think will be satisfactory.

Strategy evaluation can be a complex and sensitive undertaking. Too much emphasis on evaluating strategies may be expensive and counterproductive. No one likes to be evaluated too closely! The more managers attempt to evaluate the behavior of others, the less control they have. Yet too little or no evaluation can create even worse problems. Strategy evaluation is essential to ensure that stated objectives are being achieved.

In many organizations, strategy evaluation is simply an appraisal of how well an organization has performed. Have the firm's assets increased? Has there been an increase in profitability? Have sales increased? Have productivity levels increased? Have profit margin,

FIGURE 9-1

A Comprehensive Strategic-Management Model

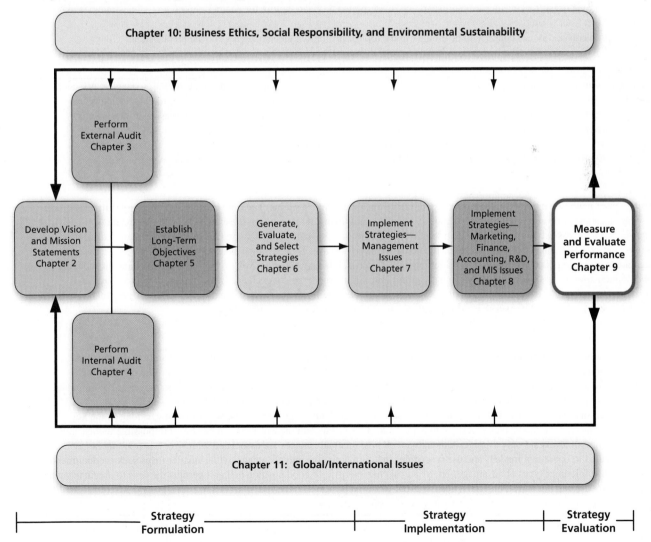

Source: Fred R. David, "How Companies Define Their Mission," *Long Range Planning* 22, no. 3 (June 1988): 40.

return on investment, and earnings-per-share ratios increased? Some firms argue that their strategy must have been correct if the answers to these types of questions are affirmative. Well, the strategy or strategies may have been correct, but this type of reasoning can be misleading because strategy evaluation must have both a long-run and short-run focus. Strategies often do not affect short-term operating results until it is too late to make needed changes.

It is impossible to demonstrate conclusively that a particular strategy is optimal or even to guarantee that it will work. One can, however, evaluate it for critical flaws. Richard Rumelt offered four criteria that could be used to evaluate a strategy: consistency, consonance, feasibility, and advantage. Described in Table 9-1, *consonance* and *advantage* are mostly based on a firm's external assessment, whereas *consistency* and *feasibility* are largely based on an internal assessment.

Strategy evaluation is important because organizations face dynamic environments in which key external and internal factors often change quickly and dramatically. Success today is no guarantee of success tomorrow! An organization should never be lulled into complacency with

TABLE 9-1 Rumelt's Criteria for Evaluating Strategies

Consistency

A strategy should not present inconsistent goals and policies. Organizational conflict and interdepartmental bickering are often symptoms of managerial disorder, but these problems may also be a sign of strategic inconsistency. Three guidelines help determine if organizational problems are due to inconsistencies in strategy:

- If managerial problems continue despite changes in personnel and if they tend to be issue-based rather than people-based, then strategies may be inconsistent.
- If success for one organizational department means, or is interpreted to mean, failure for another department, then strategies may be inconsistent.
- If policy problems and issues continue to be brought to the top for resolution, then strategies may be inconsistent.

Consonance

Consonance refers to the need for strategists to examine *sets of trends*, as well as individual trends, in evaluating strategies. A strategy must represent an adaptive response to the external environment and to the critical changes occurring within it. One difficulty in matching a firm's key internal and external factors in the formulation of strategy is that most trends are the result of interactions among other trends. For example, the daycare explosion came about as a combined result of many trends that included a rise in the average level of education, increased inflation, and an increase in women in the workforce. Although single economic or demographic trends might appear steady for many years, there are waves of change going on at the interaction level.

Feasibility

A strategy must neither overtax available resources nor create unsolvable subproblems. The final broad test of strategy is its feasibility; that is, can the strategy be attempted within the physical, human, and financial resources of the enterprise? The financial resources of a business are the easiest to quantify and are normally the first limitation against which strategy is evaluated. It is sometimes forgotten, however, that innovative approaches to financing are often possible. Devices, such as captive subsidiaries, sale-leaseback arrangements, and tying plant mortgages to long-term contracts, have all been used effectively to help win key positions in suddenly expanding industries. A less quantifiable, but actually more rigid, limitation on strategic choice is that imposed by individual and organizational capabilities. In evaluating a strategy, it is important to examine whether an organization has demonstrated in the past that it possesses the abilities, competencies, skills, and talents needed to carry out a given strategy.

Advantage

A strategy must provide for the creation and/or maintenance of a competitive advantage in a selected area of activity. Competitive advantages normally are the result of superiority in one of three areas: (1) resources, (2) skills, or (3) position. The idea that the positioning of one's resources can enhance their combined effectiveness is familiar to military theorists, chess players, and diplomats. Position can also play a crucial role in an organization's strategy. Once gained, a good position is defensible—meaning that it is so costly to capture that rivals are deterred from full-scale attacks. Positional advantage tends to be self-sustaining as long as the key internal and environmental factors that underlie it remain stable. This is why entrenched firms can be almost impossible to unseat, even if their raw skill levels are only average. Although not all positional advantages are associated with size, it is true that larger organizations tend to operate in markets and use procedures that turn their size into advantage, while smaller firms seek product/market positions that exploit other types of advantage. The principal characteristic of good position is that it permits the firm to obtain advantage from policies that would not similarly benefit rivals without the same position. Therefore, in evaluating strategy, organizations should examine the nature of positional advantages associated with a given strategy.

Source: Adapted from Richard Rumelt, "The Evaluation of Business Strategy," in W. F. Glueck (ed.), *Business Policy and Strategic Management* (New York: McGraw-Hill, 1980), 359–367. Used with permission.

success. Countless firms have thrived one year only to struggle for survival the following year. Organizational trouble can come swiftly, as evidenced by the many Fortune 400 companies listed in Table 9-2 that had negative profits for 2010.

The world's largest cellphone maker, Nokia Corp., based in Finland, watched its profits drop 21 percent in the last quarter of 2010 alone as rival firms gained market share and customer loyalty on Nokia. Nokia's operating margins on devices and services dropped in 2011 to below 7 percent from 12.1 percent early in 2010. Nokia is hoping their recent partnership with Microsoft will be a lifesaver.

Strategy evaluation is becoming increasingly difficult with the passage of time, for many reasons. Domestic and world economies were more stable in years past, product life cycles were longer, product development cycles were longer, technological advancement was slower, change

TABLE 9-2   Fortune 400 Companies That Had Negative Profits in 2010

Fortune Rank	Company	2010 Profits ($)
5	Fannie Mae	− 14.01 B
9	Bank of America	− 2.24 B
20	Freddie Mac	− 14.03 B
85	Sprint Nextel	− 3.47 B
118	AMR	− 471 M
128	Tesoro	− 29 M
138	Manpower	− 263 M
148	US Steel	− 482 M
209	Qwest Communications	− 55 M
216	Smithfield Foods	− 101 M
236	First Data	−1.02 B
257	Wiliams	− 1.10 B
277	Caesars Entertainment	− 831 M
292	Energy Future Holdings	− 2.81 B
293	Regions Financial	− 539 M
294	Kinder Morgan	− 41 M
298	Western Refining	− 17 M
305	Boston Scientific	− 1.10 B
309	Elbridge Energy Partners	− 198 M
314	Masco	− 1.04 B
327	Eastman Kodak	− 687 M
333	Charter Communications	− 237 M
341	Dole Food	− 34 M
345	Owens-Illinois	− 47 M
361	Commercial Metals	− 205 M
363	Pantry	− 166 M
371	Omnicare	− 106 M
374	Virgin Metal	− 218 M
380	MGM Resorts Int.	− 1.44 B
381	Spectrum Group Int.	− 1.1 M
383	AK Steel Holding	− 128 M
385	TravelCenters of America	− 66 M
391	CC Media Holdings	− 479 M
399	Mutual of Omaha Ins.	− 45 M

Source: Based on company documents.

TABLE 9-3   A Few Big Company Household Names That Disappeared Over Past Years

Compaq

Compaq was one of the largest sellers of PCs in the world until, under duress, the company was acquired by Hewlett-Packard and their name dissolved.

E.F. Hutton

"When E.F. Hutton speaks, people listen," claimed the well-known slogan from the 1970s and 1980s. But money laundering and fraud scandals caused people to stop listening. What barely remains of the once proud firm is today part of Citigroup.

PaineWebber

Founded in 1880 by William Alfred Paine and Wallace G. Webber, PaineWebber by 1990 had 200 brokerage branch offices in 42 states and six offices in Asia and Europe. But in 2000, it merged with UBS AG to become UBS PaineWebber. Then in 2003, "PaineWebber" was dropped and replaced with UBS Wealth Management USA.

Eastern Airlines

Eastern Airlines once dominated much of the domestic travel industry along the profitable East Coast U.S. corridor, but deteriorating labor relations forced the firm into bankruptcy, and it ceased operations in 1991.

Woolworth's

Founded in 1879, Woolworth's became the model for five-and-dime stores throughout the United States. The rise of Wal-Mart and K-mart ended Woolworth's reign.

Arthur Andersen

Arthur Andersen was once a member of the "Big 8" accounting firms, which later became the "Big 5." Andersen's downfall was its role as Enron's auditor, whereby it had approved a whole host of illegal accounting.

TransWorld Airlines (TWA)

Founded in 1930, TWA once dominated airline travel in the United States but eventually declared bankruptcy and was absorbed into American Airlines in 2001.

Source: Based on http://www.walletpop.com/2011/01/10/remember-them-15-most-memorable-companies-that-vanished/

occurred less frequently, there were fewer competitors, foreign companies were weak, and there were more regulated industries. Other reasons why strategy evaluation is more difficult today include the following trends:

1. A dramatic increase in the environment's complexity
2. The increasing difficulty of predicting the future with accuracy
3. The increasing number of variables
4. The rapid rate of obsolescence of even the best plans
5. The increase in the number of both domestic and world events affecting organizations
6. The decreasing time span for which planning can be done with any degree of certainty[1]

A fundamental problem facing managers today is how to control employees effectively in light of modern organizational demands for greater flexibility, innovation, creativity, and initiative from employees.[2] How can managers today ensure that empowered employees acting in an entrepreneurial manner do not put the well-being of the business at risk? The costs to companies in terms of damaged reputations, fines, missed opportunities, and diversion of management's attention are enormous.

When empowered employees are held accountable for and pressured to achieve specific goals and are given wide latitude in their actions to achieve them, there can be dysfunctional behavior. For example, Nordstrom, the upscale fashion retailer known for outstanding customer service, was subjected to lawsuits and fines when employees underreported hours worked in order to increase their sales per hour—the company's primary performance criterion.

The Process of Evaluating Strategies

Strategy evaluation is necessary for all sizes and kinds of organizations. Strategy evaluation should initiate managerial questioning of expectations and assumptions, should trigger a review of objectives and values, and should stimulate creativity in generating alternatives and formulating criteria of evaluation.[3] Regardless of the size of the organization, a certain amount of *management by wandering around* at all levels is essential to effective strategy evaluation. Strategy-evaluation activities should be performed on a continuing basis, rather than at the end of specified periods of time or just after problems occur. Waiting until the end of the year, for example, could result in a firm closing the barn door after the horses have already escaped.

Evaluating strategies on a continuous rather than on a periodic basis allows benchmarks of progress to be established and more effectively monitored. Some strategies take years to implement; consequently, associated results may not become apparent for years. Successful strategies combine patience with a willingness to promptly take corrective actions when necessary. There always comes a time when corrective actions are needed in an organization! Centuries ago, a writer (perhaps Solomon) made the following observations about change:

> There is a time for everything,
> A time to be born and a time to die,
> A time to plant and a time to uproot,
> A time to kill and a time to heal,
> A time to tear down and a time to build,
> A time to weep and a time to laugh,
> A time to mourn and a time to dance,
> A time to scatter stones and a time to gather them,
> A time to embrace and a time to refrain,
> A time to search and a time to give up,
> A time to keep and a time to throw away,
> A time to tear and a time to mend,
> A time to be silent and a time to speak,
> A time to love and a time to hate,
> A time for war and a time for peace.[4]

Managers and employees of the firm should be continually aware of progress being made toward achieving the firm's objectives. As critical success factors change, organizational members should be involved in determining appropriate corrective actions. If assumptions and expectations deviate significantly from forecasts, then the firm should renew strategy-formulation activities, perhaps sooner than planned. In strategy evaluation, like strategy formulation and strategy implementation, people make the difference. Through involvement in the process of evaluating strategies, managers and employees become committed to keeping the firm moving steadily toward achieving objectives.

A Strategy-Evaluation Framework

Table 9-4 summarizes strategy-evaluation activities in terms of key questions that should be addressed, alternative answers to those questions, and appropriate actions for an organization to take. Notice that corrective actions are almost always needed except when (1) external and internal factors have not significantly changed and (2) the firm is progressing satisfactorily toward achieving stated objectives. Relationships among strategy-evaluation activities are illustrated in Figure 9-2.

Reviewing Bases of Strategy

As shown in Figure 9-2, *reviewing the underlying bases of an organization's strategy* could be approached by developing a revised EFE Matrix and IFE Matrix. A *revised IFE Matrix* should focus on changes in the organization's management, marketing, finance/accounting, production/operations, R&D, and management information systems strengths and weaknesses. A *revised EFE Matrix* should indicate how effective a firm's strategies have been in response to key opportunities and threats. This analysis could also address such questions as the following:

1. How have competitors reacted to our strategies?
2. How have competitors' strategies changed?

TABLE 9-4   A Strategy-Evaluation Assessment Matrix

Have Major Changes Occurred in the Firm's Internal Strategic Position?	Have Major Changes Occurred in the Firm's External Strategic Position?	Has the Firm Progressed Satisfactorily Toward Achieving Its Stated Objectives?	Result
No	No	No	Take corrective actions
Yes	Yes	Yes	Take corrective actions
Yes	Yes	No	Take corrective actions
Yes	No	Yes	Take corrective actions
Yes	No	No	Take corrective actions
No	Yes	Yes	Take corrective actions
No	Yes	No	Take corrective actions
No	No	Yes	Continue present strategic course

3. Have major competitors' strengths and weaknesses changed?
4. Why are competitors making certain strategic changes?
5. Why are some competitors' strategies more successful than others?
6. How satisfied are our competitors with their present market positions and profitability?
7. How far can our major competitors be pushed before retaliating?
8. How could we more effectively cooperate with our competitors?

Numerous external and internal factors can prevent firms from achieving long-term and annual objectives. Externally, actions by competitors, changes in demand, changes in technology, economic changes, demographic shifts, and governmental actions may prevent objectives from being accomplished. Internally, ineffective strategies may have been chosen or implementation activities may have been poor. Objectives may have been too optimistic. Thus, failure to achieve objectives may not be the result of unsatisfactory work by managers and employees. All organizational members need to know this to encourage their support for strategy-evaluation activities. Organizations desperately need to know as soon as possible when their strategies are not effective. Sometimes managers and employees on the front lines discover this well before strategists.

External opportunities and threats and internal strengths and weaknesses that represent the bases of current strategies should continually be monitored for change. It is not really a question of whether these factors will change but rather when they will change and in what ways. Here are some key questions to address in evaluating strategies:

1. Are our internal strengths still strengths?
2. Have we added other internal strengths? If so, what are they?
3. Are our internal weaknesses still weaknesses?
4. Do we now have other internal weaknesses? If so, what are they?
5. Are our external opportunities still opportunities?
6. Are there now other external opportunities? If so, what are they?
7. Are our external threats still threats?
8. Are there now other external threats? If so, what are they?
9. Are we vulnerable to a hostile takeover?

Measuring Organizational Performance

Another important strategy-evaluation activity is *measuring organizational performance*. This activity includes comparing expected results to actual results, investigating deviations from plans, evaluating individual performance, and examining progress being made toward meeting stated objectives. Both long-term and annual objectives are commonly used in this process. Criteria for evaluating strategies should be measurable and easily verifiable. Criteria that predict results may be more important than those that reveal what already has happened. For example, rather than simply being informed that sales in the last quarter were 20 percent under what was

FIGURE 9-2

A Strategy-Evaluation Framework

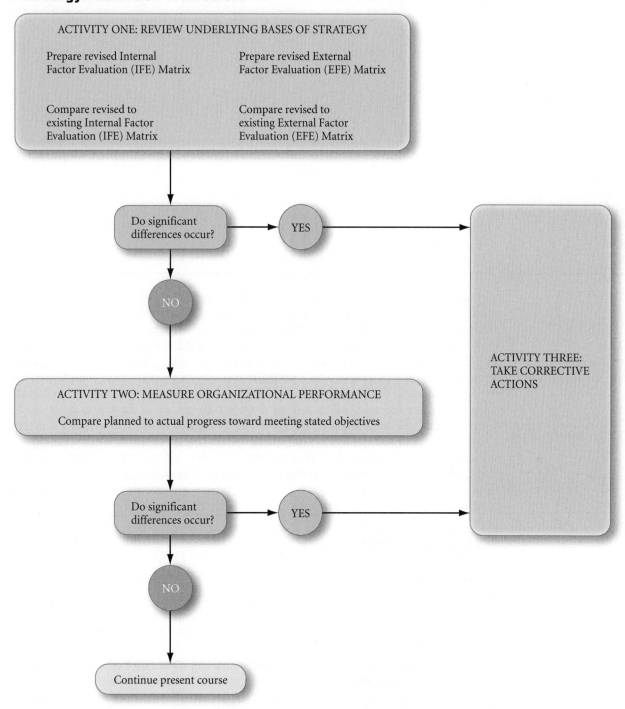

expected, strategists need to know that sales in the next quarter may be 20 percent below standard unless some action is taken to counter the trend. Really effective control requires accurate forecasting.

Failure to make satisfactory progress toward accomplishing long-term or annual objectives signals a need for corrective actions. Many factors, such as unreasonable policies, unexpected turns in the economy, unreliable suppliers or distributors, or ineffective strategies, can result in unsatisfactory progress toward meeting objectives. Problems can result from ineffectiveness (not doing the right things) or inefficiency (poorly doing the right things).

TABLE 9-5   A Sample Framework for Measuring Organizational Performance

Factor	Actual Result	Expected Result	Variance	Action Needed
Corporate Revenues				
Corporate Profits				
Corporate ROI				
Region 1 Revenues				
Region 1 Profits				
Region 1 ROI				
Region 2 Revenues				
Region 2 Profits				
Region 2 ROI				
Product 1 Revenues				
Product 1 Profits				
Product 1 ROI				
Product 2 Revenues				
Product 2 Profits				
Product 2 ROI				

Many variables can and should be included in measuring organizational performance. As indicated in Table 9-5, typically a favorable or unfavorable variance is recorded monthly, quarterly, and annually, and resultant actions needed are then determined.

Determining which objectives are most important in the evaluation of strategies can be difficult. Strategy evaluation is based on both quantitative and qualitative criteria. Selecting the exact set of criteria for evaluating strategies depends on a particular organization's size, industry, strategies, and management philosophy. An organization pursuing a retrenchment strategy, for example, could have an entirely different set of evaluative criteria from an organization pursuing a market-development strategy. Quantitative criteria commonly used to evaluate strategies are financial ratios, which strategists use to make three critical comparisons: (1) comparing the firm's performance over different time periods, (2) comparing the firm's performance to competitors', and (3) comparing the firm's performance to industry averages. Some key financial ratios that are particularly useful as criteria for strategy evaluation are as follows:

1. Return on investment (ROI)
2. Return on equity (ROE)
3. Profit margin
4. Market share
5. Debt to equity
6. Earnings per share (EPS)
7. Sales growth
8. Asset growth

But some potential problems are associated with using quantitative criteria for evaluating strategies. First, most quantitative criteria are geared to annual objectives rather than long-term objectives. Also, different accounting methods can provide different results on many quantitative criteria. Third, intuitive judgments are almost always involved in deriving quantitative criteria. For these and other reasons, qualitative criteria are also important in evaluating strategies. Human factors such as high absenteeism and turnover rates, poor production quality and quantity rates, or low employee satisfaction can be underlying causes of declining performance. Marketing, finance/accounting, R&D, or management information systems factors can also cause financial problems.

Some additional key questions that reveal the need for qualitative or intuitive judgments in strategy evaluation are as follows:

1. How good is the firm's balance of investments between high-risk and low-risk projects?
2. How good is the firm's balance of investments between long-term and short-term projects?

3. How good is the firm's balance of investments between slow-growing markets and fast-growing markets?
4. How good is the firm's balance of investments among different divisions?
5. To what extent are the firm's alternative strategies socially responsible?
6. What are the relationships among the firm's key internal and external strategic factors?
7. How are major competitors likely to respond to particular strategies?

Taking Corrective Actions

The final strategy-evaluation activity, *taking corrective actions,* requires making changes to competitively reposition a firm for the future. As indicated in Table 9-6, examples of changes that may be needed are altering an organization's structure, replacing one or more key individuals, selling a division, or revising a business mission. Other changes could include establishing or revising objectives, devising new policies, issuing stock to raise capital, adding additional salespersons, differently allocating resources, or developing new performance incentives. Taking corrective actions does not necessarily mean that existing strategies will be abandoned or even that new strategies must be formulated.

> The probabilities and possibilities for incorrect or inappropriate actions increase geometrically with an arithmetic increase in personnel. Any person directing an overall undertaking must check on the actions of the participants as well as the results that they have achieved. If either the actions or results do not comply with preconceived or planned achievements, then corrective actions are needed.[5]

No organization can survive as an island; no organization can escape change. Taking corrective actions is necessary to keep an organization on track toward achieving stated objectives. In his thought-provoking books *Future Shock* and *The Third Wave,* Alvin Toffler argued that business environments are becoming so dynamic and complex that they threaten people and organizations with *future shock,* which occurs when the nature, types, and speed of changes overpower an individual's or organization's ability and capacity to adapt. Strategy evaluation enhances an organization's ability to adapt successfully to changing circumstances.

Taking corrective actions raises employees' and managers' anxieties. Research suggests that participation in strategy-evaluation activities is one of the best ways to overcome individuals' resistance to change. According to Erez and Kanfer, individuals accept change best when they have a cognitive understanding of the changes, a sense of control over the situation, and an awareness that necessary actions are going to be taken to implement the changes.[6]

Strategy evaluation can lead to strategy-formulation changes, strategy-implementation changes, both formulation and implementation changes, or no changes at all. Strategists cannot escape having to revise strategies and implementation approaches sooner or later. Hussey and Langham offered the following insight on taking corrective actions:

TABLE 9-6   Corrective Actions Possibly Needed to Correct Unfavorable Variances

1. Alter the firm's structure
2. Replace one or more key individuals
3. Divest a division
4. Alter the firm's vision and/or mission
5. Revise objectives
6. Alter strategies
7. Devise new policies
8. Install new performance incentives
9. Raise capital with stock or debt
10. Add or terminate salespersons, employees, or managers
11. Allocate resources differently
12. Outsource (or rein in) business functions

Resistance to change is often emotionally based and not easily overcome by rational argument. Resistance may be based on such feelings as loss of status, implied criticism of present competence, fear of failure in the new situation, annoyance at not being consulted, lack of understanding of the need for change, or insecurity in changing from well-known and fixed methods. It is necessary, therefore, to overcome such resistance by creating situations of participation and full explanation when changes are envisaged.[7]

Corrective actions should place an organization in a better position to capitalize upon internal strengths; to take advantage of key external opportunities; to avoid, reduce, or mitigate external threats; and to improve internal weaknesses. Corrective actions should have a proper time horizon and an appropriate amount of risk. They should be internally consistent and socially responsible. Perhaps most important, corrective actions strengthen an organization's competitive position in its basic industry. Continuous strategy evaluation keeps strategists close to the pulse of an organization and provides information needed for an effective strategic-management system. Carter Bayles described the benefits of strategy evaluation as follows:

Evaluation activities may renew confidence in the current business strategy or point to the need for actions to correct some weaknesses, such as erosion of product superiority or technological edge. In many cases, the benefits of strategy evaluation are much more far-reaching, for the outcome of the process may be a fundamentally new strategy that will lead, even in a business that is already turning a respectable profit, to substantially increased earnings. It is this possibility that justifies strategy evaluation, for the payoff can be very large.[8]

The Balanced Scorecard

Introduced earlier in the Chapter 5 discussion of objectives, the Balanced Scorecard is an important strategy-evaluation tool. It is a process that allows firms to evaluate strategies from four perspectives: financial performance, customer knowledge, internal business processes, and learning and growth. The *Balanced Scorecard* analysis requires that firms seek answers to the following questions and utilize that information, in conjunction with financial measures, to adequately and more effectively evaluate strategies being implemented:

1. How well is the firm continually improving and creating value along measures such as innovation, technological leadership, product quality, operational process efficiencies, and so on?
2. How well is the firm sustaining and even improving upon its core competencies and competitive advantages?
3. How satisfied are the firm's customers?

A sample Balanced Scorecard is provided in Table 9-7. Notice that the firm examines six key issues in evaluating its strategies: (1) Customers, (2) Managers/Employees, (3) Operations/Processes, (4) Community/Social Responsibility, (5) Business Ethics/Natural Environment, and (6) Financial. The basic form of a Balanced Scorecard may differ for different organizations. The Balanced Scorecard approach to strategy evaluation aims to balance long-term with short-term concerns, to balance financial with nonfinancial concerns, and to balance internal with external concerns. It can be an excellent management tool, and it is used successfully today by Chemical Bank, ExxonMobil Corporation, CIGNA Property and Casualty Insurance, and numerous other firms. The Balanced Scorecard would be constructed differently, that is, adapted to particular firms in various industries with the underlying theme or thrust being the same, which is to evaluate the firm's strategies based upon both key quantitative and qualitative measures.

TABLE 9-7 An Example Balanced Scorecard

Area of Objectives	Measure or Target	Time Expectation	Primary Responsibility
Customers			
1.			
2.			
3.			
4.			
Managers/Employees			
1.			
2.			
3.			
4.			
Operations/Processes			
1.			
2.			
3.			
4.			
Community/Social Responsibility			
1.			
2.			
3.			
4.			
Business Ethics/Natural Environment			
1.			
2.			
3.			
4.			
Financial			
1.			
2.			
3.			
4.			

The Balanced Scorecard Institute has a Certification Program that includes two levels of certification: *Balanced Scorecard Master Professional (BSMP)* and *Balanced Scorecard Professional (BSP)*, both of which are offered in association with George Washington University and are achievable through public workshop participation. The website for this program is http:// www.balancedscorecard.org/.

Published Sources of Strategy-Evaluation Information

A number of publications are helpful in evaluating a firm's strategies. For example, *Fortune* annually identifies and evaluates the Fortune 1,000 (the largest manufacturers) and the Fortune 50 (the largest retailers, transportation companies, utilities, banks, insurance companies, and diversified financial corporations in the United States). *Fortune* ranks the best and worst performers on various factors, such as return on investment, sales volume, and profitability. *Fortune* annually publishes its strategy-evaluation research in an article entitled "America's Most Admired Companies." Eight key attributes serve as evaluative criteria: people management; innovativeness; quality of products or services; financial soundness; social responsibility; use of corporate assets; long-term investment; and quality of management. Every year, *Fortune*

TABLE 9-8 **The Most and Least Admired Company in Various Industries (2011)**

Industry	Most Admired	Least Admired
Pharmaceuticals	Abbott Laboratories	Pfizer
Metals	Alcoa	Hebel Iron and Steel
Computers	Apple	NEC
Food Production	Archer Daniels Midland	Pilgrim's Pride
Chemicals	BASF	ChemChina
Industrial and Farm Equipment	Caterpillar	Alstom
Specialty Retailers	Costco Wholesale	Office Depot
Food and Drug Stores	CVS/Caremark	Supervalu
Petroleum Refining	Exxon Mobil	PDVSA
Electronics	General Electric	Tyco International

Source: Based on information accessed March 15, 2011, at the websites http://money.cnn.com/magazines/fortune/mostadmired/2010/champions/ and http://money.cnn.com/magazines/fortune/mostadmired/2010/industries/42.html.

publishes additional strategy-evaluation research in an article entitled "The World's Most Admired Companies." *Fortune's* 2011 evaluation in Table 9-8 reveals the firms most admired (best managed) in their industry. The most admired company in the world in 2011 was Nike, followed by Anheuser-Busch, Nestle, and Procter & Gamble.[9]

BusinessWeek, Industry Week, and *Dun's Business Month* periodically publish detailed evaluations of U.S. businesses and industries. Although published sources of strategy-evaluation information focus primarily on large, publicly-held businesses, the comparative ratios and related information are widely used to evaluate small businesses and privately owned firms as well.

Characteristics of an Effective Evaluation System

Strategy evaluation must meet several basic requirements to be effective. First, strategy-evaluation activities must be economical; too much information can be just as bad as too little information, and too many controls can do more harm than good. Strategy-evaluation activities also should be meaningful; they should specifically relate to a firm's objectives. They should provide managers with useful information about tasks over which they have control and influence. Strategy-evaluation activities should provide timely information; on occasion and in some areas, managers may daily need information. For example, when a firm has diversified by acquiring another firm, evaluative information may be needed frequently. However, in an R&D department, daily or even weekly evaluative information could be dysfunctional. Approximate information that is timely is generally more desirable as a basis for strategy evaluation than accurate information that does not depict the present. Frequent measurement and rapid reporting may frustrate control rather than give better control. The time dimension of control must coincide with the time span of the event being measured.

Strategy evaluation should be designed to provide a true picture of what is happening. For example, in a severe economic downturn, productivity and profitability ratios may drop alarmingly, although employees and managers are actually working harder. Strategy evaluations should fairly portray this type of situation. Information derived from the strategy-evaluation process should facilitate action and should be directed to those individuals in the organization who need to take action based on it. Managers commonly ignore evaluative reports that are provided only for informational purposes; not all managers need to receive all reports. Controls need to be action-oriented rather than information-oriented.

The strategy-evaluation process should not dominate decisions; it should foster mutual understanding, trust, and common sense. No department should fail to cooperate with another in evaluating strategies. Strategy evaluations should be simple, not too cumbersome, and not too restrictive. Complex strategy-evaluation systems often confuse people and accomplish little. The test of an effective evaluation system is its usefulness, not its complexity.

Large organizations require a more elaborate and detailed strategy-evaluation system because it is more difficult to coordinate efforts among different divisions and functional areas. Managers in small companies often communicate daily with each other and their employees and do not need extensive evaluative reporting systems. Familiarity with local environments usually makes gathering and evaluating information much easier for small organizations than for large businesses. But the key to an effective strategy-evaluation system may be the ability to convince participants that failure to accomplish certain objectives within a prescribed time is not necessarily a reflection of their performance.

There is no one ideal strategy-evaluation system. The unique characteristics of an organization, including its size, management style, purpose, problems, and strengths, can determine a strategy-evaluation and control system's final design. Robert Waterman offered the following observation about successful organizations' strategy-evaluation and control systems:

> Successful companies treat facts as friends and controls as liberating. Morgan Guaranty and Wells Fargo not only survive but thrive in the troubled waters of bank deregulation, because their strategy evaluation and control systems are sound, their risk is contained, and they know themselves and the competitive situation so well. Successful companies have a voracious hunger for facts. They see information where others see only data. Successful companies maintain tight, accurate financial controls. Their people don't regard controls as an imposition of autocracy but as the benign checks and balances that allow them to be creative and free.[10]

Contingency Planning

A basic premise of good strategic management is that firms plan ways to deal with unfavorable and favorable events before they occur. Too many organizations prepare contingency plans just for unfavorable events; this is a mistake, because both minimizing threats and capitalizing on opportunities can improve a firm's competitive position.

Regardless of how carefully strategies are formulated, implemented, and evaluated, unforeseen events, such as strikes, boycotts, natural disasters, arrival of foreign competitors, and government actions, can make a strategy obsolete. To minimize the impact of potential threats, organizations should develop contingency plans as part of their strategy-evaluation process. *Contingency plans* can be defined as alternative plans that can be put into effect if certain key events do not occur as expected. Only high-priority areas require the insurance of contingency plans. Strategists cannot and should not try to cover all bases by planning for all possible contingencies. But in any case, contingency plans should be as simple as possible.

Some contingency plans commonly established by firms include the following:

1. If a major competitor withdraws from particular markets as intelligence reports indicate, what actions should our firm take?
2. If our sales objectives are not reached, what actions should our firm take to avoid profit losses?
3. If demand for our new product exceeds plans, what actions should our firm take to meet the higher demand?
4. If certain disasters occur—such as loss of computer capabilities; a hostile takeover attempt; loss of patent protection; or destruction of manufacturing facilities because of earthquakes, tornadoes, or hurricanes—what actions should our firm take?
5. If a new technological advancement makes our new product obsolete sooner than expected, what actions should our firm take?

Too many organizations discard alternative strategies not selected for implementation although the work devoted to analyzing these options would render valuable information.

Alternative strategies not selected for implementation can serve as contingency plans in case the strategy or strategies selected do not work. U.S. companies and governments are increasingly considering nuclear-generated electricity as the most efficient means of power generation. Many contingency plans certainly call for nuclear power rather than for coal- and gas-derived electricity.

When strategy-evaluation activities reveal the need for a major change quickly, an appropriate contingency plan can be executed in a timely way. Contingency plans can promote a strategist's ability to respond quickly to key changes in the internal and external bases of an organization's current strategy. For example, if underlying assumptions about the economy turn out to be wrong and contingency plans are ready, then managers can make appropriate changes promptly.

In some cases, external or internal conditions present unexpected opportunities. When such opportunities occur, contingency plans could allow an organization to quickly capitalize on them. Linneman and Chandran reported that contingency planning gave users, such as DuPont, Dow Chemical, Consolidated Foods, and Emerson Electric, three major benefits: (1) It permitted quick response to change, (2) it prevented panic in crisis situations, and (3) it made managers more adaptable by encouraging them to appreciate just how variable the future can be. They suggested that effective contingency planning involves a seven-step process:

1. Identify both beneficial and unfavorable events that could possibly derail the strategy or strategies.
2. Specify trigger points. Calculate about when contingent events are likely to occur.
3. Assess the impact of each contingent event. Estimate the potential benefit or harm of each contingent event.
4. Develop contingency plans. Be sure that contingency plans are compatible with current strategy and are economically feasible.
5. Assess the counterimpact of each contingency plan. That is, estimate how much each contingency plan will capitalize on or cancel out its associated contingent event. Doing this will quantify the potential value of each contingency plan.
6. Determine early warning signals for key contingent events. Monitor the early warning signals.
7. For contingent events with reliable early warning signals, develop advance action plans to take advantage of the available lead time.[11]

Auditing

A frequently used tool in strategy evaluation is the audit. *Auditing* is defined by the American Accounting Association (AAA) as "a systematic process of objectively obtaining and evaluating evidence regarding assertions about economic actions and events to ascertain the degree of correspondence between these assertions and established criteria, and communicating the results to interested users."[12]

Auditors examine the financial statement of firms to determine whether they have been prepared according to generally accepted accounting principles *(GAAP)* and whether they fairly represent the activities of the firm. Independent auditors use a set of standards called generally accepted auditing standards *(GAAS)*. Public accounting firms often have a consulting arm that provides strategy-evaluation services.

The new era of international financial reporting standards *(IFRS)* appears unstoppable, and businesses need to go ahead and get ready to use IFRS. Many U.S. companies now report their finances using both the old generally accepted accounting standards (GAAP) and the new IFRS. "If companies don't prepare, if they don't start three years in advance," warns business professor Donna Street at the University of Dayton, "they're going to be in big trouble." GAAP standards comprised 25,000 pages, whereas IFRS comprises only 5,000 pages, so in that sense IFRS is less cumbersome.

This accounting switch from GAAP to IFRS in the United States is going to cost businesses millions of dollars in fees and upgraded software systems and training. U.S. CPAs need to study global accounting principles intensely, and business schools should go ahead and begin teaching students the new accounting standards.

At the American Institute of CPAs (AICPA) annual conference in December 2010, Security Exchange Commission (SEC) Chairman Mary Schapiro indicated that an important IFRS decision would likely come in late 2011. She mentioned that the wide-ranging Dodd-Frank Act would have little or no bearing on the IFRS decision, and that the SEC would allow a "minimum of four years" for any transition to IFRS. When the SEC does incorporate IFRS into the U.S. domestic reporting system, the first time U.S. issuers would report under that system would be approximately 2015 or 2016. Implementation dates may still be staggered thereafter.

The U.S. Chamber of Commerce supports the change, saying it will lead to much more cross-border commerce and will help the United States compete in the world economy. Already the European Union and 113 nations have adopted or soon plan to use international rules, including Australia, China, India, Mexico, and Canada. So the United States likely will also adopt IFRS rules, but this switch could unleash a legal and regulatory nightmare. A few U.S. multinational firms already use IFRS for their foreign subsidiaries, such as United Technologies (UT). UT derives more than 60 percent of its revenues from abroad and is already training its entire staff to use IFRS. UT has redone its 2007 through 2009 financial statements in the IFRS format.

Movement to IFRS from GAAP encompasses a company's entire operations, including auditing, oversight, cash management, taxes, technology, software, investing, acquiring, merging, importing, exporting, pension planning, and partnering. Switching from GAAP to IFRS is also likely to be plagued by gaping differences in business customs, financial regulations, tax laws, politics, and other factors. One critic of the upcoming switch is Charles Niemeier of the Public Company Accounting Oversight Board, who says the switch "has the potential to be a Tower of Babel," costing firms millions when they do not even have thousands to spend.

Others say the switch will help U.S. companies raise capital abroad and do business with firms abroad. Perhaps the biggest upside of the switch is that IFRS rules are more streamlined and less complex than GAAP. Lenovo, the China-based technology firm that bought IBM's personal computer business, is a big advocate of IFRS. Lenovo's view is that they desire to be a world company rather than a U.S. or Chinese company, so the faster the switch to IFRS, the better for them. The bottom line is that IFRS is coming to the United States, sooner rather than later, so we all need to gear up for this switch as soon as possible.[13]

Twenty-First-Century Challenges in Strategic Management

Three particular challenges or decisions that face all strategists today are (1) deciding whether the process should be more an art or a science, (2) deciding whether strategies should be visible or hidden from stakeholders, and (3) deciding whether the process should be more top-down or bottom-up in their firm.[14]

The Art or Science Issue

This textbook is consistent with most of the strategy literature in advocating that strategic management be viewed more as a science than an art. This perspective contends that firms need to systematically assess their external and internal environments, conduct research, carefully evaluate the pros and cons of various alternatives, perform analyses, and then decide upon a particular course of action. In contrast, Mintzberg's notion of "crafting" strategies embodies the artistic model, which suggests that strategic decision making be based primarily on holistic thinking, intuition, creativity, and imagination.[15] Mintzberg and his followers reject strategies that result from objective analysis, preferring instead subjective imagination. "Strategy scientists" reject strategies that emerge from emotion, hunch, creativity, and politics. Proponents of the artistic view often consider strategic planning exercises to be time poorly spent. The Mintzberg philosophy insists on informality, whereas strategy scientists (and this text) insist on more formality. Mintzberg refers to strategic planning as an "emergent" process whereas strategy scientists use the term "deliberate" process.[16]

The answer to the art versus science question is one that strategists must decide for themselves, and certainly the two approaches are not mutually exclusive. In deciding which approach is more effective, however, consider that the business world today has become increasingly complex and more intensely competitive. There is less room for error in strategic planning. Recall that Chapter 1 discussed the importance of intuition, experience, and subjectivity in strategic planning, and even the weights and ratings discussed in Chapters 3, 4, and 6 certainly require good judgment. But the idea of deciding on strategies for any firm without thorough research and analysis, at least in the mind of this writer, is unwise. Certainly, in smaller firms there can be more informality in the process compared to larger firms, but even for smaller firms, a wealth of competitive information is available on the Internet and elsewhere and should be collected, assimilated, and evaluated before deciding on a course of action upon which survival of the firm may hinge. The livelihood of countless employees and shareholders may hinge on the effectiveness of strategies selected. Too much is at stake to be less than thorough in formulating strategies. It is not wise for a strategist to rely too heavily on gut feeling and opinion instead of research data, competitive intelligence, and analysis in formulating strategies.

The Visible or Hidden Issue

An interesting aspect of any competitive analysis discussion is whether strategies themselves should be secret or open within firms. The Chinese warrior Sun Tzu and military leaders today strive to keep strategies secret, as war is based on deception. However, for a business organization, secrecy may not be best. Keeping strategies secret from employees and stakeholders at large could severely inhibit employee and stakeholder communication, understanding, and commitment and also forgo valuable input that these persons could have regarding formulation and/or implementation of that strategy. Thus strategists in a particular firm must decide for themselves whether the risk of rival firms easily knowing and exploiting a firm's strategies is worth the benefit of improved employee and stakeholder motivation and input. Most executives agree that some strategic information should remain confidential to top managers, and that steps should be taken to ensure that such information is not disseminated beyond the inner circle. For a firm that you may own or manage, would you advocate openness or secrecy in regard to strategies being formulated and implemented?

An excellent example of a totally transparent company is Great Little Box, located in Richmond, British Columbia, in Canada. All 213 employees of that company know exactly how profitable the firm is; 15 percent of all pretax earnings are split equally among everyone at that firm. Employees at Great Little Box work harder because they can readily see how their work matters, and they actively try to increase the company's profits—and their own income. In contrast, *CFO Magazine* reports that only 1 percent of American companies use open-book finances.[17] Among *Inc. Magazine's* 500 fastest growing companies in the United States, fully 40 percent are like Great Little Box in that they use open-book management and clearly visible profit sharing practices.

There are certainly good reasons to keep the strategy process and strategies themselves visible and open rather than hidden and secret. There are also good reasons to keep strategies hidden from all but top-level executives. Strategists must decide for themselves what is best for their firms. This text comes down largely on the side of being visible and open, but certainly this may not be best for all strategists and all firms. As pointed out in Chapter 1, Sun Tzu argued that all war is based on deception and that the best maneuvers are those not easily predicted by rivals. Business and war are analogous.

Some reasons to be completely open with the strategy process and resultant decisions are these:

1. Managers, employees, and other stakeholders can readily contribute to the process. They often have excellent ideas. Secrecy would forgo many excellent ideas.
2. Investors, creditors, and other stakeholders have greater basis for supporting a firm when they know what the firm is doing and where the firm is going.
3. Visibility promotes democracy, whereas secrecy promotes autocracy. Domestic firms and most foreign firms prefer democracy over autocracy as a management style.
4. Participation and openness enhance understanding, commitment, and communication within the firm.

Reasons why some firms prefer to conduct strategic planning in secret and keep strategies hidden from all but the highest-level executives are as follows:

1. Free dissemination of a firm's strategies may easily translate into competitive intelligence for rival firms who could exploit the firm given that information.
2. Secrecy limits criticism, second guessing, and hindsight.
3. Participants in a visible strategy process become more attractive to rival firms who may lure them away.
4. Secrecy limits rival firms from imitating or duplicating the firm's strategies and undermining the firm.

The obvious benefits of the visible versus hidden extremes suggest that a working balance must be sought between the apparent contradictions. Parnell says that in a perfect world all key individuals both inside and outside the firm should be involved in strategic planning, but in practice particularly sensitive and confidential information should always remain strictly confidential to top managers.[18] This balancing act is difficult but essential for survival of the firm.

The Top-Down or Bottom-Up Approach

Proponents of the top-down approach contend that top executives are the only persons in the firm with the collective experience, acumen, and fiduciary responsibility to make key strategy decisions. In contrast, bottom-up advocates argue that lower- and middle-level managers and employees who will be implementing the strategies need to be actively involved in the process of formulating the strategies to ensure their support and commitment. Recent strategy research and this textbook emphasize the bottom-up approach, but earlier work by Schendel and Hofer stressed the need for firms to rely on perceptions of their top managers in strategic planning.[19] Strategists must reach a working balance of the two approaches in a manner deemed best for their firms at a particular time, while cognizant of the fact that current research supports the bottom-up approach, at least among U.S. firms. Increased education and diversity of the workforce at all levels are reasons why middle- and lower-level managers—and even nonmanagers—should be invited to participate in the firm's strategic planning process, at least to the extent that they are willing and able to contribute.

A recent example of "top-down strategic planning" is the approach used by former Hewlett-Packard CEO Leo Apotheker. A recent *Wall Street Journal* article describes how Mr. Apotheker was working with the H-P Board of Directors to develop a new strategic plan for the company.[20] CEO Apotheker made public the new H-P Strategic Plan at the firm's March 2011 shareholders' meeting. Apotheker, in conjunction with the H-P Board, crafted the new strategy aimed at placing greater emphasis on software, networking, storage, and cloud computing—rather than traditional personal computers and accessories.

Special Note to Students

Just Google the words "balanced scorecard images" and you will see more than 100 actual Balanced Scorecards being used as a tool by various organizations to gain and sustain competitive advantage. Note the variation in format. In performing your case analysis, develop and present a Balanced Scorecard that you recommend to help your firm monitor and evaluate progress toward stated objectives. Effective, timely evaluation of strategies can enable a firm to adapt quickly to changing conditions, and a Balanced Scorecard can assist in this endeavor. Couch your discussion of the Balanced Scorecard in terms of competitive advantage versus rival firms.

Conclusion

This chapter presents a strategy-evaluation framework that can facilitate accomplishment of annual and long-term objectives. Effective strategy evaluation allows an organization to capitalize on internal strengths as they develop, to exploit external opportunities as they emerge, to recognize and defend against threats, and to mitigate internal weaknesses before they become detrimental.

Strategists in successful organizations take the time to formulate, implement, and then evaluate strategies deliberately and systematically. Good strategists move their organization forward with purpose and direction, continually evaluating and improving the firm's external and internal strategic positions. Strategy evaluation allows an organization to shape its own future rather than allowing it to be constantly shaped by remote forces that have little or no vested interest in the well-being of the enterprise.

Although not a guarantee for success, strategic management allows organizations to make effective long-term decisions, to execute those decisions efficiently, and to take corrective actions as needed to ensure success. Computer networks and the Internet help to coordinate strategic-management activities and to ensure that decisions are based on good information. A key to effective strategy evaluation and to successful strategic management is an integration of intuition and analysis:

> A potentially fatal problem is the tendency for analytical and intuitive issues to polarize. This polarization leads to strategy evaluation that is dominated by either analysis or intuition, or to strategy evaluation that is discontinuous, with a lack of coordination among analytical and intuitive issues.[21]

Strategists in successful organizations realize that strategic management is first and foremost a people process. It is an excellent vehicle for fostering organizational communication. People are what make the difference in organizations.

> The real key to effective strategic management is to accept the premise that the planning process is more important than the written plan, that the manager is continuously planning and does not stop planning when the written plan is finished. The written plan is only a snapshot as of the moment it is approved. If the manager is not planning on a continuous basis—planning, measuring, and revising—the written plan can become obsolete the day it is finished. This obsolescence becomes more of a certainty as the increasingly rapid rate of change makes the business environment more uncertain.[22]

Key Terms and Concepts

Advantage (p. 288)
Auditing (p. 300)
Balanced Scorecard (p. 296)
Consistency (p. 288)
Consonance (p. 288)
Contingency Plans (p. 299)
Feasibility (p. 288)
Future Shock (p. 295)

GAAS, GAAP, and IFRS (p. 300)
Management by Wandering Around (p. 291)
Measuring Organizational Performance (p. 292)
Reviewing the Underlying Bases of an Organization's Strategy (p. 291)
Revised EFE Matrix (p. 291)
Revised IFE Matrix (p. 291)
Taking Corrective Actions (p. 295)

Issues for Review and Discussion

1. Do an Internet search using the keywords "Balanced Scorecard Images." Pick out two images among the hundred available. Compare and contrast the two images/processes as to effectiveness.

2. Do an Internet search using the keywords "GAAP to IFRS" to update yourself on this important transition coming soon in the United States.

3. How does an organization know if it is pursuing "optimal" strategies?

4. Discuss the nature and implications of the upcoming accounting switch from GAAP to IFRS in the United States.

5. Ask an accounting professor at your college or university the following question and report back to the class: "To what extent would my learning the IFRS standards

on my own give me competitive advantage in the job market?"

6. Give an example of "consonance" other than the one provided by Rumelt in the chapter.

7. Evaluating strategies on a continuous rather than a periodic basis is desired. Discuss the pros and cons of this statement.

8. How often should an organization's vision/mission be changed in light of strategy evaluation activities?

9. Compare Mintzberg's notion of "crafting" strategies with this textbook's notion of "gathering and assimilating information" to formulate strategies.

10. Why has strategy evaluation become so important in business today?

11. BellSouth Services is considering putting divisional EFE and IFE matrices online for continual updating. How would this affect strategy evaluation?

12. What types of quantitative and qualitative criteria should be used to evaluate a company's strategy?

13. As owner of a local, independent supermarket, explain how you would evaluate the firm's strategy.

14. Under what conditions are corrective actions not required in the strategy-evaluation process?

15. Identify types of organizations that may need to evaluate strategy more frequently than others. Justify your choices.

16. As executive director of the state forestry commission, in what way and how frequently would you evaluate the organization's strategies?

17. Identify some key financial ratios that would be important in evaluating a bank's strategy.

18. Strategy evaluation allows an organization to take a proactive stance toward shaping its own future. Discuss the meaning of this statement.

19. Explain and discuss the Balanced Scorecard.

20. Why is the Balanced Scorecard an important topic both in devising objectives and in evaluating strategies?

21. Develop a Balanced Scorecard for a local fast-food restaurant.

22. Do you believe strategic management should be more visible or hidden as a process in a firm? Explain.

23. Do you feel strategic management should be more a top-down or bottom-up process in a firm? Explain.

24. Do you believe strategic management is more an art or a science? Explain.

Notes

1. Dale McConkey, "Planning in a Changing Environment," *Business Horizons*, September–October 1988, 64.

2. Robert Simons, "Control in an Age of Empowerment," *Harvard Business Review*, March–April 1995, 80.

3. Dale Zand, "Reviewing the Policy Process," *California Management Review* 21, no. 1 (Fall 1978): 37.

4. Eccles. 3:1–8.

5. Claude George Jr., *The History of Management Thought* (Upper Saddle River, New Jersey: Prentice Hall, 1968), 165–166.

6. M. Erez and F. Kanfer, "The Role of Goal Acceptance in Goal Setting and Task Performance," *Academy of Management Review* 8, no. 3 (July 1983): 457.

7. D. Hussey and M. Langham, *Corporate Planning: The Human Factor* (Oxford, England: Pergamon Press, 1979), 138.

8. Carter Bayles, "Strategic Control: The President's Paradox," *Business Horizons* 20, no. 4 (August 1977): 18.

9. Adam Lashinsky, "The World's Most Admired Companies," *Fortune*, March 16, 2009, 81–91.

10. Robert Waterman, Jr., "How the Best Get Better," *BusinessWeek*, September 14, 1987, 105.

11. Robert Linneman and Rajan Chandran, "Contingency Planning: A Key to Swift Managerial Action in the Uncertain Tomorrow," *Managerial Planning* 29, no. 4 (January–February 1981): 23–27.

12. American Accounting Association, *Report of Committee on Basic Auditing Concepts*, 1971, 15–74.

13. Edward Iwata, "Will Going Global Extend to Accounting?" *USA Today*, January 6, 2009, B1.

14. John Parnell, "Five Critical Challenges in Strategy Making," *SAM Advanced Management Journal* 68, no. 2 (Spring 2003): 15–22.

15. Henry Mintzberg, "Crafting Strategy," *Harvard Business Review*, July–August 1987, 66–75.

16. Henry Mintzberg and J. Waters, "Of Strategies, Deliberate and Emergent," *Strategic Management Journal* 6, no. 2: 257–272.

17. Jody Heymann, "Bootstrapping Profits by Opening the Books," *Bloomberg Businessweek*, September 27–October 3, 2010, 62.

18. Parnell, 15–22.

19. D. E. Schendel and C. W. Hofer (Eds.), *Strategic Management* (Boston: Little, Brown, 1979).

20. Ben Worthen and JoAnn Lublin, "New H-P CEO Reprograms Strategy," *Wall Street Journal*, January 15–16, 2011, B5.

21. Michael McGinnis, "The Key to Strategic Planning: Integrating Analysis and Intuition," *Sloan Management Review* 26, no. 1 (Fall 1984): 49.

22. McConkey, 72.

Current Readings

Haynes, Katalin Takacs, and Amy Hillman. "The Effect of Board Capital and CEO Power on Strategic Change." *Strategic Management Journal* 31, no. 11 (November 2010): 1145–1163.

Kaplan, Robert S., David P. Norton, and Bjarne Rugelsjoen. "Managing Alliances with the Balanced Scorecard." *Harvard Business Review*, January–February 2010, 114–124.

Lansiluoto, Aapo, and Marko Jarvenpaa. "Greening the Balanced Scorecard." *Business Horizons* 53, no. 4 (July–August 2010): 385–396.

Shaojie, Anna Cui, Roger J. Calantone, and David A. Griffith. "Strategic Change and Termination of Interfirm Partnerships." *Strategic Management Journal* 32, no. 4 (April 2011): 402–423.

Simons, Robert. "Stress-Test Your Strategy: The 7 Questions to Ask." *Harvard Business Review*, November 2010, 92–101.

ASSURANCE OF LEARNING EXERCISES

Assurance of Learning Exercise 9A

Examine 100 Balanced Scorecards

Purpose

The Army Surgeon General and Commander of the U.S. Army Medical Command use the Balanced Scorecard as "the principal tool by which they improve operational and fiscal effectiveness and better meet the needs of patients and stakeholders." This exercise will give your experience evaluating many different formats for the Balanced Scorecard. It will also give you exposure to many different organizations that currently utilize the Balanced Scorecard as part of their strategic planning.

Instructions

Step 1	Do a Google search using the terms "balanced scorecard images." Review the many different formats of the Balanced Scorecard currently being used by organizations. Decide upon three formats that you believe are particularly effective.
Step 2	Do a Google search using the terms "balanced scorecard adopters." Review the many different organizations currently using the Balanced Scorecard as part of their strategic planning. Select three different companies or organizations. Compare and contrast their use of the Balanced Scorecard technique.
Step 3	Prepare a three page Executive Summary of your Balanced Scorecard analysis and recommendations.

Assurance of Learning Exercise 9B

Prepare a Strategy-Evaluation Report for Walt Disney

Purpose

This exercise can give you experience locating strategy-evaluation information. Use of the Internet coupled with published sources of information can significantly enhance the strategy-evaluation process. Performance information on competitors, for example, can help put into perspective a firm's own performance.

Instructions

Step 1	Visit http://marketwatch.multexinvestor.com, http://moneycentral.msn.com, http://finance.yahoo.com, and www.clearstation.com to locate strategy-evaluation information regarding Walt Disney's performance last quarter and analysts' thoughts on Disney's overall strategy going forward. How has Disney's percent of revenues and profits changed since 2010 and how do you think it will change going forward? Why?

Step 2   Summarize your research findings by preparing a strategy-evaluation report for your instructor. Include in your report a summary of Disney's strategies and performance in 2011 and a summary of your conclusions regarding the effectiveness of Disney's strategies.

Step 3   Based on your analysis, do you feel that Disney is pursuing effective strategies? What recommendations would you offer to Disney's chief executive officer?

Assurance of Learning Exercise 9C

Evaluate My University's Strategies

Purpose

An important part of evaluating strategies is determining the nature and extent of changes in an organization's external opportunities/threats and internal strengths/weaknesses. Changes in these underlying critical success factors can indicate a need to change or modify the firm's strategies.

Instructions

As a class, discuss positive and negative changes in your university's external and internal factors during your college career. Begin by listing on the board new or emerging opportunities and threats. Then identify strengths and weaknesses that have changed significantly during your college career. In light of the external and internal changes that were identified, discuss whether your university's strategies need modifying. Are there any new strategies that you would recommend? Make a list to recommend to your department chair, dean, president, or chancellor.

"NOTABLE QUOTES"

"If you have integrity, nothing else matters. If you don't have integrity, nothing else matters."
—*Alan K. Simpson*

"If business is not based on ethical grounds, it is of no benefit to society and will, like all other unethical combinations, pass into oblivion."
—*C. Max Killan*

"Good ethics is good business."

"Do unto others as you would have them do unto you."

"Be joyful when you do things to conserve, preserve, and enhance the natural environment."

Business Ethics/ Social Responsibility/ Environmental Sustainability

CHAPTER OBJECTIVES

After studying this chapter, you should be able to do the following:

1. Explain why good ethics is good business in strategic management.

2. Explain how firms can best ensure that their code of business ethics guides decision making instead of being ignored.

3. Explain why whistle-blowing is important to encourage in a firm.

4. Discuss the nature and role of corporate sustainability reports.

5. Discuss specific ways that firms can be good stewards of the natural environment.

6. Explain ISO 14000 and 14001.

7. Discuss recent trends in bribery law.

ASSURANCE OF LEARNING EXERCISES

Assurance of Learning Exercise 10A
How Does My Municipality Compare to Others on Being Pollution-Safe?

Assurance of Learning Exercise 10B
Evaluate Disney's Standards of Business Conduct

Assurance of Learning Exercise 10C
Compare and Evaluate Sustainability Reports

Assurance of Learning Exercise 10D
The Ethics of Spying on Competitors

Assurance of Learning Exercise 10E
Who Prepares a Sustainability Report?

Although the three sections of this chapter (Business Ethics, Social Responsibility, and Sustainability) are distinct, the topics are quite related. Many people, for example, consider it unethical for a firm to be socially irresponsible. *Social responsibility* refers to actions an organization takes beyond what is legally required to protect or enhance the well-being of living things. *Sustainability* refers to the extent that an organization's operations and actions protect, mend, and preserve rather than harm or destroy the natural environment. Polluting the environment, for example, is unethical, irresponsible, and in many cases illegal. Business ethics, social responsibility, and sustainability issues therefore are interrelated and impact all areas of the comprehensive strategic-management model, as illustrated in Figure 10-1.

A sample company that adheres to the highest ethical standards and that utilizes excellent strategic planning to go from "near bankruptcy" to prosperous in one year is General Motors Corp. GM has an outstanding commitment to corporate sustainability as described at their website: http://www.gm.com/corporate/responsibility/environment/.

Excellent Strategic Management Showcased

GENERAL MOTORS (GM) CORP.

Headquartered in Detroit, Michigan, GM's 2010 revenues increased 29.6 percent to $135 billion. The fantastic results marked a dramatic turnaround from bankruptcy two years earlier. GM's CEO Daniel Akerson says he expects even stronger results for 2011 even though high gas prices are prompting a shift toward more fuel-efficient vehicles that typically produce slimmer profits. GM has reduced the U.S. government portion of its ownership from 61 percent a year earlier to 26.5 percent in early 2011. The U.S. government recovered $23 billion of its $49.5 billion bailout funding. GM eliminated four of its eight brands and hundreds of dealers in the Unites States in 2010 as the company's 2010 revenue rose 30 percent to $135.6 billion.

GM is a highly ethical firm that does an excellent job on social responsibility and environmental sustainability issues. For example, GM spent $200 million in the last quarter of 2010 to give its 45,000 U.S. union employees average profit-sharing payments of $4,200 a worker. That 2010 amount per worker was an all-time record. In February 2011 alone, GM sold 207,028 vehicles, up 46 percent from the prior year. In comparison, Ford sold 156,232 vehicles, up 14 percent from the prior year.

GM in 2011 reclaimed its No.1 spot as the world's largest manufacturer of cars and light trucks. Toyota took away that distinction three years ago. However, the Japanese automaker's sales have been hurt by a series of recalls that began over a year ago as well as the recent earthquake and tsunami off the northeast coast of Japan. GM's recent success has been based to a large extent on its sales in China, where by most accounts it and its local joint venture partners are the top sellers of cars and light trucks. GM's domestic sales recently rose 27 percent to 232,538 from a year earlier, and its market share increased to 19.2 percent, up from 16.6 percent a year ago.

GM reported its highest quarterly profit (first quarter 2011) in more than a decade, helped by fuel-efficient cars and smaller SUVs that were in demand as gas prices rose. GM thrived in the quarter by selling small cars like the new Chevrolet Cruze, and efficient crossover vehicles such as the Chevrolet Equinox and GMC Terrain. Revenue rose 15 percent to $36.2

billion, driven by a 25-percent jump in U.S. auto sales and a 10-percent gain in China, which has emerged as GM's biggest market.

The U.S. Treasury Department is trying to figure out the right time to sell the remaining 500 million GM shares owned by the government. GM took nearly $50 billion in U.S. government aid to help it survive in 2009. The U.S. government has been repaid about half that amount and needs to sell its remaining shares for roughly $53 each to get all its money back.

Perhaps GM's biggest problem today is the GM Europe division, which incurred a loss of $1.8 billion in 2010. CEO Akerson is hurrying to restructure GM's Opel division in Europe. Opel is doing poorly even though that division generates $24 billion in annual sales. Profits are possible in 2011 for GM's Opel division, which has trailed Volkswagen AG in all measures for more than a decade. VW's profits increased 700 percent in 2010. Part of GM Europe's problem and Opel's problem in particular are European labor unions. For example, Opel has needed for years to close its aging factory in Bochum, Germany, but keeps it open only as part of a deal with labor unions to cut wages.

Source: Company documents. Also, Sharon Terlep, "GM Rebounds With Best Year Since 1999," *Wall Street Journal*, February 25, 2011, B1. Also, Sharon Terlep, "GM Hastens Tuneup of Opel," *Wall Street Journal*, February 28, 2011, B1.

FIGURE 10-1

A Comprehensive Strategic-Management Model

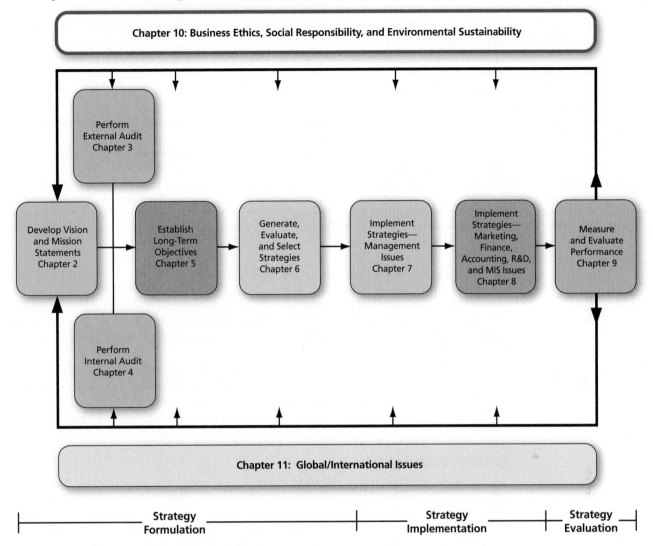

Source: Fred R. David, "How Companies Define Their Mission," *Long Range Planning* 22, no. 3 (June 1988): 40.

Business Ethics

The Institute of Business Ethics (IBE) recently did a study titled "Does Business Ethics Pay?" and concluded that companies displaying a "clear commitment to ethical conduct" consistently outperform companies that do not display ethical conduct. Philippa Foster Black of the IBE stated: "Not only is ethical behavior in business life the right thing to do in principle, it pays off in financial returns." Table 10-1 provides some results of the IBE study.

Good ethics is good business. Bad ethics can derail even the best strategic plans. This chapter provides an overview of the importance of business ethics in strategic management. *Business ethics* can be defined as principles of conduct within organizations that guide decision making and behavior. Good business ethics is a prerequisite for good strategic management; good ethics is just good business!

A rising tide of consciousness about the importance of business ethics is sweeping the United States and the rest of the world. Strategists such as CEOs and business owners are the individuals primarily responsible for ensuring that high ethical principles are espoused and practiced in an organization. All strategy formulation, implementation, and evaluation decisions have ethical ramifications.

TABLE 10-1   Seven Principles of Admirable Business Ethics

1. Be Trustful: Customers want to do business with a company they can trust. Customers can recognize when trust is at the core of a company. Simply defined, trust is assured reliance on the character, ability, strength, and truth of a business.

2. Keep an Open Mind: The leaders of an organization must be open to new ideas. Continually ask for opinions and feedback from both customers and employees to assure a good ethics culture.

3. Meet Obligations: Do everything possible to gain the trust of past customers and clients, particularly if something has gone awry. Reclaim any lost business by honoring all commitments and obligations.

4. Have Clear Documents: Make certain that all print materials such as advertising brochures and business documents are clear, precise, professional, and, most importantly, do not misrepresent or misinterpret.

5. Become Community Involved: Be actively involved in community-related issues and activities, continually demonstrating that your business is a responsible community citizen.

6. Maintain Accounting Control: View accounting and record keeping not only as a means for monitoring the progress of your company but as a resource for identifying and stopping any "questionable" activities.

7. Be Respectful: Treat others with the utmost of respect. Regardless of different positions, titles, ages, or beliefs, always treat others with professional respect and courtesy. Follow the Golden Rule: Do unto others as you would have them do unto you.

Source: Based on http://sbinformation.about.com/od/bestpractices/a/businessethics.htm.

Newspapers and business magazines daily report legal and moral breaches of ethical conduct by both public and private organizations. Being unethical can be very expensive. For example, some of the largest payouts for class-action legal fraud suits ever were against Enron ($7.16 billion), WorldCom ($6.16 billion), Cendant ($3.53 billion), Tyco ($2.98 billion), AOL Time Warner ($2.5 billion), Nortel Networks ($2.47 billion), and Royal Ahold ($1.09 billion).

Other business actions considered to be unethical include misleading advertising or labeling, causing environmental harm, poor product or service safety, padding expense accounts, insider trading, dumping banned or flawed products in foreign markets, not providing equal opportunities for women and minorities, overpricing, moving jobs overseas, and sexual harassment.

Code of Business Ethics

A new wave of ethics issues related to product safety, employee health, sexual harassment, AIDS in the workplace, smoking, acid rain, affirmative action, waste disposal, foreign business practices, cover-ups, takeover tactics, conflicts of interest, employee privacy, inappropriate gifts, and security of company records has accentuated the need for strategists to develop a clear *code of business ethics*. Internet fraud, hacking into company computers, spreading viruses, and identity theft are other unethical activities that plague every sector of online commerce.

Merely having a code of ethics, however, is not sufficient to ensure ethical business behavior. A code of ethics can be viewed as a public relations gimmick, a set of platitudes, or window dressing. To ensure that the code is read, understood, believed, and remembered, periodic ethics workshops are needed to sensitize people to workplace circumstances in which ethics issues may arise.[1] If employees see examples of punishment for violating the code as well as rewards for upholding the code, this reinforces the importance of a firm's code of ethics. The website www.ethicsweb.ca/codes provides guidelines on how to write an effective code of ethics.

An Ethics Culture

An ethics "culture" needs to permeate organizations! To help create an ethics culture, Citicorp developed a business ethics board game that is played by thousands of employees worldwide. Called "The Word Ethic," this game asks players business ethics questions, such as how do you deal with a customer who offers you football tickets in exchange for a new, backdated IRA? Diana Robertson at the Wharton School of Business believes the game is effective because it is interactive. Many organizations have developed a code-of-conduct manual outlining ethical expectations and giving examples of situations that commonly arise in their businesses.

Harris Corporation and other firms warn managers and employees that failing to report an ethical violation by others could bring discharge. The Securities and Exchange Commission (SEC) recently strengthened its whistle-blowing policies, virtually mandating that anyone seeing unethical activity report such behavior. *Whistle-blowing* refers to policies that require employees to report any unethical violations they discover or see in the firm.

Whistle-blowers in the corporate world receive up to 25 percent of the proceeds of legal proceedings against firms for wrongdoing. In the largest such whistle-blower payout ever, a quality-assurance manager, Cheryl Eckerd, with GlaxoSmithKline PLC received $96 million in 2010 for her role in helping the government secure a criminal guilty plea and a $750 million payment from that company to settle manufacturing deficiencies. Whistle-blower payouts are becoming more and more common. Pfizer paid out $2.3 billion in a whistle-blower settlement case earlier and Eli Lilly paid out $1.4 billion. Most firms have internal whistle-blowing incentives and policies and try to keep such matters internal, but recent laws and court cases are shifting disclosure and settlements outside the firm.[2]

An accountant recently tipped off the IRS that his employer was skimping on taxes and received $4.5 million in the first IRS whistle-blower award. The accountant's tip netted the IRS $20 million in taxes and interest from the errant financial-services firm. The award represented a 22 percent cut of the taxes recovered. The IRS program, designed to encourage tips in large-scale cases, mandates awards of 15 to 30 percent of the amount recouped. "It's a win-win for both the government and taxpayers. These are dollars that are being returned to the Treasury that otherwise wouldn't be," said lawyer Eric Young.

One reason strategists' salaries are high is that they must take the moral risks of the firm. Strategists are responsible for developing, communicating, and enforcing the code of business ethics for their organizations. Although primary responsibility for ensuring ethical behavior rests with a firm's strategists, an integral part of the responsibility of all managers is to provide ethics leadership by constant example and demonstration. Managers hold positions that enable them to influence and educate many people. This makes managers responsible for developing and implementing ethical decision making. Gellerman and Drucker, respectively, offer some good advice for managers:

All managers risk giving too much because of what their companies demand from them. But the same superiors, who keep pressing you to do more, or to do it better, or faster, or less expensively, will turn on you should you cross that fuzzy line between right and wrong. They will blame you for exceeding instructions or for ignoring their warnings. The smartest managers already know that the best answer to the question "How far is too far?" is don't try to find out.[3]

A man (or woman) might know too little, perform poorly, lack judgment and ability, and yet not do too much damage as a manager. But if that person lacks character and integrity—no matter how knowledgeable, how brilliant, how successful—he destroys. He destroys people, the most valuable resource of the enterprise. He destroys spirit. And he destroys performance. This is particularly true of the people at the head of an enterprise. For the spirit of an organization is created from the top. If an organization is great in spirit, it is because the spirit of its top people is great. If it decays, it does so because the top rots. As the proverb has it, "Trees die from the top." No one should ever become a strategist unless he or she is willing to have his or her character serve as the model for subordinates.[4]

No society anywhere in the world can compete very long or successfully with people stealing from one another or not trusting one another, with every bit of information requiring notarized confirmation, with every disagreement ending up in litigation, or with government having to regulate businesses to keep them honest. Being unethical is a recipe for headaches, inefficiency, and waste. History has proven that the greater the trust and confidence of people in the ethics of an institution or society, the greater its economic strength. Business relationships are built mostly on mutual trust and reputation. Short-term decisions based on greed and questionable ethics will preclude the necessary self-respect to gain the trust of others. More and more firms believe that ethics training and an ethics culture create strategic advantage.

Ethics training programs should include messages from the CEO or owner of the business emphasizing ethical business practices, the development and discussion of codes of ethics, and procedures for discussing and reporting unethical behavior. Firms can align ethical and strategic decision making by incorporating ethical considerations into long-term planning, by integrating ethical decision making into the performance appraisal process, by encouraging whistle-blowing or the reporting of unethical practices, and by monitoring departmental and corporate performance regarding ethical issues.

Bribes

Bribery is defined by *Black's Law Dictionary* as the offering, giving, receiving, or soliciting of any item of value to influence the actions of an official or other person in discharge of a public or legal duty. A *bribe* is a gift bestowed to influence a recipient's conduct. The gift may be any money, good, right in action, property, preferment, privilege, emolument, object of value, advantage, or merely a promise or undertaking to induce or influence the action, vote, or influence of a person in an official or public capacity. Bribery is a crime in most countries of the world, including the United States.[5]

The U.S. Foreign Corrupt Practices Act that governs bribery is being enforced more strictly. Eight of the top 10 largest settlements ever under the law occurred in 2010. The Las Vegas Sands Corp. is currently under bribery investigation regarding its three casinos in Macau. Macau has four times the gambling revenue of Las Vegas.

Royal Dutch Shell PLC recently paid $30 million in bribery penalties related to its association with Panalpina, which paid about $85 million in bribery fines. The U.S. Foreign Corrupt Practices Act and a new provision in the Dodd-Frank financial-regulation law allows company employees or others who bring cases of financial fraud, such as bribery, to the government's attention to receive up to 30 percent of any sum recovered. Bribery suits against a company also expose the firm to shareholder lawsuits.

Headquartered in Springdale, Arkansas, Tyson Foods recently paid $5.2 million in criminal and civil penalties to resolve bribery allegations involving two meat inspectors in Mexico. Tyson General Counsel David Van Bebber said, "While we are disappointed mistakes were made, corrective action has been taken and the improper payments were discontinued."

The United Kingdom instituted a new Bribery Law in April 2011 that forbids any company doing any business in the United Kingdom from bribing foreign or domestic officials to gain competitive advantage. The new British law is more stringent even than the similar U.S. Foreign Corrupt Practices Act. The British Bribery Law carries a maximum 10-year prison sentence for those convicted of bribery. The new law stipulates that "failure to prevent bribery" is an offense and stipulates that facilitation payments, or payments to gain access, are not a valid defense to prevent bribery.

Great Britain's new Bribery Act applies even to bribes between private businesspersons, and if the individual who makes the payment does not realize the transaction was a bribe, he/she is still liable. The new bribery law is being enforced by Britain's Serious Fraud Office (SFO) and boosts the maximum penalty for bribery to 10 years in prison from seven, and sets no limits on fines. More and more nations are taking a tougher stance against corruption, and companies worldwide are installing elaborate programs to avoid running afoul of the FCPA or the SFO.

In China, Zeng Jinchun was recently executed for accepting bribes of more than $4.7 million. Zeng had allegedly been accepting money over a nine-year period in return for awarding mining contracts and job promotions. A Chinese court found that Zeng was unable to account for about $1.4 million of his assets. A former secretary of the Chenzhou Municipal Commission for Discipline Inspection of the Communist Party of China, Mr. Zeng was executed by firing squad. The execution followed a pledge a day earlier by Communist Party officials in Beijing to "root out corruption that has caused civil unrest around the country."

Paying bribes is considered both illegal and unethical in the United States, but in some foreign countries, paying bribes and kickbacks is acceptable. Tipping is even considered bribery in some countries. Important antibribery and extortion initiatives are advocated by many organizations, including the World Bank, the International Monetary Fund, the European Union, the Council of Europe, the Organization of American States, the Pacific Basin Economic Council, the Global Coalition for Africa, and the United Nations.

The U.S. Justice Department recently increased its prosecutions of alleged acts of foreign bribery. Businesses have to be much more careful these days. For years, taking business associates to lavish dinners and giving them expensive holiday gifts and even outright cash may have been expected in many countries, such as South Korea and China, but there is now stepped-up enforcement of bribery laws. The SEC and Justice Department are investigating several pharmaceutical companies, including Merck, AstraZeneca PLC, Bristol-Myers Squibb, and GlaxoSmithKline PLC, for allegedly paying bribes in certain foreign countries to boost sales and speed approvals. Four types of violations are being reviewed: bribing government-employed doctors to purchase drugs; paying company sales agents commissions that are passed along to government doctors; paying hospital committees to approve drug purchases; and paying regulators to win drug approvals.

The SEC and the Justice Department are also investigating Hewlett-Packard for allegedly paying Russian government officials bribes to secure a $44.5 million information technology network. Similarly, the engineering giant Siemens AG is being investigated on bribery charges related to a $27 million traffic-control system installed in Moscow, Russia.

The U.S. Foreign Corrupt Practices Act (FCPA) prohibits U.S. companies from paying or offering to pay foreign government officials or employees of state companies to gain a business advantage. The oil-service company Schlumberger, which has major offices in Houston, Texas, is being investigated on bribery charges for violating these laws in Yemen. Under the U.S. Dodd-Frank Act, passed in 2010, employees are encouraged to report possible acts of bribery and whistle-blowers are rewarded between 10 percent and 30 percent of any financial sanctions against companies.

Royal Dutch Shell PLC and several other companies recently paid a combined $236 million settlement due to allegations that they or their contractors bribed foreign officials to assist in importing equipment and materials into various countries. At the center of this settlement was Panalpina World Transport Ltd., which admitted that it paid over the last few years $27 million in bribes on behalf of its clients, including Shell, to officials in Nigeria, Brazil, Azerbaijan, Russia, Turkmenistan, Kazakhstan, and Angola.

Love Affairs at Work

With 280 retail stores in 20 countries, American Apparel Inc. and its CEO, Dov Charney, currently face a $260 million lawsuit alleging that Mr. Charney pressured a teenage employee into performing sex acts in order to keep her job. The employee, New York City resident Irene Morales, now 20, alleges that Mr. Charney, 42, invited her to his New York apartment shortly after her 18th birthday and demanded fellatio as soon as she walked in the door. The alleged nonconsensual sex continued for eight months, until Morales resigned from her job as manager of an American Apparel store in the city's Chelsea neighborhood. The lawsuit contends that Morales was promised job security and advancement in exchange for sex. Also is 2011, four other women, Alyssa Ferguson, Marissa Wilson, Tesa Lubans-Dehaven, and Kimbra Lo, came forward with similar claims against CEO Charney. The 19-year-old, former American Apparel sales associate Lo said: "My main priority is to stop what's going on and to expose this man for who he is." Asked for details of her allegations, she stated: "When I went over to his house he attacked me. I made it very clear for him to stop. I said, 'No, please don't touch me,' and he became more aggressive. I didn't feel there was a way for me to leave safely. I was terrified." Mr. Charney's lawyer, Peter Schey, says: "I think all of these claims are contrived. The allegations are false. I think this is an effort to shake down American Apparel. These claims should be resolved in confidential arbitration."

Among colleges and universities, the federal Office of Civil Rights (OCR) has stepped up its investigation of sexual harassment cases brought forward by female students against professors. Yale University has been in the news in this regard as well as numerous other institutions currently being investigated. At no charge to the student, the OCR will investigate a female student's claim if evidence is compelling.

A recent *Wall Street Journal* article recapped current American standards regarding boss-subordinate love affairs at work.[6] Only 5 percent of all firms sampled had no restrictions on such relationships; 80 percent of firms have policies that prohibit relationships between a supervisor and a subordinate. Only 4 percent of firms strictly prohibited such relationships, but 39 percent of firms had policies that required individuals to inform their supervisors whenever a romantic relationship begins with a coworker. Only 24 percent of firms required the two persons to be in different departments.

In Europe, romantic relationships at work are largely viewed as private matters and most firms have no policies on the practice. However, European firms are increasingly adopting explicit, American-style sexual harassment laws. The U.S. military strictly bans officers from dating or having sexual relationships with enlistees. At the World Bank, sexual relations between a supervisor and an employee are considered "a de facto conflict of interest which must be resolved to avoid favoritism." World Bank president Paul Wolfowitz recently was forced to resign due to a relationship he had with a bank staff person.

A recent *Bloomberg Businessweek* article reports that in the sluggish job market, employees are filing sexual harassment complaints as a way to further their own job security. Many of these filings are increasingly third party individuals not even directly involved in the relationship but alleging their own job was impacted. Largely due to the rise of third party discrimination claims, the EEOC recovered $376 million on behalf of office romance victims in 2009.[7]

Social Responsibility

Fortune annually lists the most admired and least admired companies globally on social responsibility. *Fortune*'s 2011 top three most admired socially responsible companies are Statoil, Ferrovial, and Walt Disney. The top three least admired companies are Kirin Holdings, Carlsberg, and Asahi Breweries.[8] Chinese firms dominate the least admired list.

Wal-Mart was very socially responsible in the wake of the earthquake and tsunami that devastated Japan in 2011. Following the catastrophe, Wal-Mart mobilized a local relief effort to deliver supplies such as water and flashlights to survivors. Wal-Mart has a history of helping immensely in times of crisis—the retailer was also able to get supplies to people who needed them following Hurricane Katrina.

Some strategists agree with Ralph Nader, who proclaims that organizations have tremendous social obligations. Nader points out, for example, that ExxonMobil has more assets than most countries, and because of this such firms have an obligation to help society cure its many ills. Other people, however, agree with the economist Milton Friedman, who asserts that organizations have no obligation to do any more for society than is legally required. Friedman may contend that it is irresponsible for a firm to give monies to charity.

Do you agree more with Nader or Friedman? Surely we can all agree that the first social responsibility of any business must be to make enough profit to cover the costs of the future because if this is not achieved, no other social responsibility can be met. Indeed, no social need can be met by the firm if the firm fails.

Strategists should examine social problems in terms of potential costs and benefits to the firm and focus on social issues that could benefit the firm most. For example, should a firm avoid laying off employees so as to protect the employees' livelihood, when that decision may force the firm to liquidate?

Social Policy

The term *social policy* embraces managerial philosophy and thinking at the highest level of the firm, which is why the topic is covered in this textbook. Social policy concerns what responsibilities the firm has to employees, consumers, environmentalists, minorities, communities, shareholders, and other groups. After decades of debate, many firms still struggle to determine appropriate social policies.

The impact of society on business and vice versa is becoming more pronounced each year. Corporate social policy should be designed and articulated during strategy formulation, set and administered during strategy implementation, and reaffirmed or changed during strategy evaluation.[9]

Firms should strive to engage in social activities that have economic benefits. Merck & Co. once developed the drug ivermectin for treating river blindness, a disease caused by a fly-borne parasitic worm endemic in poor tropical areas of Africa, the Middle East, and Latin America.

In an unprecedented gesture that reflected its corporate commitment to social responsibility, Merck then made ivermectin available at no cost to medical personnel throughout the world. Merck's action highlights the dilemma of orphan drugs, which offer pharmaceutical companies no economic incentive for profitable development and distribution. Merck did however garner substantial goodwill among its stakeholders for its actions.

Social Policies on Retirement

Some countries around the world are facing severe workforce shortages associated with their aging populations. The percentage of persons age 65 or older exceeds 20 percent in Japan, Italy, and Germany—and will reach 20 percent in 2018 in France. In 2036, the percentage of persons age 65 or older will reach 20 percent in the United States and China. Unlike the United States, Japan is reluctant to rely on large-scale immigration to bolster its workforce. Instead, Japan provides incentives for its elderly to work until ages 65 to 75. Western European countries are doing the opposite, providing incentives for its elderly to retire at ages 55 to 60. The International Labor Organization says 71 percent of Japanese men ages 60 to 64 work, compared to 57 percent of American men and just 17 percent of French men in the same age group.

Sachiko Ichioka, a typical 67-year-old man in Japan, says, "I want to work as long as I'm healthy. The extra money means I can go on trips, and I'm not a burden on my children." Better diet and health care have raised Japan's life expectancy now to 82, the highest in the world. Japanese women are having on average only 1.28 children compared to 2.04 in the United States. Keeping the elderly at work, coupled with reversing the old-fashioned trend of keeping women at home, are Japan's two key remedies for sustaining its workforce in factories and businesses. This prescription for dealing with problems associated with an aging society should be considered by many countries around the world. The Japanese government is phasing in a shift from age 60 to age 65 as the date when a person may begin receiving a pension, and premiums paid by Japanese employees are rising while payouts are falling. Unlike the United States, Japan has no law against discrimination based on age.

Japan's huge national debt, 175 percent of gross domestic product (GDP) compared to 65 percent for the United States, is difficult to lower with a falling population because Japan has fewer taxpaying workers. Worker productivity increases in Japan are not able to offset declines in number of workers, thus resulting in a decline in overall economic production. Like many countries, Japan does not view immigration as a good way to solve this problem.

Japan's shrinking workforce has become such a concern that the government just recently allowed an unspecified number of Indonesian and Filipino nurses and caregivers to work in Japan for two years. The number of working-age Japanese—those between ages 15 and 64—is projected to shrink to 70 million by 2030. Using foreign workers is known as *gaikokujin roudousha* in Japanese. Many Filipinos have recently been hired now to work in agriculture and factories throughout Japan.

Environmental Sustainability

The Global 100 most sustainable corporations in the world are determined every year by the Corporate Knights Inc., an independent, Canadian organization based in Toronto, Ontario. Table 10-2 reveals Corporate Knights top 20 companies among the 100 identified in 2011 as being the best in the world for their sustainability efforts. Note that General Electric was determined to be the best in the world. Note that the United Kingdom led all countries with 5 companies in the top 20. Note the extension on the company names, such as Ag for Germany and Plc for the United Kingdom. These extensions denote where the firms are from.

The strategies of both companies and countries are increasingly scrutinized and evaluated from a natural environment perspective. Companies such as Wal-Mart now monitor not only the price its vendors offer for products, but also how those products are made in terms of environmental practices. A growing number of business schools offer separate courses and even a concentration in environmental management.

TABLE 10-2   The Top 20 Companies in the World on Sustainability

Company	Country
1. General Electric (GE) Corp. (#1)	USA
2. PG & E Corp.	USA
3. Tnt Nv	Netherlands
4. H&M Hennes & Mauritz Ab	Sweden
5. Nokia Corp.	Finland
6. Siemens Ag	Germany
7. Unilever Plc	United Kingdom
8. Vodafone Group Plc	United Kingdom
9. Smiths Group Plc	United Kingdom
10. Geberit	Switzerland
11. Henkel Ag	Germany
12. Inditex Sa	Spain
13. Procter & Gamble Co.	USA
14. Toyota Motor Corp.	Japan
15. Westpac Banking Corp.	Australia
16. Enbridge Inc.	Canada
17. Koninkiijke Phillips Electronics Na	Netherlands
18. Diageo Plc	United Kingdom
19. Nippon Yusen Kk	Japan
20. Royal Dutch Shell Plc	United Kingdom

Source: Based on http://www.global100.org/list/global-100-2010-review-results.html.

Businesses must not exploit and decimate the natural environment. Mark Starik at George Washington University says, "Halting and reversing worldwide ecological destruction and deterioration is a strategic issue that needs immediate and substantive attention by all businesses and managers. According to the International Standards Organization (ISO), the word *environment* is defined as "surroundings in which an organization operates, including air, water, land, natural resources, flora, fauna, humans, and their interrelation." This chapter illustrates how many firms are gaining competitive advantage by being good stewards of the natural environment.

Employees, consumers, governments, and society are especially resentful of firms that harm rather than protect the natural environment. Conversely people today are especially appreciative of firms that conduct operations in a way that mends, conserves, and preserves the natural environment. Consumer interest in businesses preserving nature's ecological balance and fostering a clean, healthy environment is high.

No business wants a reputation as being a polluter. A bad sustainability record will hurt the firm in the market, jeopardize its standing in the community, and invite scrutiny by regulators, investors, and environmentalists. Governments increasingly require businesses to behave responsibly and require, for example, that businesses publicly report the pollutants and wastes their facilities produce.

In terms of megawatts of wind power generated by various states in the United States, Iowa's 2,791 recently overtook California's 2,517, but Texas's 7,118 megawatts dwarfs all other states. Minnesota also is making substantial progress in wind power generation. New Jersey recently outfitted 200,000 utility poles with solar panels, which made it the nation's second-largest producer of solar energy behind California. New Jersey is also adding solar panels to corporate rooftops. The state's $514 million solar program will double its solar capacity to 160 megawatts by 2013. The state's goal is to obtain 3 percent of its electricity from the sun and 12 percent from offshore wind by 2020.

What Is a Sustainability Report?

Wal-Mart Stores is one among many companies today that annually provides a sustainability report that reveals how the firm's operations impact the natural environment. This document discloses to shareholders information about Wal-Mart's labor practices, product sourcing, energy efficiency, environmental impact, and business ethics practices.

It is good business for a company to provide a sustainability report annually to the public. With 60,000 suppliers and over $350 billion in annual sales, Wal-Mart works with its suppliers to make sure they provide such reports. Wal-Mart monitors not only prices its vendors offer for products, but also the vendors' social-responsibility and environmental practices. Many firms use the Wal-Mart sustainability report as a benchmark, guideline, and model to follow in preparing their own report.

The Global Reporting Initiative recently issued a set of detailed reporting guidelines specifying what information should go into sustainability reports. The proxy advisory firm Institutional Shareholder Services reports that an increasing number of shareholder groups are pushing firms to provide sustainability information annually.

Wal-Mart encourages and expects its 1.35 million U.S. employees to adopt what it calls Personal Sustainability Projects, which include such measures as organizing weight-loss or smoking-cessation support groups, biking to work, or starting recycling programs. Employee wellness can be a part of sustainability.

Wal-Mart is installing solar panels on its stores in California and Hawaii, providing as much as 30 percent of the power in some stores. Wal-Mart may go national with solar power if this test works well. Also moving to solar energy is department-store chain Kohl's Corp., which is converting 64 of its 80 California stores to use solar power. There are big subsidies for solar installations in some states.

Home Depot, the world's second largest retailer behind Wal-Mart, recently more than doubled its offering of environmentally friendly products such as all-natural insect repellent. Home Depot has made it much easier for consumers to find its organic products by using special labels similar to Timberland's (the outdoor company) Green Index tags. Another huge retailer, Target, now offers more than 500 choices of organic certified food and has 18 buildings in California alone powered only by solar energy. The largest solar power plant in North America is the one in Nevada that powers Nellis Air Force Base outside Las Vegas.[10]

Managers and employees of firms must be careful not to become scapegoats blamed for company environmental wrongdoings. Harming the natural environment can be unethical, illegal, and costly. When organizations today face criminal charges for polluting the environment, they increasingly turn on their managers and employees to win leniency. Employee firings and demotions are becoming common in pollution-related legal suits. Managers were fired at Darling International, Inc., and Niagara Mohawk Power Corporation for being indirectly responsible for their firms polluting water. Managers and employees today must be careful not to ignore, conceal, or disregard a pollution problem, or they may find themselves personally liable.

Lack of Standards Changing

A few years ago, firms could get away with placing "green" terminology on their products and labels using such terms as *organic, green, safe, earth-friendly, nontoxic,* and/or *natural* because there were no legal or generally accepted definitions. Today, however, such terms as these carry much more specific connotations and expectations. Uniform standards defining environmentally responsible company actions are rapidly being incorporated into our legal landscape. It has become more and more difficult for firms to make "green" claims when their actions are not substantive, comprehensive, or even true. Lack of standards once made consumers cynical about corporate environmental claims, but those claims today are increasingly being challenged in courts. Joel Makower says, "One of the main reasons to truly become a green firm is for your employees. They're the first group that needs assurance than any claims you make hold water."[11]

Around the world, political and corporate leaders now realize that the "business green" topic will not go away and in fact is gaining ground rapidly. Strategically, companies more than ever must demonstrate to their customers and stakeholders that their green efforts are substantive and set the firm apart from competitors. A firm's performance facts and figures must back up their rhetoric and be consistent with sustainability standards.

Federal Regulations

Strict regulations now require firms to conserve energy. Federal government buildings are being refitted with energy-efficient improvements. Alternative-energy firms are busy with new customers every day as the federal stimulus package includes adding alternative-energy infrastructure. Venture capitalists and lenders are funding new "clean technology" business start-ups, including solar power, wind power, biofuels, and insulation firms. Such firms are boosting marketing efforts, expanding geographically, and hiring more staff. Venture capital investments in clean technology companies are increasing dramatically.

General Electric achieved $20 billion in sales by 2011 in eco-friendly technologies that include cleaner coal-fired power plants, a diesel-and-electric hybrid locomotive, and agricultural silicon that cuts the amount of water and pesticide used in spraying fields. GE has a goal to improve its energy efficiency by 30 percent between 2005 and 2012.

The Environmental Protection Agency recently reported that U.S. citizens and organizations annually spend more than about $200 billion on pollution abatement. Environmental concerns touch all aspects of a business's operations, including workplace risk exposures, packaging, waste reduction, energy use, alternative fuels, environmental cost accounting, and recycling practices.

Managing Environmental Affairs in the Firm

The ecological challenge facing all organizations requires managers to formulate strategies that preserve and conserve natural resources and control pollution. Special natural environment issues include ozone depletion, global warming, depletion of rain forests, destruction of animal habitats, protecting endangered species, developing biodegradable products and packages, waste management, clean air, clean water, erosion, destruction of natural resources, and pollution control. Firms increasingly are developing green product lines that are biodegradable and/or are made from recycled products. Green products sell well.

Managing as if "health of the planet" matters requires an understanding of how international trade, competitiveness, and global resources are connected. Managing environmental affairs can no longer be simply a technical function performed by specialists in a firm; more emphasis must be placed on developing an environmental perspective among all employees and managers of the firm. Many companies are moving environmental affairs from the staff side of the organization to the line side, thus making the corporate environmental group report directly to the chief operating officer. Firms that manage environmental affairs will enhance relations with consumers, regulators, vendors, and other industry players, substantially improving their prospects of success.

Environmental strategies could include developing or acquiring green businesses, divesting or altering environment-damaging businesses, striving to become a low-cost producer through waste minimization and energy conservation, and pursuing a differentiation strategy through green-product features. In addition, firms could include an environmental representative on their board of directors, conduct regular environmental audits, implement bonuses for favorable environmental results, become involved in environmental issues and programs, incorporate environmental values in mission statements, establish environmentally oriented objectives, acquire environmental skills, and provide environmental training programs for company employees and managers.

Should Students Receive Environmental Training?

Most corporate recruiters indicate that it is important to hire students with an awareness of social and environmental responsibility. According to Ford Motor Company's director of corporate governance, "We want students who will help us find solutions to societal challenges and we have trouble hiring students with such skills."

The Aspen Institute contends that most business schools currently do not, but should, incorporate environmental training in all facets of their core curriculum, not just in special elective courses. The institute reports that the University of Texas, the University of North Carolina, and the University of Michigan, among others, are at the cutting edge in providing environmental coverage at their respective MBA levels. Companies favor hiring graduates from such universities.

Findings from research suggest that business schools at the undergraduate level are doing a poor job of educating students on environmental issues. Business students with limited knowledge on environmental issues may make poor decisions, so business schools should address environmental issues more in their curricula. Failure to do so could result in graduates making inappropriate business decisions in regard to the natural environment. Failing to provide adequate coverage of natural environment issues and decisions in their training could make those students less attractive to employers.[12]

Reasons Why Firms Should "Be Green"

Preserving the environment should be a permanent part of doing business for the following reasons:

1. Consumer demand for environmentally safe products and packages is high.
2. Public opinion demanding that firms conduct business in ways that preserve the natural environment is strong.
3. Environmental advocacy groups now have over 20 million Americans as members.
4. Federal and state environmental regulations are changing rapidly and becoming more complex.
5. More lenders are examining the environmental liabilities of businesses seeking loans.
6. Many consumers, suppliers, distributors, and investors shun doing business with environmentally weak firms.
7. Liability suits and fines against firms having environmental problems are on the rise.

Be Proactive, Not Reactive

More firms are becoming environmentally proactive—doing more than the bare minimum to develop and implement strategies that preserve the environment. The old undesirable alternative of being environmentally reactive—changing practices only when forced to do so by law or consumer pressure—more often today leads to high cleanup costs, liability suits, reduced market share, reduced customer loyalty, and higher medical costs. In contrast, a proactive policy views environmental pressures as opportunities and includes such actions as developing green products and packages, conserving energy, reducing waste, recycling, and creating a corporate culture that is environmentally sensitive.

New required diesel technology has reduced emissions by up to 98 percent in all new big trucks, at an average cost increase of $12,000 per truck. "Clean air is not free," says Rich Moskowitz, who handles regulatory affairs for the American Trucking Association, which supports the transition.[13]

ISO 14000/14001 Certification

Based in Geneva, Switzerland, the International Organization for Standardization (ISO) is a network of the national standards institutes of 147 countries, with one member per country. ISO is the world's largest developer of sustainability standards. Widely accepted all over the world, ISO standards are voluntary because ISO has no legal authority to enforce their implementation. ISO itself does not regulate or legislate.

Governmental agencies in various countries, such as the Environmental Protection Agency (EPA) in the United States, have adopted ISO standards as part of their regulatory framework, and the standards are the basis of much legislation. Adoptions are sovereign decisions by the regulatory authorities, governments, and/or companies concerned.

ISO 14000 refers to a series of voluntary standards in the environmental field. The ISO 14000 family of standards concerns the extent to which a firm minimizes harmful effects on the environment caused by its activities and continually monitors and improves its own environmental performance. Included in the ISO 14000 series are the ISO 14001 standards in fields such as environmental auditing, environmental performance evaluation, environmental labeling, and life-cycle assessment.

ISO 14001 is a set of standards adopted by thousands of firms worldwide to certify to their constituencies that they are conducting business in an environmentally friendly manner. ISO 14001 standards offer a universal technical standard for environmental compliance that more and more firms are requiring not only of themselves but also of their suppliers and distributors.

The ISO 14001 standard requires that a community or organization put in place and implement a series of practices and procedures that, when taken together, result in an *environmental management system (EMS)*. ISO 14001 is not a technical standard and as such does not in any way replace technical requirements embodied in statutes or regulations. It also does not set prescribed standards of performance for organizations. Not being ISO 14001 certified can be a strategic disadvantage for towns, counties, and companies because people today expect organizations to minimize or, even better, to eliminate environmental harm they cause.[14] The major requirements of an EMS under ISO 14001 include the following:

- Show commitments to prevention of pollution, continual improvement in overall environmental performance, and compliance with all applicable statutory and regulatory requirements.
- Identify all aspects of the organization's activities, products, and services that could have a significant impact on the environment, including those that are not regulated.
- Set performance objectives and targets for the management system that link back to three policies: (1) prevention of pollution, (2) continual improvement, and (3) compliance.
- Meet environmental objectives that include training employees, establishing work instructions and practices, and establishing the actual metrics by which the objectives and targets will be measured.
- Conduct an audit operation of the EMS.
- Take corrective actions when deviations from the EMS occur.

Electric Car Networks Are Here

GE is buying 25,000 electric vehicles between 2011 and 2015 to use in its fleet-services business, converting over half of the firm's total fleet of vehicles to electric. GE sells the popular WattStation electric-car recharger. The purchase included 12,000 GM Chevrolet Volt vehicles in 2011, and several thousand each year thereafter. The Volt can go 50 miles on a single charge before a gas generator needs to kick in for power. Ford now offers the electric Focus, Toyota Motor offers the electric RAV4, and Nissan Motor offers the 100-mile-range Leaf electric car.

Staples recently ordered 41 electric trucks from Smith Electric Vehicles of Kansas City, Missouri, and plans to order another 40. The Staples trucks have a top speed of 50 mph, can carry 16,000 pounds, and cost about $30,000 more than a comparable diesel truck—but Staples expects to recover that expense in 3.3 years. Other companies ordering electric trucks include Frito-Lay, FedEx, and AT&T.

The company Better Place is building a network of 250,000 electric car recharging stations in the San Francisco/Oakland Bay Area. Each station is about the size of a parking meter. The company has already built such networks in Denmark, Israel, and Australia. City officials in the Bay Area expect that region to lead the United States in electric cars in the near future. The stations are essential because most electric cars need recharging after about 40 miles. Better Place is also building about 200 stations in the Bay Area where electric car batteries can be switched out within 15 minutes, so no waiting is needed for recharging. Even with petroleum prices at low levels, expectations are for the United States and other countries to switch to electric cars quite aggressively over the next 10 years—for pollution minimization reasons and to take advantage of government incentives and eventual mandates.

The Chinese auto maker BYD Co. recently unveiled the country's first all-electric vehicle for mass market. The company's F3DM vehicle runs off batteries that can be charged from a regular electrical outlet. BYD is now selling this car in the United States. BYD is headquartered in Shenzhen.

Hawaii is creating an electric car network for the islands to greatly reduce the state's near-complete dependence on oil for its energy needs. The firm Better Place is creating 70,000 to 100,000 recharging points throughout the islands to support plug-in electric cars. Under the Hawaii Clean Energy Initiative, the state intends to cut its dependence on oil to 30 percent by 2030. Hawaiians pay very high electricity prices because costly oil is burned to produce power. Electric cars have a driving range of 40 miles between charges, which is suitable for Hawaii.[15]

Table 10-3 reveals the impact that bad environmental policies have on two of nature's many ecosystems.

TABLE 10-3   Songbirds and Coral Reefs Need Help

Songbirds

Be a good steward of the natural environment to save our songbirds. Bluebirds are one of 76 songbird species in the United States that have dramatically declined in numbers in the last two decades. Not all birds are considered songbirds, and why birds sing is not clear. Some scientists say they sing when calling for mates or warning of danger, but many scientists now contend that birds sing for sheer pleasure. Songbirds include chickadees, orioles, swallows, mockingbirds, warblers, sparrows, vireos, and the wood thrush. "These birds are telling us there's a problem, something's out of balance in our environment," says Jeff Wells, bird conservation director for the National Audubon Society. Songbirds may be telling us that their air or water is too dirty or that we are destroying too much of their habitat. People collect Picasso paintings and save historic buildings. "Songbirds are part of our natural heritage. Why should we be willing to watch songbirds destroyed any more than allowing a great work of art to be destroyed?" asks Wells. Whatever message songbirds are singing to us today about their natural environment, the message is becoming less and less heard nationwide. Listen when you go outside today. Each of us as individuals, companies, states, and countries should do what we reasonably can to help improve the natural environment for songbirds.[16] A recent study concludes that 67 of the 800 bird species in the United States are endangered, and another 184 species are designated of "conservation concern." The birds of Hawaii are in the greatest peril.

Coral Reefs

Be a good steward of the natural environment to save our coral reefs. The ocean covers more than 71 percent of the earth. The destructive effect of commercial fishing on ocean habitats coupled with increasing pollution runoff into the ocean and global warming of the ocean have decimated fisheries, marine life, and coral reefs around the world. The unfortunate consequence of fishing over the last century has been overfishing, with the principal reasons being politics and greed. Trawl fishing with nets destroys coral reefs and has been compared to catching squirrels by cutting down forests because bottom nets scour and destroy vast areas of the ocean. The great proportion of marine life caught in a trawl is "by-catch" juvenile fish and other life that are killed and discarded. Warming of the ocean due to carbon dioxide emissions also kills thousands of acres of coral reefs annually. The total area of fully protected marine habitats in the United States is only about 50 square miles, compared to some 93 million acres of national wildlife refuges and national parks on the nation's land. A healthy ocean is vital to the economic and social future of the nation—and, indeed, all countries of the world. Everything we do on land ends up in the ocean, so we all must become better stewards of this last frontier on earth in order to sustain human survival and the quality of life.[17]

Special Note to Students

No company or individual wants to do business with someone who is unethical or is insensitive to natural environment concerns. It is no longer just cool to be environmentally proactive, it is expected, and in many respects is the law. Firms are being compared to rival firms every day on sustainability and ethics behavior, actually every minute on Facebook, Twitter, Myspace, LinkedIn, and YouTube. Issues presented in this chapter therefore comprise a competitive advantage or disadvantage for all organizations. Thus you should include in your case analysis recommendations for your firm to exceed stakeholder expectations on ethics, sustainability, and social responsibility. Make comparisons to rival firms to show how your firm can gain or sustain competitive advantage on these issues. Reveal suggestions for the firm to be a good corporate citizen and promote that for competitive advantage. Be mindful that the first responsibility of any business is to stay in business, so utilize cost/benefit analysis as needed to present your recommendations effectively.

Conclusion

In a final analysis, ethical standards come out of history and heritage. Our predecessors have left us with an ethical foundation to build on. Even the legendary football coach Vince Lombardi knew that some things were worth more than winning, and he required his players to have three kinds of loyalty: to God, to their families, and to the Green Bay Packers, "in that order." Employees, customers, and shareholders have become less and less tolerant of business ethics violations in firms, and more and more appreciative of model ethical firms. Information sharing across the Internet increasingly reveals such model firms versus irresponsible firms.

Consumers across the country and around the world appreciate firms that do more than is legally required to be socially responsible. But staying in business while adhering to all laws and regulations must be a primary objective of any business. One of the best ways to be socially responsible is for the firm to proactively conserve and preserve the natural environment. For example, to develop a corporate sustainability report annually is not legally required, but such a report, based on concrete actions, goes a long way toward assuring stakeholders that the firm is worthy of their support. Business ethics, social responsibility, and environmental sustainability are interrelated and key strategic issues facing all organizations.

Key Terms and Concepts

Bribe (p. 314)
Bribery (p. 314)
Business Ethics (p. 311)
Code of Business Ethics (p. 312)
Environment (p. 318)
Environmental Management System (EMS) (p. 322)

ISO 14000 (p. 321)
ISO 14001 (p. 321)
Social policy (p. 316)
Social responsibility (p. 310)
Sustainability (p. 310)
Whistle-Blowing (p. 313)

Issues for Review and Discussion

1. Explain why whistle-blower payouts by the federal government to informants are becoming more and more common.
2. Compare and contrast the British Bribery Law with the American Bribery Law.
3. Compare procedures in the corporate world versus a university setting in terms of how sexual harassment complaints are investigated outside the organization.
4. Compare the EEOC with the OCR in terms of mission and scope of operations.
5. AOL has 93 lobbyists on its payroll and spent $15.4 million on lobbying in Washington, DC in 2010. Is this ethical?
6. If you owned a small business, would you develop a code of business conduct? If yes, what variables would you include? If no, how would you ensure that ethical business standards were being followed by your employees?
7. What do you feel is the relationship between personal ethics and business ethics? Are they or should they be the same?
8. How can firms best ensure that their code of business ethics is read, understood, believed, remembered, and acted on, rather than ignored?
9. Why is it important *not* to view the concept of whistle-blowing as "tattle-telling" or "ratting" on another employee?
10. List six desired results of "ethics training programs" in terms of recommended business ethics policies/procedures in the firm.
11. Discuss bribery. Would actions such as politicians adding earmarks in legislation or pharmaceutical salespersons giving away drugs to physicians constitute bribery? Identify three business activities that would constitute bribery and three actions that would not.
12. How could a strategist's attitude toward social responsibility affect a firm's strategy? On a 1 to 10 scale ranging from Nader's view to Friedman's view, what is your attitude toward social responsibility?
13. How do social policies on retirement differ in various countries around the world?
14. Firms should formulate and implement strategies from an environmental perspective. List eight ways firms can do this.
15. Discuss the major requirements of an EMS under ISO 14001.

Notes

1. Joann Greco, "Privacy—Whose Right Is It Anyhow?" *Journal of Business Strategy*, January–February 2001, 32.
2. Ashby Jones and JoAnn Lublin, "New Law Prompts Blowing Whistle," *Wall Street Journal*, November 1, 2010, B1.
3. Saul Gellerman, "Why 'Good' Managers Make Bad Ethical Choices," *Harvard Business Review* 64, no. 4 (July–August 1986): 88.
4. Peter Drucker, *Management: Tasks, Responsibilities, and Practices* (New York: Harper & Row, 1974), 462, 463.
5. www.wikipedia.org.
6. Phred Dvorak, Bob Davis, and Louise Radnofsky, "Firms Confront Boss-Subordinate Love Affairs," *Wall Street Journal*, October 27, 2008, B5.
7. Spencer Morgan, "The End of the Office Affair,"

Bloomberg Businessweek, September 20–26, 2010, 74.
8. Based on http://money.cnn.com/magazines/fortune/mostadmired/2011/best_worst/best4.html.
9. Archie Carroll and Frank Hoy, "Integrating Corporate Social Policy into Strategic Management," *Journal of Business Strategy* 4, no. 3 (Winter 1984): 57.
10. Antonie Boessenkool, "Activists Push More Firms on Social Responsibility," *Wall Street Journal*, January 31, 2007, B13; Kris Hudson, "Wal-Mart Wants Supplies, Workers to Join Green Effort," *Wall Street Journal*, February 2, 2007, A14; Jayne O'Donnell and Christine Dugas, "More Retailers Go for Green—The Eco Kind," *USA Today*, April 18, 2007, 3B.
11. Kerry Hannon, "Businesses' Green Opportunities Are Wide, But Complex," *USA Today*, January 2, 2009, 5B.

12. R. Alsop, "Corporations Still Put Profits First, But Social Concerns Gain Ground," *Wall Street Journal*, 2001, B14; Jane Kim, "Business Schools Take a Page from Kinder, Gentler Textbook," *Wall Street Journal*, October 22, 2003, B2C; Beth Gardner, "Business Schools Going Green," *Wall Street Journal*, June 6, 2007, B5A.

13. Forest Reinhardt, "Bringing the Environment Down to Earth," *Harvard Business Review*, July–August 1999, 149–158; Christine Rosen, "Environmental Strategy and Competitive Advantage," *California Management Review* 43, no. 3 (Spring 2001): 8–15; Chris Woodyard, "Cleaner Diesel Engine Rules Take Effect," *USA Today*, December 29, 2006, 1B.

14. Adapted from the www.iso14000.com website and the www.epa.gov website.

15. Jim Carlton, "Electric-Car Network Planned," *Wall Street Journal*, November 21, 2008, B2. Also, "BYD to Introduce China's First Electric Car," *Wall Street Journal*, December 15, 2008, B2. Rebecca Smith, "Hawaii Makes Big Bet on Electric Cars," *Wall Street Journal*, December 3, 2008, A2.

16. Tom Brook, "Declining Numbers Mute Many Birds' Songs," *USA Today*, September 11, 2001, 4A.

17. John Ogden, "Maintaining Diversity in the Oceans," *Environment*, April 2001, 29–36.

Current Readings

Arino, Africa, and Peter Smith Ring. "The Role of Fairness in Alliance Formation." *Strategic Management Journal* 31, no. 10 (October 2010): 1054–1087.

Delmas, Magali A., and Maria J. Montes-Sancho. "Voluntary Agreements to Improve Environmental Quality: Symbolic and Substantive Cooperation." *Strategic Management Journal* 31, no. 6 (June 2010): 575–601.

Esty, Daniel C. "The Sustainability Imperative." *Harvard Business Review*, May 2010, 42–73.

Flynn, Francis J., and Scott S.Wiltermuth. "Who's With Me? False Consensus, Brokerage, and Ethical Decision Making in Organizations." *Academy of Management Journal* 53, no. 5 (October 2010): 1074.

Gentile, Mary C. "Keeping Your Colleagues Honest." *Harvard Business Review*, March 2010, 114–120.

Gilley, K. Matthew, Christopher J. Robertson, and Tim C. Mazur. "The Bottom-Line Benefits of Ethics Code Commitment." *Business Horizons* 53, no. 1 (January–February 2010): 31.

Golicic, Susan L., Courtney N. Boerstler, and Lisa M. Ellram. "'Greening' the Transportation in Your Supply Chain." *MIT Sloan Management Review* 51, no. 2 (Winter 2010): 47–56.

Haanaaes, Knut, Martin Reeves, Balu Balagopal, David Arthur, Nina Kruschwitz, and Michael S. Hopkins. "First Look: The Second Annual Sustainability & Innovation Survey." *Sloan Management Review* (Winter 2011): 77–85.

Hopkins, Michael S. "Bad Banking. Good Ethics. Discuss." *MIT Sloan Management Review* 51, no. 2 (Winter 2010): 96–104.

Hopkins, Michael S. "How SAP Made the Business Case for Sustainability." *MIT Sloan Management Review* 52, no. 1 (Fall 2010): 69–74.

Hopkins, Michael S. "How Sustainability Fuels Design Innovation." *MIT Sloan Management Review* 52, no. 1 (Fall 2010): 75–83.

Hopkins, Michael S. "The Four-Point Supply Chain Checklist (or, How Sustainability Creates New Opportunity)." *MIT Sloan Management Review* 51, no. 4 (Summer 2010): 65–70.

Lev, Baruch, Christine Petrovits, and Suresh Radhakrishnan. "Is Doing Good for You? How Corporate Charitable Contributions Enhance Revenue Growth." *Strategic Management Journal* 31, no. 2 (February 2010): 182– 200.

Lubin, David A., and Daniel C. Esty. "The Sustainability Imperative." *Harvard Business Review*, May 2010, 42.

Lueneburger, Christoph, and Daniel Goleman. "The Change Leadership That Sustainability Demands." *MIT Sloan Management Review* 51, no. 4 (Summer 2010): 49–57.

McNutty, Eric J., and Rupert Davis. "Should the C-Suite Have a 'Green' Seat?" *Harvard Business Review*, December 2010, 133–137.

Mishina, Yuri, Bernadine J. Dykes, Emily S. Block, and Timothy G. Pollock. "Why 'Good' Firms Do Bad Things: The Effects of High Aspirations, High Expectations, and Prominence on the Incidence of Corporate Illegality." *The Academy of Management Journal* 53, no. 4 (August 2010): 701–722.

Surroca, Jordi, Josep A. Tribo, and Sandra Waddock. "Corporate Responsibility and Financial Performance: The Role of Intangible Resources." *Strategic Management Journal* 31, no. 5 (May 2010): 463–490.

Tenbrunsel, Ann. "Ethical Breakdowns." *Harvard Business Review*, April 2011, 58–67.

Unruh, Gregory, and Richard Ettenson. "Growing Green: Three Smart Paths to Developing Sustainable Products." *Harvard Business Review*, June 2010, 94–102.

Unruh, Gregory, and Richard Ettenson. "Winning in the Green Frenzy." *Harvard Business Review*, November 2010, 110–117.

ASSURANCE OF LEARNING EXERCISES

Assurance of Learning Exercise 10A

How Does My Municipality Compare to Others on Being Pollution-Safe?

Purpose

Sometimes it is difficult to know how safe a particular municipality or county is regarding industrial and agricultural pollutants. A website that provides consumers and businesses excellent information in this regard is http://scorecard.goodguide.com/. This type of information is often used in assessing where to locate new business operations.

Instructions

Go to http://scorecard.goodguide.com/. Put in your zipcode. Print off the information available for your city/county regarding pollutants. Prepare a comparative analysis of your municipality versus state and national norms on pollution issues. Does your locale receive an A, B, C, D, or F?

Assurance of Learning Exercise 10B

Evaluate Disney's Standards of Business Conduct

Purpose

Different companies have different standards of business conduct. One way to evaluate a firm's standards is to compare company documents to a leading rival firm. A major rival firm for Disney is CBS Corporation. Walt Disney has a 25 page Standards of Business Conduct document posted on their corporate website at http://corporate.disney.go.com/index.html. Rival firm CBS Corporation has a 25-page Business Conduct Statement posted at http://www.cbscorporation.com/. This exercise gives you practice comparing and evaluating standards of business conduct.

Instructions

Step 1   Go to the two websites just listed and print the Standards of Business Conduct information for (1) Disney and (2) CBS Corp. Read the two statements.

Step 2   On a separate sheet of paper, list three aspects that you like most and three aspects that you like least about (1) the Disney statement and (2) the CBS statement. In other words, compare the two statements. Conclude by indicating which statement of conduct you like best. Why do you think it is best?

Step 3   Explain why having a code of business ethics is not sufficient for ensuring ethical behavior in an organization. What other means are necessary to help ensure ethical behavior? Give the class an example of a breach of ethical conduct that you recall in your work experience.

Assurance of Learning Exercise 10C

Compare and Evaluate Sustainability Reports

Purpose

Sustainability Reports are increasingly becoming expected or even required by business organizations. This exercise will give you practice comparing and evaluating Sustainability Reports. Disney provides a Corporate Responsibility Report at http://corporate.disney.go.com/responsibility/environment.html. At rival CBS Corp., at http://www.cbscorporation.com/ourcompany.php?id=212, the company provides a document called The Green Report.

Instructions

Step 1   Go to the two respective company websites indicated above and print off the two documents cited. Compare and contrast the documents. List three aspects of each document that you like most and three aspects that you like least about each company's sustainability report. Which company's document do you like best? Why do you think it is best?

Step 2 Explain why having a Sustainability Report is not sufficient for ensuring excellent natural environment behavior. What other means besides the document itself are needed to assure ethical behavior in regard to preserving the natural environment?

Step 3 Prepare a two-page Executive Summary that provides an overview of the Disney document versus the CBS document as well as your assessment of the strengths and weaknesses of each document.

Assurance of Learning Exercise 10D

The Ethics of Spying on Competitors

Purpose
This exercise gives you an opportunity to discuss in class ethical and legal issues related to methods being used by many companies to spy on competing firms. Gathering and using information about competitors is an area of strategic management that Japanese firms do more proficiently than American firms.

Instructions
On a separate sheet of paper, number from 1 to 18. For the 18 spying activities listed as follows, indicate whether or not you believe the activity is ethical or unethical and legal or illegal. Place either an *E* for ethical or *U* for unethical, and either an *L* for legal or an *I* for illegal for each activity. Compare your answers to those of your classmates and discuss any differences.

1. Buying competitors' garbage
2. Dissecting competitors' products
3. Taking competitors' plant tours anonymously
4. Counting tractor-trailer trucks leaving competitors' loading bays
5. Studying aerial photographs of competitors' facilities
6. Analyzing competitors' labor contracts
7. Analyzing competitors' help-wanted ads
8. Quizzing customers and buyers about the sales of competitors' products
9. Infiltrating customers' and competitors' business operations
10. Quizzing suppliers about competitors' level of manufacturing
11. Using customers to buy out phony bids
12. Encouraging key customers to reveal competitive information
13. Quizzing competitors' former employees
14. Interviewing consultants who may have worked with competitors
15. Hiring key managers away from competitors
16. Conducting phony job interviews to get competitors' employees to reveal information
17. Sending engineers to trade meetings to quiz competitors' technical employees
18. Quizzing potential employees who worked for or with competitors

Assurance of Learning Exercise 10E

Who Prepares a Sustainability Report?

Purpose
The purpose of this activity is to determine the nature and prevalence of Sustainability Reports among companies in your state.

Instructions
Contact by phone at least five different plant managers or owners of large businesses in your area. Seek answers to the following questions. Present your findings in a written report to your instructor.

1. Does your company prepare a Sustainability Report? If yes, please describe the nature and scope of the report.
2. Are environmental criteria included in the performance evaluation of managers? If yes, please specify the criteria.
3. Are environmental affairs more a technical function or a management function in your company?
4. Does your firm offer any environmental workshops for employees? If yes, please describe them.

"NOTABLE QUOTES"

"Sad but true, U.S. businesspeople have the lowest foreign language proficiency of any major trading nation. U.S. business schools do not emphasize foreign languages, and students traditionally avoid them."
—*Ronald Dulek*

"America's economy has become much less American."

"In God we trust. All others bring data."
—*Edward Deming*

Global/International Issues

11

CHAPTER OBJECTIVES

After studying this chapter, you should be able to do the following:

1. Explain the advantages and disadvantages of entering global markets.

2. Discuss protectionism as it impacts the world economy.

3. Explain when and why a firm (or industry) may need to become more or less global in nature to compete.

4. Discuss the global challenge facing American firms.

5. Compare and contrast business culture in the United States with many other countries.

6. Describe how management style varies globally.

7. Discuss communication differences across countries.

8. Discuss Africa as the newest hotspot for business entry.

ASSURANCE OF LEARNING EXERCISES

Assurance of Learning Exercise 11A
Compare Business Cultures Across Countries

Assurance of Learning Exercise 11B
Staples Wants to Enter Africa. Help Them.

Assurance of Learning Exercise 11C
Does My University Recruit in Foreign Countries?

Assurance of Learning Exercise 11D
Assess Differences in Culture Across Countries

Assurance of Learning Exercise 11E
How Well Traveled Are Business Students at My University?

As illustrated in Figure 11-1, global considerations impact virtually all strategic decisions. The boundaries of countries no longer can define the limits of our imaginations. To see and appreciate the world from the perspective of others has become a matter of survival for businesses. The underpinnings of strategic management hinge on managers gaining an understanding of competitors, markets, prices, suppliers, distributors, governments, creditors, shareholders, and customers worldwide. The price and quality of a firm's products and services must be competitive on a worldwide basis, not just on a local basis. As indicated in the boxed insert, Amazon.com is an example global business that formulates and implements excellent strategies.

Among the 30 companies in the Dow Jones Industrial Average, the 10 that obtained the largest share of their sales abroad expected to see their revenues grow by an average of 8.3 percent in 2011.[1] By contrast, the 10 companies that do the least business outside the United States expect average revenue gains of just 1.6 percent. Shareholders expect substantial revenue growth, so doing business globally is one of the best ways to achieve this end.

Although exports of goods and services from the United States were valued at $1.6 trillion in 2009, that accounted for only 11 percent of U.S. gross domestic product. Therefore the United States is still largely a domestic, continental economy, and what happens inside the U.S. largely

Excellent Strategic Management Showcased

AMAZON.COM

Headquartered in Seattle, Washington, Amazon.com is the largest online retailer in the United States, with nearly three times the Internet sales revenue of the runner up, Staples, Inc. Amazon's 2010 revenues rose to $34.2 billion, up from $24.5 billion the prior year—an incredible 40 percent increase in revenues in one year. Amazon has no stores. Company profits increased to $1.1 billion in 2010. Amazon.com has formulated and is implementing one of the best global strategic plans in the world. Amazon has separate websites in Canada, the United Kingdom, Germany, France, Italy, Japan, and China.

Founded in 1994 by current CEO Jeff Bezos, Amazon started as an online bookstore but soon diversified, selling DVDs, CDs, mp3 downloads, computer software, video games, electronics, apparel, furniture, food, and toys. For 2010, Amazon ranked #5 in *Fortune*'s annual Most Admired Companies after ranking #2 the prior year. Amazon recently entered the movie streaming business. Success of the Kindle has won CEO Jeff Bezos tons of respect as Amazon now sells six Kindle e-books for every 10 printed books.

Amazon was recently named "the world's top brand" by the communications research firm Millward Brown. The report "Value-D: Balancing Desire and Price for Brand Success" found that 81 percent of consumers regard brand as an important reason to purchase, while only 7 percent of consumers make purchases based on price alone. "It's clear that Amazon is doing a great job balancing its brand perception with its pricing strategy," said Eileen Campbell, global CEO of Millward Brown. Other brands that made the top 10 list of most successful brands are, in order, Colgate, Nokia, Pampers, Visa, Coca-Cola, Microsoft, McDonald's, Nescafe, and Lidl. Just below the Amazon.com brand are the following top U.S. brands: Crest, Coca-Cola, Folgers, Bud Light, Wal-Mart, Microsoft, Colgate, Dell, and HP.

Amazon recently informed the California Board of Equalization that it would cut ties to its California affiliates if any of four bills looking to force Internet retailers to collect sales tax are passed. Amazon says if any bill is passed, the company would be "compelled to end its advertising relationships" with over 10,000 California-based participants in Amazon Associates, its affiliate program. Amazon has already dropped its affiliates in Colorado, North Carolina, and Rhode Island over similar tax bills. Whether to tax Internet sales is a hot topic for debate in America.

Amazon in 2011 joined the online movie and TV streaming market by offering its Amazon Prime users unlimited, commercial-free, instant streaming of 5,000 movies and TV shows. Amazon Prime includes free shipping and costs $79 a year. That new video streaming strategy puts Amazon in direct competition with Netflix. To become even more competitive with Netflix, Amazon may soon expand it's offerings by paying for more content, offer several current hit movies per month free, secure exclusive content that Netflix does not have, integrate with more available consumer electronic devices, and acquire the company Hulu. Amazon has already purchased Lovefilm.

Source: Based on company documents and http://smallbusiness.aol.com/2011/03/17/amazon-com-named-worlds-top-brand/?icid=maing%7Cmain5%7Cdl6%7Csec3_lnk1%7C50943.

FIGURE 11-1

A Comprehensive Strategic-Management Mode

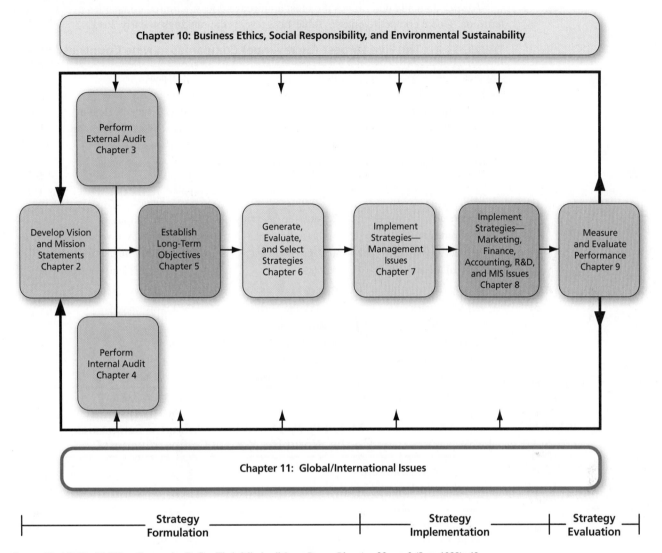

Source: Fred R. David, "How Companies Define Their Mission," *Long Range Planning* 22, no. 3 (June 1988): 40.

determines the strength of the economic recovery. In contrast, as a percent of GDP, exports comprise 35.3 percent of the German economy, 24.5 percent of the Chinese economy, and 156 percent of the Singapore economy. Singapore's number is so high because they import oil and other products and then re-export them globally. The point here is that the United States has substantial room for improvement in doing business globally based on the 11 percent exports to GDP number.

A world market has emerged from what previously was a multitude of distinct national markets, and the climate for international business today is more favorable than in years past. Mass communication and high technology have created similar patterns of consumption in diverse cultures worldwide. This means that many companies may find it difficult to survive by relying solely on domestic markets.

It is no exaggeration that in an industry that is, or is rapidly becoming global, the riskiest possible posture is to remain a domestic competitor. The domestic competitor will watch as more aggressive companies use this growth to capture economies of scale and learning. The domestic competitor will then be faced with an attack on domestic markets using different (and possibly superior) technology, product design, manufacturing, marketing approaches, and economies of scale.[2]

As a point of global reference, the five largest companies in nine different countries are listed in Table 11-1. The largest of all 45 companies listed is Wal-Mart Stores, headquartered in Bentonville, Arkansas, and employing 2.1 million people worldwide.

Fortune annually determines the most admired and least admired companies in the world in terms of "global competitiveness." Table 11-2 reveals the rankings in early 2011.

TABLE 11-1   The Five Largest (by revenue) Companies in Nine Countries (2011)

Britain	India	Japan
1. BP	1. Indian Oil	1. Toyota Motor
2. HSBC Holdings	2. Reliance Industries	2. Japan Post Holdings
3. Lloyds Banking Group	3. State Bank of India	3. Nippon TeleG & TeleP
4. Aviva	4. Bharat Petroleum	4. Hitachi
5. Royal Bank of Scotland	5. Hindustan Petroleum	5. Honda Motor
Australia	Brazil	China
1. BHP Billiton	1. Petrobras	1. Sinopec
2. Wesfarmers	2. Itausa-Investmentos	2. State Grid
3. Woolworths	3. Banco Bradesco	3. China National Petroleum
4. Commonwealth Bank	4. Banco do Brasil	4. China Mobile Communi.
5. National Australia Bank	5. Vale	5. Ind. & Com. Bank of China
USA	Canada	Germany
1. Wal-Mart Stores	1. Manulife Financial	1. Volkswagen
2. ExxonMobil	2. Royal Bank of Canada	2. Allianz
3. Chevron	3. Power Corp. of Canada	3. E.ON
4. General Electric	4. George Weston	4. Daimier
5. Bank of America	5. Sun Life Financial	5. Siemens

Source: Based on http://money.cnn.com/magazines/fortune/global500/2010/countries/US.html.

TABLE 11-2   *Fortune*'s Most and Least Admired Companies in the World for "Global Competitiveness"

MOST ADMIRED
1. McDonald's
2. Google
3. Nestlé
4. Nike
5. Yum Brands
6. Walt Disney
7. Colgate-Palmolive
8. IBM
9. Accenture
10. Manpower

LEAST ADMIRED
1. Asahi Breweries
2. Kirin Holdings
3. Winn-Dixie Stores
4. Hovnanian Enterprises
5. Carlsberg
6. Great Atlantic & Pacific Tea
7. Bob Evans Farms
8. Dongfeng Motor
9. D.R. Horton
10. Lennar

Source: http://money.cnn.com/magazines/fortune/mostadmired/2011/best_worst/best9.html.
Also, http://money.cnn.com/magazines/fortune/mostadmired/2011/best_worst/worst9.html.

Multinational Organizations

Organizations that conduct business operations across national borders are called *international firms* or *multinational corporations*. The strategic-management process is conceptually the same for multinational firms as for purely domestic firms; however, the process is more complex for international firms due to more variables and relationships. The social, cultural, demographic, environmental, political, governmental, legal, technological, and competitive opportunities and threats that face a multinational corporation are almost limitless, and the number and complexity of these factors increase dramatically with the number of products produced and the number of geographic areas served.

More time and effort are required to identify and evaluate external trends and events in multinational corporations than in domestic corporations. Geographic distance, cultural and national differences, and variations in business practices often make communication between domestic headquarters and overseas operations difficult. Strategy implementation can be more difficult because different cultures have different norms, values, and work ethics.

Multinational corporations (MNCs) face unique and diverse risks, such as expropriation of assets, currency losses through exchange rate fluctuations, unfavorable foreign court interpretations of contracts and agreements, social/political disturbances, import/export restrictions, tariffs, and trade barriers. Strategists in MNCs are often confronted with the need to be globally competitive and nationally responsive at the same time. With the rise in world commerce, government and regulatory bodies are more closely monitoring foreign business practices. The U.S. Foreign Corrupt Practices Act, for example, monitors business practices in many areas.

Before entering international markets, firms should scan relevant journals and patent reports, seek the advice of academic and research organizations, participate in international trade fairs, form partnerships, and conduct extensive research to broaden their contacts and diminish the risk of doing business in new markets. Firms can also offset some risks of doing business internationally by obtaining insurance from the U.S. government's Overseas Private Investment Corporation (OPIC).

Advantages and Disadvantages of International Operations

Firms have numerous reasons for formulating and implementing strategies that initiate, continue, or expand involvement in business operations across national borders. Perhaps the greatest advantage is that firms can gain new customers for their products and services, thus increasing revenues. Growth in revenues and profits is a common organizational objective and often an expectation of shareholders because it is a measure of organizational success.

Potential advantages to initiating, continuing, and/or expanding international operations are as follows:

1. Firms can gain new customers for their products.
2. Foreign operations can absorb excess capacity, reduce unit costs, and spread economic risks over a wider number of markets.
3. Foreign operations can allow firms to establish low-cost production facilities in locations close to raw materials and/or cheap labor.
4. Competitors in foreign markets may not exist, or competition may be less intense than in domestic markets.
5. Foreign operations may result in reduced tariffs, lower taxes, and favorable political treatment.
6. Joint ventures can enable firms to learn the technology, culture, and business practices of other people and to make contacts with potential customers, suppliers, creditors, and distributors in foreign countries.
7. Economies of scale can be achieved from operation in global rather than solely domestic markets. Larger-scale production and better efficiencies allow higher sales volumes and lower-price offerings.
8. A firm's power and prestige in domestic markets may be significantly enhanced if the firm competes globally. Enhanced prestige can translate into improved negotiating power among creditors, suppliers, distributors, and other important groups.

The availability, depth, and reliability of economic and marketing information in different countries vary extensively, as do industrial structures, business practices, and the number and nature of regional organizations. There are also numerous potential disadvantages of initiating, continuing, or expanding business across national borders, such as the following:

1. Foreign operations could be seized by nationalistic factions.
2. Firms confront different and often little-understood social, cultural, demographic, environmental, political, governmental, legal, technological, economic, and competitive forces when doing business internationally. These forces can make communication difficult in the firm.
3. Weaknesses of competitors in foreign lands are often overestimated, and strengths are often underestimated. Keeping informed about the number and nature of competitors is more difficult when doing business internationally.
4. Language, culture, and value systems differ among countries, which can create barriers to communication and problems managing people.
5. Gaining an understanding of regional organizations such as the European Economic Community, the Latin American Free Trade Area, the International Bank for Reconstruction and Development, and the International Finance Corporation is difficult but is often required in doing business internationally.
6. Dealing with two or more monetary systems can complicate international business operations.

The Global Challenge

Few companies can afford to ignore the presence of international competition. Firms that seem insulated and comfortable today may be vulnerable tomorrow; for example, foreign banks do not yet compete or operate in most of the United States, but this too is changing. China's largest commercial bank, Industrial & Commercial Bank of China Ltd., recently acquired an 80 percent stake in Bank of East Asia Ltd.'s U.S. subsidiary, putting the Chinese bank in position to become the first Beijing-controlled financial institution to operate retail banks in the United States.

America's economy is becoming much less American. A world economy and monetary system are emerging. Corporations in every corner of the globe are taking advantage of the opportunity to obtain customers globally. Markets are shifting rapidly and in many cases converging in tastes, trends, and prices. Innovative transport systems are accelerating the transfer of technology. Shifts in the nature and location of production systems, especially to China and India, are reducing the response time to changing market conditions. China has more than 1.3 billion residents and a dramatically growing middle class anxious to buy goods and services. Yum Brands, which owns KFC and Pizza Hut, reported in 2011 that its China division overtook the U.S. in profits generated. GM sales in China exceeded GM's U.S. sales for the first time ever in 2010. Wynn and Las Vegas Sands report their net revenue in China growing more than triple their U.S. properties. China is the fastest-growing market for pocket book maker Coach and the second-largest market for Dell.

Business in Brazil is booming, with that country having more than a 7 percent growth in GDP in 2011. The capital of Brazil, Rio de Janeiro, is making massive preparations for the 2016 Summer Olympics, including a $5 billion investment program to extend the subway system, improve railroads, and construct new highways. Two firms in Rio that are growing exponentially are Petrobras, the world's fourth-largest oil producer, and Vale, the world's largest iron-ore mining company. Rio de Janeiro is Brazil's second largest manufacturing center in the country, but its scenic beauty and elaborate port facilities are world renown.

More and more countries around the world are welcoming foreign investment and capital. As a result, labor markets have steadily become more international. East Asian countries are market leaders in labor-intensive industries, Brazil offers abundant natural resources and rapidly developing markets, and Germany offers skilled labor and technology. The drive to improve the efficiency of global business operations is leading to greater functional specialization. This is not limited to a search for the familiar low-cost labor in Latin America or Asia. Other considerations include the cost of energy, availability of resources, inflation rates, tax rates, and the nature of trade regulations.

Many countries became more protectionist during the recent global economic recession. *Protectionism* refers to countries imposing tariffs, taxes, and regulations on firms outside the country to favor their own companies and people. Most economists argue that protectionism harms the world economy because it inhibits trade among countries and invites retaliation.

Advancements in telecommunications are drawing countries, cultures, and organizations worldwide closer together. Foreign revenue as a percentage of total company revenues already exceeds 50 percent in hundreds of U.S. firms, including ExxonMobil, Gillette, Dow Chemical, Citicorp, Colgate-Palmolive, and Texaco.

A primary reason why most domestic firms do business globally is that growth in demand for goods and services outside the United States is considerably higher than inside. For example, the domestic food industry is growing just 3 percent per year, so Kraft Foods, the second largest food company in the world behind Nestlé, is focusing on foreign acquisitions.

Shareholders and investors expect sustained growth in revenues from firms; satisfactory growth for many firms can only be achieved by capitalizing on demand outside the United States. Joint ventures and partnerships between domestic and foreign firms are becoming the rule rather than the exception!

Fully 95 percent of the world's population lives outside the United States, and this group is growing 70 percent faster than the U.S. population. The lineup of competitors in virtually all industries is global. General Motors, Ford, and Chrysler compete with Toyota and Hyundai. General Electric and Westinghouse battle Siemens and Mitsubishi. Caterpillar and John Deere compete with Komatsu. Goodyear battles Michelin, Bridgestone/Firestone, and Pirelli. Boeing competes with Airbus. Only a few U.S. industries—such as furniture, printing, retailing, consumer packaged goods, and retail banking—are not yet greatly challenged by foreign competitors. But many products and components in these industries too are now manufactured in foreign countries. International operations can be as simple as exporting a product to a single foreign country or as complex as operating manufacturing, distribution, and marketing facilities in many countries.

Globalization

Globalization is a process of doing business worldwide, so strategic decisions are made based on global profitability of the firm rather than just domestic considerations. A global strategy seeks to meet the needs of customers worldwide, with the highest value at the lowest cost. This may mean locating production in countries with the lowest labor costs or abundant natural resources, locating research and complex engineering centers where skilled scientists and engineers can be found, and locating marketing activities close to the markets to be served.

A *global strategy* includes designing, producing, and marketing products with global needs in mind, instead of considering individual countries alone. A global strategy integrates actions against competitors into a worldwide plan. Today, there are global buyers and sellers and the instant transmission of money and information across continents.

It is clear that different industries become global for different reasons. The need to amortize massive R&D investments over many markets is a major reason why the aircraft manufacturing industry became global. Monitoring globalization in one's industry is an important strategic-management activity. Knowing how to use that information for one's competitive advantage is even more important. For example, firms may look around the world for the best technology and select one that has the most promise for the largest number of markets. When firms design a product, they design it to be marketable in as many countries as possible. When firms manufacture a product, they select the lowest-cost source, which may be Japan for semiconductors, Sri Lanka for textiles, Malaysia for simple electronics, and Europe for precision machinery.

Corporate Tax Rates Globally

Corporate tax rates vary considerably across countries and companies. Tax rates in countries are important in strategic decisions regarding where to build manufacturing facilities or retail stores or even where to acquire other firms. Japan recently cut its corporate tax rate by five percentage points, leaving the United States with the highest corporate tax rate among all nations in the world. Having the highest corporate tax rates is not a good position for the United States since it competes with other nations as a location for investment. High corporate tax rates deter investment in new factories and also provide strong incentives for corporations to avoid and evade taxes.

Since the 1980s, most countries have been steadily lowering their tax rates, but the United States has not cut its top statutory corporate tax rate since 1993. Top combined statutory rates among developed countries, excluding the United States, fell from an average of about 48 percent in the early 1980s to 25.5 percent in 2010. The main wave of reforms occurred in the mid- to late-1980s, but the average fell almost 9 percent from 2000 to 2010.

Even within countries there is significant variation in federal taxes paid. For example, General Electric paid almost no federal income taxes in the United States in 2010, thanks to various tax breaks and some innovative but legal accounting measures. GE paid nearly zero even though $5.1 billion of GE's total $14.2 billion in profits came from operations in the United States. Carnival, the world's largest cruise line company, is incorporated in Panama and paid an effective tax rate of 1.4 percent from 2005 through 2010. In comparison, the rate for Agilent Technologies was 10.7 percent over the same period, and it was 17.7 percent for Pfizer.

Forbes recently examined the 20 most profitable U.S. companies and found that the average 2010 income tax rate within the group was 25.4 percent.[3] America's three biggest oil companies, ExxonMobil, Chevron, and ConocoPhillips, all paid more than 40 percent—higher than the statutory U.S. rate of 35 percent. Exxon, with a 45 percent rate, paid $21.6 billion in worldwide income taxes for 2010. Wal-Mart Stores paid $7.1 billion (at a rate of 32.4 percent) in 2010 income taxes.

As indicated in Table 11-3, the top national statutory corporate tax rates in 2010 among sample countries ranged from 8.5 percent in Switzerland to 35 percent in the United States. Note the countries that have a flat tax, which often, upon adoption, triggers a surge in foreign direct investment.

TABLE 11-3 Corporate Tax Rates Across Countries in 2011 (from high to low)

Country	Statutory Corporate Income Tax Rate (%)
United States	35
France	34.43
Belgium	33
New Zealand	30
Spain	30
Australia	30
Mexico	30
Norway	28
United Kingdom	28
Italy	27.5
Finland	26
Netherlands	25.5
Portugal	25
Austria	25
Denmark	25
Greece	24
Ukraine	23 (flat tax)
Korea	22
Turkey	20
Czech Republic	19 (flat tax)
Hungary	19
Slovak Republic	19 (flat tax)
Poland	19
Canada	18
Chile	17
Russia	16 (flat tax)
Germany	15.83
Iceland	15
Ireland	12.5
Bulgaria	10 (flat tax)
Serbia	10 (flat tax)
Switzerland	8.5

Source: Varied sources on the Internet from a March 1, 2011 Google search for "Corporate Tax Rates Globally."

Other factors besides the corporate tax rate obviously affect companies' decisions of where to locate plants and facilities and whether to acquire other firms. For example, the large, affluent market and efficient infrastructure in both Germany and Britain attract companies, but the high labor costs and strict labor laws there keep other companies away. The rapidly growing GDP in Brazil and India attracts companies, but violence and political unrest in Middle East countries deter investment. The United States perhaps should lower its rate to reward companies that invest in jobs domestically. Lowering the U.S. corporate tax rate should also reduce unemployment and spur growth domestically.

United States versus Foreign Business Cultures

To compete successfully in world markets, U.S. managers must obtain a better knowledge of historical, cultural, and religious forces that motivate and drive people in other countries. In Japan, for example, business relations operate within the context of *Wa,* which stresses group harmony and social cohesion. In China, business behavior revolves around *guanxi,* or personal relations. In South Korea, activities involve concern for *inhwa,* or harmony based on respect of hierarchical relationships, including obedience to authority.[4]

In Europe, it is generally true that the farther north on the continent, the more participatory the management style. Most European workers are unionized and enjoy more frequent vacations and holidays than U.S. workers. A 90-minute lunch break plus 20-minute morning and afternoon breaks are common in European firms. Guaranteed permanent employment is typically a part of employment contracts in Europe. In socialist countries such as France, Belgium, and the United Kingdom, the only grounds for immediate dismissal from work is a criminal offense. A six-month trial period at the beginning of employment is usually part of the contract with a European firm. Many Europeans resent pay-for-performance, commission salaries, and objective measurement and reward systems. This is true especially of workers in southern Europe. Many Europeans also find the notion of team spirit difficult to grasp because the unionized environment has dichotomized worker–management relations throughout Europe.

A weakness of some U.S. firms in competing with Pacific Rim firms is a lack of understanding of Asian cultures, including how Asians think and behave. Spoken Chinese, for example, has more in common with spoken English than with spoken Japanese or Korean. U.S. managers consistently put more weight on being friendly and liked, whereas Asian and European managers often exercise authority without this concern. Americans tend to use first names instantly in business dealings with foreigners, but foreigners find this presumptuous. In Japan, for example, first names are used only among family members and intimate friends; even longtime business associates and coworkers shy away from the use of first names. Table 11-4 lists other cultural differences or pitfalls that U.S. managers need to know about.

TABLE 11-4 Cultural Pitfalls That May Help You Be a Better Manager

- Waving is a serious insult in Greece and Nigeria, particularly if the hand is near someone's face.
- Making a "good-bye" wave in Europe can mean "No," but it means "Come here" in Peru.
- In China, last names are written first.
- A man named Carlos Lopez-Garcia should be addressed as Mr. Lopez in Latin America but as Mr. Garcia in Brazil.
- Breakfast meetings are considered uncivilized in most foreign countries.
- Latin Americans are on average 20 minutes late to business appointments.
- Direct eye contact is impolite in Japan.
- Don't cross your legs in any Arab or many Asian countries—it's rude to show the sole of your shoe.
- In Brazil, touching your thumb and first finger—an American "Okay" sign—is the equivalent of raising your middle finger.
- Nodding or tossing your head back in southern Italy, Malta, Greece, and Tunisia means "No." In India, this body motion means "Yes."
- Snapping your fingers is vulgar in France and Belgium.
- Folding your arms across your chest is a sign of annoyance in Finland.
- In China, leave some food on your plate to show that your host was so generous that you couldn't finish.
- Do not eat with your left hand when dining with clients from Malaysia or India.
- One form of communication works the same worldwide. It's the smile—so take that along wherever you go.

U.S. managers have a low tolerance for silence, whereas Asian managers view extended periods of silence as important for organizing and evaluating one's thoughts. U.S. managers are much more action oriented than their counterparts around the world; they rush to appointments, conferences, and meetings—and then feel the day has been productive. But for many foreign managers, resting, listening, meditating, and thinking is considered productive. Sitting through a conference without talking is unproductive in the United States, but it is viewed as positive in Japan if one's silence helps preserve unity.

U.S. managers place greater emphasis on short-term results than foreign managers. In marketing, for example, Japanese managers strive to achieve "everlasting customers," whereas many Americans strive to make a onetime sale. Marketing managers in Japan see making a sale as the beginning, not the end, of the selling process. This is an important distinction. Japanese managers often criticize U.S. managers for worrying more about shareholders, whom they do not know, than employees, whom they do know. Americans refer to "hourly employees," whereas many Japanese companies still refer to "lifetime employees."

Rose Knotts recently summarized some important cultural differences between U.S. and foreign managers.[5] Awareness and consideration of these differences can enable a manager to be more effective, regardless of his/her own nationality.

1. Americans place an exceptionally high priority on time, viewing time as an asset. Many foreigners place more worth on relationships. This difference results in foreign managers often viewing U.S. managers as "more interested in business than people."
2. Personal touching and distance norms differ around the world. Americans generally stand about three feet from each other when carrying on business conversations, but Arabs and Africans stand about one foot apart. Touching another person with the left hand in business dealings is taboo in some countries.
3. Family roles and relationships vary in different countries. For example, males are valued more than females in some cultures, and peer pressure, work situations, and business interactions reinforce this phenomenon.
4. Business and daily life in some societies are governed by religious factors. Prayer times, holidays, daily events, and dietary restrictions, for example, need to be respected by managers not familiar with these practices in some countries.
5. Time spent with the family and the quality of relationships are more important in some cultures than the personal achievement and accomplishments espoused by the traditional U.S. manager.
6. Many cultures around the world value modesty, team spirit, collectivity, and patience much more than competitiveness and individualism, which are so important in the United States.
7. Punctuality is a valued personal trait when conducting business in the United States, but it is not revered in many of the world's societies. Eating habits also differ dramatically across cultures. For example, belching is acceptable in some countries as evidence of satisfaction with the food that has been prepared. Chinese culture considers it good manners to sample a portion of each food served.
8. To prevent social blunders when meeting with managers from other lands, one must learn and respect the rules of etiquette of others. Sitting on a toilet seat is viewed as unsanitary in most countries, but not in the United States. Leaving food or drink after dining is considered impolite in some countries, but not in China. Bowing instead of shaking hands is customary in many countries. Some cultures view Americans as unsanitary for locating toilet and bathing facilities in the same area, whereas Americans view people of some cultures as unsanitary for not taking a bath or shower every day.
9. Americans often do business with individuals they do not know, unlike businesspersons in many other cultures. In Mexico and Japan, for example, an amicable relationship is often mandatory before conducting business.

In many countries, effective managers are those who are best at negotiating with government bureaucrats rather than those who inspire workers. Many U.S. managers are uncomfortable with nepotism and bribery, which are practiced in some countries. The United States has gained a reputation for defending women from sexual harassment and minorities from discrimination, but not all countries embrace the same values.

American managers in China have to be careful about how they arrange office furniture because Chinese workers believe in *feng shui,* the practice of harnessing natural forces. U.S. managers in Japan have to be careful about *nemaswashio,* whereby Japanese workers expect supervisors to alert them privately of changes rather than informing them in a meeting. Japanese managers have little appreciation for versatility, expecting all managers to be the same. In Japan, "If a nail sticks out, you hit it into the wall," says Brad Lashbrook, an international consultant for Wilson Learning.

Probably the biggest obstacle to the effectiveness of U.S. managers—or managers from any country working in another—is the fact that it is almost impossible to change the attitude of a foreign workforce. "The system drives you; you cannot fight the system or culture," says Bill Parker, president of Phillips Petroleum in Norway.

Communication Differences Across Countries

Americans increasingly interact with managers in other countries, so it is important to under-stand foreign business cultures. Americans often come across as intrusive, manipulative, and garrulous; this impression may reduce their effectiveness in communication. *Forbes* provided the following cultural hints from Charis Intercultural Training:

1. Italians, Germans, and French generally do not soften up executives with praise before they criticize. Americans do soften up folks, and this practice seems manipulative to Europeans.
2. Israelis are accustomed to fast-paced meetings and have little patience for American informality and small talk.
3. British executives often complain that American executives chatter too much. Informality, egalitarianism, and spontaneity from Americans in business settings jolt many foreigners.
4. Europeans feel they are being treated like children when asked to wear name tags by Americans.
5. Executives in India are used to interrupting one another. Thus, when American executives listen without asking for clarification or posing questions, they are viewed by Indians as not paying attention.
6. When negotiating orally with Malaysian or Japanese executives, it is appropriate to allow periodically for a time of silence. However, no pause is needed when negotiating in Israel.
7. Refrain from asking foreign managers questions such as "How was your weekend?" That is intrusive to foreigners, who tend to regard their business and private lives as totally separate.[6]

Business Culture Across Countries

Mexico—Business Culture

Mexico is an authoritarian society in terms of schools, churches, businesses, and families. Employers seek workers who are agreeable, respectful, and obedient, rather than innovative, creative, and independent. Mexican workers tend to be activity oriented rather than problem solvers. When visitors walk into a Mexican business, they are impressed by the cordial, friendly atmosphere. This is almost always true because Mexicans desire harmony rather than conflict; desire for harmony is part of the social fabric in worker–manager relations. There is a much lower tolerance for adversarial relations or friction at work in Mexico as compared to the United States.

Mexican employers are paternalistic, providing workers with more than a paycheck, but in return they expect allegiance. Weekly food baskets, free meals, free bus service, and free day care are often part of compensation. The ideal working condition for a Mexican worker is the family model, with people all working together, doing their share, according to their designated roles. Mexican workers do not expect or desire a work environment in which self-expression and initiative are encouraged. Whereas U.S. business embodies individualism, achievement, compe-tition, curiosity, pragmatism, informality, spontaneity, and doing more than expected on the job, Mexican businesses stress collectivism, continuity, cooperation, belongingness, formality, and doing exactly what you're told.

In Mexico, business associates rarely entertain each other at their homes, which are places reserved exclusively for close friends and family. Business meetings and entertaining are nearly always done at a restaurant. Preserving one's honor, saving face, and looking important are also exceptionally important in Mexico. This is why Mexicans do not accept criticism and change easily; many find it humiliating to acknowledge having made a mistake. A meeting among employees and managers in a business located in Mexico is a forum for giving orders and directions rather than for discussing problems or participating in decision making. Mexican workers want to be closely supervised, cared for, and corrected in a civil manner. Opinions expressed by employees are often regarded as back talk in Mexico. Mexican supervisors are viewed as weak if they explain the rationale for their orders to workers.

Mexicans do not feel compelled to follow rules that are not associated with a particular person in authority they work for or know well. Thus, signs to wear earplugs or safety glasses, or attendance or seniority policies, and even one-way street signs are often ignored. Whereas Americans follow the rules, Mexicans often do not.

Life is slower in Mexico than in the United States. The first priority is often assigned to the last request, rather than to the first. Telephone systems break down. Banks may suddenly not have pesos. Phone repair can take a month. Electricity for an entire plant or town can be down for hours or even days. Business and government offices may open and close at odd hours. Buses and taxis may be hours off schedule. Meeting times for appointments are not rigid. Tardiness is common everywhere. Effectively doing business in Mexico requires knowledge of the Mexican way of life, culture, beliefs, and customs.

In Mexico, when greeting others, it is customary for women to pat each other on the right forearm or shoulder, rather than shaking hands. Men shake hands or, if close friends, use the traditional hug and back slapping upon greeting. If visiting a Mexican home, bring a gift such as flowers or sweets. Avoid marigolds, as they symbolize death. Arrive up to 30 minutes late, but definitely not early. Avoid red flowers which have a negative connotation. White flowers are an excellent choice. If you receive a gift, open it immediately and react enthusiastically. At dinner, do not sit until you are invited to and wait to be told where to sit. This is true in most foreign countries and in the United States. Do not begin eating until the hostess starts. Only men give toasts in Mexico. It is also polite to leave some food on your plate after a meal. For business appointments, as opposed to home visits, it is best to arrive on time, although your Mexican counterparts may be up to 30 minutes late. Do not get irritated at their lack of punctuality.

Mexicans often judge or stereotype a person by who introduces them and changing that first impression is very difficult in business. Expect to answer questions about your personal background, family, and life interests—because Mexicans consider trustworthiness and character to be of upmost importance. Mexicans are very status conscious, so business titles and rank are important. Face-to-face meetings are preferred over telephone calls, letters, or e-mail. Negotiations in Mexico include a fair amount of haggling, so do not give your best offer first.

Japan—Business Culture

The Japanese place great importance on group loyalty and consensus, a concept called *Wa*. Nearly all corporate activities in Japan encourage *Wa* among managers and employees. *Wa* requires that all members of a group agree and cooperate; this results in constant discussion and compromise. Japanese managers evaluate the potential attractiveness of alternative business decisions in terms of the long-term effect on the group's *Wa*. This is why silence, used for pondering alternatives, can be a plus in a formal Japanese meeting. Discussions potentially disruptive to *Wa* are generally conducted in very informal settings, such as at a bar, so as to minimize harm to the group's *Wa*. Entertaining is an important business activity in Japan because it strengthens *Wa*. Formal meetings are often conducted in informal settings. When confronted with disturbing questions or opinions, Japanese managers tend to remain silent, whereas Americans tend to respond directly, defending themselves through explanation and argument.

Americans have more freedom to control their own fates than do the Japanese. Life in the United States and life in Japan are very different; the United States offers more upward mobility to its people. This is a great strength of the United States, as indicated here:

America is not like Japan and can never be. America's strength is the opposite: It opens its doors and brings the world's disorder in. It tolerates social change that would tear most other societies apart. This openness encourages Americans to adapt as individuals rather than as a group. Americans go west to California to get a new start; they move east to Manhattan to try to make the big time; they move to Vermont or to a farm to get close to the soil. They break away from their parents' religions or values or class; they rediscover their ethnicity. They go to night school; they change their names.[7]

Most Japanese managers are reserved, quiet, distant, introspective, and other oriented, whereas most U.S. managers are talkative, insensitive, impulsive, direct, and individual oriented. Americans often perceive Japanese managers as wasting time and carrying on pointless conversations, whereas U.S. managers often use blunt criticism, ask prying questions, and make quick decisions. These kinds of cultural differences have disrupted many potentially productive Japanese–American business endeavors. Viewing the Japanese communication style as a prototype for all Asian cultures is a stereotype that must be avoided.

In Japan, a person's age and status are of paramount importance, whether in the family unit, the extended family, or a social or business situation. Schoolchildren learn early that the oldest person in the group is to be honored. Older folks are served first and their drinks are poured for them. Greetings in Japan are very formal and ritualized. Wait to be introduced because it may be viewed as impolite to introduce yourself, even in a large gathering. Foreigners may shake hands, but the traditional form of greeting is to bow. The deeper you bow, the more respect you show, but at least bow the head slightly in greetings.

In gift giving in Japan, chocolates or small cakes are excellent choices, but do not give lilies, camellias, lotus blossoms, or white flowers because they all are associated with funerals. Do not give potted plants as they encourage sickness, although a bonsai tree is always acceptable. Give items in odd numbers, but avoid the number 9. Gifts are not opened when received. If going to a Japanese home, remove your shoes before entering and put on the slippers left at the doorway. Leave your shoes pointing away from the doorway you are about to walk through. If going to the toilet in a Japanese home, put on the toilet slippers and remove them when you exit.

In Japan, when you finally are seated for dinner, never point your chopsticks. Learn how to use chopsticks before you visit Japan and do not pierce your food with chopsticks. Japanese oftentimes slurp their noodles and soup, but mixing other food with rice is inappropriate. Instead of mixing, eat a bit of rice and then a bit of food. To signify that you do not want more rice or drink, leave some in your bowl or glass. Conversation over dinner is generally subdued in Japan, because they prefer to savor their food.

Unlike Americans, Japanese prefer to do business on the basis of personal relationships rather than impersonally speaking over the phone or by written correspondence. Therefore, build and maintain relationships by sending greeting, thank you, birthday, and seasonal cards. You need to be a good "correspondent" to effectively do business with the Japanese. Punctuality is very important so arrive on time for meetings and be mindful that it may take several meetings to establish a good relationship. The Japanese are looking for a long-term relationship. Always give a small gift as a token of your appreciation, and present it to the most senior person at the end of any meeting.

Like many Asian and African cultures, the Japanese are nonconfrontational. They have a difficult time saying 'no,' so you must be vigilant at observing their nonverbal communication. Rarely refuse a request, no matter how difficult or nonprofitable it may appear at the time. In communicating with Japanese, phrase questions so that they can answer yes. For example, do you disagree with this? Group decision making and consensus are vitally important. The Japanese often remain silent in meetings for long periods of time and may even close their eyes when they want to listen intently.

Business cards are exchanged in Japan constantly and with excitement. Invest in quality business cards and keep them in pristine condition. Do not write on them. Have one side of your card translated in Japanese and give it to the person with the Japanese side facing the recipient. Business cards are generally given and received with two hands and a slight bow. Examine any business card you receive very carefully.

Brazil—Business Culture

In both Brazil and America, men greet each other by shaking hands while maintaining steady eye contact. Women greet each other with kisses in Brazil, starting with the left and alternating cheeks. Hugging and backslapping are also common greetings among Brazilian close friends. If a woman wishes to shake hands with a man, she should extend her hand first. Brazilians speak Portuguese. If going to someone's house in Brazil, bring the hostess flowers or a small gift. Orchids are nice, but avoid purple or black, as these are mourning colors. Arrive at least 30 minutes late if your invitation is for dinner and arrive up to an hour late for a party or large gathering. Never arrive early. Brazilians dress with a flair and judge others on their appearance, so even casual dress is more formal than in many other countries. Always err on the side of over-dressing in Brazil rather than under-dressing.

Avoid embarrassing a Brazilian by criticizing an individual publically. That causes that person to lose face with all others at a business meeting, and the person making the criticism also loses face, as they have disobeyed the unwritten Brazilian rule. It is considered acceptable, however, to interrupt someone who is speaking. Face-to-face, oral communication is preferred over written communication. As for business agreements, Brazilians insist on drawing up detailed legal contracts. They are more comfortable doing business with and negotiating with people than companies. Therefore, wait for your Brazilian colleagues to raise the business subject. Never rush the prebusiness relationship-building time. Brazilians take their time when negotiating. Use local lawyers and accountants for negotiations, because Brazilians resent an outside legal presence.

Appointments are commonly cancelled or changed at the last minute in Brazil, so do not be surprised or get upset. In the cities of Sao Paulo and Brasilia, arrive on time for meetings, but in Rio de Janeiro arrive a few minutes late for a meeting. Do not appear impatient if you are kept waiting, because relationship building always takes precedence over adhering to a strict schedule. Brazilians pride themselves on dressing well, so men should wear conservative, dark-colored business suits or even three-piece suits for executives. Women should wear suits or dresses that are elegant and feminine with good, quality accessories. And ladies, manicures are expected.

Germany—Business Culture

Business communication in Germany is very formal, so the home is a welcome, informal place. Germans take great pride in their home, which is generally neat and tidy inside and out. Only close friends and relatives are invited into the sanctity of a person's house, so consider that an honor if you get that invitation, and bring a gift, such as chocolates or yellow roses or tea roses—but not red roses, which symbolize romantic intentions. Also do not bring carnations, lilies, or chrysanthemums, which in Germany symbolize mourning. If you bring wine to a German's home, it should be imported, French or Italian. Always arrive on time but never early, and always send a handwritten note the following day to thank your hostess for her hospitality.

When it's time to have dinner, remain standing until invited to sit down. As is custom in many countries, you may be shown to a particular seat. Table manners in Germany are strictly Continental with the fork being held in the left hand and the knife in the right while eating. Do not begin eating until the hostess starts or someone says "guten appetit" (good appetite). Wait for the hostess to place her napkin in her lap before doing so yourself and do not rest your elbows on the table. Cut as much of your food with your fork as possible, since this compliments the cook by indicating the food is tender. Break bread or rolls apart by hand, but if a loaf is in the middle for all, then touch only what you extract to eat. This sanitary practice is a must in all countries including the United States. Finish everything on your plate and indicate you have finished eating by laying your knife and fork parallel across the right side of your plate, with the fork over the knife.

Germans are like Americans in that they do not need a personal relationship to do business. They are more interested in a businessperson's academic credentials and their company's credentials. A quick, firm handshake is the traditional greeting, even with children. At the office, Germans do not have an open-door policy and often work with their office door closed, so knock and wait to be invited to enter. Appointments are mandatory and should be made one to two weeks in advance. Germans are often very direct to the point of bluntness. Punctuality is extremely important in Germany, so if you are going to be delayed, telephone immediately and offer an explanation. It is very rude to cancel a meeting at the last minute and this could jeopardize your whole business relationship. German meetings adhere to strict agendas, including starting and ending times. Germans maintain direct eye contact while speaking.

There is a strict protocol to follow in Germany when entering a room—the eldest or highest-ranking person enters first and men enter before women if their age and status are roughly equivalent. Germans are detail oriented and want to understand every innuendo before coming to an agreement. Business decision making is autocratic and held at the top of the company. Final decisions will not be changed and are expected to be implemented by lower-level managers and employees with no questions asked. Americans are more flexible in many respects than Germans.

Egypt—Business Culture

In Egypt, greetings are based on both social class and religion, so follow the lead of others. Handshakes, although limp and prolonged, are the customary greeting among Egyptians of the same sex. Handshakes are always given with a hearty smile and direct eye contact. Once a relationship has developed, it is common to greet with a kiss on one cheek and then the other, while shaking hands, men with men and women with women. In greetings between men and women, the woman will extend her hand first. Otherwise, a man should bow his head in greeting.

If you are invited to an Egyptian's home, remove your shoes before entering, just as you would do in China and Japan. As a gift, bring chocolates, sweets, or pastries to the hostess. Do not give flowers, which are usually reserved for weddings or the ill, unless you know that the host will appreciate them. Always give gifts with the right hand or both hands if the gift is heavy. Gifts are not opened when received. Never sit at a dinner table until the host or hostess tells you where to sit. Eat with the right hand only and compliment the host by taking second helpings. Always show appreciation for the meal. Putting salt or pepper on your food is considered an insult to a cook. This is true to a lesser extent even in the United States. Leave a small amount of food on your plate when you have finished eating. Otherwise your Egyptian host may keep bringing you more food.

Egyptians prefer to do business with those they know and respect, so expect to spend time cultivating a personal relationship before business is conducted. Who you know is more important than what you know in Egypt, so network and cultivate a number of contracts. You should expect to be offered coffee or tea whenever you meet someone in Egypt, as this demonstrates hospitality. Even if you do not want the drink, always accept the beverage because declining the offer is viewed as rejecting the person.

In Egypt, appearance is important, so wear, conservative clothes and present yourself well at all times. For Egyptians, direct eye contact is a sign of honesty, so be prepared for overly intense stares. Hierarchy and rank are very important. Unlike in Germany, Egyptian business people do have an open-door policy, even when they are in a meeting, so you may experience frequent interruptions as others wander into the room and start a different discussion. It is best that you not try to bring the topic back to the original discussion until the new person leaves. Business meetings generally start after prolonged inquiries about health, family, etc.

Egyptians must know and like you to conduct business. Personal relationships are necessary for long-term business. The highest-ranking person makes decisions, after obtaining group consensus. Decisions are reached after great deliberation. In Egypt, business moves at a slow pace and society is extremely bureaucratic—even in the post-Hosin Mubarak era. Egyptians respect age and experience and engage in a fair amount of haggling. They are tough negotiators and do not like confrontation or having to say "no." Egyptian women must be careful to cover themselves appropriately. Skirts and dresses should cover the knee and sleeves should cover most of the arm. Women are daily gaining more rights, however, throughout the Middle East, and that is a good thing. In late 2011, women in Saudi Arabia were finally granted the right to vote, but women still are not allowed to drive cars in that country.

China—Business Culture

In China, greetings are formal and the oldest person is always greeted first. Like in the United States, handshakes are the most common form of greeting. Many Chinese will look toward the ground when greeting someone. The Chinese have an excellent sense of humor. They can easily laugh at themselves if they have a comfortable relationship with the other person. In terms of gifts, a food basket makes an excellent gift, but do not give scissors, knives, or other cutting utensils, as these objects indicate severing of the relationship. Never give clocks, handkerchiefs, flowers, or straw sandals, as they are associated with funerals. Do not wrap gifts in white, blue, or black paper. In China, the number 4 is unlucky, so do not give four of anything. Eight is the luckiest number, so giving eight of something is a great idea.

If invited to a Chinese person's home, consider this a great honor and arrive on time. Remove your shoes before entering the house and bring a small gift to the hostess. Eat heartily to demonstrate that you are enjoying the food. Use chopsticks and wait to be told where to sit. You should try everything that is offered and never eat the last piece from the serving tray. Hold the rice bowl close to your mouth while eating. Do not be offended if a Chinese person makes slurping or belching sounds; it merely indicates that they are enjoying their food.

The Chinese rarely do business with companies or people they do not know. Your position on an organizational chart is extremely important in business relationships. Gender bias is generally not an issue. Meals and social events are not the place for business discussions. There is a demarcation between business and socializing in China, so try to be careful not to intertwine the two.

Like in the United States and Germany, punctuality is very important in China. Arriving late to a meeting is an insult and could negatively affect your relationship. Meetings require patience because mobile phones ring frequently and conversations tend to be boisterous. Never ask the Chinese to turn off their mobile phones as this causes you both to lose face. The Chinese are nonconfrontational and virtually never overtly say "no." Rather, they will say "they will think about it" or "they will see." The Chinese are shrewd negotiators, so your initial offer or price should leave room for negotiation.

India—Business Culture

According to UN statistics, India's rate of female participation in the labor force is 34.2 percent, which is quite low, especially since women make up 42 percent of college graduates in India. But Indian women with a college degree are expected to let their careers take a back seat to caring for their husband, children, and elderly parents. "The measures of daughterly guilt are much higher in Indian women than in other countries," says Sylvia Ann Hewlett, president of the Center for Work-Life Policy, a Manhattan think tank, who headed a recent study on the challenges Indian women face in the workplace.[7] Sylvia says, "Since taking care of elderly parents usually becomes a reality later in a woman's career, it takes them out of the workplace just when they should be entering top management roles." That is why gender disparities at Indian companies unfortunately grow more pronounced at higher levels of management.

Like in many Asian cultures, people in India do not like to say "no," verbally or nonverbally. Rather than disappoint you, they often will say something is not available, or will offer you the response that they think you want to hear, or will be vague with you. This behavior should not be considered dishonest. Shaking hands is common in India, especially in the large cities among the more educated who are accustomed to dealing with westerners. Men may shake hands with other men and women may shake hands with other women; however, there are seldom handshakes between men and women because of religious beliefs.

Indians believe that giving gifts eases the transition into the next life. Gifts of cash are common, but do not give frangipani or white flowers as they represent mourning. Yellow, green, and red are lucky colors, so use them to wrap gifts. Since Hindus consider cows to be sacred, do not give gifts made of leather to Hindus. Muslims should not be given gifts made of pigskin or alcoholic products. Gifts are usually not opened when received.

Before entering an Indian's house, take off your shoes just as you would in China or Japan. Politely turn down the host's first offer of tea, coffee, or snacks. You will be asked again and again. Saying no to the first invitation is part of the protocol. Be mindful that neither Hindus nor Sikhs eat beef, and many are vegetarians. Muslims do not eat pork or drink alcohol. Lamb, chicken, and fish are the most commonly served main courses. Table manners are somewhat formal, but much Indian food is eaten with the fingers. Like most places in the world, wait to be told where and when to sit at dinner. Women in India typically serve the men and eat later. You may be asked to wash your hands before and after sitting down to a meal. Always use your right hand to eat, whether using utensils or your fingers. Leave a small amount of food on your plate to indicate that you are satisfied. Finishing all your food means that you are still hungry, which as true in Egypt, China, Mexico, and many countries.

Indians prefer to do business with those with whom they have established a relationship built upon mutual trust and respect. Punctuality is important. Indians generally do not trust the legal system, and someone's word is often sufficient to reach an agreement. Do not disagree publicly with anyone in India.

Titles such as professor, doctor, or engineer are very important in India, as is a person's age, university degree, caste, and profession. Use the right hand to give and receive business cards. Business cards need not be translated into Hindi but always present your business card so the recipient may read the card as it is handed to them. This is a nice, expected gesture in most countries around the world.

Nigeria—Business Culture

With the largest population of any country in Africa and located on the west coast bordering the Gulf of Guinea, Nigeria is a democratic country with English as its official language. With a growing economy, Nigeria's constitution guarantees religious freedom. Christians in Nigeria live mostly in the south, whereas Muslims live mostly in the north. Native religions in which people believe in deities, spirits, and ancestor worship are spread throughout Nigeria, as are different languages. Christmas and Easter are national holidays. Muslims observe Ramadan, the Islamic month of fasting, and the two Eids. Working hours in the north often vary from the south, primarily because Muslims do not work on their holy day—Friday.

Endowed with vast quantities of natural resources and being the sixth largest oil-producing nation on the planet, Nigeria has a well-educated and industrious people who are proud of their country. Nigerians are fond of the expression, "When Nigeria sneezes, the rest of Africa catches a cold (except South Africa)." Nigeria re-elected its president in April 2011, a zoology professor-turned-president, Goodluck Jonathan.

In Nigeria, extended families are still the backbone of social and business systems. Grandparents, cousins, aunts, uncles, sisters, brothers, and in-laws all work as a unit through life. Hierarchy and seniority within extended families are very important; the oldest person in a group is revered and honored, and is greeted and served first. In return, however, the most senior person has the responsibility to make good decisions for the extended family.

The most common greeting in Nigeria is a handshake with a warm, welcoming smile. Muslims will not generally shake hands with members of the opposite sex. Nigerians do not use first names readily, so wait to be invited to do this before engaging. Gift giving is common and even expected, but gifts from a man to a woman must be said to come from the man's mother, wife, sister, or other female relative, never from the man himself. Never rush a greeting because that is extremely rude; rather, spend time inquiring about the other person's general well-being. Foreigners who take the time to get to know a Nigerian as a person are often welcomed into the Nigerian's inner circle of family and close friends. Nigerians are generally outgoing and friendly, especially in the southwest, where the Yoruba often use humor even during business meetings and serious discussions.

To combat the AIDS epidemic in sub-Saharan Africa, the World Bank is now paying young girls cash to stop accepting gifts and cash from older men in exchange for sex. This "sugar daddy" relationship is common in many African countries and is fueling the AIDS problem, since the percent of men aged 30–34 that test positive for HIV is upward of 30 percent in countries such as Zimbabwe. The World Bank has a billboard in the Mbare vegetable market in Harare, Zimbabwe, that reads, "Your future is brighter without a sugar daddy."

Business Climate Across Countries/Continents[9]

The business climate for various countries is conveniently summarized at http://globaledge.msu.edu/countries/. This site provides comparative information for 183 countries in terms of per capita GDP, inflation rate, ease-of-doing-business ranking, and population, as well as narrative that describes the business situation in those countries. Business information about a select few countries is presented in this chapter.

African Countries

By 2020, McKinsey & Co. predicts that consumer spending in Africa will double to nearly $1.8 trillion, up from about $860 million in 2008—which will be equivalent to adding a consumer market the size of Brazil.[10] The expected growth has many firms globally acquiring firms in Africa, such as India's No. 2 tire maker, Apollo Tyres, recently buying South Africa's Dunlop Tyres for $62 million. Apollo plans to triple sales to $6 billion by 2015, with 60 percent of that revenue coming from outside India. Nearly 100 firms in India acquired firms in Africa between 2005 and 2011.

The McKinsey Global Institute reports that approximately 40 percent of Africans now live in urban areas and the number of households with discretionary income should increase 50 percent by the end of this decade.[11] Graham Allan, CEO of Yum Restaurants International, recently said, "A lot of companies, especially Chinese ones, have invested in Africa; we share the general view that Africa over the next 10 to 20 years will have massive potential." McKinsey & Co. says the number of consumers who can spend beyond bare necessities is greater now in Africa than India. From 2000 to 2009, foreign direct investment in Africa increased 600 percent to $58.56 billion.

Wal-Mart recently acquired South African retailer Massmart Holdings for $4.6 billion, providing the company with 290 stores in 13 African countries: Ghana, Nigeria, Zambia, Botswana, Namibia, South Africa, Lesotho, Mozambique, Zimbabwe, Mauritius, Malawi, Tanzania, and Uganda. The Wal-Mart acquisition paves the way for many firms now viewing Africa as a deal-making destination. For example, HSBC Holdings is trying to acquire a majority stake in Nedbank Group, South Africa's fourth-largest bank, and Nippon Telegraph and Telephone in Japan is buying Africa's largest technology company, Dimension Data. Huge purchases such as these have been a wake-up call to the rest of the world, which now views Africa as a growing, attractive new market.

Table 11-5 provides a summary of the economic situation in 12 African countries. Note that Angola is rated lowest in terms of doing business, whereas South Africa is rated highest. Recent regime changes in Egypt, Tunisia, Libya, and Algeria may spur further investment in Africa as democracy and capitalism strengthens. Many multinational companies are now gaining first mover advantages by engaging Africa at all levels. For example, Nokia and Coca-Cola have distribution networks in nearly every African country. Unilever has a presence in 20 of Africa's 50 countries. Nestlé is in 19 African countries, Barclays is in 12, Societe Generale is in 15, and Standard Chartered Bank is in 14. Africa has about 10 percent of the world's oil reserves, 40 percent of its gold ore, and 85 percent of the world's deposits of chromium and plantinum. Africa's population is young, growing, and moving into jobs in the cities. Forty percent of Africans today live in the cities, a proportion close to China and India. The general stereotype of Africa is rapidly changing from subsistence farmers avoiding lions, to millions of cell-phone carrying consumers in cities purchasing products.

TABLE 11-5 Sampling of African Countries—Ease-of-Doing-Business Rankings

	GDP per Capita ($)	Inflation Rate (%)	Population in Millions	Ease of Doing Business Among all Countries	Capital City
South Africa	10,116	07.2	49	34 out of 183	Pretoria
Tunisia	7,956	03.7	11	55 out of 183	Tunis
Ghana	1,463	19.6	24	67 out of 183	Accra
Egypt	5,425	10.1	79	94 out of 183	Cairo
Kenya	1,551	20.5	39	98 out of 183	Nairobi
Ethiopia	869	11.0	86	104 out of 183	Addis Ababa
Morocco	4,263	02.0	32	114 out of 183	Rabat
Uganda	1,166	12.6	33	122 out of 183	Kampala
Mozambique	838	03.5	22	126 out of 183	Maputo
Nigeria	2,099	11.5	150	137 out of 183	Abuja
Sudan	2,155	12.3	41	154 out of 183	Khartoum
Angola	5,820	13.1	13	163 out of 183	Luanda

Source: Based on information at http://globaledge.msu.edu/countries and other sources. Obtained March 1, 2011.

Africa has the world's largest deposits of platinum, chrome, and diamonds—and many Chinese companies in particular are investing there. Africa's largest food retailer, Shoprite Holdings, has more than 1,000 stores in 17 countries. Shoprite is a potential acquisition target being considered by European retailers Carrefour and Tesco. Diageo PLC sells Guinness beer, Smirnoff vodka, Baileys liqueur, and Johnnie Walker whiskey in more than 40 countries across Africa. Nestlé SA now has more than 25 factories in Africa.

From 2011 to 2014, Yum Brands is doubling the number of Kentucky Fried Chicken outlets in Africa to 1,200 and aims to double its revenue from the continent to $2 billion. "Africa wasn't even on our radar screen 10 years ago, but now we see it exploding with opportunity" says David Novak, Yum's chairman and CEO. Yum Brands is excited about Africa's growing middle class, vast population, and improving political stability of most African governments. Yum Brands is especially targeting Nigeria, Namibia, Mozambique, Ghana, Zambia, and South Africa. The company says it wants to reach more of Africa's one billion people than its current customer base of 180 million. But KFC currently has about 45 percent of South Africa's fast-food market, followed by Nando's with 6 percent and McDonald's with 5 percent.

Ghana recently became Africa's newest oil producing nation when the 1.5-billion-barrel Jubilee field began pumping oil. Although Ghana's estimated four billion barrels of reserves are about a third those of Nigeria, Ghana has a stable political and economic situation. Ethiopia is also doing very well economically. SABMiller PLC recently invested $20 million in a manufacturing plant in Ethiopia's large city, Ambo. That factory today produces 40,000 glass bottles of mineral water per hour. Ambo sells for about $6 a bottle in New York restaurants. Ambo water is part of the SABMiller portfolio that includes 45 African beers.[12]

Nairobi, Kenya, is the center of several major telecom companies trying to gain market share in the rapidly growing African cellphone business. Vodafone Safaricom Ltd. dominates the Kenyan telecommunications sector with 77 percent market share, but India's Bharti Airtel Ltd. boosted its market share in the last year to almost 20 percent. There are currently over 440 million mobile subscribers in Africa generating over $15 billion in telecom revenue annually. All of Africa is coming online, representing huge opportunities for countless companies. McKinsey & Co. estimates that within five years another 220 million Africans that today can meet only basic needs will join the middle class as consumers.[13] There are over 950 million people who live in Africa.

China

Although the United States is the world's largest economy with a gross domestic product (GDP) of about $14.62 trillion annually, China recently passed Japan to become the world's second-largest economy with a GDP of about $5.75 trillion annually, compared to Japan's $5.4 trillion. China, however, is still an emerging economy, as indicated by a per-capita GDP of $4,000, compared to the United States and Japan per-capita GDPs of $47,000 and $42,000 respectively. China's economic (GDP) growth of over 9 percent annually for several decades is, however, much faster than either the United States or Japan. Premier Wen Jiabao recently proclaimed that China's annual GDP growth will be held to 7.0 percent if possible to constrain inflation. Goldman Sachs predicts that China will overtake the United States as the world's largest economy by 2027.

China's rapid growth has created substantial pollution, extensive inequality, and deeply embedded corruption. In fact, China's communist government is concerned that political unrest in the Middle East may spread to China in a "Jasmine Revolution," as the masses in China barely make enough to survive. The World Bank estimates that more than 100 million Chinese citizens, nearly the size of Japan's entire population, live on less than $2 a day—but China's middle class is growing rapidly.

For many decades, low wage rates in China helped keep world prices low on hundreds of products—but that is changing, because all 31 Chinese provinces and regions recently boosted their minimum wage for the second consecutive year. Analysts expect demand for workers in China to outstrip supply by 2014, and this is contributing to rapidly rising wage rates and worldwide inflation. Commercial and industrial development in China's west has turned interior cities such as Chongqing into production centers that compete for labor with coastal factories. According to Credit Suisse in Hong Kong, pay to migrant laborers who fuel China's export industry rose 40 percent in 2010 and 30 percent in 2011, and similar increases are expected in 2012. Average monthly pay in 2009 in Shenzhen on the southern China coast was $235, compared to Seoul's $1,220, Taipei's $888, Ho Chi Minh City's $100, Jakarta's $148, and $47 in Dhaka, Bangladesh.[14]

China has become the biggest trading partner for Australia, Japan, Korea, India, Russia, and South Africa and has replaced the United States as the top export market for Brazil. The world's two fastest-growing major economies, China and India, recently announced that the two countries will more than double their bilateral trade between 2010 and 2015 to $100 billion.[15] China is opening its large consumer markets more to Indian goods. China may soon support India having a permanent seat on the United Nations Security Council. China has long opposed a permanent seat for India. The increased cooperation between China and India is good news for companies worldwide doing business in that part of Asia.

As indicated in Table 11-6, China ranks 79th out of 183 countries in terms of doing business, for a variety of reasons ranging from human rights issues to substantial disregard for copyright/patent/trademark rules of law. Best Buy and Home Depot are example companies that are closing stores in China. Both firms have not competed well in China due to being too "high priced" compared to home-grown, similar businesses. The Chinese are very price conscious.

China is gaining a stronger and stronger foothold into Japanese businesses. The five largest recent Chinese investments in Japan are Mitsubishi UFJ Financial (92 billion yen), Canon (74.5 billion yen), Sumitomo Mitsui (57.9 billion yen), Nippon T&T (49.2 billion yen), Mitsubishi (47.8 billion yen), Takeda Pharm (45.4 billion yen), and Sony (41.6 billion yen). The Japanese investment adviser Chibagin Asset Management says China state funds have recently more than doubled their investment in Japan to 1.62 trillion yen in 90 companies.

Note also in Table 11-6 that Singapore is rated the best country on the planet for doing business.

Philippines

A highly educated, English speaking country, the Philippines overtook India in early 2011 in call-center jobs, employing 350,000 compared with India's 330,000.[16] Call centers in the Philippines produced $7.4 billion in revenue in 2011, and that figure is growing about 15 percent annually. The Philippines recently also overtook Indonesia as the world's biggest supplier of voice-based call-center services.[17] Citigroup and Chase are just two companies outsourcing

TABLE 11-6 Sampling of Asian Countries—Ease-of-Doing-Business Rankings

	GDP per Capita ($)	Inflation Rate (%)	Population in Millions	Ease of Doing Business Among all Countries	Capital City
Singapore	49,321	00.2	5	1 out of 183	Singapore
South Korea	27,658	02.8	49	16 out of 183	Seoul
Japan	34,129	- 1.3	127	18 out of 183	Tokyo
Thailand	8,086	- 0.9	66	19 out of 183	Bangkok
Malaysia	14,215	00.5	26	21 out of 183	Kuala Lumpur
Taiwan	-	- 0.9	23	33 out of 183	Taipei
China	5,971	01.0	1,500	79 out of 183	Beijing
Pakistan	2,538	14.2	175	83 out of 183	Islamabad
Indonesia	3,994	05.0	241	121 out of 183	Jakarta
Russia	15,923	11.9	140	123 out of 183	Moscow
India	2,946	10.7	1,160	134 out of 183	New Delhi
Philippines	3,513	03.2	98	148 out of 183	Manila

Source: Based on information at http://globaledge.msu.edu/countries and other sources. Obtained March 1, 2011.

customer calls, back-office work, and other operations to the Philippines. A major reason why the Philippines is an attractive place for call centers is the country's overall business culture to "deliver absolutely fantastic service." An associate professor at the City University of Hong Kong, Jane Lockwood, says "Filipinos go out of their way, not just in call centers, but in tourism and events management, to ensure people are well looked after."[18]

As indicated in Table 11-6, the Philippines has about 98 million people, making the country the world's 12th largest in population. Located in Southeast Asia, the Philippines was a founding member of the United Nations and is very active in that organization. Filipinos love Americans who rescued them in WWII. Thousands of Filipinos today work all-night shifts to accommodate the normal 8 am-to-5 pm business time zone in the United States. Philippines president Benigno Aquino recently indicated that services outsourced to the Philippines from around the world will generate up to $100 billion in 2020, representing 20 percent of the global offshoring market share.

Unemployment is at 6.9 percent in the Philippines, but under-employment—defined as people who work only part-time or with minimal incomes—is 18 percent. The average per capita income of Filipinos is about $1,790 a year, so hundreds of thousands of Filipinos work outside the country. In fact, the Philippines' economy depends greatly on outside workers sending monies back to the country and also traveling to and from the country.

The television advertising market in the Philippines is nearly $4 billion annually, larger than India's and on par with Indonesia's.[19] Television is the most enjoyed media among the Philippines 7,100 island people, whereas newspapers are the most important media outlet in India. Television ads comprise 75 percent of advertising spending in the Philippines.

Among major emerging economies, the Philippines has only a 9 percent Internet penetration rate among its population, which is very low compared to China (28.9%), Nigeria (28.4%), Mexico (28.3%), and Russia (29.0%). But the Philippines' 9 percent rate is above the Internet penetration rate among Indonesia's population (8.7%) and India's population (5.1%).[20] These percentages reveal the percentage of the country's people that could shop online.

Taiwan

Located off the southeast coast of mainland China, Taiwan has a dynamic, capitalist, export-driven economy with gradually decreasing state involvement in investment and foreign trade. Many large, government-owned banks and industrial firms are being privatized in Taiwan. Real annual growth in GDP has averaged about 8 percent during the past three decades. Exports have provided the primary impetus for industrialization. The trade surplus is substantial, and foreign reserves are the world's fifth largest. As indicated in Table 11-6, Taiwan is rated 33rd among all countries in the world for doing business.

Taiwan's total trade in 2010 reached an all-time high of $526 billion, according to Taiwan's Ministry of Finance. Both exports and imports for the year reached record levels, totaling U.S. $274 billion and $251 billion, respectively. Agriculture constitutes only 2 percent of Taiwan's GDP, down from 35 percent in 1952. Some brands from Taiwan that are leaders globally include: Acer, HTC, ASUS, TrendMicro, MasterKong, Want-Want, Maxxis, Giant, Synnex, Transcend, Uni-President, Advantech, D-Link, ZyXel, Merida, Johnson, Gigabyte, CyberLink, Genius, and Depo.

India

President Obama recently said "India's progress in just two decades is one of the most stunning achievements in human history." India grew its GDP 8 percent in 2009–2010 and is on track for GDP growth of 8.6 percent in 2010–2011. With a medium age of 25, India has perhaps the youngest population among all large countries on the planet. About one third the geographic size of the United States, India's 1.21 billion people live in the world's largest democracy.

Note in Table 11-6 that India is rated 134 out of 183 in attractiveness for doing business, partly because that country still requires foreign firms to form a joint venture with an Indian firm in order to do business. Also note in Table 11-6 India's high inflation and low per capita GDP. India has been slow to allow 3G wireless, which allows for high-speed Internet access on cellphones. As the rest of Asia rolled out 4G in 2010/2011, India rolled out 3G in January 2011—and the signal quality is not that good, definitely not good enough to stream a movie.

4G will not become available in India until 2012. Japan and South Korea got 3G back in 2005, and China got 3G in 2009. Also, India's bureaucracy slows down all business. Telecom authorities for example are divided into several dozen areas and this creates problems. Still only one percent of India's population has access to broadband connections. G.V. Giri, an analyst in Mumbai with IIFL Securities, says, "People in India have been starved for high-speed Internet connections. The number of people in India with broadband access will however grow from 10 million in early 2011 to 100 million by 2014."

Various economic reports predict that by 2015, India will outpace China's annual GDP growth rate of 8.5–9.5 percent. Various trends in India lead to this conclusion, including a young, increasingly educated labor force, relatively few retired people to care for, a high savings rate, massive structural reforms the government continues to undertake, and increased infrastructure spending. The United Nations estimates that India's age dependency ratio (the number of working age people supporting children and the elderly) will decrease substantially, from 55.6 percent in 2010 to 47.2 percent in 2025; the lower the number the better. China, by contrast, has already reaped the benefit of a large working age population, which will soon begin to age and decline: its dependency ratio will rise from 39.1 percent in 2010 to 45.8 percent in 2025. The Indian government is slowly improving the country's education system, but an enormous amount of work remains. Only 74 percent of Indian men and 48 percent of Indian women are literate, compared to 96 percent of men and 88 percent of women in China. India's "knowledge economy" employs only about 2.23 million people out of 750 million available.

Prime Minister Manmohan Singh's government has instituted education reforms, so the number of Indian children out of school has dropped greatly from 18 million in 2000. Dropout ratios in primary schools have improved as well. However, at present only 12 percent of India's citizens enter higher education, and the government hopes to increase this to 21 percent by 2017. The Indian Institutes of Technology—a group of universities focused on engineering and technology—are world renowned but offer only a miniscule 7,000 places to students each year. There is elaborate red tape required to establish and operate any business in India. Also, India's tax code is archaic and many new sectors are not even open to foreign direct investment.

India's 2011 census revealed that the country will surpass China as the most populated country in 2030. The new census revealed that India's highest density growth and population is in the northwest and east-central areas of the country. India has a literacy rate now of 74 percent, up from 65 percent a decade ago.

Germany

Germany's economy in 2010 grew at 3.6 percent, the highest rate in more than two decades, as the country's cars, machinery, and other products were in high demand in Asia, especially China. As Europe's debt crisis has pushed the euro lower, German goods are more competitive abroad. The economic and fiscal crises in Greece, Ireland, Portugal, and Spain have only limited direct impact on Germany's $3.24 trillion economy. There is a growing north-south divide in Europe, with the north doing much better economically than the south. Germany's budget deficit was 3.5 percent in 2010, the first time in years that the country has exceeded the 3 percent limit set by EU budget rules, but that percent is well below the deficit in the U.S., UK, and Japan—so overall the German economy is very healthy. Note in Table 11-7 that Germany ranks 22nd out of 183 countries in ease of doing business.

German automobile producers such as Daimler AG, BMW AG, and Volkswagen AG have fallen behind rivals such as GM, Renault SA, and Nissan Motor in mass-producing electric cars. The German companies are playing catch up in this key area of industrial growth, partly because the German government has committed just $688 million in state support for electric battery research and infrastructure projects, such as car-charging stations. That amount is only a small fraction of the U.S. (and Chinese) government support for electric cars. Since one out of seven German jobs is connected to the country's car markers and domestic suppliers, this issue is very important. More than 15 percent of German exports stem from the automobile industry. Germany also fallen way behind in electric car lithium-ion battery development and production.

TABLE 11-7 Sampling of European Countries—Ease-of-Doing-Business Rankings

	GDP per Capita ($)	Inflation Rate (%)	Population in Millions	Ease of Doing Business Among All Countries	Capital City
United Kingdom	35,468	2.10	62	4 out of 183	London
Sweden	36,961	-0.50	9	14 out of 183	Stockholm
Germany	35,374	0.00	83	22 out of 183	Berlin
France	33,058	0.10	64	26 out of 183	Paris
Czech Republic	24,643	1.10	11	63 out of 183	Prague
Turkey	13,417	6.50	77	65 out of 183	Ankara
Italy	31,283	0.60	59	80 out of 183	Rome
Ukraine	7,277	12.30	46	145 out of 183	Kyiv

Source: Based on information at http://globaledge.msu.edu/countries and other sources. Obtained March 1, 2011.

The European Union is a single economic bloc with free movement of people, goods, and services among its 27 nations, but in matters such as taxes and labor costs, each country sets its own rules. Businesses entering Europe for the first time need to carefully research the various countries. Belgium, for example, has the highest labor costs in Europe with 53 percent of workers there being unionized, but that percent is only the fifth highest in Europe. In terms of employer-paid social security costs as a percentage of total labor costs, Belgium is at 30.8 percent, followed by France at 28.4 percent, Spain at 25.0 percent, Germany at 22.9 percent, and the Netherlands at 21 percent. A nonmember, the United Kingdom, is at 17.1 percent.

Germany has one of Europe's fastest aging and shrinking populations. Germany now faces shortages of skilled labor and aggressive recruiting from abroad for the country's top engineering and scientific talent.[21] More people emigrate from Germany than re-locate to Germany, especially highly educated professionals—partly because Germany has a restrictive labor code and inward-looking hiring practices. Germany might need to follow the lead of Italy, which has the same, albeit more severe, problem but has enacted excellent new laws and incentives to both keep and attract young, highly educated professionals.

Mexico

More and more companies such as Electrolux and Whirlpool have recently reduced their capital expenditures in Mexico because of spiraling drug-related violence. Electrolux AB recently chose Memphis, Tennessee, over locations in Mexico for its new $190 million appliance factor that will employ 1,200. Fights between rival drug cartels have claimed more than 31,000 lives in the past four years, including more than 11,000 in 2010.[22] Other crimes such as robbery, extortion, and kidnapping are climbing. Terex Corp. of Westport Connecticut recently said, "We won't put a factory in Mexico until some of this violence gets addressed. We just can't put our people at risk."

Based in Perrysburg, Ohio, Owens-Illinois Inc. recently said, "The escalating violence in Mexico has led us to be more cautious. We take the safety and security of our employees very seriously." Whirlpool recently chose Cleveland, Tennessee, over Mexico to build its new oven and cooktop factor that employs more than 1,600. J.P. Morgan's chief economist for Mexico, Gabriel Casillas, says drug-related violence in Mexico probably cost the country some $4 billion in foreign direct investment in 2010. Mexico's troubled interior states of Durango, Sinaloa, and Michoacan, as well as the border regions, have seen a drop in foreign investment to roughly $1.9 billion in 2010 from an average of about $5 billion in prior years. The drug-related death toll in Mexico climbed to 15,273 in 2010, the highest casualty rate in years. The most violent city in Mexico is Ciudad Juarez.

As indicated in Table 11-8, Mexico has fallen to 35th out of 183 countries in terms of doing business. Note Mexico's population is about 112 million people, more than three times Canada's population.

TABLE 11-8 **Sampling of North and South American Countries—Ease-of-Doing-Business Rankings**

	GDP per Capita ($)	Inflation Rate (%)	Population in Millions	Ease of Doing Business Among all Countries	Capital City
United States	46,350	00.7	308	5 out of 183	Washington, DC
Canada	39,078	00.2	34	7 out of 183	Ottawa
Mexico	14,570	03.6	112	35 out of 183	Mexico City
Argentina	14,313	07.7	41	115 out of 183	Buenos Aires
Brazil	10,304	04.2	199	127 out of 183	Brasilia
Chile	14,436	01.7	17	43 out of 183	Santiago
Ecuador	8,014	04.3	15	130 out of 183	Quito
Bolivia	4,277	04.3	10	149 out of 183	La Paz
Peru	8,509	01.2	30	36 out of 183	Lima
Venezuela	12,818	27.3	27	172 out of 183	Caracus

Source: Based on information at http://globaledge.msu.edu/countries and other sources. Obtained March 1, 2011.

Special Note to Students

Even the smallest businesses today regularly serve customers globally and gain competitive advantages and economies of scale doing so. Many iconic American businesses, such as Tupperware, obtain more than 80 percent of their revenue from outside the United States. Therefore, in performing a strategic management case analysis, you must evaluate the scope, magnitude, and nature of what your company is doing globally compared to rival firms. Then, determine what your company should be doing to garner global business. Continuously throughout your presentation or written report, compare your firm to rivals in terms of global business and make recommendations based on careful analysis. Be "prescriptive and insightful" rather than "descriptive and mundane" with every slide presented to pave the way for your specific recommendations with costs regarding global reach of your firm.

Conclusion

The population of the world surpassed 7 billion persons in 2011. Just as they did for centuries before Columbus reached America, businesses will search for new opportunities beyond their national boundaries for centuries to come. There has never been a more internationalized and economically competitive society than today's model. Some U.S. industries, such as automobiles, textiles, steel, and consumer electronics, are in complete disarray as a result of the international challenge.

Success in business increasingly depends on offering products and services that are competitive on a world basis, not just on a local basis. If the price and quality of a firm's products and services are not competitive with those available elsewhere in the world, the firm may soon face extinction. Global markets have become a reality in all but the most remote areas of the world. Certainly throughout the United States, even in small towns, firms feel the pressure of world competitors.

This chapter has provided some basic global information that can be essential to consider in developing a strategic plan for any organization. The advantages of engaging in international business may well offset the drawbacks for most firms. It is important in strategic planning to be effective, and the nature of global operations may be the key component in a plan's overall effectiveness.

Key Terms and Concepts

Feng Shui (p. 339)
Global Strategy (p. 335)
Globalization (p. 335)
Guanxi (p. 337)
International Firms (p. 333)

Inhwa (p. 337)
Multinational Corporations (p. 333)
Nemaswashio (p. 339)
Protectionism (p. 334)
Wa (p. 337)

Issues for Review and Discussion

1. Exports from the United States comprise about 11 percent of GDP, compared to about 35 percent of Germany's GDP. What are implications of this for American firms doing business globally?
2. Make a good argument for keeping the statutory corporate tax rate in the United States the highest in the world. Make the counter argument.
4. A company is planning to begin operations in Switzerland. That company's EFEM Matrix includes 20 factors. How much weight (1.0 to 0.01) would you place on the corporate tax rate factor? Discuss.
3. To what extent would/should a country's growth in GDP equate to a firm's expected growth in revenues from doing business in that country? Discuss.
4. Explain how awareness of business culture across countries can enhance strategy implementation.
5. Describe the business culture in Brazil.
6. Describe the business culture in Germany.
7. Describe the business culture in Egypt.
8. Describe the business culture in China.
9. Describe the business culture in India.
10. List in prioritized order the top four countries in Africa that are safe, worthwhile, and potentially lucrative for opening new business operations. Give a rationale for each.
11. What are several especially attractive aspects of the Philippines for beginning business operations in that country? What are some drawbacks?
12. Do some research on Singapore to determine whether you agree that the country merits its #1 ranking globally in attractiveness for doing business.
13. To what extent do you feel political unrest in the Middle East will spread outside the region? Would that be a good or bad thing for global business? What countries do you feel may experience political unrest? Why?
14. About 53 percent of people in Belgium are members of a labor union. Compare and contrast the labor union situation across European countries and comment on the positive or negative impact this factor has on attracting business investment into those countries.
15. Explain why consumption patterns are becoming similar worldwide. What are the strategic implications of this trend?
16. What are the advantages and disadvantages of beginning export operations in a foreign country?
17. What are the major differences between U.S. and multinational operations that affect strategic management?
18. Why is globalization of industries a common factor today?
19. Compare and contrast U.S. versus foreign cultures in terms of doing business.
20. List six reasons that strategic management is more complex in a multinational firm.
21. Do you feel that protectionism is good or bad for the world economy? Why?
22. Why are some industries more "global" than others? Discuss.
23. *Wa, guanxi,* and *inhwa* are important management terms in Japan, China, and South Korea, respectively. What would be analogous terms to describe American management practices?
24. Why do many Europeans find the notion of "team spirit" in a work environment difficult to grasp?
25. In China, *feng shui* is important in business, whereas in Japan, *nemaswashio* is important. What are analogous American terms and practices?
26. Describe the business culture in Mexico.
27. Describe the business culture in Japan.
28. Compare tax rates in the United States versus other countries. What impact could these differences have on "keeping jobs at home"?
29. Discuss requirements for doing business in India.

Notes

1. Justin Lahart, "Divided by Two-Track Economy," *Wall Street Journal*, September 8, 2010, B1.
2. Frederick Gluck, "Global Competition in the 1990s," *Journal of Business Strategy* (Spring 1983): 22–24.
3. http://finance.yahoo.com/taxes/article/112560/what-top-companies-pay-taxes-forbes.
4. Jon Alston, "Wa, Guanxi, and Inhwa: Managerial Principles in Japan, China and Korea," *Business Horizons* 32, no. 2 (March–April 1989): 26.
5. Rose Knotts, "Cross-Cultural Management: Transformations and Adaptations," *Business Horizons*, January–February 1989, 29–33.
6. Lalita Khosla, "You Say Tomato," *Forbes*, May 21, 2001, 36.
7. Mehul Srivastava, "Keeping Women on the Job in India," *Bloomberg Businessweek*, March 7–13, 2011, 11–12.
8. Stratford Sherman, "How to Beat the Japanese," *Fortune*, April 10, 1989, 145.
9. Based on information at http://www.kwintessential.co.uk/resources/country-profiles.html.
10. Mehul Srivastava and Subramaniam Sharma, "Corporate India Finds Greener Pastures—in Africa," *Bloomberg Businessweek*, November 8–14, 2010, 61–62. Also, McKinsey has excellent information for developing strategies to engage Africa at the website www.mckinsey.com/mgi. Also, there is an excellent *Harvard Business Review* article on engaging Africa (May 2011, pp. 117–122).
11. Julie Jargon, "KFC Savors Potential in Africa," *Wall Street Journal*, December 8, 2010, B1. Peter Wonacott, "A Continent of New Consumers Beckons," *Wall Street Journal*, January 13, 2011, B1.

12. Peter Wonacott, "SABMiller Taps Ethiopia's Holy Water," *Wall Street Journal*, January 13, 2011, B1.

13. Sarah Childress, "Telecom Giants Battle for Kenya," *Wall Street Journal*, January14, 2011, B1.

14. Sophie Leung and Simon Kennedy with Cotton Timberlake and Chris Burritt, "Global Inflation Starts With Chinese Workers," *Bloomberg Businessweek*, March 7–13, 2011, 9–10.

15. Arpan Mukherjee and Abhrajit Gangopadhyay, "India, China Aim to Double Trade," *Wall Street Journal*, December 17, 2010, A15.

16. Michelle Yun and Kathy Chu, "Philippines May Answer Call," *USA Today*, January 10. 2011, 1–2B.

17. Ibid.

18. James Hookway, "Dollar's Fall Rocks Far-Flung Families," *Wall Street Journal*, February 25, 2011, A12.

19. James Hookway, "High Drama for Philippine TV," *Wall Street Journal*, March 3, 2011, B10.

20. Amol Sharma, "Dot-Coms Begin to Blossom in India," *Wall Street Journal*, April 12, 2011, B1.

21. Vanessa Fuhrmans, "Exodus of Skilled Labor Saps Germany," *Wall Street Journal*, March 11, 2011, A12.

22. Nicholas Casey and James Gagerty, "Violence Limits Mexico's Allure," *Wall Street Journal*, December 17, 2010, B1. Jose de Cordora and David Luhnow, "In Mexico, Death Toll in Drug War Hits Record,' *Wall Street Journal*, January 13, 2010, A8.

Current Readings

Abdelal, Rawi. "The Promise and Peril of Russia's Resurgent State." *Harvard Business Review*, January–February 2010, 125–130.

Becht, Bart. "Building a Company Without Borders." *Harvard Business Review*, April 2010, 103–109.

Bozionelos, Nikos, and Ioannis Nikolaou. "What Accounts for Job Satisfaction Differences Across Countries?" *The Academy of Management Perspectives* 24, no. 1 (February 2010): 82–83.

Cappelli, Peter, Harbir Singh, Jitendra V. Singh, and Michael Useem. "Leadership Lessons from India." *Harvard Business Review*, March 2010, 90–98.

Cappelli, Peter, Harbir Singh, Jitendra Singh, and Michael Useem. "The India Way: Lessons for the U.S." *The Academy of Management Perspectives* 24, no. 2 (May 2010): 6–24.

Chan, Christine M., Shige Makino, and Takehiko Isobe. "Does Subnational Region Matter? Foreign Affiliate Performance in the United States and China." *Strategic Management Journal* 31, no. 11 (November 2010): 1226–1243.

Chironga, Mutsa, Acha Leke, Susan Lund, and Arend van Wamelen. "Cracking the Next Growth Market: Africa," *Harvard Business Review*, May 2011, 117–122.

D'Andrea, Guillermo, David Marcotte, and Gwen Dixon Morrison. "Let Emerging Market Customers Be Your Teachers." *Harvard Business Review*, December 2010, 115–122.

Guler, Isin, and Mauro F. Guillèn. "Home Country Networks and Foreign Expansion: Evidence from the Venture Capital Industry." *The Academy of Management Journal* 53, no. 2 (April 2010): 390.

Henisz, Witold J., and Bennet A. Zelner. "The Hidden Risks in Emerging Markets." *Harvard Business Review*, April 2010, 88–95.

Hermelo, Francisco Diaz, and Roberto Vassolo. "Institutional Development and Hypercompetition in Emerging Economies." *Strategic Management Journal* 31, no. 13 (December 2010): 1457–1473.

Hewlett, Sylvia Ann, and Ripa Rashid. "The Battle for Female Talent in Emerging Markets." *Harvard Business Review*, May 2010, 101–107.

Hout, Thomas M., and Pankaj Ghemawat. "China vs the World: Whose Technology Is It?" *Harvard Business Review*, December 2010, 94–103.

Huang, Yasheng. "Debating China's Economic Growth: The Beijing Consensus or The Washington Consensus?" *The Academy of Management Perspectives* 24, no. 2 (May 2010): 31–47.

Javidan, Mansour, Mary Teagarden, and David Bowen. "Making It Overseas." *Harvard Business Review*, April 2010, 109–114.

Martin, John A., and Kevin J. Davis. "Stacked Deck: Can Governance Structures Explain CEO Compensation Differences Across Countries?" *The Academy of Management Perspectives* 24, no. 1 (February 2010): 78.

Morrison, Allen, and Cyril Bouquet. "Are You Giving Globalization the Right Amount of Attention?" *MIT Sloan Management Review* 52, no. 2 (Winter 2011): 15–16.

Numagami, Tsuyoshi, Masaru Karube, and Toshihiko Kato. "Organizational Deadweight: Learning From Japan." *The Academy of Management Perspectives* 24, no. 4 (November 2010): 25–37.

Spencer, Jennifer, and Carolina Gomez. "MNEs and Corruption: The Impact of National Institutions and Subsidiary Strategy." *Strategic Management Journal* 32, no. 3 (March 2011): 280–300.

Tharenou, Phyllis, and Natasha Caulfield. "Will I Stay or Will I Go? Explaining Repatriation by Self-Initiated Expatriates." *Academy of Management Journal* 53, no. 5 (October 2010): 1009–1028.

Tse, Edward. "Is It Too Late to Enter China?" *Harvard Business Review*, April 2010, 96–102.

Xia, Jun. "Mutual Dependence, Partner Substitutability, and Repeated Partnership: The Survival of Cross-Border Alliances." *Strategic Management Journal* 32, no. 3 (March 2011): 229–253.

ASSURANCE OF LEARNING EXERCISES

Assurance of Learning Exercise 11A

Compare Business Cultures Across Countries

Purpose

Walt Disney does business in over 100 countries. Various websites give excellent detail that compare and contrast business culture across countries. One excellent website is http://www.kwintessential. co.uk/resources/country-profiles.html, where you can click on more than 100 countries and obtain a synopsis of a country's business culture. (Note: The culture part of this chapter is partly based on information at this website.) After clicking on a country at that website, you may scroll down to reach the section titled "Business Etiquette and Protocol." This exercise gives you experience gaining information about business culture in virtually any country. Being knowledgeable of various countries' business culture can make you a more effective manager or communicator with people or organizations in that country. This information is especially critical to firms such as Walt Disney that do business globally.

Step 1   Go to the website named above. Click on any two countries located on different continents. Scroll down to the "Business Etiquette and Protocol" section of each country. Print this material.

Step 2   Come to class prepared to give an oral presentation that compares the business culture in the two countries you selected.

Assurance of Learning Exercise 11B

Staples Wants to Enter Africa. Help Them.

Purpose

Staples, Inc. is the largest office supply company in the world. Staples has found ways to survive and actually thrive in the face of online competitors such as Amazon, Wal-Mart, and Costco that also sell a wide array of office supplies. Staples' retail, online, and mail order delivery presence gives it a competitive edge and now, having just increased its dividend payout, Staples wants Africa.

    More and more companies every day decide to begin doing business in Africa. Research is necessary to determine the best strategy for being the first mover in many African countries (i.e., being the first competitor doing business in various countries).

Instructions

Step 1   Print off a map of Africa.
Step 2   Print off demographic data on 10 African countries.
Step 3   Gather competitive information regarding the presence of office-supply firms doing business in Africa.
Step 4   List in prioritized order eight countries in which you would recommend Staples to build stores. Country 1 is your best, and country 2 is your next best. Based on your research, indicate how many Staples stores you would recommend building over the next three years in each country. List in prioritized order three cities in each of your eight African countries where you believe Staples should build most of its stores.

Assurance of Learning Exercise 11C

Does My University Recruit in Foreign Countries?

Purpose

A competitive climate is emerging among colleges and universities around the world. Colleges and universities in Europe and Japan are increasingly recruiting U.S. students to offset declining enrollments. Foreign students already make up more than a third of the student body at many U.S. universities. The purpose of this exercise is to identify particular colleges and universities in foreign countries that recruit U.S. students.

Instructions

Step 1   Select a foreign country. Conduct research to determine the number and nature of colleges and universities in that country. What are the major educational institutions in that country? What programs are those institutions recognized for offering? What percentage of undergraduate and graduate students attending those institutions are U.S. citizens? Do these institutions actively recruit U.S. students? Are any of the schools of business at the various universities AACSB-International accredited?

Step 2   Prepare a report that summarizes your research findings. Present your report to the class.

Assurance of Learning Exercise 11D

Assess Differences in Culture Across Countries

Purpose

Americans can be more effective in dealing with businesspeople from other countries if they have some awareness and understanding of differences in culture across countries. This is a fun exercise that provides information for your class regarding some of these key differences.

Instructions

Step 1   Identify four individuals who either grew up in a foreign country or who have lived in a foreign country for more than one year. Interview those four persons. Try to have four different countries represented. During each interview, develop a list of eight key differences between American style/custom and that particular country's style/custom in terms of various aspects of speaking, meetings, meals, relationships, friendships, and communication that could impact business dealings.

Step 2   Develop a 15-minute PowerPoint presentation for your class and give a talk summarizing your findings. Identify in your talk the persons you interviewed as well as the length of time those persons lived in the respective countries. Give your professor a hard copy of your PowerPoint presentation.

Assurance of Learning Exercise 11E

How Well Traveled Are Business Students at My University?

Purpose

It would be interesting to know how traveled students are at your university and also how those students consider their travels to be helpful in becoming an effective businessperson. Generally speaking, the more one has traveled, especially outside the United States, the more tolerant, understanding, and appreciative one is for diversity. Many students even state on their resume the extent to which they have traveled, both across the United States and perhaps around the world.

Instructions

Administer the following survey to at least 30 business students, including your classmates in the strategic management course. Analyze the results. Give a 15-minute presentation to your class regarding your findings. Turn in a written report of your findings to your professor.

The Survey

1. How many states in the United States have you visited?
2. How many states in the United States have you lived in for at least three months?
3. How many countries outside the United States have you visited?
4. List the countries outside the United States that you have visited.
5. How many countries outside the United States have you lived in for at least three months?
6. List the countries outside the United States that you have lived in for at least three months.
7. To what extent do you feel that traveling across the United States can make a person a more effective businessperson? Use a 1 to 10 scale, where 1 is "Cannot Make a Difference" and 10 is "Can Make a Tremendous Difference."
8. To what extent do you feel that visiting countries outside the United States can make a person a more effective business person? Use a 1 to 10 scale, where 1 is "Cannot Make a Difference" and 10 is "Can Make a Tremendous Difference."
9. To what extent do you feel that living in another country can make a person a more effective businessperson? Use a 1 to 10 scale, where 1 is "Cannot Make a Difference" and 10 is "Can Make a Tremendous Difference."
10. What three important ways so you feel that traveling or living outside the United States would be helpful to a person in being a more effective businessperson?

Source: Granite/Shutterstock.com

"NOTABLE QUOTES"

"Two heads are better than one."

—Unknown Author

"One reaction frequently heard is 'I don't have enough information.' In reality strategists never have enough information because some information is not available and some is too costly."

—William Glueck

"I keep six honest serving men. They taught me all I know. Their names are What, Why, When, How, Where, and Who."

—Rudyard Kipling

"Don't recommend anything you would not be prepared to do yourself if you were in the decision maker's shoes."

—A. J. Strickland III

"A picture is worth a thousand words."

—Unknown Author

How to Prepare and Present a Case Analysis

CHAPTER OBJECTIVES

After studying this chapter, you should be able to do the following:

1. Describe the case method for learning strategic-management concepts.
2. Identify the steps in preparing a comprehensive written case analysis.
3. Describe how to give an effective oral case analysis presentation.
4. Discuss special tips for doing a case analysis.

ASSURANCE OF LEARNING EXERCISES

Oral Presentation—
Step 1 Introduction (2 minutes)

Oral Presentation—
Step 2 Mission/Vision (4 minutes)

Oral Presentation—
Step 3 Internal Assessment (8 minutes)

Oral Presentation—
Step 4 External Assessment (8 minutes)

Oral Presentation—
Step 5 Strategy Formulation (14 minutes)

Oral Presentation—
Step 6 Strategy Implementation (8 minutes)

Oral Presentation—
Step 7 Strategy Evaluation (2 minutes)

Oral Presentation—
Step 8 Conclusion (4 minutes)

The purpose of this section is to help you analyze strategic-management cases. Guidelines for preparing written and oral case analyses are given, and suggestions for preparing cases for class discussion are presented. Steps to follow in preparing case analyses are provided. Guidelines for making an oral presentation are described.

What Is a Strategic-Management Case?

A *strategic-management case* describes an organization's external and internal conditions and raises issues concerning the firm's mission, strategies, objectives, and policies. Most of the information in a strategic-management case is established fact, but some information may be opinions, judgments, and beliefs. Strategic-management cases are more comprehensive than those you may have studied in other courses. They generally include a description of related management, marketing, finance/accounting, production/operations, R&D, information systems, and natural environment issues. A strategic-management case puts the reader at the scene of the action by describing a firm's situation at some point in time. Strategic-management cases are written to give you practice applying strategic-management concepts. The case method for studying strategic management is often called *learning by doing*.

Guidelines for Preparing Case Analyses

The Need for Practicality

There is no such thing as a complete case, and no case ever gives you all the information you need to conduct analyses and make recommendations. Likewise, in the business world, strategists never have all the information they need to make decisions: information may be unavailable or too costly to obtain, or it may take too much time to obtain. So in analyzing strategic-management cases, do what strategists do every day—make reasonable assumptions about unknowns, clearly state assumptions, perform appropriate analyses, and make decisions. *Be practical.* For example, in performing a projected financial analysis, make reasonable assumptions, appropriately state them, and proceed to show what impact your recommendations are expected to have on the organization's financial position. Avoid saying, "I don't have enough information." Always supplement the information provided in a case with Internet and library research.

The Need for Justification

The most important part of analyzing cases is not what strategies you recommend but rather how you support your decisions and how you propose that they be implemented. There is no single best solution or one right answer to a case, so give ample justification for your recommendations. This is important. In the business world, strategists usually do not know if their decisions are right until resources have been allocated and consumed. Then it is often too late to reverse a decision. This cold fact accents the need for careful integration of intuition and analysis in preparing business policy case analyses.

The Need for Realism

Avoid recommending a course of action beyond an organization's means. *Be realistic.* No organization can possibly pursue all the strategies that could potentially benefit the firm. Estimate how much capital will be required to implement what you recommended. Determine whether debt, stock, or a combination of debt and stock could be used to obtain the capital. Make sure your recommendations are feasible. Do not prepare a case analysis that omits all arguments and information not supportive of your recommendations. Rather, present the major advantages and disadvantages of several feasible alternatives. Try not to exaggerate, stereotype, prejudge, or overdramatize. Strive to demonstrate that your interpretation of the evidence is reasonable and objective.

The Need for Specificity

Do not make broad generalizations such as "The company should pursue a market penetration strategy." Be specific by telling *what, why, when, how, where*, and *who*. Failure to use specifics is the single major shortcoming of most oral and written case analyses. For example, in an internal audit say, "The firm's current ratio fell from 2.2 in 2011 to 1.3 in 2012, and this is considered to be a major weakness," instead of "The firm's financial condition is bad." Rather than concluding from a Strategic Position and Action Evaluation (SPACE) Matrix that a firm should be defensive, be more specific, saying, "The firm should consider closing three plants, laying off 280 employees, and divesting itself of its chemical division, for a net savings of $20.2 million in 2012." Use ratios, percentages, numbers, and dollar estimates. Businesspeople dislike generalities and vagueness.

The Need for Originality

Do not necessarily recommend the course of action that the firm plans to take or actually undertook, even if those actions resulted in improved revenues and earnings. The aim of case analysis is for you to consider all the facts and information relevant to the organization at the time, to generate feasible alternative strategies, to choose among those alternatives, and to defend your recommendations. Put yourself back in time to the point when strategic decisions were being made by the firm's strategists. Based on the information available then, what would you have done? Support your position with charts, graphs, ratios, analyses, and the like—not a revelation from the library. You can become a good strategist by thinking through situations, making management assessments, and proposing plans yourself. *Be original.* Compare and contrast what you recommend versus what the company plans to do or did.

The Need to Contribute

Strategy formulation, implementation, and evaluation decisions are commonly made by a group of individuals rather than by a single person. Therefore, your professor may divide the class into three- or four-person teams and ask you to prepare written or oral case analyses. Members of a strategic-management team, in class or in the business world, differ on their aversion to risk, their concern for short-run versus long-run benefits, their attitudes toward social responsibility, and their views concerning globalization. There are no perfect people, so there are no perfect strategies. Be open-minded to others' views. *Be a good listener and a good contributor.*

Preparing a Case for Class Discussion

Your professor may ask you to prepare a case for class discussion. Preparing a case for class discussion means that you need to read the case before class, make notes regarding the organization's external opportunities/threats and internal strengths/weaknesses, perform appropriate analyses, and come to class prepared to offer and defend some specific recommendations.

The Case Method versus Lecture Approach

The case method of teaching is radically different from the traditional lecture approach, in which little or no preparation is needed by students before class. The *case method* involves a classroom situation in which students do most of the talking; your professor facilitates discussion by asking questions and encouraging student interaction regarding ideas, analyses, and recommendations. Be prepared for a discussion along the lines of "What would you do, why would you do it, when would you do it, and how would you do it?" Prepare answers to the following types of questions:

- What are the firm's most important external opportunities and threats?
- What are the organization's major strengths and weaknesses?
- How would you describe the organization's financial condition?
- What are the firm's existing strategies and objectives?
- Who are the firm's competitors, and what are their strategies?
- What objectives and strategies do you recommend for this organization? Explain your reasoning. How does what you recommend compare to what the company plans?
- How could the organization best implement what you recommend? What implementation problems do you envision? How could the firm avoid or solve those problems?

The Cross-Examination

Do not hesitate to take a stand on the issues and to support your position with objective analyses and outside research. Strive to apply strategic-management concepts and tools in preparing your case for class discussion. Seek defensible arguments and positions. Support opinions and judgments with facts, reasons, and evidence. Crunch the numbers before class! Be willing to describe your recommendations to the class without fear of disapproval. Respect the ideas of others, but be willing to go against the majority opinion when you can justify a better position.

Strategic-management case analysis gives you the opportunity to learn more about yourself, your colleagues, strategic management, and the decision-making process in organizations. The rewards of this experience will depend on the effort you put forth, so do a good job. Discussing business policy cases in class is exciting and challenging. Expect views counter to those you present. Different students will place emphasis on different aspects of an organization's situation and submit different recommendations for scrutiny and rebuttal. Cross-examination discussions commonly arise, just as they occur in a real business organization. Avoid being a silent observer.

Preparing a Written Case Analysis

In addition to asking you to prepare a case for class discussion, your professor may ask you to prepare a written case analysis. Preparing a written case analysis is similar to preparing a case for class discussion, except written reports are generally more structured and more detailed. There is no ironclad procedure for preparing a written case analysis because cases differ in focus; the type, size, and complexity of the organizations being analyzed also vary.

When writing a strategic-management report or case analysis, avoid using jargon, vague or redundant words, acronyms, abbreviations, sexist language, and ethnic or racial slurs. And watch your spelling! Use short sentences and paragraphs and simple words and phrases. Use quite a few subheadings. Arrange issues and ideas from the most important to the least important. Arrange recommendations from the least controversial to the most controversial. Use the active voice rather than the passive voice for all verbs; for example, say "Our team recommends that the company diversify" rather than "It is recommended by our team to diversify." Use many examples to add specificity and clarity. Tables, figures, pie charts, bar charts, timelines, and other kinds of exhibits help communicate important points and ideas. Sometimes a picture *is* worth a thousand words.

The Executive Summary

Your professor may ask you to focus the written case analysis on a particular aspect of the strategic-management process, such as (1) to identify and evaluate the organization's existing mission, objectives, and strategies; or (2) to propose and defend specific recommendations for the company; or (3) to develop an industry analysis by describing the competitors, products, selling techniques, and market conditions in a given industry. These types of written reports are sometimes called *executive summaries*. An executive summary usually ranges from three to five pages of text in length, plus exhibits.

The Comprehensive Written Analysis

Your professor may ask you to prepare a *comprehensive written analysis*. This assignment requires you to apply the entire strategic-management process to the particular organization. When preparing a comprehensive written analysis, picture yourself as a consultant who has been asked by a company to conduct a study of its external and internal environment and to make specific recommendations for its future. Prepare exhibits to support your recommendations. Highlight exhibits with some discussion in the paper. Comprehensive written analyses are usually about 10 pages in length, plus exhibits. Throughout your written analysis, emphasize how your proposed strategies will enable the firm to gain and sustain competitive advantage.

Steps in Preparing a Comprehensive Written Analysis

In preparing a **written** case analysis, you could follow the steps outlined here, which correlate to the stages in the strategic-management process and the chapters in this text. (Note—The steps in presenting an **oral** case analysis are given on pages 367–369, are more detailed, and could be used here).

Step 1 Identify the firm's existing vision, mission, objectives, and strategies.

Step 2 Develop vision and mission statements for the organization.

Step 3 Identify the organization's external opportunities and threats.

Step 4 Construct a Competitive Profile Matrix (CPM).

Step 5 Construct an External Factor Evaluation (EFE) Matrix.

Step 6 Identify the organization's internal strengths and weaknesses.

Step 7 Construct an Internal Factor Evaluation (IFE) Matrix.

Step 8 Prepare a Strengths-Weaknesses-Opportunities-Threats (SWOT) Matrix, Strategic Position and Action Evaluation (SPACE) Matrix, Boston Consulting Group (BCG) Matrix, Internal-External (IE) Matrix, Grand Strategy Matrix, and Quantitative Strategic Planning Matrix (QSPM) as appropriate. Give advantages and disadvantages of alternative strategies.

Step 9 Recommend specific strategies and long-term objectives. Show how much your recommendations will cost. Clearly itemize these costs for each projected year. Compare your recommendations to actual strategies planned by the company.

Step 10 Specify how your recommendations can be implemented and what results you can expect. Prepare forecasted ratios and projected financial statements. Present a timetable or agenda for action.

Step 11 Recommend specific annual objectives and policies.

Step 12 Recommend procedures for strategy review and evaluation.

Making an Oral Presentation

Your professor may ask you to prepare a strategic-management case analysis, individually or as a group, and present your analysis to the class. Oral presentations are usually graded on two parts: content and delivery. *Content* refers to the quality, quantity, correctness, and appropriateness of analyses presented, including such dimensions as logical flow through the presentation, coverage of major issues, use of specifics, avoidance of generalities, absence of mistakes, and feasibility of recommendations. *Delivery* includes such dimensions as audience attentiveness, clarity of visual aids, appropriate dress, persuasiveness of arguments, tone of voice, eye contact, and posture. Great ideas are of no value unless others can be convinced of their merit through clear communication. The guidelines presented here can help you make an effective oral presentation.

Organizing the Presentation

Begin your presentation by introducing yourself and giving a clear outline of topics to be covered. If a team is presenting, specify the sequence of speakers and the areas each person will address. At the beginning of an oral presentation, try to capture your audience's interest and attention. You could do this by displaying some products made by the company, telling an interesting short story about the company, or sharing an experience you had that is related to the company, its products, or its services. You could develop or obtain a video to show at the beginning of class; you could visit a local distributor of the firm's products and tape a personal interview with the business owner or manager. A light or humorous introduction can be effective at the beginning of a presentation.

Be sure the setting of your presentation is well organized, with seats for attendees, flip charts, a transparency projector, and whatever else you plan to use. Arrive at the classroom at least 15 minutes early to organize the setting, and be sure your materials are ready to go. Make sure everyone can see your visual aids well.

Controlling Your Voice

An effective rate of speaking ranges from 100 to 125 words per minute. Practice your presentation aloud to determine if you are going too fast. Individuals commonly speak too fast when nervous. Breathe deeply before and during the presentation to help yourself slow down. Have a cup of water available; pausing to take a drink will wet your throat, give you time to collect your thoughts, control your nervousness, slow you down, and signal to the audience a change in topic.

Avoid a monotone voice by placing emphasis on different words or sentences. Speak loudly and clearly, but don't shout. Silence can be used effectively to break a monotone voice. Stop at the end of each sentence, rather than running sentences together with *and* or *uh*.

Managing Body Language

Be sure not to fold your arms, lean on the podium, put your hands in your pockets, or put your hands behind you. Keep a straight posture, with one foot slightly in front of the other. Do not turn your back to the audience; doing so is not only rude, but it also prevents your voice from projecting well. Avoid using too many hand gestures. On occasion, leave the podium or table and walk toward your audience, but do not walk around too much. Never block the audience's view of your visual aids.

Maintain good eye contact throughout the presentation. This is the best way to persuade your audience. There is nothing more reassuring to a speaker than to see members of the audience nod in agreement or smile. Try to look everyone in the eye at least once during your presentation, but focus more on individuals who look interested than on those who seem bored. To stay in touch with your audience, use humor and smiles as appropriate throughout your presentation. A presentation should never be dull!

Speaking from Notes

Be sure not to read to your audience because reading puts people to sleep. Perhaps worse than reading is merely reciting what you have memorized. Do not try to memorize anything. Rather, practice unobtrusively using notes. Make sure your notes are written clearly so you will not flounder when trying to read your own writing. Include only main ideas on your note cards. Keep note cards on a podium or table if possible so that you won't drop them or get them out of order; walking with note cards tends to be distracting.

Constructing Visual Aids

Make sure your visual aids are legible to individuals in the back of the room. Use color to highlight special items. Avoid putting complete sentences on visual aids; rather, use short phrases and then orally elaborate on issues as you make your presentation. Generally, there should be no more than four to six lines of text on each visual aid. Use clear headings and subheadings. Be careful about spelling and grammar; use a consistent style of lettering. Use masking tape or an easel for posters—do not hold posters in your hand. Transparencies and handouts are excellent aids; however, be careful not to use too many handouts or your audience may concentrate on them instead of you during the presentation.

Answering Questions

It is best to field questions at the end of your presentation, rather than during the presentation itself. Encourage questions, and take your time to respond to each one. Answering questions can be persuasive because it involves you with the audience. If a team is giving the presentation, the audience should direct questions to a specific person. During the question-and-answer period, be polite, confident, and courteous. Avoid verbose responses. Do not get defensive with your answers, even if a hostile or confrontational question is asked. Staying calm during potentially disruptive situations, such as a cross-examination, reflects self-confidence, maturity, poise, and command of the particular company and its industry. Stand up throughout the question-and-answer period.

Tips for Success in Case Analysis

Strategic-management students who have used this text over 13 editions offer you the following tips for success in doing case analysis. The tips are grouped into two basic sections: (1) Content Tips and (2) Process Tips. Content tips relate especially to the content of your case analysis, whereas the Process tips relate mostly to the process that you and your group mates undergo in preparing and delivering your case analysis/presentation.

Content Tips

1. Use the www.strategyclub.com website resources. The software described there is especially useful.
2. In preparing your external assessment, use the S&P Industry Survey material in your college library.
3. Go to http://finance.yahoo.com or http://moneycentral.msn/investor/home.asp and enter your company's stock symbol.
4. View your case analysis and presentation as a product that must have some competitive factor to favorably differentiate it from the case analyses of other students.
5. Develop a mind-set of *why*, continually questioning your own and others' assumptions and assertions.
6. Because strategic management is a capstone course, seek the help of professors in other specialty areas when necessary.
7. Read your case frequently as work progresses so you don't overlook details.
8. At the end of each group session, assign each member of the group a task to be completed for the next meeting.
9. Become friends with the library and the Internet.
10. Be creative and innovative throughout the case analysis process.
11. A goal of case analysis is to improve your ability to think clearly in ambiguous and confusing situations; do not get frustrated that there is no single best answer.
12. Do not confuse symptoms with causes; do not develop conclusions and solutions prematurely; recognize that information may be misleading, conflicting, or wrong.
13. Work hard to develop the ability to formulate reasonable, consistent, and creative plans; put yourself in the strategist's position.
14. Develop confidence in using quantitative tools for analysis. They are not inherently difficult; it is just practice and familiarity you need.
15. Strive for excellence in writing and in the technical preparation of your case. Prepare nice charts, tables, diagrams, and graphs. Use color and unique pictures. No messy exhibits! Use PowerPoint.
16. Do not forget that the objective is to learn; explore areas with which you are not familiar.
17. Pay attention to detail.
18. Think through alternative implications fully and realistically. The consequences of decisions are not always apparent. They often affect many different aspects of a firm's operations.
19. Provide answers to such fundamental questions as *what, when, where, why, who*, and *how*.
20. Do not merely recite ratios or present figures. Rather, develop ideas and conclusions concerning the possible trends. Show the importance of these figures to the corporation.
21. Support reasoning and judgment with factual data whenever possible.
22. Your analysis should be as detailed and specific as possible.
23. A picture speaks a thousand words, and a creative picture gets you an A in many classes.
24. Emphasize the Recommendations and Strategy Implementation sections. A common mistake is to spend too much time on the external or internal analysis parts of your paper. The recommendations and implementation sections are the most important part of the paper or presentation.
25. Throughout your case analysis, emphasize how your proposed strategic plan will enable the firm to gain and sustain competitive advantage.

Process Tips

1. When working as a team, encourage most of the work to be done individually. Use team meetings mostly to assimilate work. This approach is most efficient.
2. If allowed to do so, invite questions throughout your presentation.
3. During the presentation, keep good posture, eye contact, and voice tone, and project confidence. Do not get defensive under any conditions or with any questions.

4. Prepare your case analysis in advance of the due date to allow time for reflection and practice. Do not procrastinate.
5. Maintain a positive attitude about the class, working *with* problems rather than against them.
6. Keep in tune with your professor, and understand his or her values and expectations.
7. Other students will have strengths in functional areas that will complement your weaknesses, so develop a cooperative spirit that moderates competitiveness in group work.
8. When preparing a case analysis as a group, divide into separate teams to work on the external analysis and internal analysis.
9. Have a good sense of humor.
10. Capitalize on the strengths of each member of the group; volunteer your services in your areas of strength.
11. Set goals for yourself and your team; budget your time to attain them.
12. Foster attitudes that encourage group participation and interaction. Do not be hasty to judge group members.
13. Be prepared to work. There will be times when you will have to do more than your share. Accept it, and do what you have to do to move the team forward.
14. Think of your case analysis as if it were really happening; do not reduce case analysis to a mechanical process.
15. To uncover flaws in your analysis and to prepare the group for questions during an oral presentation, assign one person in the group to actively play the devil's advocate.
16. Do not schedule excessively long group meetings; two-hour sessions are about right.
17. Push your ideas hard enough to get them listened to, but then let up; listen to others and try to follow their lines of thinking; follow the flow of group discussion, recognizing when you need to get back on track; do not repeat yourself or others unless clarity or progress demands repetition.
18. Develop a case-presentation style that is direct, assertive, and convincing; be concise, precise, fluent, and correct.
19. Have fun when at all possible. Preparing a case is frustrating at times, but enjoy it while you can; it may be several years before you are playing CEO again.
20. In group cases, do not allow personality differences to interfere. When they occur, they must be understood for what they are—and then put aside.
21. Get things written down (drafts) as soon as possible.
22. Read everything that other group members write, and comment on it in writing. This allows group input into all aspects of case preparation.
23. Adaptation and flexibility are keys to success; be creative and innovative.
24. Neatness is a real plus; your case analysis should look professional.
25. Let someone else read and critique your presentation several days before you present it.
26. Make special efforts to get to know your group members. This leads to more openness in the group and allows for more interchange of ideas. Put in the time and effort necessary to develop these relationships.
27. Be constructively critical of your group members' work. Do not dominate group discussions. Be a good listener and contributor.
28. Learn from past mistakes and deficiencies. Improve upon weak aspects of other case presentations.
29. Learn from the positive approaches and accomplishments of classmates.

Sample Case Analysis Outline

There are musicians who play wonderfully without notes and there are chefs who cook wonderfully without recipes, but most of us prefer a more orderly cookbook approach, at least in the first attempt at doing something new. Therefore the following eight steps may serve as a basic outline for you in presenting a strategic plan for your firm's future. This outline is not the only approach used in business and industry for communicating a strategic plan, but this approach is time-tested, it does work, and it does cover all of the basics. You may amend the content, tools, and concepts given to suit your own company, audience, assignment, and circumstances, but it helps to know and understand the rules before you start breaking them.

Depending on whether your class is 50 minutes or 75 minutes and how much time your professor allows for your case presentation, the following outlines what generally needs to be covered. A recommended time (in minutes) as part of the presentation is given for an overall 50-minute event. Of course, all cases are different, some being about for-profit and some about not-for-profit organizations, for example, so the scope and content of your analysis may vary. Even if you do not have time to cover all areas in your oral presentation, you may be asked to prepare these areas and give them to your professor as a "written case analysis." Be sure in an oral presentation to manage time knowing that your recommendations and associated costs are the most important part. You should go to www.strategyclub.com and utilize that information and software in preparing your case analysis. Good luck.

Current Readings

Kearney, Eric, Diether Gebert, and Sven Voelpel. "When Diversity Benefits Teams: The Importance of Team Members' Need for Cognition." *Academy of Management Journal*, June 2009, 581–598.

STEPS IN PRESENTING AN ORAL CASE ANALYSIS

Oral Presentation—Step 1

Introduction (2 minutes)

a. Introduce yourselves by name and major. Establish the time setting of your case and analysis. Prepare your strategic plan for the three years 2012–2014.
b. Introduce your company and its products/services; capture interest.
c. Show the outline of your presentation and tell who is doing what parts.
d. Let your audience know that the primary motivation/rationale/intent of every slide is to reveal how the firm can best gain and sustain competitive advantage.

Oral Presentation—Step 2

Mission/Vision (4 minutes)

a. Show existing mission and vision statements if available from the firm's website, or annual report, or elsewhere.
b. Show your "improved" mission and vision and tell why it is improved.
c. Compare your mission and vision to a leading competitor's statements.
d. Comment on your vision and mission in terms of how they support the strategies you envision for your firm.

Oral Presentation—Step 3

Internal Assessment (8 minutes)

a. Give your financial ratio analysis. Highlight especially good and bad ratios. Do not give definitions of the ratios and do not highlight all the ratios.
b. Show the firm's organizational chart found or "created based on executive titles." Identify the type of chart as well as good and bad aspects. Unless all white males comprise the chart, peoples' names are generally not important because positions reveal structure as people come and go.
c. Present your improved/recommended organizational chart. Tell why you feel it is improved over the existing chart.
d. Show a market positioning map with firm and competitors. Discuss the map in light of strategies you envision for firm versus competitors' strategies.
e. Identify the marketing strategy of the firm in terms of good and bad points versus competitors and in light of strategies you envision for the firm.
f. Show a map locating the firm's operations. Discuss in light of strategies you envision. Also, perhaps show a Value Chain Analysis chart.
g. Discuss (and perhaps show) the firm's website and Facebook page in terms of good and bad points compared to rival firms.
h. Show your "value of the firm" analysis.
i. List up to 20 of the firm's strengths and weaknesses. Go over each one listed without "reading" them verbatim.
j. Show and explain your Internal Factor Evaluation (IFE) Matrix.

Oral Presentation—Step 4

External Assessment (8 minutes)

a. Identify and discuss major competitors. Use pie charts, maps, tables, and/or figures to show the intensity of competition in the industry.
b. Show your Competitive Profile Matrix. Include at least 12 factors and two competitors.
c. Summarize key industry trends citing Standard & Poor's *Industry Survey* or Chamber of Commerce statistics, etc. Highlight key external trends as they impact the firm, including trends that are economic, social, cultural, demographic, geographic, technological, political, legal, governmental, and to do with the natural environment.
d. List up to 20 of the firm's opportunities and threats. Make sure your opportunities are not stated as strategies. Go over each one listed without "reading" them verbatim.
e. Show and explain your External Factor Evaluation (EFE) Matrix.

Oral Presentation—Step 5

Strategy Formulation (14 minutes)

a. Show and explain your SWOT Matrix, highlighting each of your strategies listed.
b. Show and explain your SPACE Matrix, using half of your "space time" on calculations and the other half on implications of those numbers. Strategy implications must be specific rather than generic. In other words, use of a term such as "market penetration" is not satisfactory alone as a strategy implication.
c. Show your Boston Consulting Group (BCG) Matrix. Again focus on both the numbers and the strategy implications. Do multiple BCG Matrices if possible, including domestic versus global, or another geographic breakdown. Develop a product BCG if at all possible. Comment on changes to this matrix as per strategies you envision. Develop this matrix even if you do not know the profits per division and even if you have to estimate the axes information. However, make no wild guesses on axes or revenue/profit information.

d. Show your Internal-External (IE) Matrix. Because this analysis is similar to the BCG, see the preceding comments.
e. Show your Grand Strategy Matrix. Again focus on implications after giving the quadrant selection. Reminder: Use of a term such as "market penetration" is not satisfactory alone as a strategy implication. Be more specific. Elaborate.
f. Show your Quantitative Strategic Planning Matrix (QSPM). Be sure to explain your strategies to start with here. Do not go back over the internal and external factors. Avoid having more than one 4, 3, 2, or 1 in a row. If you rate one strategy, you need to rate the other because that particular factor is affecting the choice. Work row by row rather than column by column on preparing the QSPM.
g. Present your Recommendations Page. This is the most important page in your presentation. Be specific in terms of both strategies and estimated costs of those strategies. *Total your estimated costs.* You should have 10 or more strategies. Divide your strategies into two groups: (1) Existing Strategies to Be Continued, and (2) New Strategies to Be Started.

Oral Presentation—Step 6

Strategy Implementation (8 minutes)

a. Show and explain your EPS/EBIT analysis to reveal whether stock, debt, or a combination is best to finance your recommendations. Graph the analysis. Decide which approach to use if there are any given limitations of the analysis.
b. Show your projected income statement. Relate changes in the items to your recommendations rather than blindly going with historical percentage changes.
c. Show your projected balance sheet. Relate changes in your items to your recommendations. Be sure to show the retained earnings calculation and the results of your EPS/EBIT decision.
d. Show your projected financial ratios and highlight several key ratios to show the benefits of your strategic plan.

Oral Presentation—Step 7

Strategy Evaluation (2 minutes)

a. Prepare a Balanced Scorecard to show your expected financial and nonfinancial objectives recommended for the firm.

Oral Presentation—Step 8

Conclusion (4 minutes)

a. Compare and contrast your strategic plan versus the company's own plans for the future.
b. Thank audience members for their attention. Genuinely seek and gladly answer questions.

Name Index

Subject Index